Contemporary Political Studies 1997

by Jeffrey Stanyer

County Government in England and W
(Routledge & Kegan Paul) 1967

Understanding Local Government
(Fontana) 1976

Administering Britain
(Fontana) [with B.C.Smith] 1976

A History of Devon County Council, 1889-1989
(Devon Books) 1989

Centre and Periphery: Brittany and Cornwall & Devon Compared
(Exeter University Press) [edited with M.Havinden & J.Quéniart] 1991

Contemporary Political Studies 1994
(PSA) [edited with P.Dunleavy] 1994

Contemporary Political Studies 1995
(PSA) [edited with J.Lovenduski] 1995

Contemporary Political Studies 1996
(PSA) [edited with I.Hampsher-Monk] 1996

by Gerry Stoker

The Politics of Local Government
(Macmillan) 1988, 1991

Re-making Planning: The Politics of Urban Change in the Thatcher Years
(Macmillan) [with T.Brindley & Y.Rydin] 1989, 1996

The Future of Local Government/Local Government in the 1990s
(Macmillan) [edited with J.Stewart] 1989, 1995

Local Government in Europe
(Macmillan/St.Martinis Press) [edited with R.Batley] 1991

Cities in the 1990s
(Longman) (with S.Young) 1993

Theories of Urban Politics
(Sage) [edited with D.Judge & H.Wolman] 1995

Theory and Methods in Political Science
(Macmillan) [edited with D.Marsh] 1995

Rethinking Local Democracy
(Macmillan) [edited with D.King] 1996

Privatisation of Urban Services in Europe
(Cassell) [edited with D.Lorrain] 1997

CONTEMPORARY POLITICAL STUDIES 1997
Volumes I & II

Jeffrey Stanyer

Senior Lecturer in Politics
University of Exeter

Gerry Stoker

Professor of Government
Strathclyde University

THE POLITICAL STUDIES ASSOCIATION
OF THE UNITED KINGDOM

CONTEMPORARY POLITICAL STUDIES 1997

Volume I

edited on behalf of
The Political Studies Association
of the United Kingdom

by

Jeffrey Stanyer
&
Gerry Stoker

Introduction
Jeffrey Stanyer

Proceedings of the Annual Conference
held at the University of Ulster,
Jordanstown, Belfast,
April 8th-10th, 1997

Political Studies Association
of the United Kingdom
1997

PSA
Political Studies Association

First published in Great Britain in 1997 by
THE POLITICAL STUDIES ASSOCIATION
OF THE UNITED KINGDOM
official address:
PSA National Office,
Department of Politics,
The University of Nottingham,
Nottingham NG7 2RD.

British Library Cataloguing in Publication Data
A catalogue record for this book is
available from the British Library
ISBN 0 9523150 8 4

Typeset in LaTeX by Jeffrey Stanyer.

Printed and bound in Great Britain by Short Run Press Ltd, Exeter.

Cover Design by Delphine Jones, Graphic Design Unit, University of Exeter.

THE POLITICAL STUDIES ASSOCIATION OF THE UNITED KINGDOM

Contents

INTRODUCTION

by Jeffrey Stanyer

With these two volumes PSA passes Brian Lara's 501, but of course it has taken the Association four innings. As the project heads towards the high hundreds readers might like to reflect on what the copy editor & type setter has learned.

The main problems are first, that the ASCII-ing process is often not carried out at all or carried out badly. Sometimes it is necessary to remove one by one over 500 disruptive 'leftovers' from the commercial package originally used; in some cases all opening (but not closing) quotation marks have disappeared, whilst all genitive elisons are capital 'Us'. Sometimes every tenth group of words is run together, and the same process dispenses with some of the letters. The hardest error to deal with is the complete removal of all footnotes and references – this because instructions for preparation of the manuscript have not been followed.

Secondly, there is a considerable amount of bad typing, particularly with the use of spaces, which the computer treats as characters. The difference between a properly prepared manuscript and a poor one in terms of extra work created is of a multiplicative order – five and six times as long in time taken to create the proofs.

The third problem is often not the fault of the paper-giver. A substantial proportion have not received from their convenor the instructions for preparing the disc to be sent to Exeter. A small number do not know that the paper has to be submitted on disc. There is often no agreement about the exact title of a panel.

There are clearly some writers who are wedded to a particular style of presentation and do not wish to comply with the principles and rules chosen for these Proceedings. The system prescribed is designed to make type-setting less burdensome and to reduce the length of papers without serious affecting their quality. The type-setter has actually met Lorenz butterflies – an extra comma at the beginning produces another page at the end. The reader may ask him or herself how much it is worth to learn 500 times that Oxford University Press is in Oxford and thus, with Cambridge, Manchester, Chicago ..., perhaps have to pay for several pages of extra printing.

Most of the the authors who have received the instructions have got used to the idea that footnotes should be typed at the place where the footnote number will appear in the text, but virtually no-one seems to understand that tables and figures do not pass successfuly through the ASCII process (thus a good hard copy is vital) and, worse, that the printed page is considerably smaller than A4.

The most enjoyable part of editing the Proceedings is being exposed to such a wide variety of ideas, approaches and research findings. Members of the profession who want to get a sense of how the subject is developing should pay attention to the contents of the volumes and forget about this editor's complaints, at least until next year.

JS, 21/3/97

Panels & Papers

The papers listed here are those that were sent to the editors in time to be printed. Other papers will be brought to the Conference by the authors and will be available for purchase from the Papers Room. Sessions for which no advance papers were expected and the panels which produced none are not listed here.

Unfortunately, at the time of going to press full information about allocation of papers to panels was not available to the type-setter and some papers have had to be simply printed at the end of Volume II. Their allocation to a panel will be announced at the beginning of the Conference, along with a full and revised timetable.

First Session Tuesday, 14.00-15.15pm

The Communist Manifesto 150 Years On (Mark Cowling)

Rational Choice (Andrew Hindmoor)

Politics of Transition in East and South East Asia (Donna James)

Evolutionary Theory and the State (Peter Kerr)

Changing Environmentalism in the 1990s (William Maloney)

Comparative Local Government (Howard Elcock)

Second Session Tuesday, 15.45-17.00pm

Urban Regimes in Theory and Practice (Peter John)

Kevin Ward (Manchester), 'Rigourising Regime Theory' [181-197]

Joyce Liddle (Sunderland), 'A Regeneration Regime in the North East of England? Inter-Agency Partnerships and the Case of Siemens U.K.' [198-219]

Hegel (Tony Burns)

Howard Williams (Aberystwyth), 'Hegel's Philosophy of History and the *Philosophy of Right*' [220-227]

Tony Burns (Nottingham Trent), 'Hegel's Interpretation of the Philosophy of Heraclitus: Some Observations' [228-239]

Communitarianism and the Future of Social Policy (Adrian Little)

Gordon Hughes (The Open University), 'Radical Communitarianism, Community Safety and Social Justice' [240-248]

Adrian Little (Nene College), 'Welfare and Community in Post-Industrial Socialist Theory: Beyond Employment' [249-260]

Linda Watson-Brown (Stirling), 'Single Parents and Civic Competence – Back to Basics' [261-271]

Political Utopianism (Lucy Sargisson)

Lucy Sargisson (Nottingham Trent), Contemporary Feminist Utopianism: The Equality/Difference Dilemma' [272-282]

Historical Perspectives on Political Communication in Britain (Dominic Wring)

Jenie Betteridge (Westminster), 'Broadcasting the Post-War Elections: Changing Media, Changing Rules, Changing Politics' [283-294]

Dominic Wring (Nottingham Trent), '"Emancipation throgh Education" or Persuasion via Mass Communication: the Philosophical Debate over Labour Party Campaigning' [295-304]

Fourth Session Wednesday, 11.00-12.15pm

Irish Politics I (Alan Greer)

Rachel Ward (Salford), 'The Influence of Women on the Northern Ireland Peace Process' [615-623]

Current Issues in Local Democracy (Mark McAteer)

Neil McGarvey (Strathclyde), 'Unravelling Two Coalitions for Local Governance Reform' [624-635]

Fifth Session Wednesday, 14.00-15.15pm

Constraints on Public Policy (Helen Butler)

Colin McCaig (Sheffield), 'Constraints on Action: the Case of the Labour Party in Opposition' [636-643]

Michael Squires (Sheffield), 'Constraints in Pursuing a Policy of Rail Closures' [644-649]

Helen Butler (Sheffield), 'Constraints on Prime Ministerial/Foreign Secretary Policy-Making: the Case of Attlee and Bevin, 1945-1951' [650-658]

Frameworks of Participation (Marc Stears)

Marc Stears (Nuffield College, Oxford), 'Individual Freedom and Democracy in Industry, 1918-1925' [659-672]

Eugenia Low (St John's College, Oxford), 'A Tale of Two Citizenships: Hnery Jones, T.H.Marshall and Conceptions of Citizenship in Twentieth-Century Britain' [673-683]

Policy Networks as Exogenous Factors (Michael Cavanagh)

Michael Cavanagh (Strathclyde), 'The Norsok Process and the Norwegian Offshore Safety Policy' [684-693]

The Global Development and Spread of Policies and Political Institutions (Colin Hay)

Jonathan Davies (York), 'Developing a Comparative Approach to Urban Regime Theory in the United Kingdom' [694-703]

Comparative Perspectives on Political Corruption I (Martin Bull)

Neil Collins (Magee College) & Colm O'Raghallaigh (Smurfit Group), 'Typologising Political Corruption and an Application to the Irish Case' [704-715]

Political Theory (Ian Forbes)

Alan Apperley (Wolverhampton), 'Surveying the Inner Citadel: Liberalism and Personal Autonomy' [716-723]

Ofer Cassif (London School of Economics), 'Nationalism and the Case of Distorted Liberalism' [724-732]

Reforming the Public Sector (Gerry Stoker)

Stephanie Hoopes (Sussex), 'Politicians as Departmental Budget Manipulators: the British Case' [733-749]

Irish Politics II (Alan Greer)

Jon Tonge (Salford), 'The Political Agenda of Sinn Fein: Change without Change?' [750-760]

The Politics of Defence in Post-Soviet Russia (Jenny Mathers)

Edwin Bacon (Birmingham), 'Russia's Security Council: Institutional Continuity during Transition' [761-771]

Sixth Session Thursday, 9.15-10.30am

Citizenship and the European Union (Michael Harris)

Nicola Piper (Sheffield), 'The Impact of Racism and Nationalism on Non-European Union Nationals' Citizenship: a Comparative Analysis of Britain and Germany' [772-780]

Scottish Élite Responses to Devolution (Dimitrios Christopoulos & Stephen Herbert)

Dimitios Christopoulos (The West of England) & Stephen Herbert (University of Glasgow), 'Scottish Élite Responses to the Prospect of Devolution' [781-801]

The Politics of Investment Policy (David Marsh)

Matthew Watson (Birmingham), 'The Changing Face of Macro-economic Stabilisation: from Growth through Indigenous Investment to Growth through Inward Investment' [802-815]

The European Union and the 1996 IGC (Andreas Kintis)

Richard Whitman (Westminster), 'The CFSP and the IGC: Enhancing Capabilities or Reconciling Differences?' [816-828]

Lee Miles (Hull), 'Trouble in Store: Swedish Priorities for the IGC' [829-837]

Art as Protest (James Connelly)

Colin Beaven (Southampton Institute), 'Popular Song and Unpopular Protest: the Political Cabaret of Georg Kreisler' [838-849]

James Connelly (Southampton Institute), 'Art, Magic and Propaganda in the Principles of Art' [850-861]

Policy Studies: Theory and Practice (Nick Robinson)

Thomas Butcher (Warwick), 'Direct Community Participation in Urban Regeneration: The Single Regeneration Process' [862-870]

Nick Robinson (Derby), 'Empirically Suspect and a Methodological Mess? Policy Networks as a Tool to Study Agenda Setting' [871-883]

Paul Cairney (Strathclyde), 'Advocacy Coalitions and Policy Change' [884-895]

Seventh Session Thursday, 11.00-12.15pm

Policy Networks in Theoretical Perspective (David Marsh)

Robert Watt (Birmingham), 'A Historical Relationship between Agency and Structure: Synthesising Actor Network, Policy Network and Advocacy Coalition Interpretations of Policy-Making' [896-904]

The European Union and Economic Policy (Charlie Jeffrey)

Erik Jones (Nottingham), 'The Low Politics of Monetary Integration' [1010-1023]

Fabio Franchino (Brighton), 'Institutions and Models of Trade Policy: a Difficult Marriage' [1024-1039]

David Barling (Thames Valley), 'Regulatory Conflict and the Marketing of Agricultural Biotechnology in the European Community' [1040-1048]

Papers to be Assigned to Panels

Simon Bennett (Leicester), 'Paradigmatic Disasters' [1049-1066]

Michael Harris (Middlesex), 'Clarifying Citizenship' [1067-1081]

Russell Griffiths (Salford), 'An Environmental Interpretation of the Political Thought of Thomas Robert Malthus (1766-1834)' [1082-1091]

Colin Hay (Birmingham & Harvard), 'Political Time and the Temporality of Crisis' [1092-1102]

Jo K.Iwasaki (London School of Economics), 'Examining the Process of the 1994 Japanese Electoral Reform' [1103-1118]

Ed Page (Warwick), 'Harming Future Generations' [1119-1129]

Andrew Taylor (Huddersfield), 'Marketing the New Conservatism: the Case of the Industrial Charter' [1130-1139]

John Varty (Sussex), 'Liberalism, Republicanism, Civil Society: Adam Ferguson and the Importance of Being Active' [1140-1147]

David Whyte (Liverpool John Moores), 'Moving the Goalposts: the Deregulation of Safety in the Post-Piper Alpha Offshore Oil Industry' [1148-1160]

Chris Woodard (Warwick), 'Responsibility, Desert and Liberal Theories of Justice' [1161-1168]

Page numbers : Volume 1; 1-582
Page numbers : Volume 2; 583-1168

List of Panel Convenors

List of Paper-Givers

List of Paper-Givers (continued)

Perspectives on British Territorial Politics

Claire Reid Mackie
University of Strathclyde

'London Calling: BBC Scotland and the Territorial Divide'

BBC Scotland occupies a unique place within the British Broadcasting Corporation. In an organisation divided into regional units, it is the original 'National Region', a title which highlights its diffuse task. It has to represent the needs of the different areas of Scotland, from the Outer Isles to the Borders, covering Scottish issues for a Scottish audience, yet it also has to mediate these issues for a wider United Kingdom audience and, at the same time, reflect the centralised nature of the BBC itself. Not surprisingly, these multiple demands can place great strain on the relationship between the London-based headquarters and the broadcasters at the periphery. This paper will use the perspective of territorial politics to explore the difficult role of BBC Scotland and consider the extent to which the pressure for constitutional change mirrors the difficulties facing the BBC today.

It will argue that the BBC's reasons for defining Scotland as a national region relate to the continuation of a 'Scottish distinctiveness' in political, social, cultural, legal and economic terms, a type of autonomy which Paterson[1] argues has permeated Scottish life and culture since the Treaty of Union of 1707. Yet this distinctiveness is not homogenous: within Scotland there exist diverse regional identities which BBC Scotland, through its public broadcasting remit, must cater for and explore.

At the same time, BBC Scotland is also answerable to the network centre in London, which has the power to override Scottish advice or decisions and impose its own solution - witness the debacle over the Panorama interview with John Major, scheduled to be broadcast three days before the May 1995 local government elections in Scotland, which was eventually banned by the Scottish courts. Finally BBC Scotland must maintain its role as part of the wider BBC, contributing to the construction of an image of the whole United Kingdom as a nation.[2] Clearly this last task may be at odds with its earlier assignment of reflecting Scottish distinctiveness and it is here, I will argue, that many of BBC Scotland's problems with the London-based centre occur.

Before investigating this relationship, however, it is first necessary to explore the concept of 'Scottish distinctiveness'. This needs to be explained against the background of the United Kingdom in general. Rose argues that the United Kingdom is best visualised as four disparate identities, brought together by historical processes, which have maintained their Union through

---

[1] L.Paterson, *The Autonomy of Modern Scotland*, Edinburgh University Press, 1994.

[2] S.Hall, in W.Stevenson (ed), *All Our Futures: the changing role and purpose of the BBC*, BFI Publishing, 1993.

tradition and pragmatism.[3] As a result, therefore, it is not only Scotland which is distinctive. There are differences - sometimes substantial ones - between Wales, Northern Ireland and even the regions of England. What makes Scottish distinctiveness different, however, is that some of the issues and processes which contribute to its special status are themselves unique to Scotland.

Chief among these are the separate legal system of Scots law, the Church of Scotland (once very influential, but now declining in importance) and an educational tradition which differed significantly from its counterpart in England and Wales. The media is the fourth institution of civil society noted by Midwinter et al as helping to bolster the sense of identity and self-perception which constitute what the authors term 'Scottish difference'.[4]

Paterson argues that the separate tradition of Scots law, guaranteed by the Treaty of Union, was one of the key reasons why Scotland was able to maintain an autonomous relationship with the rest of Great Britain and, latterly, the United Kingdom.[5] By reinforcing the divide between public law and private life, the British state and Scottish civil society developed along separate tracks, occasionally crossing but more often than not proceeding along different lines. The influence of the Enlightenment, supported and shaped by Scottish thinkers such as Hume and Smith, also helped mould political and social expectations.

The rise of the welfare state and the growth of bureaucracy created a more interventionist state, but Paterson argues that the United Kingdom state continued to maintain its legitimacy by offering a type of autonomy to Scotland in the form of distinctive organisations, linked to the added 'carrot' of state benefits. These included the Scottish Office, which constitutes a Scottish bureaucracy in its own right; the growth of quangos and government agencies with Scottish bases or links; local government to cater for local communities and the availability of a wide range of welfare benefits, from the NHS to social security.

The range and scope of these distinctive institutions and processes in Scotland has led to claims that it constitutes a political system in its own right,[6] but this has been challenged by a number of commentators.[7] It is argued instead that Scotland, together with Wales and Northern Ireland, constitutes part of a wider British political system, which requires constant attention from the Westminster government to maintain legitimacy and consent for the Union.[8] But underpinning this debate is a particular view of the United Kingdom as a unitary state.[9]

---

[3] R.Rose, *Understanding the United Kingdom: the territorial dimension in government*, Longman, 1982.

[4] A.Midwinter et al, *Politics and Public Policy in Scotland*, Macmillan, 1991.

[5] Paterson, *The Autonomy of Modern Scotland*.

[6] J.G.Kellas, *The Scottish Political System*, fourth edition, Cambridge University Press, 1989.

[7] See A.Brown et al, *Politics and Society in Scotland*, Macmillan, 1996; Paterson, *The Autonomy of Modern Scotland*; Midwinter et al, *Politics and Public Policy in Scotland*.

[8] A.Gamble, in P.Dunleavy et al (eds), *Developments in British Politics 4*, Macmillan, 1993.

[9] J.Mitchell, 'Conceptual Lenses and Territorial Government in Britain', in U.Jordan

Mitchell argues that most political scientists, and indeed politicians, perceive Britain from within a unitary framework. Urwin and Rokkan define this as a centralised state which enjoys symmetrical control over all territorial areas and which deals with administration in a standardised way. Clearly this does not chime with the many attempts, as outlined above, to cater for Scottish distinctiveness, although it does help to explain the entirely different experience of Wales within the United Kingdom state.

Instead Mitchell, drawing on the work of Urwin & Rokkan on state formation, proposes that Scottish distinctiveness can be more adequately explained by visualising the United Kingdom as a union state, where historical rights and structures continue to be accommodated by the centre to give some territorial areas a degree of autonomy. The union state viewpoint, compared to the rigidity of the unitary approach, would appear to provide a more comprehensive explanation of why Scottish distinctiveness has been tolerated and, at times, even encouraged by the United Kingdom state. But this approach has itself been adapted, Mitchell argues, by the changes which have taken place in the wider Union.

The United Kingdom political system has been particularly susceptible to strain in the past 30 years, with economic decline, political change and ideological struggle all helping to fray the bonds of Union. The rise of the SNP in the 1960s, the failure of the devolution referendum of the 1970s, the growing centralisation and concentration of government power in the 1980s, disastrous policy decisions like the poll tax and the continued widening of social and economic inequalities have all contributed to heightened pressure in the 1990s for constitutional change.

Although the explosion of Next Steps agencies, NHS Trusts and quangos has helped to dilute the centralisation of power, the lack of accountability inherent in these organisations, together with the number of government-backed appointees, has strengthened claims of a democratic deficit and failed to increase public confidence. The European Union has proved another destabilising influence, both in terms of loss of parliamentary sovereignty and government unity at Westminster, and by offering an alternative outlook to Scots who wanted to turn their backs on the Union. Attempts by the Conservatives to strengthen Scottish distinctiveness, such as allowing the Scottish Grand Committee to become peripatetic and call in Cabinet ministers for questioning, appear to have failed to head off the calls for change. Mitchell asserts that Scotland can now be characterised as a 'dynamic union state',[10] where the situation is moving into a state of flux. Change of some sort looks likely but its nature and type is, however, still uncertain.

One area of Scottish distinctiveness which has not yet been discussed, yet which is integral to the whole debate, is the issue of identity. The organisations and processes mentioned above help maintain a sense of identity which

& W.Kaiser (eds), *Political Reform in Twentieth Century Britain*, German Historical Institute, 1997, following D.Urwin & S.Rokkan (eds), *The Politics of Territorial Identity: Studies in European Regionalism*, SAGE, 1982.

[10] Mitchell, 'Political Reform in Twentieth Century Britain', p.13.

is unique to Scotland and the Scots. This identity is both individually-held and culturally widespread. It pervades, shapes and maintains Scottish society in every dimension: economically, socially, culturally, politically. Supporting this identity is the role of myth, 'beliefs about themselves or their society which people hold but whose power and significance is independent of their truth'.[11] These beliefs can be centuries old or a product of recent events, passed down in song or story or given new life through the lens of Hollywood, but Scottish identity is a powerful prop which is particularly susceptible to the influence of all branches of the media.

Too often, discussions of the importance of the media in Scottish territorial politics have been conducted on the basis of the number of quality and tabloid papers printed in the country, or the amount of coverage given to Scottish stories in the London-based media.[12] While these issues are relevant, they are not detailed enough for the purposes of this paper. I wish to concentrate instead on the issue of identity and the role played by BBC Scotland in mediating Scottish distinctiveness.

The 'National Region' in Perspective

The BBC as a whole was described in the *Annan Report* as 'arguably the single most important cultural organization in the nation',[13] feted for harmonising the distinct national and regional identities within the United Kingdom into an 'imagined community'.[14] As Hall notes, the BBC 'was one of the principal means by which 'the nation' was produced as a symbolic unity out of its many differences, conflicting identities and diversities'.[15]

Interestingly, this was accomplished not by smothering distinctiveness, but by accommodating it. During the early years, the BBC did attempt to impose a paternalistic, élitist culture that was backed by the Reithian ethic 'to inform, educate and entertain', but as public service broadcasting developed, so attitudes changed. The BBC acknowledged that the audience was not homogenous, that listeners did have different tastes, different backgrounds, different political affiliations. The BBC did not simply reflect these differences but contained them by becoming a focus for 'the creation and mobilization of a sense of national identity'.[16]

At the same time, however, public service broadcasters also have a responsibility to ensure that programmes are made for minority groups, whether it is a minority through gender, race, class, religion, region, or through taste, age, or preferred interests. Against the background of Scottish distinctiveness and the public service imperative, it was inevitable that the BBC would have to set in place some method of catering for the needs

---

[11] Midwinter et al, *Politics and Public Policy in Scotland*, p.5.

[12] Kellas, *The Scottish Political System*; Midwinter et al, *Politics and Public Policy in Scotland*.

[13] Committee on the Future of Broadcasting, Cmnd 6753, HMSO, 1977.

[14] B.Anderson, *Imagined Communities*, Verso, 1983.

[15] S.Hall, in *All Our Futures: the changing role and purpose of the BBC*, p.32.

[16] C.Lury, in R.Bocock & K.Thompson (eds), *Social and Cultural Forms of Modernity*, Polity Press, 1992, p.392.

of its Scottish audience. The 'National Region' was its response.

When the BBC was formed in the 1920s, all programmes were produced by local stations set up in major towns and cities throughout the country with minimal central control from London. This was due to technological constraints which provided a mere 25-mile reception band around its transmitters. As the technology became more sophisticated and radio sets became more widespread, reception improved and London began to supply programmes which were relayed down landlines to be broadcast on local transmitters. The London centre strengthened its control, specifying how announcers on local stations should sound in a first attempt to impose a recognisable BBC 'brand'. The introduction of simultaneous broadcasting, where two programmes could be broadcast on different frequencies at the same time, also sparked the launch of the Regional Scheme. This divided the United Kingdom up into different areas, based as much upon the location of transmitters as upon particular regional or cultural identities. Certain areas, like Scotland, met both criteria.[17]

Under the Regional Scheme, the local stations were expected to relay both the National Programme, consisting of items mostly produced in London, and the Regional Programme, which was intended to let the characteristics of the local stations shine through. In fact, London-based or produced programmes tended to dominate throughout, a situation which the BBC is still trying to remedy today.[18] This 'national' (United Kingdom-wide) perspective, which the BBC carries through its network programming, embodies the Corporation's role as 'social cement'.[19] All the BBC's regions therefore have a multi-layered task: to cover local issues in-depth for local audiences (which may themselves have wide regional variations and cultural differences) and to provide information on major local stories for network news bulletins or programmes. At the same time, the region has to represent the national community of the United Kingdom to its own territorial area, acting as social cement by creating an imagined link between the metropolitan centre and the local audience.

The tension caused by this dual role is particularly damaging to a national region like BBC Scotland, which is responsible both for bolstering Scottish identity and, at the same time, attempting to represent the wider national community of the United Kingdom to the Scottish people. The two aims seem to be mutually exclusive: achieving one could mean violating the other.

The problems caused by this situation have in recent years become increasingly difficult to resolve. As a result, at a time when other outposts of the BBC, such as English local radio stations, were being urged to latch on to the BBC brand name and use it at every opportunity, Radio Scotland was telling announcers to drop the 'BBC' because it was perceived as linking the station to a London-dominated, metropolitan viewpoint. The concept of 'One BBC', popular in the late 1980s and early 1990s, was rejected by the

[17] W.H.McDowell, *The History of BBC Broadcasting in Scotland, 1923-1983*, Edinburgh University Press, 1992.

[18] J.Osmond, *The Divided Kingdom*, Constable, 1988.

[19] Sir Michael Swann, a former chairman of the BBC, quoted in the *Annan Report*, 1977, p.263.

regions, including Scotland, which felt marginalised and ignored. (Recently, the pendulum has swung back in the other direction, with the regions being told they should reflect their own culture and issues and engage with their audiences as much as possible.)

BBC Scotland has argued consistently for greater autonomy in programme scheduling, particularly with news and current affairs where issues affecting only certain parts of the United Kingdom, such as education in England and Wales, are given prominent coverage while Scottish developments are either ignored or consigned to a two-sentence summary at the end of a longer report. There is also the difficulty of coping with a major story in Scotland which also makes the national news bulletins: how can the Scottish bulletins, which invariably follow the national programmes, be made distinctive when the actuality (audio recording) or picture footage is identical to both?

The BBC has attempted to cater for regional discontent by announcing plans to increase the amount of programmes produced outside London. Around one-third of its network radio and TV programmes should be made outside London by 1998, compared to previous levels of one-fifth. As part of this move, a number of 'centres of excellence' have been set up at regional headquarters throughout the Corporation. Some, like the wildlife programmes centre at Bristol, have been a valued part of the BBC for decades, but there appears little justification for other policy decisions to site the centre for children's programmes in Glasgow or music production at Cardiff. Rather than forcing London-based staff to leave the metropolis, only around 100 people will have to move under the new scheme, as most of the programmes will be produced by independent production companies which are already based outside the capitol. As a way of targeting the BBC's inbuilt London bias, this seems singularly ineffective.

The BBC's policy towards the regions seems to be a curious mix of giving with one hand and taking away with the other. The Corporation does seem to be encouraging regions to produce more programmes which will be given wider coverage: network commissions from BBC Scotland expanded from £29 million in 1995-96 to around £40 million for 1996-97. Yet at the same time, the BBC's restructuring to take account of the digital future of broadcasting[20] seems to continue a process of centralisation which began with the creation of an internal market through Producer Choice. Splitting the production and broadcasting facilities of the BBC into two separate companies is likely to increase centralised control at the expense of the autonomy of the regions.

[20] See *Extending Choice in the Digital Age*, BBC, 1996.

It can be seen that the BBC has faced a difficult task in combining its public service obligations to cater for Scottish distinctiveness with its cultural obligations to maintain and enhance an image of the United Kingdom as a 'nation'. To return to Mitchell's[21] observations on the nature of the United Kingdom state, it is perhaps worth asking whether the BBC combines elements of a unitary approach or whether it resembles the more flexible, union state concept.

The Territorial Divide

It is clearly impossible to apply all the aspects of the unitary/union state debate directly to the BBC, since the issues under discussion - the state and the Corporation - are two very different entities. But I would argue that it is possible to discuss the extent to which the unitary/union state divide mirrors the problems facing the BBC today, when the role of broadcasting is an integral part of the debate over demands for constitutional change in Scotland.

The BBC has made periodic attempts to address these issues before, notably in the 1970s when the growth of nationalism in both Scotland and Wales led to the creation of radio stations aimed specifically at both countries. Now, however, the question must be asked: is the BBC fundamentally out of step with a national region like Scotland?

To use the typography employed before, the BBC fulfils many of the characteristics of an unitary organisation: it has one definite central point, its hierarchical internal organisation encourages uniformity and, while the regions do have some autonomy, they remain in the final instance firmly under the control of the network centre (witness the Panorama debate alluded to at the start of this paper). In its dealings with England and, to a certain extent, Wales, the Corporation is working within a state system which has the same broad underpinnings. When in Scotland, however, the BBC comes up against a union state which has a basically different mode of organisation and it is in this situation, I would argue, that a mismatch may occur.

Attempts to reform the BBC and shift it towards a more flexible, less centralised structure have been shown to be less than successful. Yet the Corporation is facing a challenge which may require it to throw out many of its old ideas and adopt new attitudes and ways of working. The growth of digital broadcasting is predicted to cause a sea change in the broadcasting industry, paving the way for new forms of communication, including pick-and-mix programme schedules where viewers can choose what they want to watch when they want to watch it. Also mooted for the BBC is a 24-hour TV news channel, similar to CNN, which would have among its components a greatly strengthened role for regional news.

Digital broadcasting is potentially a valuable tool to break down the BBC's centralised decision-making structure and transfer more autonomy to the periphery, catering for regional distinctiveness in ever more responsive

[21] Mitchell, 'Untitled'.

ways. But behind the brave new world of broadcasting technology lies the old bugbear of funding and the BBC's recently-agreed licence fee structure contains no significant increases, limiting the chances for change at least into the new millenium. It is interesting to speculate, however, the extent to which any constitutional change introduced after the next election could force the BBC to reconsider its situation, especially if it involved turning licence fee funding collected in Scotland over to BBC Scotland to be used for programme-making.

In conclusion, this paper has highlighted some of the major issues of territorial politics as they relate to Scotland. It has considered the institutions and processes which make Scotland distinctive within the United Kingdom and linked these to the role of the BBC, particularly BBC Scotland. It has concluded that there appears to be a mismatch between aspects of BBC Scotland's role as a 'national region', leaving the organisation virtually unable to fulfil all its goals without significantly damaging some of its aims. BBC broadcasting in Scotland, both radio and television, has been described as 'a buttress of national [Scottish] identity',[22] yet it remains linked to the aims and ideals of the London-dominated Corporation. As Balmer notes: 'The stark reality is that BBC Scotland needs the reputation, influence, resources, and career opportunities provided by the BBC'.[23]

---

[22] Kellas, *The Scottish Political System*, p.207.

[23] J.M.T.Balmer, *The Nature of Corporate Identity: an explanatory study undertaken within BBC Scotland*, PhD thesis, University of Strathclyde, 1996, p.162.

Hegel

Gary Browning
Oxford Brookes University

'Stirner's Egoism and the Ghost of Hegel'

Introduction

Stirner's thought is recognisably Hegelian while constituting a determined assault on the principles of Hegel's system. His thought represents what Toews has styled 'the transformative translation of Hegelian terms.'[1] The radicalism of Stirner's critique of Hegel's standpoint coupled with his creative development of Hegelian notions of alienation, historical and social forms of conflict and the intrinsic freedom of the human ego, provide an ironically unique insight into the bases of Hegelian thought. The irony derives from Stirner's celebration of the unique, flesh and blood individual which he contrasts with Hegel's abstract phantom of Spirit. Stirner is trenchant in his critique of essentialist spiritual conceptions of humanity which he sees as so many forms of alienation restricting the creative powers of the human ego.

Hegel's philosophy conceives of reality as testifying to the unificatory, universal powers of Geist or spirit. A person, for Hegel, is alienated to the extent that he perceives himself to be set apart from the rest of reality be it nature or other men and women. The spiritual capacity to think and act rationally, for Hegel, expresses the generic identity of human beings, and links human beings to one another and the world they inhabit. For Stirner, the concrete individual ego is everything, and concern for what is generically human is a fetter, or what he terms a spook or ghost. Hegel's system is thereby seen as a ghost which needs to be exorcised. Stirner begins *The Ego and its Own* with a pithy statement of his position which pointedly declares its opposition to Hegel's conception of Spirit.

> 'What is not supposed to be my concern! First and foremost the good cause, then God's cause, the cause of mankind, of truth, of freedom, of humanity,of justice; further, the cause of my people, my prince, my fatherland; finally, even the cause of mind (*Geist*) and a thousand other causes. Only my cause is never to be my concern. "Shame on the egoist who thinks only of himself!" '.[2]

Stirner's opposition to Hegel is clear and its forceful expression challenges the reader to reflect upon the relative merits of Stirner's and Hegel's philosophical positions. The trenchancy of Stirner's critique of Hegel, however,

---

[1] J.Toews, 'Transformations of Hegelianism', in F.Beiser (ed), *The Cambridge Companion to Hegel*, Cambridge, 1993, p.405.

[2] M.Stirner, *The Ego and its Own*, Cambridge University Press, 1995, p.5.

should not obscure the extent to which Stirner's work discloses an understanding of Hegel's philosophy. Stirner in subjecting Hegel's philosophy to criticism maintains that Hegel's thought insofar as it privileges ideas and the common attributes of human beings resembles religion in that it derogates from the autonomy and creativity of the unique ego. This critique of Hegel, however, assumes that Hegel's philosophy is not itself a mere reiteration of religion. Stirner does not read Hegel's philosophy as maintaining an independent God as the prime mover in reality and the subject of social and historical development. In an essay of 1842, 'Art and Religion', Stirner makes clear that he does not see Hegel as a religious theorist in this sense by observing:

> 'Who will deny that Philip II of Spain is infinitely more godly than Joseph 11 of Germany, and that Hengstenberg (a Lutheran pietist critic of Hegel and the Young Hegelians) is truly godly, whereas Hegel is quite not.'[3]

The rest of this paper will be concerned to explore, on the one hand, the positive links between Stirner's philosophy and Hegel and Hegelianism, and on the other hand, the polemical critique of Hegel and affiliated Hegelian positions which is presented by Stirner. In so doing, the relevance of Hegel and the Hegelian tradition to an understanding and evaluation of Stirner's thought will be maintained. This recognition of the relevance of the Hegelian tradition to Stirner's thought runs counter to Ferguson's interpretive standpoint. She observes,

> 'While the question of Stirner's relation with Hegel is of some historical interest, the focus on the correct placing of his ideas within this historical tradition is to sidestep an actual confrontation with his arguments.'[4]

Pace Ferguson, Stirner's philosophical standpoint and methodology is intimately bound up with Hegel's and a confrontation with his ideas is promoted by comparing them with Hegel's and other Hegelians.

Stirner's Hegelianism

If Stirner is concerned to exorcise the ghost of Hegel in *The Ego and its Own*, he conducts this exorcism by Hegelian means. Stirner's master work, *The Ego and Its Own* exhibits a number of features which link it to Hegel's philosophy. Its central concern is to establish the absolute primacy of the ego, which is conceived as distinct from any determinate categorisation. While this notion of the ego runs counter to Hegel's conception of the rational and developed self, it is derived nonetheless from Hegel's account of the

[3] M.Stirner, 'Art and Religion', in L.Stepelevich (ed), *The Young Hegelians*, Cambridge University Press, 1983, p.333.

[4] K.Ferguson, 'Saint Max Revisited: A Reconsideration of Max Stirner', *Idealistic Studies*, XII/3, 1982, p.276.

self. Likewise Stirner follows Hegel and other Young Hegelians in highlighting the capacity of human beings to become enmeshed in relationships and conceptions which are forms of alienation. Again, Stirner resembles Hegel in that he sees the supersession of alienation as developing through social and historical development. The authentic ego depicted in *The Ego and Its Own* asserts its radical independence and self- determination by explicitly disowning the social obligations maintained in the principles and practices of the kind of state which Hegel outlines in the *Philosophy of Right.* While Stirner is certainly a critic of Hegel's social and political philosophy, his focus upon the set of institutions and practices with which it deals signals his respect for Hegel.

McLellan has observed that Stirner's brand of individual egoism is far removed from the standpoint of Hegel's system.[5] The distance between Hegel's conception of the self and Stirner's is immense. Stirner urges that the individual ego is unique and that to be authentic a unique ego must recognise itself to be the sole source of value. Hegel's system, in stark contrast, depicts the self to be implicated in the nature of thought, and hence the freedom of the self, for Hegel, involves the self recognising and expressing itself as Spirit, in the patterns of thought which permeate the natural and social worlds. Hegel develops this systematic conception of thought and self, however, on the basis of the self-determination of the individual ego. At the outset of the *Philosophy of Right* he identifies the fundamental aspects of the will as being on the one hand the pure indeterminacy of the ego and on the other the ego's capacity to give itself content.[6] Likewise in the opening section of the *Phenomenology of Spirit*, 'Sense Certainty', Hegel highlights the pure universality of the ego. Hegel's recognition of the absolute negativity of the ego, its resistance to any particular identification bears an affinity with what Ferguson has styled Stirner's process view of the self, according to which the ego cannot be defined in terms of a set of essentialist properties. [7]

Stepelevich in an insightful article, 'Max Stirner as Hegelian' urges that Stirner's Hegelianism should be recognised as being informed by a sure appreciation of Hegel and that it is concerned to develop in particular, Hegel's *Phenomenology of Spirit.*[8] Stepelevich takes Stirner's egoism as representing a self-conscious completion of Hegel's project in the *Phenomenology of Spirit.* Hegel's phenomenological examination of consciousness is completed in the standpoint of absolute knowledge,in which the self of self-conscious knowing recognises itself in the truth which it knows. Stepelevich suggests that the achievement of absolute knowledge thereby releases the ego from the burden of a dialectical journey through modes of thought and action in which it is alienated, permitting enjoyment of the self-determining freedom celebrated in Stirner's egoism.

---

[5]D.McLellan, *The Young Hegelians and Karl Marx*, Macmillan, 1969, p.126.
[6]G.Hegel, *Hegel's Philosophy of Right*, Oxford University Press, 1971, pp.21-22.
[7]K,Ferguson, *op cit*, p.276.
[8]L.S.Stepelevich, *Journal of the History of Ideas*,46, 1985.

Stirner's egoism evidently develops by way of a critical understanding of Hegel's *Phenomenology of Spirit*, but Stirner, notwithstanding Stepelevich's commentary, is firmly opposed to the standpoint of absolute knowledge which ushers in Hegel's system. The phenomenological achievement of the perspective of absolute knowledge, for Hegel, discloses that there is no gap between the knowing mind and its object, truth. The self recognises itself as Spirit to be the universality of thought, hence reconciling human beings to the 'highway of despair' narrated in *The Phenomenology of Spirit*, and allowing them to identify with the reason objectified in nature.[9] From the perspective of absolute knowledge the alienation of consciousness in modes of thought and action where a gap is experienced between mind and its object are transformed on being seen as necessary moments in the achievement of knowledge. For Stirner the ego likewise experiences alienating modes of thought and action, but liberation does not consist in a reconciliatory conceptual standpoint. Nor does Stirner envisage liberation as emerging from the achievement of a Feuerbachian humanism, in which supposedly essential human powers are realised. For Stirner, the ego's very identification with trans-individual notions is to suffer alienation; the unique ego must break with all forms of practical and conceptual dependence.

A crucial section of the *Phenomenology of Spirit*, as Pinkard has observed, is the dialectic of recognition in which selves confront one another in a life and death struggle which issues in the unsatisfactory relationship of lordship and bondage.[10] While selves involved in the dialectic of recognition, for Hegel, misrecognise their underlying unity, the very struggle itself attests to the social dimension of consciousness. To understand oneself, for Hegel, presupposes seeing oneself in relation to others. Stirner likewise sees the self as necessarily pitted in conflict with other selves. At the beginning of the first part of *The Ego and Its Own*, entitled 'A Human Life', Stirner intimates a close philosophical and methodological affiliation with Hegel.

> 'Accordingly, because each thing cares for itself and at the same time comes into constant collision with other things, the combat of self-assertions is unavoidable. Victory or defeat – between the two alternatives the fate of the combat wavers. The victor becomes the lord, the vanquished one the subject: the former exercises supremacy and "rights of supremacy", the latter fulfils in awe and deference the "duties of a subject".'[11]

Stirner, then, from the outset of *The Ego and Its Own* follows Hegel in seeing conflictual social inter-action as intrinsic to development. Furthermore, he also follows Hegel in seeing the achievement of freedom as being an historical development. Like Hegel he reads history teleologically in that the significance of history turns upon the developmental supersession of alienation and the realisation of the authentic ego. Hegel's philosophical understanding of history consists in viewing social and political life as

---

[9] G.Hegel, *The Phenomenology of Mind*, George Allen & Unwin, 1971.
[10] T.Pinkard, *Hegel's Phenomenology*, Cambridge University Press,1984,ch.3.
[11] M.Stirner, *The Ego and Its Own*, p.13.

gradually accommodating man's spiritual freedom, so that a modern state can recognise the freedom of all its members. Stirner in addressing the questions of how an individual ego can establish an authentic existence and of how historical development has prepared the way for the flourishing of egoism, turns to the notion of a man's life to provide a structure for his developmental account of the person and history.

For Stirner the child is captive to his or her sociological context, the youth sets itself against the immediate world of family by developing a world of ideals and principles but these very principles are the conditions which the mature ego must break from if it is to establish an authentic unique existence. Historical development, for Stirner, runs according to the same conceptual scheme. The Ancient world is a time of childhood, where individuals are immersed in their immediate contexts, but this gives way to a period of youth in which men become bewitched by their own thoughts and ideals. This spiritual age embraces the religiosity of the medieval world and the strident humanism of Young Hegelian successors to Hegel such as Bruno Bauer and Feuerbach. In Stirner's image of his contemporary age, man is entering maturity and the age of egoism, in which individuals break free from all the ideals and ghosts of their imagination and concentrate on pursuing their own ends.

In the first part of *The Ego and Its Own* Stirner deals with the aetiology of the alienated ego, but in the second part of the book he develops an account of ownness, a positive analysis of what is involved in authentic egoism. In this account Stirner endeavours to resist enshrining egoism in a set of ideals or principles.He observes, 'Ownness includes in itself everything own, and brings to honour again what Christian language dishonoured. But ownness has not any alien standard either, as it is not in any sense an idea like freedom, morality, humanity and the like: it is only a description of the – owner.'[12]

In explaining what is involved in ownness, Stirner is at pains to distance the authentic egoist from subscription to ideals and absorption in social practices. He is ready to acknowledge an association of egoists, but such an association must be determined by the free choice of egoists. If an egoist decides against continuing an association, then the association is at once at an end. For Stirner, there can be no question of obligation for an egoist. An obligation derogates from the freedom and authenticity of the egoist. In outlining how an egoist owes no allegiance to social practices and moral principles, Stirner clarifies his position by discussing principles and practices which Hegel reviews in his *Philosophy of Right.*

Leopold in his introduction to a recent edition of *The Ego and Its Own* observes how Stirner sees the state as exercising mastery over the individual in a manner evocative of Hegel's account of the master-slave relationship in *The Phenomenology of Spirit.*[13] The entire account of the egoists's rejection of the obligatoriness of moral principles and social practices, however, is to be understood as following and rejecting Hegel's account of the state

[12]M.Stirner, *The Ego and Its Own*, p.154.

[13]D.Leopold, 'Introduction' to M.Stirner, *The Ego and Its Own*, p.xxvi.

as expressing and developing man's universality. Stirner discussion of property, the law, the market, public administration, crime, conscience and the monarchy is a critical commentary upon Hegel's treatment of these practices and principles. Hegel conceives of the rational organisation of these practices and principles as demanding and expressing effective social co-operation and co-ordination. Stirner, in contrast, sees the prescriptiveness and the accumulation of power in these social institutions and practices as wholly unacceptable to a free, egoist. The differences between Stirner and Hegel however, should not obscure the methodological and thematic affinities in their thought. Both theorists see man as progressing through stages of conflict and alienation and both understand freedom in contemporary society as explicable in terms of an individual's orientation to a set of moral principles and social and practices.

Stirner Contra Hegelianism

Stirner's philosophy takes autonomy as its goal and alienation as its defining alter ego. Its critique of historical modes of life and current political and social ideologies resembles Hegel's diagnosis of distorted forms of consciousness which do not recognise the active and constitutive role of consciousness in experience. For Stirner, however, Hegel's critique of modes of consciousness which posit truth as something distinct or alien from consciousness remains implicated in the alienation of the power and autonomy of the ego. For Stirner, Hegel's philosophical understanding of reality whereby the thought of consciousness is taken as pervading reality, detracts from the ego's autonomy in that the assertiveness of the ego is alienated by limiting it to what can be universalised in thought. This commitment to universality is taken by Stirner as tantamount to denying the supremacy of the actual, particular ego. Stirner observes, 'With him (Hegel) reality, the world of things, is altogether to correspond to the thought, and no concept is to be without reality. This caused Hegel's system to be the most objective, as if in it thought and thing celebrated their union, but this was simply the extremist case of violence of thought, its highest pitch of despotism and sole dominion, the triumph of mind, and with it the triumph of philosophy.'[14]

For Stirner Hegel's system subordinates the actual man, the egoist, to the despotism of thought, just as it subjugates the world to a procession of categories. Stirner rejected this in favour of what Brazill has termed, '... an extravagant titanism in which the ego became in effect its own absolute.'[15] Stirner saw all attempts to frame ideals and principles to order and restrain the self-assertiveness of the ego as so many forms of alienation . Stirner thought that Hegel's philosophy, and the theories of his Young Hegelian successors such as the Bauer brothers and Feuerbach, resembled religion in that true freedom in their theories was taken to be adherence to general patterns of thought and conduct. The absolute independence of the individual was denied. For Stirner, just as religion subordinated the ego to

[14]M.Stirner, *The Ego and Its Own*, pp.69-69.

[15]W.J.Brazill, *The Young Hegelians*, Yale University Press, 1970, p.69.

the demands of an alien God, so he saw Hegel's thought as subordinating actual men to ideas and Spirit (Geist). The ego, for Stirner, is to generate its own commitments ; subscription to another's code or to a political scheme which allocates the individual a specific role justified by general criteria fractures the sense of integrity and wholeness of the egoist. Alienation is the inevitable fate of any compromise with the world and others.

In the second part of *The Ego and Its Own* Stirner elaborates his own positive philosophy of ownness by means of a running critique of Hegel's political philosophy. As signalled previously, Stirner discusses and criticises key elements of Hegel's political thought, notably property, rights, contract, morality, and forms of ethical life-the family, civil society and the state. Stirner makes plain his disagreement with Hegel's entire enterprise in *The Philosophy of Right* in completely disavowing the notion of a social basis for 'right'. He observes:

> 'Right is the spirit of society ... All existing right is foreign law; some one makes me out to be in the right, "does right by me". But should I therefore be in the right if all the world made me out so? And yet what else is the right that I obtain in the state,in society, but a right of those foreign to me.'[16]

For Stirner a perspective which sees human beings gaining freedom by assuming ethical obligations in social intercourse is one which abrogates the freedom of the ego. While Hegel sees rights of personality and property as being maintained and confirmed in a social setting underpinned by the authority of the state, Stirner sees the dependence of the individual on a social organisation such as the state as highlighting the alienation involved in these 'rights'. For Stirner, the legal context of property rights undermines the individual who is not free to do what he will with his property. The egoist, for Stirner, will not and should not suffer the state to interfere in the slightest with his property. Mediation of the state between an individual and his property in Stirner's perspective abrogates the autonomy of the egoist.

Stirner's unequivocal refusal to see freedom in the authority of the state leads him to deny the obligatoriness of the law. Whereas Hegel sees crime as a token of the individual's freedom to choose which is secured ultimately by a community's laws, Stirner denies the immorality of crime. For Stirner, the characterisation of an act as criminal is merely a social designation which the egoist need not recognise. The state, for Stirner, acts like a master and its internal organisation which Hegel takes to be of supreme importance, is of no consequence. For Stirner, 'Every state is a despotism, be the despot one or many...'[17] Likewise Stirner puts no faith in Hegel's estimate of the state's capacity to ameliorate the problem of pauperism. The state, for Stirner, is in fact implicated in the prevalence of pauperism, because the operations of the market and unequal property holdings, conditions permitting pauperism, are promoted by the state's maintenance of the social and legal context for

[16] M.Stirner, *The Ego and Its Own*, p.166.
[17] *Ibid*, p.175.

economic transactions. Stirner is equally sceptical of socialist or communist projects for the redistribution of property. Reliance on the state, for Stirner, is the problem rather than the solution.

Against the power and authority of the state Stirner poses the power of the unique individual ego. The authentic egoist for Stirner admits of no binding ties with others. The individual egoist might enter into a union with other egoists but he will not submit to a 'common' will. If he wishes to break with the conditions of union at any point he will do so. Just as Stirner is against the state and its laws, so he is against any kind of social institution which limits or conditions individual conduct. Notably, he opposes the family which Hegel sees as playing an important educative role in preparing individuals for ethical commitments. Stirner perceives the family as constricting the individual. Marriage, for Stirner, in theory and practice is not a binding commitment or a 'love' which transcends individuality; it is a relationship entered into by an individual to promote his or her interests and desires. Likewise, he is against all practices and institutions in relation to which individuals are socialised into accepting binding ethical commitments.

While much of the force of the arguments in *The Ego and Its Own* is directed against Hegel and his philosophy, Stirner also takes issue with rival Young Hegelian theorists. The Young Hegelians aspire to develop Hegel's thought by exposing and superseding the persisting conditions of alienation which they see as continuing to be sustained by Hegel's philosophy. For Stirner, however, Young Hegelians like Bruno Bauer and Ludwig Feuerbach conceive of real human experience in essentialist, universal terms which are just as fanciful and distorting of actual experience as Hegel's idealism. Stirner's break with Hegel is at the same time a separation from contemporaries who retain what he takes to be an untenable Hegelian essentialism.

Toews observes that Stirner sees Bruno Bauer's privileging of the play of critical self-consciousness as illicitly universalist in that it represents '... the final form of the domination of real human existence by culturally produced "objective", "universal" values...'[18] Stirner also plays the transformative method, coined and operated by Feuerbach, against Feuerbach himself. Religion and religious language are seen by Feuerbach as constituting an inverted world whereby the active creative powers of man are transposed onto a God, generally conceived as external and supposedly responsible for human beings. The transformative method is employed by Feuerbach to change matters so that what affects to be subject (including thought in Hegel's philosophy) can be transformed into the object and vice versa. Hence man, the species, is to assume the role of subject, and become self-determining.

For Stirner, however, Feuerbach's invocation of the powers of the species derogates from the powers of actual men and women. He observes, 'Man is something only as my quality like masculinity or femininity'.[19] In 'Stirner's Critics', which Stirner wrote in answer to Feuerbach's criticisms of *The Ego*

[18] J.Toews, *op cit*, p.404.

[19] M.Stirner, *The Ego and Its Own*, p.163.

and Its Own, Stirner provides a powerful critique of Feuerbach's standpoint. 'Because he is this unique Feuerbach, he is also at the same time a male, a human being, a living being,a Frenchman and so forth. But he is also more than all that.'[20]

Just as Stirner criticises Feuerbach for his continuing entanglement in an essentialism whereby the individual is alienated, so he castigates Bruno Bauer for allegedly continuing to play with the ghosts of essentialised man. Like Marx, though from a different perspective, Stirner criticises Bauer's review of the Jewish question. He notes that Bauer wants to do away with the particularism of racial allegiances to establish a formal equality between men. In characterising Bauer's standpoint, Stirner observes, 'Man is man in general, and in so far every one who is a man. Now everyone is to have the eternal rights of man, and, according to the opinion of communism, enjoy them in the complete 'democracy', or, as it ought more correctly to be called- anthropocracy. But it is I alone who have everything that I procure for myself; as man I have nothing'.[21]

Stirner and Hegel

A study of Stirner's critique of Hegel is instructive in a number of ways. It reveals what is assumed and what is criticised explicitly about Hegel by a notable Young Hegelian who is well-versed in Hegel's philosophy. It also discloses the Hegelian roots of Stirner's own philosophy. Hegel is assumed by Stirner to identify human beings, due to their reflective capacities, as the creators of meaning and to envisage their freedom as the point or goal of social and historical development. Hegel is criticised by Stirner for identifying human beings in terms of their general reflective capacities rather than focussing upon the pure individuality of a particular individual.

Stirner understands the identification of individuals in general conceptual terms as a form of the alienation of the free creative powers of the individual, which Stirner sees it as his critical task to expose so as to signal the path of authentic individual freedom. The methodological rationale of Stirner's most famous work, is to explicate the history of alienation and the development of freedom and to criticise the major social institutions and practices of the contemporary world. The course of *The Ego and Its Own*, thereby exhibits an affinity with Hegel's philosophy in that Hegel is concerned to trace the story of the historical emergence and development of human freedom, amidst discordance and forms of alienation.

Analysis of Stirner's critique of Hegel, and other Young Hegelians, also raises important questions about the nature of freedom and the evaluation of social and political practice. Stirner's critique of each and every ethical and social obligation as symptomatic of alienation insofar as it not reducible to the absolute choice of a particular individual challenges the communitarian standpoint of Hegel and many subsequent social theorists. Hegel's identification of freedom with the individual's subscription to the principles and

[20] M.Stirner, 'Stirner's Critics', in *Philosophical Forum*, 8, p.78.

[21] M.Stirner, *The Ego and Its Own*, p.162.

practices of a rationalised version of the modern state appears vulnerable to Stirner's critical onslaught.

Stirner's process view of the self, which informs Hegel's own understanding of subjectivity, captures its resistance to exhaustive categorisation in terms of social roles. A self is always something more than its particular activities; it is itself a source of creativity. This creative dimension of the self does not fit neatly with features of the rational state Hegel outlines. A patriarchal family is despotic towards women and children, a non-democratic state undermines self-determination and the ubiquitous role assigned the civil service in clearing up the loose ends of market transactions derogates from the creative powers of ordinary individuals.

Critics from Marx onwards, however, are surely right in observing that Stirner does not allow sufficiently for the sociality of human beings. While Stirner undoubtedly undermined the contemporary credibility of Feuerbach's humanism by his astringent critique of its essentialism, Feuerbach's retaliatory strike on Stirner, 'The Essence of Christianity in relation to *The Ego and Its Own*' does contain some telling criticisms of Stirner's work. Feuerbach signals the unsustainability of Stirner's radical individualism in observing, 'I am dependent on Thou. No Thou – no I.'[22]

Stirner's egoism represents a reductio ad absurdam version of radical individualism. An individual's subscription to a set of particular social practices and principles is an appropriate object of criticism, but social commitments are not reducible to those acceptable to changing perceptions of individual interest. If individuals, universally, appraised their commitments to practices and principles according to estimates of their own changing interests, there would be no effective basis for social co-operation in practices. In turn, the conditions for the cultivation of individuality would be undermined. The dialectic of recognition observed in Hegel's *Phenomenology of Spirit* is designed to clarify the inter-subjective character of individual agency. The relationship of mastery and slavery, which Stirner invokes as testifying to the necessarily conflictual element in a social world composed of self-assertive egos is shown by Hegel to be fatally flawed. It is shown to be flawed by Hegel because it neither exemplifies nor generates a sufficiently inter-subjective perspective. The slave is merely at the mercy of another's desires, whereas the master is not recognised and respected as a free agent; his power is merely obeyed. The freedom of an individual is not a question of physical power or individual skill; it is a social condition in which individuals develop their freedom in reciprocal recognition of one another's qualities.[23]

---

[22] L.Feuerbach, 'The Essence of Christianity in relation to *The Ego and Its Own*', in *Philosophical Forum*, *op cit*, p.88.

[23] G.Hegel, *The Phenomenology of Mind*, pp.228-240.

Hegel

Robert Bruce Ware
Keble College, Oxford

'Description and Prescription in Hegel's Approach to Plato'

Acknowledgements

The author is grateful for the thoughtful criticism of Gary Browning and John Torrance.

Introduction

Many of those who have contributed to Hegel's rehabilitation have followed Taylor's influential treatment by emphasizing Hegel's debt to Aristotle.[1] Yet especially in the wake of Inwood's study, other commentators have sought to balance this interpretation by exploring Hegel's relationship to Plato.[2] Both the importance and the complexity of this project follow from Hegel's choice of Plato's *Republic* as a key illustration for his own metaphilosophy. His dramatic depiction of Plato's masterpiece against the backdrop of the ageing Aegean culture serves as a pivotal reference for the role that philosophy plays in the process of historical transformation. The exegesis of Hegel's relationship to Plato has therefore focused upon metaphilosophical issues. Hegel has been charged with neglecting the novelty and aesthetic lustre of Plato's political thought in favour of his own metaphysical and metaphilosophical agenda. And whether or not that agenda was politically retrogressive, most scholars have viewed it as metaphilosophically retrospective.[3] Hegel is said to have recognized only the descriptive role of philosophy, while denying its prescriptive competence. According to Inwood, for example, Hegel was '(u)nable to resist the temptation to regard Plato as describing Greek society rather than recommending its reform ... '[4] In his view, 'The main reason for Hegel's failure to criticize Plato's state

[1] See L.Dickey, *Hegel*, Cambridge University Press, 1987; Z.Pelczynski (ed), 'Introduction', *The State and Civil Society*, Cambridge University Press, 1984.

[2] See M.Inwood, *Hegel*, Routledge, 1983; S.Rosen, *G.W.F.Hegel*, Yale University Press, 1974; M.Rosen, *Hegel's Dialectic and its Criticism*, Cambridge University Press, 1982.

[3] See S.Avineri, *Hegel's Theory of the Modern State*, Cambridge University Press, 1972, pp.99, 234-8; R.Berki, 'Perspectives in the Marxian critique of Hegel's political philosophy', in Z.A.Pelczynski (ed), *Hegel's Political Philosophy: problems and perspectives*, Cambridge University Press, 1971, p.200; J.N.Findlay, *Hegel: A Re-examination*, Oxford University Press, 1958, p.345; G.Heiman, 'The source and significance of Hegel's corporate doctrine', in Pelczynski, pp.111-2; S.Smith, *Hegel's Critique of Liberalism: Rights in Context*, University of Chicago Press, 1991, pp.222-3; D.P.Verne 'Hegel's account of war', in Pelczynski, p.170.

[4] M.Inwood, 'Hegel, Plato and Greek " Sittlichkeit" ', in Z.Pelszynski (ed), *The State and Civil Society*, p.54.

effectively was perhaps his reluctance to concede that Plato was an innovator, proposing an ideal which was not put into practice.'[5] Going somewhat further Browning argues

> 'that the Hegelian system's assimilation of distinctive theoretical perspectives is only achieved by distorting them to trace patterns determined by the logic of its own organizing principles. Plato's philosophy, in form and content, however, can only be construed as lacking freshness by abstracting from its innovative, paradoxical radicalism so that it subscribes to a preconceived vision of political philosophy as necessarily backward looking and descriptive. The externality of this Hegelian vision of Plato casts doubt on a prevalent, current reading of Hegel in which he is interpreted as framing an "open" system, the dialectical patterns of which are seen as arising out of internal linkages between concepts and areas of experience rather than being dictated by a preconceived schematic model.'[6]

Contending that Hegel's interpretation of Plato provides a critical test for the validity of his philosophical system,[7] Browning views Hegel as a failure. However, I will argue that recent efforts to understand Hegel's relationship to Plato have been hindered by their failure to understand Hegel's metaphilosophy, to recognize the active role that it allows to philosophy, and to appreciate its transcendence of the traditional opposition of description and prescription.[8] This discussion begins with an examination of Hegel's metaphilosophy before turning to its illustration in his interpretation of Plato. It argues that Hegel is prepared to assign Plato a more significant role, both in subsequent historical development, and in the development of his own system, than the secondary literature has often allowed.

ii

Philosophy, for Hegel, is the wisdom of historical maturity. Only that which is fully developed can be comprehended philosophically, and only when an epoch comes to a close does it finally produce a thinker to translate the essence of its actual life into the language of ideas. Hence, as Hegel explains in a well-known passage, a philosophy is necessarily a product of its age.

> 'Whatever happens, every individual is a child of his time; so philosophy too is its own time apprehended in thoughts. It is just as absurd to fancy that a philosophy can transcend its contemporary world as it is to fancy that an individual can overleap his own age, jump over Rhodes. If his theory really goes

[5] M.Inwood, 'Hegel, Plato and Greek " Sittlichkeit" ', p.54.

[6] G.Browning, 'Hegel,s Plato: The Owl of Minerva and a Fading Political Tradition', *Political Studies*, 36, 1988, pp.484-5.

[7] G.Browning, 'Hegel's Plato: The Owl of Minerva and a Fading Political Tradition', pp.476-7.

[8] See R.Ware, '*Sittlichkeit* and Self-consciousness', Proceedings of the Annual Meeting of the American Political Science Association, 1995.

> beyond the world as it is and builds an ideal one as it ought to be, that world exists indeed, but only in his opinions, an unsubstantial element where anything you please may, in fancy, be built.'[9]

Hegel's ostensibly open acknowledgement of his own philosophical limitations reflects his views on the historicity of reason.[10] According to Hegel, the philosopher's rational faculty is a reflection of a deeper ontological reason which differs significantly from the common sense conception of the term. In contrast to ordinary notions of rationality, Hegelian reason necessarily expresses itself throughout the development of the world. It cannot be derived *a priori* but must evolve through time. The movement of reason can be traced retrospectively through reflection on the course of human history, but there can be no fully accurate prediction of its future.

As a consequence, the insight of any philosopher is restricted to an evaluation of his own historical epoch within the context of its antecedents, and despite the traditional aspirations of utopian thinkers, philosophy cannot provide a precise blue-print for future development. Instead, the proper task of the philosopher is to provide his generation with an adequate comprehension of itself as the product of its past.

Many commentators have examined what they have thought to be the conservative implications of this view, and have interpreted Hegel to mean that philosophy can play no part in reforming the world.

This interpretation can be traced as least as far back as 1857 to Haym's influential claims that Hegel had reduced philosophy to 'the scientific dwelling of the spirit of Prussian restoration'[11] providing 'the absolute formula' for 'political conservatism, quietism and optimism'.[12] Haym's interpretation set the tone for more than a century, and has been echoed by commentators such as Avineri, Findlay and Taylor.[13] On their view, Hegel required that philosophy must acquiesce in existing arrangements and content itself with pointing out that rationality which has already been realized in things as they stand. Inwood, for example, interprets Hegel as requiring philosophy to forsake prescription in favour of a placidly descriptive role.

> 'Philosophers *qua* philosophers should not attempt to change, or to prescribe changes in their own society, because they arrive on the scene too late. Philosophy, for example, plays no essential part in the reconciliation of the individual with his society. This has occurred independently of the emergence of philosophy, so that the most it can do is to describe, at some level or other, the achievement of such a reconciliation by the activities of non-philosophical men.'[14]

---

[9] G.W.F.Hegel, *Philosophy of Right*, Oxford University Press, 1977, pp.12-13.
[10] See Avineri, *Hegel's Theory of the Modern State*, pp.127-8.
[11] R.Haym, *Vorlesung uber Hegel und seine Zeit*, Berlin, Rudolph Gaertner, 1857, p.359.
[12] R.Haym, *Vorlesung uber Hegel und seine Zeit*, p.365.
[13] C.Taylor, *Hegel*, Cambridge University Press, 1975.
[14] Inwood, *Hegel*, p.108.

Yet this interpretation is at odds with recent readings of Hegel's metaphilosophy.[15] It is also inconsistent with important passages in Hegel's preface to the *Philosophy of Right* (PR), as well as in his Lectures on the Philosophy of History (PH) and his *Lectures on the History of Philosophy* (HP). In the introduction to HP, Hegel reiterates that the content of any philosophy is drawn from the preceding historical epoch, and that each philosophy is consequently a product of its time. Yet at the same time, each philosophy provides the critical transition that produces the new form of spiritual development characterizing the subsequent age. By grasping the essence of the preceding epoch, such a philosophy has already differentiated itself from that epoch. Thus while it draws its content from the preceding age, Hegel remarks that it already stands above that epoch in form.

> 'But if Philosophy does not stand above its time in content, it does so in form, because as the thought and knowledge of that which is the substantial spirit of its time, it makes that spirit its object ... Through knowledge, Spirit makes manifest a distinction between knowledge and that which is; this knowledge is thus what produces a new form of development. The new forms at first are only special modes of knowledge, and it is thus that a new Philosophy is produced: yet since it already is a wider kind of spirit, it is the inward birth-place of the spirit which will later arrive at actual form.'[16]

In its self-conscious comprehension of the preceding epoch, a philosophy is thus the inward act of conception that produces the new form of development. This new development begins as a form of philosophical knowledge that arrives subsequently at a realized content. Initial support for this interpretation may be drawn unexpectedly from the language of a passage at the close of the preface to the PR which is often taken to support the conservative reading of Hegel's metaphilosophy

> 'One word about giving instructions as to what the world ought to be. Philosophy, in any case, always comes on the scene too late to give it. As the thought of the world, it appears only when actuality is already there cut and dried after its process of formation has been completed. The teaching of the concept, which is also history's inescapable lesson, is that it is only when actuality is mature that the ideal first appears over against the real and that the ideal apprehends this same real world in its substance and builds it up for itself into the shape of an intellectual realm. When philosophy paints its grey in grey, then has

[15]See H.Broad, *Hegel's Philosophy of Politics*,Westview Press, 1992; S.Houlgate, *Freedom, Truth and History*, Routledge, 1991; J.Ritter, *Hegel and the French Revolution*, MIT Press, 1982; M.Tunick, *Hegel's Political Philosophy*, Princeton University Press, 1982; A.Wood, *Hegel's Ethical Thought*, Cambridge University Press, 1990.

[16]G.W.F.Hegel, *Lectures on the History of Philosophy*, translated by Haldane & Simson, The Humanities Press, 1974, 1, pp.54-5.

> a shape of life grown old. By philosophy's grey in grey it cannot be rejuvenated, but only understood. The owl of Minerva spreads its wings only with the falling of the dusk.'[17]

Hegel's choice of *Dámmerung*, which means both 'dusk' and 'daybreak', underscores his conception of philosophical self-consciousness, not as a static condition so much as a dialectical process. For as nothing can be philosophically comprehended without being fully developed, so it cannot be fully comprehended without being thereby transcended. Thus, Hegel's conclusion that philosophy cannot rejuvenate an old world does not deny its ability to initiate a new one. Nostalgia for Hellas will not bring back the polis, but a philosophical comprehension of the polis can contribute to the development of subsequent political forms. For while the owl of Minerva spreads its wings with the falling of the dusk, it must alight again at dawn, and those great leaps between each historical era are just as surely initiated through this reflective flight of the intellect. Again, at the end of PR, Hegel remarks that

> 'The history of mind (*Geist*) is its own act. Mind is only what it does, and its act is to make itself the object of its own consciousness. In history its act is to gain consciousness of itself as mind, to apprehend itself in its interpretation of itself to itself. This apprehension is its being and its principle, and the completion of apprehension at one stage is *at the same time the rejection of that stage and its transition to a higher stage.* To use abstract phraseology, the mind apprehending this apprehension anew, or in other words, returning to itself again out of its rejection of this lower stage of apprehension, is the mind of the stage higher than that on which it stood in its earlier apprehension.'[18]

The transition to the higher form of ethical life begins when the existing set of institutions, conventions and laws finds a philosophical description which succeeds in revealing its inherent limitations, thereby elevating them to the consciousness of social actors who subsequently may seek to transcend those limitations through the transformation of the society. Hegel regards this transformation as implicit within those universal principles of rational thought in relation to which the existing order comes to appear as limited and particular.

> 'The transition from one phase of the spirit to another can only take place insofar as an earlier universal is overcome (*aufgehoben*) and recognized in its particularity through the activity of thought. The higher universal which supersedes it is, so to speak, the next variety of the previous species, and is already inwardly present within it, although it has not yet come into its

[17] G.W.F.Hegel, *Philosophy of Right*, pp.12-13.
[18] G.W.F.Hegel, *Philosophy of Right*, #343, emphasis added.

own; and it is this which makes the present reality unstable and fragmentary.'[19]

Because philosophical self-consciousness is the product of limitations in an existing mode of life it cannot erase those difficulties and rejuvenate a dying culture, but it can, and necessarily does, lead to the birth of a new form. Since this self-consciousness initiates the movement from one stage of development to the next, the comprehension of the ageing epoch is an important part in the transition to that which follows. The theoretical project of bringing these problems to the surface, is the first step in the practical process of resolving and transcending them. Thus the traditional dichotomy of description and prescription is inapplicable to Hegel's metaphilosophy. Because of the reciprocal interconnection between historical transformation and self-consciousness[20] practical prescription begins when philosophical description draws attention, albeit inadvertently, to limitations inherent in the existing order. Philosophy's active role in heralding this transformation is emphasized by Hegel in his *Lectures on the Philosophy of World History.*

> 'In its active operations, the national spirit at first knows only the ends of its determinate reality, but not its own nature. But it is nevertheless endowed with an impulse to formulate its thoughts. Its supreme activity is thought, so that when it reaches the height of its powers, its aim is to comprehend itself. The ultimate aim of the spirit is to know itself, and to comprehend itself not merely intuitively but also in terms of thought. It must and will succeed in its task; but this very success is also its downfall, and this in turn heralds the emergence of a new phase and a new spirit.'[21]

Self-consciousness with regard to one stage begins the transition to the next. Knowledge plays an important role in this process since it is the source from which a higher form emerges, while the preceding spiritual content is both preserved and transformed within it. This point is made with greater force a few pages later when Hegel describes the dialectical development of spirit.'

> 'Its movement and progression do not repeat themselves, for the changing aspect of the spirit as it passes through endlessly varying forms is essentially progress. This progress is evident even when the national spirit destroys itself by the negativity of its thought, because its knowledge, its thinking apprehension of being is the source and matrix from which a new form and indeed

[19] G.W.F.Hegel, *Lectures on the Philosophy of World History: Introduction*, Cambridge University Press, 1975, pp.81-2, emphasis added.

[20] See Ware, '*Sittlichkeit* and Self- consciousness', Hegel's Metaphilosophy and Historical Metamorphosis', *History of Political Thought*, 17/2, 1996; *Consciousness and Contradiction: Subjective Freedom and Cultural Fragmentation in Hegel's Philosophy*, DPhil Thesis, Oxford University, 1994.

[21] Hegel, *Lectures on the Philosophy of World History: Introduction*, p.56.

> a higher form, whose figure both conserves and transfigures it – emerges.'[22]

Thus, while the achievement of philosophical self-consciousness cannot rejuvenate the old actuality, it can do much to anticipate and inspire its successor. For insofar as he grasps the spirit of his age, a philosopher also reveals the limitations that are the cause, at once of its decline and of its transition to the next; and insofar as it grasps these inherent limitations, a philosophy may serve as much to motivate as to indicate the general direction of subsequent development which occurs in response to these limitations. It is these problems with which the subsequent vision must grapple, and the philosophical view resulting from the contradictions of the earlier epoch will tend to retain its prominence for as long as it takes this new view to form. As the candidate world-view begins to take shape, its recognition will depend on its capacity to encompass and propose solutions to this same set of problems. Yet the full articulation of this subsequent vision is the work of the age which follows; it is not a task of philosophy. Because philosophy draws its content only from the preceding age it can do no more than provide an indication as to the general direction of this development, and a utopian philosophy is therefore a contradiction in terms: to the extent it is utopian it is not philosophy but fiction.

iii

According to Hegel, Plato's *Republic* captured the essence of the Greek polis and raised to an ideal level the institutions and manners that characterized actual Greek life. Though the *Republic* was not modelled after any single city, and while it criticized most existing city-states, it nevertheless represented a distillation of the basic ideals of the polis. Hegel remarks that 'even Plato's *Republic* which passes proverbially as an empty ideal is in essence nothing but an interpretation of the nature of Greek ethical life'.[23] This ideal encapsulation of the polis was, however, a mark of its decline since Plato could not have achieved his insight until this form of life had run its course. And in accord with Hegel's metaphilosophy, the epilogue of the preceding epoch is a prologue for that which follows. Thus in finally comprehending the essence of the polis, Plato was already standing outside it. Hegel's words bear close attention for they are indicative of his view that Plato comprehended the underlying contradictions of his age: 'Plato was conscious that there was breaking into his own life in that time a deeper principle which could appear in it directly only as a longing still unsatisfied, and so only as something corrupting.'[24]

This was the principle of subjective freedom which would be developed throughout the Christian era.[25] The immanent world revolution would

[22] Hegel, *Lectures on the Philosophy of World History: Introduction*, p.61.
[23] Hegel, *The Philosophy of Right*, p.10.
[24] Hegel, *The Philosophy of Right*, p.10.
[25] Hegel, *Lectures on the History of Philosophy*, 2, p.114.

require a change in human self-conception springing from Christian revelation and centring on the Christian doctrine of conscience. According to this doctrine moral worth would depend not simply on compliance with the law (since that would be merely Pharisaical) but on the conscientious acceptance of the law, along with the ensuing demand that the law must be a fulfilment of self-conscious conviction. From this point on, the law would no longer have the immediate objectivity (and timeless authority) which it enjoyed in the polis, but would instead be mediated through the subjective will. In this respect Hegel understands Plato's political philosophy as heralding the birth of a new age characterized by 'the subjective self-will of individuals, morals; individuals do not act out of respect, reverence for the state, the fatherland, but from their own conviction, according to a moral reflection they grasp a decision from themselves and determine themselves in accordance with it – the modern principle of subjective freedom'.[26]

This subjective longing was first expressed in the teachings of the Sophists and Socrates, and it is underscored in the *Republic* insofar as Plato strives to suppress it. Through his efforts to shore up the traditional life of the polis against the new subjectivism, Plato focused upon its inherent contradiction: the unreflective parochialism of the city-state was incapable of incorporating the universalism of the rational self-consciousness to which it gave rise. Thus it was also in the polis that cognitive and collective expressions of universality were first differentiated from one another. Hegel trades upon this distinction in his discussion of substantive and subjective forms of freedom.

> 'Firstly, there is the universal substance of the state, the ... independent spirit of the nation; and secondly, there is individuality as such, the realm of subjective freedom. The question is whether the real life of individuals is one of unreflecting habit and custom in relation to the basic unity, or whether these individuals are reflecting personalities and subjects who exist for themselves. In this connection, we must distinguish between *substantial* freedom and subjective freedom ... Where there is merely substantial freedom, commandments and laws are regarded as firmly established in and for themselves, and the individual subject adopts an attitude of complete subservience towards them. Besides, these laws need not accord with the will of the individual, and the subjects are therefore like children, who obey their parents without will or insight of their own. But as subjective freedom arises and man descends from the realm of external reality into his own spirit, reflection creates an antithesis which contains the negation of reality.'[27]

With the discovery of subjective freedom and the decline of the polis these two poles fell apart, and Hegel understands world history as the painful and labourious process of their gradual reconciliation within a new and higher

[26] Hegel, *Lectures on the History of Philosophy*, 2, p.98.

[27] Hegel, *Lectures on the Philosophy of World History: Introduction, pp.197-8.*

level universality that integrates subjective freedom within the organic unity of the state.[28] Beyond the limited effort of Socrates, Plato was the first to recognize that the difficulty lay in the rise of this subjectivism and its reconciliation with the traditional objective order. By means of its focus on this fundamental difficulty, Plato's philosophy thus provides an implicit indication of the cultural development that would occur subsequently in response to the problem. In Hegel's words

> 'This movement of the individual, this principle of subjective freedom, is sometimes ignored by Plato, and sometimes even intentionally disparaged, because it proved itself to be what had wrought the ruin of Greece; and he considers only how the state may best be organized, and not subjective individuality. In passing beyond the principle of Greek morality, which in its substantial liberty cannot brook the rise of subjective liberty, *the Platonic philosophy at once grasps the above principle, and in so doing proceeds still farther.*'[29]

Hegel remarks that Plato might have resolved the contradiction of the polis if he had been able to incorporate subjective freedom in a new vision of Greek life: 'To combat, he needs must have sought aid from that very longing itself.' But this would be the work of the next two millennia, and would encompass Hegel's own philosophy. In Hegel's view, Plato's philosophy successfully identified key limitations in the society of his day, an achievement of self-consciousness that was the first step in a long process of political transformation occurring in response to those limitations. The entire scope of this project was thus beyond Plato; yet Plato's analysis pointed to the significance of this new principle.

> 'But this aid had to come from on high and all that Plato could do was to seek it in the first place in a particular external form of that same Greek ethical life ... *still his genius is proved by the fact that the principle on which the distinctive character of his state turns is precisely the pivot on which the impending world revolution turned at that time.*'[30]

The significance of this is seen in the influence that Platonism had in shaping Christian doctrine, and the lingering role that it played in the development of the Christian world for the next 1500 years. Hegel understands Plato to have grasped the essence of his age in such as way as to underscore its limitations, and thereby to have provided the first vague anticipation of the age that would follow. This, in turn, has much to say about Hegel's own political philosophy and the significance of subjective freedom within it.

---

[28] Hegel, *Lectures on the Philosophy of World History: Introduction, p.198.*

[29] Hegel, *Lectures on the History of Philosophy*, 2, p.109, emphasis added.

[30] Hegel, *The Philosophy of Right*, p.10.

iv

According to received views the decline of Greek society left Plato with two alternatives. Either he could recognize that the city-state belonged to the past, join with the disruptive forces and piece together a new society from the elements which had contributed to the destruction of the old; or else he could use all of his powers to uphold the city-state. Browning and Inwood attribute the former objective to Plato and rebuke Hegel for attributing the latter. On either of these views, however, Plato appears as a failure, for either he sought refuge in an impotent ideal or he railed against the tide.

Yet the preceding interpretation of Hegel's metaphilosophy suggests that this choice was not actually available to Plato. Plato could not have revived the city-state because its time was past. But on the other hand, he could not hope to piece together the framework for a new society since, at least in its content, every philosophy is a child of its time. No philosopher can provide a detailed blue print of the future. In Hegel's view, however, Plato's accomplishment was a synthesis of these apparent alternatives. Far from resurrecting the city-state, Plato could aspire to nothing more than a comprehension of the polis as the embodiment of Greek culture and thought. Nevertheless, the full achievement of this philosophical comprehension, would inevitably focus upon the limitations of Hellenic culture and would thereby provide an implicit indication of the direction that subsequent cultural development would take in response to those problems. Viewed in this light, Plato's work becomes a brilliant success, for, at least according to Hegel, this is precisely what he accomplished.

Plato came to understand the traditional culture of Greece well enough to realize that it was incapable of incorporating the new spirit of subjectivism. It had long relied upon an unreflective allegiance to an established order, which had been accepted as the embodiment of divine, or universal, wisdom, and was, as a consequence, deeply vulnerable to any dichotomy capable of establishing a rift between the notions of a universal truth, on the one hand, and a divergent subjective perception on the other.[31] The Greek spiritual crisis thus turned on the opposition of the subjective to the universal – as that separation originated within, and developed out of, Eleatic philosophy – and Plato could not have comprehended either that culture or its crisis without bringing this opposition to a head.[32] In grasping the essence of the Greek polis, as he did particularly in his *Republic* , Plato singled out the principle of subjective freedom as representing a challenge which the traditional order could not hope to meet and which was therefore developing itself only through the deterioration of that order. Yet, it must be emphasized that Hegel develops this point only after stressing the role of philosophy in criticising existing political arrangements.

> 'This insight can be reached through philosophy alone. Revolutions take place in a state without the slightest violence when the insight becomes universal ... Thus the main thought which

[31] Which is the nature of the Eleatic dichotomy.

[32] Ware, *Consciousness and Contradiction*, chapter 3.

> forms the groundwork of Plato's *Republic* is the same which is to be regarded as the principle of the common Greek morality, namely, that established morality has in general the relation of the substantial, and therefore is maintained as divine. This is without question the fundamental determination. The determination which stands in contrast to this substantial relation of the individual to established morality, is the subjective will of the individual, reflective morality. This exists when individuals, instead of being moved to action by respect and reverence for the institutions of the state and of the fatherland, from their own convictions, and after moral deliberation, come of themselves to a decision, and determine their actions accordingly. This principle of subjective freedom is a later growth, it is the principle of our modern days of culture; it however, entered also into the Greek world, but as the principle of the destruction of the Greek ethical life ... Plato recognized and caught up the true spirit of his times, and brought it forward in a more definite way, in that he desired to make this new principle an impossibility in his *Republic* .'[33]

Through the severity of his attempt to restrict subjective freedom, Plato illuminated that principle as the challenge which fatally exceeded the capacity of the established order, and hence as the limitation which was implicit within it from the start. Beyond the limited effort of Socrates, Plato was the first to recognize that the difficulty lay in the rise of this subjectivism and in its reconciliation with substantive universality – conceived either culturally, politically or epistemologically. By means of his comprehension of this fundamental difficulty Plato's philosophy provides an implicit indication as to the direction that the world would take in subsequently coming to terms with this problem. In his HP Hegel remarks that

> 'this movement of the individual, this principle of subjective freedom, is sometimes ignored by Plato, and sometimes even intentionally disparaged, because it proved itself to be what had wrought the ruin of Greece; and he considers only how the state may best be organized, and not subjective individuality. In passing beyond the principle of Greek morality, which in its substantial liberty cannot brook the rise of subjective liberty, *the Platonic philosophy at once grasps the above principle, and in so doing proceeds still farther.*'[34]

Consequently, in the form and content of Plato's work, Hegel is able to locate certain basic information about the nature of subjectivity which would be fully revealed only later. Private property, for example, was forbidden to Plato's ruling class. Hegel links this abolition of property to Plato's restriction of subjective freedom, thereby deriving an important insight as

[33] Hegel, *Lectures on the History of Philosophy*, 2, p.98-9.
[34] Hegel, *Lectures on the History of Philosophy*, 2, pp.109.

to the nature of this connection, a connection which would subsequently rise to a new prominence, both in the development of social thought and in the formulation of Hegel's own political philosophy. It is through his possessions that an individual is able to express and realize himself,[35] and because he was trying to restrict subjectivism, this is precisely the difficulty which property presented for Plato. 'Personal property,' says Hegel, 'is a possession which belongs to me as a certain person, and in which my person as such comes into existence, into reality; on this ground Plato excludes it.'[36] By criticizing property, family and personal relations, Plato exposed the substantive limitations of the polis and foreshadowed the significance of each of these spheres for subsequent historical developments occurring in response to the rise of subjective freedom.

> 'In his *Republic* , Plato displays the substance of ethical life in its ideal beauty and truth; but he could only cope with the principle of self-subsistent particularity, which in his day had forced its way into ethical life by setting up in opposition to it his purely substantial state. He absolutely excluded it from his state, even in its very beginnings in private property and the family, as well as in its more mature form as the subjective will, the choice of a social position and so forth.'[37]

Because 'the family is nothing but an extended personality',[38] Plato places restrictions on it that are similar to those on property: 'According to the conception of subjective freedom, however, the family is just as necessary, yea, sacred to the individual, as property.'[39] Inwood finds it 'odd that Hegel should interpret this as a measure devised to stabilize Greek *Sittlichkeit*, since elsewhere he regards the family as one of the pillars of ethical life'.[40] Yet Inwood seems to overlook the fact that PR provides a role for the family only within the context of a modern state which incorporates subjective freedom. Thus the fact that Plato's efforts to restrict subjective freedom led to the abolition of the family serves to illustrate Hegel's metaphilosophy insofar as the family subsequently could be understood by Hegel as a feature of the modern state.

But it is above all in Plato's effort to restrict subjectivism through social stratification that Hegel finds the significance of freedom in modern society: 'It specially harmonises with this particular quality of excluding the principle of subjectivity that Plato in the first place does not allow individuals to choose their own class; this we demand as necessary to freedom'.[41]

---

[35]Inwood, 'Hegel, Plato and Greek "Sittlichkiet" ', p.51.

[36]Hegel, *Lectures on the History of Philosophy*, 2, p.111. Furthermore, Hegel adds that 'Plato in a like manner altogether abolished in his state the principle of private property. For in it individuality, the individual consciousness becomes absolute.' (Hegel, *The Philosophy of Right*, p.110).

[37]Hegel, *The Philosophy of Right*, p.124.

[38]Hegel, *Lectures on the History of Philosophy*, 2, p.111.

[39]Hegel, *Lectures on the History of Philosophy*, 2, p.112.

[40]Inwood, 'Hegel, Plato and Greek "Sittlichkeit" ', p.52.

[41]Hegel, *Lectures on the History of Philosophy*, 2, p.109.

Thus his insistence that Plato's *Republic* is more than utopian does not mean that Hegel has overlooked its inherent radicalism. In his sequel to the citation above, Hegel regards Plato's exclusion of subjective freedom as rendering his *Republic* more than an empty ideal because it foreshadows real spiritual and philosophic development.

> 'It is this defect which is responsible both for the misunderstanding of the deep and substantial truth of Plato's state and also for the usual view of it as a dream of abstract thinking, as what is often called a mere ideal'. The principle of the self-subsistent inherently infinite personality of the individual, the principle of subjective freedom, is denied its right in the purely substantial form which Plato gave to mind in its actuality. This principle dawned in an inward form in the Christian religion and in an external form (and therefore in one linked with abstract universality) in the Roman world. It is historically subsequent to the Greek world, and the philosophic reflection which descends to its depth is likewise subsequent to the substantial Idea of Greek philosophy.'[42]

Yet while Hegel regards subjective freedom as a hidden centerpiece for Platonic philosophy it cannot at this stage be anything more than implicit. As the philosophical distillation of its own epoch, Platonic philosophy could not have hoped fully to expound the principle of subjective freedom. In accord with Hegel's metaphilosophy it could do no more than illuminate that principle as the inherent conundrum of the age. Yet, in doing so, it offered an implicit indication as to the direction of future development which would occur in response to this dilemma, and which would gradually provide for its resolution. A thorough evaluation of that development could not be provided until it had actually occurred, and hence, Platonic philosophy could have provided no more than a vague anticipation of its course. According to Hegel, the substantial freedom of the Hegelian state could not have been realized in Plato's *Republic* because it could not be realized in the polis.

> 'The development of particularity to self-subsistence is the moment which appeared in the ancient world as an invasion of ethical corruption and as the ultimate cause of that world's downfall. Some of these ancient states were built on the patriarchal and religious principle, others on the principle of an ethical order which was more explicitly intellectual, though still comparatively simple; in either case they rested on primitive unsophisticated intuition. Hence they could not withstand the disruption of this state of mind when self-consciousness was infinitely reflected into itself; when this reflection began to emerge, they succumbed to it, first in spirit and then in substance, because the simple principle underlying them lacked the truly infinite power to be found only in that unity which allows both

[42] Hegel, *The Philosophy of Right*, p.124.

> sides of the antithesis of reason to develop themselves separately in all their strength and which has so overcome the antithesis that it maintains itself in it and integrates it in itself.'[43]

Within the Greek world half of this relationship was actualized in abstraction from the other. The state encompassed and determined its individual citizens, but the limitations and particularity of the state were not in turn the focus of the individual's reflection. Yet it was the latter function that Socrates proclaimed, not as the citizen's right, but as his duty, and this proclamation of the individual self-consciousness was the demise of that unreflective order upon which the polis depended. As a student of Socrates, Plato was aware of the failure of that ethos to meet the standards of subjective rationality; yet he could accommodate those demands only by means of a reason that served as a substantive principle informing every aspect of the political community. Hegel argues that this one-sided focus on objective freedom was the essential limitation of ancient rationality, a limitation that was revealed by Plato insofar as he could accept the rule of reason only in the form of the philosopher king. Plato could introduce reason into his state only by denying the exercise of subjective reason and freedom to all but the ruler. Yet while the polis was doomed by the contradiction of objective and subjective freedom, Plato was not completely aware of its ramifications. Instead, his efforts in the *Republic* reveal that contradiction most clearly for later readers, thereby lending that contradiction its rationally most comprehensible form.

Since it was philosophy that initially produced the diremption of the individual from the polis, Plato sought to segregate philosophers from society. Whereas the philosophers were allowed to achieve that universality of rational thought that Socrates had advocated, their lives were carefully regimented and restrained so as to render them incapable of realizing that individuality that would otherwise result from their subjective universality. Ordinary citizens of the *Republic* were in less danger of individuality since they were denied the privileges of philosophy and universal thought in relation to which the laws and norms of the state must inevitably appear as limited particulars. Nevertheless they were protected from the pernicious influence of poets and playwrights which might inspire criticism of social norms, the latter being further reinforced by myths designed for that purpose.

Thus a re-examination of Hegel's metaphilosophy shows that his interpretation of Plato has been misconstrued. Hegel did not view Plato's role as purely descriptive. Rather Hegel understood Plato to have grasped the essential nature of Greek society in such a way as to indicate its inherent contradictions, and thereby to provide an early indication of that development that would occur in the course of subsequent efforts to resolve those contradictions. Far from underestimating the 'innovative, paradoxical radicalism' of Plato's work, Hegel understood it as implicitly anticipating the individualism and subjective freedom of modern society in much the way

[43] Hegel, *The Philosophy of Right*, #185.

as a negative anticipates the photographic print. And insofar as the former determines the latter it may be understood, like Plato's political philosophy, as performing both descriptive and prescriptive roles.

Multiculturalism and Immigration in Europe

Andrew Geddes
University of Liverpool

'Fortress Europe: Immigration Policy Fact or Phantom?'

Introduction

For over twenty years there has been a strident rhetoric of immigration control in West European countries accompanied in many instances by increasingly restrictive legislation. More recently, it has become apparent that, since the Single European Act and ratification of the Treaty on European Union, the European Union has acquired increased responsibility for immigration and asylum policy designed to restrict movement of non-European Union citizens. Taken together, do these trends mean that European Union citizens now reside behind the ramparts of 'fortress Europe'?

If the term is to have more than rhetorical value it needs to be operationalised rather more specifically than is sometimes the case. This paper suggests three criteria for assessing the usefulness of the term. First, it implies a move towards restrictive immigration policies – but this alone is insufficient. Second, it is emblematic of a move beyond national-based restriction to increased regulatory competence at supranational European level. Third, the 'fortress' reflects an ideological shift from ethnocentric to eurocentric racism founded on an exclusionary notion of 'Europeanness'. This paper takes each of these aspects of the putative fortress in turn and argues that, although immigration policies in many European countries are restrictive and illiberal, the notion of 'fortress Europe' is an overstatement.

Restrictive Policies

The ability to regulate movement of people is a good indicator of state power (or sovereignty) construed in Weberian zero-sum terms which implies maintenance of effective regulation over who can or cannot enter a country. Over the last twenty years West European countries – particularly what Freeman calls 'post-guestworker' countries, such as Britain, France and Germany – have sought ever tighter restrictions on immigration.[1] In this endeavour they have been less successful than advocates of control had hoped because numbers of immigrants and, more recently, asylum-seekers, have remained relatively high. This has prompted the formulation of two hypotheses which are seen as encapsulating a contemporary paradox underpinning the politics of immigration.[2] First, a 'convergence hypothesis' notes similarities in response to immigration in receiving countries measured in terms of policy

---

[1] G.Freeman, 'Modes of immigration politics in liberal democratic states', *International Migration Review*, 24/4, 1994.

[2] W.Cornelius et al (eds), *Controlling Immigration: A Global Perspective*, Stanford University Press, 1994.

instruments, public reactions to immigration (generally hostile) and social integration policies. At the same time, a 'gap hypothesis' addresses the lacuna between restrictive policy goals and outcomes. As the gap between restrictive goals and actual outcomes increases it is argued that the end result is greater public hostility towards immigrants (with knock-on effects for settled immigrants and their children). Indeed, Castles has remarked upon an apparent breakdown of migration regulation in the 1990s as a result of the increased numbers of asylum-seekers fleeing war, famine, ethnic persecution or ecological disasters, but who do not fall within the definition of political persecution provided by the 1951 Geneva Convention.[3] The asylum crisis has had particular effects on Germany because of its geographical position at the crossroads of Europe and the liberal asylum provisions of the 1949 Basic Law (amended in July 1993 in an attempt to curb numbers). Moreover, Castles argued that European countries entered a new phase of mass migration in the 1990s and that the impact has been felt most keenly in new countries of immigration in Southern Europe, such as Italy, Greece, Spain and Portugal, which had traditionally been countries of emigration. These countries constitute the southern ramparts of the putative European fortress. The impact of immigration-related issues on these countries is new both in the sense that immigration is a relatively recent phenomenon and also because state power to regulate movement of people is brought into question at a time when supranational political authority is developing in Europe.

Both legal and clandestine immigration play an important part in economic development in southern Europe, so a key test for 'fortress Europe' is whether such countries will be complicit in its construction. There are grounds for supposing that southern European countries may be unable to establish tightly restrictive immigration policies because of under- developed administrative capacities which make it difficult to police external frontiers.

Immigrant workers also perform an important economic function because they are an often cheap and easily exploitable source of labour who constitute a reserve army which, amongst other things, can militate against high wage increases. A Spanish immigration policy-maker remarked that: 'Other European Community members talk about the need for a zero immigration policy, but this is completely unrealistic for Spain ... We want them to recognize Spain's objective need for foreign labour. Spaniards won't do certain kinds of jobs, and we need to channel foreign labour to meet those needs'.[4]

An economistic viewpoint would link relations of production and the regulation of scarcity in capitalist societies with a dialectic of inclusion and exclusion which is viewed as central to an understanding of immigrant workers social position in contemporary European societies. Social inclusion or exclusion are generated because the regulation of scarcity in capitalist society necessitates signification and categorization in order to typify individuals

[3] S.Castles, 'Migrations and minorities in Europe. Perspectives for the 1990s: eleven hypotheses', in J.Wrench & J.Solomos (eds), *Racism and Migration in Western Europe*, Berg, 1993.

[4] Quoted in W.Cornelius, 'Spain: the uneasy transition from labour exporter to labour importer', in W.Cornelius et al (eds), *op cit.*

and consign them to a place in the social order. One aspect of signification is categorization based on phenotypical and cultural differences, and attendant development of racist ideologies, to justify subordination of immigrant workers on the basis of supposed 'racial' inferiority. These general processes of inclusion and exclusion are diffused through national political and institutional contexts which prompt generation of other exclusionary criteria – language, religion etc – by which immigrants are judged not to 'belong' to the nation.[5]

An alternative viewpoint challenges this economistic analysis by directing attention towards structural components of liberal democracy which, it is argued, promote a tendency towards expansive and inclusionary immigration politics.[6] This viewpoint has particular relevance for new European countries of immigration in southern Europe. The structural features of liberal democracy identified are: free constitutions founded on individual rights; competitive party systems; and regular elections which lead to optimal policies derived from the preferences of individual voters who are assumed to be utility maximisers with perfect information. However, the model is corrupted by information assymetries which generate a 'temporal illusion' during the early stages of immigration. One aspect of this temporal illusion arises from the general public's belief that immigration will only be temporary. In this respect, Freeman argues that publics have been

> 'sold a bill of goods ... which were élite driven and packaged with what turned out to be, in retrospect, seriously misleading promises'.[7]

Meanwhile, advocates of expansive immigration policies, such as business, who can see the advantages of a cheap source of labour, are well organised and able to ensure that policies remain expansive. At the same time, mainstream political parties seek a consensus which minimizes the potential for conflict over immigration issues and attempts to diminish populist exploitation. Thus, particularly in its early stages, immigration is seen as producing 'concentrated benefits' and 'diffuse costs' within a clientelist relationship between the advocates of expansion and government. Because of 'temporal illusion' opposition to immigration during its early states is likely to be weak and badly organised. In longer-standing countries of immigration there has been more overt conflict about immigration prompting anti-immigration and racist political mobilisation. Even so, the politics of immigration are still seen as fundamentally liberal democratic, expansive and inclusive because they are based on a Tocquevillian sympathy for immigrants who are viewed as people like ourselves trying to make their way in the world (although it is also noted that the 'asylum crisis' has prompted a partial policy reversal). It has also been argued that the trend towards

[5] F.Bovenkerk et al, 'Comparative studies of migration and exclusion on the grounds of "race" and ethnic background in Western Europe: a critical appraisal', *International Migration Review*, 25/2, 1991.

[6] Freeman, *op cit.*

[7] Freeman, *op cit.*

inclusiveness is founded on the 'embedded liberalism' of the post-Second World War era and the consequent development of rights-based regimes which emphasise human rights and social justice from which immigrants and their children benefit.[8]

These contrasting perspectives have two important implications for 'fortress Europe'. First, nation states may be unwilling or unable (or both) to effectively regulate movement of people, and some European Union member states are likely to be more unwilling or unable than others. These factors imply that the ramparts of the fortress appear a little less formidable and that the demand for migrant labour is likely to remain stronger in southern Europe than in longer-standing countries of immigration.

Second, the analysis of capacity to regulate immigration tells us interesting things about state power. In particular, it prompts qualification of the Weberian perspective on sovereignty construed as a zero-sum game and measured by a state's ability to control its borders and its people irrespective of intervening factors, such as the international environment. In contrast, state power could be construed as the ability to achieve desired outcomes. Thus, interdependence means that desired outcomes may be more readily attainable through cooperation or integration in key policy sectors with other states. Consequently, in this non-zero sum context the ability to attain preferred outcomes is reflective of relations with other social actors and other states, rather than just a state's power over its people and its borders.[9] This means that a government that holds and achieves restrictive immigration policy objectives in an integrated European policy framework, within which Weberian notions of state sovereignty are compromised, can be judged as more successful than a state that fails to attain restrictive immigration policy objectives by acting unilaterally and clinging to a zero-sum notion of state power. To use a term familiar to analysts of European integration: states may attain their objectives across a range of policy issues by 'pooling' their sovereignty. This leads us to the second part of our analysis of the notion of 'fortress Europe': the development of regulatory capacity at supranational level in recognition of interdependence on immigration and asylum policy issues.

The European Union and Fortress Europe's External Frontier

If it were to be the case that the European Union's southern Member States were unwilling or unable to restrict immigration, then other European Union member states could seek to impose a restrictive policy on them by 'pooling' sovereignty and eliminating free rider problems in an integrated single market within which internal frontiers have been abolished. European Union membership has impacted upon Italian policy because, as Martiniello notes: '(m)igration policy is largely inspired by the European policies' and 'other

[8] J.Hollifield, *Immigrants, States and Markets*, Harvard University Press, 1992.

[9] G.Marks et al, 'European integration from the 1980s: state-centric v. multi-level governance', *Journal of Common Market Studies*, 34/3, 1996.

European countries ... considered Italy as the weak point of the European belt to be constructed'.[10] Spain's 1985 immigration law was 'almost entirely the result of external pressure associated with Spain's entry into the European Community'.[11] It would seem that southern European countries have been obliged to cooperate with the construction of a European citadel that forces adoption of tighter restrictions on entry of non-European Union citizens than the states may have chosen for themselves. This appears to be good evidence of the emergent fortress Europe; but things may not be as clear cut as they first appear because an examination of the current condition of European Union immigration and asylum policy prompts the questioning of supranational regulatory capacity.

The development of European Community/European Union responsibility for immigration and asylum policy is linked to a paradox engendered by the liberalisation contained within the (then) European Community's single market programme. The attainment of the free movement of people objective (although 'people' actually means European Union citizens, not all people) implied the abolition of internal frontiers and generated policy spillover which impelled cooperation on a range of what were seen as internal security issues, including immigration and asylum. However, member states preferred intergovernmental cooperation on immigration and asylum policy rather than creation of a common policy. Between 1986 and 1991 the member states developed largely ineffective informal intergovernmental arrangements within which member states were hidebound by the need for unanimity. Moreover, this form of intergovernmental cooperation meant the adoption of conventions in international law, which are not directly enforceable by international judicial authority, as opposed to supranational law which is directly enforceable by the European Court of Justice. The result of these inadequate arrangements was that the two most substantive measures brought forward, the Dublin Convention on asylum and the External Frontiers Convention, have, at the time of writing, either not been ratified in all member states (Dublin) or not even signed by all member states (the EFC).

The TEU sought to counteract the weakness of informal intergovernmentalism by creating a Justice and Home Affairs (JHA) 'pillar' which recognised immigration and asylum as matters of common interest and introduced a Treaty obligation to cooperate within a single institutional structure. Articles K.1.1-3 outline European Union responsibilities for asylum policy, rules governing the crossing of external frontiers, and immigration policy and policy regarding nationals of third countries. The Council acts by unanimity when deciding on conventions, joint actions or joint positions. There is also a 'double lock 'mechanism because Council decision's to establish conventions in international law must also be ratified by national parliaments.

It has been argued that the JHA pillar accentuates the European Union's

[10] M.Martiniello, 'Italy: the late discovery of immigration', in D.Thranhardt (ed), *Europe: A New Immigration Continent*, Munster, Lit.

[11] W.Cornelius, 'Spain: from labour exporter to labour importer', *op cit*.

'democratic deficit' because, for example, the Councils' endemic secrecy means that most immigration and asylum-related discussions are beyond the purview of both national legislatures and the European Parliament (which has only the right to be informed about JHA decisions, Article K.6).[12]

In its 1994 Communication on Immigration and Asylum policies the Commission outlined an approach to the development of European Union immigration policy based on three inter-related elements:

- (i) action on migration pressure;
- (ii) controlling immigration flows by formulating basic principles on issues such as admission policy;
- (iii) strengthening integration policies for the benefit of legal immigrants by, for example, promoting free movement for third-country nationals within the European Union on the basis of a residence permit.

However, the Commission noted that even though:

> 'The general political climate remains favourable to the development of a comprehensive approach. No international forum ... has yet proved capable of making such a policy operational.'[13]

It appears that the European Union does not yet have common immigration and asylum policies because the influence of supranational institutions remains weak and member states retain the upper hand. Increased European Union responsibility for immigration and asylum issues is secured in the main through intergovernmental arrangements within which unanimity is the decisional modus operandi in almost all areas. Intergovernmentalism is a brake on the development of a common European immigration and asylum policy because unanimity allows recalcitrant member states to block development. For example, the United Kingdom is far from convinced that southern European countries have the capacity to adopt the highly restrictive framework that successive British governments have put in place since 1962. Interestingly, from the British government's perspective, an integrated European Union immigration policy is unlikely to lead to a fortress Europe. In fact, the fear seems to be that its operationalisation by creation of common immigration and asylum policies would have precisely the opposite effect because of what are seen as lax or ineffective controls in certain member states. It is far from assured that even if a common policy was to emerge it would or could be properly enforced to satisfy the advocates of restriction. Rhetorical commitment to the lofty goals and aspirations of European integration has often exceeded the ability of states to properly implement supranational commitments. Moreover, supranational authorities do not possess the capacity to oversee implementation and must rely on the

[12] A.Geddes, 'Immigrant and ethnic minorities and the European Union's democratic deficit', *Journal of Common Market Studies*, 32/2, 1995.

[13] Commission, *Communication on Immigration and Asylum Policy*, COM (94) 23, OOPEC.

good will of administrative authorities in member states. However, newer countries of immigration have tended to lack the administrative capacity to effectively police external frontiers, in part because of the relatively recent development of immigration pressures. As a result, a future European Union immigration and asylum policy could be weakened by inability to secure adequate enforcement, as well as by unwillingness to rigidly enforce a restrictive policy that may confound labour market requirements in some member states.

The ongoing Intergovernmental Conference may increase the scope of European Union responsibility for immigration and asylum policy by, for example, bringing more issues within the remit of supranational authority. The German and Dutch governments, among others, have argued that the JHA pillar should be brought closer to the Community pillar, which would mean fuller involvement for the Commission, Court and Parliament. There already exists a potential 'bridge' from the JHA pillar to the Community because Article 100c of the Treaty (already covering visa policy) could be extended to cover other immigration and asylum issues, provided all member states agree.

An example of the kind of immigration and asylum provisions that could emerge within the European Union as a result of the removal of internal frontiers is provided by the Schengen countries who have decided to move faster towards attainment of free movement objectives. Internal frontiers were abolished in 'Schengenland' on March 26 1995. At the time of writing nine European Union member states are participants in Schengen, whilst Austria, Denmark, Finland, Sweden and the Commission have observer status and the United Kingdom and Ireland remain outside of the agreement. Associated with the Schengen arrangements is the Schengen Information System. The SIS is significant in that it represents the move towards an internal security policy, or put another way, the 'securitization' of the European interior. It could be argued that it is the development on an internal European security policy – with Schengen as its laboratory – that provides most insight into an emergent Eurocentrism that could fuel exclusionary or racist tendencies in the European Union.

From Ethnocentric to Eurocentric Racism?

The creation of 'fortress Europe' implies a move from ethnocentric to eurocentric racism, perhaps founded on bogus presumptions of 'European' superiority construed in phenotypical or cultural terms. This movement towards eurocentric racism signifies the creation of a symbolic space of 'Europeanness' guarded by the ramparts of the fortress. Eurocentrism is functional to the creation of 'fortress Europe' because an exclusive and exclusionary ideology reinforces the economic and political-institutional processes which underpin the development of the fortress. Eurocentrism is also likely to have marked effects on already settled immigrants and their descendants who may find themselves not in accord with supposed 'European' phenotypical or cultural norms.

Eurocentric racism could derive from false assumptions of European superiority originating from the significance racists have often attached to phenotypical differences, particularly of skin colour. However, analysts of racism argue that it is equally significant to examine the development of a 'new racism' based on supposed cultural differences. The 'new racists' eschew what they would see as cruder variants of racism which impute significance to phenotypical difference and, instead, argue that cultural differences lead to incompatibilities between peoples. Thus, it is not that people are 'racially' different, but that they are culturally incompatible. To do so is to risk what Enoch Powell referred to in 1968 as the 'rivers of blood' that would run as a result of black people settling in Britain. In France, the leader of the National Front, Jean Marie Le Pen denies that he is a racist by contending that he has nothing against immigrants, he just thinks that should live in their 'own country'. A complication, of course, is that for many 'immigrants' France is their own country because they are French citizens. At the same time, analysts of the 'new' cultural racism would contend that Le Pen's cultural essentialism implies that: groups of people are fundamentally different; that these differences can be delineated in cultural terms; that cultures are static rather than dynamic phenomena; and that markedly distinct cultural groups cannot live peacefully together. It is then argued that the essentialism and the emphasis on categorization of the 'new racism' renders it almost indistinguishable from older racism. It is also the case that Le Pen denies being a racist but makes speeches containing remarks that clearly appeal to racists. For example, he referred to the holocaust as a detail of history and his 'Durafour crematoire' remark made a tasteless link between a Jewish Gaullist politicians name and gas ovens.[14]

If the ideological space of 'fortress Europe' has been demarcated and defined in 'racial' or 'cultural' terms then we have support for the notion of eurocentric racism. However, politicians such as Le Pen and the leaders of other extreme right-wing neo-fascist parties, such as Jörg Haider in Austria, seem more representative of a resurgent ethnocentrism than Eurocentrism. They may allude to a form of occidentalism, usually as part of their Islamophobia, but are also strongly opposed to European integration. Le Pen may speak of 'western values' but at the heart of his appeal is the traditional nationalistic and racist slogan of 'France for the French'. The racist right in Europe appears markedly ethnocentric and increasingly anti-European Union. The reason for this is clear: both immigration and European integration threaten the extreme-right's conceptualisation of 'the nation' and 'its people'.

There may be more to be gained from an assessment of the 'securitized' European interior in a search for an exclusionary Eurocentrism rather than analysing the ramparts of the European Union's external frontier, which may not be as strong as sometimes supposed, or the activities of the extreme right. The abolition of external frontiers within a properly integrated single market means new forms of security and control. The SIS – the intended

[14] J.Marcus, *The National Front and French Politics. The Resistible Rise of Jean Marie Le Pen*, Macmillan, 1995.

forerunner of a European Information System – is representative of this trend. Within this new security apparatus, immigrants and asylum-seekers are labelled as security problems alongside international criminals. The development of the European Union's internal security capacity is occurring with very little public debate and little scope for democratic oversight at either national or supranational level. It may be that it is as important to assess developments inside the fortress – and their implications for immigrants and asylum-seekers – than it is to focus on the ramparts of the supposed fortress. The development of a symbolic space of Europeanness and attendant security apparatus within an integrated and border free single market also has implications for already-settled immigrants and their children. Those who do not hold the nationality of a member state are largely excluded from free movement provisions. Others, who do hold the nationality of a member state and are, therefore, European Union citizens, may find it difficult to exercise free movement rights because of racist discrimination.

However, it is also worth noting that racists are increasingly acting in Europe- and world-wide concert and that the European Union may be a forum within which, amongst other things, cross-border dissemination of racist materials can be combatted. Racists have begun to avail themselves of new technologies such as the internet. In 1996, the US neo-Nazi, Gary Lauck, was imprisoned for sending neo-nazi material to Germany from the USA – he was arrested when making a visit to Denmark and deported to Germany to face charges. The European Union has recently taken tentative steps towards tackling dissemination of racist material across between European Union member states. However, there is still a long way to go because, as it stands, the Treaty of Rome forbids discrimination on the grounds of nationality but does not allow for redress when discrimination occurs on grounds of ethnic origin or skin colour. The absence of such legislation means that the symbolic space of Europeanness is prey to forms of Eurocentrism from which racist ideologies founded on exclusive notions of European identity can emerge, alongside more 'traditional' ethnocentric racism.

Conclusion

A threefold definition of fortress Europe has been developed encompassing restrictive immigration policies, the establishment of political-institutional capacity at supranational level to police the fortress and the development of an ideology of Europeanness underpinning eurocentric racism. This threefold definition provides grounds for thinking that the term 'fortress Europe' may be an overstatement. This does not mean that immigration and asylum policies are fundamentally liberal and inclusive, or that effective measures have been introduced to promote better integration of immigrants and their children and tackle racism. In all too many cases legislation has been illiberal and draconian. However, the rhetoric of control – which can be very harmful to immigrants in European countries – appears to exceed the reality of restriction during what has been described as a global migration crisis.

Problems associated with this crisis have been common to most European countries of immigration, but they have had particular effects in new countries of immigration which may be both unwilling and unable to impose restrictions on immigration. Indeed, the southern ramparts of the putative 'fortress' may actually belie such a characterisation.

'Fortress Europe' also implies European-level immigration and asylum policies. It should not be assumed that such policies will necessarily emerge, or, if they do, that they could be effectively implemented. Finally, the development of a eurocentric racism was assessed. Even though there is resurgent ethnocentrism which makes itself manifest in racist and anti-immigrant political mobilisation the forces of ethnocentrism are strongly opposed to both immigration and European integration because both threaten the far-right's idea of the nation. It is perhaps more significant to note the creation of a securitized European interior as a result of the abolition of internal frontiers within Schengenland. The European Union does, though, also provide a forum within which ethnocentric racism could be challenged.

Political Discourse and Practical Politics: Frameworks for Analysis

Richard Heffernan
London School of Economics and Political Science

'Ideology, Practical Politics and Political Consensus: Thinking about the Process of Political Change in the United Kingdom'

The Phenomenon of Political Change

The past is a chronological continuum, a process, one marked by a series of staging posts characterised by even the most elementary of attempts at periodisation. British politics since 1900 can be divided into distinctive periods suggested, for example, by electoral cycles and outcomes, party alternation in office, or by the rise and fall of public doctrines projected as political ideology. Analysis of political change should focus on the ebb and flow of political ideologies and their impact upon public policy. The political discontinuities of the United Kingdom in the twentieth century (the periods around the snapshot elections of 1906, 1945 and 1979) cannot be understood without an understanding of the movement of ideas that gave rise to them, the impact these ideas had on the political climate of the time, and, perhaps more importantly, understanding the process of transition from one distinctive political era to another.

In recent years the familiar landscape of British public policy has been fundamentally altered in a process summed up in the phrase 'the era of big government is over'. In a phenomena unconfined to the United Kingdom policy instruments such as full employment, public enterprise, established styles of business regulation, progressive income tax structures and traditional forms of public management have almost become things of the past, 'policy dinosaurs', in the words of Christopher Hood, species of public policy replaced by new 'life forms'; deregulation, neoclassical economics, flatter taxes and new public management.[1] In common with other sets of political actors in comparable countries the Thatcher and Major governments led the way in the United Kingdom in recasting the industrial and economic form of the social democratic state by dismantling many of its corporatist features.

The history of political economy is characterised by the duality of collectivism and individualism, a process of trend and cycle illustrated by the rise and decline of public doctrines expressed as ideological politics.[2] In a grand historical sweep Milton Friedman has classified the period since 1800 as the Age of Adam Smith, the Age of Maynard Keynes and the Age of

---

[1] C.Hood, *Explaining Economic Policy Reversals*, Open University Press, 1994.

[2] W.H.Greenleaf, *The British Political Tradition*, Volume 1: 'The Rise of Collectivism', Volume II: 'The Ideological Heritage' , Methuen 1983; A.V.Dicey, *Lectures on the Relation Between Law and Opinion in England during the Nineteenth Century*, Macmillan edition, 1963.

Hayek.[3] The twentieth century has witnessed the polarity of collectivism and individualism, a process typified by the rise of a semi-collectivist social democracy, one informed by statist welfare politics and Keynesian politics which was ultimately reconfigured by the revival of market liberalism. Here, the process of political change within British politics can be classified into the pre-social democratic Keynesian era lasting up to 1940; the social democratic Keynesian era lasting up to 1975; and the neo-liberal post-social democratic Keynesian era after 1975.

Where the social democratic era presupposed that the role of the state was to directly regulate the market in a social interest, neo-liberalism, as a revived form of market individualism, conceives the role of the state as being to empower the market in an economic interest and (when possible) in a social interest. Its rise and consolidation as a dominant political ideology has brought about fundamental political change in practical politics, part of an anti-corporatist strategy which over time came to be characterised by privatisation, deregulation and commercialisation of the state sector and an acceptance of the primacy of market forces in the governance of the economy and state-centred activity.[4] In a continuing process the state has been recast since 1975 in as close a neo-liberal (that is, non-social democratic) guise as has proved politically possible and/or administratively practicable: (1) The state is no longer considered a mechanism to radically reform economic relations; (2) Egalitarianism has been abandoned. Redistribution of income and wealth is no longer a stated objective; (3) High rates of progressive taxation are explicitly ruled out; (4) A commitment to increased levels of social expenditure has been excised; (5) The privatisation of state owned industries and utilities and the withdrawing of the state from direct control over economic activity is an accepted fact of life.

Political change is therefore closely related to the rise of new (or, more likely, updated or repackaged) political ideas that capture the imagination of key elements of the electorate and, more significantly, political and administrative élites. Such has been the power of the neo-liberal political agenda that political actors have found themselves persuaded of the need to 'modernise' their appeal to 'accommodate' to changing circumstances. This is an exceptional example of political change, a dramatic shift in which contemporary politics are enacted within a set of parameters enclosing a space on

[3]Quoted in A.Gamble, 'Ideas and Interests in British Economic Policy', *Contemporary British History*, 10/2, 1996, p.19.

[4]The following are extremely useful: A.Gamble, *The Free Economy and the Strong State*, Macmillan 2nd edition, 1994; A.Gamble, 'The Politics Of Thatcherism', *Parliamentary Affairs*, 42, 1989; D.Kavanagh, *Thatcherism and British Politics*, Oxford University Press, 1990. Also S.Letwin, *The Anatomy of Thatcherism*, Harper Collins, 1992; J.Douglas, 'The Changing Tide: Some Recent Studies of Thatcherism', *British Journal of Political Science*, 19, 1989; B.Jessop et al, *Thatcherism: A Tale of Two Nations*, Polity Press, 1988; R.Levine (ed), *The Ideology of the New Right*, Cambridge University Press 1986; D.King, *The New Right*, Macmillan, 1987. An interesting historical account of the antecedents of the 'New Right' is included in R.Desai, 'Thinking the Unthinkable: Thinking up Thatcherism, *New Left Review*, 203 January-February, 1994; R.Cockett, *Thinking the Unthinkable: Think Tanks and the Economic Counter-Revolution*, Harper Collins, 1993. A contrary view is to be found in D.Marsh, 'Explaining "Thatcherite" Policies: Beyond Uni-Dimensional Explanations', *Political Studies*, 43/4, 1995.

the centre right of politics, reflecting a political agenda which structures the set of political ideas regarded as given, unchallengeable and therefore politically acceptable. The displacement of Keynesian social democracy charts the passage of neo-liberalism from being a vilified heterodoxy to becoming a predominant orthodoxy, a shift that has taken place within a political generation.[5]

This neo-liberal ideological disposition informs the political ideas which, as normative recommendations, form part of a belief system eventually translated into public policy. Contemporary politics is structured around an altered discourse, one that reflects a different set of practical priorities and a new conception of the purpose of government and the role of the state. From this perspective the politics of, say, 1995 are dramatically different from those of 1975. Here, a series of contestable political beliefs have over time become translated into a set of assumptions common to some extent to all political élites. Neo-liberal political attitudes have pervaded the body politic, colonising intellectual territory inch by inch, suggesting that individual choices exercised within a system of economic market exchange are more preferable to collective political decision making enacted through an interventionist state.

In an explanation of political change political ideas influence the 'policy goals; policy means; policy outcomes; political style; the presentation of policy to the electorate; and even the range of policies excluded from the political agenda' that characterise the form government takes.[6] Political change is often explained by the rise of new ideas that come to demonstrate their economic, political and administrative viability: here ideology is seen to be an engine of change. A study of the course and causes of political change should consider the prevailing conditions that encourage an alteration in the role and purpose of government (what it does; why it does things; how it does them) takes place. If distinctive political ideas are capable of determining the set of policies presented in the form of public or administrative choices then, rather than an abstract conception, the dominant political discourse forms an series of ideological propositions, a set of normative recommendations, constructing a broadly informed belief system that has far reaching social implications when realised as public policy.[7]

[5] Toward the end of the 1979 Election Campaign, the then Labour Prime Minister, Jim Callaghan, all but resigned to impending defeat, remarked to his adviser Bernard Donoughue: 'You know there are times, perhaps once every thirty years there is a sea change in politics. It then does not matter what you say or do. There is a shift in what the public wants and what it approves of. I suspect there is now such a sea change – and it is for Mrs Thatcher'. B.Donoughue, *Prime Minister*, Jonathan Cape, 1987 p.191. This oft-quoted observation is close to becoming a modern cliché.

[6] C.Hay, *Restating Social and Political Change*, Open University Press, 1996 p.45.

[7] Ideological prescriptions affect the political-economic-social context within which government operates. This structures what political actors and governmental institutions actually do and so impacts upon the outputs of the state. Of course, a pragmatic response to social and economic pressures may serve to modify the impact that a political ideology might have. Equally, the reception climate that greets a ideological project is an important factor. For one agenda to succeed, others have to fail; for change to prosper, the status quo has to be discredited. The failure of Keynesianism paved the way for the resurgence of market liberalism much as the limitations of individualism prepared the

A study of political change therefore involves an examination of the processes by which ideas are transmitted as part of the process by which political ideas (when operationalised as doctrine or ideology) become widely accepted as administratively viable and politically practical. Anthony Seldon has recently argued that the interplay of ideas, individuals, circumstances and interests provides four possible causes for policy change. Utilising Galbraith's notion of a prevailing 'conventional wisdom', he suggests that 'the preponderance of one idea or another at any given point in time conditions the entire way in which judgements are made by policy élites'.[8] The idea of a 'paradigm-shift' in scientific enquiry was developed by Thomas Kuhn who distinguished between set structured forms of scientific discourse which utilised different frameworks of both analysis, exposition and understanding. These distinctive forms of activity established patterns of behaviour and defined what scientists did. Thus distinctive paradigms (for example Aristotelian and Newtonian physics) structured all forms of scientific enquiry. These established patterns of analysis took the form of 'normal science' (standardised and routine activity working within an established framework); scientists continued to work in this framework and followed the unwritten 'rules' and 'regulations' set out by the discipline within which they worked.[9]

Kuhn counterposed 'normal science' with 'revolutionary science', a form of scientific enquiry established when anomalies generated within 'normal science' create a crisis in the existing paradigm (and so create a change in the scientific perception of a number of scientists) which is resolved by a process of change from the old to a new paradigm (paradigm-shift). Once established the new paradigm becomes the basis for contemporary scientific enquiry characterised by the collective acceptance of the ideas and attitudes upon which it is based. Scientists return to normal science within that new paradigm.[10] Shifting paradigms in political activity (as expressed in economic doctrine or a definition of the role and scope of the state) involves an alteration in the dominant ideology which finds expression in the activities of political institutions and political and administrative actors. Here, dominant ideas are applied to practical politics in order to define problems and offer ways to resolve them. Over time, given success (dependent upon opportunity, circumstance and the impact of contingency factors), these dominant ideas can forge a new (or revamped) political structure (both an altered ideological discourse and different policy agendas) which refashion the way in which the world is interpreted and how it is assumed it should be managed. Only when translated into practical politics does ideology have a significant impact upon political affairs.

---

way for social democratic collectivism.

[8] A.Seldon, 'Ideas are nor Enough', in D.Marquand & A.Seldon (eds), *The Ideas That Shaped Post-War Britain*, Harper Collins, 1996, pp.263, 266.

[9] T.Kuhn, *The Structure of Scientific Revolutions*, Chicago University Press, 1970 edition.

[10] *Ibid.*

Consensus Politics as a Reflection of Political Change

Political change, as an evolutionary process with various stages in its formation, is manifested in an alteration in what David Marquand describes as the set of 'commitments, assumptions and expectations' shared by political actors which transcend party conflicts and characterise a political consensus within which policy is enacted.[11] The notion of consensus politics is commonly (although not uncontroversally) defined as a situation where political actors will broadly accept or actively endorse a series of policy options they regard as given, unchangeable and therefore politically acceptable.[12] The concept, despite the criticism it has encountered in recent years,[13] does not assume complete and total agreement between parties across political issues. Indeed it presupposes that a adversary style of politics will continue and may well prosper.

By the mid-1990's, the term consensus has fallen into some academic disrepute (in both the field of political history and in political science), and there is a need to reconfigerate the idea as a worthwhile and relevant contribution to the explanation of political change. A theory of consensus politics suggests that political activity is structured around a dominant discourse, one not simply reflected by a policy coincidence but by a broad associative agreement on general principles which inform the policy decisions parties make. 'Settlement' is a preferable term to that of 'consensus'. It effectively captures the idea consensus is meant to denote, namely that a 'consensus as settlement' determines what is commonly accepted (or reluctantly acknowledged) as normative judgements about the possible role of government. This reflects the policy limitations acknowledged by political actors operating in an environment not of their own choosing and not of their own making. Political change is thus defined as the transition from one dominant political paradigm to another.

A political consensus is best defined as a shared adherence to a limited series of methods and objectives common to government rather than a commonly held direction of purpose. It is a form of conformity (if not outright compliance) with an established political agenda, an acceptance of common political values which define what governing actors can expect to do and what they should aspire to do. Political actors can come over

---

[11] D.Marquand, *The Unprincipled Society*, Fontana, 1988 p.18.

[12] For an introduction to this debate see D.Kavanagh & P.Morris, *Consensus Politics from Attlee to Major*, Basil Blackwell 2nd edition, 1994: P.Addison, *The Road to 1944*, Pimlico 1994; D.Kavanagh, 'Whatever Happened to Consensus Politics?', *Political Studies*, 1985; A.Seldon, 'Consensus: A Debate too Long?', *Parliamentary Affairs*, 47 1994. An alternative view is presented by B.Pimlott, 'The Myth of Consensus', in L.M.Smith (ed), *The Making of Britain; Echoes of Greatness*, Macmillan 1988.

[13] Cf H.Jones & M.Kandiah (eds), *The Myth of Consensus? New Views of British History 1945-1964*, Macmillan 1996; A.Butler, 'The End of Post-War Consensus', *Political Quarterly*, 64, 1993. Also N.Rollings 'Poor Mr Butskell: A Short Life, Wrecked by Schzophrenia', *Twentieth Century British History*, 5/2, 1994; R.Lowe, 'The Second World war, Consensus and the Foundatyions of the Welfare State', *Twentieth Century British History*; K.Jeffreys, 'The Churchill Coalition and Wartime Politics, 1940-1945', Manchester 1991; P.Addison, 'Consensus Revisited', *Twentieth Century British History*, 1993.

time and through experience to internalise a set of political values that constrain and shape their behaviour rather then overtly determine their actions. Agreement is thus an implicit acceptance of a parameter in the form of a held assumption constructed over time and through experience. The 'consensual settlement' within which policy is enacted, reflects a series of contestable political beliefs that have over time become translated into a set of assumptions common to some extent to governing and would be governing political actors. This idea of consensus is an implicit 'agreement' on the role of public administration, one existing as a 'framework', which reflects the preparedness of political actors to accept a prevailing political orthodoxy based upon a set of prescriptive and conceptual political ideas. While partisanship rather than common identity is the feature of the British political scene, public disagreement is all too often only a cover for political agreement; where parties actually violently disagree with one another is on who shall form the next government. A consensual settlement underpins the prevailing paradigm within which political actors operate. A political settlement thus shapes a 'climate of opinion', not simply (or even significantly) the opinions and attitudes of the mass electorate but those of key opinion formers and other political players. This 'climate of opinion' is informed by the predominant values which set the boundaries of the acceptable for public policy.[14] Certain policy approaches or political values may be deemed illegitimate because they conflict (or simply challenge) these core values: Here only 'safe' questions may be raised which do not threaten existing attitudes on the direction of policy and the ideological appeal that underpins it. A dominant set of prescriptive ideas come to inhibit political actors; they structure political activity and serve to define the limits of possibility. This is where the settlement between governing and would be governing political actors comes to pass.

A consensus is therefore an arrived at unstated accommodation between parties on the various foundations of policy (what is government for; what can actors do; and, perhaps more importantly, what should actors expect to do). It is this framework which constructs the set of 'parameters which bounded the set of policy options regarded by senior politicians and civil servants as administratively practicable, economically affordable and politically acceptable' to which Kavanagh and Morris refer in their definition of consensus.[15] This framework lies at the heart of consensus politics and determines the ends identified and the means employed by government and would be governing actors. Governing Objectives are a broad and imprecise concept but Governing Assumptions, unwritten rules guiding and structuring policy choice and the behaviour of governing actors, are generated by a dominant set of ideological prescriptive ideas. They serve to define what is possible/what is not possible; what is permissible/what is not permissable and which come to be subscribed to be major political actors. Actors are

[14] As characterised in the post-war consensus by the mixed economy, demand management, the centrality of public expenditure to the public good, full employment and the welfare state.

[15] D.Kavanagh & P.Morris, *Consensus Politics from Attlee to Major*, Basil Blackwell, 2nd edition, 1994, pp.13-14.

therefore constrained not to agree but to accept the ideas based framework within which policy is to be enacted. Marked by an assessment of what is necessary to comply with the status-quo, it is as far from harmony as could be imagined. It characterises what is considered to be feasible (and not necessarily desirable) and so defines what is considered to be possible as is illustrated by an 'essential bias' in policy selection.[16]

A Framework for Evaluating Political Change

A consensual settlement is almost a mock theory of governance, one which guides what governments (and, as importantly, what prospective governments) can and should do (and what they consider themselves able to do). Dramatic political change may be defined as the transition from one consensual settlement to another.[17] A consensus as settlement is the product of a dominant agenda, a pre-set paradigm and not merely a purposeful agreement between willing parties. Consensus exists as a set of constraints which are deemed to limit what actors can and cannot do. Consensus politics can therefore be seen, in Paul Addison's phrase, as 'an exercise in containment', a process reflecting a political agenda derived from a variety of sources which commits both governing and would be governing actors to 'certain common principles' which are enshrined in policy.[18]

The contemporary neo-liberal consensus (the post-Thatcher settlement) imposes significant constraints upon present day political actors through the free-market view of economic realities which dramatically restricts the range of strategic options political and administrative actors consider to be available to government. As with the post-war consensus, this consensual settlement is a reflection of an emergent paradigm not a purposeful agreement commonly accepted by political actors (as implied by the term consensus). This example of political change both reflects and generates the dominant 'political agenda' which serves to define the dominant set of political ideas, attitudes and values that arise within political discourse. As an abstract reflection of political activity, the 'agenda' may be described as the broad appeal, or dominant political discourse, which defines the attitudes political actors are likely to strike when they attempt to engage with

---

[16] As Colin Hay suggests: 'It would seem then as though there is certainly a case to be made for the existence of post-war consensus in Britain if by consensus we understand: the acceptance by the major parties of the parameters defined by a state regime; a degree of political convergence unusual in Britain by recent historical standards; or, more likely, a combination of the two'. C.Hay, *Restating Social and Political Change*, Open University Press, 1996, p.48.

[17] It is important to emphasises that continuity as well as discontinuity is a feature of any political scene. The transition from a political discourse based upon a semi-collective social democratic ideology to one characterised by a fidelity to a revived market liberalism does not involve a total break from the politics of the earlier period. Elements of the former paradigm continue to exist thus marking a process of continuity. Thus is characterise in the field of defence and foreign policy and, in the domestic field, by the state's perennial obligations to provide some form of welfare for its citizens such as education, housing, social insurance, and health care. Social democratic or neo-liberal, capitalism remains capitalism.

[18] P.Addison, *The Road to 1945*, Pimlico 1994.

those issues promoted to public attention. A dominant political agenda is a framework of political ideas which reinforce a set of attitudes which find expression in political, economic and social policy.

A political agenda presents value-based ideas as suggestions which are capable of influencing political opinion and not just the set of policies presented in the form of administrative choices. Hard definitions of what constitutes such an agenda are rarely forthcoming. For the most part 'agenda setting', 'agenda building' and 'agenda managing' are vague and unsubstantial concepts. The existing political science literature on political agenda setting is weak and undeveloped. For the most part it is somewhat out of date, United States based and cast in a pluralist universe, heavily skewed in favour of such notions as 'bottom up' policy development.[19] A model of agenda formation may however have a wider application within political science in exploring the concept of political change as informed by ideological change realised in public policy. Political change is therefore related to the idea of settlement which marks the transition from one dominant paradigm to another as ultimately reflected in the form of a shared political agenda common to converging political élites. Far reaching political change engenders an altered consensual settlement which establishes the process of governance.

This framework of analysis suggests that: (1) a dominant political agenda exists which overshadows subordinate, less influential agendas; (2) that a series of political ideas have made a significant contribution to this form of political change; and (3) that this dominant political agenda can advance a set of political actors who have been able to determine élite (not necessarily popular) political opinion and influencing the set of policies (the ideological predisposition that informs policy choice). Of course contingency, circumstances and structural explanations all play a not insignificant part in the promotion of political change. War, as Orwell remarked, is a harbinger of dramatic changes in public policy: environments do impact upon political actors and the circulation of prescriptive political ideas.[20]

In the *General Theory*, Keynes famously suggested that the world is ruled by ideas[21] but in reality dominant ideas, rather than simply arise, are spon-

[19]Cf R.W.Cobb & CD Elder, *Participation in American Politics: The Dynamics of Agenda Building*, John Hopkins University Press, 1972; J.Kingdom, *Agendas, Alternatives and Public Policies*, 2nd edition, HarperCollege 1995; J.Kingdom, 'How Do Issues Get on Public Policy Agendas', in W.J.Wilson (ed), *Sociology and the Public Agenda*, Sage 1993.

[20]The environment may be defined as a series of arenas encompassing such interrelated dimensions as: (1) governmental-institutional (the form of the state, the rules of the constitutional system, election law and system, electoral cycles); (2) political-ideological (the form of party competition, the number of parties, the form of ideological engagement, the climate of opinion); (3) electoral (electoral outcomes, public opinion, policy orientations on the part of electors, electoral pressures); (4) socio-economic (economic conditions and social factors). These all impact upon political and administrative actors and provide the arenas within which ideology and doctrine are constructed and disseminated.

[21]In a phrase which has now become quite a cliché, Keynes suggested that '[T]he ideas of economists and political philosophers, both when they are right and when they are wrong, are more powerful than is commonly understood. Indeed the world is ruled by little else. Practical men who believe themselves to be quite exempt from any intellectual

sored and transmitted. They have different impacts at specific times, and either fail or succeed in winning distinct audiences at the level of the political élite and/or the mass. In understanding the process of change typified by the eclipse of social democracy and the rise of neo-liberalism the moment(s) of transition from one to the other must be located and the dynamics of change identified. A theory of political agenda setting applicable to the realm of political ideas may offer a way forward to explore this phenomena. The concept needs to be properly defined before it can be widely applied in political science but, shorn of pluralist preconceptions, may usefully illuminate the dynamics of political change (and, for that matter, periods of stability between periods of change).

Ideological prescriptions, impact upon the political mode which informs the architectural form of the state and its relationship to the economy and civil society. Specifically, they affect the method by which the state defines the objectives to which it intervenes in these spheres and the manner in which it does so. The ideology of the public sphere is not necessarily reducible to the dominant political mode because subordinate agendas continue to attract support at the same time as they are overshadowed by the dominant discourse; 'Hayek's ideas' were in circulation during the 'time of Keynes' even through they were not articulated at the level of the state and did not form part of the dominant political agenda. The process of paradigm shift (as typified by the transition from a social democratic ideological discourse to one informed by neo-liberalism) is one of gradual disengagement form the practices of the past combined with their partial retention in some form. Here, a social democratic polity can be seen to have been neo-liberalised; not all past policies have been abandoned as the survival of the Beveridgian welfare state testifies. The past, from this perspective, can be more than prologue; refashioned by a newly dominant élite discourse, it may continue to exert an influence over what the state does and, just as crucially, the expectations that civil society has of it.

Political change is characterised as an alteration in the ideological suppositions that govern policy formation – a reflection of the impact a paradigmatic shift can have on social 'belief systems'. Political actors, both when they are constrained by and when they reshape their environments, are capable of both reaction and proaction. Political change (as intended by actors) can be a response to an altered policy universe, one provoked by an acknowledgment that a fundamental shift has been engineered in the form of political debate and in the ideological agenda that governs it. A detailed and empirical analysis of the impact of ideological discourse upon practical politics can therefore provide a framework for exploring the process of political change. This can tell us much about how an ideologically based political agenda can influence attitudes involving the purpose of government, the role of the state and, ultimately, the form that public policy takes. Identifying the moment(s) of transition in the form of dominant ideological agenda is one thing, understanding the process of transition, quite another.

---

influences, are usually the slaves of some defunct economist'. J.M.Keynes, *The General Theory of Employment, Money and Interest*, Macmillan, 1936, p.383.

Political Discourse and Practical Politics: Frameworks for Analysis

James Stanyer
London School of Economics and Political Science

'The 1996 British Party Conferences as News Events: Assessing the Contribution of the Broadcasters to Conference News Agendas'

Introduction

Recent agenda setting research in political communications has been primarily concerned with the general election period (Nossiter et al 1995; Semetko et al, 1991). The British party conferences a media event of some significance in the intervening years have been virtually ignored. This is surprising considering that they attract not only substantial amounts of live coverage but also daily coverage in the press, on radio and on terrestrial and satellite television news. While the live coverage of each conference on the BBC attracts only small audiences the evening news programmes attract large audiences and are therefore important for the political parties. That the political parties set the news agenda for the duration of each conference seems uncontested within the literature. In fact for McNair they are a classic example of a pseudo event (1995) or a Nuremberg rally (Scammell, 1995). Indeed the conference news agendas do reflect the issues raised by timetabled speeches and debates. But the news broadcasters contribution is not merely one of reflection. As with recent studies of the formation of election agendas there needs to be a recognition of the 'active role that the media play in constructing ... coverage' (Semetko et al, p.3). The news broadcasters are autonomous actors at the party conferences and play an active valuelaiden role in constructing what the elector sees on television. This is particularly the case at the beginning of conferences where the news agendas are dominated not by issues initiated in the course of conference proceedings but by issues the news broadcasters see as particularly newsworthy. Taking the first days terrestrial evening news coverage of the 1996 Liberal Democrat and Conservative party conferences on ITV, BBC 1, Channel Four and BBC 2 the paper endeavours to identify the contribution they make.

Variables Specific to Conference Agenda Formation

There are significant differences compared to the general election period that need to be considered when examining the formation of conference news agendas. Firstly, that political parties are heterogeneous organisations. Therefore studies of conference news agenda formation have to examine intra rather than inter party activity. It is therefore necessary to use an organisational framework in order to identify the contributors. The structure of the parties can be understood as a series of concentric circles

(Heffernan & Stanyer 1996). At the centre is the Inner Core Élite comprising of the leader, his immediate entourage, personal advisers; leadership insiders and selected members of the front bench, and party officials. Then there is an Outer Core Élite comprising

(a) the Cabinet and Shadow Cabinet;

(b) other front bench spokespersons;

(c) in Labour's case the NEC.

Further out there is a Peripheral Élite comprising

(a) the Parliamentary Party (back bench MP's);

(b) party officials.

Then the External Power Brokers comprising

(a) trade union élites;

(b) organised activists.

And finally the Unorganised activists, Inactive Members and Supporters. So rather than 'a struggle that pits ... candidates and parties in contention for agenda domination' (Semetko et al 1991, p.176) it is a struggle between various sections within a party, as well as the much emphasised struggle of 'political campaign management's against news organisation teams' (Semetko et al 1991, p.176) although this is less obvious than at election times. Therefore the building blocks of any report are the contributions provided by the various sections within any party.

Secondly, conference agendas are no less complex and mutli layered than election agendas. Conferences can be seen as a series of agendas on numerous issues. As such conference provides an ideal opportunity for various sections of the parties to get their message across via the news broadcasters. The conferences provide the parties with timetabled opportunities to present policy. Conference agendas can be divided firstly, into those that are produced formally through a series of composites and motions submitted to conference for debate and from speeches. The formal agenda varies throughout and each day. Secondly, the conferences act as a loci for the debate of salient issues within the political parties that are not part of the formal timetable. These informal agendas are ones that are usually but not exclusively initiated externally to the conferences themselves but nevertheless are contentious and of importance to the party as a whole.

Thirdly, the Inner Core Élites have some advantages over other groups and actors within the party. Formal Conference agendas have tended to be dominated by them. They make a series of policy statements in a number of speeches over the period of the conference week. Such use of the formal conference proceedings is well planned. In fact more time as been allocated by the Inner Core Élites to speechifying in recent conferences (Wintour, *Guardian*, October 1995). Although the Inner Core Élites may not however have ultimate power within their parties to set the formal agenda they do have a large impact in the formulation of the weeks agenda in the period prior to the start of the conferences. But even if the Inner Core Élites may not be able to prevent an issue coming before conference they can at least prepare in advance for any negative publicity that might arise from it. While the Inner Core Élites have a dominant position in controlling formal agenda their position is challenged by members of the of other groups. These outsider groups may use existing mechanisms to set formal conference agendas but more often they seek to actively contribute to the conferences' informal agendas.

Fourthly, in addition to the series of formal and informal agendas conferences are also a source of a wide range of perspectives on these agendas provided by all the actors and groups present. Because of the significance of conference as a publicity opportunity for the Inner Core Élite, they cannot afford to have informal agendas overshadowing the issues they want to initiate. They cannot ignore them and are forced to engage with them. They have to offer a perspective to the broadcasters and in fact the broadcasters seek out such perspectives. Perspectives can be seen as a contribution to an already existing agenda they are a 'set of views, arguments, explanations and policy suggestions' (Schlesinger et al 1983, p.2). As such the Inner Core Élites views on issues are one of many possible perspectives on issues. At conferences, therefore, the struggle tends not to be about the struggle to control the news agenda but a struggle to initiate a dominant perspective on that agenda. Schlesinger et al (1983) identify three main forms of perspectives, the official, the alternative and the oppositional. These can be appropriated and allotted in terms of conferences to the various sections of the parties identified already. The official perspective is the Inner Core Élite line on a given issue which can be disseminated by any member of the party. The alternative and oppositional perspectives are those that deviate from the official line or are against it. Finally, the news broadcasters are in a one to one relationship with the parties for the duration of the conference and this allows them 'off the hook' of bi-partisanship. In fact these set of unique points do not act to diminish the contribution of the news broadcasters but in some circumstances enhance it .

Contribution of the Broadcasters

It is not the simply the case 'that the conferences [are] "events of the political parties" and the BBC [has] no business interfering with or reshaping the events' (Semetko et al, p.4) The broadcasters both ITN and the BBC in the various news bulletins while not directly impacting on the formal agendas formation do nevertheless actively contribute to the agenda they project within their news reports. The broadcasters 'posses considerable discretionary power on how to frame the daily news report' (Semetko et al, p.xvii). The broadcasters as Semetko et al (1991) argue are able to provide an independent input into the formation of campaign agendas so why not conference agendas too. Such discretionary power is evident in the broadcasters' ability to 'expand the agenda beyond the issues of the day' (Semetko et al, p.xvii) and in their ability to determine the prominence of the report within the overall running order of the bulletin. But also importantly it can be seen in the contribution to the framing of reports on the conferences in general and on the informal agendas in particular.

The news broadcasters firstly, give a certain life and a legitimacy to informal agendas. Without the broadcasters and the wider news media many informal agendas may stay rooted in the conferences' fringe. In this area therefore broadcasters make a larger contribution to the news agenda than they do to the formal agenda of the conference hall. Taking Blumler & Gurevitch's conception of a 'continuum from "agenda setting" to "agenda reflecting" with "agenda shaping" and "agenda amplifying" falling in between the two extremes' (1995, p.96). The news broadcasters actively choose whether or not to reflect informal conference agendas; whether to amplify those agendas, shape them or even set them. Secondly, in addition to giving legitimacy to the informal agendas the broadcaster have discretionary power in deciding the weight and credence given to the various perspectives on those agendas. They bring these perspectives that are provided in different parts of the conference together into a package. Thirdly, news broadcasters provide contextualising remarks within the narrative of the news report about the nature of the agendas and the range of perspectives on it.

The broadcast journalists are therefore faced at any conference with a series of choices about which agenda and perspectives on it they want to reflect or amplify, such choices are the product of their discretionary power. Their discretion lies in their ability to decide whether or not to reflect or amplify the formal agenda and the perspectives associated with that or the informal agenda and perspectives on that. Or move towards a combination of the two. In short they 'tell the ... story not as the (Inner Core Élite) wish it to be presented but as reporters see it' (Semetko et al, p.3).

While possessing discretion the news broadcasters are also committed to conferences as a source of news. The broadcasters Blumler & Gurevitch (1995) have two different orientations or attitudes to parliament as a source of news and that these orientations are role differentiated. They distinguish three groups of broadcasters role, firstly the journalists and correspondents, secondly the editors, managers and channel controllers at the periphery of parliamentary broadcasting and thirdly the higher executives and policy makers within the organisations. They suggest far from being randomly dispersed there is a 'tendency for broadcasters in certain roles to adapt one set of attitudes while incumbents of others exhibit different orientations' (1995, p.52). Focusing on one of the three groups identified namely the journalists and correspondents. Blumler & Gurevitch argue that their orientation towards parliament is primarily 'sacerdotal', that is one that considers that parliamentary developments 'deserve a regular and prominent airing as an inherent right and regardless of news value calculations' (1995, p.50). The opposite orientation and one held by those less involved in news gathering is the 'pragmatic'. This is

> 'the treatment of politicians activities based on ... the assessments of their intrinsic newsworthiness and that consequently the prominence given to the stories reporting these activities, the amount of time or space allocated to them will be determined by a strict consideration of news values' (1995, p.89).

The journalists are not just oriented towards parliament as a source of news such an orientation is transposed every summer recess to the party conferences. In addition they are also oriented towards the political parties Inner Core Élites as the most important actors at the conferences and towards issues within the parties. Nossiter et al (1995) highlight the domination of televisions' election coverage by party leaders, the party leaders are the actors that are most frequently seen in the news. This observation is held up in study of conference news.[1] While the journalists are sacerdoatally oriented towards the Inner Core Élite they are pragmatically oriented towards the other sections of the party. The Inner Core Élites perspective is always sort but the use of the perspectives of other groups or actors are determined by their newsworthiness. The further one moves out along the series of concentric circles the more pragmatically oriented the broadcast journalist are towards those groups or actors. Only the most newsworthy are used as sources for reports. The Peripheral Élite or External Power Brokers receive coverage according to what Blumler & Gurevitch would call a '... consideration of news values' (1995, p.89). The broadcast journalists also have a set of attitudes towards the series of issues which form part of the informal agendas of conference. They are pragmatically oriented towards certain issues that have a particular salience within each party. The issue of Europe at the Conservative conference or relationships with Labour at the Liberal Democrats' conference. These salient party issues that form part of the informal agenda act as the main thrust of some of the news reports with the perspectives on these agendas being sought out by the journalists.

So the news reports act as a reciprocal for a series of agendas. The broadcast journalists decide the gravitas and priority each perspective on these agendas receives. However while autonomous they have certain attitudes which means that the are predisposed to seek out the official perspective of the Inner Core Élite. But the perspectives of the other groupings within the parties will only be used because of their newsworthiness. The more the perspective contradicts the official line the more newsworthy and more likely it is to be used.

The news reports from the first day's six evening news bulletins at the 1996 Liberal Democrat and Conservative annual conferences were all typically a package of several agendas both originating from official conference proceedings and from outside the conference venue. In political communications literature they would be referred to as agendas initiated by a mix of sources (Nossiter et al 1995; Semetko et al 1991) but such classification does not adequately expand upon the broadcasters role in their formation

[1] Except in Newsnight's report from the Liberal Democrats' and ITN 5.40's from the Conservatives' both party leaders appeared and spoke in every report.

The division between what has been described as the formal and the informal agendas of conferences in all reports on these two days leant heavily towards the latter.[2] In fact the Conservative conference proper had not started and so there was no mention of any announcements from the hall. The formal agenda was however presented through a series of trailed policy announcements to be made that evening or the next day.[3] It is difficult and not necessary to determine the origin of these informal agendas but just to note that they are part of wider news agendas which continue through out the year and are transposed by the news broadcasters to the conferences. There was a striking amount of similarity in the prioritising these external agendas in all six news bulletins on the opening days of both conferences. At the Liberal Democrats' all six news bulletins' reports focused on the informal agenda of their present and possible future relations with the Labour party before or after the next general election. At the Conservatives' two defections and a resignation were used as pegs for the agendas of Europe, conference unity and sleaze. The bulletin's reports from both conferences gathered together a series of different perspectives on these issues. These perspectives were indexed as a series of quotes (Lance Bennett 1990) with the official, alternative and oppositional perspectives juxtaposed with one another in order to convey the nature of the debate.

All six conference reports from the Liberal Democrats' Brighton conference were framed in the form of three distinct perspectives around the party's future relations with Labour. The official Inner Core Élite perspective was represented through the indexing of quotes from Paddy Ashdown. These quotes were either a product of an answer to a direct question as both ITN's reports or as in the case of the others taken from a short speech made by Ashdown on the fringe. The official 'nothing is ruled in nothing is ruled out' perspective in each report was contrasted with two alternative perspectives that favourably disposed to doing a deal and that opposed. The former alternative perspective was presented through a quote by a member of the Liberal Democrats' Peripheral Élite Lord Rodgers. Rodgers' 'vote to get rid of this government vote Liberal Democrat as a first preference but vote Labour if that is the best way of doing so' delivered in a speech to fringe meeting was used by all bulletins except the BBC six where the correspondent chose to index the voice of another member of the Inner Core Élite whose perspective the narrative suggested diverged from the official line. The no deal perspective again was presented in counter point to this. Firstly, as what may be described as scepticism in reports from Channel Four news, the BBC Nine and Newsnight in the form of Charles

---

[2] Of the first day's reports from the Liberal Democrats' conference the informal agendas accounted for 69% of the report on the ITN 5.40; 28% of the BBC Six's; 83% of Channel Four's; 46% of the BBC Nine's; 47% of New at Ten's and 100% of Newsnight's.

Of the first day's reports from the Conservatives' conference the informal agendas accounted for 59% of the report on the ITN 5.40; 59% of the BBC Six's; 64% of Channel Four's; 68% of the BBC Nine's; 62% of New at Ten's; and 95% of Newsnight's.

[3] All of the first day's reports from the Conservatives' conference trailed announcements which accounted for 24% of the report on the ITN 5.40; 9% of the BBC Six's; 11% of Channel Four's; 20% of the BBC Nine's; 14% of News at Ten's; and 5% of Newsnight's.

Kennedy's opinions on the break down of trust between the two parties on the question of a Scottish referendum. Secondly a stronger version of this alternative perspective appeared in both of ITN's reports in the form of two quotes from delegates condemning any deals. Channel Four's and Newsnight's reports further reinforced the scepticism with more hard-line condemnation provided by delegates. The extent to which the perspectives differed was further underlined by some of the correspondents' own summary commentary. Hugh Pym on the ITN 5.40 suggested '... there are now conflicting views of how to deal with Labour both before and after the general election' and further on News at Ten he suggested 'there was no concealing the continuing tension over how to deal with Labour'. Similarly John Sergeant on the BBC Six suggested '... within the leadership there are differences on the thorny question of how far they should go in linking up with Labour'. And Robin Oakley on the BBC Nine that 'The Lib Dems remain uncertain on how seriously they should take Tony Blair's flirtations'. But there was no obvious summary commentary at the end of either of the reports on Channel Four news or Newsnight.

On the unofficial opening of the Conservatives' conference all six evening news reports highlighted the series of events that had occurred in Bournemouth linking these events to the ongoing issues of Europe, conference unity and sleaze. Each report went through these events in a shopping list fashion. The defection of Lord McAlpine to the Referendum party, and later the resignation of senior ministerial aide James Cran brought the issue of Europe to the fore. The official Inner Core Élite perspective was in essence reactionary and represented through the indexing of the voice of the Party Chairman on the first four of the six evening news reports with Channel Four using additional comments by the Chairman of the 1922 Committee. All the reports except the ITN 5.40 and Newsnight juxtaposed this official perspective with an alternative perspective provided by Peripheral Élite member John Redwood. The BBC borrowed material directly from an interview with Redwood on that evening's Panorama and ITN and Channel Four News sought out their own quotes. Both Channel Four and Newsnight buttressed this perspective with quotes from arriving representatives. Reports from the BBC Nine onwards also dealt with Cran's resignation, the official perspective that he resigned because of constituency matters was challenged in each report by journalists referring to unnamed sources suggesting that his Euro-scepticism was the real cause. Ian Greer's interview in *The Times* and his sponsoring of the conference fringe guide raised the separate issue of sleaze on the 5.40, Channel Four, News at Ten. With Channel Four soliciting the perspective of party representatives and News at Ten that of the Inner Core Élite.

The reactionary official perspective to these events and the issues they raised was further indexed with a series of quotes from John Major on his arrival at the conference presented in all the reports except on the ITN 5.40. The Prime Minister's response on the BBC dealt with John Redwood's comments specifically but they also along with the other bulletins referred to his annoyance with the questioning. The series of events and divergence of perspectives around the issues they threw up was again underlined by the journalists contextualising remarks. Tom Bradby on the ITN 5.40 suggested 'The Tories desperately need a display of unity and purpose at this conference and they need to shift the agenda quickly away from sleaze and Europe'; John Sergeant that the 'Tories are off to a distinctly unsteady start'; Robin Oakley that 'Party managers hope after such an uncomfortable start to the conference they can get the Tory act together ... '; Jackie Ashley that the party are 'fighting to play down rows over Europe and sleaze'. But again there was no obvious summary commentary at the end of either of the reports on Channel Four News or Newsnight.[4]

Conclusion

These two examples highlight that the news broadcasters have the discretionary power to contribute towards the framing of the day's news agenda. Such a contribution can be seen firstly, in the BBC and ITN's pragmatically derived preference for the informal agenda as a source of news. This agenda was seen as the most newsworthy and subsequently received the most attention within all the reports. Their contribution can be seen secondly in the choices the journalists made over which protagonists represented the various perspectives on these agendas. The leaders and other members of the Inner Core Élite symbolically represented the official perspectives and like wise members of the Peripheral Élite symbolically represented the alternative perspectives. With the delegates acting as a resource to bolster either perspective. Their contribution could also be seen thirdly in the gathering of the perspectives from different locations at different times of the day and the juxtaposing of them, the official against the alternatives. While the official perspectives became main ones around which others were juxtaposed, in all the reports analysed they were not dominant in terms of the number of times they were indexed.[5] There seemed no consistent attempt

[4]The lack of contextualising remarks in the reports of these two bulletins may in a large part be due to the fact that they provided on both days interviews and follow-up reports where the informal agendas were discussed at greater length.

[5]In reports from the Liberal Democrats' conference the ITN 5.40 quoted 5 sources, 2 inner core élite providing the official perspective 1 peripheral élite and 2 delegates providing an alternative perspective; the BBC Six quoted 5 sources, 2 inner core élite and 1 delegate providing an official perspective 1 peripheral élite providing an alternative; Channel Four News quoted 6 sources, 2 inner core élite 1 providing the official perspective and the other along with 1 peripheral élite and 3 delegates providing the alternative perspective; BBC Nine quoted 4 sources, 3 inner core élite 2 providing the official perspective and 1 with 1 peripheral élite member the alternative; News at Ten quoted 5 sources, 2 inner core élite providing the official perspective and 1 peripheral élite and 2 delegates the alternative perspective; and Newsnight quoted 5 sources, 2 inner core élite provided an alternative perspective along with 1 peripheral élite member and 2 delegates.

In reports from the Conservatives' conference the ITN 5.40 quoted 2 sources, both inner core élite providing the official perspective; the BBC Six quoted 4 sources, 2 inner core élite providing the official perspective and 1 peripheral élite providing an alternative perspective; Channel Four News quoted 10 sources 3 inner core élite providing the official perspective and 2 peripheral élite and 5 representatives providing alternative perspectives; the BBC Nine quoted 3 sources, 2 inner core élite providing the official perspective and 1 peripheral élite providing an alternative perspective; News at Ten quoted 4 sources, 2

to balance the opposing perspectives either in terms of time or number of times indexed. May be this was because the broadcasters were freed of their legal requirement to balance party opinion as with election coverage. In addition fourthly, their contribution could also be seen in the contextualising remarks provided within the reports. Those highlighted from the Liberal Democrats' conference sought to 'unmask' the divisions over the informal agenda within the party. Those in reports from the Conservatives' conference tended towards the prescriptive.

The journalists have a decisive role in framing news reports on the conferences by selecting the informal agendas over the formal and by determining the weight allotted to each perspective within the news report through the indexing of quotes from various party sources. Taking Blumler & Gurevitch's (1995) agenda continuum the news broadcasters more than reflect and amplify the informal agendas at the start of the conferences. Through a process of selection and juxtaposing of perspectives on those agendas they shape the informal agenda creating a debate of symbolically polarised opinions.

References

J.G.Blumler & M.Gurevitch, *The Crisis of Public Communication*, Routledge, 1995.

R.Heffernan & J.Stanyer, *Strengthening the Centre: The Labour Party, Political Communications and the Enhancement of Leadership Power*, a paper delivered to the EPOP Conference, September, 1996.

W.Lance Bennett, 'Towards a theory of press-state relations in the United States', *Journal of Communication*, 40, 1990.

T.J.Nossiter et al, 'Old values verses News values: the British 1992 general election campaign on television', in I.Crewe & B.Gosschalk (eds), *Political Communications: The General Election of 1992*, Cambridge University Press, 1995.

B.McNair, *An Introduction to Political Communications*, Routledge, 1995.

M.Scammell, *Designer Politics: How Elections are Won*, Macmillan, 1995.

P.Schlesinger et al, *Televising Terrorism: Political Violence in Popular Culture*, Comedia Publishing Group, 1983.

H.Semetko et al, *The Formation of Campaign Agendas*, Lawrence Erlbaum Associates, 1991.

inner core élite providing the official perspective and 2 peripheral élite providing alternative perspectives; and Newsnight quoted 6 sources, inner core élite providing the official perspective and 4 representatives providing alternative perspectives.

Political Discourse and Practical Politics: Frameworks for Analysis

Andrew Chadwick
London School of Economics

'Ideologies, Communication and Public Discourse'

Acknowledgements

I would like to thank Rodney Barker and Len Tivey for their advice and encouragement. Any errors or shortcomings are, of course, my own.

Introduction

Political ideologies are an inescapable fact of political life. Yet, as with most inescapable facts, controversy has raged over how they should be studied. Analyses of ideologies have, unsurprisingly, varied dramatically. This short essay suggests elements for a tentative framework; one which aims to strike a balance between presenting a set of generally applicable assumptions, and a recognition that any framework must engage with particularistic evidence from the historical context under investigation, especially the processes through which ideological communication occurs.[1] It therefore seeks to address several neglected practical issues. Elements from a variety of perspectives may be combined to provide a distinctive framework of 'public discourse', one that: appreciates the importance of ideological communication through the media; provides justifications for specific sources of evidence to be used for ideological analysis; places ideologies in the context of political conflict; and enables a 'panoramic' rather than a 'detail' approach.

Ideologies and Communication

Communication is a crucial element of ideology. If ideas are to win support, they must be communicated to audiences, and audiences must be receptive to those ideas. The participants in the process of ideological communication are entwined in relationships which differ according to the specific case in point, but it is possible to generalise about the effects of communication for the role of ideologies. Within the political studies community, the debate over the implications of poststructuralism has largely been confined to political theory. Recent debates in the field of history have, however, been

[1] In this case, early twentieth century Britain – the period under investigation in the author's current research. 'Framework' here is taken as a set of explicit working assumptions. It does not refer to a 'theory', from which hypotheses can be drawn and 'tested', rather it serves to highlight the reasons why certain decisions are taken regarding the selection of evidence – decisions which need to be stated and justified.

moved by a desire to provide a view of ideas which may be used in the concrete study of parties, pressure groups and protest movements. Historians influenced by the 'linguistic turn' in social theory have attempted to apply generalisations about the constitutive role of language in the creation of political identity, in which processes of communication are seen as central.

Patrick Joyce, for example, argues that it is necessary to give more prominence to 'the actual terms in which contemporaries talked about the social order, and to the means through which they communicated their perceptions'.[2] This points toward a 'recognition of the contested and constructive role of argument and ideas in the establishment of successful political strategies.'[3] But there is some debate over the precise meaning of 'language' in the new history. Does it refer to 'bodies of utterance of a relatively formal, public sort, often associated with institutions': the sphere of the printed word, the pamphleteer, political intellectual, newspaper columnist, or platform speaker? Or does it refer to the 'symbolic, less formal and less public, often assumed and unspoken ways in which the social world is given form by people'?[4] The ambiguity surrounding the meaning of political language in the new history presents several important difficulties, but by far the most damning criticism is that the new approach does not live up to its expectations because it has paid too much attention to formal language, and not enough attention to the broader symbolic notion of language. It is asserted that much of the work inspired by the linguistic turn seems to focus on coherent public ideologies, which are seen as linked directly to the fortunes of existing political institutions, such as pressure groups and political parties.[5]

These are serious criticisms of the historical-linguistic approach, but the usefulness of the notion of political languages is by no means destroyed by them. In the absence of opinion polls, caused either by the historical period or pollsters' priorities, not to mention the impossibility of interviewing the dead, expressed language is the only means by which political scientists are able to explore the role and meaning of ideologies. The concept of a political language implies that meanings are constructed and shared by élites and non-élites, engaged in symbiotic relationships. Political languages are to be seen as perpetually undergoing contestation and redefinition. Ideas are seen as an important source of collective and individual identity, and are therefore the focus of political research.

---

[2] P.Joyce, *Visions of the People: Industrial England and the Question of Class 1848-1914*, Cambridge University Press, 1991, pp.1, 12, 17-18.

[3] J.Lawrence & M.Taylor, 'The Poverty of Protest: Gareth Stedman Jones and the Politics of Language – a reply', *Social History*, 18/1, 1993, p.12.

[4] P.Joyce, *Visions of the People*, pp.1, 12, 17-18.

[5] J.Lawrence & M.Taylor, 'The Poverty of Protest', p.13; N.Kirk, 'The Continuing Relevance and Engagements of Class', *Labour History Review*, 60/3, 1995. Steinberg, for instance, objects to this approach on the grounds that it assumes that political institutions and élites actually create political identities, a perspective which has much in common with the old 'social control' analysis of élite theory, or even 'hegemony' in Gramscian Marxism. M.W.Steinberg, 'Culturally-Speaking: finding a commons between post-structuralism and the Thompsonian perspective', *Social History*, 21/2, 1996, p.199.

Yet the most important aspect of the notion of political language is that it suggests communication. As Joyce argues: 'the events, structures, and processes of the past are indistinguishable from the forms of documentary representation, the conceptual and political appropriations, and the historical discourses that construct them.'[6] In short, recent developments in the field of history are suggestive for a framework for the analysis of ideologies which places communication at its centre.

Three Forms of Ideological Communication: A Taxonomy

The rather vague definitions of political language as they are used in recent historical studies does nevertheless suggest the need for a basic taxonomy of ideological communication. In the study of political ideologies more generally many begin by asserting the importance of ideas simply because they exist. This is a start, but it does not go very far in the direction of deciding precisely which sorts of ideas are more important for the purposes of a particular framework. The problem may be defined as one of levels of abstraction and communication. It is possible to define three types of ideological communication, each of which may be seen in terms of three basic criteria: the characteristic style of argument; the media of ideological communication; and the core assumptions most commonly employed by those who study them. This provides at least three types of ideological communication: ideology as political philosophy; ideology as public discourse; and ideology as symbolic discourse.

Ideology as Political Philosophy

First, there is ideology communicated as 'political philosophy', in which certain concepts enjoy status because they can be seen as 'perennial'.[7] Arguments about the nature of 'the state', for example, rely on a distinctive mode of reasoning about 'the state' which has a long ancestry. Political philosophers are at one remove from the political arena, and enjoy the fruits of idle speculation. Ideological communication at this level occurs mainly through narrowly circumscribed channels, such as works of political philosophy, whose main audience is seen as highly literate, highly educated and familiar with the demands of the idiom. Ideological communication as it pertains to political philosophy is therefore confined to a small minority during any given period. (This does not, however, mean that the concepts discussed are always so confined: ideology as political philosophy may radiate out into other areas of ideological communication). It is most often assumed that ideologies as political philosophy are independent variables, that they influence political activity, and that it is therefore acceptable to assume all of this, and study ideologies in their 'purest' forms. Debate exists

---

[6] P.Joyce & C.Kelly, 'History and Post-Modernism', *Past & Present*, 133, 1991, p.208.

[7] M.Bevir, 'Are There Perennial Problems in Political Theory?', *Political Studies*, 42/4, 1994.

over the exact method to be employed: for instance, should the approach attempt to discern the 'core elements' of an ideology, or understand it as a tension between two extremes, such as libertarianism and collectivism?[8] But the fundamental assumption is that ideologies are to be studied in terms of their internal structures ('in their own right') and that, in order to do this, it is necessary to focus on the most elaborate and demanding expressions of such ideologies.[9] Those who study ideology as political philosophy generally pay very little attention to the processes of communication between producers and audiences.

Ideology as Public Discourse

Second, there is ideology communicated as 'public discourse'. At this level, ideas are articulated, much debate and discussion takes place, but these debates are seen as supremely political interventions and as elements of particular political strategies. They may have been the product of quiet reflection, or they may have been written with the fierce heat of a polemic, but they are all politically motivated in the sense that they are primarily written for the times in which they are produced: they are public and are caught within a political and historical context. Ideological communication here occurs through a wide variety of channels, especially regular, mass communications, whose main audience is seen as reasonably literate and educated, and as having access to such media. Ideological communication of this type usually, but not always, involves greater numbers of people than ideology as political philosophy.

When it comes to the framework of analysis, it may often be assumed that ideologies as public discourse arise out of 'real' politics, that their success or failure is dependent upon the success or failure of particular institutions, groups, or classes, and that they rise and fall with the particular agent with which they are identified.[10] Yet this assumption is not strictly necessary to such an approach. A different view of public discourse, one which assumes that the distinction between 'real' politics and ideology is too rigid, may be employed. In this latter perspective, politics is in large part a linguistic activity, and an understanding of any political activity is incomplete if it does not refer to the discourses that surround and construct it. In other words, public discourse is intrinsic to political activity, and important methodological implications follow. Moreover, the public discourse type demands that attention to processes of ideological communication be incorporated into the framework for analysis of ideology.

---

[8]For an example of the 'core ideas' approach, see B.C.Parekh, *The Concept of Socialism*, Croom Helm, 1975. For an example of the 'tension between two extremes' approach see W.H.Greenleaf, *The British Political Tradition*: Volume II: *The Ideological Heritage*, Methuen, 1983.

[9]R.Barker, 'A Future for Liberalism or a Liberal Future?', in J.Meadowcroft (ed), *The Liberal Political Tradition: Contemporary Reappraisals*, Edward Elgar, 1996, p.184.

[10]R.Barker, 'A Future for Liberalism or a Liberal Future?', p.184.

Ideology as Symbolic Discourse

Third, there exists what can be termed ideology communicated as 'symbolic discourse'. This is the realm of language in which symbolic practices, ranging from the spectacular to the relatively mundane (processions, banners, the wearing of particular colours, the burning of flags, iconography, and so on), contribute towards shared beliefs. Most ideological expression at this level is either direct, or mediated through unobtrusive forms. Like public discourse, ideological communication of this type usually involves large numbers of people. Indeed, the prevalence of symbolic discourse, due to its informal and relatively unrestricted nature, suggests an assumption that it involves greater numbers than 'public discourse' as I define it. When it comes to the framework of analysis, the populist ethos of some social science, such as 'history from below' or ethnographic approaches to social movements, take pride in digging up ideologies as expressed through symbolic discourse. As with public discourse, symbolic public discourse requires attention to the forms of ideological communication in a way that political philosophy does not. However, as will be shown below, there are very good reasons for arguing that the extent to which ideology is communicated in this way varies substantially from period to period.

These three types of ideological expression: political philosophy, public discourse and symbolic discourse, have radically different implications for the study of ideologies. They require different sets of assumptions about evidence and explanation, and yet it is precisely these assumptions which are rarely made explicit. In the rest of this essay the notion of 'public discourse' will be elaborated upon, indicating the usefulness of this concept for a framework for the study of ideology in general, and for the analysis of early twentieth century Britain in particular.

Public Discourse

Basing a framework for the study of ideology on the level of ideological communication as public discourse has several implications. First, it is desirable that in the historical period under investigation, the ideas were in the public domain. This introduces an important, yet often overlooked, distinction between public and private. There are immense problems with treating evidence from private sources in the same way as published opinion. Published opinions, by their very nature, are written in the hope of consolidating or reconstituting the political beliefs of audiences.[11] As such they differ from private papers in that such written beliefs were never meant for immediate public consumption and therefore cannot be taken as interventions in the public debates of the time. The research on early Labour ideology is peppered with references to the diary of Beatrice Webb, but if such a source is taken as evidence of the ideology of Fabian socialism, then this clearly involves an assumption that the distinction between ideas

[11] G.Stedman Jones, *Languages of Class: Studies in English Working-Class History 1832-1982*, Cambridge University Press, 1983, especially the Introduction and Chapter Three: 'Rethinking Chartism'.

in the public domain, and ideas in private, is one not worth making. The argument here, however, is that such a distinction is crucial to the notion of public discourse, because ideas in this view must be communicated and disseminated in order to exert an influence on debate.[12] Put bluntly, the public discourse framework has an uncompromising focus on *public* debate.

Second, public discourse involves special attention to the mediated printed word with specific political content: books, journals, newspapers, pamphlets, and leaflets. If analysis is focused at this level, and not solely upon ideology communicated as political philosophy, it encompasses a wider range of writers than small, renowned groups of intellectuals. At the same time, whilst it is recognised that symbolic discourse is an important sphere of ideological communication, the less mediated nature of this level makes it less relevant to periods in which mediated political communication becomes the norm. An important characteristic of public discourse is that it is regularised, accessible communication involving a national community. The concept of public discourse therefore makes it possible to delineate which sources are to be considered important.

Third, although ideology communicated as political philosophy and symbolic discourse are not the main focus, the concept of public discourse does not preclude discussion of them. It does, however, seek to place them in the context of a broader range of sources. It is therefore necessary to look at high and low, élite and mass, official and unofficial, sophisticated and simple.

Fourth, public discourse makes it explicit that the ideologies under analysis are embedded in political conflict. It does not privilege certain ideas simply because they were expressed elaborately, or were written by an intellectual. Instead, it assumes that focusing on these kinds of texts can bring us closer to those ideas that were more relevant to the everyday political experiences of those involved in the process of ideological communication. (It must be stressed, however, that this does not imply that only popular ideas should be discussed). In widening the range of evidence, public discourse moves away from a 'detail' and towards a 'panoramic' approach. The meaning of these terms is significant.[13] Public discourse attempts to provide a panoramic perspective on political ideologies.

---

[12]It should be stressed, however, that this public-private distinction does not rest upon the classic liberal distinction between public and private spheres. It does not, therefore, seek to privilege what takes place in the public sphere at the expense of the private sphere. It simply states that there is a distinct mode of ideological communication – public discourse – which is best captured by attention to publicly communicated political ideas.

[13]In the visual arts, 'detail' refers to the 'extended treatment of or attention to particular items; a part of a whole; a small and subordinate part; a portion considered independently of the parts considered together; a minor part (as the cornice, caps of the buttresses, capitals of a building) or the small elements of a photographic image corresponding to those of the subject'. In contrast, 'panorama' refers to 'a picture exhibited a part at a time by being unrolled before the spectator; an unobstructed or complete view of a region in every direction; a comprehensive presentation of a subject; or a mental picture of a series of images or events'. (*Webster's English Dictionary*, 1996).

Public Discourse in Historical Context

The public discourse framework requires attention to the forms of communication in any particular historical period. In this case, it will be explored in relation to early twentieth century Britain. One influential theory for understanding the role of communication in democracies is Habermas's concept of the 'public sphere'. Although there has been a heavy normative emphasis in the work influenced by this approach, there have nevertheless been attempts to apply Habermas's framework to concrete instances of communication.[14] Habermas argued that the public sphere developed in Western Europe during the eighteenth century, reached its high point during the mid-nineteenth century, and subsequently declined during the later nineteenth and early twentieth centuries. He therefore locates the development of particular forms of communication, providing a dynamic perspective that indicates how the structures which facilitate public discourse have changed over time. The communications media in any period therefore assume a central position. Yet the obvious notion that the media through which ideologies are constructed and transmitted change dramatically over time is frequently overlooked in approaches to the study of ideologies. Late twentieth century ideological communication, for instance, occurs through a wide variety of media, but it would be highly controversial to assume that print media are now the sole means by which political actors seek to promote political ideas. Thus, a framework for the analysis of ideologies in 1997 is bound to consider broadcast media as a major site of ideological conflict, construction and transmission. This, of course, has little relevance for 1900.

The neglect of this simple point is one of the reasons why those who study ideologies in action have often found it difficult to answer the criticism: why did you look at that particular expression of ideology? If this is a question which deserves an answer, the study of ideologies must involve some explanation of the sources of ideological expression, and the hierarchies of evidence which are a crucial component of any research. This is especially important for the public discourse framework because the structure and role of media in ideological communication are subject to dramatic change across time. The public discourse framework therefore requires the prioritising of the media of ideological communication in any given period.

In calling for a new 'cultural history of politics', in which print, symbolic, and ritualised forms of communication are given equal attention in the framework of analysis, James Vernon uses the concept of the public sphere in a distinctive sense – as popular, collective, and rich with symbolic characteristics. Vernon argues that in the mid-nineteenth century informal popular involvement in politics was extremely high: politics as spectacle was equal in importance to politics as rational discussion. The 'public sphere', as he defines it, depends explicitly on the physical characteristics of publicness: the street, the platform, the speech, and the outdoor meeting. Situating the

---

[14] J.Habermas, *The Structural Transformation of the Public Sphere: An Inquiry Into a Category of Bourgeois Society*, MIT Press, 1989. Although it has to be said that normative considerations are rarely excluded from such work. Reasons of space preclude detailed discussion of the concept of the public sphere.

decline of this popular public sphere from the mid- nineteenth century onwards, Vernon argues that it was displaced by an individualised, élitist and restrictive form of political communication, one which exhibited a 'rational' style, but in so doing, excluded those who had previously participated in spectacular politics: the illiterate poor and most women. By the end of the nineteenth century, in this view, the open, participatory politics of the street had been marginalised by the closed, disciplinary politics of the printed word.[15] For Vernon, this development marked the end of a golden era, and led to the 'rational and disciplined use of literacy within the family and its private home.'[16]

Although Vernon's general adherence to the public sphere approach is rather loose, and his argument about the backward march of democracy is open to doubt, his indication of the dominance of print by the end of the nineteenth century is indisputable. The chief modes of ideological communication between the 1880s and the 1930s – between the relative decline of the oral and symbolic culture of the pre-nineteenth century period, and the emergence of the popular consumption of radio – were the press, periodicals, pamphlets and related literature. The act of reading became heavily burdened with the responsibility of political communication. Other writers have arrived at the same conclusion, pointing not so much to the end of a style of symbolic politics, as to the simple fact of the increase in the mass consumption popular press by the late Victorian period.[17] In both perspectives print became the dominant means of political communication, and the forms of print culture were genuinely diverse. The period from the 1880s to the 1930s was a unique 'window' of print culture in Britain. Early twentieth century British politics was dominated by the printed word in its countless manifestations. Long before television, and before radio, the printed word in a variety of forms provided the dominant opportunity for reaching larger audiences than those who could be gathered in the physical presence of a politician. Analysis of the printed word, then, should be the dominant focus of any study of early twentieth century ideology in Britain.

But if ideological communication during the early twentieth century is assumed to have taken place primarily through the printed word, then are we not committing the errors which Vernon highlighted: namely, that print culture excluded vast numbers of people? Does the attention to print culture as the focus of study not contradict the panoramic quality of public discourse outlined above? This is not the case for at least two reasons.

First, there is the matter of literacy. In the taxonomy outlined above, ideology communicated as political philosophy assumes that the relationship between producers and audiences is tightly restricted by the demands of the idiom, and ideology communicated as symbolic discourse is not dependent upon literacy at all. Public discourse, on the other hand, at least requires that levels of literacy were such that the dominant media of ideological

[15] J.Vernon, *Politics and the People: A Study in English Political Culture, 1815-1867*, Cambridge University Press, 1993, p.105.

[16] J.Vernon, *Politics and the People*, p.142.

[17] See A.J.Lee, *The Origins of the Popular Press in England, 1855-1914*, Croom Helm, 1976.

communication in a period were easily accessible. In the mid-nineteenth century, literacy levels stood at 33 per cent for married men and 49 per cent for married women. By 1914, over 99 per cent of married men and women were literate. Even where illiteracy might have precluded the reading of political texts, the residual practice of communal reading, whereby literature would be shared among family, friends and neighbours, ensured that by the early twentieth century there was clearly a potential mass, national readership for all forms of printed political literature.[18] By the opening of the twentieth century, the vast majority had been brought within the pale of print culture.

Second, and equally important for the panoramic view provided by public discourse is the existence of a plurality of media. Arguments have varied over the effects of changes in the structure of ownership and control of the press during the nineteenth and early twentieth centuries. Support for Vernon may be found in Curran's view that censorship by the state in the early nineteenth century was replaced by censorship by the market in the late nineteenth century, edging out the oppositional radical press of the early nineteenth century in favour of a watered down, commercialised radicalism increasingly subject to the control of the official Liberal Party in alliance with industrial entrepreneurs.[19] Yet Curran's analysis, whilst convincing in its depiction of a general trend, requires important qualifications. The commercialised radicalism of the late nineteenth century was no less important for providing an arena for the critical voices of subordinate groups.[20] The existence of myriad radical and socialist papers needs consideration, as does the wide range of monthly reviews which had their heyday during this period.[21] Such papers enjoyed a particularly close relationship with their readers, one characterised by reciprocity, interaction and reinforcement.[22] Rather than the 'depopularisation' of politics by the end of the nineteenth century, it is possible to argue that, even though ideological communication underwent changes, the 'popular' element of politics was not lost – it

[18]D.Vincent, *Literacy and Popular Culture in England 1750-1914*, Cambridge University Press, 1989, pp.1-3. Literacy as defined by the ability to sign the marriage register. This is of course a relatively crude index of literacy, but given the shortage of available evidence, it forms the backbone of Vincent's wide-ranging study. Indeed, Vincent suggests that this measurement is useful because it provides a standard for long term comparison. On the question of whether the ability to sign one's name is indicative of the ability to read, Vincent argues that most learned to read before they could write. Writing was therefore a good indicator of the acquisition of basic reading skills (p.17). On communal reading see also J.Vernon, *Politics and the People*, p.145.

[19]J.Curran, 'The Press as an Agency of Social Control: An Historical Perspective', in G.Boyce et al (eds), *Newspaper History*, Constable, 1978, pp.51-75; J.Curran, 'Rethinking the Media as a Public Sphere', in P.Dahlgren & C.Sparks (eds), *Communication and Citizenship: Journalism and the Public Sphere*, Routledge, 1991 p.40.

[20]V.Berridge, 'Popular Sunday Papers and Mid-Victorian Society', in G.Boyce et al (eds), *Newspaper History*, p.249. See also A.J.Lee, 'The Radical Press', in A.J.A.Morris (ed), *Edwardian Radicalism 1900-1914*, Routledge & Kegan Paul, 1974.

[21]D.Hopkin, 'The Socialist Press in Britain, 1890-1910'; J.Mason, 'Monthly and Quarterly Reviews, 1865-1914', both in G.Boyce et al (eds), *Newspaper History*.

[22]V.Berridge, 'Content Analysis and Historical Research on Newspapers', in M.Harris & A.J.Lee (eds), *The Press in English Society from the Seventeenth to the Nineteenth Centuries*, Associated University Presses, 1986.

may even have been enhanced. A pluralistic public sphere of print communications existed, one in which the 'mainstream' press was accompanied by a diverse range of marginal and oppositional newspapers, journals and pamphlets, all supported by a variety of literate reading publics. These two contextual factors, the high level of literacy, and the relatively pluralistic structure of the media, suggest that, while communication undoubtedly changed from oral to print-based patterns, this transition did not do too much damage to the interactive relationship between producers and audiences.

Multiple and Overlapping Public Spheres

The concept of the public sphere therefore indicates the importance of print culture for the early twentieth century, but it is still a blunt instrument for conceptualising ideological communication. The demise of a single, relatively undifferentiated sphere of communication is difficult to portray empirically. Habermas charts the collapse of the public sphere in the late nineteenth century, but it is arguable that it was precisely this period which saw the emergence into West European politics of many new and different groups and ideologies, in particular feminism and socialism. The dissemination of these ideologies was carried out vigorously through channels of public discourse. It is difficult, for example, to imagine the early Labour Party in isolation from the various labour and socialist newspapers of the time. The single public sphere as a framework is therefore too restrictive, because it misses the emergence of new political groups, each with their own distinctive infrastructures of communication. A single public sphere obscures the differences between groups, and has the potential to ignore ideological conflict.[23] Utilising a panoramic perspective necessitates sensitivity towards such minority ideologies. The clash of relatively marginal ideological currents must be incorporated into the broader landscape.

Recently, Susan Herbst has attempted to develop a theoretical perspective on public expression 'outside the mainstream' by adapting the concept of the public sphere.[24] Whilst it is concerned primarily with marginalised groups, one of the implications of her work is that, in order to develop a multi- layered notion of ideological conflict, it is necessary to explore how groups, movements and parties develop and make use of their own distinctive channels of communication. This theory can therefore illuminate all forms of political communication in which a party or group seeking to influence public debate constructs its own network of communication. Herbst uses three main concepts: 'linguistic space', 'community-building' and 'communication environments' to describe the communication relationships which groups, movements and parties develop in order to advance

---

[23]M.P.Ryan, 'Gender and Public Access: Women's Politics in Nineteenth Century America', in C.Calhoun (ed), *Habermas and the Public Sphere*, MIT Press, 1991. See also G.Eley, 'Nations, Publics and Political Cultures: Placing Habermas in the Nineteenth Century', in C.Calhoun (ed) *Habermas and the Public Sphere*.

[24]S.Herbst, *Politics at the Margin: Historical Studies of Public Expression Outside the Mainstream*, Cambridge University Press, 1994.

their own ideologies, and which lead to the emergence of multiple public spheres.

Linguistic space specifies the channels set up by group leaderships in order to communicate to their supporters, for their supporters in turn to communicate back, and for both leaders and supporters to communicate to the wider public.[25] The opening up of linguistic space facilitates the development of ideology by providing relatively stable, regular opportunities for communication. Whilst it may refer to the organised output of an established institution such as a political party, linguistic space does not assume that ideological communication is always formally attached to such institutions. In this view, many different participants contribute to ideological debate: they do not have to be formal representations of organised opinion. Herbst's second concept – community- building – specifies the functions of public spheres for providing cohesion for groups and their supporters. It is suggested that processes of communication serve to draw boundaries around the group, constituting insiders and outsiders, defending the group's beliefs from external attack in the process.[26] This particular view needs to be modified, however, because it does not seem to allow for the possibility of cross-fertilisation between groups and parties. If all groups simply provided their supporters with their own communication networks, then there would be little chance of building alliances based on ideological affinities with other groups. It is therefore necessary to amend Herbst's theory by adding the notion of overlapping public spheres, which refers to the process whereby groups seek to build ideological bridges based on common preoccupations and practical measures. In the early twentieth century, for example, the development of both socialist and feminist ideology cannot be understood without reference to liberalism. Finally, the concept of the 'communication environment' refers to the power groups have to shape the patterns of communication in a particular field.[27] Drawing upon elements from Steven Lukes' theory of power and Foucault's notion of discourse, Herbst suggests that the powerful in this sense have the ability to set the boundaries of the communication environment, to decide who is able or unable to communicate and to influence the content of political ideology.

Herbst's theory is complementary to the concept of public discourse outlined above. It suggests that there are reciprocal relationships between élites and supporters, and it points to the ways in which groups and parties, large and small, seek to disseminate their ideas. In pointing to the infrastructures of communication set in place by parties and groups, the idea of multiple, overlapping public spheres is an important dimension.

Conclusion

The public discourse framework is an attempt to suggest a practical orientation for the study of political ideologies by highlighting the problem of

[25] S.Herbst, *Politics at the Margin*, p.2.
[26] S.Herbst, *Politics at the Margin*, pp.22-23.
[27] S.Herbst, *Politics at the Margin*, p.30.

evidence and the positive aspects of a panoramic approach. For this reason, broader epistemological questions have been underplayed. Such approaches have, of course, long been the lifeblood of ideological analysis, but the translation of abstract theorising into a set of criteria for the concrete study of political phenomena has sometimes proved elusive. There is a need to bridge the divide between a concern with 'ideology' and the analysis of ideologies; an enterprise that would benefit from contributions from a whole range of theoretical perspectives. It is safe to assume, however, that problems similar to those raised by the public discourse framework need to be addressed in any empirical work on ideologies that places value on the presentation of core assumptions.

The Communist Manifesto: 150 Years On

John Hoffman
University of Leicester

'The Communist Manifesto and the Idea of Permanent Revolution'

Introduction

The *Manifesto* does not actually use the slogan of the permanent revolution (although elsewhere Marx does). But it does enunciate the idea which lies behind the slogan and in a way which captures the ambiguities which have dogged the idea ever since.

I shall argue that in essence the theory of permanent revolution implies that capitalism and communism, democracy and socialism, liberalism and emancipation are indissolubly linked. Hence the theory is crucial to Marxism as a whole and is expounded in the *Manifesto.* However the term is often taken to mean that the link between a 'bourgeois revolution' which establishes capitalism, and a 'proletarian revolution' which seeks to introduce a communist society, involves a process of revolutionary struggle within a relatively short timescale. One revolution is followed immediately by another.

I shall call this version of the permanent revolution the 'immediacy thesis' and I will argue that although the immediacy thesis does receive textual support within the *Manifesto* (and elsewhere in Marx's writings), it is in conflict both with the general argument of this document and with Marx's overall political theory.

Permanent Revolution and the Immediacy Thesis

As far as the *Manifesto* in general is concerned, a communist revolution is only possible because 'the weapons with which the bourgeoisie fells feudalism to the ground are turned against the bourgeoisie itself'.[1] It is the bourgeoisie which supplies the proletariat 'with its own elements of political and general education': 'it furnishes the proletariat with weapons for fighting the bourgeoisie'.[2] This 'weapons' argument contains, I would suggest, the essence of the permanent revolution idea – the notion that capitalism and communism are indissolubly linked. That Marx and Engels regarded this idea as distinctive to their particular theory of communism can be seen from Part III of the *Manifesto* where the other variants of communism and socialism around in 1848 are criticised either because they reject the revolutionary character of the bourgeoisie, or because they are uncritical towards

[1] K.Marx & F.Engels, *Collected Works*, volume 6, Lawrence & Wishart, 1976, p.490. All further citations from the *Manifesto* will be presented as *MECW*, 6.

[2] *MECW*, 6, p.493. See also J.Hoffman, 'Karl Marx and Friedrich Engels: The Communist Manifesto', in M.Forsyth et al, *The Political Classics*, Oxford University Press, 1993, pp.176-80.

capitalism. Marx and Engels believe that it is necessary and possible to be *both* critical of capitalism and to accept the revolutionary part played historically by the bourgeoisie.

I shall call this linkage between capitalism and communism the general idea of permanent revolution. There is however a rather different version of the theory also presented in the *Manifesto*, and it is this version which I tag the immediacy thesis. In Part IV we see both versions of the theory existing side by side.

The general idea is reiterated in relation to Germany. In the case of Germany – still under absolute semi-feudal rule in 1848 – communists, the *Manifesto* tells us, fight with the bourgeoisie 'whenever it acts in a revolutionary way'. However in doing so, they continue to instil in workers 'the hostile antagonism between bourgeoisie and proletariat', using as 'weapons' against the bourgeoisie, the social and political conditions which the bourgeois revolution introduces.[3]

It is also argued in Part IV that the German workers may straightaway use bourgeois weapons against the bourgeoisie 'in order that, after the fall of the reactionary clases in Germany, the fight against the bourgeoisie itself may *immediately* begin'.[4] But this comment in itself is not sufficient to assert the immediacy thesis, for this requires (as we see in the passage which follows) that a revolution against capitalism will immediately follow the bourgeois revolution itself. It is not merely that the struggle against the bourgeoisie begins immediately after a bourgeois revolution, but rather that (in the celebrated formulation of Part IV) 'the bourgeois revolution in Germany will be but the prelude to an immediately following proletarian revolution'.[5]

The difference between what I have called the immediacy thesis and the general idea of the permanent revolution should now be clear. It is not simply a question of there being a link between capitalism and communism or even that after the bourgeois revolution, a struggle against the bourgeoisie may begin straightaway. It is a question of a struggle culminating in a seizure of proletarian power (that is, a proletarian revolution) immediately following the bourgeois revolution.

This immediacy thesis is, I want to argue, in tension with the wider notion of permanent revolution presented in the *Manifesto* (and in Marx and Engels's writings more generally). It is however a thesis of great historic importance, since it is the immediacy thesis which is often seen as providing the Russian Revolution of 1917 with its Marxist credentials.

---

[3] *MECW*, 6, pp.518-19.
[4] *MECW*, 6, p. 519. Italics mine.
[5] *MECW*, 6, p.519.

The Idea and the Single Stage Revolution

There is general agreement that the slogan of the permanent revolution was first used by Jacobins during the French Revolution of 1789. Marx and Engels explicitly acknowledge this[6] and there can be no doubt that this historical origin explains the term's prestige among the radical revolutionaries with whom Marx and Engels allied in the 1848 period. As an expression of popular sovereignty, the slogan implied the demolition of absolutist rule. But it also pointed to a movement beyond political and legal equality and towards social and economic equality. Hence the idea of a revolution which is 'permanent'. It is here that ambiguities begin. For the notion implies, on the one hand, that revolution is a process. On the other hand, the question has to be asked: is a process intelligible unless it is divided into distinct 'phases' and 'stages'?

In tackling this problem, Marx added something of his own to the Jacobin formulation, for he and Engels were not uncritical of Jacobin political thought. While they saw the Jacobins as heroic and audacious revolutionaries who had attempted to take the logic of liberalism to its radical extremes, these revolutionaries were imprisoned within an idealist philosophical framework which ascribed political development to abstract will power rather than to maturing social conditions. This idealist political outlook, in Marx and Engels's view, made it impossible to articulate the distinct phases which a revolutionary process requires.[7]

For this reason I would argue that neither of the two versions of the permanent revolution found in the *Manifesto* – the general argument and the immediacy thesis – can be described as Jacobin in character since both distinguish between a bourgeois revolution and a proletarian revolution. This point also explains why it was that although the Jacobin tradition was continued in the nineteenth century by Auguste Blanqui , Blanquists did not espouse the idea of permanent revolution precisely because they rejected the notion of a bourgeois revolution as a politically desirable objective distinct from a socialist or communist one.

When Buonarotti (one of Blanqui's predecessors) referred to a 'regenerative revolution' that required 'strong and wise revolutionary hands' to ensure its consummation, he saw the revolution as fundamentally communist in character. It is true that Blanqui could refer to introducing commuism 'step by step', but this is a 'process' view within a communist revolution.[8] It does not imply that one kind of revolution is to be followed by another.

Even the compressed timescale implied by the immediacy thesis distinguishes between two distinct phases of the revolutionary process. In both versions of the permanent revolution presented in the *Manifesto*, the no-

---

[6] Marx & Engels, *Collected Works*, volume 3, Lawrence & Wishart, 1975, p.156 and *Collected Works*, volume 4, Lawrence & Wishart, 1975, p.122. In 1884 Engels noted that the French revolutionary, Marat, like Marx and Engels, 'did not want the revolution declared finished but continuing in permanence'. Cited by R.Hunt, *The Political Ideas of Marx and Engels*, volume 1, Macmillan, 1975, p.185).

[7] For references and commentary see M.Johnstone, 'Marx, Blanqui and Majority Rule', *Socialist Register 1983*, Merlin, p.302.

[8] Johnstone, 'Marx, Blanqui and Majority Rule', pp.299, 301.

tion of distinctness, separation and differentiation is linked to the idea of unity, process and fusion. The concept of a distinctive bourgeois revolution separate from and preceding a proletarian one, derives from Marx's view of revolution as a process tied to maturing material conditions so that even before Marx had formulated the idea of permanent revolution in the *Manifesto*, his argument cannot be described as Blanquist or Jacobin in character.

Marx identifies Jacobinism with an abstract politics which seeks to suppress the real contradictions developing in civil society. Even when Marx speaks only of a communist revolution (as in 1844) , his argument emphasises revolution as the product of developing material conditions within society itself. It is not something which can be imposed by a dedicated élite. The Jacobin strategy of 'declaring the revolution to be permanent' is seen as a political drama which necessarily ends with the re-establishment of religion, private property and civil society.[9]

When Marx does come to accept the need for political organisation, the logic which informs his argument is quite different from that of Blanqui. He explicitly rejects Weitling's (Blanquist) argument that humanity is 'always ripe for communism' and insists that communism can only be established if revolutionaries move through differentiated and distinct stages of development. Against Weitling, Marx argues in 1846 that it is 'the bourgeoisie which must attain power to begin with'.[10]

The point is that the idea of permanent revolution as expounded in the *Manifesto* (in both its versions), rejects the notion of communism as a single stage revolution. It is revealing therefore that when Willich's group within the Communist League breaks with Marx in September 1850, his faction abandons the theory of permanent revolution and reverts to a one step revolutionary strategy involving the immediate seizure of power. If 'genuine' or 'true' revolution only has a communist character, then it seems clearer not to call it 'permanent', since the idea of permanent revolution implies some differentiation between different phases of the revolution, and that a distinct (and positive) recognition should be given to the revolution of the bourgeoisie.[11]

This is why Cunliffe's analysis of the 'tensions' within the *Manifesto* is problematic. Although Cunliffe focuses his argument upon the passage in the *Manifesto* which deals with a proletarian revolution immediately following a bourgeois one, he concerns himself exclusively with the prospects for proletarian revolution in Germany. While it is true that proletarian revolution is necessary for the idea of permanent revolution, it is not sufficient,

[9] Marx & Engels, *Collected Works*, volume 3, p.156; *Collected Works*, volume 4, p.183. Fernbach argues that the reference to the German proletariat 'somersalting' into communism presages the tactic of permanent revolution (D.Fernbach, 'Introduction', *The Revolutions of 1848*, Penguin, 1973, p.36), but Hunt is right to discount this view since the idea of permanent revolution in Marx implies the linkage between for two revolutions rather than a focus simply on one. See Hunt, Political Ideas of Marx and Engels 1, p.178; also Johnstone, 'Marx, Blanqui and Majority Rule', p.302; 313.

[10] Hunt, *Political Ideas of Marx and Engels*, volume 1, pp.155, 179.

[11] Hunt, *Political Ideas of Marx and Engels*, volume 1, p.246.

since essential to the idea is the differentiation between two types of revolution, however closely linked they might be. Cunliffe refers to the *Manifesto*'s 'laconic reference' to an impending bourgeois revolution in Germany[12] but fails to see that it is precisely the role of the bourgeois revolution which lies at the heart of the controversy generated by Marx's idea of permanent revolution. What makes the revolution permanent is the fact that it does not embrace the proletarian revolution alone.

The Unfortunate Verschmelzung

Hunt has argued that the immediacy thesis arises as a tactically contrived amalgamation or *Verschmelzung* between Marxian and Blanquist ideas.[13] The logic of Marxism (as Hunt rightly stresses) requires a bourgeois revolution in order to create the basis for communism. This involves (as Marx points out in 1847) the destruction of absolute monarchy and explicit patriarchalism; the development of political centralisation, and the proletarianisation of the propertyless classes – in short 'the material basis that the proletariat requires for its liberation'.[14] The problem is that the implementation of this bourgeois revolution implies a timescale that cannot be reconciled with the immediacy thesis.

The *Manifesto* itself suggests that the proletariat would only acquire the political skills and theoretical confidence to challenge the bourgeoisie over a lengthy process of time. Although we are told that 'at its birth' it begins its struggle with the bourgeoisie, the proletariat goes through 'various stages of development'. These can (at least in part) be enumerated as follows: an infantile experience of Luddism – smashing machinery rather than challenging relationships – fighting the absolute monarchy (alongside the bourgeoisie), forging trade unions, forming a working class political party able to intervene in political debate and exploit divisions within the bourgeoisie, and enlisting the support of ideologically sophisticated bourgeois renegades. All this is necessary if the proletariat is to emerge as the independent movement of the immense majority.[15] If we assume (as the *Manifesto* seems to) that these developments are necessary for a proletarian revolution, then it is difficult to see how such a revolution could immediately follow a bourgeois one. The maturation process for proletarian supremacy is clearly a protracted one.

Hunt's argues that the members of the Communist League had accepted the need for a 'democratic' (that is to say, accountable rather than conspiratorial) political organisation, but were not really convinced that two distinct revolutions were necessary. Hence, as he points out, even where they accepted the notion of a 'democratic revolution', they interpreted this in Blanquist fashion. The democratic revolution is not (as it is in Marx)

[12] J.Cunliffe, 'Marx's Politics – the Tensions in the Communist Manifesto', *Political Studies*, 30/4, 1982, p.573.

[13] Hunt, *Politial Ideas of Marx and Engels*, p.189.

[14] Cited by Hunt, *Political Ideas of Marx and Engels*, volume 1, p.180.

[15] *MECW*, 6, p.492, 494-95.

the bourgeois revolution which creates the material basis for a 'higher' communist struggle. Rather it is synonymous with the communist revolution itself. Within a single upheaval, a 'community of goods' is to be immediately introduced.[16]

The immediacy thesis which separates the two revolutions but states that one immediately follows the other, is neither 'fish nor fowl'. It seeks, Hunt argues, to reconcile the irreconcilable – the desire for an immediate communist revolution with the argument that a prior bourgeois revolution is necessary. It is designed to placate radical sympathies by sugaring the classical Marxist pill so that a distinct bourgeois revolution is to be tolerated on the grounds that a proletarian revolution 'immediately follows'.[17] The distinction between the two revolutions is preserved alongside a highly problematic sense of immediacy.

Not only is this particular version of permanent revolution in tension with the argument of the *Manifesto* as a whole, but it is inconsistent with positions taken in other texts in this period. For example, Engels in 1847 declared that the workers in Germany would not be mature enough to form a ruling class 'for a long time', and in his preliminary draft of the *Manifesto*, he argued that a communist revolution would be 'slowest and most difficult to carry out in Germany'.[18] These views certainly accord with the argument of the *Manifesto* and what I have called the general idea of permanent revolution, but they are clearly in conflict with the immediacy thesis.

During the 1848 revolution Marx and Engels offered critical support for the bourgeois revolution, and when they became convinced that the bourgeoisie were too weak to provide political leadership, they argued that the tasks of the bourgeois revolution should be carried through by a radical popular alliance. Johnstone notes that Marx and Engels saw their campaigning paper, the *Neue Rheinische Zeitung*, as an 'organ of democracy' and not emphatically as an organ of communism.[19]

After the collapse of the revolution in Germany, Marx and Engels continued to believe (until September 1850) that fresh revolution was imminent. Hence they judged that a political alliance with radicals was still necessary. This accounts for the positive references made to Blanqui and his 'revolutionary socialism' in the *Class Struggles in France*, and for the fact that in Marx's address to the Communist League in March 1850, there is, to quote Hunt, 'an exact rerun of the *Manifesto*'s *Verschmelzung*'. The need for a tactically contrived formula designed to mask two incompatible versions of revolution is repeated (and for the same reasons) in a statement which explicitly refers to permanent revolution by name. On the one hand a bourgeois revolution (identified here with 'petty bourgeois democracy') is insisted upon, but on the other we are told that this preponderating influence will only last 'for a moment'. Moreover the March Address also argues that German workers will not be able to attain power without going

[16] Hunt, *Political Ideas of Marx and Engels*, volume 1, p.186.

[17] Hunt, *Political Ideas of Marx and Engels*, volume 1, pp.190, 246.

[18] Hunt, *Political Ideas of Marx and Engels*, volume 1, p.179; Johnstone, 'Marx, Blanqui and Majority Rule', p.303.

[19] Johnstone, 'Marx, Blanqui and Majority Rule', p.303.

through 'a lengthy revolutionary development': a reference which embraces the general idea of permanent revolution (and thus the wider logic of Marxist theory) rather than the immediacy thesis.[20]

What further complicates the picture is the fact that although Blanquists proper did not (as we have already noted) support the idea of permanent revolution, Blanquist-minded radicals within the Communist League certainly did, at least until the middle of 1850. Incensed by Marx's argument in 1849 that an industrial revolution (bourgeois in character) was necessary for communism, Gottschalk, a fellow member of the Communist League, contrasted bourgeois rule with the theory of permanent revolution, accusing Marx of not believing in the latter![21]

In 1848 therefore permanent revolution could mean one of three things: the demand for communism now; the 'immediacy thesis', and a notion that bourgeois and proletarian revolutions were linked over a prolonged period of time. The first of these does not square with either version of the permanent revolution in the *Manifesto*, and by denying the role of phases, it is hard to see why a one step theory of communist revolution should be conceived of as 'permanent' at all. However the phrase about 'an immediately following proletarian revolution' does occur in the *Manifesto* (although only in the *Manifesto*), but the immediacy thesis is atypical. Hunt argues that after 1850 this thesis (which he identifies with the slogan of permanent revolution itself) is never repeated again in Marx's writing.[22] As for the general idea of permanent revolution – the notion that the bourgeois and communist revolutions are linked – it has to be said that this did not commend itself to all socialists, but it is the immediacy thesis which has tended to preoccupy both the critics and the exponents of the permanent revolution.

Lenin, Trotsky and the Bolshevik Revolution

In April 1917 Lenin links support for the *Manifesto* with the argument that with the destruction of Tsarism, the bourgeois democratic revolution in Russia is complete. A new form of state – a proletarian state – has now become possible and preparation for a a proletarian revolution should begin.[23]

It is plausible to infer that in invoking what he sees as the Marxism of the *Manifesto*, Lenin is also identifying the Russian Revolution with the immediacy thesis. The argument seems to be this. Not only does Russia have a developed proletariat, but as in the *Manifesto*'s prediction for Germany in 1848, a bourgeois revolution (the removal of the Tsar in February) can be 'immediately followed' by a proletarian revolution (the events of October). The Russian Revolution thereby receives its Marxist imprimatur.

---

[20]Hunt, *Political Ideas of Marx and Engels*, volume 1, pp.234, 244; for the text of the March Address, see Marx & Engels, *Collected Works*, volume 10, Lawrence & Wishart, 1978, pp.277-87.

[21]Hunt, *Political Ideas of Marx and Engels*, pp.220-21.

[22]Hunt, *The Political Ideas of Marx and Engels*, p.246.

[23]V.Lenin, *Collected Works*, volume 24, Progress, 1964, pp.57, 84, 87.

In 1950 E.H.Carr presented the *Manifesto* as 'a living document whose centenary cannot be celebrated otherwise than in the light, and in the shadow of the Russian Revolution'. The Revolution constituted 'the culminating moment of the *Communist Manifesto*'. Taylor cites the famous formula of the immediacy thesis and comments pithily: 'this prophecy proved incorrect so far as Germany was concerned, but it came surprisngly to life during the Russian Revolution of 1917'.[24]

If the Russian Revolution can be interpreted as an event which accords with the *Manifesto*'s immediacy thesis, then the question arises: how do Lenin's arguments in 1917 square with his earlier position? Before 1917 Lenin (like Rosa Luxemburg in this respect) had seen revolution in Russia as involving two distinct and chronologically separate stages. Both he and Luxemburg argued that the bourgeois revolution in Russia would have to made against the bourgeoisie, and Lenin identified the dictatorship of the proletariat and peasantry (the slogan he embraced in 1905) as a radical form of the bourgeois revolution. It would seem therefore that he did not accept the immediacy thesis since (in Carr's view) he refrained from suggesting that the bourgeois revolution would be immediately followed by the socialist revolution.[25]

It is true that Lenin also speaks in 1905 of an 'uninterruped revolution', arguing that 'from the democratic revolution, we shall at once, and precisely in accordance with the measure of our strength, begin to pass to the socialist revolution', and there is a good deal of argument as to whether this particular formulation was characteristic of Lenin's thought before 1917.[26] But the notion of an 'uninterrupted revolution' does not necessarily imply an immediacy thesis since it could simply mean (as in the *Manifesto*) that the proletariat develops its political skills and confidence through an 'uninterrupted' process of turning bourgeois 'weapons' against the bourgeoisie. In other words, the revolutionary process can be 'uninterrupted' or 'permanent' without being chronologically compressed, and Geras is therefore correct to emphasise that before 1917, Lenin assumed that the interval between the bourgeois and socialist revolutions would be a relatively lengthy one.[27]

In 1917 however his position changes, and (as suggested above) we are entitled to infer that Lenin embraces the 'immediacy thesis' as presented in the *Manifesto.* Can it be said (as so many commentators have) that in doing so, he had come round to supporting Trotsky's own (and much discussed) theory of permanent revolution? There are notable similarities between the positions of the two revolutionaries in 1917. It is true that

[24]E.H.Carr, *Studies in Revolution*, Macmillan, 1950, p.19; Hoffman, 'Karl Marx and Friedrich Engels; the Communist Manifesto' p.198; A.J.P.Taylor, 'Introduction', *The Communist Manifesto*, Penguin, 1967, p.35.

[25]E.H.Carr, *The Bolshevik Revolution*, volume 1. Penguin, 1966, pp.20, 60.

[26]Lenin, *Collected Works*,, volume 9, Progress Publishers, 1964, p.237. Also N.Geras, 'Rosa Luxemburg after 1905', *New Left Review*, 89, pp.32, 36; M.Liebman, *Lenin under Leninism*, Jonathan Cape, 1975, p.188; N.Harding, *Lenin's Political Thought*, volume 1, Macmillan, 1977, p.198.

[27]Geras, 'Rosa Luxemburg after 1905', p.32.

it was later argued by Stalin and his supporters that Trotsky sought to skip the different phases of the revolution so that his permanent revolution simply stands for the communist revolution alone. This view is occasionally echoed in academic literature.[28]

But Trotsky insisted that his theory of permanent revolution did distinguish between the bourgeois and the socialist revolution. However it has to be said that the distinction he makes between the two is a complicated one. Take his comment that 'the class dialectics of the bourgeois revolution would bring the proletariat to power and without its dictatorship not even democratic tasks could be solved'. This suggests that the two revolutions can be differentiated but in a way which does not really make them separate! Geras argues that while Trotsky accepts a logical distinction between the two revolutions, such a distinction cannot be transposed 'into a simple chronological succession within the real, historical process'.[29]

The two revolutions are distinct but in the case of Russia at least, it is not possible to have one without the other. A revolutionary government, Trotsky argues, would not be able to implement its minimum programme without moving towards communism, since the introduction of a eight hour day and full employment – both theoretically within the remit of the democratic phase – could only be carried through by way of socialist revolution. The workers must in practice therefore 'ignore the logical boundary line which should confine it to a democratic dictatorship'.[30] Trotsky directly invokes Marx's support for his argument. He refers to the immediacy thesis in the *Manifesto*, arguing that Marx's error was factual, not methodological since the revolution of 1848 did not turn into a socialist revolution 'but that is why it also did not achieve democracy'.[31] This suggests that because the bourgeois revolution is immediately followed by the proletarian revolution, one cannot really occur without the other. The emphasis is upon fusion rather than differentiation, although a logical distinction between the two revolutions is still maintained.

In one of the clearest formulations of his position, Trotsky comments that 'while the traditional view was that the road to the dictatorship of the proletariat led through a long period of democracy, the theory of the permanent revolution established the fact that for backward countries the road to democracy passed through the dictatorship of the proletariat'.[32] While it does seem to me that Lenin's position in 1917 is similar to that of Trotsky's, it is not identical. It is true that Lenin now accepts that proletarian revolution is possible in a backward country. At the same time his position appears to allow for more 'chronology' in the immediacy thesis than Trotsky does, since Lenin argues in April 1917 that the bourgeois revolution

[28]N.Harding, *Lenin's Political Thought*, volume 1, p.198, and (at least implicitly) Cunliffe, 'The Tensions in the Communist Manifesto', p.571.

[29]L.Trotsky, *The Permanent Revolution* and *Results and Prospects*, Pathfinder Press, 1969, p.180; Geras, 'Rosa Luxemburg after 1905', p.26.

[30]L.Trotsky (1905) Penguin, 1971, p.331; also Trotsky, *Permanent Revolution*, pp.78-80.

[31]Trotsky, *Permanent Revolution*, p.131.

[32]Trotsky, *Permanent Revolution*, p. 132.

had been completed before a proletarian revolution could occur. However I have to concede that against this argument are the quotations assembled by Geras which suggest that in Lenin's view, the second revolution had carried the first to its conclusion.[33]

The position is complex and ambiguous. At times Lenin does appear to argue that a logical and chronological distinction between the two revolutions can be maintained. One revolution was completed before a second could occur so that 'on the whole', Lenin argues, the traditional Bolshevik position had been confirmed by events.[34] Might it also be suggested that Lenin gives slightly more weight to the bourgeois revolution as a separate event when he argues later that the Constituent Assembly deserved to be dissolved because it was insufficiently representative of the popular will. For Trotsky, on the other hand, the Constituent Assembly reflected an opportunist majority of a 'counter- revolutionary democracy'.[35] It remains true that both justify an authoritarian event and both sought to defend the revolution in terms of an immediacy thesis which made it inevitable that the USSR would suppress rather than build upon the liberal tradition associated with the bourgeois revolution.

Here Gramsci's comparative analysis of Lenin and Trotsky is instructive. The young Gramsci had argued that Lenin had gone over to Trotsky's view in November 1917 but in the *Prison Notebooks* his position is more nuanced. Here he argues that the theory of permanent revolution was a 'scientifically evolved expression' of the Jacobin experience during the French Revolution which had been embraced by Marx and Engels just before the revolutions of 1848.[36] The theory had later been developed by Trotsky in abstract, literary form but applied by Lenin in 1917 in a form which was concrete and historically sensitive – as 'something which sprang from all the pores of the particular society which had to be transformed'. With Trotsky, there was a Jacobin temperament 'without an adequate political content' but with Lenin, this Jacobin temperament derived from 'new historical relations, and not from a literary and intellectualistic label'.[37]

Gramsci's reference to Jacobinism is contentious, but it is clear that he opposed the immediacy thesis (which he saw as synonymous with the idea of permanent revolution itself) on the grounds that it belonged to the period before a modern liberal democracy had developed. The theory of permanent revolution as Gramsci interpreted it, underplays the importance of 'consent' in politics and has been transcended in political science by the formula of 'civil hegemony'.[38] What makes Gramsci's argument particularly interesting here is the suggestion that even the immediacy thesis is suspectible to

[33] Geras, 'Rosa Luxemburg after 1905', p.39.

[34] Lenin, *Collected Works*, volume 24, p.44; J,Hoffman, *The Gramscian Challenge*, Basil Blackwell, 1984, p.147.

[35] Lenin, *Collected Works*, volume 26, p.487; L.Trotsky, *Terrorism and Communism*, University of Michigan Press, 1961, p.43; Hoffman, *The Gramscian Challenge*, p.157.

[36] A.Gramsci, *Selections from the 'Prison Notebooks'*, Lawrence & Wishart, 1971, pp.242-43. For further references and commentary, see Hoffman, *The Gramscian Challenge*, p.145.

[37] Gramsci, *Prison Notebooks*, p.85.

[38] Gramsci, *Prison Notebooks*, p.243.

(slightly) different interpretations, and that Trotsky's position was somewhat more abstract than Lenin's. Lovell confirms the difference when he argues that Lenin's strategy fell somewhere between Plekhanov's 'two stage revolution' and Trotsky's theory of permanent revolution which, Lovell tells us, 'respectively separated and telescoped the bourgeois and socialist stages of the revolution'.[39]

Three positions around the problem of separation and unity in relation to the idea of permanent revolution deserve distinguishing. The first is the notion that the bourgeois and socialist revolutions are simply separate. In my view this position is not Marxist and cannot be identified with any version of permanent revolution. The second is that the argument that the two revolutions while separate, are also linked so that they are phases or stages within a (relatively protracted) revolutionary process: I have called this the general idea of permanent revolution. The third is the immediacy thesis which asserts the linkage within a compressed timescale, but which historically has lent itself to slightly different versions. One of these argues that the two revolutions are both chronological and logically separate (arguably Lenin's view), while the other contends that the revolutions are simply logically separate so that 'chronologically speaking', one revolution is not possible without the other.

A Critical Evaluation

The idea of permanent revolution seeks to portray revolution as a process with distinct phases. How distinct the phases and how compressed the timescale between them is open to controversy, but the idea seems to assume that we can reconcile the notion of revolution as a process and the notion of revolution as a discrete event.

Here it seems to me that Marx and Engels never really shed what Hunt calls their reverence for the French Revolution 'as a model'.[40] Revolution as a discrete event implies a seizure of power – the implementation of a new social order which radically and sharply breaks from the old – and this is clearly what Engels had in mind when he described a revolution as 'the most authoritarian thing there is'. Ironically Marx also seems to have the same conception when he commented that if British workers used their legal power and liberties, they could avoid a revolution.[41]

Marxists generally hold to the notion of revolution as a discrete event – a seizure of power – and this, as Macpherson has pointed out, creates grave dificulties for the kind of consensus necessary to sustain a participatory democracy. Revolutions provoke counter-revolutions; they concentrate power, and Lovell has argued, they are 'intrinsically illiberal' events.[42] It is difficult to see how, in terms of the *Manifesto*'s argument, we could move

[39] D.Lovell, *From Marx to Lenin*, Cambridge University Press, 1984, p.160.

[40] Hunt, *Political Ideas of Marx and Engels*, p.144.

[41] K.Marx & F.Engels, *Selected Correspondence*, Progress Publishers, 1955, p.334. Engels's comment is discussed in Hoffman, *The Gramscian Challenge*, p.168.

[42] D.Lovell, *From Marx to Lenin*, p.67; C.B.Macpherson, *The Life and Times of Liberal Democracy*, Oxford University Press, 1977, pp.99-101.

from 'more or less veiled civil war' involving the overthrow of one class by another to an emancipated world in which the concentrated force of the state has become redundant and the freedom of each is a condition for the freedom of all.[43]

The notion of a classless and stateless society is an attractive one particularly if one links it to an explicit acknowledgement of, and toleration for, all identities whether of an ethnic, gendered, religious or regional kind. But, as I have argued elsewhere, the notion of reaching such a society through war, revolution, state and proletarian dictatorship is not credible. If the immediacy thesis makes the attainment of a self-governing society especially problematic, the wider argument within the *Manifesto* still emphasises the primacy of class struggle, the need for revolution and a logic of polarisation which works against the realisation of emancipation.[44]

On the other hand, if we interpret the notion of revolution as a process and not as a discrete event, we can avoid the authoritarian and illiberal implications which the concept of revolution seems to imply. With this reading, revolution simply becomes synonymous with 'change' and 'critique' – a scepticism towards established orders. It does not involve a divisive seizure of power. If this is what is meant by 'permanent revolution', then the idea is supportable and appealing.

While revisionist socialism (as articulated say in Bernstein's classic *Evolutionary Socialism*) rejects the notion of revolution as a discrete event, it is also in danger of rejecting the importance of critique as well. Bernstein expresses rather complacent views about liberalism, colonialism, the state and class division[45] and his stance demonstrates the problem of simply rejecting the permanent revolution thesis.

It would be better in my view to try to construct a version of the idea of permanent revolution which would bring it closer to Marx's admirable 'ideal' of an association in which the free development of each is the free development of all.

---

[43] *MECW*, 6, pp.495, 506.

[44] J.Hoffman, *Beyond the State*, Polity Press, 1995, pp.140-44.

[45] E.Bernstein, *Evolutionary Socialism*, Schocken Books, 1961.

The Communist Manifesto – 150 Years On

Paul Wetherly
Leeds Metropolitan University

'A Capitalist State? Re-examining the Classical Marxist View of the State in Capitalist Society'

The State of the Manifesto

The Communist Manifesto contains probably the best-known and most often-quoted statement on the subject of the state to be found in Marx's writing. Here it is claimed that

> 'each step of the bourgeoisie was accompanied by a corresponding political advance of that class. ... the bourgeoisie has ... conquered for itself, in the modern representative state, exclusive political sway. The executive of the modern state is but a committee for managing the common affairs of the whole bourgeoisie.' (Marx & Engels 1967)

According to Miliband this is 'the classical Marxist view on the subject of the state' (Miliband 1965, p.283).

The Manifesto appears to make a rather simple and bold claim: political or state power has been conquered or taken over by the capitalist class (thus suggesting deliberate political action by the class) and is used exclusively (ie to the exclusion of other classes) to defend and advance the interests of the class. Hence the Manifesto may be seen as putting forward a class (or class-theoretical) analysis of politics and, more specifically, an 'instrumental' view of the state: 'the state and its bureaucracy are class instruments' (Held 1984, pp.52-3). Understood as a general claim, this interpretation also supports a strong form of economic determination insofar as it suggests a correspondence between the economic and political dimensions of a capitalist society; between the economic and political constitution of classes. For it is claimed that the economically dominant class is also, thereby, politically dominant; that a capitalist economy has as its counterpart a capitalist state. The Manifesto view of the state thus exemplifies the 'cardinal principle' of marxism; that the character of the legal and political superstructure is explained in terms of the nature of the economic structure.

This simple view of the state appears to present the antithesis of the liberal conception. For Marx 'the state is not an independent structure or set of institutions above society, that is, a "public power" acting for the "public". On the contrary, it is deeply embedded in socio-economic relations and linked to particular interests'(Held 1984, p.52). So deeply embedded and firmly linked, indeed, that there appears to be no scope whatever for independent action by the state (the executive is 'but', that is 'nothing more than', a committee for managing the bourgeoisie's affairs) or for other interests in society to be represented (the bourgeoisie has 'exclusive political sway'). The state represents the interests of the capitalist class and that is all.

However the Manifesto view of the state is perhaps more subtle than is at first apparent: the reference to the common affairs of the whole bourgeoisie may suggest an important distinction between the common interests of the whole class and the particular (divergent and possibly conflicting) interests of units (that is, individual firms) or 'fractions' of capital. Thus the notion of 'class interests' is intimately related to our understanding of the concept 'the bourgeoisie'. Recognition of the fractioned and diverse nature of the dominant class clearly complicates any simple instrumental conception of the state. An additional subtlety is introduced by the consideration that (except for the 'but' in Marx's formulation) it is consistent with an instrumental conception that the state does not manage the affairs of the bourgeoisie exclusively. That is, the instrumental (for the bourgeoisie) actions of the state might not be a complete description of what it does. It is not, after all, inconsistent with the idea that the bourgeoisie is in charge of the state that not everything the state does benefits that class. This allows the possibility that the state might also respond to other social interests. Nevertheless the instrumental conception does imply that this responsiveness is circumscribed: other interests cannot be allowed to conflict with those of the dominant class.

Marx's Ambiguous Legacy

The Manifesto may express the 'classical' view on the subject of the state, yet it is not the only view to be found in Marx and it is important to place it in the context of Marx's other writings. Taken as a whole, these constitute an ambiguous legacy. We start from the fact that there is in Marx no comprehensive and systematic treatment of the theory of the state, rather a variety of themes and perspectives is suggested in his writing. Miliband discerns, in addition to the instrumentalist approach expressed in the Manifesto, a 'secondary view .. of the state as independent from and superior to all social classes, as .. the dominant force in society rather than the instrument of a dominant class' (Miliband 1965, p.283) (exemplified by The Eighteenth Brumaire of Louis Bonaparte). Similarly Held (1984, pp.52-3) suggests that

> 'there are at least two strands in Marx's account of the relation between the classes and the state ... the first ... stresses that the state ... may take a variety of forms and constitute a source of power which need not be ... under the unambiguous control of the dominant class in the short term. By this account, the state retains a degree of power independent of this class ... [it is] ... 'relatively autonomous'. The second strand ... is without doubt the dominant one ... the state and its bureaucracy are class instruments ...'

For Elster (1985, p.402) the 'central question' in Marx's approach to the state is posed in similar terms: whether the state is autonomous from or reducible to the interests of the economically dominant class. Elster distinguishes three approaches to the state in Marx: instrumentalism, abdication (or abstention), and class balance theories. The latter two are united by the conception of the state as autonomous from the capitalist class so that Elster's typology closely matches that of Miliband and Held. Elster makes the distinctive claim, however, that 'Marx made the autonomy of the state into the cornerstone of his theory' (1985, p.426).

It appears that there is a fundamental tension within Marx's thought between seeing the state as an instrument of or autonomous from the dominant class. In Elster's account the autonomy of the state may sometimes arise from the voluntary abstention or abdication from power by the bourgeoisie motivated by a calculation that their interests are best served if they remain outside politics. In this case the bourgeoisie can, apparently, choose to take power back into their own hands if their strategic calculation alters and the 'instrumental state' and 'autonomous state' views are thus reconciled (the second view becomes, in effect, a special case of the first). However Elster says that sometimes 'the struggle between two opposed classes allows the state to assert itself by divide and conquer.' In this case, as with Miliband's reference to the state as 'the dominant force in society' and Held's characterisation of the state as 'independent' of the dominant class, the two views appear much harder to reconcile. The tension within Marx's thought might be resolved by the claim that the instrumental view refers to the 'normal' relation between the state and the dominant class and, consequently, that the 'Bonapartist' state is 'exceptional.' This view would be predicated on a claim that the bourgeoisie normally retains the upper hand in its struggle with the working class.

The normal-exceptional distinction seems to preserve the instrumental view as the cornerstone of Marx's theory of the state. State autonomy becomes an interesting but marginal case – the exception to the rule of the capitalist class. However the concept of (relative) autonomy suggests that the state is not simply reducible to the interests of the dominant class and this opens up a number of interesting theoretical avenues. Miliband's reference to the state as the dominant force in society and Elster's notion of the state asserting itself imply the need to investigate what Poggi refers to as the supply of state actions based upon 'the push of interests lodged inside the state' (1990, p.120). This moves us away from a 'black box' conception of the state which passively transforms inputs in the form of class interests into functional policy outputs towards a conception of the state as a subject with its own interests (a conception found in Marx's early writing (Jessop 1984, pp.4-5)). In other words, it moves us away from a 'society-centred' to a 'state-centred' understanding of the state, or to a synthesis of these approaches. The concession that the state is not reducible to the interests of the dominant class also permits the possibility of the state responding to other interests, particularly those of the working class, or even of the working class using the state as an instrument to pursue its own interests (this is a plausible interpretation of Marx's analysis of the Factory Acts in volume one of *Capital* (see Mishra 1975)).

Using a simple class-theoretical analysis – based upon a two-class model of the economic structure – and a strategic actor understanding of the state based upon a concept of competing interests it is thus possible, once the simple instrumental view is relaxed, to see the state as the vector of three distinct sets of interests: the dominant and subordinate classes and the state itself. The dichotomy between the instrumental and autonomous state is clearly inadequate to capture the feasible alternatives: there is a variety of theoretical positions in-between these two extreme formulations (Geras 1987; Wetherly 1995).

Within a class-theoretical approach additional complexity can be introduced into the model by a more complex view of strategic actors and their interests, and by allowing for the influence of other class and non-class social forces. Following Miliband we might conceive the subordinate class in terms of fractions with competing interests similar to the fractions of the dominant class. For example Gough (1979, p.60), in a discussion of the origins of the Welfare State, places particular emphasis on the role of 'the core of the "labour movement" ... the unionised, predominantly manual, working class' (see Wetherly 1988 for a discussion of 'fractions of labour). Similarly we might conceive the state system in terms of diverse interests. In each case we move away from seeing the state and classes as unified actors towards the idea of dominant fractions. Further, the simple two class model of bourgeoisie and proletariat may be extended by the recognition of other classes which may be conceived as external to the capital-labour relation (for example, landlords, the petty bourgeoisie) or occupying an intermediate position between capital and labour (for example, supervisors). Finally 'non-class' social forces or movements may be defined in terms of issues which are not directly connected to relations of production (for example, movements for democratic reform such as Chartism).

The 'class-theoretical' approach, which focuses on the relation between the state and classes and appears to be exemplified by the Manifesto, involves a strategic actor conception of political power: the disposition of political power is the outcome of the balance between organised interests – the bourgeoisie, interests within the state, the working class, other class and non-class forces. The emphasis is on the role and effectiveness of agency conceived primarily in terms of classes as 'collective actors.' The Manifesto asserts that the state is an instrument wielded by the capitalist class in its own interests, whereas other writings of Marx suggest an alternative disposition of power in which the state is autonomous in some degree from the capitalist class. However there is another side to the theory of the state in Marx which involves a structural or 'capital-theoretical' approach.

> 'Marxist political economy is a theory which encompasses a 'structural' view of the economy and a conflict theory of class struggle,' (Gough 1979, p.56).

In the Preface to *A Contribution to the Critique of Political Economy* the theory of the state is located as an element of the theory of history. Here Marx characterises the relationship between the economic and political realms in terms of the famous 'base and superstructure' metaphor.

> 'The sum total of ... relations of production constitutes the economic structure of society, the real basis, on which rises a legal and political superstructure ... At a certain stage of their development, the material productive forces of society come in conflict with the existing relations of production ... From forms of development of the productive forces these relations turn into their fetters. Then begins an epoch of social revolution. With the change of the economic foundation the entire immense superstructure is more or less rapidly transformed.'

There is no mention here of the relation between the state and classes, and no strategic actors. Rather the relationship is conceived as structural: between the economic structure, which comprises the relations of production, and the legal and political (super)structure, which includes the state. It is this passage, above all, which expresses the principle of economic determination, the idea that the character of the state is to be explained in terms of the nature of the economic structure. There appear to be two distinct theoretical claims involved here which are often compounded. The first is the conceptualisation of the economy as a structure which entails that the economy exhibits its own dynamic, its own 'laws of motion', in virtue of its structural characteristics, specifically the nature of the relations of production. In this view the economic structure has a logic of its own which is prior to individuals and notions of agency in the explanatory order: 'here individuals are dealt with only in so far as they are personifications of economic categories, embodiments of particular class-relations and class-interests'. This claim is related to (but does not entail) the second, that there is a structural *relationship* between the economic and political dimensions of society, that the nature of the economic structure supplies a principle of explanation of the character of the state (economic determination).

It may be argued that a major strength of marxism is the recognition of the role of both agency and structure in social theory, but there seems to be ambiguity in Marx: sometimes agency is forefronted (as in the Manifesto) and sometimes structure (the Preface). It is clearly important to clarify the relationship between these two explanatory principles, to set out a coherent and plausible understanding of their combination. There are two approaches to this problem. The first, exemplified by Gough (1979) and Miliband (1977), is to see them as commensurable principles in terms of the level of concreteness of social reality at which they operate so that the theoretical and empirical task is to assess their relative weights in contributing to specific outcomes. The second approach, taken by Cohen (1978) (1988), sees these two principles as non-equivalent in the sense that one is more fundamental than the other; in particular structural explanation may be viewed as more fundamental and operating at a higher level of abstraction than class struggle explanation.

The principle of economic determination raises again the question of state autonomy – how far there is scope for action by the state independent of economic structural determinations -and how far the state exerts a causal influence upon the economic base. In other words, to what extent does economic determination involve a simple one-directional determinism or reductionism? In general, economic determination need not entail that the state has no scope for independent action or no causal effect on the economic structure, but involves the assertion of causal asymmetry: the principal direction of causality is from the economic to the political dimension, the base explains the superstructure more than vice-versa. Again, the theoretical alternatives are not *either* economic determination *or* state autonomy but a conception of relative autonomy.

In sum, Marx's legacy is thoroughly ambiguous. This is not to say that there are no important and distinctive unifying themes running through Marx's writing: the most important of these is the society-centred approach to the state which emphasises the relationship between state and society and rejects any notion of the state as an independent set of institutions. More specifically the key idea of Marx – the cardinal principle – is economic determination, that is that explanations of politics and the state are to be found (more than vice versa) in economics. Finally, to use Poggi's terms (1990), Marx's image is of a partisan rather than a serviceable state – political power is closely aligned with, and subordinate to, economic power. However, as we have seen, the ambiguity in Marx can be seen as running along two dimensions. The first is the structure-agency dimension or, in other words, the distinction between class- and capital-theoretical approaches. This ambiguity is encapsulated in Held's apt characterisation of Marx's approach: the state is both 'deeply embedded in socio-economic relations *and* linked to particular interests' (1983, p.52, emphasis added) but no link is made between the workings of these explanatory principles. They are linked by the theoretical claim which they both purport to sustain – the partisan model of the capitalist state. But here we find Marx running along the second dimension of ambiguity – between a determinist thrust (the state as instrument of the bourgeoisie or as superstructural effect of economic structural causes) and a recognition that there is scope for independent action by the state.

Appraising the Classical Marxist View – the 'Base' and 'Superstructure' Metaphor

The principle of economic determination, explanation of 'politics' by or in terms of 'economics', involves seeing the state (primarily) as a point of reference and the nature of the economic structure as the principle of explanation, the state as effect of an economic cause. This principle, to be coherent, seems to rely on the economic 'base' being clearly distinguished from the political and legal 'superstructure' in order that the two can be conceived as independent and dependent variables. This problem can be considered in terms of the 'institutional differentiation' (Burnham 1994, p.2) of the state: the set of institutions that comprises the state is 'so differentiated from the rest of society as to create identifiable public and private spheres' (Dunleavy & O'Leary 1987, p.2).

> 'Capitalism is often seen as the first mode of production in which there is a clear institutional separation between the economic and the extra-economic.' (Jessop 1990, p83).

Differentiation is, as Poggi observes, implicit in the definition of the state as a distinct organisation, or set of institutions, and is 'at a maximum when the organisation in question performs all and only political activities' (Poggi 1990, p.20).

This conception of institutional differentiation is at the heart of key problems in marxist state theory. The possibility of a plausible theory of economic determination appears to be challenged both by this alleged differentiation and by claims to the contrary that the economic structure cannot function, or even be conceptualised, apart from the political realm.

The convention of institutional differentiation problematises economic determination because it allows the state system to be conceived as a potentially autonomous set of institutions governed by its own internally generated operating criteria and exercising political power in pursuit of its own specific interests. According to Jessop, a crucial feature of capitalism as a distinctive economic structure is that extra-economic coercion is abstracted from the process of exploitation which is secured through voluntary exchange between capital and labour.

> 'This permits the autonomization or self-closure of the economic sphere ... But it also secures one of the necessary conditions for the legal system and the state to become autonomous – each with their own distinctive forms and modes of self-reference, self-organization and self-reproduction .... This mutual autonomization of the economic, political and legal realms permits distinctive organizational principles, modes of calculation and operational practices to develop in each of these systems.' (Jessop 1990, pp.83-4).

The question can be posed in terms of the relationship between forms of social power, specifically political or state power and economic power. Thus Poggi (1990) analyses this relationship as one of rivalry with each form of power seeking to extend its control over others. This conception is highly abstract and raises questions about the cohesiveness of these rival forms of power, and agency. However at this level of abstraction we can pose as the key issue in the relationship between the political and economic realms, between political and economic power, 'the limits of independent action by state power' (Moore quoted in Jessop 1990, p.85) or, in other words, the extent to which the state is autonomous. There is no incompatibility between the separation of the economic and the political and the 'functional subordination' (Poggi 1990, p.120) of political to economic power (or vice-versa). In other words differentiation does not entail autonomy. However, given the potential for self-reference, self-organisation and self-reproduction by the state, the task for marxist theory is to demonstrate how the potential for autonomy or 'independent action' is in fact constrained. In other words marxist theory must elucidate plausible mechanisms through which political power is subordinated to economic power.

It may seem difficult to sustain the claim that 'state' and 'economy' are institutionally differentiated in the face of the growth of the state and its intervention in social and economic life – what Poggi refers to as the 'compenetration of the political and societal realms' (1990, p.122). Thus it is notoriously difficult to clearly distinguish the public and private spheres which differentiation is supposed to create and to locate the boundary between them. Indeed Poggi argues that state intervention - partly driven by a search for legitimacy through state-managed economic growth – means that private concerns become public: it seems, in consequence, that institutional separation has largely ceased to operate (Poggi 1990, p.121).

The growth of the 'interventionist' state, and particularly the 'welfare state', appears to present a challenge to Marx's legacy on a number of levels. The sheer scale of the modern state and the range of its social and economic interventions constitutes an enormous weight for the single explanatory vector of economic determination to bear: it seems difficult to reduce the 'entire immense superstructure' of the modern welfare state to the 'common affairs of the bourgeoisie' or economic structural constraints. Here again we should note that Marx's characterisation is easier to reconcile with a view of the state as an essentially coercive instrument but is harder to sustain in the face of the growth of state welfare. Related to this, marxism has to counter the claim that the welfare state, far from simply managing the affairs of a capitalist class, in fact represents a response to social and economic problems and to human needs, a response which has, even, fundamentally transformed the very nature of capitalism.

Whereas Poggi emphasises that the differentiation of state and society has largely become inoperative due to the growth of state intervention in the twentieth century – there was institutional differentiation but there is no longer – it might be argued more fundamentally that politics is an intrinsic, constitutive, dimension of a capitalist economy; in other words, that capitalism as an economic structure has political conditions of existence. In this view the capitalist economy is never, historically, already given, fully functioning according to its own internal dynamic and ready to do the work of generating political effects, of explaining the state. Rather the state is there at the beginning and plays a part in creating the capitalist economy and its development. The character of the capitalist economy, the nature of the economic structure, is always itself in part determined by the actions of the state. This poses a more fundamental challenge to marxism and the idea of economic determination, for the marxist cause-effect relationship appears to be reversed. Rather than the state being an effect of the economic structure it seems that the economic structure is itself an effect of political action.

For example, it can be argued that capitalist relations of production, enshrined as property rights, are constituted in legal and political forms (Lukes 1983). Given that law enters into the very definition of the economic structure it seems difficult to sustain the base-superstructure distinction and hence to explain the character of the superstructure in terms of the nature of the economic structure. Cohen (1978) discusses this 'problem of legality' and shows that although the economic structure is conventionally understood in terms of property *rights* (and thus defined in legal, that is, superstructural, terms), the base-superstructure distinction can be sustained by a distinction between (basic) powers and (superstructural) rights. The economic structure comprises relations of effective control or *power* which can be abstracted from the matching property rights which are conferred by the state.

This argument seems to succeed in sustaining an analytical distinction between base and superstructure – we can conceive relations of production in terms of naked power even if in practice they are usually clothed in legal property relations. On the basis of this distinction the underlying relations of power or control might figure in explanation of matching rights. However in order to carry out this work of explanation it seems that relations of effective control or power (of which production relations properly so called consist, according to Cohen) have to be capable of existing independently of and prior to property relations which they explain. Yet if property rights are part of a package of *conditions of existence* of relations of production, as their very prevalence might suggest, then relations of production cannot exist independently: the economic structure presupposes government or the state.

This argument in relation to property rights can be put more generally. Poggi claims that a distinctive feature of political power in relation to other forms of social power (normative and economic) is its 'paramountcy'.

> 'It can be claimed for political power that it has a functional priority over others, for only insofar as it discharges those tasks [of securing internal and external security] can individuals go about their business – and that includes the exercise of whatever other form of social power they possess – in a (relatively) peaceable and orderly manner.' (Poggi 1990, p.9).

The performance of these quintessential political tasks secures what may be termed extra-economic or external conditions of existence insofar as it involves no direct intervention or inputs into the economic realm. In addition the state discharges tasks which are constitutive of the economic realm, such as the securing of property rights; and others, such as the provision of infrastructure and the reproduction of labour power, which involve the provision of direct inputs into the economy. The performance of these tasks by the state suggests that the economy is not self-sufficient and it seems to follow that 'economics' cannot do the job of explaining 'politics'. Thus according to Jessop

> 'the claim that the economic is determinant ... is misleading ... [because] it ignores the extent to which the economic realm lacks the self-sufficiency needed for it to play such a determining role.' (1990, p.84)

To do the job of explaining the political (or any other realm) the economic must, in this view, be shown to be self-sufficient. Against Poggi it might be argued that the claimed paramountcy of political power can be turned on its head and appear equally plausible. In other words it can equally be asserted that economic power has a functional priority over others for only insofar as material production is carried on can a political (or any other realm) exist, for political activities depend on a flow of resources procured through economic activity. However this argument does not establish the self-sufficiency (let alone explanatory capacity *vis-à-vis* politics) of the economic realm. Rather it seems only (but importantly) to establish against the claimed paramountcy of politics a chronic *interdependency* of the economic and political realms. The economic and political realms may be differentiated but neither is self-sufficient.

Those wishing to sustain the conception of the economy as a self-sufficient realm and some form of economic determination may rely on the theoretical strategy of abstraction, deploying a highly simplified model of the economic structure, such as the highly abstract model of the capitalist mode of production and circuit of capital in marxism. Alternatively, and more pragmatically, they may emphasise the essentially limited scope of state intervention. The point of both arguments is that they allow the encroachment of politics into economics while alleging that this does not disturb the essential character and functioning of the economy. On this basis it might be argued that the economy can indeed be analysed as if it is a self-sufficient realm, and, furthermore, that this analysis can provide a principle of economic determination. The rationale of the method of abstraction is that it involves 'extracting the essentials' (Fine 1975, p.13), uncovering basic relationships which underlie and explain more complex observed phenomena. Thus the 'law of value' can be analysed in simplified form. The point of the pragmatic argument is that the economy is still *predominantly* capitalist and, as such, governed by these laws. The problem with these arguments is that they fail to recognise that the laws of supply and demand and of value, even in their most abstract forms, are themselves politically conditioned, sanctioned or created. Thus the 'rules of the game' which govern commodity and exchange relations are made and enforced by the state: without the state there would be no game (not even the simplified version).

It might be argued that while there are inescapable political conditions of existence of the economic sphere the task that politics performs is essentially to *create* the autonomization or self-closure of the economy. This might be argued where state intervention is in the form of what Jessop (1984, p.233) terms 'formal facilitation' wherein

> 'the state maintains the general external conditions of capitalist production: these include a formally rational monetary

> system, a formally rational legal system, and a formally rational system of administration.' (1984, p.233)

The argument would be that the securing of these general external conditions allows commodity and exchange relations to function with a high degree of self-closure or self-sufficiency. These general conditions are necessary for a capitalist or market order to function, but once it gets going the economy exhibits its own dynamic within the framework that these conditions provide. Of course the economy could not be seen as strictly self-sufficient because we still need an explanation for the state creating the conditions in which the economy can operate autonomously in the first place and, further, its continued functioning would depend on the continual renewal of these conditions by the political realm. The economy can only reproduce itself so long as the state undertakes the tasks that constitute formal facilitation, and the state might, conceivably, withdraw from these tasks at some point. The self-sufficiency of the economy would, then, be seen to be enhanced if it can plausibly be argued that the state does not have an option to withdraw. And it could be argued that this option disappears as the capitalist order develops and becomes the dominant mode of organising economic life. Alongwith this dominance the economy's dependence on the state is turned around and becomes the state's dependence on the economy – the state now has no alternative but to sustain the external conditions of capitalist production as alternative, rival modes of organising economic life have been obliterated. The state gets locked into providing the conditions of existence of capitalism because, although without the state there would have been no game in the first place, it is now the only game in town.

However the modern state is involved in forms of intervention in the economy which extend beyond 'formal facilitation'. Indeed the general trend has been towards increasing intervention by the state. The conception of the state providing the general external conditions or starting conditions which allow the capitalist economy to get going and thence to develop according to its own autonomous dynamic seems unable to account for this growing intervention. A number of marxist writers, in particular, have argued that as capitalism develops it generates new needs for state intervention (O'Connor 1973; Gough, 1979). This argument is also put forward by Poggi who, in a discussion of the causes of the growth of the state, claims that

> 'in the course of the twentieth century the dependency of private economic forces on positive state action .... became a systemic feature of industrial capitalism.' (1990, p.116).

This *systemic* link between the economic and political realms indicates that not only is the capitalist economy not self-sufficient but that there is a tendency to progressive weakening of the capacity of the economy for self-sufficiency as it develops. In Jessop's view this must render any claim that the economic is determinant increasingly misleading. However it can be argued, against Jessop, that economic determination can be reconciled with a recognition of the dependency of the economy on state action. This can be achieved by a form of explanation of 'politics' by 'economics' wherein the powerful effect which intervention by the political realm has in sustaining the economy is precisely what it is intended to capture. It has been argued by Cohen (1978) (1988) that Marx's theory of history involves economic determination of this type, and the explanation of the 'legal and political superstructure' by the 'economic base' is expounded as a form of functional explanation. Indeed Cohen maintains that economic determination can be reconciled with the powerful effect of politics in stabilising the economy only if it is construed as a functional explanation. This view fully recognises, indeed starts from the fact, that the economy lacks self-sufficiency but has, on the contrary, 'system needs' or 'functional requirements'. It follows that the claim that the economic is determinant is not judged, as Jessop alleges, on the basis of the self-sufficiency of the economic realm but on the admissibility of functional explanation in social science and the plausibility of the specific functional explanations to which historical materialism is 'unrevisably' (Cohen 1978) committed. (See Wetherly and Carling 1992 for discussion of Cohen, and Wetherly 1992 for discussion of the admissibility of functional explanation.)

In a functional explanation political intervention which stabilises (or, more generally, secures a functional prerequisite of) the economy occurs because it has (or would have) that effect. In historical materialism the nature of the economic structure is alleged to functionally explain the character of the legal and political superstructure. The superstructure is not a residual category comprising all non-economic phenomena, but only those non-economic institutions (to follow Cohen's restriction) which are functionally explained by the economic structure. This means that 'state' and 'superstructure' are not synonymous terms, and historical materialism might not provide explanations for the entire state system. It seems clear that while a functional form of economic determination does not require the economy to be self-sufficient (the whole point is that it is not), it does require that the nature of the economic structure be expounded free of political terms. In other words there has, at some basic level, to be differentiation of economics and politics. The base cannot explain the superstructure if it cannot be distinguished from it, if superstructural terms enter into the very definition of the base. To return to the 'problem of legality', if it is the case that property rights constitute a condition of existence of capitalist relations of production, then a functional explanation, in order to succeed, must show that property rights can be explained by their capacity to establish relations of effective control over forces of production rather than merely to stabilise a structure that already exists. This seems to be a more difficult explanation to mount, but is not precluded by the logic of functional explanation.

Reconstructing a Marxist Theory of the State

Although Miliband has described the Manifesto as containing the classical Marxist view on the subject of the state it is not so much the particular form of class analysis as the more general principle of economic determination which is distinctive of the marxist perspective: the claim that political power is subordinate to economic power. As such the theory of the state is properly located in Marx's writing as an element of the theory of history and the classical view is to be found in the Preface. Here the principle of economic determination is expressed in the form of the 'base-superstructure' metaphor and we have argued, following Cohen, that this is to be construed as a functional explanation. However the theory of the state is relatively neglected by Cohen. Thus marxism stands in need of a fully elaborated theory of the state with functional explanation at its heart consistent with the theory of history. Such a theory might be developed from the following starting points and parameters:

- 1. Economic determination constitutes the cardinal principle of marxism.
- 2. There is institutional differentiation of the state from the economic structure.
- 3. The state is a potentially autonomous subject capable of exercising power in pursuit of its own interests.
- 4. The economic structure has crucial political conditions of existence.
- 5. Functional explanation reconciles the principle of economic determination with recognition of the powerful (and necessary) effects of state action.
- 6. Concepts of state and superstructure are not coterminous, that is, only those aspects of the state belong in the superstructure which are functionally explained by the nature of the economic structure.
- 7. Functional explanation trades on a notion of system need, that is, conditions that must be met if the economic structure is to be reproduced. Thus state actions are functionally explained in terms of the 'needs of capital'.
- 8. The theory of the state must elucidate the causal mechanisms whereby the potentially autonomous state is in fact constrained by the nature of the economic structure.
- 9. The causal mechanisms will be elaborated in terms of class-theoretical and capital-theoretical approaches and clarify the relations between them and between concepts of needs of capital and class interest.
- 10. The theory of the state as an integral part of the theory of history, functionally construed, requires 'a form of determinacy which is not equivalent to economic reductionism' (Hall 1977, p.23) or determinism but is understood probabilistically, as involving tendencies of mechanisms. In this view the state is relatively autonomous but the theory seems to require that economic primacy is a strong tendency. In other words the autonomy of the state must be severely constrained by mechanisms of economic determination of a powerful kind and the element of contingency allowed must be minimal.

References

P.Burnham, 'The Organisational View of the State', *Politics*, 14/1, 1994.

G.A.Cohen, *Karl Marx's Theory of History. A Defence*, Oxford, 1978.

G.A.Cohen, *History, Labour and Freedom*, Oxford, 1988.

P.Dunleavy & B.O'Leary, *Theories of the State*, MacMillan, 1987.

J.Elster, *Making Sense of Marx*, Cambridge, 1985.

B.Fine, *Marx's Capital*, MacMillan, 1975

N.Geras, 'Post-Marxism?', *New Left Review*, 163, 1987.

I.Gough, *The Political Economy of the Welfare State*, MacMillan, 1979.

S.Hall, 'The "Political" and the "Economic" in Marx's Theory of Classes', in A.Hunt (ed), *Class and Class Structure*, Lawrence & Wishart, 1977.

D.Held, 'Central perspectives on the modern state', in G.McLennan et al (eds), *The Idea of the Modern State*, Open University Press, 1984.

B.Jessop, *The Capitalist State*, Blackwell, 1984.

B.Jessop, *State Theory*, Polity, 1990.

S.Lukes, 'Can the Base be Distinguished from the Superstructure?', in D.Miller & L.Siedentop (eds), *The Nature of Political Theory*, 1983.

K.Marx, *The Eighteenth Brumaire of Louis Bonaparte*, Progress, 1930.

K.Marx, *Capital*, volume 1, Lawrence & Wishart, 1954.

K.Marx, *A Contribution to a Critique of Political Economy*, Lawrence & Wishart, 1970.

K.Marx & F.Engels, *The Communist Manifesto*, Penguin, 1967.

R.Miliband, 'Marx and the State', in R.Miliband & J.Saville (eds), *The Socialist Register*, Merlin Press, 1965.

R.Miliband, *Marxism and Politics*, Oxford, 1977.

R.Mishra, 'Marx and Welfare', *Sociological Review*, 23/2, 1975.

J.O'Connor, *The Fiscal Crisis of the State*, St Martin's Press, 1973.

G.Poggi, *The State. Its Nature, Development and Prospects*,Polity, 1990.

P.Wetherly, 'Class Struggle and the Welfare State', *Critical Social Policy*, 22, 1988.

P.Wetherly, 'Mechanisms, Methodological Individualism and Marxism: a Response to Elster', in P.Wetherly (ed), *Marx's Theory of History: The Contemporary Debate*, Avebury, 1992.

P.Wetherly & A.Carling, 'An Analytical Outline of Historical Materialism', in P.Wetherly (ed), *op cit.*

P.Wetherly, Marxism, History and the State, PhD thesis, 1995

Rational Choice

David Chapman
Democracy Design Forum

'Electoral Systems Designed to Protect the Ethnic Minorities and their Use in Northern Ireland and Eastern Europe'

Introduction

In ethnically divided countries, democracy rarely functions well. The problem appears to be that, under any of the usual electoral systems, parties tend to divide on ethnic lines, and become more or less mono-ethnic, that is, they appeal to and draw votes from only one ethnic group. This obviously makes government more difficult. Coalitions tend to be divided and unstable, and any ethnic minority whose party is not included in the government will tend to be neglected and oppressed.

Several new electoral systems are therefore put forward, designed to provide each party with strong *electoral* incentives to seek the votes of and respond to each ethnic group, that is, to become more of a *pan-ethnic party.* Such pan-ethnic parties, more moderate and more similar in their policies, can be expected to provide more stable government, and better protection of the ethnic minorities.

There are two basic systems, the Association System, and the Distributed Vote, which are set out below. Each uses a different principle to provide the pan-ethnic incentive, for parties to respond to each ethnic group. However, as will be explained, the two systems can be beneficially combined.

The Association System

The basic structure of the Association System, is that parties join together into two-party 'associations'. A party does not *have* to join an association, but if it does not, it effectively loses half of its seats, that is, it gets a percentage of seats equal to one-half of its percentage of first-preference votes. Any association thus formed gets seats according to the total of first-preference votes of the two parties it contains. Each party in the association then gets a share of the association's seats according to the number of voters who prefer it to the *other* party in the association, *except that* the party cannot get less than a certain guaranteed minimum, which again is a percentage of seats equal to one-half of the party's percentage of first-preference votes.

For example, let us suppose that in Northern Ireland, the two main Protestant-oriented parties, the DUP and the UUP, form an association. How big a share of the association's seats the DUP will get, will depend on how many of the Catholics, and of those Protestants who give their first preferences to neither of these two parties, prefer the DUP to the UUP.

Thus the DUP (and also the UUP) will have an incentive which it did not have before, to appeal to Catholics and to moderate Protestants.

Thus the operation of the Association System has these two main features:

- (1) it gives each party, whether in an association or not, a guaranteed minimum percentage of seats equal to one-half of its percentage of first-preference votes;

- (2) it gives any party which joins an association, the chance of greatly increasing its seats above its minimum (normally to about twice its minimum, but possibly to about three times its minimum), by competing with the other party in the association, for the non-first-preference votes of the rest of the voters, the ones who do not vote first preference for either party in the association.

Thus each party is given the incentive to appeal more widely, to sections of electors *and to ethnic groups* to which it did not appeal before, since under the new system it is now able to increase its seats by doing so.

A more detailed account of the Association System is as follows. The parties join up into two-party associations as described above. The ballot paper carries the names of the parties, and any two parties which are in the same association are indicated, and placed close together on the ballot paper.

The elector is asked to give an XX-vote (that is, by writing in an 'XX') to the party which he or she most prefers. The electors are also asked to give an X-vote ('X') to that party they prefer, in *any other association* in which they have a preference between the two parties in it. If an elector X-votes for *both* parties in the same association, then both these X-votes are disregarded. If an elector XX-votes for one party and X-votes for the other party in the same association, then the X-vote is disregarded.

The seats are allocated between the parties by a two-stage process:

- (1) each association gets seats according to the first-preference votes (that is, XX-votes) cast for the two parties in it;

- (2) in each association, each of the two parties in it gets a share of the association's seats according to the number of voters who prefer it to the *other* party in the association, that is, who give the party *either an XX-vote or an X-vote.*

The first stage, the allocation of seats between the associations, is as follows. If in any association the party with fewer XX-votes has at least two-thirds as many votes as the party with more votes, then the association gets seats in proportion to the total XX-votes of the two parties. If the smaller party has *less* than two-thirds as many votes as the other party, the association gets seats in proportion to 2.5 times the votes of the smaller party.

However, there are three exceptions to this. First, if, for any association, there are any areas of the country in which one or both of the parties have not run a candidate, then the seats of the association are reduced proportionately (for example, if these areas without candidates contain one-third of the electorate, the association loses one-third of its seats). Second, there is a *maximum* limit on an association's number of seats: it must not get more than one-half of the total seats. Third, there is a *minimum* limit to an association's seats: it must not get less than the sum of the two parties' guaranteed minimum percentages of seats, that is, one-half of the sum of the two parties' percentages of XX-votes.[1]

The second stage of the process is that the seats of each association are allocated between its two parties, each getting a share of the seats according to the votes cast for it, both XX-votes and X-votes. Thus for any one association, the percentage of votes for any one of the two parties in it is calculated, as follows: the party's XX-votes and X-votes, *divided* by the sum of the two parties' XX-votes and X-votes, *multiplied* by 100.

Each party is then given a percentage of the association's seats equal to the following: twice the party's percentage of votes *minus* 50%; provided this would not result in one or other of the two parties getting fewer seats than its guaranteed minimum of seats (that is, a percentage of the total seats equal to one-half of its percentage of the total XX-votes.) If this formula would give one of the two parties of the association fewer seats than its guaranteed minimum, then that party gets its guaranteed minimum, and the other party gets the remaining seats of the association.[2]

To illustrate this Association System, let us consider a possible scenario

---

[1]The purpose of these provisions is as follows: (1) to give each party the incentive, if it is to avoid losing seats, to stand as a nation-wide party, placing its candidates in all areas of the country, and competing with the other party in the association in all areas of the country; (2) to give a large party the incentive to split (perhaps into two roughly equal parties which come together to form one association), so that it can avoid the one-half maximum limit on an association's seats; (3) to give each party the incentive to join in association with another party which is expected to get at least two-thirds as many XX-votes as it gets itself, and which therefore is likely to be able to compete effectively with the first party for X-votes as well.

[2]For example, suppose that two parties, A and B, join in an association. A obtains XXs from 25% of the voters, and Xs from 10%, while B obtains XXs from 20%, and Xs from 25%. Let us suppose that all associations get seats in proportion to their respective totals of their parties' XXs. Thus the A+B association gets 25 + 20 = 45% of seats. A gets (0.25 + 0.10)/(0.25 + 0.10 + 0.20 + 0.25) = 43.75% of the XXs and Xs of the association, and B gets 56.25%. Thus A receives 0.45 x ((2 x 0.4375) − 0.5) = 16.875% of seats (provided this is more than A's guaranteed minimum of 25/2 = 12.5% of seats, which it is); and B receives 0.45 x ((2 x 0.5625) − 0.5) = 28.125% of seats (provided this is more than B's guaranteed minimum of 20/2 = 10% of seats, which it is). Thus B, which got fewer first-preference votes than A, ended up with considerably more seats, because it got more lower-preference votes.

But let us suppose that party A gets only 3% of X-votes, instead of 10% of them. Then A gets (0.25 + 0.03)/(0.25 + 0.03 + 0.20 + 0.25) = 38.36% of the XXs and Xs of the association, and B gets 61.64%. Thus A receives 0.45 x ((2 x 0.3836) − 0.5) = 12.02% of seats (unless this is less than A's guaranteed minimum of 12.5% of seats, which it is). Thus A receives its minimum of 12.5% of seats, and B receives 45 − 12.5 = 32.5% of seats. Thus by not getting enough X-votes from the electors who first-prefer neither A or B, party A has effectively lost half its seats.

of its use in Northern Ireland. To avoid losing half its seats, any party (let us call it P) must join an association. To maximise its seats, P therefore seeks as an 'associate', a party which (1) is unlikely to get less than two-thirds as many XX-votes as P does itself, and (2) is unlikely to be preferred to P by any more than a bare majority of voters. If P cannot find an acceptable associate, P is likely to split itself into two parties of similar size, which can then form an association.

The extreme Catholic Sinn Fein expects that, if it joins an association with any other party, only a small percentage will prefer it to its associate, and so it splits into two parties, which form an association. The moderate Catholic SDLP cannot find an associate of the required size, and so splits into two parties which form an association. A new Centre Party is formed by moderate politicians from both communities, and forms an association with the non-sectarian Alliance Party. A reduced UUP (having lost support to the Centre Party) forms an association with the DUP. In each association, the two parties will be competing strongly for the X-votes of those electors who give neither of them first preference, since a party which does not compete, is likely to lose about half of its seats to the other party. Thus formerly mono-ethnic parties will need to appeal to, and adopt a policy responsive to, the other ethnic group, the UUP and DUP to the Catholic electors, the ex-Sinn Fein and ex-SDLP parties to the Protestants. Even the already pan-ethnic Alliance and Centre parties will need to broaden their appeal, to be more responsive to the concerns not only of the moderate voters, but also of the voters more to either extreme, both those who are Catholics and those who are Protestants.

Thus in conclusion, the Association System will give the parties a strong incentive to converge towards each other in policy, each to adopt a similar moderate policy responsive to each section of electors and to each ethnic group. Thus although the system is likely to increase the number of parties, the fact that these parties are moderate ones, similar to each other both in policy and in the groups to which they seek to appeal, can be expected to facilitate the formation of a coalition government, and this government can be expected to be stable and effective, and responsive to each ethnic group.

The Territorial List Scheme

The Association System as so far described, has done no more than determine each party's number of seats. But to qualify as a complete electoral system, it must also allocate the seats won by a party between its candidates, and allocate these candidates to the areas of the country for which they are to have responsibility. It would be possible to do this by means of party lists in multi-member constituencies, just as in the usual forms of Party List PR. However, this paper proposes an alternative scheme of party lists in *single-member* territories, which will be referred to as the *Territorial List Scheme*. The advantages claimed for this scheme are (1) that it would give much better contact between the individual MPs (Members of Parliament) and the electors each one represents, and (2) that it would promote greater unity and cohesion in each party. This party cohesion is important for the Association System, which aims to transform the currently more or less mono-ethnic parties, into *pan-ethnic* parties, responsive to each ethnic group. This transformation is more likely to be achieved, if each party can function as coherent and disciplined team of MPs, united behind the objective of obtaining votes from each ethnic group, and so maximising the party's seats. Thus the Territorial List Scheme is put forward as an important part of the Association System, and its rules are as follows.

Shortly before the general election, each party registers its provisional list of candidates, which normally will include the party's MPs of the immediately previous term. A separate *candidate selection ballot* is then carried out for each party, under the auspices of the electoral authority. In this ballot, all persons on the party's provisional list are placed as candidates on the ballot paper, and only persons on this provisional list may vote, voting for as many candidates as they like. The ballot is secret. To be accepted on to the party's final list, a person must obtain votes from at least one-half of the members of the provisional list. Further persons may be voted on to the final list, by the assenting vote of a majority of those already on the final list, in secret ballot.

The final list of candidates is then placed in the order in which they are to receive seats, again by vote of the candidates on that list, in another secret ballot. In this, the voting is preferential, that is, the person votes by writing '1' for a first preference, '2' for a second preference, and so on, for as many candidates as they wish. The candidates on the list are then placed in order by successive applications of the Alternative Vote method.[3]. That is, one candidate is chosen by AV, to occupy the first place on the list. From the remaining candidates, one is chosen by AV to occupy the second place, and so on.

Under the Territorial List Scheme, the country is divided into small electoral areas referred to as 'tracts', there being let us say twice as many tracts as MPs to be elected. From these tracts, each party creates a number of 'territories', a territory being a cluster of tracts, as many as the party chooses, in which the party places one of its candidates. The party may not overlap its territories, that is, it may not put more than one candidate in the same tract. But the territories may be of any size, as is decided by the party. Presumably the party will choose to create a number of territories which is not more than the minimum number of seats it expects to obtain, and will create them of such size that they cover the whole country, so that every tract in the country can be the responsibility of one of its elected MPs. The party can be expected to put on its list enough additional candidates *without* territories, to fill the seats it gets in excess of this minimum number, and to fill any vacancies which might occur during the course of the

[3]By the Alternative Vote, the candidate with fewest first-preference votes is excluded, and his votes are transferred, each vote going to its next preference. The candidate then with fewest votes is similarly excluded, and his votes are transferred, and so on, until one candidate has more than half the total votes held by all the non-excluded candidates, and is elected.

legislative term due to death or retirement.[4]

Thus the general effect of the scheme will be that large parties will create small territories, and many of them, and small parties will create large territories. Each tract of the country will have an elected MP of each party to take responsibility for it, while the territory of each MP will not be any bigger than is necessary for the MP's party to be sure of covering the whole country. Thus this scheme would appear to maximise the degree of contact between the individual MPs and the electors each one represents.

In order to strengthen the parties, it is important that a substantial amount of state funding should be paid to the parties as a regular income throughout the legislative term, each party getting a share in proportion to its seats. This party income should be paid, not to the individual MPs of the party, but to the party's team of MPs as a whole, or to an organisation they set up to receive it. The object of this subsidy is to help establish each party as an independent team of MPs, able to finance its own campaigning, and as far as possible without financial or other ties to outside groups, in particular without ties to any one ethnic group. Such an independent team will be better able to seek and attract votes from all ethnic groups, and so increase its seats.

Another factor helping to establish each party as an independent and coherent team, is the procedure for drawing up the party list. For the individual MPs of a party will be fully aware that they will face a candidate selection ballot before the next election, at which the other MPs of the party can, in secret ballot, with no risk to themselves, and without need to explain or justify, simply expel them without appeal from the party's list, or place them so low down on the list that they are very unlikely to get a seat. Thus any MP who wants to be re-elected will have a strong incentive to cooperate with the rest of the party team, in their efforts to develop and promote a policy which will get votes from each section and each ethnic group, and so increase the party's seats. If a party has split into two parties to form its own association (as Sinn Fein or the SDLP might do), then this factor, and also the party subsidy, will enable each of the two new parties to establish itself as an independent team, competing with the other party for votes and seats. Thus in conclusion, the provisions of the Territorial List Scheme can be expected to strengthen and unify each party, building up its independence, and encouraging its MPs to cooperate as a team, responsive to each ethnic group.

The Distributed Vote

The Association System is one general method for protecting the ethnic minorities. Another is that of the *Distributed Vote.* The principle here is that the system rewards a party for getting an even *distribution* of votes as

[4]However, if it did happen that a party over-estimated the seats it would get, and so had some territories in which its candidate was not elected, it could assign each tract of these territories to one of its elected MPs, as an additional responsibility, so as to ensure that its MPs covered all tracts in the country.

between the different ethnic groups, and penalises it for getting an uneven distribution. For example, suppose that in Northern Ireland, party A gets the votes of 20% of the Catholics, and 24% of the Protestants, while party B gets the same number of votes as A, but all from the Protestants. The Distributed Vote principle requires that A should get more seats than B.

There are two ways to implement this principle – *Tract DV* and *Set DV*. Under Tract DV, the country is divided into small 'tracts', as with the Territorial List Scheme, except that the tracts will tend to be smaller, and of irregular size and shape. The reason is that the boundaries of each tract are drawn so that it contains as high as possible a percentage of electors of one or other of the ethnic groups, that is, so that the tract is as *mono-ethnic* as possible. For example, in Northern Ireland, each tract should be drawn so as to consist of as high a percentage as possible, either of Protestants, or of Catholics. Then for each party, its 'minimum percentage' is found, that is, its percentage of the votes in that one-fifth of tracts in which the party obtains its *lowest* percentages of votes (one-fifth of tracts being defined as a set of tracts containing one-fifth of all electors). Each party then receives seats in proportion to its minimum percentage, except that no party must get a percentage of seats which is less than one-half of its percentage of votes.[5]

The effect of this Tract DV system is that if for example a party gets very few votes from the Catholics, it will get a very low percentage in those tracts which are mainly or entirely Catholic. Thus its 'minimum percentage', its percentage in its worst one-fifth of tracts, will be very low, and it will lose seats, perhaps as many as one-half of its seats, if its minimum percentage is low enough.

Tract DV thus gives each party the incentive to get votes as evenly as possible from all tracts, and hence, *in so far as each ethnic group has tracts in which it is concentrated*, it gives each party the incentive to get votes from each ethnic group. However, if an ethnic group is small, and dispersed more or less evenly over most tracts, Tract DV will not provide any extra incentive above the normal, for a party to seek its votes. For this reason, another form of the system, referred to as *Set DV*, is put forward, which is likely to be more effective in protecting such small ethnic groups.

In Set DV, the electors are registered on separate ethnic electoral rolls, each roll containing one ethnic group.[6] The country is divided into tracts, but in this case, unlike under Tract DV, the tracts are given any convenient boundaries, and no attempt is made to make them mono-ethnic. A 'set' is defined as a set of electors in one or more tracts, *who are all registered on*

[5]For example, suppose that parties A, B and C respectively have overall percentages of votes of 30, 40 and 30, and minimum percentages of 20, 15 and 5. If all got seats in proportion to their minimum percentages, seats would be 50%, 37.5% and 12.5%, giving C less than half its percentage of votes. Therefore C gets 30/2 = 15%, and A and B share the remaining 100 − 15 = 85% in proportion to their minimum percentages, getting 48.6% and 36.4% respectively. Thus B, the party with most votes, gets fewer seats than A because in its worst tracts it gets a lower percentage than A does, while C effectively loses half its seats by getting a very low percentage in its worst tracts.

[6]This has already been done in some countries, for example in Fiji, where there is a Fijian roll, an Indo-Fijian roll, and a 'general' roll for other races.

the same ethnic roll. If an ethnic roll has only a small percentage of the electors in some area, then for that roll electors from several tracts will be included in one set. A party's 'minimum percentage' is then defined as its percentage of the votes in that one-fifth of *sets* in which the party obtains its *lowest* percentages of votes. Each party then receives seats in proportion to its minimum percentage, except that again no party must get a percentage of seats which is less than one-half of its percentage of votes.

The effect of Set DV is that if a party gets a much lower percentage of votes from any one ethnic roll than it gets from the electors as a whole, then it will get a low percentage in the sets of that roll. Thus it will get a low minimum percentage, and so will lose seats, perhaps one-half of its seats, if its minimum percentage is low enough. This gives the party the incentive to appeal to each ethnic group, *irrespective of whether the group is concentrated in some localities, or is spread out widely over the country.* Thus Set DV offers stronger protection to a numerically small and spread-out ethnic minority, than would Tract DV.

The Distributed Vote principle can be used alone as described above, but it is better to use it in combination with the Association System. In such a combined system, one of the forms of Distributed Vote is used, to determine what share of an association's seats should be given to either of the two parties in the association.[7] Thus, as compared with either the Distributed Vote or the Association System used alone, the combined system can be expected to greatly strengthen the incentive of each party to obtain votes from each ethnic group.

Use of the proposed systems in Northern Ireland and Eastern Europe

The use of these systems in Northern Ireland has already been extensively discussed. But which of these systems should be used? The conflict does not appear to be severe enough to require the use of the system with the strongest pan-ethnic incentive, the Association System with Set DV. The use of the Association System with Tract DV would seem to be desirable, provided it is found to be politically acceptable, and if not, the use of the Association System alone is suggested.

If the system is to be used only in Northern Ireland, the minority protected would be the Catholics. But it might be possible to have in parallel with such a Northern Ireland assembly, an all-Ireland federal assembly and government, presumably one with very limited powers. This assembly would be elected by the same system, in order to make it more acceptable to the Protestants, who would then be the minority whose interests were to be protected.

[7] If for example Set DV is used, then for each of the two parties in the association, its percentage of the XX-votes and X-votes in each set is found. From these percentages, each party's minimum percentage is calculated, as before. Each party receives a share of the association's seats, in proportion to its minimum percentage, unless this would give one of them less than its guaranteed minimum of seats.

The use of one of these systems should be considered for electing a federal assembly for the whole of Bosnia. Bosnia appears already to have been divided into almost mono-ethnic areas. Thus the Set DV version of the Association System could be used, regarding the electorate of all the Muslim areas as one ethnic roll, and the electorates of the Serb and the Croat areas as the other two ethnic rolls. Thus in the special situation of Bosnia, Set DV can be employed, without the necessity of registering individual electors on different ethnic rolls.

This system will give each party a powerful incentive to appeal to each of the three ethnic groups. For if in any one of them a party gets a low percentage of votes, it could lose as much as half its seats. Thus it might be expected that each party would energetically seek the votes of and respond to each ethnic group. A coalition government formed from such parties could be expected to follow a moderate policy, a compromise between the interests of the different ethnic groups. Thus the proposed system should be seriously considered, as it might well offer in this difficult situation, a better chance of stable and generally acceptable government than do any of the conventional systems.

The same system is suggested, for any other country where the different ethnic groups are segregated in mono-ethnic or nearly mono-ethnic areas.

However, in most ethnically divided countries, there are few or no mono-ethnic areas, but instead one or more ethnic minorities are spread over much or all of the country. For example, Romania has a Romani or Gypsy minority of about 10 per cent, spread over much of the country, as well as other minorities. In this situation also, the Association System with Set DV appears the most suitable, but here it will be necessary to register the electors of each ethnic minority individually on separate ethnic rolls.

Conclusion

This paper offers a range of new electoral systems, which, though designed for situations of ethnic division, can nevertheless be expected to provide stable and effective government, responsive to the electors' needs, both when ethnic divisions exist, and in more normal situations where ethnic divisions are absent. For in general these systems exert over time on each party and each candidate a steady incentive towards moderation, towards a policy responsive to the needs of each section of electors, and towards a centre position, not only on the ethnic dimension, but also on any other dimension – such as the left-wing/right-wing dimension – which is of importance to the electors. Thus unlike the usual forms of proportional representation, these systems encourage the parties to converge towards each other, both in policy, towards this moderate centre position, and *in the groups to which they seek to appeal.* Given such parties, moderate and similar to each other in policy, it seems likely that a stable and effective coalition government could be formed from them, one which was widely acceptable to the electorate, and responsive to each ethnic group.

Politics of Transition in East and Southeast Asia

Duncan McCargo
University of Leeds

'The politics of scandal: the case of the Thai press'

Acknowledgements

I gratefully acknowledge financial support from the ESRC, the British Academy , and the Department of Politics, University of Leeds, which enabled me to carry out fieldwork in Thailand for the research on which this paper is based. The present paper derives from a major project on the politics of the media in Thailand and Pacific Asia, for which I hold a four year ESRC Research Fellowship.

Introduction

In May 1995, the Thai government led by Democrat leader Chuan Leekpai collapsed during a no-confidence debate over a scandal concerning land reform irregularities. The press, especially some elements of the Thai language press, played a crucial role in the downfall of the Chuan government.[1] Despite significant state control over the electronic media, Thailand has a flourishing and extremely free press. Leading Thai language newspapers such as the popular *Thai Rath* (which claims sales of a million copies for its colourful blend of sensationalism, crime and politics)[2] and the more serious *Matichon* are widely read and highly influential. This paper contends that Thai politics can be viewed as a 'politics of scandal', in which political developments are closely related the emergence (and subsequent disappearance) of political controversies and scandals in the press.[3] It further argues that the Thai press functions as a political actor in its own right (not simply as a 'mirror', 'agenda-setter', or 'watchdog'),[4] participating actively in a dialogue with elected politicians and other actors. The paper reaches this conclusion by exploring a number of questions with relation to the Thai language press: What constitutes 'political news'? Where does political news come from? How is it assembled in the newsroom? What are the relationships between political reporters, columnists and editors ? How do newspaper people relate to politicians and other political actors? How does the presentation of political news have an impact upon political developments in Thailand?

---

[1] For background on media and politics in Thailand, see Duncan McCargo, 'The buds of May', *Index on Censorship*, 22/4, 1993; Gordon Fairclough, 'Free to air', *Far Eastern Economic Review*, 16/November, 1995.

[2] For an interesting if somewhat unreliable account of Thai Rath and its late owner, see Nicholas Coleridge, *Paper tigers*, Mandarin, 1994, pp.430-37.

[3] For a recent general account of Thai politics, see Pasuk Phongpaichit & C.Baker, *Thailand: economy and politics*, Oxford University Press, 1995.

[4] For a useful discussion of alternative concepts of the media's political role, see S.J.Pharr, 'Media as trickster in Japan: a comparative perspective', in S.J.Pharr & E.Krauss (eds), *Media and politics in Japan*, University of Hawaii Press, 1996, pp.19-43.

Paper takes on government: *Thai Rath* and the Democrats

The demise of the relatively liberal Chuan Leekpai government in May 1995 has been widely seen as a setback for Thai politics, since subsequent prime ministers (Banharn Silpa-archa 1995, and Chavalit Yongchaiyudh 1996) were closely associated with money-based provincial politics.[5] Yet *Thai Rath* had been opposed to the 1992-95 government (led by the Democrat Party under Chuan Leekpai) virtually from the outset. The anti-Democrat stance of *Thai Rath* had to be seen in the context of the position adopted by the newspaper during the April-May 1992 government of Suchinda Kraprayoon. As Army commander-in-chief, Suchinda was one of the leaders of the 23 February 1991 military coup. Following a general election in March 1992 which was supposed to usher in democratic 'normalisation', non-MP Suchinda was selected as prime minister by civilian politicians from political parties with strong personal and financial ties to the military. Most of the Thai press had opposed Suchinda's premiership, giving sympathetic coverage to protest movements initiated by various groups, and involving hunger strikes by activist Chalard Vorachat and former Bangkok governor Chamlong Srimuang. But for *Thai Rath*, which enjoyed close ties with many of the leading figures in the Suchinda government, backing the opposition movement was difficult. *Thai Rath* had initially been very sympathetic to Suchinda, although it had changed its position as the crisis unfolded.[6]

When Suchinda fell from power, following huge demonstrations in central Bangkok on 17 and 18 May – which culminated in the at least fifty unarmed civilians losing their lives when the army opened fire – fresh elections were called. The new Democrat-led government was composed mainly of parties which had opposed Suchinda. *Thai Rath* 's best connections were now with opposition parties such as Chart Thai, Chart Pattana, and Social Action. Yet the core issue was not these personal ties, so much as the attitude which new prime minister Chuan Leekpai adopted towards *Thai Rath*.

Partly as a function of his combination of lowly origins and immense wealth, Kamphol expected the great and the good of Thai society to appear at his birthday party on 27 December each year. The party, held in a banqueting hall at his home, was usually attended by several hundred guests. No invitations, however, were issued. Instead, those whose presence was expected at the party were informed by the relevant *Thai Rath* reporter. Senior politicians, including the prime minister of the day, would always be expected by Kamphol to attend. Their attendance was an indication of their willingness to 'suhok' Kamphol, to pay their respects to him and acknowledge his importance. To fail to attend would be to snub Kamphol, and thus to invite his wrath. As Abhisit Vejjajiva – who served as government spokesman under Chuan from September 1992 to December 1994 – explained:

[5] On the demise of Chuan in relation to wider political trends, see D.King & J.LoGerfo, 'Thailand: toward democratic stability', *Journal of Democracy*, 7/1, 1996, pp.102-117.

[6] See Pajaree Tanasomboonkit, MA dissertation, Faculty of Communication Arts, Chulalongkorn University, 1995 (in Thai).

> '*Thai Rath* has been a very, very influential force in politics, and you just have to witness this birthday party with all the biggies, from every circle, not just political, who have to pay respects to him. Chuan is not that kind of man ... he doesn't think it's necessary for him to do that, and he thinks that he has to do things in a straightforward way; if they didn't like it they would criticise him, and if they stepped over the line he'd take them to court, and that's what happened.'[7]

Anand Panyarachun had also refused to attend Kamphol's parties, but Anand (who served two short terms as prime minister in 1991 and 1992) was an unelected appointee who did not have to contend with party political opposition. Despite three requests to attend Kamphol's birthday party in 1992, Chuan failed to show up, preferring to keep another engagement in the South. A similar pattern followed in 1993 and 1994. Thus from early on in Chuan's premiership, he found himself at loggerheads with *Thai Rath*. This conflict was also symbolised in his decision to sue *Thai Rath* columnist Santi Viriyarangsarit (known as 'Typhoon') for suggesting in his 11 May 1993 column that Chuan was dictatorial, and implying that he had ordered violent action to be taken against farmers protesting in Kamphaeng Phet province.[8] It was unusual for a serving prime minister to sue a newspaper, especially such a powerful one as *Thai Rath*, and Chuan's decision amounted to a declaration of hostilities. From early 1993 onwards, *Thai Rath* was looking for an issue which it could use to mount a major campaign against the Democrats. When that issue presented itself in the form of the Sor Por Kor land reform scandal, *Thai Rath* did not hesitate to put the boot in, 'locking' the story onto its front page for six months. As Abhisit put it:

> 'By the time of the land reform issue, anybody who follows politics could expect to see that they saw in *Thai Rath*. Of course they would do that because they don't like the Democrats. So in a way by sort of declaring an open war, *Thai Rath* didn't have the status of being a neutral and straightforward newspaper, and so people who had read *Thai Rath* would have that in mind.'

It is impossible to prove that the presence of several former close associates of Chart Thai Party leader Banharn Silpa-archa among the senior editorial team of *Thai Rath* had anything to do with the 'open war' declared by the paper on the Democrat administration. The picture was complicated by the fact that important figures at the newspaper retained close personal ties with the Democrats. Nevertheless, the onslaught against the Democrats mounted by Thai Rath over the land reform issue was a formidable one. Coverage of the story, which began on 23 November 1994, was 'locked' onto the front page and carried in immense detail. When the Chuan government collapsed on 19 May 1995, Palang Dharma Party leader Chamlong Srimuang remarked in a radio interview that any story which ran

[7] Abhisit Vejjajiva, interview, 31 January 1996.
[8] *Bangkok Post*, 15 May 1993.

on the front page of the newspapers every day for six months had to have some basis to it.

The nature of the 'basis' for *Thai Rath* 's campaign against the Democrats lies in the structure of the political coverage of *Thai Rath* and other Thai-language dailies, a structure best seen in terms of dichotomies: news versus comment, juniors versus seniors, reporters versus columnists, inside the system versus outside the system, and Bangkok versus the provinces.

News versus comment

An important distinction in the context of the Thai language press is the distinction between news and comment. 'News' especially political news, is narrowly defined as literal descriptions of actual events, plus the statements of people involved. The majority of the text in political news stories comprises drect or indirect quotations. Most political reporters are not employed to gather information, so much as to collect quotations.

The Thai concept of what constitutes a 'front page' political story often differs from that used in other countries. The front pages of most Thai newspapers consist almost entirely of large headlines, with sub-headings and the first few words of a story. The rest of the story then appears on an inside page, sometimes running on to a third page. Political news stories follow a definite formula, with a series of quotations linked by phrases such as 'Mr Chuan still insists that', and 'the permanent secretary also stated that'. A story about the Democrat party might begin with a series of statements from Democrats (not necessarily in order of seniority), then quote various responses from rival political parties, followed by statements from academics or well known public figures not directly involved in the party political fray. These news stories have no conclusion: the quotations simply come to an abrupt end. Many news stories had virtually no kernel of factual content, consisting almost entirely of verbal responses to the the statements of others, pyramids of accusation and counter-accusation. Under these conditions, stories could be spun out almost indefinitely by newspaper reporters and editors. Thus scandals (such that over as land reform in 1995) could be run on front pages for months on end, without any significant new development having occurred.

Junior versus seniors

Underlying the structure of political coverage in the Thai language press is a hierarchical relationship between juniors and seniors. This relationship exists in two parallel worlds: the political world beyond the newspaper, and journalistic world inside the newspaper. In the political world, reporters do not operate on terms of relative equality with politicians. With the exception of a handful of senior reporters, those working on the political 'beats' at places such as parliament and government house were mostly under 25, and had been working as reporters for no more than two or three years. They were generally referred to by both editors and politicians alike as 'dek', kids, and received little or no training for their work.

A typical front page political news story contained material from eight, ten, or even twelve different reporters. The quotations gathered were either faxed or phoned in to political 'rewriters', whose task was to string the material into some kind of story. At *Thai Rath*, some rewriters literally employed scissors and paste to create a news story out of faxed material sent in from reporters,[9] typing up connecting material themselves. Most political reporters lived in fear of 'tok khao', missing an important item of news. Partly out of habit, and partly because they were not always confident of their ability to spot the important issue, reporters preferred to fax in everything they had collected. Thai reporters were taught that inserting any sort of explanation or background material into a story was tantamount to putting in the personal opinions of the writer, something absolutely forbidden. Any such material could only be expressed within the confines of a column. Although political news stories did have a 'beginning' – usually a statement by a well known public figure – they lacked either a middle (a core 'praden', a central issue), or an 'end' in the form of a concluding paragraph summarising the development, and looking forward to the next stage.

However, the business of political rewriting was not necessarily always a purely mechanical process. At least one *Thai Rath* insider argued that it was possible to tell from reading *Thai Rath* 's front page stories which of the three political rewriters had been on duty that day. Rewriters were more than passive compilers of material: they could page or telephone reporters to follow up stories and supply more detailed quotations. Indeed, they could also telephone sources of their own and solicit quotations from them; these might include personal friends, and drinking or gambling buddies with whom they enjoyed close relations. Of *Thai Rath* 's three political rewriters, one was very close to several figures in the Chart Thai Party and other 'ex-devil' parties, whilst another had a broader range of connections in parties such as Chart Pattana and Chart Thai. Two of the three had formerly worked for Ban Muang, the newspaper owned by Chart Thai politician Banharn Silpa-archa, who became prime minister in July 1995. The political rewriters were supervised by the front page editor.

Front page editors did not have the final word on decisions, however. A former front page editor for a leading daily explained that he would select front page stories partly on the basis of hints from the newspaper's owners that he should 'look out' for particular stories.[10] One example of a general policy over-riding day-to-day news considerations was a decision in late 1994 to 'lock' the Sor Por Kor land reform scandal onto the front page of *Thai Rath*, meaning that this story would be run every day regardless of whether there had been any important development. This continued for around six months, until the Democrats lost power in mid-May 1995.

The inside pages of Thai language newspapers contained considerable amounts of political 'comment', mainly by regular columnists. Unlike re-

[9]Since my fieldwork in April 1995, the process has been computerised.

[10]Interview, 29 March 1995.

porters, who were juniors in both the political and newspaper worlds, columnists were seniors or 'big people' (phu yai). As phu yai, they could operate on terms of relative equality with political figures. Indeed, some well-known columnists might be more powerful than the average politican. Most political columns consisted almost entirely of opinion, with very little factual material. Most political news consisted of the comments of people 'outside' in the wider political world (mainly MPs, party leaders, and ministers), whilst most political columns contained the comments of those 'inside' the newspaper, and those closely associated with it. In other words, Thai language newspapers established and perpetuated a constant political dialogue between two groups of commentators, both of whom have the status of 'insiders' in the Thai political order. Almost all political coverage in Thai newspapers was opinion. News consisted of the opinions of phu yai outside the newspaper. Comment consisted of the opinions of phu yai inside the newspaper.

There were often close personal ties between politicians and columnists, ties which sometimes brought financial and other benefits to the columnists concerned. Some columnists – like two of the three political rewriters at *Thai Rath* – were also senior figures inside the newspaper, holding positions on the political desk, the front page desk, or as editors. Others worked full-time for the newspaper but were responsible solely for their columns, whilst a third group were regular freelance contributors.

The political column is an institution in Thailand. Given the highly literal and incompletely informative character of political news stories, Thais are reliant upon political columms for guidance as to the significance of news items, and hints as to what is actually going on. At the same time, political columnists are unreliable narrators. Just as political news stories are simply compilations of the opinions of others, political columns are simply the opinions of columnists, many of who set out to write in an entertaining, declamatory fashion which is brazenly partisan. The model for most political columnists was MR Kukrit Pramoj, founder of the Social Action Party, and prime minister in the seventies. In the daily 'Suan Phlu' column which he wrote for *Siam Rath*, the newspaper he founded and owned, Kukrit would sound off about political developments in an over-blown fashion. The column contributed to Kukrit's larger-than-life political persona, and exemplified the model of columnist as consummate political insider, using the inside page of a newspaper to initiate controversies, leak information, start rumours and speculation, reproach political opponents, and generally cause trouble.

Reporters versus columnists

Mutually beneficial arrangements between politicians and columnists are commonplace in Thailand. Politicians sometimes make expensive gifts to columnists (perhaps a luxury car or even a house) in return for favourable coverage; in some cases this extended to offering columnists regular 'salaries'. Given the low pay which pervades the journalistic profession in Thailand

– senior political staff at *Thai Rath* in 1995 were earning in the region of 15-20,000 baht per month, and some other papers paid less – many newspaper staff were understandably susceptible to the temptations of such offers. The most well-known group of columnists associated with a leading politician was the so-called '18 Orahan', many of whose members were formerly journalists on Banharn Silpa-archa's newspaper *Ban Muang*. By 1995, they had partially dispersed to other newspapers, including *Thai Rath* (reputed to employ 8 or 9 of them), *Daily News*, and *Naew Na*. Most politicians and ministers sought to build up circles of supportive journalists. The means they used varied; whereas politicians such as Chamlong Srimuang cultivated reporters who had considerable personal and political faith in him,[11] and Chuan Leekpai maintained contacts with a circle of friendly journalists over many years, other less scrupulous politicians showered reporters and columnists with favours.

Unlike reporters, columnists had considerable license to comment on issues of the day. The voices of columnists on the inside pages of newspapers competed with the voices of politicians and other important figures quoted extensively in front page stories. Columnists (especially those writing well-known columns in big-selling or influential papers) were public figures in their own right. Conversation among politicians, government officials, and journalists would often turn to the latest column by Chalam Khiew (*Thai Rath* columnist Weerajak Konthong) Plaew Si Ngern (*Siam Post* senior editor and former *Thai Rath* columnist Rojana Ngamman), Wipak Chapphan ('Jodpai Matichon', page 3 of *Matichon Daily*), and Than Phu Noi (*Siam Post* columnist and founder of *Arthit Weekly* Chatcharin Chaiwatsu).

A newspaper such as *Thai Rath* was not simply a monolith characterised by centralised control. This was only one part of the story. As Thai academic Chaiyan Rajchagool puts it:

> 'A common characteristic among popular newspapers is the inclusion of a wide variety of edictorial columns in order to cover a broad readership. Some columns may be radically progressive, whereas others may be downright conservative. By including these opposing views in one paper, these dailies create the facade that they are in fact "liberal". But with close inspection, one can easily pin-point the over-all outlook of a paper by its distribution of space to certain topics and political parties.'[12]

Thai Rath epitomised this kind of 'omnidirectional' newspaper, designed to appeal to a wide variety of readers, by supporting different political parties and interest groups through its spread of columns.

---

[11] See Duncan McCargo, *Chamlong Srimuang and the new Thai politics*, Hurst, forthcoming.

[12] Chaiyan Rajchagool, 'Caution advised while reading your paper', *The Nation*, 19 June 1995.

Inside the system versus 'outside the system'

The *Thai Rath* political team had around twenty members. A striking feature of the political team was its focus upon gathering news from traditional centres of state power in the capital. The main emphasis was on four institutions: Government House (the office of the prime minister, the five or so deputy prime ministers, and the three or so ministers attached to the PM's office), Parliament, the military, and the Interior Ministry. There were no roving political reporters whose job it was to pursue important stories: the job of reporters was to 'cover' specific physical locations, usually leaving them only to follow the movements of associated big shots. The result was a highly conservative political coverage; the views of prominent politicians and senior establishment figures were reported at considerable length, while those of non-governmental figures or ordinary members of the public were marginalised. Despite the view taken by many academics that Thailand's 'bureaucratic polity' had long since been modified by the rise of party politicians, new social forces, and alliances between business and politics, political reporting reflected a notion of politics more appropriate to the 1960s than to the 1990s. Some reporters were also assigned to cover news concerning extra-parliamentary groups such as the student movement, labour unions, and pro-democracy NGOs, but these secondary tasks were frequently re-assigned, and were not taken very seriously by the reporters concerned unless a specific demonstration was taking a place or a high profile issue emerged. Extra-parliamentary politics was generally referred to as 'nok rabob', 'outside the system', a phrase which suggested an illegitimate quality. Extra-parliamentary politics only became important in the eyes of Thai newspapers when it threatened to challenge or subvert the established political order.

Bangkok versus the provinces

Another characteristic of the political news-gathering operation was its Bangkok focus. Metropolitan reporters only ventured out of Bangkok in pursuit of political stories for two main purposes: accompanying politicians such as the prime minister on provincial trips, and covering parliamentary elections. Although a national newspaper such as *Thai Rath* maintained reporters in every province in the country, provincial reporters did not enjoy the same status as Bangkok-based reporters. Provincial reporters were not full-time salaried employees of the newspaper, but semi-freelance 'stringers' who were paid by the story. Insofar as they covered political and other issues, provincial reporters tended to act as the mouthpieces of local government officials. Despite the fact that 90% of Thai politicians represented provincial constituencies, and that important political issues such as the 1995 land reform scandal were essentially provincial stories, very little political news was generated in the provinces.

Conclusion

The structure of political news-gathering in the Thai press has created a dialogue between two groups of 'big shots': politicians and political columnists. Political news consists almost entirely of summarising and commenting upon the utterances of big shots. So long as Thai newspapers can engage in a continuous political conversation with other actors, they are able to influence the nature of that conversation, helping to determine which political issues (and scandals) remain uppermost. A concerted campaign by a leading newspaper such as *Thai Rath* can contribute to the demise of a government, as prime minister Chuan Leekpai found to his cost in May 1995. While an unfettered and dynamic press can enhance civil society at the expense of entrenched bureaucratic and military power, such a press can also operate for illiberal ends where the news agenda is influenced by close personal relationships between newspaper owners, editors and conservative élites.

Politics of Transition in East and South East Asia

William A. Callahan
University of Durham

'Harmony or Hegemony in Greater China?
reading China's actions in the South China Sea'

Introduction

The Spratly Islands in the South China Sea are interesting because they provide multiple challenges to the system of world politics both empirically and conceptually. In other words, these unassuming islets are a loud hiccup in the discourse of the 'Pacific Century', which is one of the few positive statements of 'post cold war' discourse.[1] They are problematic to the solidarity of 'Asia' because the main source of conflict is not from outside actors – either via European imperialism or the Cold War. For the first time in a century, the problem is clearly between fellow Asian states.

The South China Seas disputes are thus taken to be an exemplary post Cold War conflict: China, Taiwan, Vietnam, the Philippines, Malaysia and Brunei each have made claims of sovereignty on this archipelago. By examining how such territorial disputes have arisen, and how they are being resolved, we can start to see both which way China is going – towards harmony or hegemony – and how it will affect the world. Thus, I will argue that this concerns much more than who ultimately gets the deeds to the Spratly Islands, but more importantly, how the dispute is resolved is most important. As even the most mainstream analysts note, the South China Sea struggles have broad geopolitical implications beyond territory or oil, but are indicative of 'post cold war trends'.[2]

On the one hand, it is a case study for the norms of international politics. The disputes arise not from an ideological war as in the recent past, but constitute an economic struggle: the main attractions of the islets are the natural resources – oil and gas. Thus the South China Sea disputes challenge international law, and specifically the Law of the Sea, to sort out sovereignty claims. Indeed, both academics and foreign policy élites seem to use sovereignty's traditional definition of 'territory, population, and authority'. This is the obvious tool to use; except when you come to the South China Sea that is. Closer examination shows that it is a space where territorial sovereignty does not make sense.

Firstly, there is no territory in the South China Sea. Most of the reefs are under water most of the year; to build bases on them, the various army engineers have to construct stilts, and pour lots of concrete. Secondly, there is

---

[1]For a critical view of 'the Pacific Century' see Arif Dirlik (ed), *What is in a Rim? Critical Perspectives on the Pacific Rim Idea*, Westview Press, 1993.

[2]M.J.Valencia, *China and the South China Sea Disputes: Conflicting Claims and potential solutions in the South China Sea*, Adelphi 298, Oxford University Press, 1995, p.6.

no population, except for the literally 'floating population' of fishermen and pirates. The Chinese have to engage in elaborate narratives of travelogues, history, and archaeology to prove their claims of a Chinese population on the islets.[3] Thirdly, there is no authority in the region, either symbolically or materially. Actually it is an area of a very obvious lack of authority, for it is the most active region in the world for piracy.[4] Symbolically, to name is to control.[5] The overdetermination of names thus shows a lack of single sovereign authority: the names of the islands, reefs and atolls are not set, for each country has its own collection of names. For example, the Chinese call the Spratlys *Nansha*, or South Sand Islands. This recalls Sun Yatsen's famous metaphor of Chinese national instability: China is like a plate of sand, that could blow away at any time.

The presence of absence in these three categories is neatly summed up by the 1995 CIA Factbook's entry on Spratly Islands: most of the common sense categories for nation-states don't make sense; NA (not applicable) is the most common datum.[6] So each of the states has to work very hard to imagine sovereignty; to imagine communities where there are no communities at all. Thus, one could argue that the South China Sea disputes challenge the very notion of sovereignty. Resolving the problems is not just a nuts and bolts problem of dividing up the goods, but a theoretical problem of understanding how power and authority work in world politics where space is multiple, and where the sovereign claims overlap.

More than being simply a battle between the Chinese and Vietnamese navies, I will argue that there is a significant – albeit unspoken – struggle between concepts of space. Simply put, the contest is between the master narrative of a horizontal map of geopolitics on the one hand, more vertical mappings of ironic world politics on the other. Thus it is necessary to switch our conceptual focus because the horizontal map of unitary state sovereignties is not very helpful in making sense of the South China Sea dispute. Even *The Asian Wall Street Journal* doubts the utility of the Law of the Sea itself: 'It seems that what the Law of the Sea Treaty has accomplished is to intensify, rather than diminish, off shore territorial disputes.'[7]

But rather than making a simple reversal of 180 degrees, it is more helpful to reorient ourselves by ninety degrees to start imagining a vertical map of space.[8] I will argue that in switching from geography to cosmography, we can see how sovereignty becomes multiple, and shared around intersecting peripheries such as the South China Sea. Such a vertical imagining of communities effaces the boundaries between domestic and international relations, and thus alters political space as well.

---

[3]Monique Chemillier-Gendreau, *La Souveraineté sur les archipels Paracels et Spratlys*, Editions L'Harmattan, 1996; Chen Hurng-yu, 'A comparison between Taipei and Peking in their policies and concepts regarding the South China Sea', *Issues and Studies*, 29/9, 1993.

[4]'Treacherous Shoals', *Far Eastern Economic Review*, 13 August 1992, p.14.

[5]Tzvetan Todorov, *The Conquest of America*, Harper & Row, 1984.

[6]<http://www.odci.gov/cia/publications/95fact/pg.html>

[7]'Subic Memories' (editorial) , *Asian Wall Street Journal*, 17-18 February 1995, p.6.

[8]The discussion of vertical spaces owes much to Michael J.Shapiro, 'Moral Geographies and the Ethics of Post-Sovereignty', *Public Culture*, 6, 1994.

Comparing two sets of maps can help us start the switch from horizontal to vertical, and from singular sovereignty to ironic space. Horizontal maps are familiar to us. Mark Valencia, an expert on the South China Seas who is based at the East West Center in Honolulu, produces maps which noteworthy for their attention to detail. His Map 2 shows the chaotic and overlapping nature of the South China Sea claims in what he elsewhere calls a 'crazy quilt' pattern. Map 3 tries to bring order to this chaos by drawing borders on the map to divide up the territory between the various claimant states. This the solution is characteristic of a horizontal conception of space; you resolve the conflict by constituting homogeneous space, and then dividing it with a simple line boundary.

Yet Valencia and others keep failing to solve the disputes because the landscape is not singular, but ironic and multilayered: the Chinese, Taiwanese, Vietnamese, Filipino, and Malaysian claims overlap. The problems of the South China Sea, in this way, are quite similar to the situation in the former Yugoslavia, which Campbell argues 'serves as a powerful example of the limitations and problems associated with international relations' standard modes of representation'.[9] The various attempts to solve Bosnian problem, through a drawing of stable boundaries between the ethnic communities, keep failing because the ethnographic landscape of Muslim/Croat/Serb is not singular but ironic and multilayered.

Conversely, the verticality of Chinese space is shown quite well in the maps of the capitals of Imperial China. Jeffrey Meyer, in *The Dragons of Tiananmen: Beijing as a Sacred City* has a map of an idealised Chinese capital; it shows an orderly city organised along a regular grid pattern which is oriented on a north-south, east-west axes.[10] Yet the orderliness of Chinese capitals is not an expression of secular Protestant rationality, as is often found in the numbered grids of Manhattan and Philadelphia. (Shapiro) Rather than being homogeneous and flat, Chinese space is historical and cosmic.

To understand such worlds, it is necessary to recover a former Chinese understanding of what Tu Weiming calls a 'civilisation state', as opposed to the nation-state.[11] We can see traces of the civilisation state in this map of Beijing which is actually not laid out on a grid. Rather the imperial capital is organised in concentric circles to focus cosmic energy on the emperor. The capital, then, is not a political center, so much as a cosmic center; a nodal point between the terrestrial and the celestial. The legitimising vocabulary of the 'celestial empire' is focused on the heavens, rather than on the nation state's horizontal world: the word for the empire, *tianxia*, literally means, 'all under heaven.' There was no concept of 'China' or 'Chinese civilisation', because in this universal empire, there was only civilisation and the barbarians. In building such walls, Chinese construct their identity: As

[9] David Campbell, 'Political Prosaics, Transversal Politics, and the Anarchical World', in Michael J.Shapiro & Hayward R.Alker (eds), *Challenging Boundaries: Global Flows, Territorial Identities*, University of Minnesota Press, 1996, p.23.

[10] Jeffrey E.Meyer, *The Dragons of Tiananmen: Beijing as a Sacred City, Columbia*, University of South Carolina Press, 1991.

[11] Tu Wei-ming, 'Cultural China: The Periphery as the Center', *Daedalus*, 120/2, 1991.

Meyer tells us:

> 'The real essence of the city was its walls. "Wall" is what makes China, wall makes the city of Beijing, the Imperial City, the Forbidden City, and all subsidiary units down to country town, village, and private home. Give any Chinese some loose bricks and he will build a wall, a gate, and hire a gatekeeper to prevent the outsider from entering.'

This wall building is a discursively political act as well:

> '... the wall is the line clearly drawn between what is significant and what is insignificant, what is powerful and what is not powerful, who is kin and who is stranger, what is sacred and not sacred. The Great Wall is the symbol of China par excellence. Traditionally it marked off civilisation from barbarism; today it still marks off the "sacred land" (*shenzhou*) from the rest of the world.' [Meyer, p.4]

Thus the celestial empire is thoroughly hierarchic in its in/out distinctions. Chinese maps were drawn concentrically with China at the center of the world, Beijing at the center of China, and the emperor at the center of Beijing.

Since the main focus of political attention was vertical, the horizontal dimensions were not seen as so important. The horizontal relations with neighboring human communities were not the focus of world politics. Thus there often were not clear borders, but belts of land in which both sides refrained from occupancy and cultivation (empty space) or a zone in which the people belonged to both countries, or a buffer state (shared space). All this amounts to a different policing of cultural boundaries as well. The relations between the civilisation state and the barbarian hordes are neither those of self / other nor of equal sovereign states: the two options in European politics.

World politics was characteristically formulated in terms of family relations and rituals. The Emperor is the Father, while the kings of neighboring states were the Emperor's 'younger brothers'. In terms of world politics, this means that those barbarians who accept Chinese culture are reclassified as tributary states who had bilateral relations with the Son of Heaven in Beijing. But the submission was mostly ritual. If a ruler recognised Chinese culture as civilisation, and paid tribute to the emperor, then the emperor usually left them to run their own domestic affairs, in an ancient doctrine of 'non-interference'.

In this system, sovereignty could be multiple: more than one ruler could demand tribute of a single city on the periphery: cities in what is now Laos often paid tribute to Kunming, Bangkok, Hue and Mandalay.[12] Islands have been an important part of this system of multiple sovereignty, paying tribute to two or three empires, as well. For example, the Liu Qiu Islands, in

[12] Thongchai Winichakul, *Siam Mapped: A history of the geo-body of a nation*, University of Hawaii Press, 1994.

what is now Okinawa, paid tribute to both Beijing and Edo for nearly three centuries; they saw China as their 'father' and Japan as their 'mother'.[13] Although some scholars see this relationship as 'diplomatic evasion' which relied on 'confusion',[14] we can also see this as a positive expression of ironic world politics.

Multiple sovereignty and ironic space in the Spratly Islands

Though talk of Imperial China sounds very pre-modern – and reactionary – such an ironic, multiple conception of space is already present in the region. In July 1997, Hong Kong reverts to Chinese sovereignty. In the Basic Law, Beijing guarantees that the Hong Kong way of life would be preserved for the next fifty years. To explain how communism and capitalism could be contained in the same state, Deng Xiaoping came up with the slogan, 'one country, two systems'. Under this arrangement, Beijing's sovereignty is more of a formality than a tool of centralised control.

Using the civilisation state's practices of multiple sovereignty and ironic space also goes a long way to explain what is happening right now in the South China Sea. I argue that in switching from geography to cosmography, we can see how sovereignty becomes multiple and shared around the intersecting peripheries in places like the South China Sea: so 'one country, two systems' becomes 'one civilisation, many systems'. Many of the problems of China's actions in the South China Sea become more understandable in terms of the civilisation state. For example, both China and Taiwan base their claims not on international law, but on 'history' and 'culture', (Valencia, Chen) which is a very imperial Chinese thing to do. The evidence for this sovereignty is compiled from historical documents, travelogues, maps and archaeological digs to prove that the region has been Chinese 'since ancient times'.

Thus the Chinese élites seem to be mixing the metaphors of international law and local history, science and poetry. This is taken to be a problem, but actually it emphasises how international law has its own history and grammar – a European history and grammar. Now Vietnam is using archaeology to justify its claims as well.[15] This shows how the Confucian Chinese world order of which the Vietnamese kingdom was a part is now reasserting itself.

But most importantly, a map of the South China Sea claims clearly shows how borders overlap, and that multiple sovereignty might be a solution. As we have seen, from a horizontal point of view, sovereignty is problematic. But the vertical maps of the civilisation state allow for such pre-modern

[13] Robert K.Sakai, 'The Ryuku Islands as a Fief of Satsuma', in John King (ed), *The Chinese World Order: Traditional China's Foreign Relations*, Harvard University Press, 1968, p.14.

[14] Sakai & Ch'en Ta-tuan. 'The Investiture of Liu Ch'iu Kings in the Ch'ing Period', John King (ed), *The Chinese World Order: Traditional China's Foreign Relations*, Harvard University Press, 1968.

[15] Chemillier-Gendreau; 'Vietnam rejects China's claim to archipelagos', *The Nation*, 11 May 1996.

multiple sovereignty. Vertical maps can make sense of the contradictions in Chinese Premier Li Peng's 1990 statement (which has been echoed many times since):

> 'under the premise that China has indisputable sovereignty over the Nansha Islands, China is willing to temporarily shelve the question of sovereignty over Nansha so as to jointly develop the resources in Nansha together with ASEAN countries.' [in Chen, p.44]

Rather than 'indisputable sovereignty' and 'shelving sovereignty issues' being a contradiction, they sound like Beijing's former relationships with tributary states. Perhaps what Beijing means by 'joint development' with itself in control after all parties recognise Chinese sovereignty, is not as threatening as it sounds. Some Chinese scholars feel that while China should make foreign firms engaged in oil prospecting in the Spratly Islands admit that they are Chinese territory, if these firms are willing to recognise China's sovereignty over the islands, Beijing can allow them to continue prospecting. Once the contracts signed with Vietnam expire, then they can sign new contracts with Beijing. [Chen, p.48] The control, then, could be simply an acknowledgement of China's centrality to the region, to pay symbolic tribute to China as it were.

As most historians will tell you, the tributary relations benefited the Chinese culturally, but the tribute states economically. Hence the South China Sea claims could be sorted out magnanimously to mutual benefit, according to the idealised view of the civilisation state. The 'regional commons' that Valencia suggests, or the 'pooling sovereignty' of the Indonesian Workshops,[16] could actually work out better using the civilisation state's practice of multiple sovereignty, rather than the un-ironic abstractions of international law.

On the other hand, it is noteworthy that China and Taiwan present a united front in demanding full sovereignty along the 'historic claim line' which encompasses the entire South China Sea. This is the only issue where Taiwan co-operates with Beijing on the world stage. If we take 'Asian Values' to mean the civilisation state, then this means that other states in the region would be tributaries in this hierarchy. It is curious that the states that have been promoting 'Asian Values' – Singapore and Malaysia – are also those that trumpet their national sovereignty the loudest, even in the South China Sea. Are we witnessing a post-colonial era in Asia with nation-states involved in national development, or is it simply China's re-colonisation of the region, with a reproduction of the dominance of the (Chinese/European) imperial era now in the civilisation state?

---

[16] University of British Columbia, School of Law, <http://www.law.ubc.ca/centres/scsweb/index.html/>

Conclusion

Since most analysis of the South China Seas takes the modern mode of nation- state sovereignty for granted, in this essay I have been excavating the civilisation-state as an alternative mode of power and authority. Though I certainly do not take the civilisation state as the inevitable form of Chinese politics, I can still argue that Beijing's actions are more than just residue from Imperial China that will go away with modernisation. Thus Chinese practices promise to influence Europe not just economically – as the myth of the China market – but also influence the rest of the world conceptually. As a working version of a non-Enlightenment system, it seems to be one of the few challenges to 'globalization' and American hegemony: the nationalists in China certainly see themselves in this light. Thus a resistance to the global system comes not just from the margins, in nomadic groups and social movements as Campbell and Shapiro argue, but from alternative systems that occupy the center of a different space, a parallel space in the present.

It is easy to either romanticise or demonise the civilisation state. I am wary of that. Neither the Westphalian nation-state nor the Imperial Chinese civilisation state provide an ideal way of addressing difference – both have very violent policings of their walls. But since the civilisation state helps explain current events in the South China Sea while problematizing the present, I think it is useful to consider it as a category, as part of our bag of tricks. It could also be helpful in areas beyond China; it could help in reconceptualizing how the United States deals with its tributary states in Latin America as well.

Evolutionary Theory and the State

Hugh Ward
University of Essex

'The Possibility of an Evolutionary Explanation of the State's Role in Modes of Regulation'

Introduction

Marxist theory now typically explains the existence and the actions of the capitalist state in functional terms. By virtue of its structural position, the state functions to stabilise the capitalist mode of production, while ensuring that the system is also legitimated. This helps to overcome the contradictions of capitalism, thus serving the long-term class interests of capital. Particular state institutions, and historical and national variation in state forms, are explained by the logic of capital that is, the functional needs of the capitalist system. To use functional explanation in this way is highly problematic, though.

Consequences follow causes. To explain a cause, the functional institution X, in terms of its consequences, the functions Y it carries out, reverses this temporal sequence (Faia 1986, p.5). To get around this, social structures like the state are often anthropomorhised by postulating that they have a immanent goal which *pulls* actions in the *right direction* (Elster 1983, pp.58-9; Faia 1986, p.6). But individual agents operating within structures, not structures themselves, have goals. If individuals are aware of Y, and X is maintained for that reason, the function is manifest. Then the explanation can be recast in standard intentional forms, as in the instrumentalist versions of marxist state theory that were largely rejected in the early 1970s.

As Van Parijs notes, the problem of consequences being invoked to explain causes can be overcome by saying that it is not Y that causes X but the disposition X has to cause Y that causes X. As dispositions exist through time, they can precede a particular instance of Y (1981, pp.29-30). But what ensures that X continues to have the disposition to cause Y? Cohen argues that we can still use functional explanation in the absence of a detailed account of the mechanism involved so long as we observe the institution whenever it is functionally required (1978, chapters 9 & 10). But this simply sidelines the 'why question'.

Elster argues that the only coherent answer for latent functions is to postulate the existence a feedback loop from Y to X which explains why X continues to perform the function (1983, p.61; Faia 1986, p.5). For example, the genetic basis of functionally adaptive biological traits is maintained because any mutation likely to occur reduces the reproductive fitness of the individual concerned, so that evolutionary selection eliminates the dysfunctional mutation. Elster suggests that, uniquely, social evolution can perform the same role in social explanation (Elster 1983, pp.52-61). Van

Parijs (1981, pp.43-48) adds that evolutionary selection can sometimes be replaced by related processes of reinforcement or trial-and-error learning.

In the first section of this paper I sketch the conceptual relationship between biological and social evolution. I then give relevant examples illustrating the sort of evolutionary feedback loop that Elster and Van Parijs talk about. The central issue, though, will be whether evolutionary arguments can ground the view that the state operates in capital's long- term and general interests. The problem is that state responses may evolve as a function of short-term *particularistic* selective pressures; and it might be impossible to ignore these so as to get a better long-run result (Van Parijs 1981, chapter 6; Elster 1983, p.61). I conclude that this argument is not compelling, though.

Biological and social evolution

One mode of biological evolution involves random variation in genetically controlled traits and selection of adaptive mutations.[1] Genetic mutation is 'blind' that is, it is unaffected by the selection mechanism. A mutation is adaptive if its presence increases the chances of survival or reproduction of the organism in a given evolutionary environment, including the traits of the other individuals among whom selection is taking place. It is heuristically useful to think of an adaptive landscape. For some level(s) of the trait(s) adaption will be at a local optimum that is, 'small' changes in the trait will lead to a reduction in adaption, so the optimum is a local evolutionary equilibrium. There may also be a global optimum at which adaption is greater than or equal to that at any other peak. In a valley of the landscape all members of the population are relatively poorly adapted; so there are variations which give a selective advantage; and eventually mutation will, with very high probability, generate some individual with a more advantageous level of the trait(s). As it has an adaptive advantage, the mutation is likely to spread. Thus, in small steps, random variation and selection drives the population up gradients towards peaks. Biological evolution is path dependent. Its initial direction often depends on chance events; but having proceeded in a particular direction, it is difficult to change tack. Global optima may not be reached, because of path dependence and because a large enough mutation to jump the intervening valleys between the status-quo and the highest peak is unlikely. Evolution is *short sighted:* 'long-term' gains in adaptiveness unlikely to be reachable except through a very large number of *loss making* incremental changes will generally not happen. Only information contained in the genotype is passed on during reproduction. So the adaptive phenotypical characteristics of the rest of the organism acquired during the individual's lifetime cannot be passed on. The Lamarckian idea that such adaptions can be passed on is a heretical one in biology, but analogous ideas are important to theories of social evolution.

[1] For general accounts of the theory of evolution in modern biology see Ridley (1985), Van Parijs (1983, chapter 3), and Elster (1989, chapter 8).

Social evolution often means little more than change through time or movement through a sequence of stages (Hodgson 1993, chapter 3). Much critical commentary on evolutionary ideas in the social sciences is really directed at this sort of evolutionism (Giddens 1984). Attention is best restricted to areas where there is 'selection' of variants which are produced 'blindly' (Winter 1987b; cf. Giddens 1984, pp.231-33). For instance policy initiatives are typically made in a way that is relatively blind to the what will and will not work. Even though some degree of rational analysis is possible, there are limits on globally rational decision making (Simon 1982; Braybrooke & Lindblom 1963). Solutions are often taken from the policy 'garbage can' (March & Olsen 1984) and fitted by policy- entrepreneurs to problems that 'float by' (Kingdon 1984, chapter 4). Filters select the policies that actually get implemented. Policies may not solve the problems they set out to; they may lack support among legislators, the electorate, and in relevant policy communities; they may miss windows of opportunity in legislative or budgetary cycles; they may be declared unconstitutional (Riker 1982, chapter 8; Kingdon 1984, chapter 6; Winter 1995).

Reinforcement and trial-and-error learning are conceptually related to evolution by selection and can be considered an intrinsic part of social evolution (Van Parijs 1983, chapter 4; Hodgson 1993, p.26). The simplest form of reinforcement involves random variation in behaviour and systematic, selective reinforcement. Given the capacity to register the reinforcement and limitations on the amount of random variation, there is a tendency gradually to converge on the form of behaviour that is reinforced. Eventually this becomes habitual; so reinforcement pushes behaviour up reward gradients until (local) optima/equilibria are attained (Van Parijs 1983, pp.97-100). Humans can often spot the causal link between reinforcement and behaviour, so the process is 'short-circuited' (Van Parijs 1983, pp.126-7). There is learning-by-doing when successful anticipation of what will lead to higher rewards leads to further changes in the same direction. There is also emulation of others' success.

Knowledge is stored in relatively enduring structures such as institutional routines, social paradigms, and social norms. Because social structures of this sort are relatively stable and can be transmitted through time, they are the *cultural* analogous of the genetic code of biological evolution (Hodgson 1993, pp.42-47). The sociological commonplace is now that structures both constrain and enable action and are, in turn, modified as a deliberate and as an emergent consequence of action. In this context, agents act within *cultures*; but *cultures* are subject to evolutionary modification, by selection, reinforcement, trial-and-error learning, and emulation (cf. Giddens 1984, p.237). Modifications are then passed on to the next generation located within the relevant structure. So social evolution is often Lamarckian (Hodgson 1993, pp.40-8; Ridley 1985, pp.21-3). *Cultures* may be emulated and applied by others in different contexts, so they reproduce. New *cultures* arise by recombination, a process also important in biological evolution. For example, merger may mean the loss of some 'cultural genetic material' for each organisation concerned, but the remainder is recombined through pooling (Hodgson 1993, pp.47-48).

There are problems with defining what morbidity means when the idea of selection is used in social evolution (Faia 1986, pp.25-32). But it is plausible that the rates of morbidity of firms, governments, individual office holders, etc. are low. So if social evolution moves up gradients, reinforcement, learning, and emulation under conditions of bounded rationality will probably be a crucial (Van Parijs 1983, 100-2; cf. Elster 1989, pp.80-1). I now illustrate how some of these ideas have been put to work.

The evolutionary grounding of functional explanation: the case of technical change

Technology is central to regulation theory. Fordism is seen as based on relatively inflexible forms of automation articulated around a production line capable of producing only one product. In contrast, post-Fordism will be based on flexible forms of automation where the combination of computers, robotics and older forms of automation allows production facilities to be much more flexible. Yet regulation theory provides little or nothing by way of explanation of how the technical base of capitalism actually comes to shift. Even if functionalism is not overt, it is seldom far beneath the surface: capitalism gets the technologies it needs temporarily to patch up its crisis tendencies. While some regulation theorists have shown an interest in evolutionary arguments (Boyer 1988a, 1988b), they do not actually use the ideas of selection, reinforcement, trial-and-error learning, or emulation. Yet functional arguments can be replaced by evolutionary ones here.

Evolutionary theories of technical change derive heavily from the work of Joseph Schumpeter (Nelson & Winter 1982, pp.39-40; cf. Hodgson 1993, chapter 9). In Schumpeter's view, when a particular economic niche is created by an entrepreneur, the innovation is copied or modified by others, with a view to getting some of the short-term monopoly rents. Successful companies riding the wave of the innovation become centres of investment and growth, while other sectors decline. Thus, 'waves of creative destruction' wash over the economy (Schumpeter 1943, p.84). Nelson & Winter (1982) graft Schumpeterian ideas about technical change onto Alchian's (1950) evolutionary theory of the firm. Routines are all regular and predictable behaviour patterns (Nelson & Winter 1982, p.14). Firms are the analogue of biological phenotypes; so they *carry* the *cultural code* of routines (Nelson 1995, p.60). In contrast to the neo-classical model, firms are seen as subject to bounded rationality. They use routines to make decisions, not globally rational decision procedures. For instance, they are tied to one production technique in the short term; and they have to search for alternatives to it in the long run, using routinised search procedures that may not scan all the alternatives (Nelson & Winter 1982, p.14). Routines are hereditable for example, when a company opens a new plant in a different country (Nelson & Winter 1982, p.14). Firms – and thus the routines that they embody – are subject to selection in market competition (Nelson & Winter 1982, pp.9-10). Routines leading to low profits are eliminated, while those leading to higher profit 'reproduce': as profitable firms embodying them invest and expand their operations using the same successful routines, they spread through the population of firms (Nelson & Winter 1982, p.17).

Firms are capable of changing what they routinely do, but subject to bounded rationality (Nelson & Winter 1982, p.18). Better adapted routines are then propagated in a Lamarckian way (Nelson & Winter 1982, pp.10-11). Problem solving is, itself, governed by routines for scrutinising lower-order routines and for searching for alternatives to them; so that the existing 'cultural genes of the firm effect the way it produces mutations in routines (Nelson & Winter 1982, p.18). Although Nelson & Winter deny that the routines that survive economic selection will be profit maximising (1982, chapter 7; cf. Friedman 1953), their argument shows that evolutionary selection generates a feedback that ensures that the routines that survive are adaptive in a competitive economic environment.

This general account is applied to technological change. Production set-ups are rigid in the short term. A shift in input prices may provoke search for different technological options or alteration of the routines used to make decisions over production (Nelson & Winter 1982, pp.175-184). There is no pre-existing set of technological options to search; perceptions about the feasible options are dim, at best; information is costly; and the meaning attached to new information is dependent upon the firm's *culture*(Nelson & Winter 1982, pp.171-2). Selective pressures ensure that surviving firms achieve a 'favourable balance' between the costs and market advantages of innovation, though (Winter 1987a, p.547). Again evolution sustains a functional argument here.

Two key ideas in the burgeoning literature on technical change in evolutionary economics are: technological paradigms – a set of ideas and routines that shape technical change in the same way that scientific paradigms shape scientific work; and technological regimes, in which related and complimentary paradigms come together synergistically.[2] The idea of a regime draws explicitly on regulation theory and starts to connect with questions about the state. Changes of technological regime have far reaching effects (Freeman & Perez 1988, p.45). They are associated with a quantum leap in productivity over most, if not all, sectors of the economy; so they generate an unusually wide range of investment and product opportunities (Freeman & Perez 1988, p.48). They change engineering and managerial 'common-sense' right across the economic board, provoking numerous shifts in technological paradigm (Freeman & Perez 1988, p.49). Typically they are associated with a key new technological input-factor with low or rapidly falling relative cost, apparently unlimited availability, and clear potential for incorporation in many products and processes, micro-electronics being a current example (Freeman & Perez 1988, p.48).

Different technological regimes require qualitatively different socio-political arrangements (Freeman & Perez 1988, p.44). New technological regimes start to emerge before the old, dominant regime has decayed. They have a potential to create an investment boom which would re-invigorate the whole

[2] For reviews see Nelson 1995, the contributions in Dosi et al (eds) 1988.

economy. However, this potential is often blocked by the mal-adaption of key political and social structures; so the initial effects are to reduce growth, create uncertainty, destroy old sectors, and displace labour (Freeman & Perez 1988, p.45). However, once the requisite mode of regulation is in place, the new technological regime becomes growth-promoting. This reaccomodation occurs by political search, experimentation and adaption; and when it has been achieved, the upswing phase of the long wave starts (Freeman & Perez 1988, p.59).

Beyond mentioning that this process is a conflict laden one that proceeds at different rates in different national contexts (1988, pp.59-60), Freeman & Perez say little about it. Nelson & Winter (1982, chapter 16) and Nelson (1995), paint a more detailed picture, albeit one that is more concerned with individual technologies than with regimes. Policies evolve as a response to technology, changes in market structures, changes in values, and changes in the pressures exerted on government, as filtered through the institutional structures of society and the perceptions of legislators about what problems are important (Nelson & Winter 1982, pp.372-5). Policy change is incremental and carried out under conditions of bounded rationality, as well as being powerfully shaped by policy paradigms and theoretical perspectives (Nelson & Winter 1982, pp.372-3). Selection operates in much the same way as suggested in the models of policy evolution discussed above (Nelson & Winter 1982, pp.376-7). An active role needs to be ascribed to the state, because of its power to shape the direction of basic science, the magnitude of state procurement, and its ability to change legal structures, allowing technologies to takeoff (Nelson 1995). Nelson now talks of the co- evolution of technology and organisational structures within business, on the one hand, and the various 'supporting institutions', such as public policies and legal structures, on the other hand (1995, pp.77-84).

These arguments combine evolutionary economics with a rather crude form of pluralism. There is no conception of the unequal distribution of power between capital and labour or of strategic selectivity of the state favouring capital's interests (Jessop 1990). For instance, the marxist literature on the labour process starting with Braverman (1974) can be read as suggesting that *class-struggle* selects technical innovation. In crisis the state shapes the rules of the game, via industrial relations law and macroeconomic policy, arguably biasing selection in capital's favour. The importance of policy communities is neglected (cf. Kingdon 1984, pp.124-5), yet they have been central to technical change in areas like transport, agriculture and energy. The idea that the state's strategic, bureaucratic, and extractive interests shape technology clearly emerges from historical sociology (Mann 1986; Giddens 1985). Although Nelson (1995) gestures at the power of state professionals, statist ideas about the distinct interests of the political élite and state autonomy (Ward 1995) are ignored. The role of broader ideological currents is neglected, but it is easy to see how the new-right's view of freedom *selected* for the use of the private car, for example.

Nelson comments that 'It is clear that, somehow, in the advanced industrial nations, there have been mechanisms that have made the co-evolution of technology, industrial organisation, and institutions more broadly, move in directions that have led to sustained economic progress.' (Nelson 1995, p.83). Why should this complex co-evolutionary dance favour the reproduction of the basic economic structures of capitalism? Elsewhere I have tried to provide the outlines of an answer to such questions within a framework in which a regime of economic regulation co-evolves with a mode of rule in such a way that the state's interests are squared with those of capital (Ward 1994). In brief:

- (i) economic crisis provokes search for policies, because growth is strategically important to the state, allows extraction of a larger surplus, and legitimates the role of the political élite;
- (ii) economic growth is important to electoral outcomes, so governments carrying routines and programmes that fit the emerging technological regime will tend to be selected for;
- (iii) government policies select for successful technological and other innovations;
- (iv) as dynamic sectors are of vital interest to the state, their representatives will tend to get built into policy communities, increasingly filtering policy innovations in ways that favour the sector at the expense of sectors carrying the old technological regime;
- (v) the careers of successful policy entrepreneurs, be they politicians or bureaucrats, will flourish, while those carrying unsuccessful ideas will lose power, generating path-dependence;
- (vi) path dependence also arises as successful policy innovations are extrapolated through trial-and-error learning;
- (vii) successful innovations are emulated both from other areas of state activity, other states, and from the private sector.

It is precisely this sort of account that Van Parijs suggests cannot work!

Must evolutionary reconstruction of the marxist theory of the state fail?

As in my account, Van Parijs argues that the state faces structural constraints stemming from capitalist control of the mode of production and the state's dependence of capital for finance and the legitimacy that goes with a buoyant economy. These structures generate a selection bias: governments whose policies do not come close to maximising the level of economic activity get swept away; and there is reinforcement as governments selectively retain policies maximising their financial health and popularity (1981, pp.184-5). Governments' chances of survival and payoffs are maximised at the same point in the evolutionary landscape as economic activity and profitability levels (1981, p.185). If economic activity is largely determined by business confidence, business confidence depends on expected profit rates, and actual and expected profit rates converge in the long-term through learning in economic markets, state policies can be expected to evolve along upward gradients set by levels of business confidence (1981, pp.185-6). Successful policies become surrounded by a superstructure of sanctions for changing them, generated by institutionalisàtion and (possibly false) beliefs that they are the best available options (1981, p.186).

Van Parijs rejects this evolutionary reconstruction, because: there are numerous cases where capital actively resists what is arguably in its long-run interests; and the introduction of related measures then reduces business confidence, placing selective pressure on governments to abandon the measures (1981, pp.187-8). In Van Parijs' view, invoking selection of governments by the electorate is of little help, even if the policies concerned favour the working class: the electoral fortunes of parties largely respond to the dynamics of economic activity that is, ultimately to business confidence (1981, pp.189-9). The problem with the evolutionary reconstruction is that 'what is functional in the long term but dysfunctional in the short term will never be actualised, because the deviation which introduces that policy will be corrected before the latter has had time to produce its long-term effects' (1981, pp.188-9).

Van Parij's argument concerns the failure to arrive at a global optimum in a fixed evolutionary landscape. This is far too static. Moreover, capitalism does not require maximum levels of economic activity to survive. The key question is whether there is evolution along one of the numerous potentially possible paths out of crisis along which the contradictory tendencies of capitalism are temporarily contained, in a process of evolution that may never reach equilibrium. Are things moving up hill *fast enough*?; and has *satisfactory* altitude been reached?

Van Parijs notes that 'slacker' selection and reinforcement mechanism that do not immediately punish policies that hit business confidence might allow policies functional in relation to the long-term interests of capital to emerge (1981, p.189). However, he sees little possibility that pressures could slacken. Moreover, he regards it as unlikely that where policies only have positive effects for the state in the long term there would be the registering of the effects and connection of them to the policies concerned that is central to arguments about reinforcement and learning (1981, p.189). I will return to the question of whether longer-term perspectives can be developed. First I focus on support and selection. Statist theorists argue the state sometimes has a great deal of autonomy to ignore short-term pressures from capital and the electorate – notably in wartime and deep economic crisis (for example, Block 1977). Van Parijs' account largely (1981, pp.192-6) operates as if capital and the working class are monolithic and as if no other relevant social cleavages exist. The state can have considerable autonomy where the pressures upon it *cancel out*, or different class fractions and other groups can be played off against each other (Nordlinger 1981).

Van Parijs overstates the degree to which the electoral fortunes of parties are tied to short-term economic dynamics. Much of the short-term variance in support for governments can be accounted for in economic terms; but growth is not the only, or even the most significant, factor.[3] Controlling inflation has been an important electoral issue in some countries in recent years, for instance, and this is important to the resolution of the current crisis. Variance in economic outcomes does not explain *baseline* support coming from partisanship, non-economic concerns, and economic concerns not captured by macro- economic aggregates. This is crucial for legitimating what the state does; and the baseline can be moved.

Some say that evolutionary theory can only account for gradual change. Actually ideas about 'punctuated' evolutionary equilibria and relatively rapid change are current both in biology and political science (Jones 1994, pp.214-5). Riker's theory of the 'natural selection of issues' (1982, chapter 8) illustrates this point. It also shows how Van Parijs' short-term support trap could be escaped. The fundamental result in social choice theory is that stable majorities typically exist where politics takes place over a single issue-dimension; but majorities are almost always unstable where politics takes place over multiple issue dimensions (Riker 1982, chapter 7). In the latter case a proposal gaining majority support against the status-quo almost always exists, putting together what amounts to a coalition of minorities or creating a package-deal across the issue dimensions. Jones (1994) makes a related argument to Riker's when he suggests that politicians can alter the support landscape by manipulating the inability of voters and groups simultaneously to pay attention to all evaluative dimensions of policy, using their power to focus attention on some dimensions. Linking different single-dimensional issues together, in effect, produces a multidimensional policy space. Politicians seek latent dimensions, interlinkages, or emphases which will bring about increased support (Riker 1982, p.209); but this is difficult because they have imperfect information about voters' preferences (Riker 1982, p.209). So they try out new alternatives in the 'political market'; and some attempts succeed while others fall flat (Riker 1982, p.209). What succeeds is further extrapolated (Riker 1982, pp.209), but the initial change in the support landscape could be non-incremental. While this account take underlying preferences as fixed, Dunleavy & Ward (1981) show how state power can be used to shift underlying preferences. It is easy to see how this idea can be assimilated into an evolutionary account. To illustrate the possibilities, suppose that the economic changes and changes in the state sector over the last twenty years in Britain are functional for domestic capital. The winning electoral coalition for the package has eroded, though. So the Tory right flies the Euro-sceptical kite. They hope that this will break the winning Blairite coalition: some who are more attracted by Labour's version of the economic package will, nevertheless, be seduced by the rhetoric of sovereignty and nationalism.

The central point is that state policies are not only selected for by the support landscape, but thay can also rapidly and fundamentally transform

[3]See for example, the contributions in Norpoth et al (eds) 1991; Lewis-Beck 1990.

it. There is no reason to restrict this argument to electoral support. It applies equally to any context where winning coalitions matter (Peterson & Ward 1995) – for instance to the dynamics of support among powerful groups, such as fractions of capital or labour. Van Parijs view of business confidence reflects his monolithic view of capital. However, the interests of capitals clustering around new or emergent technologies and consumption norms may be radically different. Because they matter more for growth, the state may be more responsive to the needs of such sectors. Also, the view of capital markets of government activity is not static. Rather, because financial markets ultimately retain links to productive capital, it will be shaped by the needs of the most dynamic sectors. By a trial-and-error process of building coalitions across different dimensions of what concerns the business community, the state can *sideline* blocking coalitions centred on declining sectors and the old technological paradigm. It can reconstitute or destroy policy communities involving groups that want to block change. Again the Thatcherite era is suggestive: older manufacturing capital and organised labour lost out to a coalition of financial, export orientated and *high tech* capital; the new coalition was built around an (evolving) package-deal of privatisations, deregulation, globalisation, and constrained public expenditure growth; coalition partners got what they wanted on salient dimensions, even if they lost on others.

Van Parijs' argument treats national economies in isolation and concerns fully democratic systems. In order to sustain the argument, we really need only show that it works in one major economy. Other countries may be able partially to short-circuit the evolutionary process, avoiding down-gradients in the support landscape by emulating successful states. Beside emulation, the pattern of the successful nation may be imposed on others if that nation becomes internationally hegemonic. Although the key player in the evolution of Fordism – the US – is a polyarchy, exemplars and hegemons have not always satisfied the relevant criteria in the past (for example, 19th century Britain) and may not do so in the future (for example, the Tiger Economies?). In an authoritarian system, or in a limited élite-democracy, some of the short-term pressures on politicians to maintain support are absent. Deforming electoral rules – or as a dose of repression – may substitute for lack of popular support.

As has already been said, legal structures select for technical innovations, the routines firms operate, and policy innovations. The common law and the meaning of legislation co- evolves with the capitalist system, and they do so in ways which do not necessarily snag up on popular support, because of fundamental biases in access to the legal systems. For example, when the common law is economically inefficient, there is a greater tendency to litigate, as efficient laws make it easier to settle out of court (for example, Demetz 1967; Landes & Posner 1987). As more and more cases are bought, the law changes. Even if judges and juries do not have an eye to economic efficiency, eventually a pathbreaking judgement will occur – if only at random – which makes the law tolerably efficient. At this point litigation pressures are reduced, and the common law in the area remains relatively stable for a period. There may be a selection bias in favour of dynamic sectors and firms, because they have greater resources to go to law.

Van Parijs rejects the possibility of combining intentional explanation and evolutionary explanation within marxism, because this reduces the approach to the intentional mode (1981, pp.178-9). Yet there is no need to accept this conclusion, so long as rational foresight is subject to bounds. Some fractions of capital are capable of developing more long-term, less particularistic, views and may be prepared to see lower short-term rates of growth to achieve longer-term goals. Politicians can also conceive broader, and longer term political projects. These both influence and are influenced by business thinking. These projects crucially shape micro and meso-level policy developments, through selection of what is compatible with them. They typically recombine elements from other projects and are, in turn, evolutionarily reshaped. Any ideology that aspires to become hegemonic must resonate with enough existing popular concerns and a powerful enough supporting coalition of business and other interests to get a toe hold; and it will be modified as it goes, better to ascend support gradients. There is no reason, then, for an evolutionary perspective on the state to reject the role of shaping ideologies such as the ideas behind the New Deal, the British post-war settlement, or Thatcherism. But it must be recognised that they were not forged with fifty-fifty foresight and evolve due to selective pressures of the sort I have discussed above.

Conclusion

Lurking within instrumentalist theories of the state is the idea that some individual or group knows what capital's general interests are. One attraction of structural marxism derived from the sheer implausibility of this view. Structural marxism is threadbare, not least because of its use of functional explanation. But we cannot reject the possibility of an evolutionary reconstruction of the functionalist arguments of marxist state theory and regulation theory. To show that the account can be fleshed out theoretically and empirically will be a task of major proportions, though.

References

A.Alchian, 'Uncertainty, Evolution and Economic Theory', *Journal of Political Economy*, 58, 1950.

F.Block, 'The Ruling Class Does Not Rule', *Socialist Revolution*, 77, 1977.

J.Boyer, 'Technical Change and the Theory of Regulation', in Dosi et al (eds), 1988.

J.Boyer, 'Formalising Growth Regimes', in Dosi et al (eds), 1988.

H.Braverman, *Labour and Monopoly Capital*, Monthly Review Press, 1974.

D.Braybrooke & C.E.Lindblom, *A Strategy of Decision: Policy Evaluation as a Social Process*, Collier-Macmillan, 1963.

G.A.Cohen, *Karl Marx's Theory of History: A Defence*, Oxford University Press, 1978.

H.Demetz, 'Towards A Theory of Property Rights', *American Economic Review*, 57, 1967.

G.Dosi et al (eds), *Technical Change and Economic Theory*, Pinter, 1988.

P.Dunleavy & H.Ward, 'Exogenous Voter Preferences and Parties With State Power', *British Journal of Political Science*, 11, 1981.

J.Elster, *Explaining Technical Change*, Cambridge University Press, 1983.

J.Elster, *Nuts and Bolts for the Social Sciences*, Cambridge University Press, 1989.

M.A.Faia, *Dynamic Functionalism: Strategy and Tactics*, Cambridge University Press, 1986.

C.Freeman & C.Perez, 'Structural Crises of Adjustment, Business Cycles and Investment Behaviour', in Dosi et al (eds), 1988.

M.Friedman, 'The Methodology of Positive Economics', in his *Essays in Positive Economics*, Chicago University Press, 1953.

A.Giddens, *Constitution of Society*, Polity, 1984.

A.Giddens, *The Nation-State and Violence*, Polity, 1985.

G.M.Hodgson, *Economics and Evolution: Bringing Life Back Into Economics*, Polity, 1993.

B.Jessop, *State Theory: Putting the Capitalist State in its Place*, Polity, 1990.

B.D.Jones, *Reconceiving Decision Making in Democratic Politics*, University of Chicago Press, 1994.

J.W.Kingdon, *Agendas, Alternatives and Public Policies*, Little, Brown, 1984.

W.H.Landes & R.Posner, *The Economic Structure of Tort Law*, Harvard University Press, 1987.

M.Lewis-Beck, *Economics and Elections*, University of Michigan Press, 1990.

M.Mann, *The Sources of Social Power*, Cambridge University Press, 1986.

J.G.March & J.P.Olsen, 'The New Institutionalism: Organisational Factors in Political Life', *American Political Science Review*, 78, 1984.

R.R.Nelson, 'Recent Evolutionary Theorising About Economic Change', *Journal of Economic Literature*, 33, 1995.

R.R.Nelson & S.G.Winter, *An Evolutionary Theory of Economic Change*, Harvard University Press, 1982.

E.A.Nordlinger, *On the Autonomy of the Democratic State*, Harvard University Press, 1981.

H.Norpoth et al (eds), *Economics and Politics*, University of Michigan Press, 1991.

J.Peterson & H.Ward, 'Coalitional Stability and the New Multi-dimensional Politics of Security', *European Journal of International Relations*, 1, 1995.

M.Ridley, *The Problems of Evolution*, Oxford University Press, 1985.

W.H.Riker, *Liberalism Against Populism: A Confrontation Between the Theory of Democracy and the Theory of Social Choice*, Waveland Press, 1982.

J.A.Schumpeter, *Capitalism Socialism and Democracy*, Allen & Unwin, 1943.

H.A.Simon, *Models of Bounded Rationality*, volume 2, MIT Press, 1982.

P.Van Parijs, *Evolutionary Explanation in the Social Sciences: An Emerging Paradigm*, Tavistock, 1981.

H.Ward, 'State Exploitation, Capital Accumulation and the Evolution of Modes of Regulation', paper given at the Annual Conference of the Political Studies Association, 1993.

H.Ward, 'The Statist Approach', unpublished, 1995.

S.G.Winter, 'Natural Selection and Evolution', in J.Eatwall et al (eds), *The New Palgrave: A Dictionary of Economics*, volume 3, Macmillan, 1987.

S.G.Winter, 'Competition and Selection', in Eatwall et al (eds), 1987.

Evolutionary Theory and the State

Peter Kerr
University of Birmingham

'The Selection and Adaptation of Thatcherite State Strategy'

Summary

My aim in this paper is to demonstrate that evolutionary explanations of change are appropriate to analyses of specific periods of governmental activity. In so doing, I will focus attention upon the study of Thatcherism, which highlights the paucity of existing attempts within orthodox political science to elucidate periods of political and economic change. Firstly, I shall argue that dominant conceptions of Thatcherism fail to account for both the temporal unfolding of the Conservatives' strategy and the processes and mechanisms involved in this process. Secondly, I will suggest that an evolutionary account of change can overcome these problems by providing us with an explanatory framework which can accomodate such an analysis. Thirdly, I will task outline three of the processes which might be considered appropriate to analysing the dynamism of the Thatcherite project. Given the strict constraints of space, the views expounded here are underdeveloped. However, my overall aim is to offer a starting-point from which a more thorough analysis of state strategies and their effects upon institutional structures may be developed.

Problems in the Literature on Thatcherism

The Thatcher Governments entered office in 1979 committed, at least rhetorically, to restructuring the contours of postwar British politics. The term 'Thatcherism' has been used to denote both the *strategic* nature and the historical specificities of the Conservatives' aims and objectives. It is its special character, as a modernising *project* aimed at re-mapping the institutional parameters and practices of the British state, which makes Thatcherism an important focus for any attempt to theorise the dynamics of political, economic and, more broadly, institutional change. Here however, I will contend that the bulk of existing studies of Thatcherism can be criticised for a failure to capture both the inherent dynamism of the Thatcherite project and the processes and mechanisms which have contributed to this dyanamism.

There are of course two separate but related criticisms here. First, in recognising the strategic character of the Thatcher project (reflected in its coherent articulation of a number of vague strategic objectives), most authors have been guilty of assuming prior knowledge (on the part of themselves and, indeed, the Conservatives) of what these objectives precisely are and of what they entail at an institutional and policy level. The result is that most authors have attempted to 'fix' their definition of Thatcherism, by offering a closed conception of its precise contours and inherent characteristics. This has resulted in a tendency to overstate the unity and coherence of Thatcherism at the expense of a proper consideration of the essentially contingent, and often disjointed, nature of the Conservatives' reforms.[1] In this respect, few serious attempts have been made to consider the temporality of Thatcherism; thereby recognising the Conservatives' strategy as having evolved through a series of often ad-hoc interventions which have changed substantially and gained coherence through time.[2] Second, and related, few authors have succeeded in illuminating the highly complex and multidimensional processes which have contributed to the temporal unfolding of Thatcherism.[3] In this respect, explanations have tended to divide crudely into structuralist or intentionalist accounts which privilege singular variables (either economic, political or ideological) as the primary generative force behind the Conservatives' strategy. An important adjunct of this problem is the prevalence of ethnocentric approaches to explaining Thatcherism, derived from an overall neglect of the external factors which have shaped and constrained the development of British politics since the 1970s. In this respect, there have been few serious attempts to characterise Thatcherism as part of a wider, international response to political and economic crises within the world system.

These problems have contributed to the fact that Thatcherism has most often been presented as a singular static 'snapshot' in time (a temporal conjuncture which is most often linked directly to Mrs Thatcher's own personal term in office),[4] with primary emphasis alternating between ethno/agency-centred accounts of change or strict structural determinism. Indeed, this tendency to preclude an analysis of the essential dynamics of political change, pervades our understanding of postwar British politics as a whole. The most common way in which political scientists have endeavoured to 'fix' Thatcherism has been through repeated references to its distinctiveness in relation to, often fictionalised, past practices.[5] This has meant that the Conservatives' strategy is often measured against a series of static comparisons between Thatcherism and its presumed historical 'others' (for example conviction vs consensus, neo-liberalism vs social democracy, mone-

---

[1] Although see D.Marsh & R.A.W.Rhodes (eds), *Implementing Thatcherite Policies: Audit of an Era*, Open University Press, 1992.

[2] Exceptions include: A.Gamble, *The Free Economy and the Strong State*, Macmillan, 1988; B.Jessop et al, *Thatcherism: A Tale of Two Nations*, Polity, 1988; C.Hay, *Restating Social and Political Change*, Open University Press, 1996.

[3] For a comprehensive critique of existing uni-dimensional explanations see D.Marsh, Explaining 'Thatcherite' Policies: Beyond Uni-Dimensional Explanation', *Political Studies*, 43/4, 1995.

[4] This is revealed in the tendency for most authors to conclude that under John Major the Thatcherite strategy has exhausted itself. My own view is that Major has presided over a maturer and more radical period of 'late-Thatcherism' in which the Conservatives' have stepped up their reforming zeal. See P.Kerr et al, 'Charting Late-Thatcherism': British Politics Under Major', in S.Lancaster (ed), *Developments in Politics*, Causeway Press, 1997, forthcoming.

[5] P.Kerr & D.Marsh, 'False Dichotomies and Failed Assumptions: Revisiting and Revising the Consenesus Debate', in I.Hampsher-Monk & J.Stanyer (eds), *Contemporary Political Studies 1996*, volume 2, PSA, 1996.

tarism vs Keynesianism etc).[6] The result is a general tendency to dislocate Thatcherism from its historical precedents and the longer-term conflicts and institutional compromises which have contributed to both shaping and constraining the Conservatives' strategic calculations. Overall, this exercise in comparative statics provides us with an inanimate picture of postwar British politics in which our understanding of the evolution of state structures and governmental strategies is compromised by a series of static representations which characature change and obscure important continuities. What is missing is a proper analysis of the evolution of the state through the dynamic and dialectical interplay between structure, agency and strategy.[7]

These problems reveal the need to move towards a more elastic conception of Thatcherism capable of accounting for the contingency and variability of the Conservatives' strategy. The major problem with existing 'fixed' notions of Thatcherism is that they often pre-suppose the radicalism, and indeed the success, of the Conservatives in achieving their longer-term strategic objectives. Thus, most authors, in recognising the transformative potential of Thatcherism, have taken the transformation of institutional structures to be axiomatic. Thatcherism is thus presented as having occurred within a single temporal moment in the sense that the effects of Thatcherism are equated simply with the articulation of its broad objectives. This has led to a tendency to exagerate the achievements of the Conservatives – a tendency which gives credence to the Thatcherites' own bloated view of success. What is needed then, is a proper conception of the temporality of Thatcherism; one which re-asserts the essential struggle in which the Conservatives have had to engage in order to transfer their strategic potential into actual outcomes. This also implies a more sophisticated elucidation of the multi-dimensional set of factors (political, economic, ideational, historic, external and domestic) which have generated the Conservatives' project, as well as the delicate and constant articulation between structure, agency and strategy. Of course, this is no small challenge. However, it is one which needs to be addressed if we are to theorise the dynamics of political change. In what is to follow I will propose that it is only through the application of an evolutionary explanation that we can begin to approach the type of sophisticated understanding required to make sense of periods of intensified political change such as the Thatcher years.

Towards an Evolutionary Account of Thatcherism

Evolutionary explanation pre-supposes a heightened sensitivity to the constantly changing relationship between strategic actors and the environment within which they are forced to operate. Change is conceived of here as being both contingent and path-dependent; as a conditioned response to

[6]For a consideration of Thatcherism's manipulation of popular perceptions of its fictionalised others see S.McAnulla's contribution to these volumes, 'Fade to Grey: Symbolic Politics in the Post-Thatcher Era'.

[7]See C.Hay, 'Structure and Agency', in D.Marsh & G.Stoker (eds), *Theory and Methods in Political Science*, Macmillan, 1995.

environmental exigencies filtered through the limited capacities and strategic judgements of state actors. In this respect, an evolutionary explanation entails a proper consideration of the dialectical interplay between structure, agency and strategy by focussing our attention on the ways in which actors articulate strategies in order to negotiate the structural and strategic demands of the context which they inhabit. It is this heightened sensitivity to the *relational* and *contingent* articulation of strategy which provides an evolutionary account with the explanatory depth required to elucidate periods of intensified political change such as the Thatcher years. Thus, an evolutionary explanation of Thatcherism would necessarily preclude the type of static, ahistorical, ethnocentric and reductionist accounts which have so far dominated the literature; instead, directing our focus to the inherent dynamism of the Conservatives' strategy and to the multi-layered processes and mechanisms which have generated, facilitated and constrained it. This implies a proper consideration of the essential temporality of change which would allow us to view Thatcherism as a series of contingent interventions which have unfolded and evolved through time.

How then might we begin to construct an evolutionary explanation of Thatcherism? As indicated, we need to conceptualise the processes and mechanisms which have both facilitated and constrained the Conservatives' strategy over time. Here, I will attempt to outline briefly, and tentatively, three of the processes which might be considered appropriate to an analysis of Thatcherism: *environmental selectivity; actors' extrapolation and interpolation of strategy*; and *adaptive learning*. My aim is not to theorise the relationship between these processes; rather, it is merely to suggest a potential starting point from which to begin to capture the dynamism of the Thatcher project.

Environmental Selectivity

An informed analysis of political change must account for the inherent biases which reside in both the global and the domestic environments in which strategies are articulated. In this sense, we need to recognise that responses to crises occur within a structured context which is itself the product of previously articulated strategies and historical processes and which will necessarily favour certain responses over others. Thus, government strategies are subject to a variety of selective environmental pressures which both constrain and facilitate the articulation of future responses.

As such, any analysis of Thatcherism must take account of the environmental pressures which have conditioned the Conservatives' response to the political and economic crises of the 1970s. This necessarily entails an awareness of wider evolutionary changes within the world system of economic and inter-state relations and the selective pressures which these exerted upon Britain's particular evolutionary trajectory.

Here, it is useful to draw from the work of world systems analysts[8] and regulation theorists.[9] As Wallerstein and others have argued, the highly integrated and competitive global environment exerts pressures upon all nation states to accomodate themselves to the wider trajectories and crises of the world economy. Thus, the evolution of the world system, through developmental stages of capitalist accumulation, forces selective pressures upon nation states to develop strategies which correspond with global economic patterns. This then directs our attention to the necessary co-evolutionary tendencies which emerge between global technological paradigms and national-specific political responses.[10] Regulation theory deals specifically with these co-evolutionary cycles. Here, the focus is upon the national (and sometimes local) specific configurations of socio-economic and political structures – *regimes of accumulation* – which adapt in response to changing global technological paradigms. These analyses highlight the crucial constraints on strategic responses to crises by reminding us of the path-dependent nature of change incurred by selective environmental pressures. Yet, they also serve to illuminate the contingency and variability of the national structures within which economic regulation is embedded.

Turning our attention once again to Thatcherism, it is clear that the Thatcher Governments were engaged in the strategic re-adjustment of Britain's socio- economic and political structures in response to two key conjunctures within the world system – the weakening of US hegemony and a crisis of Fordist accumulation strategies. Whilst the former has squeezed the UK into a re- adjustment of its international political and economic alliances, the latter has forced restructuring on a domestic level to accomodate more flexible modes of growth. This has brought selective pressures for the introduction of apposite forms of institutional organisation, including the re-composition of welfare delivery as part of a transition towards what some authors have termed a Schumpterian Workfare State.[11]

Whilst it is important to consider these external variables, it is equally crucial that we assess the selective pressures exerted by domestic institutional structures and historical processes. Thus, although the world system shapes the trajectories of national responses to crises, these will still vary considerably given that governments are also constrained to act in accordance with selective pressures which are nation-specific. In this respect, we need to consider the historical specificity of Britain's own position within the world system. This entails an assessment of the pressures brought to

[8]See, for examples, I.Wallerstein, *Historical Capitalism*, Verso, 1983; *The Politics of the World Economy: The States, The Movements and the Civilisations*, Cambridge University Press, 1984; T.Hopkins et al, *The Age of Transition: Trajectory of the World-System 1945-2025*, Zed Books, 1996.

[9]See, for examples, M.Aglietta, *A Theory of Capitalist Regulation: The US Experience*, New Left Books, 1979; A.Lipietz, *Mirages and Miracles: The Crises of Global Fordism*, Verso, 1987; R.Boyer, *The Regulation School: A Critical Introduction*, Columbia University Press, 1990.

[10]H.Ward, 'Evolution and Regulation: Economism Rediscovered', Essex Papers in Politics and Government, 64, 1989.

[11]See B.Jessop, 'The Transition to post-Fordism and the Schumpterian Workfare State', in R.Burrows & B.Loader (eds), *Towards a Post-Fordist Welfare State?*, Routledge, 1994.

bear upon the Thatcher Governments by Britain's decline from a previous hegemonic position within the international economic and inter-state system.[12] Here, Thatcherism must be viewed as a conditioned response to UK decline, whilst at the same time, the weakened structures of the UK economy can be seen as conditioning the Conservatives' ability to respond effectively. Parallel consideration must be given here to the constraints imposed by previous failures to halt Britain's decline and to the correlative factors which contributed to these failures.[13] In this sense, we need to look at the configuration of class compromises and institutional practices specific to Britain's own variant of Fordist accumulation and Keynesian Welfarist modes of regulation. As Jessop has argued, these contributed in the earlier post-war period to the emergence of an essentially 'flawed' system of accumulation and a lack of core state capacities to ensure successful regulation.[14]

Extrapolation and Interpolation of Strategy

Whilst it is crucial that we retain an emphasis upon the structural conditioning of responses to crisis, it is equally important that we do not fall into a strict reductionism. In this respect, we cannot simply assume that institutional adjustments to environmental exigencies are automatic; to do so would be to fall into a crude form of functionalist explanation.[15] Thus, although strategies evolve partly in response to environmental exigencies, it is through the interventions of social and political actors that these are enacted. Actors are never passive creatures in the formulation of strategy; rather, they will invariably furbish their strategic interventions with their own sets of meanings and objectives. In this respect, we need to consider the fact that governments both *extrapolate* meaning from the information they receive from their environment and *interpolate* their own intentionality into their strategic responses. There are at least three main considerations which are important here. Firstly, although the environment exerts pressures for particular types of solutions to crises, actors' bounded rationality prevents them from gaining full knowledge of what these might be. As a result, the actors' limited awareness will inevitably force them to both elicit and insert their own interpretations of optimal responses. Secondly, and relatedly, strategic actors carry their own sets of biases and strategic heuristics. Thus, governments are not merely bounded actors; they are

[12] For an analysis of Britain's 'post-hegemonic trauma' see P.Taylor, 'Britain's Changing Role in the World-Economy', in J.Mohan (ed), *The Political Geography of Contemporary Britain*, Macmillan, 1989.

[13] For a consideration of explanations of Britain's decline, see J.Johnston's contribution to these volumes, 'Britain's Economic Decline: Beyond Idealist Fallacies Within the Literature'.

[14] B.Jessop, 'The Transition to Post-Fordism'.

[15] Although it may not be fruitful to reject functionalist explanation entirely. Indeed, as Ward argues, evolutionary explanation may prove capable of sustaining a 'weak functionalist' argument, by elucidating the processes whereby certain requirements of capital accumulation are met through the unintended consequences of actors 'groping' for soutions to crises; H.Ward, 'State Exploitation, Capital Accumulation and the Evolution of Modes of Regulation: A Defence of "Bottom-line economism" ', Paper Presented to the PSA Annual Conference, Leicester, 1993.

also intentional, motivated agents who have their own sets of goals and objectives. As a result, responses to crises are mediated, filtered and thus selected through the ideational and subjective processes of motivated government actors. Thirdly, crises themselves cannot be narrowly conceived as objective properties of the system; rather, they are essentially contested constructs which reflect the subjectivity and intentionality of the actors who narrate them.[16] Before responses to crises can be made, governments must extrapolate (through their own biases and strategic heuristics) from their environment information about the types of crises and contradictions which exist; moreover, they will, in turn, interpolate their own intentionality into their strategic responses.

Turning once again to the Conservatives' strategy, it is arguable that the Thatcher Governments compromised many of the strategic responses necessary to accommodate flexible growth by focussing upon shorter-term tactical goals. Thus, although the Thatcher Governments appeared to embrace the environmental demand for the liberalisation and deregulation of market forces, much of their energies were spent in adapting these strategies to suit narrower political and ideological objectives. The most obvious example of this has been the Conservatives' de-nationalisation programme. Although this appears to have been a response to global pressures for privatisation, the Conservatives' programme was adapted to meet short-term electoral goals (through its material effects upon key sections of the electorate and its symbolic significance as part of a popular assault upon collectivism) rather than longer-term economic requirements.[17]

A further point in relation to crises is the fact that government actors must invariably engage in the process of legitimising their strategic interventions in order to mobilise popular support and secure future responses. In this sense, strategic interventions are likely to be accompanied by some form of hegemonic politics built around the discursive articulation of crisis narratives. These constructions of crises will inevitably shape the discursive space through which subsequent responses are articulated. Thus, the discursive articulation of crisis and, hence, strategic responses, can be said to exert further selective pressures by facilitating and constraining future interventions. Here, it is appropriate to consider the damaging effects upon the governments' ability to stimulate economic growth conditioned by their narrow anti-statist neo-liberal ideology. This has arguably led the Conservatives to search for solutions which displace previous (albeit limited) state capacities for intervention without replacing these with alternative means of economic regulation.

[16] For a proper consideration of actors' construction of crises narratives see C.Hay, 'Narrating Crisis: The Discursive Construction of the Winter of Discontent', *Sociology*, 30/2, 1996.

[17] D.Marsh, 'Privatisation Under Mrs Thatcher', *Public Administration*, 69, 1991.

Overall then, the bounded rationality of actors and, indeed, the inherent biases which they carry, combine to ensure that responses to crises, and importantly, the very constructions of crises themselves are extrapolated through, and interpolated with, governments' own sets of meanings, objectives and discursive articulations.

Adaptive Learning

These considerations highlight the important point that successful adaptations to environmental exigencies cannot be presumed to be either automatic or inevitable. Here, it is perhaps appropriate to reflect upon what a 'successful' adaptation might entail. The very idea of 'success' would imply the existence of some (hypothetical) point of global equilibrium towards which strategies are impelled.[18] Speculation on such matters can be fraught with danger; for they can lead us into adopting a very crude form of functionalist explanation based upon a strict notion of structural pre-requisites. However, it may be possible to avoid this by emphasising the *relativity* of 'success'. In this sense we need to consider again that national responses to crisis-tendencies take place within a highly competitive and hierachical system of global political and economic relations. Thus, it inevitably follows that some countries must *a priori* be more successful at adapting to crises than others. From this then, it may be possible to derive a conception of globally optimal, or 'successful', solutions to crises, based upon the idea that success is conditioned by others' failure to compete within the world system.[19] My aim here is not to delineate the characteristics of an optimal response to crises; it is merely to posit the existence of a hypothetical point of long-term global optima which shapes the evolutionary trajectory of state strategies. This would enable us to conceive of multiple points of local optima to which strategic interventions are attracted in the medium-term.[20]

Here, I will contend that further selective pressures (towards global optima) are brought to bear upon strategic responses to crises through processes of strategic learning. In this respect, actors reflexively monitor both their actions and the effects of those actions. Thus, feedback mechanisms can be posited to occur as the strategy unfolds which allow the relative success of previous interventions to be monitored.[21] An important consideration here is the inherent inertia within institutional structures and the rigidity of organisational routines and institutional practices. Thus, initial government interventions will invariably prove unsuccessful in meeting desired outcomes. This means that the evolution of state structures and practices is heavily dependent upon governments' persistence and their ability

---

[18] H.Ward, 'Evolutionary Explanation', first draft copy, mimeo, 1995.

[19] Although this may simply displace the problem of defining 'success' with that of defining 'competition'. Certainly, a proper conception of global optima would have to balance social needs with economic demands; see M.Watson, 'Bounded Strategies: Local Economic Development in an Age of Fiscal Crisis', MSC dissertation presented at University of Strathclyde, 1996.

[20] H.Ward, 'Evolutionary Explanation'.

[21] *Ibid.*

to respond and adapt to previous failures. For this reason, I will contend that, if we are to explain the evolution of the state, it is as crucial to focus upon the evolution of state strategies, and their adaptive potential, as it is to concentrate upon the evolution of state structures and institutional routines. This entails a recognition that the evolution of the state is, in many ways, dependent upon the ability of strategic actors to engage in adaptive learning in order to steer strategic response towards optimal solutions.

Turning our attention once again to Thatcherism, it is clear that the Conservatives' strategy has gained some form of unity, and hence a coherence, and a radical momentum through time. Throughout the 1980s, a stream of solutions to the (narrowly perceived) crisis of the state were thrown into the political market. These included monetarism, denationalisation, contracting-out and management reform. Whilst these initial responses to environmental demands appear to have been relatively inconsistent and random, by the Conservatives' third and fourth terms their strategic interventions (backed by increased emphasis upon market-testing and quango-isation) were beginning to display a greater degree of consistency and sophistication. Whilst selective pressures were brought to bear through environmental selectivity and the Conservatives' own extrapolation and interpolation of strategy, this evolutionary process also reflects the governments' capacity, and indeed, willingness, to adapt and respond to previous failures.

Conclusion: The Temporal Unfolding of Conservative Strategy

Any reflection upon the crucial temporality of the Conservatives' strategy, indicates that the contours of Thatcherism have been progressively worked out over time. Initially formulated around a discursive commitment to reduce the role of the state through monetarist strategies, the Conservatives have consistently had to redefine the parameters within which these responses should be met. Thus, it is important when analysing Thatcherism to shift our focus from an analysis of the Conservatives' strategy as a singular static snapshot in time to a consideration of the various 'stages' of its contingent evolutionary trajectory. This entails 'periodising' Thatcherism and a recognition that current Conservative interventions differ markedly from those articulated during Mrs Thatcher's first two terms in office. The key to explaining Thatcherism then, and periods of intense political change more generally, lies in our ability to elucidate the dynamism of change and hence the processes which contribute to this dynamism. Here, I have argued that it is only through the application of an evolutionary explanation that we can begin to grasp such processes.

Changing Environmentalism in the 1990s

Brian Doherty
Keele University

'Direct Action Against Road-Building: Some Implications for the Concept of Protest Repertoires'

Protest Repertoires

Theorists of social movements have paid less attention than might have been expected to the forms of action used by protesters. While it is generally accepted that tactics and strategy do influence success, there is little challenge to the consensus that the forms of action available to protesters are limited and have changed little since the early nineteenth century. Charles Tilly has devoted more effort to this question than probably any other analyst of social movements and it is his work on the repertoires of collective action that supports this consensus. By charting the kinds of action taken by protesters from the mid-eighteenth century into the first half of the nineteenth century he has shown that in Britain in this period protests changed in focus from parochial to national issues. Second, where earlier forms of action varied from place to place and were particular to the issue raised, by the nineteenth century new, 'modular', forms of action had emerged, meaning that the same form of action could be used in different places by groups pursuing different aims. Third, whereas earlier action was bifurcated in that local issues provoked direct action but when national issues arose insurgents addressed their claims through a local patron, by the mid-nineteenth century claims were being made autonomously in the name of the people.[1]

Pre-modern forms of protest action were directly related to the person or offence being targeted, such as grain seizures, charivaris, funerals, food riots or the burning of effigies, but from the early nineteenth century turnouts, strikes, rallies, demonstrations, public meetings and petitions were claims made to a public authority made legitimate by the fact that they were collective forms of action. Moreover, actions were more communicative, seeking negotiation, where before they had more often been violent and sought redress for a moral outrage, or the failure to uphold established customs. Now, different issues could be pursued using the same methods, so public meetings could be used by a movement, but the same form might easily be used by its opponents. Tilly argues that this modular form of collective action remains dominant at the end of the twentieth century. Forms of protest action are therefore culturally circumscribed and only major structural changes, of the kind that occurred with the emergence of the modern nation state, are likely to produce future changes in the nature of such actions.

Tilly's use of the concept of repertoire to define the range of actions available to a movement also reinforces the limits on the creation of new

[1] C.Tilly 'Contentious Repertoires in Great Britain, 1758-1834', in M.Traugott (ed), *Repertoires and Cycles of Collective Action*, Duke University Press, 1995.

forms. Repertoires are shared by a group, must be learned before they can be acted out and are limited by social contacts, memory and knowledge. Only a few possible repertoires are ever used. Others, while accepting most of Tilly's arguments have acknowledged that there have been some innovations in forms of protest action. Sidney Tarrow, for instance argues in his analysis of protests in Italy in the late 1960s that new forms of action are most likely to emerge in the 'moments of madness' at the beginning of a protest cycle, in which, according to the protesters, all is possible. Tarrow says that these moments of madness do not transform the whole repertoire all at once, rather they are tested, amended and diffused through larger cycles of mobilisation:

> 'It is within these larger cycles, that new forms of contention combine with old ones, the expressive encounters the instrumental, traditional social actors adopt tactics from new arrivals, and newly invented forms of collective action become what I call 'modular'. Cycles of protest are the crucible in which moments of madness are tempered into the permanent tools of a society's repertoire of contention.'[2]

Doug McAdam has gone furthest in according a causal role to tactical innovation in the impact of a social movement. The scale of activity in the American civil rights movement, he argues, depended on the development of new tactics to outflank its opponents. Thus, bus boycotts, lunch counter sit-ins, Freedom Rides and Community-wide campaigns such as those in Birmingham and Selma, each introduced a new element into the campaign and maintained the sense of crisis and confrontation upon which the movement depended. When a new tactic was introduced movement activity as a whole rose, not simply actions involving the use of the new tactic, but once the authorities learned how to respond to the new innovation a further innovation was needed. Many of the tactics of the civil rights movement, such as the sit-in became signature actions for subsequent movements such as the New Left.[3]

From the existing state of knowledge about protest repertoires the following points can be made:

- Forms of action involving competing claims are likely to lead to conflict
- The extent of innovation in forms of action is slow,
- When new forms emerge they do so as a product of the interaction between movements and their opponents and are diffused through protest cycles

---

[2] 'Cycles of Collective Action', in M.Traugott, *Ibid*, 1995, p.92.

[3] D.McAdam, 'Tactical Innovation and the Pace of Insurgency', *American Sociological Review*, 48, 1983; D.McAdam, 'The Framing Function of Movement Tactics', in D.McAdam et al (eds), *Comparative Perspectives on Social Movements*, Cambridge University Press, 1986.

- Successful and useful forms of protest action are, or will become, modular.

Direct action in the radical ecology movement in Britain

The 1990s saw an upsurge in direct action on ecological issues in Britain, posing a challenge for the conventional pressure groups such as Greenpeace and Friends of the Earth, who were anxious about being associated with mass illegal protests over which they had no control. In large part it was the caution of the latter two groups which created the impetus for a new generation of young ecological activists, influenced by the dramatic rise in environmental concern at the end of the 1980s. For this group direct action was a rational strategy primarily because there was a crisis of representation excluding the environment from the political field. After 1991 debate about the environment receded from the political scene almost completely. At around the same time groups inspired by the American direct action network, Earth First! were established in the United Kingdom. Like the wider radical ecology movement, United Kingdom Earth First! was decentralised, existing only where there was sufficient interest in direct action to provide the basis for a local group.

The catalyst for widespread action was provided by the start of work on the extension of the M3 through Twyford Down in Hampshire in 1992. The actions of a small number of young protesters who camped at Twyford, named by the local newspaper as the Dongas after the medieval trackways that crossed the Down, inspired the first sustained campaign of direct action. The fact that the Twyford protesters had been disowned by Friends of the Earth, who were fearful of the loss of assets from any court actions arising from illegal protest actions, helped to ensure that the movement developed autonomously, following the counter-cultural and anarchistic form already established by, among others, the network of Earth First! groups. While most new movements have structural links to other existing movements, one of the striking features of the growth of the radical ecology movement in Britain has been the autonomy of the movement, and its lack of any direct roots in earlier campaigns.

The one shared target for the anti-roads movement was the Government's major road-building programme, announced in 1989. By 1995 there were around 300 local groups opposing particular road schemes, co-ordinated by a group called Alarm UK. Where the latter represented the local groups fighting roads through procedural measures before the final decision to build a road had been made, the eco-protesters mainly concentrated on attempts to stop work on roads that had already been approved. Relationships between the direct action specialists and local groups have been varied. The counter-cultural lifestyle of the ecological protesters is deliberately intended to provoke a sense of difference, which makes it sometimes difficult to work with groups concerned about creating mass local support. This has been more of a problem in affluent small towns, such as Bath, and Winchester, than in urban areas such as East London and Glasgow. But at all the major sites, eco-protesters have been able to rely to some extent on lines of support from the local community.

The Dynamic of Protest and the Evolution of Tactics

Protests at road sites are a form of siege warfare. Protesters occupy a site and build defences. The defences are in trees, houses, or underground tunnels. The besiegers outnumber the occupiers, and have greater resources. One of the principal weapons of the besiegers is the cherry-picker crane, which can hoist bailiffs to pluck protesters from trees, rooftops or rope walkways at heights of up to 200 feet. Successive protests have produced new techniques for resisting the besiegers, to the extent that when the time comes for an eviction, major hopes are invested by protesters in the effectiveness of specific forms of obstructing eviction. Yet, while the eviction represents the culmination of the campaign, it is not the only event of significance. Aside from the considerable amount of work invested in building site defences, there are also forays into enemy territory. Contractors' offices are occupied, and shareholders' meetings are disrupted. Also, since 1995 the campaign has been taken into the streets with surprise actions to reclaim urban space from traffic.

Three factors have influenced the development of tactics by protesters. First, situational factors, such as the terrain, and also the nature of the local community shape the choices available and also influence the values appealed to. Open chalk download, such as at Twyford provided fewer opportunities to defenders than the woods at Preston and the M65. Destruction of areas of outstanding natural beauty and wildlife habitats was emphasised at Newbury and other rural sites, while the destruction of an east London community, bisected by a road intended to bring commuters from outside into central London more quickly, was the main issue for those opposing the M11 Link.

Second, the discourse of protesters also influenced tactical choices. At Twyford, the Dongas used dragon symbols, and drew boundary circles, invoking the power of magic to defend their site. Through invoking Celtic spirituality they saw themselves as achieving a closer identification with the land. In order to restore the balance of nature it was argued that it is important to rediscover indigenous earth-based spirituality. Adopting a tribal identity, and in the case of the Dongas, even a nomadic way of life, was also a means of situating themselves in the global struggles of indigenous peoples against ecological destruction. Thus, after Twyford, many of the Dongas lived in mobile camps of benders, carrying possessions on carts and donkeys, along old trackways, so minimising their contamination by modernity.

There was a distinct anti-urbanism evident among some other eco-protesters. An article in the Earth First! journal, invoked the need to escape from the spiritual desolation of cities, and many Earth First! gatherings were held in isolated rural areas. This did influence how the movement developed. In the M11 campaign some of those squatting houses in Leytonstone could not understand the 'hippies' 'obsession with sitting in trees. The squatters believed that 'it made far more sense tactically to occupy houses than trees'.[4] Furthermore, 'once there were other rural campaigns to go to (first Bath, later Preston) the 'tree people' tended to move away from the urban wilderness of east London, particularly once the 'bender site' had been destroyed in July 1994'.

In fact, although evicting people from tree houses is easier than plucking them from nets or rope walkways, tree houses had some instrumental value. It is difficult to be caught by surprise action by evictors in a tree house. They also provide a base for storing supplies and allow those less experienced at climbing a means of participating in delaying eviction. The eviction of the tree houses at Newbury saw desperate and emotional confrontations with flour, urine, and disinfectant, as well as staves with rubber hoses, designed to impede chainsaws, being used to hamper the actions of bailiffs. Moreover, trees had an expressive role as well. They were given personalities, and some at Stanworth left before the eviction rather than see their tree home destroyed. The importance of trees to the identity of eco-protesters meant that even when it was tactically not necessarily the best option tree houses were still built.

The third factor that shapes the development of tactics is the ability of opponents to adapt to earlier tactics. The main initial successes at Twyford were in disrupting construction work through surprise invasions of the site. Under safety at work legislation the builders were forced to stop work, and on many days protesters were successful in climbing on bulldozers and chaining themselves onto vital machinery. In the end such tactics could be countered by increasing the number of security guards. But protesters continued to use this tactic with some success in delaying the progress of machinery and by increasing the level of security required they were increasing the costs of the road as well as keeping the road in the public eye. Neither did use of overwhelming numbers by the authorities necessarily guarantee easy success. The eviction of Claremont Road the last main squatted site on the path of the M11 in November and December 1994 was carried out by 700 police, 400 security guards and 200 bailiffs. Nevertheless the eviction took 4 days, during which the 500 occupiers were able to make themselves a major news story and score tactical successes, such as maintaining power supplies to the occupiers through a secret tunnel beyond police lines, and a scaffolding tower constructed on the rooftop of one house allowed one protester to delay the evictions single-handedly for a further day.

Whereas, by the time of the evictions at Claremont Road, protesters had accepted that the houses would be demolished, when evictions began at Newbury in January 1996, there was greater optimism that skilled defences would delay the progress of road building significantly The evictions of the 28 camps at Newbury took 11 weeks and became a regular feature of the TV news. In one sense this was a success, since the theatre of direct action forces awareness of the depth of feeling expressed by the protesters. But in other respects, the dramatic quality of the evictions reinforced the sense

[4] E-mail communication from activist with *Reclaim the Streets*.

of distance. The medieval character of the battle, with massed lines of security guards with bright tunics moving through the mist, siege engines manoeuvring slowly towards their goal, with a phalanx of police and knights in the form of police on horseback, reinforced the sense of dislocation from everyday life. While more conventional groups of locals were often portrayed acting in support of the eco-protesters, they were always on the fringes, reinforcing the image that eco-protest had become a technically skilled form of action, which not only required a difficult lifestyle, but also a degree of professionalism, that should not be attempted by amateurs.

The Government had also tried to use legal harassment against the road protesters, but initially this back-fired badly. Attempts to sue protesters at Twyford Down for the costs of the police action were unsuccessful. And when several Twyford protesters were sent to jail for breaking protest injunctions, they received significant supportive media coverage and a visit from the European Environment Commissioner Carlo Ripa de Meana. However, protest also provided opportunities to justify repressive legislation. The Criminal Justice Act, 1994, introduced new restrictions on the right to protest which made it possible for the police to prosecute protesters for criminal trespass. Moreover, the regular use of injunctions to stay away from the site of roads as a part of bail conditions did make life difficult for protesters. In March 1996 the Association of Chief Police Officers announced that they would use anti-terrorist squads to step up surveillance of environmental activists. Despite the lack of any serious incidents at any roads protests the spectre of environmental terrorism was being used to justify the need for domestic intelligence spending.

Technical Ingenuity

The most successful of the technical innovations used by protesters were lock-ons, walkways, and tripods. To 'lock-on' protesters placed their hand in a tube wide enough only for their arm and clipped their wrist onto a metal bar at the other end of the tube. When the bar and tube were embedded in concrete, it became very difficult to move them. At Claremont Road, for instance, people who appeared to be lying on mattresses in the road were actually locked-on to concrete in the road itself and were able to delay the advance of cherry-pickers for several hours. Lock-ons could even be used in trees. An empty oil barrel was hoisted into the tree and then filled with concrete and lashed down with a tube inserted to allow the protester to lock- on. Pneumatic drills have to be used to extract the tube. However, whereas at first this often took hours as bailiffs became more experienced and prepared they were able to break lock-ons more quickly. In response, protesters adapted their own tactic, adding metal and glass to hamper the drills.

Walkways were ropes strung at a height between trees or houses to allow protesters to move around above ground level. Once an eviction began, some protesters would move onto the walkways, and climb up and down, sometimes without harnesses, to avoid being plucked from them. There were many cases when the ropes were cut with protesters still on them, and on several occasions protesters fell. However, the most effective counter to walkways and to tree climbers was the introduction of a specialist team of paid climbers by the bailiffs. The recruitment of climbers caused considerable controversy in climbing clubs, but the Sheffield based group were used regularly in evictions after the evictions at Stanworth Woods near Preston in 1995. The battles in the tree tops at Newbury were dangerous and on some occasions violent, as protesters, who included some famous in climbing circles themselves, were chased across trees until eventually removed.

The use of tripods was pioneered by the urban-based group Reclaim the Streets. Tripods were scaffolding poles of around 10 metre length, formed into a tripod, clipped together from which protesters could be suspended. To move them risked causing the protester serious injury. Tripods were first used to block traffic in the rush hour in Greenwich in 1995 and were then a regular feature of Reclaim the Streets actions across the country because they provided a portable and rapidly erected barricade. However, the use of tripods was not restricted to urban actions, they were successfully used at Newbury to block the coaches due to transport security guards to the site, causing work to cancelled for the day and in perhaps the apogee of technical virtuosity in protest actions at Newbury a tripod was erected at the top of a tree and used to suspend a barrel of concrete for a protester to lock-on.

A final tactical innovation was the use of tunnels. The most extensive network of tunnels was at Fairmile in Devon in the route of the A30. The effectiveness of the tunnels depended in part on the nature of the ground. By locking-on underground, protesters hoped to make it impossible for the evictors to bring up heavy machinery, based on the risk of the tunnels collapsing. At previous evictions at Newbury and at Trollheim, also on the A30 route, protesters had been evicted from tunnels within hours, but the evictors had taken considerable safety risks, cutting off air and communication for several hours and moving heavy machinery close to the tunnels. The network at Fairmile was more extensive and sophisticated than elsewhere, and at the time of writing, three protesters remained in the tunnel, after six days.

The limitation of tunnels is the same as that of other methods used by the protesters. Their success depends upon the risks taken by the protester. By making themselves vulnerable, they require the evictors to take extra care and time, to avoid injury. However, as experience of evictions developed, the bailiffs and police became less cautious in using force and more skilled at overcoming the defences relied on by protesters. Whereas earlier, the technical devices developed by protesters had created confusion and secured delay, by 1997 the authorities were able to take them into account in their planning. Moreover, each new device has required protesters to take new risks. The tunnels at Fairmile took two years to construct and only the most committed activist would take the deliberate risk of locking-on within a home-made tunnel.

Nevertheless, for over two years from 1994 onwards, protesters were able to make every eviction of a road site a hard-fought and expensive operation. Moreover one of such theatrical quality that it guaranteed that the issue of road-building remained on the public agenda. As one activist from Reclaim the Streets commented, the momentum of the movement depended upon changing tactics. The media would not keep telling the same story again and again.

Conclusion: Tactical Ingenuity and the Impact of Roads Protests

Despite the obvious failure of direct action to halt a road scheme once construction has begun, in certain respects the direct action groups can claim qualified successes. The road programme has been substantially cut to a third of the size envisaged when it was launched in 1989. The cuts may be partly attributed to the desire in the Treasury to find cuts in public expenditure, but they also became more politically acceptable, forcing the government to reconsider its overall transport strategy in the face of widespread public debate about the environmental consequences of motor vehicles. The direct action groups are only one part of the broader anti-roads coalition, but it is probable that without their protests the issue would not have remained at the centre of national political debate.

Only tentative conclusions can be drawn in such a short paper about the implications of road protests for the concept of protest repertoires. It is evident, however, that the creativity and ingenuity of protesters has been essential to their impact. Most recent debates on social movements have concentrated on system-level causes of their emergence or on the processes of mobilisation. The direct action movement is small and did not emerge as a result of changes in the political opportunity structure.[5] It has no central organisation and no centralised pool of resources. In all respects it is a clear example of the kinds of movement defined as new in recent debates in social movement theory. The combination of nonviolent direct action and the use of the law, defined as characteristic of new social movements by Dieter Rucht in order to demarcate them in relative terms from earlier movements, applies precisely to this movement.[6] Similarly, Melucci's criteria for an antagonist movement, one that reflects the increased cultural basis of power in 'information society' also apply well to the eco- protesters.[7] The forms of action chosen by such movements are defined by their increasing symbolic content (inside-out streets, carhenges, dragon circles, and union jills), and decreases in the divisibility of their goals, the reversibility of conflicts and the calculability of their demands. Eco-protesters, take on planetary

[5]Elsewhere, I have argued that models such as political opportunity structure models do not help to explain why the movement emerged. B.Doherty, 'Paving the Way: the rise of direct action against road-building and the changing character of British environmentalism', Working Paper 21, Keele University Politics Department, 1996.

[6]D.Rucht 'The Strategies and Action Repertoires of New Movements', in R.J.Dalton & M.Kuechler (eds), *Challenging the Political Order*, Polity, 1990.

[7]A.Melucci, *Challenging Codes*, Cambridge University Press, 1996.

concerns, and local and national policy changes; cultural questions about the nature of public space and spiritual relationships with nature as well as detailed technical discourse. Their cultural codes are clearly challenges to the dominant codes.

Nevertheless, if this defined the symbolic role of the movement, its impact is largely attributable to successes in sustaining the public and media-mediated dramaturgy of direct action. Given, the small numbers of the protesters, their lack of money and minimal external support, no other conclusion is possible. Technical ingenuity has been a major factor in their success. If this has produced new element in the repertoire of protesters, it is not clear that this creativity has occurred in the way expected according to the existing theories of act on repertoires. Lock-ons, tripods, tunnels and walkways did not emerge at the beginning of a widespread protest cycle. For all the coverage of protests, very few have taken part, and these protests support Melucci's view that where cultural codes are at stake, mass mobilisation is no longer necessary, the actions of small groups can be sufficient.

The prospect of these tactics becoming modular is uncertain. It may be that if the authorities are able to develop sufficient experience in adapting to the kinds of tactics employed by road protesters, that they will no longer be useful. Certain tactics depend on legal rights that may be specific to Britain, and the exploitation of vulnerability by protesters depends on the acceptance of the need for restraint by police, bailiffs and security guards. Nevertheless, vulnerability is a powerful tool in liberal democracies, since casualties to protesters always carry heavy political costs. There is also some evidence that there has already been some diffusion of tactics. In October 1996 tree sitters were reporting on their actions in Freiburg. And the significant numbers of overseas activists who have participated in roads protests in Britain are likely to carry the repertoire to groups in other countries. Yet if such tactics do become more widespead they will only be used by radical greens. This action repertoire will not be modular in the sense that the same tactics can be used by both a movement and its opponents. The symbolic content of these forms of action and their reliance on vulnerability suggests that they are a contribution to the specific repertoire of new social movements.

Changing Environmentalism in the 1990s

Purwo Santoso
LSE & Gadjah Mada University, Indonesia

'Prospect of Environmental Control Institutions in a Developmental State: the case of Indonesia'

Acknowledgement

I would like to thank to Dr.James Putzel who has made useful comments and substantial grammatical improvement of this paper.

Introduction

The advancement of environmental discourse has led only very slowly to institutional change,[1] even though it has played a critical role in altering our collective effort in caring for the environment. The 'developmental state', as a theoretical institutional explanation for economic success[2] is used here as a starting point to analyse environmental institutions. The point is, if institutions are central to the failure or the success of a state-led process, the state's difficulty in bringing about environmental policy objective should subject to institutional explanation.

Rhetorical arguments stating that economic development and environmental protection are mutually supportive[3] have to be translated into institutional arrangements. Given the difficulty in delivering together a developmental state and sustainable development, Indonesia has deliberately sub-ordinated environmental institutions within the well established developmental state institutional arrangement. Sustainable development is not assumed to require institutions distinctive from the existing institutions. The performance of sustainable development is believed to rest on the ability of existing institutions to commit to self-reorientation.

The first part of this paper explores the notion of a sustainable developmental state. It will be followed by a discussion of the organisational feature of environmental institutions, within which the rhetoric concerning the complementarity of economic development and environmental concerns is organisationally translated into the subordination of the latter to the former. After presenting forest resources management as an illustration of the argument in the third part, the concluding part considers the prospects of developing environmental institutions.

---

[1] M.A.Hajer 'Acid Rain in Great Britain: Environmental Discourse and the Hidden Politics of Institutional Practice', in F.Fischer & M.Black (eds), *Greening Environmental Policy: The Politics of Sustainable Future*, Paul Chapman Publishing, London, 1995.

[2] T.Y.Kong, 'Form Relative Autonomy to Consensual Development: the Case of South Korea', *Political Studies*, 1995, p.630.

[3] World Commission on Environment and Development, *Our Common Future*, Oxford University Press, 1987.

Sustainable Developmental State?

Empirically, the state continue to play a central role in consolidating a systemic response to environmental problems, despite the recognition of the importance of decentralization in favour of societal decision making and that of developing forms of supra-state power.[4] The resurgence of the idea of a minimal state role advocated by neoclassical economists has been challenged by the advocates of the idea of the developmental state. The latter argues, the success of economic development in East and Southeast Asia is largely due to the ability of the state to implement appropriate measures and strategies, however they are defined,[5] including the ability to govern the market.[6] The ability of achieving policy goals has been associated with the autonomy and the strength of the state. The success of economic development, particularly industrialisation, is not explained by the extent but the way the state involve. The question is not 'how much' but 'what kind' of state's involvement.[7] The developmental state assumes the centrality of institutions, including the ability to keep the state's bureaucracy from abusing its autonomy. The failure of the developmental state is associated with predatory behaviour[8] which denotes the lack of 'ability to prevent individual incumbents from pursuing their own goals'.[9] Evans further explains the structural characteristic of predatory state as follows:

> 'Personal ties are the only source of cohesion, and individual maximization takes precedence over pursuit of collective goals. Ties to society are ties to individual incumbents, not connections between constituencies and the state as organization. Predatory states are, in short, characterized by dearth of bureaucracy as Weber defined it.'[10]

If the assertions of theorists of the developmental state's are true, the less spectacular Indonesian economic performance relative to the Newly Industrialising East Asian countries, is explained by the degree of the pervasiveness of predatory behaviour by the state. Yet, its overall performance allows us to categorize Indonesia's state as developmental state. In the period 1967- 1980 Indonesia's annual GDP growth was faster than that of the East Asian countries. Even in the subsequent period 1981-1991, when it was less that of East Asian countries, Indonesia's annual growth of GDP

---

[4]P.Wapner, 'The State and Environmental Challenges: A Critical Exploration the State-System', *Environmental Politics*, 1995.

[5]Among the proponent of this argument are: White, Gordon (ed), *Developmental States in East Asia, St.Martin, New York, 1988; S.Haggard, Pathways from the Periphery: The Politics of Growth in the Newly Industrialising Countries*, Cornell University Press, 1990.

[6]R.Wade, *Governing the Market: Economic Theory and the Role of Government in East Asian Industrialization*, Princeton University Press, 1990.

[7]P.Evens, *Embedded Autonomy: States & Industrial Transformation*, Princeton University Press, 1995, p.11.

[8]Haggard, *op cit*, p.263.

[9]*Ibid*, p.12.

[10]*Ibid*, p.12.

was better than the average of the developing countries.[11]

Many developmental states, including Indonesia, declare a commitment to sustainable development. In doing so, they have no intention to abandon developmentalism to which they have been subscribing. What is interesting to see here is how the state brings together developmentalism and some sort of environmentalism within the state's institutional structure, and to what extent the institutional structure within the state is reliable basis for pursuing a sustainable development. Given the potential contradiction between the developmental and sustainability purpose, the environmental institution within the state has been granted only marginal bureaucratic power, and has to find ways by itself for extending its leverage. The reason is simple. The decision to accommodate environmental issues within the developmental framework was taken with a full awareness of the potential conflict of policy goals, and therefore with anticipation of conflicts of interest among institutions within the state. Before the notion of sustainable development became internationally popular, meaning before the idea of mutual enhancement between economic development and environmental protection were globally accepted, Indonesia attempted to pursue that direction. The catchword was 'to dissolve environment into development'.[12] This means, the essential structure of the developmental state is retained, and an environmental framework of state's decision making is promoted. Even when the term sustainable development getting its popularity, that institutional arrangements is acceptable. Nonetheless, the insistence to retain the existing institutional structure made Indonesia's approach belongs to weak sustainability camp within the spectrum of sustainable development. The fundamental difference between the strong and the weak sustainability camps, according to Turner, lies in their assumption regarding substitutability of resources. The strong camp of sustainability disbelieves to the substitutability of resources, and presupposes the importance of institutional changing. On the other camp the proponent if a weak sustainability assume that resources is substitutable, and their concern is the maintenance of the aggregate resources, and not on the protection of the environment as such. In other words, the institutionalisation of 'developmental state committed to environmental sustainability' is only sensible on a weak or shallow sustainability perspective.[13]

While 'sustainable development' has received endorsement of most of the state on the planet, it is nonetheless practically deceiving, at least in understating the urgency of arranging and enhancing institutions for ensuring sustainability. The subscription to a shallow sustainability perspective indicated the reluctance, if not the denial, of the need for a paradigmatic shifting advocated under the banner of strong sustainability. The lack of agreement regarding the extent of policy reorientation leave the state to chose the

---

[11]The World Bank, *Indonesia: Sustaining Development*, Washington, 1994, p.2.

[12]E.Salim, *Menang Tanpa Ngasorake* [To Win Without Defeating], a retrospective note, un dated.

[13]R.K.Turner, 'Sustainability: Principles and Practice', in R.K.Turner (ed), *Sustainable Environmental Economic and Management: Principles and Practice*, Belhaven Press, 1993.

institutionally safe option, namely maintaining the status quo. The consolidation of the institutional basis for sustainable development therefore requires policy advocacy within-the- state. The challenge of advocacy is even more obvious if it is agreed that pursuing a sustainable development, in fact, means setting up an ecologically sound framework of interacting with the environment. If commitment to environmental goals is more than just accommodating international pressures, then, developmentalism must become subject to reorientation. The irony, as I will demonstrate later, is that policy reorientation does not always lead to practical reorientation. While conceptionally the complementarity between developmentalism and environmental concern is reconcilable, the state nonetheless chose a safe path of institutional development by instituting a gradualist environmental policy.

Implicit in the strategy of dissolving environment into development is being 'patient' with a lengthy process of environmental policy 'socialisation' within an advocacy-based policy reorientation. As early as 1973, the National Development Planning Document included a special chapter on the Management of Natural Resources and the Environment. The idea of writing the chapter was merely to raise awareness within sectoral agencies that environmental issues are something that they have to take into account. There was no specific environmental program except establishing a ministry in charge of environmental affairs. This program was realized in 1978 by assigning Professor Emil Salim as Minister for Development Supervision and the Environment. During the first five years of the existence of this ministry, effort was devoted to establishing an Environmental Management Act, which would form the legal basis for interfering with the course dictated by developmentalism. The devotion was primarily to environmental legislation, under the banner of advocating development policy reorientation.

Politics is not merely a matter of constrained rational competition, nor merely getting the timing right. It is also a matter of a structural reshaping of institutions within which the political process takes place.[14] In this discussion, the internal state structure and its relationship with society are the locus of the political process. In accordance with that point, the following two sections will explore the internal institutional structure by focussing on organisational format. To see a clearer political relationship within state-society interaction, the forestry sector will be presented as an illustration afterwards.

Organisational Format

The institutional basis of the developmental state had been well-established prior to the commitment to sustainable development. The institutions in this context are state-based, if not state-controlled. As the theory of institutions suggests, a commitment to new activity tend to be based on

[14] J.G.March & J.L.Olsen, *Rediscovering Institutions: The Organizational Basis of Politics*, Free Press, 1989.

the existing institutions.[15] This means that the steps toward sustainable development have to rely on the institutions designed or shaped by the developmental framework. Pursuing sustainable development, in this regard, faces a paradox. On the one hand, there is a need to direct them toward environmental goals, on the other hand the ability to do so depends on the willingness of actors framed by institutions within the state. In other words, the fate of sustainable development highly depends on the ability of the state to launch a self-reorientation.

By definition institutions shape patterns of behaviour and prescribes a well-established practice expected by other.[16] Given the heterogeneity of institutions within the state taking part in handling environmental issues, the notion of self-reorientation somehow is misleading. It is essentially the result of a conflict of interests. In Sabatier's terms, it is dependent on the ability to build a advocacy coalition within the policy community.[17]

In the Indonesian case, the developmental state's reorientation is handled very slowly and with a careful minimisation of transitional destabilisation. The guiding rule is that pursuing sustainability must not contradict the developmental-state's interests. The minimisation of risk is not only carried out through the evolutionary development of environmental institutions within the state, but also through an exclusion of fundamental reforms demanded by the advocates of strong sustainability. As least during the early period of its commitment to sustainable development, the state would only endorse a shallow sustainability. The advocates of sustainable development within the state face a tremendous challenge of pin-pointing evidence showing that within the day to day decision making process of the state, pursuing sustainability does not constrain, and even benefit, the developmental state.

The state established institutions for reorientation purposes. Based on the idea of dissolving environment into development, the ministry in charge of environmental policies was established in 1978. It was among the earlier environmental ministries (chaired by cabinet member) being established, especially in the developing countries. As a comparison, it was not until 1990 the US (under the Bush administration), has a minister for the environment as member of cabinet. That 'advancement' of organisational formation, however, shall not be exaggerated, given the marginal power and limited access to state resources that the ministry has been suffering from. The point that I want to make here is that organisational solutions to govern the potential conflict between policy goals is critical. Unlike the US which established Environmental Protection Agency (EPA) long before establishing cabinet level environmental department, Indonesia established a ministry which has been well before developing environmental agencies within the state similar to the EPA, namely the Environmental Impact Control Agency (BAPEDAL).[18] The state ministry responsible for environ-

---

[15] *Ibid.*

[16] R.E.Goodin, 'Institutions and Their Design', in R.E.Goodin (ed), *The Theory of Institutional Design*, Cambridge University Press, 1996, p.26.

[17] P.A.Sabatier & H.CJenkins-Smith (eds), *Policy Change and Learning: An Advocacy Coalition Approach*, Westview, Boulder, 1994.

[18] The establishment of BAPEDAL almost coincided with the twentieth anniversary of

ment is specifically in charge of formulating and coordinating environmental policy in every sectoral activity, and hence is cross-sectoral in nature. Unlike Great Britain which only very recently reached legal agreement on how to establish a cross- sector environmental agency,[19] Indonesia has been quick and decisive in doing so.

The idea of establishing environmental ministry in advance to the establishment of BAPEDAL is to secure developmentalism in accommodating environmentalist idea. The decisiveness, however, hides an important developmental point, ensuring that the course of development is facing minimum disturbance upon 'dissolving environment to development'. A firm insistence on developmentalism is protected by separating policy formulation and policy implementation in its organisational arrangement. The responsibility of environmental management remains intact within sectoral development policy. For example, the Ministry of Forestry (MoF) assumes a full formal responsibility in handling environmental problems along with extensive forest exploitation. The authority for exorcising industrial pollution lies within the authority of the Ministry of Industry.

The risk of encountering a clash of policy goals is avoided at the cost of delaying the institutionalisation of environmental policy coordination. Coordination of environmental policy implementation was not well advanced during the fifteen years of Emil Salim's ministerial term. The merit of his ministerial term was the extensive establishment of legal and bureaucratic instruments. As Sarwono Kusumaatmadja took over the ministerial leadership in 1993, implementation policy coordination was to become more apparent. In 1995, namely in his third year in this ministry, he pushed forward the institutional role of the State Ministry for the Environment by taking part in scrutinizing development programs from sectoral ministries, a task previously the monopoly of the National Developmental Planning Agency. Even though the ministry has been equipped with legal and bureaucratic instruments, the ministry under the Sarwono Kusumaatmadja further extended its leverage by initiating the development of economic instruments of environmental policy. It is true that this measure coincided with the resurgence of environmental economic discourse. The relevance in the Indonesian context is that, given the environmental law is 'non-political' and hence not directly related to the political interests of the state, the law is not automatically enforced. Despite the attribution of the Indonesian state as 'authoritarian', the exercise of coercion is very selective concentrating on issue which directly threaten the authority of the state. In other words, the development of economic incentives sounds promising because it does not rely on the exercise of the state's coercive power, which is not always easy to mobilise.

---

the EPA.

[19]N.Carter & P.Lowe, 'The Establishment of a Cross-sector Environment Agency', in T.S.Gray (ed), *UK Environmental Policy in the 1990s*, MacMillan, 1995.

If there is such thing as sustainable developmental state, precisely developmental state committed to sustainability', the pivotal point in bringing it about is the state's institutional arrangement, particularly the organisation of inter- organisational relationships Every country has their own way of matching ecological with organisational interconnectedness. Indonesia chose to accommodate the ecological interconnectedness by pursuing an all-encompassing sectoral environmental policy through a single ministry at the expense of permitting a division between bureaucratic authority for policy formulation and for policy implementation. In demonstrating how this arrangement performs in reorienting the developmental state toward a sustainable direction, our attention turns to a sectoral illustration from forest resource management.

Bureaucratic Reorientation: Forestry Management

Forest resource management, I think, is a good case to illustrate how bureaucracy is reorienting itself in the light of serving a developmental purpose on the one hand, and environmental protection on the other hand. Even within forest resource management, this illustration is confined to the management of production forest, within which exploitation takes place. When militarily-backed Suharto came to power in the mid-1960s the Indonesian economy was on the verge of bankruptcy, and the first thing to do was rehabilitatation by relying on foreign debt. As the second largest owner of tropical forest after Brazil, the government looked at forest resources as a means to resolve the problem of scarcity of help to restore the economy, particularly to repaying the national debt. The need for financial capital to keep the economy running, including the lack of initial capital for the state- own enterprises to launch exploitation, drove the government to use the private sector to transform forest resource capital into financial capital. As of 1967, the Forestry Act was enacted, not only allowing a private role in exploitation, including a foreign one, but also outlining a principle of sustainable forest management. It emphasized the duality of the state's responsibility – exploitation with conservation. In other words, the importance of conservation was not only recognised but also legally binding the state's action. Having underlined legality, however, it is undeniably the case that the orientation was on exploitation. Despite the urgency of obtaining foreign currency, there were long terms objectives of developing forest-based industries.

As the scale of forest exploitation increased in 1970s, the debt burden was lessened. The escalation of log exports helped to secure the country from indebtedness. So even though the amount of debt service increased from Rp.12.7 billion in 1969/1970 to Rp.62.5 billion in 1973/1974, the burden of debt to the economy has been lessening. The size of debt was equal to 77% of development spending in 1969/1970. Within five years, it was reduced to 45.2%. This economic success was made possible through the expansion exploitation in production forest. The proportion of production forest was increased from 9% in 1972 to 52% of forest land in 1979. At the same time the size of forest reserve shrinking from 79% to 30% of total forest land. As the scale of exploitation was expanding, so too the amount of the rent that the state collected. The estimated rent at the 1980 constant prices increased from US$208 million in 1970, to US$401 million five years later, and peaked to the level of US$1347 million in 1979.

Contrary to assumptions about the developmental state, such escalating contribution of forestry to the economy not really indicate the strength of state bureaucracy. The contribution of Indonesian forestry sector was important state's success in capital generation. The actual forest exploitation was primarily undertaken through mostly privately-run concessionaires, instead of by the state itself. It was achieved not particularly because of complying bureaucratic control. By 1978 there were 382 units of forest concessions allocated. The figure increased to 521 units in 1984 and 575 in 1992. Most of the concessions were given to the 'officially' private sector. The disposal of forest concessions in principle was governed by political 'competence' (for example, connection), instead of managerial competence. In granting the concessions there has been an intention to reward key (retired and active) military officers[20] and politicians who have demonstrated loyalty to the President.[21] Many of the concession holders, not surprisingly, merely act as rent seekers, leaving the exploitation of the forest to mostly historically-known dedicated businessmen of Chinese decent. From a developmental state point of view, this indicates the failure of the state to discipline itself, or the abuse of its autonomy. The fact that the state's bureaucracy was weak is obvious from the following observation.

First, until very recently the regulation of selective cutting designed to ensure the sustainability of exploitation was not implemented with rigour, and therefore sustainability of forest exploitation has been very loosely controlled by the existing bureaucratic process. Even though by 1978 there were 382 units of concessions being granted and many of the concession holders have been engaged in exploitation for almost a decade, not many of them had complied with their contract to the state to establish forest-based industries. In that year, there were only 121 sawmills and 19 plywood mills. This implies that the day-to-day bureaucratic control largely failed to direct the growth of forest-based industries. It was not until the boom of log exports in late 1970s a hard push was taken for bolstering forestry industrialisation. This means, instead of the state creating a favourable condition for promoting forestry industrialisation, the state was not seriously pursing it until favourable conditions emerged. In 1980 the government decided to embark on gradual ban of log exports over five year period. It was a political decision to push industrialisation, and not institutional strengthening or reorientation which have driven change. Through this measure, the number of sawmills were doubled from 188 units in 1980 into 331 in 1986, and the number of plywood mills tripled from 29 to 111 in the same

[20] R.Robison, *Indonesia: The Rise of Capital*, Asian Studies Association of Australia, North Sydney, 1986, p.254.

[21] R.Broad, 'The Political Economy of Natural Resources: Case Studies of the Indonesian and Philippine Forest Sector', *Journal of Developing Areas*, April 1995, p.323.

period.[22] Nonetheless, since many concession holders were not managerially competent for forestry industrialisation, this policy inevitably speeded up the process conglomeration. The rent seeker (retired) officials holding concessionary rights preferred to sell the company out rather than commit to forestry industrial development. Such a selling out, however, does not imply that the link between concessions holders and the core of political power within the state was terminated. For the sake of protecting their economic interests the tiny minority of Chinese-decent of businessmen have had to establish some type of linkage. Their relative power vis a vis regular bureaucratic control has been getting even stronger as the forestry-business community formed an industrial cartel which unites the entire chains of forest-based industries, organised under an organisational umbrella of the Indonesian Forestry Community.

Secondly, political connections between concessionary right holders and key actors within the state makes bureaucratic control run by the MoF highly deficient, even for optimising rent for the state. Gillis's calculation of the share of rent during the period of 1979-1982 uncovered that the government only managed to get between 31% to 52% of the available rent. '... forest revenue system collected only US$1.6 billion of a potential aggregate rent of $4.4 billion. The remaining $2.8 billion was left as private profit or absorbed in pay-offs to various authority.'[23] The weaknesses also manifests itself in the inadequacy of manpower and financial resources for exercising bureaucratic control. In conducting its bureaucratic supervisory role the MoF's staff has been dependent on concessionaires for field data and logistic and information. Even though that inadequacy has been gradually overcome, this has not necessarily meant the strengthening of the MoF's institutional basis, given the expansion of relative power of the conglomerating concessionaires' businesses. The decision making process governing economic and ecological resources, to a large extent, has been beyond the state's bureaucratic control supposedly undertaken by organization units within the MoF. In exercising bureaucratic control over forest resources the MoF has acted – according to King – as landlord, despite its deficiency.[24]

The proponents of the developmental state argue that one of ways the state is involved, is to help the emergence of capitalist groups. Given the weakness of the state's bureaucratic control, capitalist groups have emerged from the concessionaire scheme initiated by the state. The accumulation of concessionaire's profit from the highly lucrative business of forest harvesting has meant the formation of a small enclave of economic power within the forestry business community. The increasing number of concession units were accompanied by the increasing merger of companies holding forest concessions. As of 1991, fifteen larger merged companies were harvesting 38% (23.4 million ha out of 61.7 million ha) land disbursed for concessionaires

[22] P.T.Herzal Agrokarya Pratama, *Industri Kehutanan di Indonesia* [Forestry Industry in Indonesia], Jakarta 1991, p.8.

[23] M.Gillis, 'Indonesia', in R.Repetto (ed), *The Forest for the Tree?*, World Resource Institute, Washington, 1988, p.43.

[24] D.Y.King, 'The Political Economy of Forest Sector Reform in Indonesia', *Journal of Environment & Development*, 1996.

operation. Three of the largest private concessions were operating at some 23 to 27 times of the average size of a concessionaire's plot. King's personal communication with the MoF's official in 1994 even suggests that the fifteen largest concessionaires are conglomerates holding 55% unit of the concessions.[25]

Not every sectoral ministry has already established organizational unit for handling sectoral environmental affairs, but the division of works within the MoF represents its dual responsibility. The exploitation interest is manifested in the establishment of the Directorate General of Forest Production, and the responsibility of conserving forest resources manifested in the directorate General for Forest Conservation and Nature Protection, and the Directorate General of Conservation Regreening and land Rehabilitation. In addition there is another Directorate General responsible for Inventory and Forest Land Use. From a bureaucratic point of view, these institutional arrangements are the basis for the developmental role of the state. This organisational expression of state's dual responsibility in handling forest resources, however, is insufficient for guaranteeing sustainable forest management.

The predominance of extra-bureaucratic political processes in handling forest resources has led to the attribution to the political community in this sector of the title of a 'state within the state'.[26] A political joke in Indonesia attributes to Bob Hasan's office – the chairman of the Indonesian Forestry Community – the title of 'the office of the Ministry of Forestry'. These anecdotes express the dysfunction of the bureaucracy as formal institution for governing forest resources. This does not always mean that the pursuance of policy goals has always failed because there is also evidence that informal mechanisms are also being used for achieving official goals. But there is one thing that is certain, commitments to official goals depend on the will of private actors, and not depend on what has already been legally established.

Having established the point that political processes within the state have both formal and informal features, it is interesting to look back at the format of environmental institutions. As I have mentioned earlier, the Ministry of Forestry is the one which already established environmental agencies for serving the state's responsibility in conserving and preserving forest resources. Even so, the state's activities in the forestry sector indicates that both the agency looking after of forest exploitation and forest conservation are unable to act decisively according to officially established bureaucratic operating procedures. The pervasiveness of extra-bureaucratic based decision making permitted by the patrimonial political system makes bureaucratic control overloaded with political processes beyond the power of the bureaucrats to handle, and hence, subject to manipulation. Establishing environmental institutions in sectoral ministries appears to be

---

[25] King, *op cit*, p.224.

[26] W.Ascher, *Political Economy and Problematic Forestry Policy in Indonesia: Obstacle to Incorporating Sound Economics and Science*, Centre for Tropical Conservation, Duke University, July 1993.

insufficient for handling sectoral environmental affairs. In other words, the drive for environmental institution development should be sought from an extra-bureaucratic politics.

The prolonged 'soft' treatment to concession holders was terminated in 1993, signified by the assignment of an uneasily compromising minister, Djamaloedin Soerjohadikoesoemo. This indicates that individual incumbent do count in reshaping institutional performance. From an institutional point of view, this represents the President's commitment to sound forest management since the appointment is autonomously decided by the President. Moreover, the ability of this new minister to strengthen bureaucratic control over forest exploitation was made possible by the improvement of the bureaucratic infrastructure. The remote sensing feature of each concessions was just made available. Moreover, the early 1990s are strategic since most of the twenty year terms of concessionary right are end, and subject to scrutiny for renewal. Not to renew concessionaire's rights, is a safe policy turn in that it does not invoke a sense of withdrawal of political reward. The super profits from the first harvest have been given anyway. Nonetheless, not to renew concessions for another, at least, twenty years opens the opportunity to alter the management of the forest. Given the pervasiveness of poor management of the concessions many of them are not eligible for renewal. More than two hundred units of concessions have been denied renewal. The number will very likely increase since many more are waiting for renewal. The tragedy is that most of them then go to the state enterprises's management, the Inhutani. I consider it tragic because not only the state have not been on financial sense fairly compensated from the implementation of concessions scheme, it eventually had to take responsibility for restoring the badly exploited forest.

In summing up the illustration, the disposal of concessionary rights indicates the dependency of the state on the initial capital to launch forest exploitation. It essentially opened up the use of public resources to private interests, which historically justified as a short cut to transform natural resources capital into badly needed financial capital. The problem is that the bureaucratic dependence of the state on the privately controlled concessions has been prolonged and exacerbated by the predatory behaviour of the state's apparatus. The activities of concessionaires has been very much loosely controlled by the state's bureaucracy. Even though financial capital has been made available from log exports, the ability of the state to control these did not match the scale of activities of exploitation and the cumulative power of the concessionaires from the use of public resources. Not only does the state continue to depend on concessionaires, the relative autonomy of the state is not improved since the accumulated profits of the concessionaires has allowed them to strengthen their economic power vis a vis the state. Forestry experts are mostly confident that if the concessionaires perform their contract with the state and if the bureaucratic control is effectively implemented, the forest land under concessionaires's management will be ready for another cycle of harvest. There is a paradox in the forestry bureaucracy. The lucrativeness of the forest exploitation made it not difficult to make a great deal contribution to economic restoration and progress described earlier. It is also the lucrativeness of the exploitation which drives the trouble in policy implementation. Applied in a resource-based economy like Indonesia, the developmental state proposition creates a danger of exaggerating the institutional strength of the state.

Prospect

The relative strength of the state's bureaucracy is not something we can take for granted. This is especially so where its relative strength is primarily due to the weakness of societal control, and where political culture is not sensitive to public-private distinction. Predatory behaviour in the highly lucrative natural resources extraction (including oil) industries may remain un-checked by the state's bureaucracy because of the institutionalisation of patrimonial political culture. Institutions work differently in different cultural contexts, and state strength by itself has little correlation with economic and social performance.[27]

The seemingly good developmental state performance in the forestry sector in fact is not so much the result of the appropriateness of the state in choosing a certain kind of involvement, as it's proponent would argue, but largely due to the resource rich nature of the forest. The state has not only transformed forest resources into financial capital but also created a small group of capitalists, upon whom the dream of developing the forest industry rest on. Form a developmental point of view there is nothing wrong about it as far as it is under the state's control, directly or indirectly. The share of forest products to total exports was only 5.8%, as of 1985. The figure is much higher (21.7%) if the major commodities, oil and gas, were excluded. By 1991, the share of forest product to total exports reached 13%, and if oil and gas commodities are excluded the figure becomes 23%. The state is proud to have boost the non oil-and-gas exports, however given the foreseeable exhaustion of those commodities, it implies the appreciation of the contribution forestry capitalist group.This pride, however, is only one side of the story because a new environmental threat has escalated. The boost of forestry industrialisation in the first half of 1980s has eventually creating over capacitated installations, implies a shortage of input or demand for extending forest trees cutting. Given the lucrativeness of forest exploitation, the state in fact always has looked for way to end its dependency on societal capitalist power that it has by itself created.

From the above illustration, it is obvious that the move toward a more stringent bureaucratic control has always been waiting for a good timing or favourable conditions. Any attempt to strengthen bureaucratic control has to bear the political and economic instability it may cause. The embedded political- economic interest in forest management has determined the pace of institutional development. The prospect of environmental institutions, therefore, is not only dependent on availability of bureaucratic infrastructure such as information, adequate budget, sufficient personal, but

[27] Clark & Chan, *op cit*, p.352.

also dependent on the ability of taking advantage of favourable economic performance to advance environmental institutions. The ability to invoke the ecological precautionary principle,[28] is highly dependent on the ability of giving assurance of a political-economic precautionary principle, including the minimal disturbance to the privileged group. Institutional development of environmental agencies within the state, under the current political setting, is inevitably slow. Moreover, its potential development is threatened by the accumulation of relative power of the privileged group, as well as by the accumulation of environmental and resource depletion. The cumulative impact of environmental and resource depletion, in turn, undermined the desire to institutionalise pro-active responses since much of the currently limited bureaucratic resources are inevitably devoted to curative problem solving.

The move toward more stringent bureaucratic control, including strengthening state enterprises, sounds positive. This, however – as King has rightly criticized – is far too inadequate.[29] Given the prolonged dysfunctional nature of bureaucratic control which is the outcome of the political economic constellation, confining reform to the bureaucratic level merely indicates the persistence of the incapacity of the state. There is enough reason to suspect that a commitment to strengthening state's bureaucratic control tend not to reach a political decision to reform patrimonial politics. It is also reasonable to suspect that the bureaucratic solution become a good camouflage to deflect attention to privileging process under patrimonial politics. There are some initiatives of the state to protect the privileging scheme of forest allocation by way of launching welfare programs to local communities. These programs are politically compensating the relative deprivation of local communities by the forest exploitation regime. On of them is obliges every concessionaire to establish community development programs bureaucratically subjected to annual review. Other than attempting to improve the welfare of the local community, the program also intends to decrease dependency of local people on forest resource, implying minimisation disturbance in the concessionaires land generated by local pressure over forest resources.

From an organisational point of view, Indonesia's choice to institutionalise environmental control by reorienting the existing bureaucracy apparently is not easy to bring about. Even though bureaucratic units for forest conservation and nature protection have been established, they have much less say in ensuring the sustainability of exploitation of production forest area. Only very recently the MoF launched a conservation program in production forest are. In translating the dual responsibility of the state in managing the forest, the existing organisational arrangement has framed territorial division of responsibility between production unit and conservation unit. This division overlooks the importance of reorienting bureaucratic control over forest production toward a sustainable development. Struggle

---

[28] A.Jordan & T.O'Riordan, 'The Precautionary Principle in UK Environmental Law and Policy', in T.S.Gray (ed), *op cit*, pp.57-84.

[29] King, *op cit*, pp.229-231.

for sustainable forest management for so long has been confined on conservation area, which even tough consistently expanding its management remain suffers from the wider problem under-finance and under-staff. In other words, the establishment of an environmental unit within the MoF has not automatically advance the environmental orientation of its counterpart in the production unit. Ironically, the availability of environmental unit within the MoF is a good justification for asserting sectoral autonomy in handling environmental issue. Environmental reorientation process undertaken from other ministry, namely the state ministry responsible for environmental issue, even more difficult given the lack of leverage.

There is a paradox in the developing organisational basis for environmental reorientation of the bureaucracy. The advocacy of the state ministry responsible for environmental policy within the existing highly-sectoralised organisational arrangement has a shallow leverage. For deepening it, an organisational basis within each sectoral bureaucracy is preferable. The experience of forestry management shows that establishing an environmental unit within a ministry can cause a further divorcing the environmental from developmental purposes, and therefore failed to accomplish the mission of reorienting the exploitation process. The prospect of the state's self-reorientation is even bleaker as societal pressure is highly unarticulated. For building a winning advocacy coalition in favour of sustainability, the inter-agency power relationship is a determining factor. However, this is precisely the thing that the developmental state of Indonesia has attempted to avoid.

Conclusion

Institutional tensions arose from policy intention of pursuing sustainable development, as it appears from Indonesia's experience, is not easily mediated without compromising environmental concern. The lacking of theoretical explanation within the developmental state has made in inadequate to explain the difficulty of ensuring the developmental state operate under principles of sustainability.

As one of the least spectacular developmental states, Indonesia has been choosing to reorient its bureaucracy, instead of developing a coherent unit of bureaucracy responsible for ensuring the sustainability of the development process. By examining inter-organisational interaction, in the light of the advancement of the developmental process, it turns out that there is no such thing as a self-reorientation within the state. For advancing environmental discourse and accommodating international pressures the state allows an inter-organisational environmental advocacy to take place, yet the agency in charge of running advocacy is not sufficiently backed-up by bureaucratic and political resources. The prospects of environmental institutions are bleak, unless political back-up is provided.

Comparative Local Government

J.A.Chandler
Sheffield Hallam University

'The Liberal Roots of Intergovernmental Relations in Britain and the USA'

Introduction

Despite concern over the globalisation of culture with the spectre of high streets from Inverness to San Diego lined with McDonalds and Pizza Huts there remains a discernible nationalism within many areas of intellectual debate within the United States and Britain. Rhodes[1] observes 'British Public Administration is insular, a quality it shares with its American counterpart, but it is also unreflective' whilst Pollitt considers that

> 'the cultural bias in UK public administration remains profoundly anglophile ... on the whole, the textual identity of UK public administration is still more that of a North American satellite than of a European core state.'[2]

Local government in general, and the study of inter-governmental relations in particular, appears to be an arena where these tendencies are evident. With the important exception of Marxist theory, British grown theory on inter-governmental relations seems confined largely to Britain. Although, as Pollitt suggests, there are considerable borrowings from United States such appropriation is often used in Britain for rather different ends than in the originating Nation.

It will be argued in this paper that divergence in theoretical approaches to the study of intergovernmental relations in Britain and the United States are a consequence of a frequently overlooked difference between the two Nations in the development of the liberal-democratic theory that supposedly unites the two regimes. Although of crucial importance to the intellectual development of public administration in the two countries, it will be suggested that the importance of the diverging views on liberalism tend to be overlooked in recent British theory which shuffles off this area of concern into what is seen as the pensionable category of traditional-institutional historical studies.

Classifying approaches

The study of Intergovernmental relations in Britain has over the last thirty years been much given to differing theoretical interpretations. Following a

[1] R.Rhodes, 'From institutions to dogma: Tradition, eclecticism and ideology in the study of British public administration', *Public Administration Review*, 56/6, 1996, p.507.

[2] C.Pollitt, 'Antistatist reforms and new administrative directions: public administration in the United Kingdom', *Public Administration Review*, 56/1, 1996, p.86.

more generalised model of Rhodes,[3] Stoker[4] has classified these approaches from a British context into *institutional-historical; organisation theory; rational choice;* and *Marxist.*

Classifying approaches to the understanding of intergovernmental relations in the United States through a British taxonomy must, however, be pursued only with caution. Much analysis of sub-national government in the United States places less emphasis on intergovernmental issues which do not generally form as strong a focus as in Britain even though the federal system would appear to make this arena a far richer and more complex issue than afforded within the British centralised state. There has been no equivalent to the two Research Council funded initiatives in this sector in America where, in contrast, the Advisory Commission on Intergovernmental Relations has been wound up.

American literature retains a far greater interest in the issues of policy determination and performance with much concern devoted to measuring the output of governments. Community power also, remains a central element in United States writing on sub-national government, often as up dated regime theory, aimed at understanding power relations within the city related to issues of equality, pluralism and elitism. These are issues that have had an important impact on British research in the 1960s and early 1970s but are currently far from fashionable approaches to the analysis of local government. Analysis of intergovernmental issues in the United States are, therefore, frequently embedded in studies that have a rather different focus than that relationship and the following comparison, in general, compares British studies that concentrate predominantly on intergovernmental relations with United States studies where this is a more incidental theme.

Traditional approaches

For much of this century understanding central-local relations in Britain has been placed in a category of historical interpretation of institutional change. This approach which can be characterised by the work of the Webbs and later Herman Finer, Robson and Griffiths is argued to involve a 'distaste for theory; incorporation of ethical ideas; and a predilection for social engineering'.[5]

It is not, however, a wholly outdated approach. Bulpitt's[6] work in the 1980s depicting the historical and social context of central-local relations is sagaciously seen by Stoker as a high point in this genre.[7]

The traditional approach has been criticised for neglecting the informal

[3] R.Rhodes, 'Theory and methods in British public administration: the view from political science', *Political Studies*, 39/3, 1991.

[4] G.Stoker, 'Intergovernmental relations', *Public Administration*, 73/1, 1995.

[5] R.Rhodes, *op cit*, 1991, p.538.

[6] J.Bulpitt, *Territory and Power in the United Kingdom*, Manchester University Press, 1983; J.Bulpitt, 'The discipline of the new democracy: Mrs Thatcher's domestic statecraft', *Political Studies*, 34/1, 1986.

[7] G.Stoker, *op cit*, p.102.

links that bind local and central governments, for undervaluing the resources held by local governments and the problems faced by a government seeking to implement a policy through the medium of reluctant agents.[8] More broadly the 'traditional' public administration approach is seen as an eclectic methodology that is lacking in rigour and hence a complete and rounded appreciation of the factors affecting the intergovernmental relationship.

The 'traditional' approach in Britain can be paralleled by the mainstream of many studies of Federalism and local government in the United States where a more historical approach still informs much recent literature. Traditional text books on sub-national government in the United States frequently identify a number of historical stages in the development of federalism and there are also well established but basic models describing the nature of inter-governmental relations.[9]

These range from the obsolete dual federal view that suggests each layer of government is sovereign within its assigned constitutional sphere, through models expressing interdependence suggested by Grodzin's[10] marble cake model to creative and new federalism and Sanford's[11] characterisation of the relationship as three individuals in a rowing boat capable of progress through working together or inertia if they fail to act in accord. This historical, developmental approach continues as shall be indicated later, as an aspect of more recent approaches to sub-national government in, for example, regime theory.

Organisational theory

From the late 1970s the traditional institutional/legal approach to central-local relations in Britain is argued to have been largely replaced as the mainstream methodology by the development of organisational theory. The new focus concentrated not so much on formal institutions but on the informal relationships between the protagonists in central-local relations and considered not so much the legal aspects of the debate but the balance of power and authority, whether overt or concealed, between conflicting or collaborating interests. A central concern of the approach lies in unravelling the extent to which one sector of the governmental network can exert power and influence over the other and hence arguments using these models tend to revolve around the issue of whether local governments have discretion or are predominantly dominated by some other nexus of power. The power dependence model developed by Rhodes maintains that the relationship is based on an exchange of resources in which neither the centre nor localities prevail.[12] Whilst no one side is usually dominant in the exchange of

---

[8] G.Stoker, *op cit*, pp.103-4.

[9] D.Nice, *Federalism: The Politics of Intergovernmental Relations*, St Martin's Press, 1987.

[10] M.Grodzins, *The American System*, Rand McNally, 1966.

[11] T.Sanford, *Storm over the States*, McGraw-Hill, 1967.

[12] R.Rhodes, *Control and Power in Central-Local Relations*, Gower, 1981; R.Rhodes, *Beyond Westminster and Whitehall: the sub-central governments of Britain*, Allen & Unwin, 1988.

resources the centre had, however, a significant resource in its capacity to change the rules of the game.

The complexity of political relationships suggested by the power dependency model can be subsumed in the wider framework of network and policy community theory which perceives formal and informal decision making organisations operating within a network of complex relationships which may have sufficient stability to become a significant nexus, a policy community, within an arena of decision making. Intergovernmental relations is composed of the network of relationships between centre and locality and between local units that form into a number of policy communities that have significant influence over the process.

There was a significant move towards the use of organisational theory in the United States at the same time as this approach was becoming central to the debates in Britain. The most prominent of these models first published in 1978 is that of Deil Wright who did much to popularise the term 'inter- governmental relations' within academic discourse.[13] Wright values 'inter-governmental relations' rather than federalism to describe national and sub-national governmental interaction as a less legalistic term that can analyse informal as well as formal relationships and more clearly embrace local as well as state governments. He perceives the various spheres of government in the United States as being interlinked in many, although not all, of their actions and depicts the possible combination of relations through overlapping Venn circles.[14]

The inter-linking structures of the United States system of national-local government ensures that the power of each unit is limited as each structure is, to some extent interdependent and, in a perception reflected in the Rhodes power-dependence model, characterised by 'bargaining and exchange relationships and co-operation and competition'.[15]

Network theory, whilst not as overtly evident in United States studies of central-local relations emerges particularly through the regime theory which is predominantly a development of community power studies. Stone's study of power in the city of Atlanta concerns itself with

> 'the informal arrangements by which public bodies and private interests function together in order to make and carry out governing decisions.[16] These governing decisions, I want to emphasize, are not a matter of running and controlling everything. They have to do with managing conflict and making adaptive responses to social change.'[17]

In effect Stone recognises unofficial co-operative groups that determine the policies and stability of the political system that are akin to the idea of

[13] D.Wright, *Understanding Intergovernmental Relations*, 2nd edition, Brooks/Cole, 1982.

[14] *Ibid*, p.29.

[15] *Ibid*, p.40.

[16] C.Stone, *Regime Politics: Governing Atlanta*, Kansas University Press, 1989.

[17] *Ibid*, p.6.

policy communities. Stone and other regime theorists[18] use this insight to unravel the politics of large cities and, whilst adaptable to intergovernmental relations,[19] the role of other formal governments in the local political process is seen as but a further influence on urban politics and not a central issue in itself. The analysis also has considerable depth in that regime studies have a dynamic edge in seeking to understand stability and change in the informal relationships that underlie the governance of a polity and many studies, such as that of Stone on Atlanta, have an historical socio-economic edge.

The lack of more explicit development of organisational, power dependence and network theory in the United States is, perhaps, a reflection that these approaches on their own are limited in their power to explain the development or stability of a political relationship. Organisational theories in themselves lack a powerful means of explaining the relationships that they can often excellently describe. The theory can lead to insights into how organisations relate to one another and at any given time the resources they can marshal in pursuit of their interests. The analysis does not, however, provide insight into what these interests may be and how they emerged and developed. A power dependence model says nothing of motives and values.

Public choice and the new right

Although organisational theory has the appearance of normative neutrality, the two other major theoretical tendencies identified by Rhodes and Stoker relating to inter-governmental analysis, Marxism and public choice theory, carry a considerable weight of ideological sentiment. Within the United States the impact of public choice theory has more generally been to defend rather than denigrate the local government systems. Tiebout's early study suggesting efficiency gains from citizen mobility to localities that offer the best utility for tax payers money, promoted the value of urban conurbations composed of small competitive local governments.[20] This view has more recently been developed by Bish and the Ostroms who argue that greater individual freedom is achieved in a flexible local government system made of several generally community based jurisdictions that are allowed to establish the optimum method of co-operating with one another.[21]

In contrast, in Britain, public choice theory has been used by central Government and its advisors to increase the size of units of local government and shift their powers from the public to the private sector.[22]

---

[18] For example, S.Elkin, *City and Regime in the American Republic*, University of Chicago Press, 1987.

[19] F.Huizenga, 'Regime analysis: A rule based method for studying institutions', *Administration & Society*, 27/3, 1995.

[20] .Tiebout, 'A pure theory of local expenditures', *Journal of Political Economy*, 64, October, 1956.

[21] V.Ostrom et al, *Local Government in the United States*, Institute of Contemporary Studies Press, 1988.

[22] J.Chandler, 'Public choice and local government reform; Contrasts between Britain and the United States', in P.Dunleavy & J.Stanyer (eds), *Contemporary Political Studies 1994*, Political Studies Association, 1994.

Local government is viewed by British enthusiasts of new right values not as a means of securing individual freedom but as monopolistic state agencies that will consequently be prone to increase in size over and above their functional value and become agencies that are parasitic on the tax paying citizen.[23] The role of central government must be to check the excesses of local government. The theory, therefore, suggests a probable conflict of interest between central and local government for resources and depicts the central-local relationship as one of continual conflict.

Academic enthusiasm for adapting Niskanen's model of bureaucracy to central-local relations in Britain is further curtailed by Dunleavy's critique of the theory and the development of the bureau shaping model to explain the readiness of civil servants to accept the privatisation and decentralisation of central government.[24] The theory has for Britain some considerable explanatory power. As is observed below, the role of local government in Britain is seen, as J.S. Mill observed, as a basis for implementing the details of policy at the local level rather than determining matters of principle. Bureau shaping in the growth of government in the 19th century prompted senior civil servants and politicians to cast local government as a convenient means of securing local implementation of centrally determined polices. Given their situation local councillors and officers were seen as lesser and subordinate agents within the governmental hierarchy whose rewards should not amount to those enjoyed by actors at the centre.

State and Marxist theory

Whilst diverging use has been made of public choice theory, there appears to be far greater convergence between United States and British analysts following a broadly Marxist agenda. During the late 70s and early 80s, when Thatcherism was striving for dominance over a radicalised left in Britain, the Marxist approach gained considerable support and popularity. There had been a long established view among Marxists that local government was predominantly an instrument of the State and, as such, was either a direct means of securing legitimacy for the ruling class or securing proletarian compliance through repression. This view was primarily at the root of one of the earlier essays in the revival of Marxist analysis, Cockburn's *The Local State* which attempts to demonstrate that even an initially left inclined local authority is obliged by the nature of capital to suppress agitation for more egalitarian policies.[25] This analysis remains a strong text through the simplicity of its argument despite the development of a number of far more sophisticated Marxist interpretations of the role of local government within the British polity.

The most influential essays in the genre came from the popularising of European Marxist thought and in particular the theories on urban government developed by Castells and translated by Dunleavy in *Urban Political*

[23] M.Pirie, *Blueprint for a Revolution*, Adam Smith Institute, 1992.

[24] P.Dunleavy, *Democracy, Bureaucracy and Public Choice*, Prentice Hall, 1991.

[25] C.Cockburn, *The Local State*, Pluto Press, 1977.

Analysis into a British context.[26] The theory argues that local government has a major role in the welfare state and, therefore, serves capital as a means of securing the replication of labour. This view was then taken further by Saunders in his now rather eclipsed dual state hypothesis.[27]

A further major essay in this direction was Duncan and Goodwin's The Local State and Uneven Development.[28] Studies by Stoker among others on post-Fordism whilst not so pointedly accepting Marxist values also suggest that privatisation, managerialism and the restructuring of local government is an attempt by the central State to remodel the administrative system to secure more efficient means of production under the developing conditions of new technology.[29]

Marxist analysis has also played a not dissimilar role in the study of intergovernmental relations in the United States although it is probably less in the mainstream of central-local analysis than in Britain. There are several studies that analyse the autonomy of city governments is terms of the interests of capital and in pushing this avenue they also draw greatly on the same literature that informs British studies within this genre. Thus work by Katznelson or Harvey refers to and develops ideas from seminal Marxist urban analysts such as Castells or Lefebvre. It is also possible to establish fully comparative transatlantic studies in the genre such as the study by Gurr and King on urban development.[30] However, the rise of interest in new-right applications has tended to eclipse further work in this genre.

Liberal theory

Divergences in the approaches to inter-governmental relations in both Great Britain and America cannot simply be explained by writers on either side of the Atlantic being inspired by different thoughts but rest, arguably, on long established attitudes to local government within the two countries that have been encapsulated in much of the pre-1970s 'traditional' literature on the subject. The central value that informs and also divides orthodox approaches to local government in Britain and the United States is liberalism in its several forms.

Within the United States liberal values achieved a dominant status in the founding of the constitution and in the structuring of the political and sub-national systems of their earlier member States. Whilst there was much debate about the extent to which individual liberty could be practically achieved within a political system, there were few dissenters in the late 18th century to the view that personal freedom was desirable and whilst government regulation was necessary to prevent threats to liberty, there

---

[26] P.Dunleavy, *Urban Political Analysis*, Macmillan, 1980.

[27] P.Saunders, *Social Theory and the Urban Question*, Hutchinson, 1981.

[28] S.Duncan & M.Goodwin, *The Local State and Uneven Development*, Polity Press, 1988.

[29] G.Stoker, 'Creating a local government for a post-Fordist society', *in J.Stewart & G.Stoker (eds), The Future of Local Government*, Macmillan, 1989.

[30] T.Gurr & D.King, *The State and the City*, Macmillan, 1987.

was also a serious danger that an organised protective state was as great a threat to liberty and personal self-interest. Thus, the Federalist constitution ensured that governments had limited powers subject to checks and balances which included the balancing of States and Federal government within the constitution. Below the State level local governments became by the 19th century subject to the principle of ultra-vires in relation to State legislatures but the ethos of liberty also ensured that State governments regulated localities largely to ensure they did not tax individuals too heavily rather than set out detailed instructions as to the level of services and standards that they were to provide. Many States bequeathed powers of general competence upon their local governments.

The liberal values that sustained the network of sub-national government in the United States is most classically articulated in the writings of De Tocqueville who is still much quoted in current American writing as a fountain of wisdom on the balance between centre and locality.[31] De Tocqueville perceived the New England township as the closest ideal of liberal democracy where all citizens in a close knit community could come together and jointly determine the policies that affected them. The State or Federal government should only intervene on matters that greatly influence others outside the self sufficient community. These attitudes have, in part, ensured that local governments in the United States have robustly avoided reforms that increase the size and decrease the number of smaller cities so that the sub-national system at least in the Eastern seaboard looks not unlike the pattern established 200 years earlier.

Given the strength of demands for modernising the system arising from economic theories of management of scale and left wing reactions to the widespread inequalities that the unreformed structure harbours, the De Tocqueville liberal ethos that sustains much thinking and action in American central-local relations is still a very powerful force that is now much reinforced and modernised by the addition of certain aspects of public choice theory

British liberalism

British local government has also been greatly sustained by a liberal tradition although socio-economic circumstances in the late 18th and early 19th century have shaped this value into a far more complex and contradictory set of beliefs. Liberalism as a movement to free individual enterprise so as to ensure capital formation was as powerful pressure on the growth of the British polity as that of the United States and many early British liberals from Bentham to Tom Paine helped sustain the values of liberalism in the United States as much as in Britain.

British liberals were not, however, pushing at an open door, unlike their American counterparts once they had seen off the British monarchic colonialism. English liberals had their own wars of independence to fight against

[31] T.Dye, *Politics in States and Communities*, 3rd edition, Prentice Hall, 1977, pp.31-2; A.Syed, *The Political Theory of American Local Government*, Random House, 1966.

an entrenched political system based on the wealth of the landed aristocracy supported by the lesser ranks of the landowning squirearchy. Through the system of Lord Lieutenant, and Justice of the Peace, the landed interest could keep check on the local government of parishes and increasingly the chartered towns whose sometime democratic system, had long fallen into decay. Within the growing new industrial cities the retention of an older agrarian or craft based government prevented wealthy industrialists from maintaining organised control over the growing cities that sustained their industries. The whole system was finally intermixed with the national system for selecting the members of Parliament and the House of Lords who were the beneficiaries of the structure.

Following the Liberal breakthrough in 1832 it was, therefore, hardly surprising that among the most important subsequent reforms was the modernisation of British local government. The 1835 municipal reform act ensured that liberal industrialists could shape the industrial towns to suit the needs of industrial growth whilst the Poor Law Reform amendment laid down the means of breaking the role of parish government and restraining the activities of local magnates through central, and if Chadwick could have had his way, liberal bureaucratic inspection and control.

The values that drove the British liberals to forge larger units of local government that became increasingly subject to central controls are reflected at their most extreme in the ideas of Bentham whose ideal constitution required local administration not government with each layer of the system subject to a higher control of the democratically elected Parliament armed with the sole power to establish the general principles to be applied uniformly throughout the Nation. The zeal of Bentham was put into more practical form by J.S. Mill whose idea of central-local relations remains the most dominant and defining view in the British official mind and also that of many academic commentators. Mill saw a role for local government to ensure political participation and education but most importantly the role of local government was to secure the efficient implementation of principles determined by the much wiser counsels of the national parliament by the less capable, but on local matters alone, more knowledgeable local councillor. Despite a logic concerning individual freedom in Liberty that points Mill in the direction of the idea of subsidiarity and De Tocqueville, Mill could not escape reverting to the need for central government to have the power to shape and supervise localities.[32]

The development of liberal values in Britain into a far more reformist and less libertarian strand than in the United States is a consequence of the difficulty faced by many revolutionaries seeking a more open and egalitarian society. Liberals in Britain had to undermine the old order of traditional Tory and adullamite Whig values and could not secure this goal in the rural areas except by breaking the hold of the magistery over the system through the creation of larger centrally inspected units whilst in the cities, because gains could be reversed in a reactionary Parliament, it was quickly essential

[32] J.Chandler, 'The liberal justification of local government: Values and administrative expediency', *Political Studies*, 37/4, 1989.

to mould urban politics into a pattern that would be difficult to overturn by a Conservative regime. However, by the early 20th century the best interests of the most libertarian liberal minds in Britain had succumbed to siren voices or power that had lured Robespierre, Napoleon, Lenin, Stalin and many other lesser revolutionaries into despotism. Once the state bureaucracy had secured control over local administration, they were not willing to surrender the reins of power and, with minds that doubted the wisdom of the liberated masses, sought to retain the powers that would secure their domination over the system.

Mill's view was a reflection of attitudes forming in the mind of most liberals, progressive conservatives and above all the post-Northcote Trevelyan liberal minded Civil Servants. Indeed, from this august and austere grouping have derived an early 20th Century tradition of public sector exegesis that, in relation to local government include, Redlich & Hirst, the Webbs, Herman Finer and W.A.Robson. George Jones, John Stewart and Jim Bulpitt perhaps remain as latter day exponents of this tradition.

British liberals, unlike their United States counterparts, had indeed much to fear from the forces of reaction who established in the 19th Century a modernised aristocratic paternalist view of local government that still has some occasional resonance in current writing. In the 1830s the redoubtable Toulmin Smith romanticised parish government as the haven of order and prosperity as beneficent squires sought the welfare of their close and co-operative communities. His zeal helped ensure that Parliament rather than the bureaucracy retained the levels of control of the newly shaped rural agencies of local government. The latter discovery of German romantic thought brought a more refined philosophical justification for small decentralised autocratic local governance through writers such as Gneisst who sparked off Redlich and Hirst's powerful justification for the British liberal system of local governance.[33]

Later on this tradition is found in the controversy sparked off by Langrod in Public Administration.[34] If one should think that this set of beliefs is wholly defunct, it could be suggested that the rekindling in the 1980s of interest in citizenship and customer care, particularly in the works of Stewart and Clarke, is an awakening of these much submerged appeals to local government based on an ethos of Gemeinschaft.[35]

Conclusion

It can be suggested that many aspects of the methodological differences that divide British and United States studies of inter-governmental relations can be, at least in part, explained against the background of the different interpretations of liberalism within the two Nations.

[33] J.Redlich & F.Hirst, *Local Government in England*, Macmillan, 1903.

[34] G.Langrod, 'Local government and democracy', *Public Administration*, 31, Spring, 1953.

[35] M.Clarke & J.Stewart, *The choices for local government for the 1990s and beyond*, Longman, 1991; J.Stewart 'A future for Local Authorities as community government' in J.Stewart & G.Stoker (eds), *Local Government in the 1990s*, Macmillan, 1995.

The institutional and social-engineering proclivities that have been discerned in the traditional approach in Britain reflect the elitism of a central polity that had to battle throughout the 19th century against decentralist conservative forces in order to ensure the dominance of liberal values. This necessitated a centralist minded sate which seeks to shape the structure of local government for its own purposes and is content, within a tightly controlled framework in terms of structure and functions of the institutions, to let them pursue the process of local government as best they may.

In the United States, where decentralisation has been ideologically more acceptable and also more prone to controls from within decentralised polities rather than through pressure from above, the concern for institutional and legal regulation was never as strongly engrained in the literature. Interest, has focused far more on the nature of power within polities and the mechanisms for achieving internal regulation which is reflected in community studies and policy analysis.

A major concern of this arrangement is the issue of central-local relations reflecting the concern of the centre to retain its ascendancy over local organisations and administration. This concern when modernised in the 1970s arguably lends itself to an organisational theory approach which, although recognising the process of conflict between centre and locality, does not differ from the traditional approach in its central concern for inter-governmental relations and the connections between the various institutional elements of the State. What organisational theory and network theory provides that is new, or at least more explicitly added to the approach, is the realisation that relationships do not exist solely at the level of formal legal-institutional arrangements but are pursued through informal groupings and by less overt understandings and acknowledgements of the potential authority and power among the many elements in the central-local systems.

The differences in approaches to liberalism may also explain how theorists in the United States adopt rational choice theory for generally very different ends than British practitioners who see the theory as a further basis for continuing a relatively tight central control over local government whilst their American counterparts see the idea as a means of furthering individual liberty. Marxist values are, in contrast, far more antagonistic to the basic assumptions of liberal theory and hence can reject either the British or American variants of this traditional standpoint.

Urban Regimes in Theory and Practice

Kevin Ward
University of Manchester

'Rigourising regime theory'

Acknowledgements

I am grateful to the ESRC for their support for this research (award number R00429434350). Jamie Peck, Adam Tickell, Martin Jones and Adam Holden have all provided academic support and personal encouragement. I remain – of course – responsible for the contents of the paper.

Introduction

In this paper urban regime theory, one of the 'new' theories of the New Urban Politics (NUP) (Cox 1991) is considered to explain the institutional linkages dominating now urban economic development decision-making. A theoretical interrogation of regime theory prefigures its deployment in the city of Leeds, England. Section two sets out urban regime theory's principal features, its relevance in the United Kingdom and the way it illuminates the understanding of the regeneration process. Sections three and four construct a critique of urban regime theory, drawing upon the critical literature that has emerged during the last decade. Section five highlights the empowerment of élites in coalitions and through initiatives, such as the Single Regeneration Budget (SRB), drawing upon research carried out in Leeds. In conclusion, it is argued the Single Regeneration Budget reinforces the fragmentary policies underpinning the British central government's neoliberal agenda, casting doubt over the longevity of any regimes in formation (Bassett 1996). This paper suggests that urban regime theory draws academic attention to agency sensitive explanations of the transformation of governance. For urban regime theory to become a more rigourous conceptual tool, the structurally inscribed actions of the agents engaged in urban economic development should be considered.

Urban regime theory outlined

Urban regime theory places the city within a wider economic, political and spatial context (Mollenkopf 1983; Peterson 1981). In the last decade there has been a growth in research looking at the effects of urban political and economic restructuring (Jessop et al 1997). Urban regime theory pulls together the community-power approach that underpinned research in the United States during the 1950s and 1960s (see Dahl 1961; Hunter1953) but which had reached an academic cul-de-sac and attempts to situate the local economy in a wider political-economic context (see Elkin 1985; Fainstein &

Fainstein 1983). In *Regime Politics*, Stone clearly states the basic tenets of regime theory. Stressing 'the interplay of change and continuity" (Stone 1989, p.6), an urban regime is defined as 'the informal arrangements by which public bodies and private interests function together in order to be able to make and carry out governing decisions" (*ibid*, p.6). The regime forms through this 'meshing of interests', institutions and agents working behind a negotiated agenda. Institutions see it is in their interest to remain within the regime, the alternative being the mobilisation of resources and formation of an opposition regime. This implies that institutions are unwilling, unable or simply not empowered to act unilaterally in activities of urban economic development. That is, the call for inter-organisational organisations, such as coalitions, partnerships or regimes is a specific policy response to a perceived failure (Jessop et al 1997). Underpinning the emphasis placed on business interests is that it is necessary 'to encourage business investment in order to have an economically thriving community" (Stone 1989, p.7). The importance of politics is highlighted through the deployment of discourses of electoral legitimacy, which are used to ensure policies are successfully implemented. At the margin of these two interest groups partisanship leads to a common consensus and regime theory stresses civic cooperation. This cooperation is theorised through Stone's social-production model of urban governance. Here the power of governance is deployed to accomplish particular kinds of outcomes. This is clearly distinguishable from the community power paradigm's social-control model, where the emphasis is on exerting control.

> 'By contrasting social production with social control, ... [it is] emphasised that urban regimes do not involve comprehensive efforts to control local communities or even the belief systems of local publics; influence yes, control no" (*ibid*, p.231).

Regime theorists conceptualise power structures in an almost Foucauldian fashion as alliances, through which governance is purposive and city leaders constructed as goal-oriented agents. In contrast to the community power approach, regime theory posits the form of the power structure is contingent upon the circumstances and the participants of governance. This extends to the analysis of how regimes react to, and are effected by, political, social and economic change, and what affects their ability to survive.

Urban regime studies focus on the major urban areas of the United States and the United Kingdom, analysing power in cities, such as Atlanta, Baltimore and Detroit in the United States and Birmingham in the United Kingdom. Interviewing the urban élite, regime theorists seek to establish how public and private interests are mediated locally. Recent empirical work in the United Kingdom has problematised the existence of urban regimes, taking a step back from the taken-for-grantedness that underpins the bulk of American work (Bassett1996; John & Cole 1996). While progress has been made in the empirical application of regime theory, theoretically there has been a conspicuous silence. Urban regime theory appears to exhibit a number of weaknesses. Some stem from the way the theory was initially conceptualised by academics in the United States, while others originate from the inherent difficulties of transferring theories between different institutional contexts. These difficulties are considered (Jessop et al 1997; Stoker & Mossberger 1994; Ward 1995) and this paper will review these issues.

Problem of application I: Theoretical transfer, American to United Kingdom-style

> 'The mix of participants varies by community, but that mix is itself constrained by the accommodation of two basic institutional principles of the American political economy:
> (1) popular control of the formal machinery of government;
> (2) private ownership of business enterprise" (Stone 1989, p.6, emphasis added).

> 'It is important to point out that local authorities in Britain are more constrained in their ability to undertake local economic development activities than are local governments in most US states" (Wolman & Goldsmith 1992, p.201).

Comparative work has been undertaken by both American and United Kingdom academics. Using concrete studies from both countries to exemplify application, there have also been a small number of positive contributions to unpacking the basics of urban regime theory. Developed during the last five years, this work overlaps with studies still being undertaken on American cities. Taking the form of comparative theoretical analysis (Harding 1994; Stoker & Mossberger 1994; Wood 1996) and case study analysis (Orr & Stoker 1994; Jonas 1997) both tranches sought to identify and apply the main theoretical tenets developed in the United States. Three themes from the United States work are highlighted: regime formation (the processes leading to regime formation), sustenance (how and why regimes form/fail) and 'characteristics' (the outcomes of regimes, which have been identified through the construction of ideal types). Understanding the processes that lead to regime formation and regime sustenance is important if urban regime theory is to be successful applied in the United Kingdom. These highlight the specificity of the United States studies, rendering problematic the application of regime theory in the United Kingdom. It is the mechanisms underpinning the formation of regimes rather than superficially similar concrete outcomes that will provide urban regime analysis with theoretical power.

Although analysis of regime formation does seek to understand why institutions become involved in inter-organisational partnerships, this insight is often neglected, as the focus becomes how regimes manage once in position. Urban regime theorists have used empirical observations to build a classification of characteristics. Digaetano & Klemanski (1993a), for example, break down regime formation into four factors; context (economic conditions that afford opportunity or constrain the regime), formation (those links between coalition building and political orientation), leadership capacity (the formal and informal arrangements for governance) and organisational capacity (the financial and staffing resources that are necessary for strategy implementation). Within the literature two of the central criteria for regime formation are that private resources and the motivation to participate (using those resources) are unevenly distributed (Stone1989; Stone et al1991). The result is that regimes are heterogeneous, within a specific time period (cf Harvey 1989); their configuration attributed to 'urban' forces.

The 'bottom-up' nature of the work carried out in the United States appears to run counter to the urban landscape in the United Kingdom. Where the primacy of local government meant business-led organisations and community groups were not involved in urban economic development, the recasting of the local state over the last fifteen years has undermined this position (see Cochrane 1993; 1997). There are now both local-arms of national organisations active in urban economic development and specific local organisations. A regime's existence and formation in one context and not in another, should be of interest to those academics applying urban regime theory in the United Kingdom This is in contrast to the work in the United States where a regime's existence is taken-for-granted. Regimes are couched as resulting from specific-local circumstances, but circumstances that appear in the majority of American cities. With the United States local state playing a lesser role than its United Kingdom counterpart, so institutional and political- economic spaces exist, within which business-led organisations or private-public partnerships operate. Only in the last two decades has the situation altered in the United Kingdom, to the point where regimes may be beginning to emerge. Yet the situation in the United Kingdom is the outcome of national programmes specific to the United Kingdom. Are regimes able to be successfully created out of such a context, from a different set of institutional circumstances? Stone goes as far to say that,

> 'the creation of a regime from scratch is imaginable but not likely. The cost of co- ordination would be enormous hence the strong relevance of the problem of collective action to formation ... the problem can be solved, but this means that existing collectivities (or better yet, alliances of collectivities) are especially attractive, more so if they, in turn, can contribute resources to the overall task of co-ordination and governance.' (Stone 1989, p.236).

A second issue raised in the United States literature is how and why regimes survive. To understand the limits of regimes (in terms of decision-making power rather than scale), wider political economic context must be considered (Digaetano & Klemanski 1993b). In the United Kingdom it is important to go a stage further than making the observation that extra-local forces will affect whether a regime exists and the form it takes: the wider political economic context may actually be driving regime formation. Processes such as the competitive allocation of regeneration funds, increasing global competition for overseas investment and the creation of local neoliberal institutions have forced groups into coalitions. It is against this backdrop that the formation and sustenance of regimes in the United Kingdom may be occurring.

In the development of a comparative approach to regimes, it is important to recognise that differences in local institutional relations exist (Harding 1994; Stoker & Mossberger 1994). The diffuse nature of power in the United States is illustrated by the relative strength of cities. In the United Kingdom, by contrast, the rhetoric of decentralisation has far outstripped real change. This difference in centre-local relations between the two countries is coupled with a long-standing tradition of business involvement in American urban development. It is beyond the scope of the paper to say why this difference has emerged, but the United Kingdom central government has sought to plug this institutional space through 'top-down' policies.

Yet, an apparent institutional convergence underlies United Kingdom academic interest in American theories, such as the urban regime concept. Collinge & Hall (1997) argue that institutional differences between the United States and the United Kingdom influences how regimes develop and operate: the acquisition and use of political power is common to all liberal democracies. This claim, however, concentrates on the outcomes rather than the processes that empower regimes. The groups with power and autonomy are not the same in the United States and the United Kingdom. The United States, for example, has a strong and independent public sector, where fiscal rather than planning autonomy is prevalent and where the business sector has a long-standing history of participation. Most importantly, the structure of the state is more decentralised in the United States than in the United Kingdom, which means that localities are accustomed to acting as relatively autonomous and competitive agents. In the United Kingdom, on the other hand, there has been a centralisation of power during the 1980s (Cochrane 1993). Local authorities have been 'capped' (or had restrictions place on spending), services have been privatised, quasi-markets have been introduced into public provision, as part and parcel of the dismantling of the Keynesian welfare state (Jessop 1993; 1994). In contradiction to some claims, then, this suggests a widening of the local institutional terrain between the United States and the United Kingdom.

While there may now be institutional similarity, differences in the way these institutions interact now make concrete studies of wider theoretical interest. If, as Harding (1994) suggests, the United States literature does assume the fixity of institutional interaction then the analysis of regimes is reduced to listing characteristics. Examining the problems of comparative studies, Harding adopts a dual, 'global-local' approach to 'teases-out' the institutional change due to global restructuring, drawing out implications for urban change and considering the localised effects of economic restructuring. This is problematic, partially based as it is, on the assumption that local change is able to be read off global change. The intermeshing of the different scales and the way 'change' is mediated through the national and regional level is more complex and opaque than this approach suggests. In order to move from what Harding calls 'local government to urban governance' he advocates the prior identification of 'influentials' (individuals/groups) within the sphere of urban development. Harding suggests that this moves the foci of study from the assumption that local government and the business sector are the principal regeneration partners, the aim being to examine the extent to which strategies, agendas, aims and actions of influential actors in the business community represent a measure of the range and inclusiveness of urban governance (Harding 1994).

> 'A shared opportunity by itself is not specific and compelling enough to account for the extraordinary effectiveness and durability of the city's governing coalition. Policies that make particular incentives available stand a better chance of being sustained than do policies that simply further a generally desired goal ... use of particular, material benefits may not be the only way to co-ordinate the efforts of a governing coalition and reinforce its norms of co-operation, but it is an effective way.' (Stone 1989, p.195).

The formation and existence of regimes is outlined as emblematic of the benefits, both substantive and symbolic, that accrue to those within the regime. Regime survival is based upon achieving relatively manageable tasks rather than being underpinned by ideological dogma. Yet, while this may be true in the United States, in the United Kingdom urban regimes are a result of the national neoliberal agenda. The scope of the public sector in the United Kingdom and the extent of the local state's control over planning means there has been little cooperation between local government and business élites. As the United Kingdom local state is recast and local relations between institutions remade so, according to this argument, business élites will become more involved in development and co-operation between the two major local stakeholders will increase.

The American work on the formation and sustenance of regimes illustrates the difficulties of trans- national theoretical transfer. The American work has been shaped by that country's specific institutional characteristics. Attempting to export such a grounded construction has proved problematic (Ward 1996). While British academics, such as Gerry Stoker & Alan Harding, have made positive contributions to understanding the difficulties of comparative studies, a more fundamental problem with urban regime theory is that as a theory it is flawed almost by design. Social mechanisms that might explain why and if regimes form are ignored for more easily studied observations. Within the regime, the emphasis on management stresses the role of agency but fails to consider the structural positions of different partners.

Problem of application II: theorisation

Despite the innovative work of United Kingdom academics, urban regime theory is underpinned by two theoretical weaknesses; it is both localist and empiricist (Cox 1991). That is, regime theory has focused attempts to study the mediation of power through urban economic development and failed to consider structural factors, over-simplifying the issue of scale in either regime formation or regime sustenance (Cox 1996). Urban regime theory instead has developed through empirical observations, which themselves have limited explanatory power, even in the context of American regime formation. While the transfer of urban regime theory from one context to another has been addressed (Harding 1994; Stoker 1995; Stoker & Mossberger 1994), this work has still introduced a theoretically undeveloped concept. This is because urban regime theory does not get to grips with the processes underlying power in the contemporary United Kingdom city. Although the construction of typologies is useful, there needs to be a 'theoretical leap', to an approach that outlines the abstract preconditions for United Kingdom regime formation and which sensitises studying urban regimes to strategic actions at other scales.

Harding (1994) addresses the localised nature of the United States studies to suggest that any form of national or central government is excluded from the United States work, which tends to focus on the interaction between different local interests. Yet as Mollenkopf (1983) shows, in the 1950s and 1960s, pro- growth coalitions in the United States aimed to secure federal monies (Elkin 1985; Fainstein & Fainstein 1983). This apparent contradiction is a result of (i) the starting point of some of the United States studies (ii) a methodology that stops at city boundaries when seeking to explain local political configuration. This highlights an epistemological weakness of the approach. Put simply, regimes may appear 'bottom-up' because that is the way they have been studied.

> '[R]egime theory approaches city governance from the bottom up. The local polity, not the nation state, is the object of analysis. In short, regime theory posits that the configuration of power at the local level, which may indeed entail forming alliances with non local leaders, should be the point of departure for the study of urban governance.' (Digaetano & Klemanski 1993b; 381).

Academics have advanced the theory's explanatory power through the construction of typologies, based on case-studies (for a review see Ward 1995). While the more recent work has neatly illustrated the form taken by policies, this paper argues the factors upon which typologies are constructed are the same ones that need to be peeled away, if we are to explain why regimes form.

Despite different characteristics, the majority of the regimes studied appear to favour economic as opposed to community development. This assumes there is a non-necessary relationship between the two (on which, see Jonas 1995). Although these two forms of development may strategically overlap, Stone et al (1991) suggest that the privileging of economic development stems from the problems of co-ordinating community development. For economic development, consensus between a few peak organisation representatives is required; coordination at the top level. For community development, however, grass-roots mobilisation is also required. This involves a substantial commitment, leading to possible instability within the regime (Stone et al 1991; see also Nevin & Shiner 1995).

The construction of typologies does contextualise urban politics, placing action in its specific- local context. However, there are a number of theoretical difficulties with this approach. While the construction of typologies deepens the understanding of the breadth of possible policy alternatives, they do not, in themselves, say enough about the material processes (and discursive practices) that underpin regime formation. At what levels are the processes operating and how do they interact with other processes at different scales? In an illuminating paper, Stoker & Mossberger (1994) set out to resolve some of the problems of theoretical transfer by constructing typologies to explain difference. Noting wider factors that influence the formation and sustenance of regimes: institutional arrangements, economic differences, history, political culture, partisanship and so on, they fail to indicate fully how the factors feed into the typologies constructed. The focus on empirical case studies that tend to be theoretically weak, reducing the effectiveness of comparative studies. While concrete studies have an important place in research, attempts to theorise regime theory have so far fallen some way short of what is required. More recently Stoker has stressed that the 'groundedness' of regime theory is an advantage that should not be overstated, given that causal relationships underlying policy development are very complex. Consequently, regime theory offers a broad framework with which to guide analysis (Stoker 1995). This is a valid point. Yet, if attempts to theorise urban change are to not to be reduced to the construction of ever more sophisticated typologies there must be a concerted attempt to address these more complex questions.

As the local level may be an important element in regional, national or supranational accumulation strategies, so these different levels impact within a 'locality'. This is not to conflate issues of agency and scale, although a more structural account may prove revealing, per se, exposing the often unstated epistemological themes running through the present agency-centred approach. What is required now is an approach that isolates the mechanisms that empower the individual to act as *cause célèbre* in regeneration; this structure and debate is much rehearsed in and outside the geographical discipline (see Jessop 1996). These 'forces' constrain the form taken by regimes. If the processes at work are different in the United States to those in the United Kingdom, then 'evidence' must be sought to substantiate the claims over local dependence. Even where global processes are active and where similarities between the two nations are expected, concrete outcomes may be different reified through different conjunctural contingencies. One difference maybe that regimes in the United Kingdom may be a locally mediated- nationally prescribed response to the current period of after Fordist institutional crisis. The mechanisms behind the scripting of local institutions would appear, anecdotally at least, to be qualitatively different in the United Kingdom.

The inherently short-term character of funding arrangements and a partnership's ability to affect development within a locality both go some way to distinguishing between whether a regime exists or something less structured and piecemeal is in place (cf Painter 1997). Partnerships appear unlikely to happen 'naturally' (cf Bassett 1996; but see Eisenschitz and Gough 1993; Jessop et al 1997; Peck and Tickell 1995). Central government has sought to coerce local authorities into working alongside the new institutions, following the United States example of involving the 'downtown business élite' in regeneration policies. Yet, it is not all one way. Initiatives, such as the SRB, place new pressure upon networks. While they strengthen (existing) links between institutions, they also place additional strain upon inter-organisational relations. Partnerships previously concerned with the discursive promotion of the city are now faced with material projects that may reveal intra-coalition tensions. This shift may be a small realignment or a more fundamental shift, with new partners coopted. Urban regime theory is used to study how coalitions 'work'. For example, how are different interests managed? Particular institutional interests maybe subsumed to the perceived (but contested) greater good of the city. Although the form of regime taken is contingent on local conditions, the necessary factors for formation are often outlined through central government guidelines.

Institutional cooperation is strengthened through the use of narrative, which are deployed to pre-empt 'subversive stories' (Ewick & Silbey 1995). At present the account given by the institutions governing British cities, is that historically institutions have cooperated, leading to the formation of a regime being regarded as a 'natural' (and uncontested) development. This account goes largely unchallenged, as institutions mark territory, through the production of scripts, such as the City Pride prospectus or economic development plans. Through the use of regime theory, where the management of interests is central, this 'revisionism' is able to be challenged and alternative institutional history(s) plotted. According to Jessop (1997), narratives have three elements to them. Regimes focus on one; the selective appropriation of past events. This 'historic revisionism' privileges the 'entrepreneurial city' as the response to extra-local processes, such as increased competition for national and overseas direct investment, the increased role of 'world' cities, the allocation of funding through a competitive mechanism and so on. The form taken is dependent upon local conditions and the mechanisms through which the governing élite is seeking to image the city. This discourse may allow a regime to 'smother' decision- making in the locality, working through policies to legitimise respective roles and the existence of the regime itself.

The most thought provoking aspect of regime theory's deployment is the consideration of (i) whether regimes exist in the United Kingdom and (ii) the form regimes may take. In side-stepping charges of determinism, it is worth considering how a policy, such as the SRB, feeds into the local regime process. Unlike the United States, local government in the United Kingdom does not have the same autonomy as its American equivalent. While the autonomy of the local state may have been exaggerated in the

United States (see Elkin 1987) and understated in the United Kingdom (Cochrane 1997), change in the United Kingdom has forced a systematic and considered repositioning of the local state. This, coupled with the direct 'call- to-arms' issued by central government in the 1980s to business, puts TECs and Chambers of Commerce in a strong position. The institutional flux of governance allowed local 'characters' to become involved in the regime, filling spatial vents that may appear. Not simply a case of local entrepreneurship, this apparent 'arising' is a result of central government policy that has structurally privileged individuals who, traditionally in the United Kingdom, have not been involved in the mechanisms of urban governance. Through both formal and informal policies it is structural mechanisms that have positioned institution/agencies now governing British cities.

The Single Regeneration Budget and regimes?

There have been two rounds of the SRB. An evaluation of the first round indicates the lead partners in most bids were TECs and local authorities (Mawson et al 1995), due largely to the guidelines issued by central government. Although the community and voluntary sectors were explicitly targeted through the guidelines, the first round evidences highlights a 'discursive gap' (Clarke 1995; Community Development Foundation 1995; Mawson et al 1995). The second round, completed at the end of 1995 has yet to be evaluated fully (although see Hall et al, 1996). Research currently underway on the management of the SRB process in three major United Kingdom cities suggests SRB bids continue to be the source of dispute within partnerships. Government officers have had one-to-one meetings with institutional representatives, where disquiet is often expressed over the way one or more partner is riding 'roughshod' over other members. Yet the internal disputes over the focus of the bid or its construction are submerged in a unifying discourse adopt by regimes in dealing with external funding bodies. The problems posed when regimes become involved in material bids, where the common 'good' may often be in direct competition with individual institution's objectives, and the attempt by governing regimes to portray themselves (discursively and materially) as total; overarching, all embracing and, ultimately regimest is considered by brief reference to the way the SRB is feeding into the regime process in Leeds.

The institutional terrain of Leeds in the 1990s has been moulded by the affects of global restructuring and the intermeshing of the different scales – local/regional/national/supranational - of response. The city bears the hallmarks of central governments search for a 'local institutional fix' to the scripted national crisis. A number of Quango-like agencies are at work, either in Leeds or at the regional level, the community and voluntary groups have become sharper and more focused, as they have been brought onto (at least discursively) the local platform and local government has been 'transformed', as a result of the well-documented policies of the 1980s (Stoker 1992). Running together, these processes left those governing localities with hard decisions, the most important of which was 'how were they to position their city in the newly emerging global economy?' The script given to the localities in the late 1980s and early 1990s was in order to compete/remain competitive, they needed to form a regime, comprising of a pre-determined but contingently elastic set of actors. Although Jessop et al (1997) point out that urban regimes were only one response to crisis, cities were on the receiving end of the 'translation' and faced with little option but to attempt to position themselves alongside the other localities active within (and contributing to) the process. The Leeds response came in 1990 with the Leeds Initiative. The key institutions in Leeds came together to form a coalition, whose remit was to promote the city to the outside world and improve the environment and visual appeal of the whole city (see Haughton 1996). Similar initiatives emerged in a number of United Kingdom cities during the late 1980s and early 1990s.

> 'It's me and just one other councillor and the rest of it is totally partnership people, be it the Chamber, be it the TEC, be it the voluntary group, community groups, churches or police. Those kinds of organisations which you will probably find this is a common thread running through most partnerships (senior local councillor, Leeds). The term 'partnership people' refers to a group of institutions previously marginalised by the council. The 'others' is a metaphor for agencies who have been scripted into local economic development over the last decade. The Leeds Initiative did not mark a complete de-coupling from past trends. Haughton (1996, p.25), in outlining the role of leadership in the city, notes that "[f]or most of the twentieth century a consensus existed that leadership in Leeds was to be in the hands of the local authority". In the 'new' regime, Leeds city council has positioned itself as the 'natural' leader in urban economic development.
>
> I think there is a recognition in this place ... whilst we don't always see eye to eye then the business or the private sector community in Leeds recognise the significant role the council plays in almost everything ... If you were saying, well okay we'll start this initiative then they ... [the partnership people] ... do accept the value of the council being prominent. So I don't think there was ever any argument when we decided that we would move towards an initiative as a concept (senior local councillor, Leeds).

Haughton (1996, p.34) notes that 'most players ... [in Leeds] ... accept the inevitability and even the legitimacy of the local authority's dominant role'. This taken-for-grantedness, in part, reflects the role played by local government under the fordism/keynesianism national regime of the 1970s. It is also an example of the 'institutional repositioning' agencies have undertaken over the last decade in response to extra-local policies. The form taken by this repositioning reflects the 'tangled' (see Jessop et al 1997, p.10;

also see Thrift 1990, p.81) nature of the local/global receptor/distributor model. Where other United Kingdom cities adopted the language of local boosterism (if not the practice), the business and elected élite subsumed differences and local authorities (talked-up) private sector participation whilst simultaneously (talking down) public sector financial involvement, those in elected power in Leeds were suspicious of the 'new' regeneration discourses.

> 'There is also an issue in Leeds ... [as] ... Leeds has a very parochial view of doing things itself. It's partly cultural and ... it's a self- sufficiency argument. Leeds doesn't play nationally ... [or globally] ... anywhere; Leeds is a city state. I think there is a view that Leeds doesn't need anybody else and that's bolstered to some extent by the city having access to monies. Therefore a few million pounds from the SRB is neither here nor there if you look at numbers. [But] [o]f course if you don't play in those sort of arenas you get penalised in other events (voluntary sector representative, Leeds).

The contradictions implicit in the local authority's new role have been discussed elsewhere (Jones & Ward 1997) and reflect the complex processes of governance at work under the present national regime. Furthermore, while the insular nature of Leeds should not be overstated, institutions at work in Leeds were slow in embracing 'urban entrepreneurialism' (Harvey 1989). The cumulative affect of a historically strong local authority and a reticence about joining the rush to achieve 'world city' status, shaped the movement towards regime formation. While these local contingencies continue to affect the urban institutional terrain, the necessary conditions for Leeds becoming (belatedly) involved are extra-local.

By late 1993 and the announcement of the SRB, the Leeds Initiative had existed four years. The SRB, while further empowering those privileged through the 'remaking of the local state' (Tickell & Peck 1996), has also heightened tensions within newly emerging regimes. Within Leeds a sub-group of the Leeds Initiative was formed with the remit of 'regeneration'.

> 'What has emerged over recent months, once we have all started talking to each other about this subject ... [the SRB] ... , I mean we've been talking to each other for months, years about other things but once we have started to focus on regeneration I think the one thing that has emerged is that we really need to now talk about a regeneration strategy. And one of the things with partnerships is it takes a little while to have a true partnership because everybody turns up with their own agenda. And so there is a bit of time trying to get through that, trying to discover who's real wish list is what (senior local councillor, Leeds).

The unfolding of the SRB process locally has shaped the way the Leeds Initiative operates, leading to internal (re)alignments.

> 'I think the involvement, I mean it has taken some while to get going but the involvement and the nature of how we do it now increasingly is by involving absolutely everybody. There are problems for the city council because they've got elected members, councillors, who are there on the back of votes and therefore where this ... [the SRB] ... money is directed is a source of huge concern for them. We went through periods of dissatisfaction ... [however] ... what we've not been afraid to do is confront problems. So when this ...[the SRB bidding process] ... didn't seem to be going well then we did have people screaming and jumping up and down. So we went through the thing ... [the SRB bidding process] ... and we wrote a paper to the Leeds Initiative regeneration board saying you've got to do something different otherwise all that will happen is all these partners will simply be sitting at this table in body and all they will be doing is writing their own loose cannon bids to SRB. And when we find we have got 300 bids going in; the main partnership bid and another 299 that are coming from the partners separately, people will begin to start questioning just how good a partnership we've got going here (senior officer, quango, Leeds).

In round one the peculiarities of the SRB (Mawson et al 1995; Nevin & Shiner 1995; Ward, 1997) meant institutional linkages already in place were tested. In Leeds there were particular difficulties experienced in putting together a coordinated bid.

> 'We were better involved that the other partners but not well enough involved in my view. We were all technically involved in forming the bid itself but I mean technically. I mean there were issues about scripting beforehand. So that councillors and/or officers had been involved in deciding where all the money was going effectively and what the other partners got was a beautiful, professional presentation two months into the bidding process that said, this is how it is going to be. And everybody said bollocks!' (senior officer, private sector organisation, Leeds).

> 'If you look at the key players in the ...[Leeds] ... initiative the City Council is obviously the key player ... because it is the organisation that has the widest interest and is the only one that has got any serious money. The TEC in Leeds ... found it very hard to understand what regeneration in Leeds is about. We were saying very clearly 'now hear this', regeneration in Leeds is about social exclusion, it is disadvantage, it is about poverty and it is about the effect it has on the general economic, social and moral well being of the city. Instead they said, regeneration is about small business development ... there was a fundamental brain problem between us.' (local government officer, Leeds).

Yet, the cumulative affect is to strengthen platforms created through central government policies. Despite initial difficulties the SRB is most potent as a mechanism that ensures local participation. In Leeds, the second round has progressed with less institutional bickering. While different institutions are constantly (re)assessing their relative positions, such manoeuvring is fine tuning rather than the construction of an alternative (urban) discourse (or practice).

Concluding comments

British central government policy has deepened the territorial awareness of the different agents, through competition. Such is the acceptance of competition that 'pragmatic revisionism' now involves rewriting local history with difference subsumed to allow the 'entrepreneurial city' to be marketed to an external audience. In the SRB, community and voluntary group representatives, are involved, at least rhetorically (although the extent to which this is achieved is questioned, see Clarke 1995; Mawson et al 1995). Their involvement is required by central government guidelines and legitimises claims made by the regime to be representative of the whole community. Within the SRB process there is an observable hierarchy of partners; those afforded less power, which tend to be regime members outside the local authority, chamber of commerce, local TEC and local quasi-public organisation, are often consulted late on in the process and, in the most extreme cases, their involvement is no more than signatures on the final bid submission. Some regime theorists claim that spatial, as well as temporal, variation in regime types is identifiable (Stone 1989). Yet, the SRB process appears to reinforce claims that spatial variation is not possible (Elkin 1987) and that the entrepreneurial regime is the privileged response (Harvey 1989; Jessop 1997).

In conclusion, the SRB appears to feed into existing institutional arrangements, affecting the internal dynamics of regimes. The peeling away of discourse appears to reveal that the new powers afforded to previously marginalised institutions is at the level of implementation, rather than at the strategic level. Urban regime theory suggests that the tools deployed to manage regimes in the United Kingdom are structurally inscribed. Concrete studies that contextualise the SRB as one policy in a process will highlight the unfolding and shifting geography of regime formation in the United Kingdom. At one level are processes that affect regime formation; at the same time, policies such as the SRB are locally active, coercing institutions to subsume differences for the perceived (and discursively mediated) 'good' of the locality. The overlapping of the processes and how they they feed into each other has much to say on the way cities are governed.

Bibliography

K.Bassett, 'Partnerships, business élites and urban politics: New forms of governance in an English city?', *Urban Studies*, 33, 1996.

G.Clarke, 'A Missed Opportunity: An initial assessment of the 1995 Single Regeneration Budget approvals and their impact on voluntary and community organisations in England', National Council of Voluntary Organisations, 1995.

A.Cochrane, *Whatever happened to Local Government?*, Open University Press, 1993.

A.Cochrane, 'Rethinking urban politics for the 21st century', in A.E.G. Jonas & D.Wilson (eds), *The Urban Growth Machine: Critical Perspectives Twenty Years later*, State University of New York Press, 1998 (forthcoming).

C.Collinge & S.Hall, 'Hegemony and regime in urban governance: towards a theory of the locally networked state' in N.Jewson & S.MacGregor (eds), *Transforming cities: Contested Governance and New Spatial Divisons*, Routledge, 1997 (forthcoming).

Community Development Foundation, it Regeneration and the Community: Guidelines to the community involvement aspect of the SRB Challenge Fund, Community Development Foundation, 1995.

K.R.Cox, 'Questions of abstraction in studies in the new urban politics', *Journal of Urban Affairs*, 13, 1991.

K.R.Cox, 'Governance, urban regime analysis, and the politics of local economic development' in M.Lauria (ed), *Reconstructing Urban Regime Theory, Regulating Urban Politics in a Global Economy*, Sage, 1997.

R.A.Dahl, *Who governs?*, Yale University Press, 1961.

Department of the Environment, *Partners in Regeneration: the Challenge fund bidding guidance*, DOE, 1995.

A.DiGaetano & J.S.Klemanski, 'Urban regimes in comparative perspective: The politics of urban development in Britain', *Urban Affairs Quarterly*, 29, 1993a.

A.DiGaetano & J.S.Klemanski, 'Urban regimes capacity: A comparison of Birmingham and Detroit', *Journal of Urban Affairs*, 15, 1993b.

A.Eisenschitz & J.Gough, *The politics of local economic policy: the problems and possibilities of local initiatives*, Macmillan, 1993.

S.L Elkin, 'Twentieth century urban regimes', *Journal of Urban Affairs*, 5, 1985.

S.L.Elkin, *City and regime in the American republic*, University of Chicago, 1987.

P.Ewick & S.A.Silbey, 'Subversive stories and hegemonic tales: towards a sociology of narrative', *Law and Society Review*, 29, 1995.

S.S.Fainstein & N.I.Fainstein, 'Regime strategies, communal resistance and economic forces" in S.S.Fainstein et al, *Restructuring the city: The political economy of urban development*, Longman, 1983.

S.Hall et al, *The Single Regeneration Budget: A review of challenge fund round two*, School of public policy, University of Birmingham, 1996.

A.Harding, 'Urban regimes and growth machines: Towards a cross-national research agenda', *Urban Affairs Quarterly*, 29, 1994.

D.Harvey, 'From managerialism to entrepreneurialism: the transformation in urban governance in late capitalism', *Geografiska Annaler*, 71B, 1989.

G.Haughton, 'Local leadership and economic regeneration in Leeds', in G.Haughton & C.Williams, *Corporate City? Partnership, participation and partition in urban development in Leeds*, Avebury, 1996.

F.Hunter, *Community power structure*, University of North Carolina, Chapel Hill, 1953.

B.Jessop, 'Towards a Schumpeterian workfare state? Preliminary remarks on post-Fordist political economy', *Studies in Political Economy*, 1993.

B.Jessop, 'The transition to post-Fordism and the Schumpeterian workfare state' in R.Burrows & B.Loader (eds), *Towards a post-Fordist welfare state?*, Routledge, 1994.

B.Jessop, 'Interpretive sociology and the dialectic of structure and agency', *Theory, Culture and Society*, 13, 1996.

B.Jessop, 'The entrepreneurial city: re-imaging localities, re-designing economic governance, or re-structuring capital?', in N.Jewson & S.MacGregor (eds), *Transforming cities: Contested Governance and New Spatial divisons*, Routledge, 1997 (forthcoming).

B.Jessop et al, 'Retooling the machine: economic crisis, state restructuring and urban politics', in A.E.G.Jonas & D.Wilson (eds), *The Urban Growth Machine: Critical Perspectives Twenty Years later*, State University of New York Press, 1998 (forthcoming).

P.John & A.Cole, 'Economic policy-making networks in Leeds and Lille: emerging regimes or public sector alliances', mimeo, Department of Politics, Southampton University, 1996.

A.E.G.Jonas, 'Labor and community in the deindustrialization of urban America', *Journal of Urban Affairs*, 17, 1995.

A.E.G.Jonas, 'Regulating suburban politics: "suburban-defense transition", institutional capacities, and territorial reorganization in southern California', in M.Lauria (ed), *Reconstructing Urban Regime Theory, Regulating Urban Politics in a Global Economy*, Sage, 1997.

M.R.Jones & K.G.Ward, 'Crisis and disorder in British local economic development: Business Link and the Single Regeneration Budget', *Journal of Contingencies and Crisis Management*, 1997 (forthcoming).

M.Lauria (ed), *Reconstructing urban regime theory, Regulating Urban Politics in a Global Economy*, Sage, 1997.

J.Mawson et al, *Single regeneration budget: the stocktake*, School of public policy, University of Birmingham, 1995.

J.Mollenkopf, *The contested city*, Princeton University Press, 1983.

B.Nevin & P.Shiner, 'The Single Regeneration Budget: urban funding and the future for distressed communities', *Local Work*, 58, Centre for Local Economic Strategies, Manchester, 1995.

M.E.Orr & G.Stoker, 'Urban regimes and leadership in Detroit', *Urban Affairs Quarterly*, 30, 1994.

J.Painter, 'Regulation, regime and practice in urban politics', in M.Lauria (ed), *Reconstructing Urban Regime Theory, Regulating Urban Politics in a Global Economy*, Sage, 1997.

J.Peck & A.Tickell, 'Business goes local: dissecting the 'business agenda' in Manchester', *International Journal of Urban and Regional Research*, 19, 1995.

P.Peterson, *City limits*, University of Chicago, 1981.

G.Stoker, 'Regulation theory, local government and the transition from Fordism' in D.S.King & J.Pierre (eds), *Challenges to Local Government*, Sage, 1992.

G.Stoker, 'Regime theory and urban politics', in D.Judge et al (eds), *Theories of urban politics*, Sage, 1995.

G.Stoker & K.Mossberger, 'Urban regime theory in comparative perspective', *Environment and Planning C: Government and Planning*, 12, 1994.

C.N.Stone, *Regime politics: The governing of Atlanta, 1946-1988*, University of Kansas, 1989.

C.N.Stone et al, 'The reshaping of urban leadership in US cities: A regime analysis', in M.Gottdiener & C.Pickvance (eds), *Urban life in transition*, Sage, 1991.

N.Thrift, 'Doing regional geography in a global system: the new international financial system, the city of London and the South East of England', in R.J.Johnston et al (eds), *Regional geography: current developments and future prospects*, Routledge, 1990.

A.Tickell & J.Peck, 'The return of the Manchester Men: men's words and men's deeds in the remaking of the local state', *Transactions of the British Institute of Geographers*, 21, 1996.

K.G.Ward, *A rough guide to ... regime theory*, Business Élites and Urban Politics , Working Paper 5, University of Manchester, 1995.

K.G.Ward, 'Rereading urban regime theory: a sympathetic critique', *Geoforum*, 27, 1996.

K.G.Ward, 'The Single Regeneration Budget and the issue of local flexibility', *Regional Studies*, 31, 1997.

H.Wolman & M.Goldsmith, *Urban Politics and Policy: A Comparative Approach*, Blackwell, 1992.

A.Wood, 'Analysing the politics of local economic development: making sense of cross-national convergence', *Urban Studies*, 33, 1996.

Urban Regimes in Theory and Practice

Joyce Liddle
University of Sunderland
&
John Corcoran
University of Sunderland

'A Regeneration Regime in the North East of England? Inter-Agency Partnerships and the Case of Siemens U.K.'

Abstract

The need to attract Foreign Direct Investment into the North East of England is a major consideration for regional agencies, and since the setting up of the Northern Development Company in 1985 it has been a key feature of all regional strategies for economic regeneration. This paper considers whether or not there is an established, strategic' regime for regeneration' in the North East, particularly in relation to F.D.I.

It draws on existing urban regime literature and uses the findings from 25 in depth interviews carried out in a diverse range of agencies between January and July 1996. Using additional data obtained from key actors involved in the Siemens United Kingdom decision to locate its latest semiconductor plant in North Tyneside the case study illustrates how a regional regime operates. It also demonstrates the relative importance of key regional actors and agencies in the process and shows how, even given the 'top down' nature of the decision making process in this instance, that there was still a need, albeit at a reduced level, to involve actors from the 'regional regeneration regime'.

Introduction

The North East of England, described in 1970 by Cullingworth as,

> 'one of those unfortunate regions, a boom area of the coal age with an enormous legacy of obsolete social capital, a slower rate of economic growth, an accompanying higher rate of unemployment, a poorer standard of health and social services, and a not unrelated outward migration of population'.[1]

is, if one is to believe current literature, undergoing a major transformation. Indeed Newcastle, with its hinterland is according to Rossabeth Moss Kanter now a global growth region that is 'creating jobs faster than all but two

[1] J.B.Cullingworth, *Town and Country Planning in England and Wales*, Allen & Unwin, 1970.

other United Kingdom regions ... and characterised by companies bringing capital rather than coals to Newcastle'.[2]

Quotations abound in the local and regional press and there is a wealth of literature emanating from various agencies extolling the virtues of the region. Increasingly the region is described as 'a region in the vanguard', 'outwardly focussed', 'at the leading edge', 'looking to Europe and beyond', and a 'world class region'.[3] It is also regarded by some commentators as 'obsessed with image'[4] and keenly competing with other regions to attract F.D.I. In the absence of other forms of investment there is a strongly held belief that the attraction of foreign industry should be paramount in regional strategic thinking and action. To this end the key agencies have concerned themselves with this aspect of regional development as a strategic priority, and in their attempts to 'go it alone' have proactively and aggressively promoted the region as a means of securing vitally needed investment. The requirement for a strategic, regional response to the legacy of decline has led to the development of a regime of regional actors who operate in similar, but nevertheless distinctive ways to those described in existing urban regime literature.

Much of the regime literature focusses on describing urban change processes or international regimes, and up until quite recently American research dominated the field. There is, however, a growing body of United Kingdom work to be accessed. The absence of a strong British theoretical tradition within the area of urban and regional change has resulted in the adaption and application of American models, with only limited success. Over the past 10 years a number of specifically British research studies have set urban change processes into a wider political and economic framework. This has facilitated an interesting debate with a new emphasis on the region as the important unit of analysis. Notwithstanding the fact that the region is a quite different forum of decision making space compared to the urban, reference to urban regime literature does provide some interesting and useful comparative analyses.

The findings on which this paper are based suggest that the need to attract F.D.I. to the North East has produced a set of consciously thought out strategic and regional responses to existing and newly recognised problems. These responses are articulated by a regime of actors whose overriding aim is to regenerate the region. Before summarising some of the important aspects of existing regime literature the following short section gives a brief synopsis of definitions on the region.

Defining the Region

Regions are difficult to define, theoretically and practically, as reflected in the regionalist debate which has continued throughout the twentieth cen-

[2] R.M.Kanter, *World class, thriving at home in a global economy*, Simon & Schuster, 1995.

[3] Various Northern newspaper reports/articles (1995/1996).

[4] Interview with Mr.D.Kelly, General Manager, North of England Newspapers, 19th March 1996.

tury. There has always been the tension between those social theorists who relate unique locales with general social processes and political economists who place differentiated regions into a wider theory of analysis of capitalist uneven development. In addition, a region can be described in a variety of ways, that is, politically/economically, administratively, culturally/socially/linguistically, historically, spatially/territorially/geographically, or as a European region. Furthermore, there is a diversity between regions and within them. By their very nature, urban/regional analyses have offered only partial explanations of the phenomena.[5]

For the purposes of this paper, which is concerned with making some observations on systems of interest and regimes at the regional level, Self's definition of the region as,

> 'some area of intermediate space between national and local government which is a focus for shared demands, common needs, or important issues of decision making'.[6]

and Keating's as,

> 'political space in a functional and territorial sense in which a variety of types of intervention occur, precisely because of the weakness of the region's political and institutional articulation'.[7]

seem to provide useful starting definitions.

Changing Perceptions in Regime Theory

Stoker suggests that the theoretical debate within the field of urban/regional change has moved on from what he refers to as,

> 'the flag of convenience of urban politics with a narrow emphasis on city government and representative politics to a broader concern with how collective decisions are made through conflict and collaboration, and not solely confined to state agencies or formal representative politics.'[8]

In his view, in complex societies it is no longer appropriate to examine the notion of power as the ability of one actor to get another actor to do

---

[5] Comprehensive debates on how to define a region can be found in an extensive body of literature on the subject. See, for examples of the variety of ways, M.Keating, 'Whatever happened to regional government?', *Local Government Studies*, 11, 1985; M.Keating & R.A.W.Rhodes, *Is there a regional level of government in England?*, University of Strathclyde Studies in Public Policy, 49, 1979; D.Byrne, *The class-cultural politics of northern regionalism: A problem or solution?*, ESRC Paper, 1993; P.J.Taylor, 'A theory and practice of regions: A case of Europes', *Environment and Planning, Society and Space*, 9, 1991; P.Dunleavy, 'The limits of local government', in M.Boddy & C.Fudge (eds), *Local Socialism?*, Macmillan, 1984; L.J.Sharpe, *The rise of meso government in Europe*, Sage, 1993.

[6] P.Self, 'Regional planning in Britain', *Urban Studies*, 1, 1964.

[7] M.Keating, *op cit*.

[8] G.Stoker, 'Regime Theory and Urban Politics', in D.Judge et al (eds), *Theories of Urban Politics*, Sage, 1995

something they would otherwise not do; the issue is now more focused on the capacity to achieve tasks by concentration on leadership and partnership/regime operations. For him 'old style' urban politics with the emphasis on 'who governs?' has been replaced by growth coalitions focusing on 'who benefits?'. A broader analysis of organisations and city governments within civil society locates them in a wider political economy. The question now asked is 'how are tasks achieved?'.

Stoker concurs with Stone's definition of a regime as,

> 'the power to act to accomplish goals rather than domination and subordination. Governments need to blend their capacities with non-governmental actors to facilitate action and empower themselves'.

A regime in his view, is therefore,

> 'an informal, yet relatively stable group with access to institutional resources that enable it to have a sustained role in making governing decisions'.[9]

To add to the regime literature, with its renewed interest in a wider political economy, greater emphasis is now given to specific concepts such as governance, networks; partnerships,and growth coalitions, all of which can be located under the 'regime umbrella', or can also be defined separately.

The literature is scattered with competing definitions of all the aforementioned concepts and to add to this confusion Jessop, providing a review of the definitional literature on governance in particular, claims that,

> 'it is a rather vague term with theories at an eclectic and pre-theoretical stage of critique'.[10]

Stein, on the other hand, referring specifically to international regimes, criticises scholars who have,

> 'fallen to using the term so disparately and with such little precision that it ranges from an umbrella for all international relations to little more than a synonym for international organisations'.[11]

Regime theory, according to John,

> 'offers many lessons and models ... and cannot lightly be dismissed by an assertion of U.S. exceptionalism' ... [the defining characteristics of regimes being] 'interorganisational, sustained,

[9] C.Stone, *Regime Politics.* University Press of Kansas, 1989. See also Stoker & Mossberger who provide a useful compilation of the work of some of the notable urban regime theorists in their 'Urban Regime Typology', 1995.

[10] B.Jessop, *Conservative regimes & the transition to Post-Fordism. The cases of Britain & W.Germany*, Essex Papers in Politics & Government, 47, 1988.

[11] Stein, quoted in V.Rittberger (ed), *Regime Theory and International Relations*, Clarendon Press, 1993.

coordinative and empowering processes for powerful actors to bargain, develop trust and mutually learn to solve problems.'[12]

The aforementioned definitions give an indication of the way in which regime theory has developed as a critique of pluralism, with, according to Collinge and Hall,

> 'partnership as an important institutional form of local/regional regime'.[13]

Geddes, focussing particularly on regimes involving partnerships for poverty and social exclusion points to the major weakness of regime theory as,

> 'its overriding concern with interests, processes and outcomes within the regime, and with élites, rather than the relations between dominant and dominated groups'.

He asserts that:

> 'the problems can be overcome by resorting to the Gramscian concept of hegemony based on a viable accumulation strategy/economic growth model built around a "historic bloc" which links the interests of dominant factions of capital to subordinate classes and other social interests'.[14]

Whether one takes the neo-pluralist or neo-marxian approach to regime theory, as outlined earlier, it is clear that the growing regime literature offers some useful theoretical frameworks to explain urban and regional changes within a wider political economy.

The following section of the paper focusses on the role of public and private élites in the regional regime in the North and explores this by looking at the motivation of key participants. It then addresses the importance of F.D.I. and uses Siemens United Kingdom as an illustration of regime operation.

The Role of Élites in Regimes: public or private sector led?

Findings

The research findings on which this paper is based indicate that in the Northern region, as Hardy found in his research into urban growth coalitions and alliances there is a common economic growth agenda, which has replaced an earlier paradigm based on domination by the local public sector.[15]

---

[12] P.John & A.Cole, 'Urban Regimes in Britain and France: the case of Leeds and Lille', paper presented to the Association Française de Sciemce Politique, Université de Paris IV et IEP Paris, 1996.

[13] C.Collinge & S.Hall, *Hegemony and regime in urban governance: Towards a theory of local policy networks and partnerships*, B.S.A. Annual Conference, Leicester, 1995.

[14] M.Geddes, *Policy responses to social exclusion in the European Union: The local partnership approach*, paper to the First European Urban and Regional Studies Conference, Exeter, 1996.

[15] A.Hardy, 'The rise of urban growth coalitions, United Kingdom style?', *Environment & Planning. Government & Policy*, 9, 1991.

Although Shaw agrees with Molotch that in the USA growth coalitions had influential business interests taking the lead, more especially with property interests at the core, he rejects the notion that a similar situation is apparent in the North.[16] Whilst accepting that growth statesmen may spread the ideology that growth is in everyone's interest Shaw asserts that the situation in the North is still one based on the centrality of a public sector lead; the business sector being only one important element in the overall scenario.

It is this author's opinion it is no longer clear cut to suggest, as Shaw does, that the public sector has the primary role in economic regeneration in the North East. Undoubtedly the public agencies still play an important role, especially in funding of projects but the resources necessary for coalitions are not always solely financial. There are many other resources such as personnel, time, information, know-how, experience etc that other participants can contribute to the equation. Coalitions for economic regeneration in the Northern region have a very long history and the situation is much more complex than the three types of British growth coalition idenitified by Cooke as follows,

- (i) classic North East labour and trade union led corporatism in the era of T.Dan Smith (for Cooke this was the closest United Kingdom equivalent to the United States),
- (ii) Swindon with its trade union, railway workers, shopkeepers and professional alliances, and
- (iii) Non-municipal Lancaster with its local mangerialism comprising the University, Chamber of Commerce and City administrators.[17]

Cooke summarises that all three types of regime were dominated by political and professional representatives of the public sector, all of whom saw social justice as their major criteria for stimulus to change. Unlike the USA as described by Molotch where business élites were able to dominate the process of civic boosterism, Cooke describes most United Kingdom cities as being Labour run with no apparently motivated business class.

The findings on the North suggest a more complicated picture than the one described by Cooke in the 1960s and alluded to by Shaw in his later work. In this author's view it is too simple to assume that only labour, political, or professional representatives of the public sector have social justice as a key criteria for action. In the Northern region there are many examples of representatives from other agencies who share similar social concerns as their political and labour partners. It is therefore misleading to suggest that only the public sector agents have social justice as their guiding principle.

---

[16] K.Shaw, 'The political economy of urban regeneration in the North East: The rise of growth coalitions or corporatism revisited?', *Regional Studies*, 27, 1993; H.Molotch, 'The city as a growth machine: towards a political economy of place', *American Journal of Sociology*, 82, 1976.

[17] P.Cooke, 'Municipal enterprise, growth coalitions and social justice', *Local Economy*, 3/3, 1988.

In a long standing debate on the issue Stone & Cox have considered the privileged position of business, with Cox arguing that business representatives, who have as their primary aim, the need to make a profit, occupying a very priviledged position in any coalition.[18] Stone, with a contrary view, argues that Cox's mono-causal model of economic determinism is a unitary system of abstract analysis divorced from the reality of concrete facts.[19] In essence Cox's main argument, vehemently rejected by Stone, is that an emphasis on business and the market-led solutions to urban problems lead to a situation whereby the profit motive is regarded as the only way to bring about change in urban locales. In the United Kingdom business does have more of a role to play depending on the specific locale, than earlier theorists suggested, as there must be a reciprocal bargaining and negotiating process between business representatives and government officials if overall aims are to be achieved.

Economic regeneration in the North is characterised by a high degree of bargaining and negotiation between a wide range of actors, as shown in the stakeholder analysis. The business community has recently enhanced its role and profile in this field and a declared aim to achieve the best solutions by involving as many people from various sectors as is possible.

Hanf & O'Toole regard governance as

> 'decision making systems in which territorial & functional differentiation disaggregate effective problem solving into a collection of sub-systems of actors with specialised tasks and limited competences and resources'.

In the case of the Northern region N.D.C. is clearly still seen as the strategic body that works in collaboration with the Government Office for the North East, the North of England Assembly of Local Authorities, and the business community. It does this by disaggregating problems, differentiating tasks where necessary, and then drawing in respective players from many other agencies, as and when required.

Hanf & O'Toole also assert that

> 'independent participants work together possessing bits of information, representing different interests through separate, often conflicting courses of action. As problems cut across boundaries of separate jurisdiction and specialisation there needs to be the maintenance of informality, levels of perception on common purpose, shared history, flow of information and openness, and coordination of activities into an action arena'.[20]

Keohane suggests that,

[18] K.Cox, 'The abstract, the concrete and the argument in the new urban politics', *Journal of Urban Affairs*, 13, 1991.

[19] C.Stone, 'The hedgehog, the fox and the new urban politics: rejoinder to Kevin R.Fox', *Journal of Urban Affairs*, 13, 1991.

[20] K.Hanf & L.J.O'Toole, 'Revisiting old friends. Networks, implementation structures and the management of inter-organisational relations', *European Journal of Political Research*, 21, 1992.

> 'Co-operation does not necessarily depend on altruism, personal honour, common purpose, internalised norms, or shared beliefs in a set of values embodied in a culture. It can be about instrumentally rational actors who are involved due to the functional benefits. It is therefore purposeful and functional.'[21]

But, conversely, as Chester Barnard is quoted as saying, many years ago,

> 'Morality is the underlying and enduring principle in organisational leadership. Multi-dimensional cooperation is not a natural act. Social purpose as well as material gain and individual interests are crucial. Regimes need to be built with broad agendas in order that leaders may have a vision that the location is more than profit/investment based but considers the non-business elements of community governance.'[22]

When asked about their motivation for regime/partnership involvement in the region all respondents claim to support Barnard's view of cooperation, with a strong desire to be seen to be altruistic, share a common purpose, and a set of values embodied in the Northern culture. There is an almost messianic drive to be shown to be 'in it together'. The findings on the North suggest that business representatives and other agency representatives do purport to share a broader vision than the narrowly restricted one postulated by Cox. Whether or not this is a conspiratorial aspiration on the part of business to secure a profit whilst at the same time claiming to be socially driven is open to debate, but when questioned all representatives claim to want socially desirable outcomes to flow from profit – driven projects and initiatives.

It could be argued that the desire to secure inward investment and economic regeneration as a means of providing a 'trickle down' effect to communities in the region may merely be a cosmetic exercise. The image of the region is undoubtedly being enhanced by the building of large scale projects and the securing of inward investment but there is little evidence to suggest that the real needs of some of the impoverished communities that is, sustainable jobs and a better standards of education and social provision of services are in evidence. Examples of high profile projects to improve the image are manifold but all respondents are in agreement that they are not enough to bring about a transformation. Without exception, all respondents agreed that sustainable jobs, and stability in the regional economic base are vital for any future transformation.

For Bennett & Krebs partnerships for economic regeneration must be concerned with:

> 'turning external stimuli into internal responses by coordinated local leadership. This governance arrangement is not supported by rules, regulations, and domination but secured by

[21] Keohane (1988), quoted in V.Rittberger (ed), *Regime Theory and International Relations*, 1993.

[22] C.I.Barnard, *The Functions of the Executive*, Harvard University Press, 1968 edition.

> collectvely agreed goals by a critical mass of those involved on mode and outcomes.'[23]

There is evidence to suggest that Northern élites are able to do as Bennett & Krebs suggest but there is very little evidence to suggest that all groups affected by outcomes of actions are involved or represented in the change process. Many excluded and disadvantaged groups, such as the disabled or long term disabled, are not drawn into the economic regeneration process.[24]

If, as Rittberger claims,

> 'Governance without government obligation does not emanate from a hierarchical norm and rule setting process but from voluntary agreements to play by a set of rules which are binding in the sense that they create convergent expectations and govern behaviour. In this way governance can be distinguished from government by the rules is not backed up by the threat of physical and legitimate force. It is based on non-hierarchical normative institutions involving a stabilised pattern of behaviour of a given number of actors in recurring situations.'[25]

There is a lot of support for the notion that the Northern regional regime for enhancing economic regeneration and inward investment is a recurrent process which is based on voluntarism, is non-hierarchical, has convergent expectations, stabilised patterns, and a given number of actors. Each actor has their own rationale for involvement in the regime, as outlined in the following sections.

Participation in Regimes: the role of the public sector and labour representation

Labour and trade union involvement has always been an acceptable feature of the corporate tradition in the Northern region, and remains so, much as Mawson suggested when he described the tripartite representation of local politicians, capital and labour.[26] He, and Shaw, quite correctly assert that since the 1930s there has been a strong tripartite lobby for some form of regional infrastructure to support regional development. As Shaw & Robinson found in their review of 'Who Runs the North' local notables from all three sectors (and other sectors) are represented on many regional agencies and quangos, but with the business community more favoured under a Conservative government than labour groups.[27]

---

[23] R.J.Bennett & G.Krebs, 'Towards a partnership model of L.E.D. initiatives in Britain and Germany', *Regional Studies*, 28/2, 1994.

[24] For a clearer exposition of the way in which certain groups are excluded from the decision making process see Davoudi & Healey, 'City Challenge. Sustainable process or temporary gesture?', *Environment & Planning. Government and Policy*, 13, 1995.

[25] V.Rittberger (ed), *Regime Theory and International Relations*, 1993.

[26] J.Mawson, *Sub-national government & L.E.D.: A case study of County Durham within the northern region*, Inlogov Research Paper, University of Birmingham, 1994.

[27] K.Shaw & F.Robinson, *Who Runs the North?*, Review of non-elected public bodies in Tyne and Wear conducted for Unison and the Tyne and Wear Research and Intelligence Unit, Newcastle Upon Tyne, 1995.

Mawson refers to the way in which the strong Labour controlled local authorities still exert an influence in the region. Although it may be true that most local authorities are still Labour dominated, this is not to suggest that all of them are equally successful in responding to the needs of under-represented groups and furthering social needs of particular areas. Indeed, many respondents felt that Newcastle City Council was very inert and moribund, and as one commented 'Sir John Hall, Kevin Keegan and Newcastle Football Club have done more for the City's social needs than the local council'. Undoubtedly as both Shaw and Robinson found, Labour councils still provide some of the personnel on quango boards, but with central government pushing for more business led approaches to problems there has been a decline in the membership of councillors and trade union representatives on such bodies. The enhanced role of the business sector is shown in the following section.

The Role of the Business Sector

The business sector has always an important player in economic regeneration in the region but this role has grown in importance in recent years. Respondents were asked whether they considered there to be a new 'business cadre', and why it could be assuming a greater significance in the field. Most respondents agree that the business community has enlarged its role since the late 1980s, pushed into prominence mainly as a result of central government policies with the emphasis on management and business solutions to a range of different 'ailments'.

The setting up of the Regional Chamber of Commerce with improved membership has formalised many informal relationships, provided a focal point for a wider range of business people, and allowed more of them to become involved in economic development initiatives that they would otherwise not have been aware of. In addition, latterly, the instigation of a Northern Business Forum with its newly appointed Chief Executive, has heightened the business profile and increased the level of business involvement in regional decision making.

The Northern Business Forum was set up in May 1996 and, in addition to furthering business interests, it has set regional targets for, among other things, outputs on exports, education and training needs and the service sector. Hardy quite rightly asserts, and this is supported by evidence in the North, that alliances are based on a common economic growth agenda[28] but he also suggests that labour groups are still predominant urban players with private sector actors having a restricted capacity to act; their relationship with local authorities being based on a simple dialogue concerning the level of rate demands. In Hardy's opinion, corporate redundancies and ownership decline have led to a situation whereby the private sector has little or no cohesion, nor the organisational capacity to act. He points to the way that the C.B.I, I.O.D, and local Chambers of Commerce are dominated by

[28] Hardy, *op cit.*

small to medium sized firms, who, because of financial and organisational constraints have no ability to act.

In the North, the decline in large scale manufacturing since the Second World War has resulted in a situation where SMEs and Far Eastern inward investment constitute the largest part of the business sector (it is accepted, however, that the economic base of the region is still mainly of a service/public sector nature). The consequence of this change in economic base is that the private sector has a greater capacity to act than was previously the case. The Northern region has not been as successful in SME start-ups as other regions, but in terms of F.D.I. it is on a par with other deprived regions. One reason given for the success in attracting foreign investors is that they do not have pre-conceived ideas of what they might find in the region (unlike, as some respondents claim, investors from south of Watford Gap!) This has provided a very powerful form of leverage to attract capital investment, albeit aided by central grants to aid the regional change process.

Contrary to Hardy's idea that a typical United Kingdom style coalition has the imprint of national business, the current economic base in the North indicates a mixture of small to medium size companies started up by entrepreneurial owners who have grown the businesses and multi-national companies such as Nissan, Fujitsu and Siemens etc. In this case there is more organisational capacity to act than was previously recorded, witnessed by the greater involvement of SME entrepreneurs and senior executives from multi-nationals on regional forums. Dialogue with local authorities is continuous, cordial and, according to respondents, a reciprocal and valuable relationship. The private sector provides many forms of advice for public agencies. As an example of this the Regional Chamber has recently joined forces with Durham Constabularly and Gateshead M.B.C. to work on a large scale crime initiative to counteract criminal activities on the Team Valley trading Estate. Likewise the public agencies have a very strong, and cordial set of relationships with the business community. An example, and there are many, is the planning advice provided by local authorities and English Partnerships, or the assistance with applications for Eurofunding etc.

The reasons given for the growing importance of the business community in the region are many, including, the influx into the region of a new 'breed' of managers, leading to new styles of managing and new approaches to problem solving: the European dimension has forced them to work more closely with other sectors: a need to 'get their act together': the strategic need to provide a more professional image of the region: the business community claim to be more experienced than the public sector in managing resources and consider themselves to possess an instinct for survival, and finally they claim to have always been better than their public sector counterparts in informal networking and collaboration. Whether one agrees or not with the respondents it is clear that the profile, and associated press coverage afforded to the business community in the Northern region has risen, certainly over the past two years. There is a distinct feeling by business people that the Northern region is beginning to experience a renaissance and that they have an important part to play in it. There is, however, a growing involvement of representatives from a much wider set of interests, as described in the following section.[29]

The role of universities, sporting/cultural and trade union organisations in regimes: auxiliary or central players?

With regard to the importance attached to certain groups in coalitions for economic regeneration, Hardy recognises universities, sports and cultural organisations and trade unions as merely auxilliary elements in the equation; the public sector and business interests achieving greater prominence.[30] The findings on the north suggest that far from having an auxilliary role, the universities/sport and cultural/trade unions are of key importance in the field. There are very strong linkages between business and public sector organisations and sporting and cultural activities. Indeed, it could be argued that sporting and cultural concerns are so closely linked with economic regeneration agencies that on occasion it is difficult to separate the two. As an example, Newcastle United Football Club is owned by the foremost business man in the North, who also developed the Metro shopping centre.

Most influential business people and senior public servants have seats in the Director's box at Newcastle United Football Club, a location where endless business deals are clinched. (Nissan, Fujitsu and Siemens executives were all treated to the obligatory complimentary tickets!). Similarly, Newcastle racecourse holds the Newcastle Plate Event, another event attended by regional élites from a wide variety of organisations (media, financial, euro officials, MEPs, business and public officials). The home of county cricket in the region, Riverside Park, has a large conference centre where notables gather and informally do business. Other sporting, theatrical and cultural venues also have a strong business focus, for example, Newcastle Sailing Club, Gateshead International Athletics Stadium and, Tyne Theatre and Empire Theatre.

The Tyne Theatre has recently been bought and refurbished by a leading businessman who intends to use it as a focal point for business dealing. Similarly, the role of universities and trade unions, and the key individuals who represent them, have much more than an auxilliary role to play in economic regeneration. Vice chancellors of all universities in the region and key trade unionists in the region sit on the Boards of many forums devoted to regional regeneration. They are also well represented on the Board of the Regional Chamber of Commerce and the Northern Business Forum with the opportunity to make far reaching decisions affecting the region.

Two good examples of this decision making involvement are (i) the recently launched Services Challenge, an initiative being promoted by the

[29] This data was collected from representatives of the business community!

[30] Hardy, *op cit*.

Regional Chamber with the support of the C.B.I. to improve output measures for service sector agencies, as a way of improving the efficiency of regional agencies, and (ii) prior to the Heseltine White Papers on Competitiveness the vice-chancellors of northern universities were involved, together with senior TEC, G.O.N.E, C.B.I., trade union and other representatives in setting targets on educational and training criteria for the region for example, the number of school leavers required to stay on post 16-18, and the number of teenagers requiring vocational training etc to achieve national competitive requirements.

As has been shown the emergent findings indicate a complex and interwoven web of relationships from a very wide system of interests operate in the field of regional regeneration. Furthermore the property sector is an important feature in the picture, but as the following sections on the Siemens U.K. show, it is not a homogenous group, but a series of fragmented agencies with sometimes conflicting and contradictory aims and objectives.

A unified property sector? the case of Siemens U.K.

Hardy rejects the work of earlier writers who introduced the notion of a 'unified property sector'. In his opinion, the property sector is constituted by physical assets, such as land, buildings and infrastructure.[31] In his view, and this is supported by factual information gathered in the North, the property sector is not homogenous but fragmented. As an example of this fragmentation the Siemens F.D.I. case highlights the divisions.

The land on which the plant was to be built was previously owned by Tyne and Wear Metropolitan Authority, but since its demise became jointly owned by Gateshead and NorthTyneside Local Authorities. There was considerable conflict over which council actually owned the land to be built upon, but the matter was resolved in a cordial manner (according to an N.D.C spokesperson). The buildings surrounding the site were owned by property development companies and the infrastructure was the preserve of Northumbria Water (water supply), Northern Electric (electricity supply), and Department of Transport (roads). Land reclamation involved the Department of Environment through the new Integrated Regional Office, with some involvement of the local planning authority. As in all previous inward investment successes Northern Development Company took the strategic role in bringing together the various agencies/actors to enable as smooth a process as possible for the inward investing company.

This complicated case, and its predecessors Nissan, Fujitsu, Samsung and others verify Hardy's claims that there is no such thing as a' unified property sector'. There is an obvious need to have collaborative and coordinated efforts of a fragmented property sector, the strands of which were drawn together in this case by other regional agencies, most notably N.D.C, G.O.N.E, N.E.A. and the Regional Chamber.

All these agencies have a stake in encouraging F.D.I, as an aspect of regeneration, the importance of which will be considerted in the following

[31] Hardy, *op cit.*

sections.

A typology of interests

Hardy following on from the work of Logan &Molotch (who had stressed the importance of business élites in the U.S.A) says that in the United Kingdom after Victorian times philanthropic, industrialists or 'city bosses 'declined for a number of reasons. In his view universal franchise, suburbanisation of business élites, mobilisation of non-business interests, bureaucratisation of corporate enterprises, and internationalisation of capital had all mitigated against the philanthropist who was able to exert power and influence.[32] Whilst all of the aforementioned events are true, it is too simple to say that a business élite has been replaced by Labour groups as the dominant form of urban players.

In the case of the North, particularly across the region, there is a very complicated picture emerging. Indeed it could be argued that there is a stratified group on four levels:

GROUP 1: old monied, established Tory business people (still considered with suspicion in the region due to their insidious linkages to the Conservative Party, their current and past role in decision making and their preponderance on non-accountable Boards.

GROUP 2: entrepreneurs who have established and grown businesses in the Thatcher and Major years. Many consider themselves to be excluded from regional decision making, and also too busy trying to make the next million to have time to become involved too much

GROUP 3: owners, managers, senior executives from many of the former F.D.I. companies. They are drawn into regional decision making due to their expertise at running large multinationals and their ability to generate new ideas.

GROUP 4: entrepreneurial public bureaucrats such as university vice-chancellors, chief executives of U.D.C.s, T.E.C.s, other quangos, chief officers of Development Agencies and other economic development agencies, chief executives of local authorities and local politicians.

Any initiative concerned with economic regeneration seems to have a collection of the aforementioned groups of people, supported by other representatives, acting on behalf of their organisation or in an individual capacity. The range of actors changes over time, and in response to the particular economic regeneration need. F.D.I has been recognised as of crucial importance to the Northern Region, and the report now focusses on this important aspect of regeneration.

The importance of F.D.I.

The Northern region is in competition with all United Kingdom regions and most European regions for inward investment from overseas. N.D.C

[32] Hardy, *op cit*.

and other agencies have made a huge effort to attract foreign investment, and there has been some success in attracting a few large multinationals. The level of jobs created as a result of these successful inward investments is in dispute, but, at least in comparison with other United Kingdom regions, the region does claim to be faring as well as other regions. It compares favourably with Scotland, Wales, Northern Ireland,Midlands and Yorkshire and Humberside in securing Far Eastern investment, although there was a great deal of dismay to have been seen to lose out to South Wales on the Lucky Goldstar investment. Siemens U.K. was the last big success for the region with all agencies claiming to have been the one responsible for attracting the Company.

The picture of economic regeneration in the North had begun to change with the setting up of the Northern Development Company, followed in 1986/87 by the North East Assembly of Local Authorities, and has changed markedly over the past 5 years with the influx of inward investors, and an increasing role for the business sector. N.D.C. was initially set up with public and private sector finance, with the former providing the majority of funds for start-up, and an anticipation that it would become self financing over a period of time.

There are conflicting views on where the stimulus came from to set up the N.D.C. thus, trade union representatives and local politicians claim credit for a sustained lobby during the 1970s and early 1980s when the region was experiencing particularly poor economic recessionary conditions; the worst since the depression of the 1930s. In the opinion of labour representatives there has been continuous pressure exerted on central governments of all political persuasions to enable the region to have some form of Development Agency to rectify many of the deeply rooted economic problems.

On the other hand, the former Vice Chancellor of the Universtiy of Durham who is now the Chair of Northumbria Water also claims credit for bringing together most of the influential business and financial representatives to sit alongside local politicians and trade union representatives in an important meeting with Mrs.Thatcher and two of her Ministers in Durham Castle at a top secret meeting held in 1985. The result was that after a heated exchange of views, with Mrs Thatcher asking all representatives present to 'prove their commitment to the region' (as she thumped hard on the table, in her own inimitable style!) by matching business finance with public finances. N.D.C. was then set up with a combination of public/private sector funding. Its Board consisted of representatives from local political parties, trade unions and the business community. At that time the role of the business community was seen to be minimal in comparison to political and public sector officials, though the business representative capacity has been extended in recent years.

At around the same time as the setting up of the N.D.C. representatives of the region's local authorities began to think it apposite to set up a regional forum for the exchange of views, and the North of England Assembly of Local Authorities was formed with representation from all supporting Local Authorities. This body had a clear aim to work very closely with N.D.C.

in a strategic role; N.D.C. having been set up primarily to promote and market the region as a way of securing inward investment

The setting up of the two aforementioned agencies could be regarded as a watershed in the history of Northern economic regeneration, and even though there may be some difference of opinion on how, and why they were set up, there is little disagreement on the fact that for the first five years or so of operation, the role of the business community in economic regeneration was minimised in relation to the role of the public sector. However, over the past 5 years there have been many significant changes within the arena of economic regeneration, with the business community now taking a much larger and high profile role in regional decision making than it had hitherto done.

Siemens U.K.

An analysis of the factors which combined together to lead to the decision by Siemens, one of the worlds leading electrical and electronic engineering companies,to locate its latest semiconductor plant in the North East of England shows that important role played by regional agencies. The invesment involved which was an estimated £1.1 billion is set to generate1,800 jobs in the first phase, in a region which has suffered severely from structural decline in the past two decades. The plant will produce ASICS (Application Specific Integrated Ciricuits) which are logic chips tailor made for use in telecommunications etc. The decision was presented by the government as a confirmation of the success of its economic policies, in particular those which had contributed in the words of Ian Lang to the creation of 'our skilled and flexible labour force' and 'excellent labour relations',which could be interpreted partially as a reference to the greatly reduced bargaining power of the trade unions in British industry and the subsequent absence of the fairly rigid demarcation of labour roles which was characteristic of British manufacturing industry in the 1970's. This particular decision is of interest because it allows an analysis of the roles played by the complex network of agencies involved in enticing Siemens to locate in the United Kingdom, and subsequently to choose the North East of England as its ideal location. The most significant factors attending this particular decision are the particular practices and features which can be deemed to have assisted North Tyneside in persuading the senior management of Siemens to choose them.

There were many complex reasons underlying Siemens decision to locate the plant in North Tyneside and the case illustrates that successful inter-agency working arrangements were crucially important to the decision making process. In addition the distinct contribution of each agency in this case synthesised into a creative and flexible synergy which provided an optimal array of advantages for North Tyneside, resulting in the decision in their favour.

The case also brings into focus the issue of exactly how much power and influence regional actors wield in comparison with the role of central government. What is clear from this case is that the prime movers were arms of central government, such as the private offices of the Prime Minister and the Deputy Prime Minister, the Department of Trade and Industry (DTI) and its Invest in Britain Bureau (IBB) and the DTI Industrial Development Unit. Having won the decision in favour of the United Kingdom, these central government agenies were then able to draw the regional agencies into the process. This 'top-down' progression represents a departure from previous inward investment successes where regional agencies have been more to the fore.

Background to the decision

Siemens is one of the worlds leading companies in the field of electrical and electronic engineering, it employs over 300,000 worldwide. Although German owned, it has ambitions to become a truly global company,and has for some years has been expanding the scope of its operations throughout the world. The company's Semi-Conductors Group has moved strongly into profit in recent years,reflecting this profitability a series of new plants have come into production in the past few years,notably in Villach in Austria and in Regensburg near Dresden in Germany. Because of the rapidly changing and expanding nature of the world semi-conductors market it was necessary to add a further large production unit to Siemens capacity. The desire to look at sites in other countries was governed by the firms need to be present in major semi-conductor markets outside of Germany, and the United Kingdom being the second largest in Europe was an obvious strong contender,furthermore the company is well established in the United Kingdom, in 1993 it celebrated the 150th anniversary of its establishment in the United Kingdom.

In January 1995 an initial enquiry was made to the Invest in Britain Bureau (IBB) an arm of the DTI in London from Siemens concerning possible sites for a major wafer fabrication plant in the United Kingdom, the potential scale of the investment, a projected £1.1 billion produced a rapid response at the highest levels, (the Deputy Prime Minister Michael Heseltine was actively involved from the earliest stages). The IBB immediately entered into close co-ordination with English Partnerships. In doing this IBB greatly enhanced the strategic role of English Partnerships, by not contacting the Regional Development Agencies directly about the impending opportunity, they instead placed English Partnerships in the position of selecting suitable sites from its portfolio. This was partially a result of the stringent technical requirements of a micro-chip manufacturing plant,which requires above all a level, green field, vibration-free site with access to an industrial scale electrical supply and a pure water source. Another important factor was the extreme urgency of the case, because of the rapidly changing nature of the semi-conductor market,speed was of the essence. IBB required an agency with a national profile to provide an objective technical analysis of the case for each contending site,to have involved the regional agencies at this stage would have invited a competitive auction of contending claims as each region vied with the other for the ear of the Siemens executives. It seems likely that with the winding up of the work of the Development Corporations in 1997 will provide an opportunity for the enhanced strategic role of English Partnerships to continue, acting as it did in the Siemens case as a coordinator of the various regional development agencies, thereby reducing unnecessary competitive posturing between the agencies and fruitless duplication of effort.

English Partnerships produced a brochure identifying potentially technically suitable sites. Siemens executives were given further information on the various sites,until the contenders were narrowed down to the Hadrian Business Park on North Tyneside and the Springvale Park near Wolverhampton. Between June and July 1995 many different executives from Siemens visited the two prime sites identified by English Partnerships. It was in this period that the regional agencies in the North East and the West Midlands were drawn into the process. From this point on the pace of consultation and investigation was frenetic, from the 16th May 1995 to the 2nd August there were five site visits by senior executives from Siemens to the North Tyneside site. In the course of these visits,and in between, a whole series of considerations and queries were raised by Siemens, the ability of the local agencies to collaborate in their efforts, so as to provide Siemens with the high quality data they required to make their decision was crucial to the final decision. After a board meeting in Munich on Friday 4th August Siemens AG announced their decision to build a new semi-conductor plant in North Tyneside.

Strategic considerations

Research into the Siemens decision involved the authors in interviewing representatives of all the local and national agencies,as well as senior figures within Siemens AG. From these interviews we derived considerable insight into the strategic business considerations which persuaded Siemens to locate in the North East of England.

In the past two years in particular many German companies have felt under pressure from the strength of the Deutsch-Mark which has made it more difficult to compete in export marks. The semi-conductor chip market is one of the fastest growing markets in the world valued currently at well over US$200 billion. Since it is a truly world wide market and the product is portable and of very high added value then constraints to retain production in or near Germany have been greatly reduced. After a decade in which Siemens made large losses in semi-conductors, the signs in the past two years are that this particular area of their business is beginning to yield significant dividends. In 1993-94 semi-conductors accounted for 7 percent of group sales and 14 percent of pre-tax profit. Revenue from semi-conductor chips rose from DM 3.1bn in 1994, an increase of 43% from the previous year, to DM 4.2bn in 1995 (a further increase of 36%). (Siemens Annual Reports 1994 and 1995). Clearly this is a rapidly expanding and highly profitable market sector, for which Siemens needed to increase their productive capacity so as to continue their expansion of their market share.

The rapidly changing nature of this market also accounts for the crucial importance Siemens attached to an expeditious decision making process regarding this investment. It must also be remembered that the United Kingdom alone represents a massive market for semi-conductors being worth £3.5 billion per annum as one of our respondents within Siemens put it 'we want to be close to that market'.

In addition labour costs in Germany are now a great deal higher than in many other parts of the European Union, both in terms of hourly labour costs and also in non-wage labour costs such as employers contributions to social insurance, see Table 1.[33]

Table 1
Manufacturing Labour Costs
Differential UK-GERMANY

Country	*A*[a]	*B*[b]	*Index (UK = 100)*
Germany	23.5	25.71	201
United Kingdom	15.5	12.76	100

[a]Non Wage Labour Costs as percentage of total hourly labour costs.
[b]Total Hourly Labour Costs in US dollars 1993.

The significance of this differential in Siemens calculations was confirmed in Siemens senior managements responses to our questionaire on the relative importance of factors in Tynesides favour where it consistently was cited as 'a very important factor of crucial significance', the highest rating possible. Although it is estimated that in a capital intensive venture such as this labour costs will only represent at most about 15% of the projects total costs, this withstanding it is still a significant enough differential to ensure that the North East's low wage levels were undoubtedly an important factor in the firms considerations

To this advantage as a nation can be added the North East's additional attractiveness for Siemens as a region where workers in manufacturing industry are paid considerably below the national average, see Table 2.[34]

[33]The figures for total labour costs come from the United States Bureau of Labour Statistics; these give total hourly labour costs in manufacturing industry. These figures also show the proportion of total cost that goes in direct pay,including holiday pay and pay for time not worked. The remainder the non-wage element, mainly comprises employers social security contributions and other compulsory expenditure like pension contributions and health insurance. Source: *United States Bureau of Labour Statistics.*

[34]Full Time Manual Employees on adult rates - pay unaffected by absence. Source: *New Earnings Survey* – Part A, Department of Employment HMSO, September, 1994.

Table 2

Average Gross Weekly Earnings in Great Britain, April 1994-

region	*adult earnings*	
	Men	*Women*
South East	299.2	204.4
East Anglia	273.5	172.5
South West	271.1	173.4
West Midlands	274.2	175.4
East Midlands	273.3	169.7
Yorkshire & Humberside	277.0	172.7
North West	279.4	175.7
North	278.5	172.9
Wales	272.3	175.7
Scotland	269.5	183.1
England	282.6	183.1
Great Britain	280.7	181.9

These figures show that wage rates in manufacturing industry in the North of England are significantly below the National Average for England, a discrepancy which is more marked in the case of female labour than in the case of male labour.

As well as the competitive labour costs of the region we must also appreciate the significance of a ready pool of labour being available to employers, North Tynesides unemployment rate in October 1996 stood at a rate of 8.9 %, with the bulk of this being male unemployment (12.3% of the male labour force are unemployed). Reflecting the changing nature of the local economy with the decline of the secondary and primary production sectors and the growth of employment in the tertiary sectors the figures for female unemployment is significantly lower however at 4.3%. It is not certain at this stage what the gender composition of the Siemens workforce in North Tyneside is likely to be, however it is safe to assume that a significant number of the production staff will be females. The main impediment to a substantial proportion of the workforce being female will be the likely requirement of Siemens for the workforce to be available for shiftwork in order to meet the companies requirement of round-the-clock production which may deter women with domestic responsibilities for school age children. There is every likelihood however that single school leavers will be recruited and trained for the production work, with the company benefiting substantially from a flexible fast-learning workforce who will be satisfied to be paid wages marginally above the regional average for production staff. Since the regional average wage is sustantially below the European average pay level in any case, the company will be satisfied that it has found a location where it has the luxury of attracting a large number of eager recruits whilst incurring relatively low labour costs in comparison to other parts of the European Union. An indication of the large pool of labour Siemens will be able to choose from, is indicated by The Daily Telegraph report that on the first working day after the announcement of Siemens decision, the Monday 7th August, over 3,000 telephone enquiries had been made to the employment centre in North Shields by noon. Another important labour factor which carried significant weight with the Siemens management team was the finaincial role that Tyneside Training and Enterprise Council was willing to play in the training of the workforce required by Siemens. Furthermore regional Universites were involved very early in the process to advise on the types of skilled engineers required from the plant.

As well as the prominence given by senior Siemens personnel to labour market considerations, the other most prominent factor referred to consistently is the important role played by the financial package devised by central government and the local agencies to offset some of the costs Siemens might incur for land purchase, site preparation and buildings. Although Siemens respondents cited the financial assistance as being of great significance to the final decision, it is clear from the reseach undertaken, that this alone would not have been sufficient to sway the decision in Tynesides favour, since the financial inducements offered by the Austrian government were in fact greater in sum than those available in the United Kingdom. North Tyneside certainly qualified for for Regional Selective Assistance (RSA) as an area in need of investment to revitalise its economy, furthermore it became apparent to Siemens that more than just the RSA grant would apply in their case.

Although there were wildly speculative figures quoted in the press concerninig the size of the financial package our research indicates that the package finally offered was substantial but not excessive,and most importantly included a series of attendant commitments to assist Siemens get their new plant into production as quickly as possible. Respondents to the questions we asked confirmed that the RSA grant amounted to £30 m which represented the single largest component of the package. Agencies such as the North Tyneside City Challenge fund and the Tyneside Training and Enterprise Council (TEC) combined to offer a fund of £15 m to contribute to infrastructure development and training costs respectively. English Partnerships took financial responsibility for the site preparation, a contribution of a further £15 m. North Tyneside Council also contributed a further £150,000. In addition to the financial commitments of central government and the local agencies, there was a comprehensive set of non-financial commitments to support Siemens investment. Since the land for the site is largely on enterprise zone land, the site is therefore mostly zero-rated. Also with the arrival of Siemens North Tyneside City Challenge altered the direction of many of its programmes so as to dovetail its infrastructure programme to meet the needs of Siemens.

A regional regime in the North?

The Siemens F.D.I. case is quite different to the earlier F.D.I. successes in the Northern region because of the high profile involvement of the Prime

Minister, his Deputy and the central government agencies. It indicates that although the main regional agencies were marginalised in the initial phases their role was still of great importance in the implementation phase. N.D.C, G.O.N.E, N.E.A. and the Regional Chamber worked in a coordinated way to draft in many other actors and agencies. The picture is a very complicated one but does not negate the existence of a regional regime. If regimes can be regarded as important networks the work of Van Waarden might prove to be a conclusive application to the findings on the North East. He dilineated networks into 'open' and 'closed' systems, thus:

> 'Open systems are issue-based, open ended, ad-hoc, unstable not necessarily having mutual dependence, informal, fragmented, intricate and with no central authority. Closed systems, on the other hand, have a central authority, a stable set of participants, variable mutual committment, dependence and segmentation.[35]

The position in the North with regard to the existence of a regional regime for economic development suggests that there is a mixture of open and closed elements. There is clearly a strong, strategic lead given by N.D.C and the North of England Assembly of Local Authorities(despite the fact that both bodies were marginalised in the Siemens case). Central authority seems to rest with G.O.N.E, the Integrated Regional Office, as the main funding body from central government, and N.D.C as the regionally recognised body charged with securing inward investment. Both are generally regarded as performing a valuable role in this area. However it is too simple to assume that all economic development initiatives are public sector driven. The participants in any initiative are changeable over time, and drawn in ad hoc to deal with situations as and when they arise. The business community has developed a strong voice in the region, as have many entrepreneurial public bureaucrats, with the result that there is a collaborative process based on an intricate and fragmented, but mutually reciprocal set of arrangements. This fluidity is based on strong relationships between the various actors, many of whom have long standing personal and professional relationships going back many years. Actors and agencies are drawn into the process at different points, and at different times. The region is regarded as a continuously learning region with, what could be regarded as an almost 'virtual reality' regime for economic regeneration. The position in the northern region is, in this author's view very different to other regions of the United Kingdom.

The cohesion and mutual trust necessary for maintaining and smoothing informal relationships is very evident in the case of a regional regime for economic development in the north, and it is this factor above all others that makes the region stand out from other regions in the United Kingdom. The strategic, regional overview is a continuous and consciously thought out process enacted through an effective set of governance arrangements, or a regenerative regional regime.

---

[35] F.Van Waarden, 'Dimensions and types of policy networks', *European Journal of Policy Research*, vol (?), 1992.

Hegel

Howard Williams
University of Wales, Aberystwyth

'Hegel's Philosophy of History and the *Philosophy of Right* '[1]

Introduction

According to Hegel there is but one philosophy which manifests itself in various forms throughout the history of philosophy. This one philosophy does not make itself known in a hap-hazard way. Rather this one philosophy expresses itself in a progressive development from the pre-Socratic onwards. The task of the historian of philosophy, a task which Hegel himself undertakes in his Lectures on the History of Philosophy is to uncover this development and to point the way to the authetic philosophy. This applies also to political philosophy. The history of political philosophy should not be depicted as one accumulated mass of standpoints at variance with one another. Ultimately the history of political philosophy can be boiled down to the development and expression of the one standpoint. This one progressive standpoint is, as Hegel sees it, spirit (*Geist*) revealing itself.

This paper opens up a potentially vast topic. In every detail Hegel's approach to philosophical issues is coloured by his understanding of the history of philosophy and particular figures within it. In his approach to the history of philosophy Hegel is both extraordinarily ambitous and, oddly, extraordinarily modest. He is hugely ambitious in that he seeks to absorb into his thinking most of what he believes to be significant in the history of philosophy, but he is strangely modest in that he believes this puts him in the position not to write his own entirely novel and enterprising philosophy but rather it puts him in the position that his own philosophy is determined as the outcome of all previously philosophy. Hegel builds on past philosophy to present his own system, but that system is not, in his view, uniquely his own but rather what the culmination of philosophy requires him to present.

I do not intend to pursue in their entirety the issues raised by this contrast between Hegel's apparent humility and immodesty raise here. Instead I hope to shed some light upon the possible role of some aspects of the history of political philosophy upon Hegel's major work in political philosophy. Hegel's *Philosophy of Right* is often obscure for the modern day reader because it it is not immediately clear what he is attempting to do nor why he takes the approach he does. This is particularly so at the beginning where neither the Preface nor the Introduction, dealing as they do with relation of philosophy to practice and the foundations of the will, set a clear context. Here an insight into Hegel's use of the history of philosophy in his political philosophy may help to provide a context. In looking at Hegel's reception

[1] All citations are from *Elements of the Philosophy of Right*, translated by H.B.Nisbet & ed. A.Wood, Cambridge University Press, 1991. The page number is cited first and paragraph number second.

of previous political philosophers we can gain some clues as to the origins of his approach in the *Philosophy of Right.* And since Hegel takes the view that all philosophy is heading in the one direction of the present (evidenced in his own system) we may also gain some more substantive notion of the main themes of the work.

What I want to do is to reduce this issue to mangeable proportions by looking at one or two episodes in the *Philosophy of Right* where the history of philosophy seems particularly important. What leads me to my choice of episodes is my desire to pick on the reception which two political philosophers in particular are given in the *Philosophy of Right*, namely, Rousseau and Plato. It is my impression, although I cannot be statistically precise about this, that it is only two other philosophers, Kant and Fichte, who remotely receive the same kind of attention in the book as Rousseau and Plato. As Hegel's contemporaries, Kant and Fichte provide a great deal of the immediate context within which Hegel writes, Rousseau and Plato contribute to the wider context. Put more positively, my impression is that if Hegel is writing his political philosophy with any two past political philosophers in mind (and given his conception of philosophy he has to have such references points in mind) those two would appear to be Rousseau and Plato.

Rousseau

The first mention of Rousseau in the *Philosophy of Right* is interestingly, and perhaps symptomatically, where Hegel is introducing his notion of ethical life (Sittlichkeit). Hegel explains that subjective freedom is a moment in ethical life but it is a moment which cannot be allowed to dominate. 'The right of individuals to their subjective determination to freedom is fulfilled in so far as they belong to ethical actuality.' (196/153) Freedom, for Hegel, has to be seen in the context of the ethical whole and not apart from it. Hegel quotes with approval the story of the Greek Pythagorean philosopher who when asked by his son about how one might best live replied: 'Make him the citizen of a state with good laws'. In the addition (196/153a) Hegel comments that attempts to remove individuals from the influence of their society by allowing them to grow up in isolation cannot in the end work. Accordingly, the experiment described by Rousseau in *Emile* was bound to fail. No one can successfully isolate people from their society and least of all from the laws of their land. Right and freedom do not come to us in the asocial condition but rather from within society. Hegel sets the scene here for his dialogue with Rousseau on politics by calling into question Rousseau's attraction to an unspoiled natural condition before modern society.

The next significant mention of Rousseau in the *Philosophy of Right* begins in a much more positive vein. This arises where Hegel is discussing the will at the start of the section on the state. For Hegel the substantial will is present at the core of the state, and this is an insight he thinks Rousseau (albeit in a different form) shares. Hegel says 'it was the achievement of Rousseau to put forward the will as the principle of the state, a principle which has thought not only as its form (as with the social instinct, for example, or divine authority) but also as its content, and which is in fact thinking itself.' (277/258) Rousseau's approach to the state in the *Social Contract* was reflective and centred upon the ethical motivation of the individual. It matters for Rousseau how individuals see their relationship with the state. They have to regard themselves as consenting to the political arrangements of their society in order to be true citizens.

Rousseau is critical in the formation of Hegel's theory of the state. Hegel regards as Rousseau's great achievement the bringing of the will into the centre of political thought. But Rousseau does not understand the will in the proper way. Rousseau fails to conceive it as the rational will. The distinction between the particular will and general will is insufficient in Hegel's view. The general will is something partially forced upon the individual from the outside. Rousseau sees the general will not as the summation of all the particular wills of the society (this abstract sum would simply be the anarchical 'will of all') but rather as an approximate average of the motivations of the various particular will. In the general will each individual both gains an advantage in entering fully the wider community, and loses an advantage in losing some of his original freedom. Hegel finds this way of posing the transition to an ethical situation somewhat flawed. As Hegel sees it, no loss is involved in properly becoming members of a civil society. 'Rousseau considered the will only in the determinate form of the individual (einzelnen) will (as Fichte subsequently also did) and regarded the universal will not as the will's rationality in and for itself, but only as the common element arising out of this individual will as a conscious will.' (277/258) Hegel does not like the apparent social detachment that Rousseau brings to the account of the individual will. Hegel is a thorough communitarian in his account of the will. The will is only through the common element to which it belongs. We are individuals first only through the whole.

Hegel's opposition to Rousseau's view of the general will allows him to distance himself from the social contract view of politics. Hegel does not see the state, even from the moral point of view, as being the outcome of a contract or notional agreement. What happens with Rousseau is that

> 'the union of individuals within the state [thus] becomes a contract, which is accordingly based on their arbitrary will and opinions, and on their express consent given at their own discretion'. (277/258)

This is far too voluntarist for Hegel and the acceptance of the contract idea in practice as advocated by Rousseau had appalling consequences. Invested with Rousseau's ideas sections of the French population undertook the most hazardous adventure at the time of the Revolution. These people sought to rebuild society from the ground up based upon the idea of abstract freedom. Hegel sees the radicals of the French Revolution as excessive rationalists who attempted 'the revision of its [France's] constitution from first principles and purely in terms of thought.' The outcome was catastrophic. 'The intention behind this was to give [the constitution] what was supposed to be a purely rational basis. On the other hand, since these were only abstractions divorced from the idea, they turned the attempt into the most terrible and drastic event.' (277/258)

Hegel would argue that Rousseau with his notion of the general will was striving at a genuine political truth for the modern world. For it to be successful the modern state has to bind the particular will of the individual with the universal will of the whole. So Hegel gives credit to Rousseau for grasping the idea that there has to be a rational will at work in the modern constitution. But Hegel disputes that Rousseau has developed this rational principle properly. Hegel doubtlessly would disagree with the averaging procedure Rousseau employs to create the general will. This is far too empirical a procedure. One will cannot be measured against the other will in a simple arithmetical way. Moreover Rousseau's averaging procedure means that no individual can fully identify with the general will. With Rousseau we all have to suffer some loss of our freedom of action to bring it into being. But, as Hegel sees it, no loss at all is incurred in bringing into being a genuinely universal will. The genuinely universal will is the foundation for any particularity or individuality in society.

Hegel's universal will (ultimately the product of spirit) is somewhat at a distance therefore from Rousseau's concept of the general will. As Hegel would see it, Rousseau glimpsed incompletely and somewhat obscurely the genuine truth. Hegel's vision of a political community slightly favours the totality and Rousseau's vision slightly favours the individual. But can we conclude from this that Hegel has philosophically superceded Rousseau? Might not a case still be made for Rousseau's general will being more workable than Hegel's universal will (balanced as it is very much in favour of the state)? Rousseau at least does not cede authority in Hegel's fashion to supra-historical forces. Individuals have to make up their minds themselves with Rousseau about social issues, with Hegel the impression is often created that they should have their minds made up for them. It is ironic that Hegel seeks to attribute to Rousseau blame for the bloody outcome of the French Revolution when it is he, rather than Rousseau, who is more inclined to see individuals at the mercy of blind historical forces. Some of Rousseau's ideas may have gone into the making of the French Revolution, but Rousseau can no more be blamed for the course of the French Revolution than Hegel can be blamed for the outcome of the Bolshevik Revolution (instigated by one of his most enthusiastic readers – Lenin).

Plato

If Rousseau has an important influence on Hegel's orientation towards political philosophy Plato's influence is even more fundamental. Plato is mentioned very early on in the *Philosophy of Right* in the Preface where Hegel considers the issue of the role of the political philosopher. The whole question of the role of the political philosopher in society had been rendered problematic for Hegel at the time of publishing the *Philosophy of Right* by Jacob Fries's intervention in German politics. Fries, a professor of philosophy at Jena, was a supporter of the Burschenschaft movement, a liberal-nationalist student organization. Fries had spoken at the Wartburg Festival of the students's societies which had led to his being suspended from his post at the University. Fries was far too much of a populist in Hegel's view who threatened to bring the whole of philosophy into disrepute by his ill-timed intervention. Hegel was not wholly hostile to the liberal trends in German society and the student movements which were giving it expression, but he was undoubtedly hostile to Fries's mode of philosophical intervention in public debates.

Hegel argues for a non-activist role for the philosopher in his Preface. He does not see it as the direct task of the philosopher to change the political complexion of the world. Hegel sees the role of political philosophy as that of dispassionate analysis. He regards its role as analogous to that of the natural sciences. The role of political philosophy is to discern in the world what is already rational.

Plato is drawn into this debate because Hegel believes that, despite appearances to the contrary, Plato shares his own reflective view of political philosophy. At first sight, this is a strange view for Hegel to take. Plato seems to want to give the philosopher a central political position. In the *Republic* he takes the view that there will be no peace in the world nor sound political order until philosophers are rulers and rulers philosophers. Here Plato seems to be according high authority to philosophers in determining political policy. We might legitmately argue that Plato wants to see the state run by philosophers. But this is not how Hegel sees (or rather interprets) the *Republic.* Hegel refuses to see the *Republic* as an immediate call to arms on behalf of philosophers. Rather Hegel sees Plato's masterpiece as a belated but vain attempt to prevent Athenian politics from being subverted by false principles. In other words, Hegel's contention is that Plato knew that it was already too late for philosophy to affect the outcome of events.

> 'Even Plato's *Republic*, a proverbial example of an empty ideal, is essentially the embodiment of nothing other than the nature of Greek ethics; and Plato, aware that the ethics of his time were being penetrated by a deeper principle which, within this context, could appear immediately as an as yet unsatisfied longing and hence only as a destructive force, was obliged, in order to counteract it, to seek the help of that very longing itself. But the help he required had to come from above, and he could seek it at first only in a particular external form of Greek ethics. By this means, he imagined he could overcome the destructive force, and he thereby inflicted the gravest damage on the deeper drive behind it, namely free infinite personality. But he proved his greatness of spirit by the fact that the very principle on which the distinctive character of his Idea turns is the pivot on which the impending world revolution turned.' (20)

This is an extraordinarily difficult passage to unravel. But one of Hegel's broad themes is that in Plato's times Greek society had developed to such a point that any kind of philosophical intervention was fated to fail. So Hegel concludes that Plato was not serious about the rule of philosophers. What Plato was serious about, however, was stopping the flowering of individuality and independence in Greek society. Plato tries to employ all means at his disposal to prevent this. Inadvertently in doing this Plato reveals the true role of political philosophy. This true role is not to change society, but to outline its true working. What philosophy has to do is to show 'what is rational is actual;and what is actual is rational.' (20) Political philosophy has to reflect its own time in thought.

This interpretation of Plato is a little strained. There is no reason to believe that at the time of writing the *Republic* Plato was not perfectly serious about making philosophers into rulers. Like many political philosophers Plato had a prescription for the circumstances of politics which even under the most ideal of conditions probably would not have worked. But that the ideal that he was proposing was unattainable cannot be taken to imply that Plato's intention in the *Republic* was entirely different from what it appears to be. Hegel's attempt to uncover the one philosophy in Plato striving to emerge might be more legitimately seen as an attempt to impose upon Plato a purpose he might well not of shared. Hegel seems to want Plato to begin writing the political philosophy which is appropriate for our age rather than Plato's own.

Hegel continues in this vein. Plato is criticized for not anticipating the requirements of the modern age. The theme of Plato's attack on incipient individuality is taken up in Hegel's next remark on the great Greek philosopher. Hegel says in paragraph 46: 'The idea of Plato's republic contains as a universal principle a wrong against the person, inasmuch as the person is forbidden to own private property.' (77) For Hegel the ownership of property is essential to the development of personality. As an individual one has not only to come to own things to give proper expression to oneself but one has also properly to possess one's abilities and characteristics.

Classes in Plato and Hegel

Plato's class divisions follow the natural division of the society's members into their various metallic properties/abilities. The group which possesses gold in its make-up becomes the political class. They are the rulers. Those with souls of gold hold all the political power in the society and make decisions on behalf of the other classes. The Auxiliaries (who represent the police and military arm of the Guardians) have silver in their souls and their task is limited to the physical defence of the state. Their very specialization in the skill of fighting (war-making) will prevent them from undertaking the task of ruler properly. Those who have souls of bronze or iron belong to the manufacturing, financial and agricultural class. Their abilities suit them to these economic tasks. Since Plato describes his account of the different types of soul as a 'noble lie' he does not entirely believe that every human being has absolutely unalterable natural qualities. For the sake of the solidarity and harmony of the society it is simply important that everyone imagines they have the natural qualities for their job. As Hegel would see it, Plato is proposing an absolutely inflexible class system, one which would not do in modern times.

Hegel prefers a class system with mobility which is founded on individual choice. In this respect Plato disappoints Hegel greatly. As Hegel says when he is discussing ethical life: 'Plato, in his *Republic*, presents the substance of ethical life in its ideal beauty and truth; but he cannot come to terms with the principle of self-sufficient particularity, which had suddenly overtaken Greek ethical life in his time ... This principle is historically later than the Greek world.' (222/185) In modern civil society 'subjective opinion' quite rightly decides which estate to which you belong' but with Plato you were placed in your appropriate role by the Guardians. (238/206) As Hegel understands it, it was impossible for Plato to be familiar with the principle of autonomy which colours modern life. 'In Plato's *Republic*, subjective freedom is not yet recognized because individuals still have their tasks assigned to them by the authorities.' (286/262) The best political philosophy of the past highlights the taken for granted assumptions of the politics of the day. In seeing how politics and society are differently constituted in our own time we discover the key principles of our own society.

Hegel's strange argument about Plato is that Plato gets things right even where he gets things wrong. In wanting to exclude the subjective element Plato was attempting the impossible. The impossible was the eruption of individual self-consciousness – which was a necessary development in the growth of human freedom. But in what he sought to do Plato discerned the true nature of the Greek city-state. Athens needed to be an ethical whole, hierarchically organized.

Conclusion

Hegel can neither claim the authority of Plato nor argue that the position he takes flows from Plato's account of political philosophy. This is what he wants to do and the enterprise in this sense fails. With Rousseau there is a perhaps a stronger case for arguing that Hegel develops the logic of Rousseau's position on the general will with his idea of the universal class and the state founded upon the rational will. Rousseau and Hegel stand much closer together in terms of time than Plato and Hegel. This may make Hegel's proposed synthesis more plausible. But oddly Hegel does not want to claim the authority of Rousseau here to sustain the position nor is it wholly necessary consequence of what Rousseau says. Rousseau is perhaps too radical to become an authority for Hegel. Hegel does not press his cumulative and progressive notion of the history of philosophy too strongly in this instance.

Despite these doubts about Hegel's employment of the history of philosophy in the political philosophy of his completed system, I should still like to suggest there is something *sublime* about the way in which Hegel wants to present his position as the logical culmination of previous philosophy. What is sublime about it is not that it holds water but rather in always contrasting and comparing his views with those of previous philosophers (particularly some of the best amongst them) he makes his own position particularly clear. Just as we may know a painting of Picasso better because of what he rejects in classical painting and in the painting of his contemporaries like Braque, so we know Hegel better by what he tries to keep alive in classical philosophy, what he rejects, and sustains in his own. The dialectic may not be cumulative and progressive but it is always highly suggestive and intriguing.

Hegel

Tony Burns
Nottingham Trent University

"Hegel's Interpretation of the Philosophy of Heraclitus: Some Observations"

Introduction

It is well known[1] that Hegel was greatly impressed by the ideas of the Presocratic philosopher Heraclitus.[2] That this is so is evident from a reading of Hegel's *Lectures on the History of Philosophy.*[3] It is here where Hegel claims that 'there is no proposition of Heraclitus which I have not adopted in my Logic'; where he insists that Heraclitus' philosophy is 'not one that is past and gone', for 'its principle is essential and is to be found in the beginning of my Logic'; and where he agrees with the view, attributed to Socrates, that 'What remains to us of Heraclitus is excellent, and we must conjecture of what is lost, that it was as excellent.'[4] Given this, it is not so surprising that Howard Williams should claim that there are 'very few' aspects of Heraclitus' metaphysics 'with which Hegel does not agree' and even, perhaps, that he should go so far as to claim that Hegel 'identifies completely with the philosophy of Heraclitus.'[5] However, this immediately raises an important question, namely, how is Hegel interpreting the views of Heraclitus when he makes these enthusiastic remarks about him in his *Lectures*? It is not entirely clear how this question should be answered.

Hegel is not alone in attaching importance to the ideas of Heraclitus. Heraclitus has also had a great impact on the philosophy of both Friedrich

[1]See, for example, H.Williams, *Hegel, Heraclitus and Marx's Dialectic*, Harvester, 1989; J.Barnes, *The Pre-Socratics*, Routledge, 1989, p.57; J.Burnet, *Early Greek Philosophy*, Adam and Charles Black, 1965, fn. 1, p.144; J.N.Findlay, *Hegel: A Re-Examination*, Collier Books, 1962, p. 45; M.Heidegger, *An Introduction to Metaphysics*, Doubleday Anchor, 1961, p. 106; C.H.Kahn, *The Art and Thought of Heraclitus: An Edition of the Fragments with Translation and Commentary*, Cambridge University Press, 1979, pp. 188-9; W.Kaufmann, *Nietzsche: Philosopher, Psychologist, Antichrist*, Princeton University Press, 1974, pp.241-2; K.Popper, *The Open Society and its Enemies*, 1, Routledge, 1969, fn. 4, p.203; P.Redding, 'Hegel's Logic of Being and the Polarities of Presocratic Thought', *The Monist*, 74, 3, 1991, pp.441- 2.

[2]The editions of the fragments of Heraclitus referred to are: Kahn, *The Art and Thought of Heraclitus*; R.D.McKirahan jnr, *Philosophy Before Socrates: An Introduction With Texts and Commentary*, Hackett Books, 1994; and T.M.Robinson, *Heraclitus: Fragments: Text and Translation With Commentary*, University of Toronto Press, 1987. The fragment numbers are the standard ones employed by Diels & Kranz.

[3]G.W.F.Hegel, *Lectures on the History of Philosophy*, translated by E.S.Haldane & F.H.Simson, in 3 volumes, Routledge, 1968. Hereafter: *Lectures.*

[4]Hegel, *Lectures*, 1, pp.279, 283, 297-8.

[5]Williams, *Hegel, Heraclitus and Marx's Dialectic*, pp.4, 26, 3. In the light of Hegel's remarks, as L.Palmer has argued, it is difficult to accept J.Findlay's claim that Hegel 'altogether fails to give due importance' to Heraclitus' influence on his own thinking. See J.Findlay, 'Hegelianism and Platonism', in J.O'Malley (ed), *Hegel and the History of Philosophy*, Martinus Nijhoff, p.63; and L.Palmer, 'On Hegel's Platonism', in O'Malley (ed), p.80.

Nietzsche[6] and Martin Heidegger.[7] For example, Nietzsche insists that with respect to fundamental principles the philosophy of Heraclitus 'will always be right' and he sets 'apart with high reverence the name of Heraclitus.'[8] The fact that both Hegel and Nietzsche, in particular, should identify themselves so closely with the philosophy of Heraclitus may, at first sight, seem somewhat surprising. For some would argue that the basic principles of their respective philosophies are diametrically opposed to one another.[9] On the other hand, however, it could also be argued that this is not really so surprising after all. For the philosophy of Heraclitus is notorious for its ambiguity. Heraclitus was fond of paradox and is frequently referred to by later writers as the 'obscure', 'the dark one', or even 'the riddler'.[10]

To help clarify the relationship which exists between Hegel and Heraclitus we shall consider in some detail two opposed interpretations of the philosophy of Heraclitus itself, focusing specifically on the questions of ontology, change, and epistemology. For each of these interpretations of the philosophy of Heraclitus there is a corresponding interpretation of Hegel's attitude towards that philosophy. We will maintain that Hegel's assessment of Heraclitus, both in his *Lectures on the History of Philosophy* and elsewhere, is actually quite ambivalent and that the reason for this is that Hegel cannot make up his mind which of the two interpretations of Heraclitus that we are about to discuss he actually prefers. There is therefore, we shall argue, at least some evidence to suggest that Hegel's identification

[6] F.Nietzsche, *The Twilight of the Idols*, translated by R.J.Hollingdale, Penguin Books, 1972, pp.35-6; 'Philosophy in the Tragic Age of the Greeks', in *Early Greek Philosophy and Other Essays*, translated by M.A.Mugge, Edinburgh, 1911; also E.Blondel, 'Nietzsche: Life as Metaphor', in D.Allison (ed), *The New Nietzsche: Contemporary Styles of Interpretation*, MIT Press, 1985, pp.162, 168-9; G.Deleuze, *Nietzsche and Philosophy*, Athlone Press, 1983, pp.23-4; M.Heidegger & Eugen Fink, *Heraclitus Seminar: 1966-67*, University of Alabama Press, 1979, p.115; S.Kofman, 'Metaphor, Symbol, Metamorphosis', in D.Allison (ed), *The New Nietsche*, pp.209-11; W.Kaufmann, *Nietsche*, p.241; J.Lavrin, *Nietzsche: A Biographical Introduction*, London, 1971, p.37; F.A. Lea, *The Tragic Philosopher: Friedrich Nietzsche*, Methuen, 1956, pp.45-6, 230; M.A. Mugge, *Nietsche*, London and Edinburgh, n.d., pp.26, 55, 70.

[7] Cf. M.Heidegger, *Heraclitus Seminar: 1966-67*, p.115; M.Heidegger, *Early Greek Thinking*, translated by D.Krell & F.Cappuzzi, Harper & Row, 1975; M.Heidegger, *Introduction to Metaphysics*, Doubleday Anchor, 1961, pp.82-3, 106-7, 113-4.

[8] Nietzsche, *The Twilight of the Idols*, pp.35-6.

[9] Nietzsche, *Twilight of the Idols*, pp.25, 31-2, 36-7. For Nietzsche's antipathy to Hegel's philosophy see G.Deleuze, *Nietzsche and Philosophy*, pp.8, 156-9, 162; R.J.Hollingdale, *Nietsche*, Routledge, 1973, pp.168-9; M.Tanner, *Nietsche*, Oxford University Press, 1994, pp.9, 53. Also D.Brezeale, 'The Hegel-Nietzsche Problem', *Nietzsche-Studien*, 4, 1975, pp.146-64; S.Houlgate, 'The Hegel-Nietzsche Debate', in *Hegel, Nietzsche and the Critique of Metaphysics*, Cambridge University Press, 1986.

[10] For these descriptions of Heraclitus and some general comments regarding our sources of information in relation to his philosophy see J.Barnes, *The Pre-Socratics*, Routledge, 1989, pp.57-8; F.Copleston, *A History of Philosophy*, 1, Burns & Oates, London, 1951, pp.38-46; W.K.C.Guthrie, *A History of Greek Philosophy*, 1, Cambridge University Press, 1962, pp.403-13; E.Hussey, *The Presocratics*, Duckworth, 1972, pp.32-4; Kahn, *The Art and Thought of Heraclitus*, pp.1-9; G.S.Kirk, *Heraclitus: The Cosmic Fragments*, edited with an Introduction and Commentary, Cambridge University Press, 1962, pp.1-13; G.S.Kirk, J.E.Raven & M.Schofield, *The Presocratic Philosophers*, Cambridge University Press, 1983, pp.181-6; McKirahan, *Philosophy Before Socrates*, pp.128-30; Robinson, *Heraclitus: Fragments*, pp.2-5.

with the philosophy of Heraclitus is by no means complete and that he is in fact somewhat more critical of Heraclitus than some commentators would have us believe.

A First Interpretation of The Philosophy of Heraclitus

According to our first interpretation of the philosophy of Heraclitus, in so far as questions of ontology are concerned the thought of Heraclitus is simply a continuation of that of his predecessors, the Milesian philosophers. The earlier Presocratics all base their thinking on what later philosophers refer to as the 'appearance-reality' distinction.[11] They all assume that it is important that we make a distinction between how things appear to us and how things truly are. On the surface, things appear to us to be isolated and separate from one another, and to be constantly changing. In reality, however, this is not so. Beneath the level of surface appearances there is some underlying, primordial basic 'stuff' or substance, out of which all things are composed, and which itself never changes. There is a realm of Being which we must distinguish from that of Becoming. The difference between the respective philosophies of the earlier Presocratics lies, for the most part, in how the nature of this basic substance is characterised. For example, in the philosophy of Thales water is the basic substance, whereas for Anaximenes this substance is air. On this interpretation, Heraclitus continues this tradition by putting forward a new candidate for the status of primary substance. Hence he is most definitely a 'philosopher' and a 'metaphysician'.[12] He, also, recognises that there is a primary substance or substrate which is permanent and stable and underlies all surface appearances. Commentators do not always agree as to what, in Heraclitus' opinion, this primary substance is. Usually, however, it is suggested that this substance is 'fire'. For, in Heraclitus' own words, 'All things are an exchange for fire.'[13] On this interpretation, then, Heraclitus also acknowledges that there is a realm of Being alongside that of Becoming.

In so far as the idea of change is concerned, not surprisingly, given its assertion that Heraclitus does indeed recognise that there is a realm of Being which underpins that of Becoming, our first interpretation also asserts that Heraclitus' philosophy attaches as much importance to the principle of permanence or stability as it does to that of change. On this interpretation,

---

[11]See J.M.Moravcsik, 'Appearance and Reality in Heraclitus' Philosophy', *The Monist*, 74/4, 1991, pp.551-67.

[12]See Guthrie, *The Greek Philosophers: From Thales to Aristotle*, Methuen, 1967, pp.23-4; Moravcsik, 'Appearance and Reality in Heraclitus' Philosophy', pp.551, 562.

[13]See fr.90; McKirahan, p.124; also Barnes, *Early Greek Philosophy*, Penguin Books, 1987, p.38; J.Barnes, *The Pre-Socratics*, p.61; Burnet, *Greek Philosophy: Thales to Plato*, Macmillan, 1968, pp.49-50; Burnet, *Early Greek Philosophy*, Adam & Charles Black, 1965, pp.144-5; Findlay, *Hegel: A Re-Examination*, p.45; Kirk, Raven & Schofield, *The Presocratic Philosophers*, pp.75, 186, 188; McKirahan, *Philosophy Before Socrates*, p.129; Parker, *A Short Account of Greek Philosophy: From Thales to Epicurus*, Edward Arnold, 1967, p.37; B.Russell, *History of Western Philosophy*, Allen & Unwin, 1974, pp.59, 61; W.T.Stace, *A Critical History of Greek Philosophy*, Macmillan, 1920, p.78; P.Wheelwright, *Heraclitus*, Atheneum Press, 1974, p. 39; Williams, *Hegel, Heraclitus and Marx's Dialectic*, p.26.

it is Heraclitus' view that although things certainly do change, and this is important, nevertheless they also persist in and through this process of change. That this is Heraclitus' view is evident from the wording of the famous 'river statement' for which, in later ages, he was to become so notorious: 'Upon those who step into the same rivers, different and again different waters flow'. From this point of view, then, there could be no perceived change unless there is also some stability or persistence, some thing which changes.[14] Thus, although Heraclitus evidently does subscribe to a 'flux theory' of some sort, and perhaps even to a theory of 'constant flux', he nevertheless rejects the extreme version of such a theory that has been attributed to him from the time of Plato onwards.[15]

According to our first interpretation, this recognition of the importance of the principle of stability as well as that of change is only what is to be expected given the emphasis which Heraclitus places on the idea of the 'unity of opposites' in his philosophy generally; for 'stability' and 'change' are themselves precisely two such polar opposites. From this standpoint, then, Heraclitus' approach to the problem of change might be said to be one which is fundamentally binary or dualistic. All processes of change should be understood as being in some way related to the conflict which exists between polar opposites.[16] Moreover, all change when properly understood can be apprehended to be, not random, chaotic and completely governed by chance, but on the contrary regular, ordered and lawlike. Change is thought of as being imbued with a certain direction, purpose or goal. It is regulated by the principles of reason or logos, that is to say divine law.[17]

Regarding the problem of knowledge, our first interpretation maintains that Heraclitus considers this problem in much the same way that later philosophers do. He takes the view that genuine knowledge is knowledge of reality, or of how things truly are beneath the surface appearances of things. For, he says, 'Nature loves to hide', that is to say, a thing's 'real constitution has a tendency to conceal itself.'[18] Such knowledge is, it is claimed, associated with our apprehension of absolute truths. On this interpretation, Heraclitus has reservations about the senses and sense-perception as a possible source of such knowledge. He is of the opinion that the senses

[14]Fr.12; McKirahan, p.122. Fragment 84a, Kahn, p.53, reinforces the point: 'It rests by changing.'

[15]For this interpretation of Heraclitus' views on change see Barnes, *The Pre- Socratics*, pp.66-9; Emlyn-Jones, 'Heraclitus and the Identity of Opposites', *Phronesis*, 21, 1976, p.92, fn.1; Findlay, *Hegel: A Re-Examination*, p.45; Kirk, 'Natural Change in Heraclitus', in A.Mourelatos (ed), *The Presocratic Philosophers*, Anchor Books, 1976, p.195; Kirk, 'Popper on Science and the Presocratics', in D.Furley & R.Allen (eds), *Studies in Presocratic Philosophy*, 1, London, 1970, pp.171-6; McKirahan, *Philosophy Before Socrates*, pp.142-4; Russell, *History of Western Philosophy*, pp.59, 62-3.

[16]For the view that Heraclitus subscribes to a more moderate doctrine of 'constant flux' which is a corollary of his theory of 'opposites' see Copleston, *A History of Philosophy*, 1, p.39; Guthrie, *History of Greek Philosophy*, 1, pp.447-8; Wilde, *Marx and Contradiction*, p.8; Williams, *Hegel, Heraclitus and Marx*, p.10.

[17]Kirk, *Heraclitus: The Cosmic Fragments*, p.257; Williams, *Hegel, Heraclitus and Marx's Dialectic*, p.25.

[18]Fr.123, McKirahan, p.123; Robinson, p.71. Also fr.54; McKirahan, p.121: 'An unapparent connection is stronger than an apparent one.'

deceive us, for 'Eyes and ears are bad witnesses to people if they have barbarian souls.'[19] This does not mean, however, that genuine knowledge is impossible. This is so because there is an alternative source of knowledge, namely reason or logos (*logos*).[20] It is reason which gives us an insight into the ultimate nature of things and into absolute truth. Thus Heraclitus is a 'rationalist' philosopher.[21] This is so whether we are considering metaphysical questions or moral and political ones. In so far as the latter, in particular, are concerned, Heraclitus is of the opinion that here also there are certain truths which are timeless and universal and which are discoverable by reason. In this regard he might be said to be a forerunner of the stoic philosophy with its belief in divine or natural law. For, as with Stoicism, Heraclitus maintains that 'Right thinking is the greatest excellence', that 'wisdom is to speak the truth and act in accordance with nature', and that 'all human laws are nourished by one law, the divine law.'[22]

A First Interpretation of Hegel's Attitude Towards Heraclitus

There is certainly some evidence to support the view that Hegel subscribes to this first interpretation of the philosophy of Heraclitus. For example, with respect to questions of ontology, in the *Lectures on the History of Philosophy* he claims that Heraclitus is, like himself, most definitely a metaphysician with clear ideas of his own regarding the nature of the 'one' primary substance or reality which underpins the surface appearances of things.[23] He points out that, for this reason, Heraclitus 'is still reckoned as belonging to the Ionic school of natural philosophers' by most commentators, although these commentators cannot agree whether he considers this primary substance to be 'fire' or 'air'.[24] He even goes so far as to imply that, for

[19]Fr.107; McKirahan, p.118; and fr.56; McKirahan, p.117: 'People are deceived about the knowledge of obvious things...'; also Barnes, *Early Greek Philosophy*, p.113; Cherniss, 'The Characteristics and Effects of Presocratic Philosophy', in Furley & Allen (eds), *Studies in Presocratic Philosophy*, 1, p.21; Guthrie, *The Greek Philosophers*, pp.43-4, 88; Kahn, *The Art and Thought of Heraclitus*, pp.186-7, 293-5; T.M.Robinson, 'Heraclitus and Plato on the Language of the Real', *The Monist*, 74/4, p.484; Williams, Hegel, Heraclitus and Marx's Dialectic, p.14.

[20]Fr.1, McKirahan, p.116: 'This Logos holds always ...'; fr.50, McKirahan, p.120: 'Listening not to me but to the logos ...'.

[21]See Barnes, *Early Greek Philosophy*, pp.21-2; Copleston, *A History of Philosophy*, 1, p.43; Guthrie, *The Greek Philosophers*, pp.43-4; Kirk, *Heraclitus: The Cosmic Fragments*, p.231; Robinson, 'Heraclitus and Plato on the Language of the Real', p.484; J.M.Moravcsik, 'Heraclitean Concepts and Explanations', in K.Robb (ed), *Language and Thought in Early Greek Philosophy*, La Salle, Illinois, 1983, pp.142-7; G.Moyal, 'The Unexpressed Rationalism of Heraclitus', *Revue de Philosophie Ancienne*, 7, 2, 1989, p.187; Stace, *A Critical History of Greek Philosophy*, p.79; Williams, *Hegel, Heraclitus and Marx's Dialectic*, pp.15, 25.

[22]Fr.112; McKirahan, p.120; fr.114; McKirahan, p.122; also Cleve, *The Giants of Pre-Socratic Philosophy*, 1, Martinus Nijhoff, 1969, pp.41-2, 121; Emlyn-Jones, 'Heraclitus and the Identity of Opposites', p.106; Kahn, *The Art and Thought of Heraclitus*, pp.6, 15; Kirk, *Heraclitus: The Cosmic Fragments*, p.53, 69; McKirahan, *Philosophy Before Socrates*, p.148; Robinson, 'Heraclitus and Plato on the Language of the Real', pp.483-4.

[23]Hegel, *Lectures*, pp.283, 292.

[24]Hegel, *Lectures*, pp.285-6.

Heraclitus, it is 'reason' or logos which is the primary substance, and hence that Heraclitus may be considered to be an early proponent of his own doctrine of philosophical idealism.[25] Similarly, with respect to the problem of change, Hegel draws attention to Heraclitus' emphasis on the conflict which exists between opposites as the driving force which lies behind all processes of change. This is Heraclitus' 'great principle'.[26] He also points out, with approval, the fact that Heraclitus considers all processes of change to be regular, ordered and law-like. This being so because change always occurs in accordance with the principles of 'reason' or logos which inform the whole of reality.[27] And finally, with respect to the problem of knowledge, Hegel presents Heraclitus as being someone who, though not a sceptic, nevertheless doubts the reliability of the senses as a potential source of knowledge and who is, therefore, like himself, basically a 'rationalist', not only in matters philosophical but also in matters ethical and political.[28]

This assessment of Hegel's understanding of the philosophy of Heraclitus is reinforced by what Hegel has to say about the Heraclitean concept of Becoming, both in the *Lectures* and in the *Shorter Logic.* For example, he refers to the concept of Becoming as 'the first concrete' principle in the history of philosophy. This is so because it is a synthesis of two other principles, namely that of Being on the one hand and Nothing on the other. The principle of Becoming therefore, Hegel suggests, is one which embraces the principle of 'the unity of opposites'. It is a principle which is genuinely 'speculative' and which stands on an altogether different and 'higher' level from the principle of Being associated with the philosophy of Parmenides, which is a principle of 'the abstract understanding' only. It is for this reason, he insists, that Heraclitus' principle of Becoming represents such a monumental advance in the history of philosophy. As it is the first concrete thought term, it is also the 'first adequate vehicle of truth'.[29] From this point of view, the concept of Becoming is quite unlike that of Being. For, as Ivan Soll has pointed out, the latter is merely a 'one sided and simple abstraction', whereas the former is a 'higher' or more 'total' concept.[30]

In short, then, some of the things which Hegel says in his *Lectures* do indeed support the claim that he more or less identifies his own philosophy with that of Heraclitus. He reads Heraclitus as an early exponent of the principles of 'Hegelianism'. In his own philosophical system he merely repeats, uncritically, what Heraclitus has already said before him.

---

[25] Hegel, *Lectures*, pp.282, 293-4.

[26] Hegel, *Lectures*, pp.282, 284-5.

[27] Hegel, *Lectures*, pp.293, 296.

[28] Hegel, *Lectures*, pp.293-4, 296.

[29] Cf. Hegel, *Lectures*, p.279; also G.W.F.Hegel, *Hegel's Logic: Being Part One of the Encyclopaedia of the Philosophical Sciences*, translated by W.Wallace, Oxford University Press, 1975, s.88z, p.132. Also Q Lauer, 'Hegel as Historian of Philosophy', in O'Malley (ed), *Hegel and the History of Philosophy*, p.36; L.Palmer, 'On Hegel's Platonism', p.80; and by I.Soll, *An Introduction to Hegel's Metaphysics*, Chicago University Press, 1969, pp.137-8.

[30] Soll, *Introduction to Hegel's Metaphysics*, pp.137-8.

A Second Interpretation of the Philosophy of Heraclitus

According to our second interpretation of Heraclitus, the thinking of Heraclitus actually constitutes a radical break from that of the Milesian philosophers. This is so because it is based on an implicit rejection of the appearance-reality distinction as it is traditionally understood. From this point of view, therefore, Heraclitus has no metaphysics and is not a 'philosopher' in the traditional sense at all.[31] He rejects the very idea of a primary substance or substrate which underlies the surface appearances of things and which remains stable whilst they change. As Rex Warner puts it, Heraclitus maintains that nothing 'exists statically. There 'is no "stuff".'[32] The references which Heraclitus makes to 'fire' in the fragments are not at all to be taken literally. They are actually metaphors which Heraclitus employs to in an attempt to communicate his implicit rejection of the view that there is any underlying 'reality' which is changeless.[33] On this view, Heraclitus maintains that the world of appearances is itself the only 'reality'.[34]

From the standpoint of our second interpretation, therefore, the opinions of Heraclitus with respect to change are quite different from those presented earlier. Here it is asserted that a logical implication of Heraclitus' approach to questions of ontology is the claim that there is actually no realm of Being at all. Rather, all is Becoming.[35] Understood in this way, Heraclitus adopts a standpoint which is evidently not binary or dualistic but monistic or one-sided. It is acknowledged here, as before, that Heraclitus subscribes to a doctrine of permanent change or 'constant flux'. In this case, though, the 'flux' doctrine, is given a much more radical interpretation. It is taken

[31]See Heidegger & Fink, *Heraclitus Seminar*, pp.64-5, 67, 75; also Waugh, 'Heraclitus: The Postmodern Presocratic?', *The Monist*, 74/4, pp.613, 620.

[32]Warner, *The Greek Philosophers*, Mentor Books, 1963, p.28. See also Wheelwright, *Heraclitus*, p.34.

[33]The claim that Heraclitus' use of 'fire' is nothing more than a metaphor used to represent the idea of process or constant flux is made by Cherniss, 'The Characteristics and Effects of Presocratic Philosophy', pp.13-14; G.de Santillana, *The Origins of Scientific Thought: From Anaximander to Proclus*, Mentor Books, 1961, p.44; Popper, *The Open Society and Its Enemies*, 1, fn.7, p.206; Warner, *The Greek Philosophers*, p.28; and Williams, *Hegel, Heraclitus and Marx's Dialectic*, pp.x, 9. The importance of metaphor in Heraclitus generally is emphasised by Waugh, who offers a 'postmodern' interpretation of the thought of Heraclitus based on a reading of Nietzsche and Derrida. See 'Heraclitus: The Postmodern Presocratic?', pp.609-10, 613, 619.

[34]This is Nietzsche's understanding of Heraclitus. See *The Twilight of the Idols*, p.36. This assessment is shared by Guthrie, *History of Greek Philosophy*, 1, p.468 and by Waugh, 'Heraclitus: The Postmodern Presocratic?' p.618.

[35]For this view see Cherniss, 'The Characteristics and Effects of Presocratic Philosophy', p.14; Cleve, *The Giants of Pre-Socratic Philosophy*, 1, pp.37-8; D.Furley, *The Greek Cosmologists*, 1, Cambridge University Press, 1967, p.35; C.J.Emlyn-Jones, 'Heraclitus and the Identity of Opposites', pp.91, 110-11; Guthrie, *The Greek Philosophers*, pp.45-6; Guthrie, *History of Greek Philosophy*, 1, pp. 432, 457, 459-61; Kirk & Raven, *The Presocratic Philosophers*, p.198; McDiarmid, 'Theophrastus on the Presocratic Causes', in Furley & Allen (eds), *Studies in Presocratic Philosophy*, 1, p.186; A.P.D.Mourelatos, 'Heraclitus, Parmenides and the Naïve Metaphysics of Things', in E.N.Lee et al (eds), *Exegesis and Argument: Studies in Greek Philosophy Presented to Gregory Vlastos*, *Phronesis*, 1, 1973, p.47; Popper, *The Open Society and Its Enemies*, 1, pp.11-12; Popper, 'Back to the Presocratics', in *Conjectures and Refutations*, Routledge, 1981, pp.144-5; Stace, *A Critical History of Greek Philosophy*, p.73.

to imply that Heraclitus rejects the principle of stability, permanence or identity altogether. Thus, from this point of view, 'It is not possible to step twice into the same river.'[36] This amounts, in effect, to the view that there is *no* river, or more generally, that there are, properly speaking, no 'things' at all, in the sense in which this term is usually understood. Karl Popper expresses this idea very well when he says that, for Heraclitus, the world is composed of 'processes rather than things.'[37] The original source for this account of Heraclitus' views on change is of course Plato, whose views represent what Mourelatos has called the 'traditional' interpretation of Heraclitus' philosophy.[38]

Interpreted like this, Heraclitus' views on change have nothing at all to do with his doctrine of the unity and conflict between opposites. It is, therefore, a mistake to assume that these two aspects of Heraclitus' thought must be necessarily connected. As C.J.Emlyn-Jones has insisted, the 'causal connection of the identity of opposites with the doctrine of flux does not occur' anywhere in 'the extant fragments of Heraclitus.'[39] From this point of view, the existence of change in the world is simply a basic datum which we must recognise on the basis of our own experiences. Moreover, on this view Heraclitus is also of the opinion that change itself is something which is intrinsically disordered and chaotic. For even the 'most beautiful kosmos is a pile of things poured out at random.'[40] Again, this is Nietzsche's understanding of Heraclitus' views on change. Order and purpose are things which we ourselves impose on our experiences of change in order that we might to give them some coherence and hence make some intelligible sense out of them.[41]

---

[36]Fr. 91; McKirahan, p.122. For the claim that Heraclitus subscribes to the doctrine of 'constant flux', understood in this 'extreme' sense, see Burnet, *Early Greek Philosophy*, p.146 and *Greek Philosophy: Thales to Plato*, pp.46-9; Guthrie, *The Greek Philosophers*, pp.47, 87-8; Guthrie, *History of Greek Philosophy*, 1, p.450, fn. 3, p.452, fn. 1; Hussey, *The Presocratics*, pp.54- 5; Mourelatos, *Introduction to The Pre-Socratics: A Collection of Critical Essays*, pp.10-11; Mourelatos, 'Heraclitus, Parmenides and the Naive Metaphysics of Things', p.37, fn.56; Popper, *The Open Society and Its Enemies*, 1, p.205, fn. 2; Popper, 'Back to the Presocratics', p.148'.

[37]Popper, *The Open Society and its Enemies*, 1, pp.14, 204-5, fn. 2; 'Back to the Presocratics', p.144. Also Mourelatos, 'Heraclitus, Parmenides and the Naive Metaphysics of Things', p.47; Parker, *A Short Account of Greek Philosophy*, p.42.

[38]See Plato, *Cratylus*, 402A; *Theatetus*, 152C-153D, 179C- 183C. Mourelatos, *Introduction to The Pre-Socratics: A Collection of Critical Essays*, p.10. See also Cleve, *The Giants of Pre-Socratic Philosophy*, pp.119- 20; Furley, *The Greek Cosmologists*, pp.33-4; Guthrie, *History of Greek Philosophy*, 1, p.450; Kirk, 'Natural Change in Heraclitus', pp.189-92, 195-6; G.S.Kirk, 'Popper on Science and the Presocratics', pp.170-1; Kirk & Raven, *The Presocratic Philosophers*, p.195; McKirahan, *Philosophy Before Socrates*, pp.128-9; D.G.Stern, 'Heraclitus' and Wittgenstein's River Images: Stepping Twice into the Same River', *The Monist*, 74/4, p.580.

[39]Emlyn- Jones, 'Heraclitus and the Identity of Opposites', p.92.

[40]Fr.124; McKirahan, p.122.

[41]See F.Nietzsche, 'On Truth and Falsity in their Ultramoral Sense', in *Early Greek Philosophy and Other Essays*, pp.177-8, 180, 183-4, 186-7; *The Will to Power*, translated by W.Kaufmann & R.J.Hollingdale, Vintage Books, 1968, p.14. As Mugge has observed, Nietzsche, who was a self-confessed 'disciple of Heraclitus' always 'tried hard to look at nature without juggling into it finality or purpose'. *Nietsche*, p.26. In so far as history is concerned, Nietzsche's 'Heracliteanism' leads him to emphatically reject the idea of

As might be expected, our second interpretation presents us with a completely different picture of Heraclitus' opinions regarding the problem of knowledge from that presented by the first. According to this interpretation, it is Heraclitus' view that it is not actually possible for us to achieve what a philosopher like Plato would consider to be genuine knowledge. If by 'knowledge' we mean the apprehension of timeless and universal truths associated with a permanent reality underpinning all appearances, then, as Plato claims, for Heraclitus such knowledge is indeed, unattainable.[42] On the other hand, however, for Heraclitus at least, if not for Plato, this does not mean that there we can have no knowledge at all. For we can have knowledge of the world of everyday things which exist in time and space, and the source of such knowledge is precisely the evidence of our senses, or sense-perception. As Heraclitus himself expresses it, 'Eyes are more accurate witnesses than ears' and 'All that can be seen, heard, experienced – these are what I prefer.'[43] It is true that what we perceive is, to some extent at least, relative to our own perspective or point of view. This is a key theme in a number of the fragments.[44] Nevertheless, ideas and beliefs of this sort should certainly be accorded the status of genuine knowledge. Moreover, once again this is as true of the social world as it is of the natural. For although to God 'all things are beautiful and good and just', human beings 'have supposed some unjust and others just.' In this sphere also, therefore, it is the principle of relativism or perspectivism which rules.[45]

From the standpoint of our second interpretation, then, the references which Heraclitus makes to 'reason' or logos in the fragments should not be taken as an indication that he is a rationalist philosopher or a forerunner of stoicism. On the contrary, these phrases refer to nothing more than Heraclitus' 'account' or 'word' – that is to say, his philosophical 'world view' generally.[46] Far from being a 'rationalist' philosopher, Heraclitus

'progress'. Cf. *The Will to Power*, p.55.

[42]Plato, *Theaetetus*, 152C-153D, 179C-183C; Cornford, *Plato's Theory of Knowledge: The Theatetus and the Sophist of Plato*, Routledge, 1970, pp.36-9, 92-101; also Barnes, *Early Greek Philosophy*, p.112-13; Burnet, *Early Greek Philosophy*, p.166, fn. 1; Cherniss, 'The Characteristics and Effects of Presocratic Philosophy', p.21. Emlyn-Jones, 'Heraclitus and the Identity of Opposites', pp.93-4; Guthrie, *The Greek Philosophers*, pp.87-8; Guthrie, *History of Greek Philosophy*, 1, pp.450, 468.

[43]Fr. 101a; McKirahan, p.119; fr.55; McKirahan, p.119.

[44]E.g. fr.61, McKirahan, p.121: 'The sea is the purest and the most polluted water: to fishes drinkable and bringing safety, to humans undrinkable and destructive'; fr.59, McKirahan, p.122: 'The track of writing is straight and crooked'; fr.60, McKirahan, p.122: 'The road up and the road down are one and the same'; fr.3, McKirahan, p.125 'The sun's breadth is the length of the human foot.' See also Guthrie, *History of Greek Philosophy*, 1, pp.429-30; Kirk, 'Natural Change in Heraclitus', pp.194-5; Hussey, *The Presocratics*, p.37.

[45]Fr.102, McKirahan, p.125; see also Barnes, *The Pre-Socratics*, pp.73-4; Cherniss, 'The Characteristics and Effects of Presocratic Philosophy', p.12; Copleston, *A History of Philosophy*, 1, pp.42-3; de Santillana, *The Origins of Scientific Thought*, p.45; Popper, *The Open Society and Its Enemies*, 1, pp.16-17; Waugh, 'Heraclitus: The Postmodern Presocratic?', pp.609, 615-16, 619.

[46]See Barnes, *The Pre-Socratics*, pp.58-9; Barnes, *Early Greek Philosophy*, pp.21-2; Burnet, *Early Greek Philosophy*, fn. 1, p.133; Heidegger, *Early Greek Thinking*, pp.59-78, esp.pp.60-1; Kirk, *Heraclitus: The Cosmic Fragments*, pp.36-7; E.L. Minar, 'The Logos

is presented here, as Karl Popper puts it, as a fierce proponent of 'anti-rationalism'.[47] With respect to his general philosophy, he is in fact a fore-runner of what, precisely because it does rely heavily on a commitment to sense-perception, T.M.Robinson has gone so far as to describe as a form of 'empiricism'.[48] Similarly, with respect to matters moral and political, he subscribes to the doctrine of moral and juridical 'positivism', which might be said to be the ethical counter- part of the doctrine of empiricism.[49]

A Second Interpretation of Hegel's Attitude Towards the Philosophy of Heraclitus

There is at least some evidence that Hegel reads the philosophy of Heraclitus in a quite different way from that suggested earlier and that he does not consider Heraclitus to be a forerunner of his own philosophy in any straightforward sense. From this alternative point of view, Hegel's understanding of the philosophy of Heraclitus follows quite closely the lines indicated by the second of the two interpretations discussed above rather than the first. One observation that might be made in support of this claim has to do with Hegel's understanding of the ontology associated with Heraclitus' philosophy. It is evident from reading the *Lectures* that Hegel is not altogether happy with the idea Heraclitus is a latter day Milesian philosopher or metaphysician who considers 'fire' to be the primary substance. This unease is indicated by the fact that Hegel takes very seriously the idea that the significance of 'fire' for Heraclitus is not that it is the basic unchanging 'stuff" out of which the world is composed, but precisely that it acts as a metaphor for the idea of 'flux" or 'process", or for the idea that there is in fact no such primary substance at all. For, as Hegel puts it, 'fire is process'.[50]

Another supporting observation relates to Hegel's understanding of Heraclitus' views on change. On this issue Hegel has a tendency to attribute to Heraclitus the extreme version of the doctrine of 'constant flux', as that doctrine is interpreted by Plato. He is quite happy in the *Lectures* to appeal to Plato as a valuable source for our understanding of Heraclitus' doctrine of change. Thus he is content to follow Plato in representing Heraclitus' philosophy as a philosophy of pure Becoming. He acknowledges that the emphasis which Heraclitus places on the principle of Becoming, understood in this particular sense, is 'a great advance' in the history of philosophy. And yet at the same time he also clearly recognises that this Heraclitean doctrine also has definite limitations. For the principle of Becoming in the

of Heraclitus', *Classical Philology*, 34, 1939, p.328; Popper, 'Back to the Presocratics', p.144; T.M.Robinson, 'Heraclitus and Plato on the Language of the Real, pp.481-2, fn. 5, p.488; G.J.Seidel, *Martin Heidegger and the Presocratics: An Introduction to His Thought*, University of Nebraska Press, 1978, p.92; Waugh, 'Heraclitus: The Postmodern Presocratic?', p.616.

[47] Popper, *The Open Society and its Enemies*, 1, p.15.

[48] Robinson, 'Heraclitus and Plato on the Language of the Real', pp.484-5, fn. 10, p.489. See also Barnes, *The Pre-Socratics*, p. 77; Kirk, 'Natural Change in Heraclitus', pp.194-5.

[49] Popper, *The Open Society and Its Enemies*, 1, fn. 9, p.207.

[50] Hegel, *Lectures*, pp.286-7.

philosophy of Heraclitus remains, he insists, merely an 'abstract' principle.[51] Moreover, Hegel makes similar remarks about the philosophy of Heraclitus in his *Shorter Logic*. For example, he says there that 'the Eleatics never got beyond Being, or Heraclitus beyond Becoming.'[52] This comment suggests that, for Hegel, Heraclitus resembles the other Presocratic philosophers in that, like them, he also attaches importance solely and exclusively to just one basic principle. His standpoint is therefore a limited one because it is partial and one-sided. As J.Findlay has put it, for Hegel 'Heraclitus is the philosopher of absolute Werden and no more.'[53]

In this respect Hegel's assessment of Heraclitus and his limitations resembles very closely that presented by Plato in his *Theaetetus*. Like Hegel, Plato directly opposes the philosophy of Heraclitus, as a philosophy of pure Becoming, to that of Parmenides, which is, Plato alleges, a philosophy of pure Being. According to Plato, just as Heraclitus attaches exclusive importance to the principle of change and ignores altogether that of permanence or stability, so also Parmenides attaches exclusive importance to the principle of permanence or stability and rejects altogether the idea of change as being fundamentally illusory. In Plato's opinion, there is something to be said for each of these doctrines. What is required, therefore, is the development of a third position based on a synthesis of the principle of Being with that of Becoming.[54] It could quite plausibly be argued that this is also Hegel's view. This clearly implies, however, that Hegel's own views on change are significantly different from those of Heraclitus, as Hegel himself understands them.

Interpreted in this way, the Heraclitean principle of Becoming, as Hegel sees it, does not stand above the principle of Being associated with the philosophy of Parmenides. It operates, rather, on the same level. Hegel says that if the Parmenidean principle of Being is 'the first immediate thought' in the history of philosophy, then the Heraclitean principle of Becoming is 'the second'. Like the principle of Being, therefore, the Heraclitean principle of Becoming itself is also an 'abstract' notion and not a 'concrete' one. This means, however, that for Hegel the principle of Becoming, as employed by Heraclitus, is limited because it is partial and one-sided. It is a principle which, although certainly valuable, nevertheless cannot stand alone and needs to be incorporated as a component element in some higher totality.[55]

A further observation attesting to the differences which exist between the philosophy of Heraclitus, as Hegel interprets it, and Hegel's own philosophy, has to do with the issue of whether there is any rational principle of order which underpins processes of change. In the *Shorter Logic*, as in his

[51] Hegel, *Lectures*, p.283.

[52] Hegel, *Shorter Logic*, s.12, p.17.

[53] J.Findlay, 'Hegelianism and Platonism', p.63. That this is Hegel's understanding of Heraclitus is also maintained by F.Copleston, *A History of Philosophy*, 1, p.40; M.Heidegger & E.Fink, *Heraclitus Seminar: 1966-67*, pp.113-5, 160; M.Inwood, *A Hegel Dictionary*, Basil Blackwell, 1992, pp.44-5, 168; G.R.G.Mure, *The Philosophy of Hegel*, Thoemmes Press, 1993, p.123.

[54] Plato, *Theaetetus*, 180C-181B, Cornforth, *Plato's Theory of Knowledge*, pp.94-5.

[55] Hegel, *Lectures on the History of Philosophy*, p.283; Hegel, *Shorter Logic*, s.88z, p.132; s.89z, p.134.

Lectures on the History of Philosophy, Hegel explicitly acknowledges that the concept of Becoming 'is the first adequate vehicle of truth', and that in the history of philosophy 'this stage of the logical Idea finds its analogue in the system of Heraclitus.' Despite this, however, as P.Redding has pointed out,[56] he nevertheless insists that the Heraclitean notion of Becoming, even 'at its best', is an 'extremely poor term' which needs to 'grow in depth and weight of meaning.'[57] This is so, Hegel maintains, because this particular formulation of the principle of Becoming is associated with the notion of 'utter' or 'abstract restlessness'. Such a formulation is inadequate because it does not comprehend that any process of Becoming must have a definite 'result'. The final outcome of such a process of Becoming is 'not an empty Nothing' but, on the contrary, some particular determinate Being – some particular 'thing' which has come into Being.[58] In other words, for Hegel, as for Nietzsche, what is lacking in Heraclitus' philosophy is an appreciation that the process of change does indeed have a determinate goal, or clear sense of direction. As Hegel interprets it here, the philosophy of Heraclitus considers change to be fundamentally an irrational process.

On this account of Hegel's relationship to Heraclitus, then, Hegel does seek to incorporate Heraclitus' thinking into his own system. At the same time, however, he seeks to go beyond Heraclitus. He attempts to transcend the emphasis which Heraclitus places on the simple principle of pure Becoming. From this point of view, the decisive difference between Hegel and Heraclitus is that whereas Heraclitus, as Hegel interprets him, does indeed subscribe to an extreme doctrine of 'constant flux' or pure Becoming in the Platonic sense, Hegel himself does not do so. In Hegel's opinion, his own views on change are superior to those of Heraclitus precisely because they recognise the inadequacies of the extreme version of the 'flux' theory. Thus, as Michael Inwood has maintained, 'Hegel did not, like Nietzsche and (on Hegel's interpretation) Heraclitus, abandon being altogether in favour of unremitting flux'. He is, rather, of the opinion that whereas the philosophy of Parmenides represents the principle of Being, and that of Heraclitus represents that of Becoming, his own philosophy is superior to both in that it corresponds to the 'absolute idea', which 'sublates' all of the earlier Thoughts developed in his Logic.[59]

---

[56] P.Redding, 'Hegel's Logic of Being and the Polarities of Presocratic Thought', pp.441-2.

[57] Hegel, *Shorter Logic*, s.88z, p.132.

[58] Hegel, Shorter Logic, s. 89z, p.134.

[59] M.Inwood, *A Hegel Dictionary*, pp. 44-5, 168; see also Heidegger & Fink, *Heraclitus Seminar*, pp. 113-5, 160.

Communitarianism and the Future of Social Policy

Gordon Hughes
The Open University

'Radical Communitarianism, Community Safety and Social Justice'

Summary

This working paper builds on earlier interventions by the author into debates on contemporary appeals to community in general and on communitarianism in particular around issues of crime control[1] *It is not my main concern in this paper to go over the conceptual ground covered in these earlier papers. However, I begin with some brief remarks regarding the dominant academic response to communitarian thinking in the United Kingdom in order to help the reader understand the specific position I adopt with regard to the radical potential of communitarian thinking on the politics of law and order and social inclusion. Following this first section on the general contextualisation of both conservative and radical appropriations of community in communitarian discourses, I focus on two interrelated themes which may move the debate on communitarianism forwards from its current stage of being a limiting trench war between 'born-again' believers and 'knee-jerk' opponents. In the first theme I look at some of the political and policy implications of a radical communitarian agenda on what is increasingly known as 'community safety' rather than crime prevention in the United Kingdom.*[2] *In the second theme, I wish to live up to the true status of the committed agnostic and examine a series of challenges, both conceptual and political, which face any radical communitarian agenda on social justice and inclusion.*

Communitarianism beyond moral authoritarianism

I have argued at some length elsewhere that the radical academic response in the United Kingdom to communitarian thinking has with some notable exceptions been limiting and even knee-jerk in its critique.[3] It is contended here that there is more to communitarian thought than the admittedly dominant and populist expressions associated with the work of commentators such as Amitai Etzioni in the USA and self-consciously 'Cassandra'-like writers gathered around the Institute of Economic Affairs in the United

[1] See, for example, G.Hughes, 'Communitarianism and law and order', *Critical Social Policy*, 16/4, 1996; G.Hughes & A.Little, 'Towards Radical Communitarianism: the politics of social inclusion in the work of Jordan & Gorz', SPA Conference, Sheffield Hallam University, July, 1996.

[2] For a fuller explanation of the term community safety and its place in current political discourses on law and order see G.Hughes, 'Policing late modernity', in N.Jewson & S.Macgregor (eds), *Transforming Cities*, Routledge, 1997.

[3] See G.Hughes, *ibid*, 1996.

Kingdom, such as David Green, Melanie Phillips and Norman Dennis. This body of work may be termed moral authoritarian communitarianism given inter alia its following domain assumptions:

- 1. an emphasis on one moral community at the expense of a recognition of the plurality and diversity to identities in late modernity ;
- 2. a desire to return to a traditional and nostalgic past;
- 3. a neglect of power structures in human societies or at least a naturalisation of hierarchical relations;
- 4. a critique of personal rights and a call for duties but a failure to critique property rights;
- 5. a glorification of past solidaristic communities together with a failure to conceptualise the crucial importance of struggles versus oppression in the creation of collectivist communities;
- 6. finally a political and moral rallying call for a return to the traditional family (a new conservative 'Restoration' settlement).

All in all, within this popular variant of communitarianism, there is a vision of a unitary, homogeneous community sustained by strongly held moral certainties, celebrating in turn mono-culturalism and setting a morally prescriptive agenda for the social exclusion of marginalised and 'deviant' categories of people.

Understandably, communitarianism as a political project when understood on the basis of the above variant has been written off as 'abject and authoritarian' by radical commentators such as Campbell. Accordingly Campbell argues that

> 'Communitarianism celebrates a holy trinity of family, community and nation, as if community represented a halcyon pasture, small but perfectly formed, an immaculately conceived domain of homogenous kinships, shared interests and common histories'.[4]

Such a trenchant critique does not seem misplaced with regard to the work of Etzioni or more recently in the United Kingdom in the work of Phillips and Green.[5] The dismissal of communitarian thought per se on the basis of a very selective if influential body of work is in my view a serious error and one that could lead to a dangerous evacuation of important, contested political and ideological spaces (community/ies, civil society) by the left. Given this danger I would argue with others[6] that radical re-imaginings of community

[4] B.Campbell, 'Old fogeys and angry young men', *Soundings*, 1, 1995, p.51.

[5] M.Phillips, *All Must Have Prizes*, Little, Brown & Company, 1996; D.Green, *Community Without Politics*, IEA, 1996.

[6] See, for example, the recent contributions by J.Weeks, 'The idea of a sexual community', *Soundings*, 3, 1996; M.Kenny, 'After the deluge: politics and civil society in the wake of the New Right', *Soundings*, 4, 1996, and writers such as Jordan, Braithwaite, Gough and Stoker & Young discussed in Hughes, *op cit*, 1996.

and solidarity are necessary at the current historical juncture which in turn do not result in moral closure but instead celebrate the lived realities of diversity and plurality in late modern societies. Of course these may appear worthy but empty platitudes unless the pressing political questions of 'what is to be done' are addressed together with the recognition that any project of community-building in the wake of the New Right deluge will be complex and uncertain in outcome. The next two sections begin a consideration of these questions for radical communitarianism.

What is to be done about law and order by radical communitarians? A vignette on community safety

This section argues that there is some radical potential for local community safety strategies albeit within the context of a reactionary central government agenda in the United Kingdom. The preferred 'reading' of appeals to community in crime prevention/community safety developments in the United Kingdom during the past decade is, put simply, that communitarian appeals in crime prevention discourses have been successfully stage-managed by central government to consolidate the marginalisation of the designated 'underclass', off-load 'responsibilities' for social problems onto communities and individuals and in particular to offer a means of re-legitimation for neo-liberal government policy. In particular, it is argued that community safety initiatives have led to a 'criminalisation' of social policy whereby 'needy' communities are only likely to receive help if they accept their designation as 'criminogenic'.[7] There is little doubt that this 'criminalisation of social policy' has been a dominant strategy during the 1980s and 1990s, the importance of which social scientists would be foolhardy to down-play. However at the risk of being pilloried for recidivist Panglossian tendencies, it is important to argue that local community safety strategies may also be 'hitched up' to progressive communitarian calls for social justice and social inclusion, particularly when we move beyond a narrow criminological notion of what is to be done about crime and disorder.[8]

During the last two decades, the problem of law and order may be said to have held centre stage in both central and local politics in the United Kingdom. It would not be productive nor appropriate to enter into this whole debate here. Instead, the more modest purpose of this section is try and place the local communitarian developments regarding crime prevention and community safety in the context of the wider structuring and constraining but not necessarily determining initiatives and legislation emanating from recent national government policy.

In this part of the paper I present in brief some findings from my own research during the 1990s on both the conflicts and alliances involving local

[7]See, for example, A.Crawford, 'Appeals to Community and Crime Prevention', *Crime, Law and Social Change*, 22, 1995; D.Gilling & A.Barton, 'Crime prevention and community safety: a new home for social policy?', *Critical Social Policy*, forthcoming.

[8]For a fuller elaboration of radical communitarian strategies of social inclusion which address criminalisation see Hughes & Little, *op cit*; B.Jordan, *The Common Good*, Blackwell, 1989.

policy networks with regard to the interwoven issues of community/police consultation, community safety and democratic accountability of public service deliverers to local communities in one English county – Northamptonshire. Initially, the research focused on the development of an officer-driven 'corporate' strategy for community safety, which, in its original shape, largely ignored democratic accountability issues: a common flaw in 'top-down' communitarian initiatives in local authorities. This officer vision thus by-passed the question of the participation of elected members, never mind their 'leadership' of such community initiatives, for what may have appeared very sound professional reasons to permanent officers of local government and public services. Next, the research plotted the rise of a politicised police authority member-driven 'alternative' model of the strategy for both community safety and public consultation . The development of this latter model was in large part the result of a self-consciously reflexive and highly politicised resistance from a group of elected police authority members to perceived threats to both local government in general and to democratically accountable and participatory forms of community safety strategies in particular. It may not be too fanciful to see this development as one particular instance of what Elliot Currie would term 'community-building' as a progressive local political project in opposition to the dominant destructive trends of the centralist New Right agenda towards the most vulnerable communities on both sides of the Atlantic.[9]

As it currently stands, consultation with and the participation of the diverse communities of identity and place in Northamptonshire on community safety initiatives remain limited, as the key political participants are well aware. Although there is scope for increasing the level of public participation with localised and targeted meetings, the key players are not be too ambitious in their hopes for high levels of popular involvement. Given the sheer size and complexity of our society, any hope of a return to the direct participation of the citizenry in the communal democratic process on the Athenian lines of Ancient Greece is pure 'pie in the sky' thinking. The involvement of the citizen is a much lauded goal in public policy but it may seriously overestimate loyalty and obligation to place which for most people have been seriously eroded of late. It would again be misguided to view any community safety strategy, however well-conceived and implemented, as a panacea for such historical shifts.

However, it did appear from this research that the very looseness and emptiness of the concept of community safety offers the opportunity for creative ideological appropriation of this signifier by local, progressive communitarian alliances and networks which were able, often in small ways, to challenge centralist and moral authoritarian tendencies on the crime and disorder problem. As a backlash to the numbing mundanity of managerially-driven strategies on crime management, is it fanciful to view the appeal of the idea of community safety to local actors as a means of rekindling concerns over social solidarity and collective control over the wider social envi-

---

[9] E.Currie, *Reckoning: drugs, the cities and the American future*, Hill & Wang, New York.

ronment? A big question facing such current local policy initiatives as the Community Safety Strategy for Northamptonshire in this era of the audit is how do you measure its success. The most obvious measure would probably be that of a reduction in crime and a concomitant increase in security and safety among the people of this county, whilst avoiding a conservative moralising closure on issues of diversity and difference. This difficult issue is certainly not amenable to measurement in any short-term manner, again as acknowledged by the participants in this research. Given the complex mixture of demographic, cultural and technological factors which come into play in any explanation of the shifts in the sense of in/security and in the material reality of crime and disorder, the chances of ever 'measuring' in a quantifiable manner the impact of a community safety strategy on these rates is difficult to envisage. However, a more reasonable 'test' may be to ask how do the 'good intentions' associated with local democratically-driven community safety work end up as practical anti-despotic outcomes. On this question the research to date is able to point to some tangible outcomes across the county. Community safety with its emphasis on an elected member multi-agency committee and communities-consultative approach to the social problems of crime and safety is now clearly part of the agenda of the public services in Northamptonshire. Under the umbrella of this new rallying call, some significant policy initiatives have been emergent, for example with regard to the problems of domestic violence, racist and homophobic violence and harassment and via the diversion of offenders from custody.

A key contention of this section is that current community safety and multi-agency crime prevention initiatives are not simply reducible in terms of origins and outcomes to a 'New Right' law and order agenda. The influence of this latter agenda is of course evident in much of the processes and structures examined in brief here. Who would deny that the novel forms of governance associated with the slippery and promiscuous concept of the community carry potential for the disempowerment of the weak and marginal (as the demonised 'other'), the further consolidation of existing social divisions and modes of regulation together with a numbing silence on questions of democratic accountability and participation. However, in contrast to previous overviews on national and international trends in communitarian social control which point to a new penetrative totalitarianism,[10] this discussion suggests that local crime prevention/community safety initiatives in the United Kingdom also at times draw on, and create, agendas and projects, in the Gramscian sense, which are beyond the control of the reactionary penalism of central government. In giving contextual factors their proper place in the investigation of crime prevention trends, this discussion has sought to highlight the importance of the specificity of local circumstances and of interpreting general trends in the context of particular localities. I am not of course arguing for the triumph of the local ('good') over the central ('bad'). Once again the nature of state power today is beyond such simple dichotomies. Instead I contend that what is

[10]See S.Cohen, *Visions of Social Control*, Polity Press, Cambridge, 1985 and the critique by Hughes, 1997, *op cit.*

in the public interest regarding community safety is not an unproblematic matter bestowed from the centre but is instead capable of co-option and re-articulation by alternative voices to that of both the neo-liberal and traditional moralistic wings of the New Right bloc. In conclusion then this section has suggested that local crime prevention and community safety initiatives 'on the ground' in the United Kingdom may be viewed as offering a complex picture of constrained negotiation and struggle with the penal populism of the current central administration.

Some conceptual and political challenges for a radical communitarian agenda on social justice and inclusion

Having given a specific illustration of how communitarian ideas may be incorporated into tangible policy initiatives at the local state level by means of the example of community safety, I now wish to address change tack and air some of the major challenges, conceptual and political, which face the radical communitarian project around community empowerment and social inclusion. In no particular order of priority, special attention will be given to (1) the role of the state and economy in radical communitarianism, (2) some clarification of the relationship of civil society and community, (3) the nature of communities in the globalising context of late modernity and (4) the need for new discourses of rights in an era of growing social exclusions. It will not be argued that there are any easy answers to these questions but rather that the recognition of their importance can only help those who are willing to play this dangerous game of engaging with the debate on community rather than play the safe game of the radical sceptic.

Unlike the voluntaristic communitarianism of commentators like Etzioni, radical communitarians need to accept that there is a crucial role to be played by the state in the re-building and (re-) generation of vibrant communities. We cannot assume that communities are natural or dormant sleeping beauties simply waiting for the metaphorical kiss of the communitarian knight to become re-animated. Any re-building of communities will thus require the establishment of new bridges of trust, accountability and consent between public institutions and social groups. As Michael Kenny rightly notes we need to avoid any simple dichotomy of self-activity versus state regulation.[11] State bodies will thus need to play an active role in creating the conditions for the re-empowerment of communities, particularly those who have most ravaged by the chill winds of market imperialism.[12]

In a similar fashion, Hope has argued that the voluntaristic, anti-statist communitarianism sponsored by Etzioni cannot hope to address the wider processes of what has been termed 'counter-urbanisation' (involving the 'lifting out' of social relations from the close proximity of the residential

[11] M.Kenny, *op cit*, p.24.

[12] See also the argument of Jordan & Arnold in favour of 'public power' or the state in repairing social conflict 'through action in other spheres before attempting to open up criminal justice policy to popular participation', B.Jordan & J.Arnold, 'Democracy and Criminal Justice', *Critical Social Policy*, 44/5.

environment) alongside the bifurcatory process of increasing poverty concentration in the inner cities in the late twentieth century.[13] Radical communitarianism in the debate on the future(s) of social policy must therefore recognise the need for the state to play a key role in the manufacturing of the most vulnerable communities through such initiatives as significant social and economic investment and support for intermediary institution-building to help hold communities together. The importance of such intermediate institutions would lie not least in their capacity to act as a two-way conduit between community and wider sources of wealth and power . This does not constitute a return to the statist paternalism of the Beveridgean welfare state settlement but does acknowledge the crucial importance of the state as an 'enabling' power (to use a much abused word) in a pluralistic and differentiated society.

Much communitarian thinking of the moral authoritarian hue has ignored the realm of the economic although this is not true of radical communitarian thinkers such as those in the debate on basic income like Gorz & Jordan.[14] Again, Kenny makes an important contribution to this debate in arguing that we cannot afford to neglect the ideological, cultural and social construction of economic processes and spaces:

> 'the economy is deeply intertwined with the cultural, symbolic and political worlds; the degree of emancipation or domination which emerges from economic processes depends upon the social and cultural contexts in which markets work and the ways in which economic outcomes are regulated'.[15]

Any radical communitarian agenda on social justice and inclusion will thus need to recognise and debate the very difficult questions of the right to work in the era beyond full (male) employment and begin to develop programmes for viable work-sharing between 'job-rich' and 'job-poor' households and communities. Together with the state regulation of corporate rights and duties, debates around economic justice arguably hold one of the keys to greater social inclusion without any necessary association with stultifying conformity.

It would seem that much radical communitarian thought in the recent past has been guilty of conflating the concepts of civil society and community. The former may be best viewed as the pluralistic realm between the state and the market and is generally seen as a progressive realm in which an autonomous and non-oppressive civic culture can prosper. As such it is not entirely clear where 'it' begins and communities end if we move beyond the notion of community as a monolithic and homogeneous entity and move towards the pluralist, diverse and self-critical notion of imagined communities, as in the work of Weeks cited above. This slippage between using

[13]T.Hope, 'Community Crime Prevention', in M.Tonry & D.Farrington (eds), *Building a Safer Society*, University of Chicago Press, 1995, p.74-7 and see the similar argument in the USA by E.Currie, *op cit*.

[14]See Hughes & Little, *op cit*.

[15]Kenny, *op cit*, p.21.

civil society and community somewhat coterminously will require further debate. But we may wish to be wary about putting our faith in either civil society or community as benign realms populated by progressive alliances and agents. It is likely that the social worlds we inhabit will continue to have its 'heavies' and reactionary forces. Thus the acceptance of such differences and probability of continuing struggles between opposing groups needs to be openly acknowledged in any radical communitarian agenda on social justice and the common good.

Following on from the brief discussion of conceptual slippage between the notions of civil society and community, I now wish to raise some questions as to the empirical status of the very notion of community in the era of late modernity.[16] In much of the sociological literature on community, communities are defined as involving the reassertion of bonds and loyalties that bind individuals in their most immediate locales. Such traditional notions of community, although beloved of moral authoritarian communitarianism, are no longer sociologically feasible in late modern societies such as the United Kingdom at the end of the twentieth century. Instead recognition must be given to the processes of differentiation and pluralism of collective as well as individual identities. We may therefore ask whether community should be abandoned as a conceptual tool. Instead of this latter option, it seems wise to write of communities in the plural, and perhaps to go further by conceptualising communities as imagined but necessary fictions, the importance of which lies in the realisation that it is only through the enhancement of a collective identity that individual autonomy in turn can be realised.[17] However, perhaps the greatest challenge to the radical communitarian project on social justice and the celebration of differences may reside in relationship to the processes of globalisation and the problem of how to achieve, to paraphrase, communitarianism in one country. The challenge of welcoming the often unwanted but needy stranger, often demonised as the 'alien other', into the complex mosaic of core capitalist societies of Western Europe has not been seriously confronted in current progressive communitarian discourses and it would appear that no simple answer is possible.

Finally some discussion of the status of rights and duties needs to be considered in this series of challenges for radical communitarianism. It is important to note that the balance of rights and duties has not been seriously engaged with at the regressive end of the communitarian spectrum of thought. Writers like Etzioni and Phillips dangerously devalue the importance of rights and ignore the crucial communitarian point that rights create duties, not least the duties to protect other's rights[18] According to some radical communitarians in Europe, it is the new social movements which are at the forefront in establishing new discourses on rights. Thus Lustiger-Thaler & Shragge point to the two-pronged call in such social movements for greater rights first in terms of rights of inclusion within the political system of action

[16]On the concept of late modernity, see A.Giddens, *The Consequences of Modernity*, Polity Press, 1990.

[17]J.Weeks, *op.cit*, p.84.

[18]See in particular J.Braithwaite, *Crime, Shame and Re-integration*, Oxford University Press, 1989.

and second in terms of the overlapping discourse of counter-rights directed toward social transformation and institution-building through struggle.[19] In similar vein, de Leonardis has highlighted the simultaneous tendency for a new positive discourse on rights among new social movements alongside the massive growth of new forms of poverty, disaffiliation and marginalisation. In the context of these tendencies towards both social exclusion and new forms of belonging, de Leonardis sees some signs of a progressive communitarian sense of active citizenship in the new 'social enterprises' emergent in parts of Italy. These social enterprises are characterised by an emphasis on enterprise and work but they are primarily social institutions in that their main object is to produce well-being and are especially 'aimed at' those most in need. 'To be the subject of rights is no longer simply to be a recipient of goods and services, but a bearer of the right to exercise capabilities'.[20] Such work on the new social movements would appear to effectively counter the dangerous down-playing of the importance of rights in regressive communitarian work whilst moving beyond the traditional liberal discourse of rights as negative freedoms and also struggling to counter the still dominant tendencies towards social exclusion of vulnerable groups and communities across Europe.

Conclusion

This paper has sought to make the case for communitarianism as a potentially radical social policy and political programme. I began by distinguishing and criticising the dominant variant of communitarianism in current political discourses (moral authoritarianism). The paper then offered an admittedly limited vignette on how appeals to community (and community safety) might illustrate in a practical policy way the radical possibilities of a democratic and pluralistic communitarian project. Having made the case for, the final section of the paper focused on some of the conceptual and political challenges facing any radical communitarian agenda on social justice and social inclusion beyond that of community safety and law and order. It will no doubt be evident that there remains much unfinished business. The engagement with the politics of community may still seem too close to 'supping with the devil' for some readers. However, I would conclude by repeating that the politics of community – and the nature of communitarianism itself – remain profoundly contradictory and contested. As a site of struggle and as a realm of the imaginary, community should not be left to the suffocating appeals to neo-tribalism evident in the moral authoritarian discourse.

---

[19] H.Lustiger-Thaler & E.Shragge, 'Social movements and social welfare', in G.Drover & P.Kerans (eds), *New Approaches to Welfare*, Cambridge University Press, 1993.

[20] O.de Leonardis, 'New patterns of collective action', in Drover & Kerans (eds), *op cit.*

Communitarianism and the Future of Social Policy

Adrian Little
Nene College of Higher Education, Northampton

'Welfare and Community in Post-Industrial Socialist Theory: Beyond Employment?'

Abstract

This paper sets out to evaluate some of the developments in socialist theory in Europe which are designed to provide a fresh agenda for the Left. This process is necessary as the Left has a long industrial-productivist heritage which is a problematic foundation as we face the potential development of post-industrialism. Initially I will attempt to define post-industrial socialism by differentiating it from post-industrialism (as it has been traditionally understood) and other work-based forms of socialism. From this I shall establish that the defining characteristic of post-industrial socialism is the belief in and advocacy of 'the end of work-based society'.[1] *This idea refers to the belief that developments in labour markets suggest that if all available work were distributed more equitably then more time would be available for activities in civil society. This would need to be facilitated by the state and suggests potentially radical social and economic policies. The second half of the paper will focus on theoretical initiatives which are designed to regenerate the concept of 'community' through radical social policy. This section should demonstrate that not only is the understanding of community employed in much policy discourse rather limited and conservative, but also that the post-industrial Left has much to offer any attempt to reimagine the notions of community and civil society in a theoretically rigorous manner.*

Introduction

The notion of post-industrialism has been an often used – and yet peculiarly under theorised – concept since it emerged during the late 1950s and 1960s.[2] Daniel Bell has been one of the most prominent analysts of social change linked to post-industrialism. He suggested (in 1973) that the advent of post-industrial society was likely to come about due to changes in the class structure associated with the decline of blue collar manufacturing industry and the consequent decline of organised labour. The social organisation which would replace this scenario would be of a post-industrial nature encompassing an affluent and consumerist knowledge-based society

[1] A.Gorz, *Critique of Economic Reason*, Verso, 1989.

[2] See D.Bell, *The Coming of Post-Industrial Society*, Basic Books, 1973; C.Kerr et al, *Industrialism and Industrial Man*, Oxford University Press, 1964; and A.Touraine, *The Post-Industrial Society*, Random House, 1971. See also the work of Krishan Kumar which provides a useful analysis of this area, in particular, *Prophecy and Progress*, Pelican, 1978; and *From Post-Industrial to Post-Modern Society*, Blackwell 1995.

mirrored by a high technology, service-based economy. Bell's vision was grounded in the knowledge that structures of industrialism remained resiliently in place when he wrote his book and this fact was emphasised by the decline of literature predicting the onset of post-industrial society later in the 1970s. Alternative explanations of capitalist reproduction such as post-Fordism emerged in the 1980s and 1990s as did new strands (or reworkings) of socialist thought such as market socialism. However in the 1990s post-industrialism has re-emerged as a pertinent concept and, importantly the new commentators treat the concept as if it is presently being witnessed in Western capitalist societies.[3] This paper sets out to refute the notion that post-industrial features are dominant in contemporary capitalism and to show that the type of post-industrialism being developed amongst the European Left offers a much clearer understanding of the variety of forces at work in the reproduction of modern social organisation. Having established this position we can examine the 'communitarian' perspective developed by the major post-industrial socialist, Andre Gorz, and compare that with some of the more common viewpoints on community and communitarianism. Finally we can then briefly analyse the conception of welfare associated with the post-industrial socialist perspective on community and the implications of this theoretical position for the state and social policy.

Exploring Post-Industrial Socialism

Bell's visualisation of post-industrial society as outlined above is highly questionable. Some of the features he highlights have undoubtedly developed to some extent but others look even more distant than when Bell predicted them in the 1970s. Arguably the status of citizenship has been subsumed by the ubiquitous logic of consumerism,[4] but there is little evidence that Western capitalist societies as a whole have become particularly affluent. Rather the available resources are not as widely distributed as they might be so that the increased resources in society are shared by decreasingly small sections of the population. This leads not to 'an affluent society' but rather a fragmented, divided society riven by social exclusion in which the affluence created is hived off and distributed within a small, compartmentalised élite. This situation has arisen because Bell's prediction that a high technology, white collar, service-based economy would emerge has fallen wide of the mark. Whilst service-sector employment has increased, there is little evidence that this work has been technologically sophisticated or highly skilled. Thus he was wrong to perceive that the tertiarisation of the economy would result in an affluent society because 'in contrast to Bell's thesis, low-status blue collar and service occupations show no signs of disappearing'.[5] Thus his perspective seriously underestimated the distinc-

[3]See G.Esping-Andersen (ed), *Changing Classes: Stratification and Mobility in Post-Industrial Societies*, Sage/ISA, 1993; 'Equality and Work in the Post-Industrial Life-Cycle', in D.Miliband (ed), *Reinventing the Left*, Polity Press, 1994.

[4]See M.Cahill, *The New Social Policy*, Blackwell, 1994.

[5]G.Ritzer, *The McDonaldisation of Society*, Pine Forge Press, 1993, p.153.

tion between the wealth in society which may be very poorly distributed and the lived experience of the mass of individuals who suffer from the social inequalities, insecurity and marginalisation which characterise contemporary capitalist societies. To this extent, Lodziak argues that 'theorists of the post-industrial society embrace a flawed conception of power which enables them to misconstrue the relation between the social totality and the individual'.[6]

Undoubtedly much has changed in the labour market since Bell's social forecast first appeared and this has had profound effects on social organisation. However it is highly debatable whether these changes can be equated with any kind of mature post-industrialism. For instance Bell was far too quick to equate the downfall of trade unionism with the decline of work as a central issue in the organisation of capitalist societies when he suggested that 'the crucial fact is that the "labor issue" *qua* labor is no longer central, nor does it have the sociological and cultural weight to polarize all other issues along that axis'.[7] In this suggestion Bell wrongly confuses the importance of the issue of work (and the lack thereof) with the decline of organised labour. On the contrary, the decline of trade unions has (not surprisingly) taken place alongside – and as a result of – the increased centrality of work as a key category in social life. In other words, as work becomes increasingly less available so the role of trade unions becomes less central whilst, at the same time, the possession of work becomes an ever more important mode of social inclusion and citizenship. In this sense organised labour is at its strongest when there is a highly ordered and disciplined labour market in which there is a clear constituency for trade unions to represent. The labour market of today is flexible, transitory and disorganised with a strong growth of part-time and non-unionised labour, often in the service sector. In this scenario work and unemployment are increasingly important as harbingers of economic citizenship whereas the representation of workers through trade unionism becomes increasingly tenuous.

The rhetoric of mainstream advocates of the post-industrial society looks all the more misguided as contemporary capitalist societies witness the new divisions in the labour market between core and peripheral workers and non-workers. These new divisions result in a situation whereby much new work is in the tertiary sector which is frequently lowly paid with little job security and yet simultaneously a large number of individuals remain marginalised from the economy (and society as a whole) through the absence of sufficient jobs. This explains why many on the Left have been sceptical of any attempt to embrace post-industrialism because it does little to challenge the logic of capital accumulation or the fragmentation of the labour market. Thus Wilde contends that 'developments in the forces of production and alterations in the specific forms of production relations do not constitute a departure from the logic of the capital accumulation process'.[8] From this perspective the increasing fragmentation of the labour market should not be viewed as the

[6]C.Lodziak, *The Power of Television*, Pinter, 1986, p.193.

[7]D.Bell, *The Coming of Post-Industrial Society*, Basic Books, 1973, p.164.

[8]L.Wilde, *Modern European Socialism*, Dartmouth, 1994, p.100.

inevitable result of the post-industrialisation of the economy but rather as the outcome of neo-liberal policies which prioritise 'efficiency' in the labour market and the leanest possible labour force. Moreover Lee contends that the divisions in the labour market are produced by the primacy of 'efficiency' (which is a key by-product of industrialism rather than post-industrialism) and as a result contemporary times should not be dubbed 'post-industrial' but 'rather the era of mass permanent unemployment'.[9]

Lee correctly identifies that post-industrial visions of highly technological, service economies in which affluent consumers abound cannot be equated with contemporary Western capitalism, but fails to acknowledge that post-industrialism can also exist in a more radical format than the kind of 'conservative' social forecast propounded by Bell. For example, Dobson, drawing on the work of Michael Marien, outlines the difference between what he calls 'dominant post-industrialism' which is seen as 'an affluent, technological, service society'[10] and more progressive visions of post-industrialism inspired by political ecology. It is this kind of radical post-industrialism which is the main concern here, although the intellectual heritage of the key ideas involved can just as easily be attributed to what Offe calls the 'left-libertarian' ideological orientation as to political ecology.[11] Andre Gorz points to the type of policies which the Left, informed by radical anthropocentric environmentalism, should follow in the development of post-industrial socialism:

> 'To exist politically, an ecological Left, has ... an urgent need for mediations between the existing industrial system, its wage-workers and its jobs, on the one hand, and, on the other, post-industrial forms of society which comply both with ecological demands and individuals' aspirations to liberate themselves from work as it exists and find in work as great a potential for self-determination as possible. We have to start out from what work is and what it really means today in order to transform it, reduce it, and expand the scope for autonomous activities, production for one's own use and self-realization for everyone.[12]

Clearly then for radical post-industrialists, a post-industrial society requires qualitative societal changes as well as alterations in the mode of production. Whilst the latter does have a wide and powerful influence on social and economic life, it does not necessarily define social relations in a deterministic fashion. Thus whilst the move towards a service based economy – the process of tertiarisation – is taking place, attitudes towards work and employment have not altered at a similar pace. In other words, moves towards a redefinition of the way we work have not been accompanied by a recognition that there is a possibility that this redefinition could facilitate

---

[9] K.Lee, 'To De-Industrialize – Is it so Rational?', in A.Dobson & P.Lucardie (eds), *The Politics of Nature*, Routledge, 1993, p.108.

[10] A.Dobson, *Green Political Thought*, Routledge, 1990, pp.5-7.

[11] C.Offe, 'A Non-Productivist Design for Social Policies', in P.Van Parijs (ed), *Arguing for Basic Income*, Verso, 1992, p.70.

[12] A.Gorz, *Capitalism, Socialism, Ecology*, Verso, 1994, p.64.

an understanding that the prospect of 'the end of work-based society', that is, genuine post-industrialism, could come onto the agenda. If this scenario is valid – and the pace of technological change suggests that it could be – then, as Gorz points out, dialogue on a social level is necessary to prepare and plan for the future. On a similar note Sherman argues that:

> 'The new industrial revolution is different from the first in that we are partially aware of what is happening ... [T]echnology is changing, employment is changing, products and services are changing – but the one key change has not occurred. As happened eventually in the course of the nineteenth century, we need a revolution in attitudes to match that in industry.'[13]

Progress towards a post-industrial society, therefore, requires more than *changes to the kind of work we perform.* It necessitates debate and planning about how to translate changes in working patterns into *the organisation of society and everyday life.* A post-industrial society cannot be deterministically fashioned by an increase in employment in the service sector of the economy, it can only be created by investigating the nature of the new economy and understanding the opportunities that it generates and then changing social organisation appropriately. Post-industrialism has hitherto been characterised by commentators such as Bell as the advent of the knowledge-based society without recognising that knowledge can be restricted to a rather small section of the society. Thus the forces of post-industrialism in the economy are open to manipulation and can be extremely divisive when applied to society in general. Obviously socialist post-industrialism must aim to create a society in which divisions and inequalities are minimised. This has not been the case with the new economy which has encouraged social polarisation and marginalisation for many who do not benefit from flexible labour markets. Thus post-industrial socialism opposes the technological determinism employed as much by Bell as the Marxists he attempted to negate.[14] Rather post-industrial socialism advocates democratic dialogue between employers and employees, the state and local communities and institutions of civil society, individuals and their communities, and women and men.[15] This kind of dialogue is designed to encourage debate about work and human activity in general and to negotiate, amongst other things, how that work is going to be distributed.

Post-industrial socialism then is an ambitious project which asks questions of the very nature of democracy and advanced capitalism. It is concerned with challenging the nature of changes in the economy and their effects on social realities. In this sense it should not be conflated with contemporary literature which confuses moves towards post-industrial economies with the altogether different notion of post-industrial societies.[16] Post-industrial socialism also stands in contrast to those who focus on issues relat-

[13] B.Sherman, *Working at Leisure*, Methuen, 1986, p.276.

[14] W.Clement & J.Myles, *Relations of Ruling*, McGill-Queen's University Press, 1994, pp.26-7.

[15] A.Gorz, *Farewell to the Working Class*, Pluto Press, 1982, pp.85-7.

[16] See W.Clement & J.Myles, *Relations of Ruling*, McGill-Queen's University Press,

ing to post-industrialism and class mobility. Gershuny, for instance, concentrates on occupational mobility and employs empirical data to demonstrate relatively high mobility into and out of low-level service occupations'.[17] This does not mean that these jobs do not exist in large numbers, it merely (and not surprisingly) indicates that people change jobs with increased frequency in the new economy. Gershuny's evidence says little about unemployment and he openly admits that, whilst the United Kingdom may not have a steady group of individuals who are part of a low-level service-related class, it may well be a dualistic society. It is precisely this kind of dualised and polarised society that post-industrial socialism stands against. Gershuny's line of thought is reflected by Blossfeld, Giannelli and Mayer who argue that there is high mobility between categories of unskilled employment in Germany suggesting that 'unskilled service jobs can be regarded as a "collecting vessel" for redundant manual workers'.[18] The argument against a new post-industrial service class is continued by Jacobs who states that 'the good news is that the bottom of the post-industrial society is far from closed ... the bad news is that the economic distance from bottom to top is growing'.[19] Similarly Myles et al, in celebrating mobility from low-level service employment in Canada, state that '[O]ccupational skill levels have risen over the postwar period, but despite rising skill levels, low-wage employment has grown faster than average or high-paying jobs'.[20]

All of the authors above concentrate on the belief that there is not a new class created by post-industrial economies and at the same time all admit that there is increased social polarisation. The notion that there is mobility within different categories of low-level employment does not negate the post-industrial socialist view that polarisation and marginalisation is increasing as a result of the new economy. Moreover if that economy determines society at the moment, then it is determining social fragmentation rather than an affluent, knowledge-based society. This does not mean that this situation is the inevitable result of a post-industrial economy, rather post-industrial socialists believe that society can be improved along with the new economy if the political will to do so exists. Yet many analysts of post-industrialism continue to suggest that the real polarisation that does exist 'applies ... not to skills but to the attributes of jobs' whilst simultaneously noting that 'inequalities of earnings, and the proportion of people in precarious jobs have risen sharply. The unskilled and new labour-force entrants are the

---

1994; G.Esping-Andersen (ed), *Changing Classes*, Sage/ISA, 1993; G.Esping-Andersen, 'Equality and Work in the Post-Industrial Life-Cycle', in D.Miliband (ed), *Reinventing the Left*, Polity Press, 1994.

[17] J.Gershuny, 'Post-Industrial Career Structures in Britain', in G.Esping-Andersen (ed), *Changing Classes*, Sage/ISA, 1993, p.139.

[18] H-B.Blossfeld et al, 'Is There a New Service Proletariat? The Tertiary Sector and Social Inequality in Germany', in G.Esping-Andersen (ed), *Changing Classes*, Sage/ISA, 1993, p.134.

[19] J.A.Jacobs, 'Careers in the U.S. Service Economy', in G.Esping-Andersen (ed), *Changing Classes*, Sage/ISA, 1993, p.223.

[20] Myles et al, 'Does Post-Industrialism Matter? The Canadian Experience', in G.Esping-Andersen (ed), *Changing Classes*, Sage/ISA, 1993, p.189.

two groups that have been most severely affected'.[21] This would appear to suggest that polarisation with regards to skills is likely to increase. If more jobs are becoming precarious and insecure, it seems pertinent to suggest that the contemporary 'post-industrial' economy will not close the deficit between the securely-employed and the growing marginalised group living in insecurity.

For post-industrial socialists, the economy needs to be controlled and subject to planning to eradicate the insecurity and inequalities that it produces at the moment. This presupposes a radical reappraisal of the way in which governments (attempt to) manage their economies. Planning is anathema to most political and economic thinking in contemporary times, although clearly governments do operate economic plans on a regular basis. For example the annual budget in the United Kingdom is an examination of previous economic performance and a projection of economic planning for the future (for example, plans to cut public spending). Similarly all companies operate on the basis of economic planning to survive.[22] This is not to say that planning is always accurate and reliable but it does (by necessity) take place. Clarification and democratisation of economic planning is important for post-industrial socialism because, like all proposals aimed at regenerating socialism, it must outline what role market mechanisms will play in the socialist alternative to current arrangements.[23] For theorists like Gorz, though, the development of a more transparent economic system must be coupled with a more thorough understanding of the notion of community and a much clearer outline of the relationship between social and economic policy.

Post-Industrial Socialism, Community and Civil Society

The idea of community has been resurrected and popularised in the 1990s, not least through the work of Amitai Etzioni and it has found a variety of constituencies across the political spectrum.[24] Etzioni's brand of communitarianism, which is based upon visions of a unitary, homogeneous community sustained by strong moral convictions in society, has been termed 'moral authoritarian communitarianism' by Hughes.[25] From this perspective, and despite Etzioni's claims that his communitarian programme would not be puritan or oppressive, it can be argued that 'moral authoritarian communi-

---

[21] G.Esping-Andersen, 'Equality and Work in the Post-Industrial Life-Cycle', in D.Miliband (ed), *Reinventing the Left*, Polity Press, 1994, pp.175-76.

[22] A.Gorz, 'On the Difference Between Society and Community, and Why Basic Income Cannot by Itself Confer Full Membership of Either', in P.Van Parijs (ed), *Arguing for Basic Income*, Verso, 1992.

[23] This is an argument for what Tomlinson calls a 'socialism with markets approach' which he differentiates from market socialism. See J.Tomlinson, 'Market Socialism', in B.Hindess (ed), *Reactions to the Right*, Routledge, 1990. For thorough commentary on recent developments in market socialism, see C.Pierson, *Socialism after Communism*, Polity Press, 1995.

[24] See A.Etzioni, *The Spirit of Community*, Fontana, 1994.

[25] G.Hughes, 'Communitarianism and Law and Order', *Critical Social Policy*, 16/4, 1996.

tarianism' represents a mono-cultural and morally prescriptive agenda for social exclusion and marginalisation. Much of the debate surrounding communitarianism has been centred on a differentiation between it and liberalism in the exposition of contemporary political philosophy.[26] At the same time, however, there has also been a growth of literature which is explicitly concerned with radical notions of democracy and simultaneously develops a much broader conception of community.[27] It is from this perspective that post-industrial socialism should be approached for, unlike 'moral authoritarian' communitarianism and traditional liberalism, it is a programme for fundamental political change organised around radical participatory democracy and regenerated citizenship and community. All of this is to be facilitated in post-industrial socialist thought by a reduction in working hours and consequently a new politics of time.[28]

The initial starting point when examining post-industrial socialist approaches to community is to note that theories of 'the community' are broadened to encompass a range of communities which make up society. In other words society and community are not synonymous but rather the former is made up of the institutions (whether national or international) which enshrine our social framework and organisation whereas the latter consists of the smaller groupings which represent a variety of interests within society and usually operate in the domain of civil society.[29] Thus in Andre Gorz's model of post-industrial socialism there are three different sectors of activity which individuals require to experience full citizenship. Gorz's theory – based as it is upon the advancement of a more pluralistic, radical democracy – tries to envisage a scenario whereby individuals can become:

- (A) members of society at large which is manifested by work in the public sphere;
- (B) members of a range of communities in which collective self-determination is the organising principle; and
- (C) autonomous to the extent that self-determined activities take precedence over A and B in the sense that the combination of time spent in the other sectors is relatively freely chosen.

Gorz, in a large body of work,[30] has argued that a tripartite division of society as above indicates the different levels of society which individuals

[26]See, for example, S.Mulhall & A.Swift, *Liberals and Communitarians*, Blackwell, 1992; W.Kymlicka, *Liberalism, Community and Culture*, Clarendon, 1989; E.Frazer & N.Lacey, *The Politics of Community: A Feminist Critique of the Liberal-Communitarian Debate*, Harvester Wheatsheaf, 1993; S.Avineri & A.de-Shalit (eds), *Communitarianism and Individualism*, Oxford University Press, 1992.

[27]See C.Mouffe (ed), *Dimensions of Radical Democracy*, Verso, 1992; C.Mouffe, *The Return of the Political*, Verso, 1993.

[28]See A.Gorz, *Capitalism, Socialism, Ecology*, Verso, 1994; A.Little, *The Political Thought of Andre Gorz*, Routledge, 1996; C.Lodziak, *Manipulating Needs*, Pluto Press, 1995.

[29]See A.Gorz, 'On the Difference Between Society and Community, and Why Basic Income Cannot by Itself Confer Full Membership of Either', in P.Van Parijs (ed), *Arguing for Basic Income*, Verso, 1992.

[30]See A.Little, *The Political Thought of Andre Gorz*, Routledge, 1996.

need to enter if full citizenship is to be genuinely encountered. In other words, individuals must be guaranteed social insertion through a right to work. At the same time we must understand that a right to work for all cannot be realised through a traditional model of full employment which assumes that everyone who is fit to work does so full-time throughout a working life-course which ends at a specific age. Post-industrial socialists argue that such a model is no longer either efficient or desirable and that a more effective answer would be a policy initiative which ensured that, whilst individual citizens had a right to work, they also had a right not to work for certain periods in which they wanted to concentrate on activities in either the micro-social or autonomous spheres. Thus, using the work of Gorz and Conrad Lodziak,[31] we can proceed towards a break down of social activity in Table 1 around which a post-industrial socialist framework can be identified:

Table 1
Post-Industrial Socialism and the Division of Social Activity

Sphere of Activity	*Type of Activity*	*Organising Principle*	*Status Conferred*
A.Macrosocial	Work for wages, the public sphere	Social insertion	Social citizenship
B. Microsocial	Voluntary, co-operative work	Collective self-determination	Non-work/local citizenship
C.Autonomous	Freely chosen activities	Individual self-determination	Individual freedom

From this formulation we can roughly equate the macrosocial sphere with the domain of the state and markets, the microsocial sphere with civil society/communities and the autonomous sphere becomes the domain whereby individuals organise their own time in the spheres of work for wages, voluntary (but sometimes necessary) work in the home or a community and self-ordained activities (for example, leisure). Now clearly everyday life is more complex than any model of this kind could indicate but this does move us beyond the limited Leftist responses to pluralist challenges identified by Walzer.[32] The latter claims that the Left has traditionally either a) glorified the state and the political community as the ultimate site of action or b) resorted to a utopian economistic belief in the primacy of co-operative work as the unifying feature of the relationship between the state, civil society and individuals. Thus Walzer, in rejecting both these critiques of pluralism (along with individualist and nationalist perspectives), advocates

[31] *Manipulating Needs*, Pluto Press, 1995.

[32] 'The Civil Society Argument', in C.Mouffe (ed), *Dimensions of Radical Democracy*, Verso, 1992, pp.91-94.

a potential regeneration of civil society as the venue in which individuals can participate pluralistically in social life. He believes this provides a large-scale framework for 'a project of projects' under which citizens can regain lost powers and influence over politics and the economy through small- scale activities and decisions in civil society. This would spawn 'a new recognition ... that the good life is in the details'.[33] Walzer's argument suggests that civil society can become the location through which market organisations and state organisations compete and co-operate freed from the values which previously characterised them such as economic rationality or bureaucracy. In this scenario the state could set a framework for a value-free civil society – an arena where a variety of bodies and institutions (including bodies of the state and market-oriented firms) operate under the focused gaze of the ultimate arbiter, consumer choice.[34] However all of this seems to ignore power differentials between consumers and presupposes the absence of vested economic interests.

Nonetheless much of Walzer's argument is useful for post-industrial socialists insofar as it identifies the importance of the state in fostering conditions for civil society to flourish whilst simultaneously understanding that democratic civil society requires associations with political agency. Thus Gorz has formulated a theory of post-industrial socialism whereby the macrosocial sphere would become the domain of the state (and the provision of universal social policy) and the microsocial sphere would be the space in which universal rights and obligations could be experienced in particularistic ways in different communities.[35] However post-industrial socialists tend not to concur with Walzer's faith in the value freedom of certain institutions. Thus Gorz argues that civil society can only flourish when it is safeguarded from the economic rationality which permeates market mechanisms, for instance. From this perspective, Walzer's notion of market mechanisms operating in civil society is worrying because it suggests that this non-market sector could become imbued with the economic rationality that governs markets.[36] This is also where the post-industrial dimension of Gorz's thought adds a different dimension to socialist thought on relationship between the state and civil society. The state has a key role in planning and regulating markets in the tightly defined area where economic rationality is to prevail (the domain of work for wages). At the same time it is to perform this role through close mediation with communities (or associations) which exist in the broader realm of civil society. From the post-industrial socialist perspective, it seems suitable to identify the bodies acting in civil society as communities precisely because they are supposed to be governed by principles of mutualism, voluntarism and co-operation

[33]'The Civil Society Argument', p.107.

[34]'The Civil Society Argument', p.100.

[35]This stands against some of Spicker's claims about the exclusivity between universalism and particularism. See P.Spicker, 'Understanding Particularism', *Critical Social Policy*, 39, 1994.

[36]For a fuller definition of Gorz's theory of economic rationality see A.Little, *The Political Thought of Andre Gorz*, Routledge, 1996, chapter 5, and A.Gorz, *Capitalism, Socialism, Ecology*, Verso, 1994, chapter 6.

rather than economic rationality.[37]

According to Gorz, the task of empowering civil society necessitates action by the state to empower individuals by reducing the primacy of paid work in gaining the resources which are fundamental to social insertion. Membership of and participation in communities and institutions in civil society could be facilitated by a universal scheme to provide benefits for all to enable each individual to become less reliant on paid labour to gain resources. In this sense the state has a pivotal role to play in ensuring that the requisite conditions exist for civil society to flourish. This is a much more socialistic argument for pluralism than that of Walzer because it highlights the (often overlooked) centrality of paid work (and the lack of it) in contemporary debates on citizenship and realises that the foundations of civil society need to be rebuilt. The notion of a basic income guarantee need not however generate socialistic outcomes and could be used as a subsidy for low paying employers and continued marginalisation if set at too low a level.[38] For this reason post-industrial socialists including Gorz and Offe have sought to propose that the state not only has an obligation to provide universal social policy but also that individuals have a right to a job which can only come about through reduced working hours. This requires state action to cap the working week and gradually aim at reducing working hours for all in the interests of allowing everyone the opportunity to work. In other words radical social policy must also be accompanied by radical economic policies to overhaul the labour market. The time out of work saved by a state policy of reduced working hours could then be used by individuals to engage in community or self-ordained activities.[39] It seems clear that notions of welfare and community are central to post-industrial socialist thought but that they cannot be assumed to exist in their present form. On the contrary they must be manufactured by state policies (social and economic) to generate suitable conditions for universal welfare to be established and then to allow individuals to participate in the domain of community and society at large.

[37]This is not necessarily the case with 'associations' which could be bodies imbued with economic rationality as could be the case with Walzer's reading of the civil society debate. More detail on the debate on associational democracy can be found in E.O.Wright (ed), *Associations and Democracy*, Verso, 1995.

[38]See A.Little, 'Flexible Working and Socialist Theories of Welfare', *Imprints: A Journal of Analytical Socialism*, 1/3, forthcoming; the most thoroughgoing debate on basic income can be found in P.Van Parijs (ed), *Arguing for Basic Income*, Verso, 1992.

[39]For an analysis of the economics of the end of the work-based society, see A.Gorz, *Capitalism, Socialism, Ecology*, Verso, 1994, chapter 9, and further evaluation of moves towards a less work-orientated society see C.Offe & R.Heinze, *Beyond Employment: Time, Work and the Informal Economy*, Polity, 1992.

Conclusion

Post-industrial socialism is, as yet, a developing perspective in political thought as the social, economic and political factors and ideas which brought it into existence continue to evolve.[40] In terms of welfare and community, it can be closely identified with the basic income debate which is concerned with a universal social policy provision irrespective of work requirements. However theorists such as Keane, Offe and Gorz have also suggested that this radical social policy needs to be accompanied by a move 'beyond employment' which, Gorz argues, is facilitated by a policy of reduced working hours and a right to work for everyone. In turn this involves a new politics of time in which the domain of states and markets is minimised and civil society is expanded and regenerated. In this scenario a pluralistic socialism comes to the fore in which a range of communities enjoy collective self-determination liberated from the intrusive presence of economic rationality and state bureaucracy – in this sense it is a communitarian agenda precisely because communities are accorded a primary status in the formation of political identity. However the key remains 'the end of work-based society' and, whilst that is the principle which differentiates post-industrial socialism from other strands of thought on welfare, communities and civil society, it is also the major obstacle to the realisation of the ideas of its advocates because despite the flexible labour market of the new economy, the underlining rationality is rooted in industrialism. In this sense the quantity of work may diminish in the new economy but society may become even more work-based.

[40] Whilst I have identified the work of Andre Gorz and Claus Offe as being particularly influential in the development of post-industrial socialism, a range of authors (especially those involved in the basic income debate such as Bill Jordan and Philippe Van Parijs) have contributed ideas which will lead to a more concrete identification of the new agenda.

Communitarianism and the Future of Social Policy

Linda Watson-Brown
University of Stirling

'Single Parents & Civic Competence – Back to Basics'

Introduction

This paper will present a brief analysis of recent political pronouncements, proposals and legislation on single parents. There will be reference to additional areas of discussion – the extent to which gender socialisation and stereotypes impose themselves upon women at an early age with consequent feelings of inadequacy when later forced into dealing with bureaucracy and officialdom; and the extent to which women may be consistently more disadvantaged than men in areas of 'moral' welfare policies. Women – like the poor – may possess a particularly difficult variety of situational dependency, indeed a helplessness to affect many important social factors in their lives (Bremner, 1968, p.15). Their dependency, lack of competence when dealing with officialdom, and socialization defines them as a similarly unresourceful outgroup as the poor. It is this lack of competence which, following on from Almond & Verba (1963; 1980), may represent yet another layer of the challenge to issues of citizenship and democracy for a particular sector of our society.

Government Action & The Child Support Agency

In 1990, the government, through the Department of Social Security, announced: 'Government cannot ensure that families stay together. But we can and must ensure that proper financial provision for children is made by their parents whenever it can be reasonably expected' (HMSO, 1990, foreword). In essence, the government had decided that changes had to be made to the child maintenance system. The White Paper that first proposed these changes of the Child Support Act 1991 made it clear that it was the unconditional responsibility of the parents of a child to provide for it throughout childhood (HMSO, 1990, passim). The idea was to establish an agency, which would be charged with the task of implementing a formula to determine how much the absent parent should pay towards the upkeep of the child(ren). The existing court-based system, under which maintenance payments were made as part of divorce settlements, was seen as increasingly arbitrary and unenforceable. It also failed to take account of the children born to mothers who were never married to the child's father. The new system promised a fair way of ensuring that maintenance was paid on time and regularly, and was at a level which provided for the needs of the child without forcing the absent parent into poverty.

The initiative was part of a scheme designed under the Thatcher administrations – the passing of the Act itself, the setting up of the agency, the maintenance formulae and all details were laid down by her successors. The government's given justification for the changes was suggested to be a moral one. Many mothers, it was implied, were struggling under conditions of adversity because they had been abandoned by the father of their children. Many wanted to go out to work but were trapped by dependence on state welfare that made it economically impossible for them to do so. The government would therefore chase the absent fathers, and extract maintenance payments (if necessary directly from their wage packet) in order to enforce their responsibilities. This underlined the government's belief that state dependence was not natural or healthy.

Millar & Whiteford observe that this was the perfect moral high ground from which to launch an attack against a growing part of the social security system. Single parents had become, it appeared, increasingly reliant on benefit. In 1976, 43 per cent of all lone parents were in receipt of benefit. By 1989, this had gone up to 67 per cent. There had been an absolute rise in numbers receiving benefit from 210,000 in 1971 to 607,000 in 1986. The cost of funding these benefits rose from £1.4 billion in the early 1980s to £3.2 billion in the late 1980s (DSS figures, 1990, at constant 1991 prices). This seemed to be caused by a fall in single parent employment rates: in the late 1970s, about 48 per cent of lone mothers were working, but by the mid-1980s it had fallen to 39 per cent. On top of the moral issues of state dependency was a political opportunity to bring down spending on the social security budget, an area in which the Thatcher government had suffered a conspicuous lack of success.

Before the system began, its disruptive potential began to become clear. Average maintenance payments were predicted to rise from £25 a week to £48. The Chief Executive of the CSA at the time, Ros Hepplewhite, announced that maintenance payments could run at up to £166.10 a week. She said: 'This is not an agency dealing with a small and irresponsible element of society; this is a major social change.' The aim for the CSA was to eventually supervise maintenance arrangements between all parents living apart. From April 5 1993, all couples seeking to make maintenance arrangements would have to approach the agency, whether they were drawing welfare at that time or not. The CSA would have the power to examine divorce statements retrospectively, and its formula would ignore 'clean break' settlements. Lone parents on Income Support, Family Credit or Disability Working Allowance are expected, unless exempt, to co-operate with the Agency. This involves both supplying information on the child's father and authorising the Agency to contact him.

The National Council for One Parent Families stated in its annual report of the year of implementation: 'All too often [the] statistics [are] moulded to suit the purposes of those attempting to spread gloom about the breakdown of the family and the spiralling welfare bill for single parents ... In particular, we challenge(d) the myth that the average lone parent is a feckless teenager who has deliberately become pregnant to get a council house and state benefits' (NCOPF, 1993, p.3).

In 1992, 21 per cent of all families with dependent children in Great

Britain were headed by a lone parent – one in five families. Between one in five and one in six dependent children were living in a one-parent family. Approximately 90 per cent of which were headed by lone mothers. The proportion of families headed by a lone parent rose from eight per cent in 1971 to 21 per cent in 1992. This was due to an increase in families headed by a single, divorced or separated mother. 73% of one-parent families result from divorce, separation or death. Only just over a third of lone mothers are single (that is, never married). Only one fifth of lone parents in Britain were under 25. The number of births outside marriage continues to rise and has more than doubled over the past decade. In 1992, births outside marriage were 31.2 per cent of all live births, compared to 30.2% in 1991 and 14.4% in 1982. In contradiction to the impression given in response to these statistics, the number of births to teenage mums actually declined significantly in 1992. The number of births to unmarried teenagers dropped five per cent to 31.7 births per 1,000 women from the previous recent high of 33.3 in 1990. In August 1993 there were 1,040,000 lone parents claiming Income Support. In 1992, nearly half of lone mothers got an income of less than £100 per week compared with only four per cent of married couples, while the number of lone parents getting over £350 was 11% compared with 59% of married couples. Lone fathers were likely to be better off than lone mothers with only 23% receiving less than £100 per week.

While the numbers of women working has increased steadily over the past ten years, the trend for lone parents is in the opposite direction. In 1992, 17 per cent of lone mothers with dependent children worked full-time and 24 per cent worked part-time. Whilst most of the lone parents who were recently surveyed by the National Council for One Parent Families expressed a desire to work at some stage, many cited the lack of affordable child care and the 'benefits trap' as key obstacles to getting a job. Many leading lone parent organisations and children's charities have expressed grave doubts about the legislation, and continue to do so. The arguments mainly surround the questions of how many lone parents are either no better off or are caught in a deeper poverty trap as a result of the legislation, the issue of whether the welfare of children is actually the paramount consideration, and whether the second families of 'Absent Parents' have suffered because of larger maintenance assessments.

Campaigns & Reports Against the CSA

In 1994, the Child Poverty Action Group summarised the main points of the legislation, giving the results of monitoring of the impact of the Act in terms of its effects on families and proposing that the Act did not put children first. The monitoring showed seven main points,: that many families are worse off due to loss of linked benefits; that the requirement to co-operate is having an adverse effect on women – many are not aware of their rights and the penalty puts enormous pressure on women to comply, often against their better judgement; that the maintenance formula has caused hardship in some cases, especially those with second families; that the failure to take into account clean break settlements has caused breakdown of previously amicable arrangements; that many parents with care are not getting maintenance after assessments are made or are experiencing long delays; that the new system is causing disruption to family relationships and is reopening painful issues; and, that maintenance has to be viewed within a wider policy of support for families – better benefits, training and education, provision of child care and flexible working conditions.

The campaign against the CSA has been dominated by the impact the Act is having on absent parents who are in the main men. Dramatic headlines of men being left with little or nothing to live on, some allegedly forced to commit suicide, has been a potent weapon in the campaign to change the maintenance calculation formula. Such an approach has been fairly successful as in response to this the Social security Advisory Committee researched the operation of the Act and recommended changes in the formula which were accepted by the Government. Very little, in comparison, has been heard of the effect of the CSA on lone parents who are in the main women – one of the big differences is that lone parents have been forced to live on poverty levels of income for many years.

One Parent Families and Poverty

Elsewhere, I have considered the premise that the process of gender socialization encourages and persuades young people throughout childhood and adolescence to conform to expectations of gender fostered by society for the continuation of traditional stereotypes with the result that adult experiences are coloured in particular ways – namely, that the roles imposed upon women at an early age leave them with a feeling of inadequacy if later forced into dealing with bureaucracy and officialdom, and that, subsequently, women are consistently and considerably more disadvantaged than men in areas of welfare policies. To connect these topics and demonstrate their relationship, let us first consider the situation of the sector of society brought into question by such hypotheses.

Clearly, there are many mixed and varied definitions within this particular section – what is poverty? Are single-parents to be considered a homogeneous mass? Are there distinct differences between men and women as lone parents? Firstly, a definition of 'poverty' must be arrived at. Are we speaking of absolute poverty (the conception of existing without access to the minimum requirements necessary for life, or survival)? Of relative poverty (a measure determined in relation to the standard of living enjoyed by the rest of society)? Or official poverty (based upon government statistics and levels of available welfare support, and largely rooted in the Townsend study of 1979)? We must also consider the significant factors which obscure the visibility of a great deal of poverty in Britain today – for example, the poverty of women (Glendinning & Millar, 1987, p.8-15). It has always been considerably more difficult for women in households to be treated as individuals within the boundaries of social research. Conventional studies of poverty tend to concentrate on the resources of collective units which are less complicated to deal with, therefore, families and households are focused upon rather than separate members of these groups. For the purposes of this research, it is clearly relative poverty which is of interest.

Alongside this consideration, must be an analysis of gendered poverty. Both definitions are subjective to some extent, which leads to the many party and interest group pronouncements debating both causes and effects. Some believe that poverty no longer exists in Britain and has therefore ceased to be a real problem. For example, ex-Secretary of State for Social Security, John Moore MP, in a renowned speech during the Conservative Party's third consecutive term of office, remarked upon a 'bizarre' radio announcement that one-third of the United Kingdom population is living in poverty or on the margins of poverty. 'It is utterly absurd to speak as if one in three people in Britain today is in dire need' (Moore, 1989, p.4). Moore described such claims as 'false and dangerous'. He continued:'... by almost every material measure it is possible to contrive ... not only are those with lower incomes not getting poorer, they are substantially better off than they have ever been before' (Moore, 1989, pp.13-14). As a precursor to the lack of understanding in this area which has been apparent in recent years, there are few more appropriate commentaries.

The Feminization of Poverty

The lives of women are often determined by the relevance and importance they place on the needs of others which leads them into poverty. Their traditional role as carers shape their work patterns, their occupation types and even their welfare benefits. As a result, caring for children, spouses, parents and the home pushes many women into dependence on male partners – or, eventually as an extension of this, the state (Oppenheim, 1993). Clear connections can be seen between the pre-adult socialization of children and the actual adult lives which result. The majority of women with children under five years of age do not have paid, contracted employment (whether they are married or not). Of the women who do work, they are concentrated in part-time, low status, poorly paid occupations. On average, women's wages remain considerably lower than those of men, often due to domestic responsibilities. There are additional considerations of gender socialization to be accounted for. Many women themselves believe that the 'proper place' for them is within the home, as a wife or mother. They are subjected to a barrage of societal images of men as wage-earners and providers. This image proposes that married women should only work for 'pin-money'. While it is often this 'pin-money' which prevents a family from official poverty statistics, the status of women in society results in poor wages and associated benefits. A woman may only work part-time in order to look after her child(ren) during the day, to provide family meals and keep the home together. She may decide to work in the evening, or when the child(ren) are at school, thus entering into the mire of low pay and dispensability with which such workers are faced.

Within this ghetto of gendered poverty, Annual Family Expenditure Surveys consistently reveal that lone parent families constitute a large part of 'the poor'. Lone parent households have fewer consumer durables than two-parent households, substantially fewer cars, freezers, and telephones. They are also more likely than two-adult families to be living in rented accommodation. When all of these obvious indicators of low-income lifestyles are considered alongside the numbers of lone parents dependent on the State, poverty becomes alarmingly synonymous with single parenthood. In many cases, lone parents discover that poverty is an unavoidable part of the welfare benefits package. The risk of poverty for these family units is very much greater than for two parent families and the extent of poverty is likely to be much more extreme.

The issue is not a 'marginal' one – one in seven families with dependent children is a one-parent family and nine out of ten lone parents are women. Of these women, the greatest number are separated and divorced mothers (58 per cent), followed by single mothers (19 per cent), and then widowed mothers (13 per cent). Only ten per cent of lone parents in Britain are men. Official definitions exclude the social and moral hypocrisy which colours the acceptability of many lone parents who are in their situation through a variety of causes – the main reason for the increase in one-parent families is the rise in the divorce rate. In Scotland, one in four marriages ends in divorce, compared to one in three in England and Wales. While unmarried motherhood and widowhood lead all lone parents into one homogeneous classification, there are many differences in public attitudes toward the various categories. These variations within one-parent families also make the idea of a universal policy for the group somewhat unrealistic – 'It may be wrong for example to discount the differences between an unmarried mother of nineteen, living with her parents, and a widow of 45 living in her own home' (Popay, Rimmer & Rossiter, 1985, p.5).

Family Values

'The Family' is no longer a universal image which can be applied to all households with children (despite the efforts of many). For some, the changes in family structure and responsibilities are obviously seen as threatening to their defined values of society.

> ' "The Family" evokes a constellation of social, moral and religious values concerned with the structure and quality of family life and its relationship to outside institutions and individuals. Assumptions about "normal' family life, about what is good or bad, based on these values, implicitly and explicitly underlie behaviour and policy in many different fields. One parent families represent an obvious and visible challenge to many of these values and formal and informal attitudes towards such families, reflecting this, are often ambiguous and sometimes actually unsympathetic.' (Popay, Rimmer & Rossiter, 1985, p.18)

Reinhold has noted that 'family' is an 'ideologically potent category ... mobilized as a natural, normal relation', when it is not at all natural, but, an ongoing site of struggle (Reinhold, 1994, p. 63). This view is echoed by numerous writers who support the idea that the concept of 'the family' wields enormous ideological power, hence its recurrent use in political debate. Yet the diversity of family forms apparent in modern society has led many to analyse the intrinsic uncertainty of the term – the term, although familiar, requires explanation (Zinn, 1993, p.474). The many 'truths' which make up the image of 'the family' are extremely flimsy. The stereotypical nuclear family unit is by no means the 'norm' in British contemporary society, and yet it is constantly resurrected by politicians, commentators, and the media to reflect and represent all that is good about our culture. Indeed, in many instances, all that is not family, is deviant, unnatural, even pathological.

Gittins (1985) has noted that 'the family' as an ideological stereotype is produced and maintained for the very purpose of exerting types of social control. The fact that such 'families' may not demographically exist is virtually irrelevant. The myth of the family has been constructed not because it is the norm, but in order that it will become the norm, largely for the benefit of policy makers, state controllers, welfare agencies, and the legislature. Thus, 'the family' becomes part of a discourse of control. However, if we are to accept that this idea of the family is a convenient and oft-used one in our society, we should not lose sight of the contradictions which still emerge within it. As an ideological tool, it is a useful one. As McLennan has noted: 'Ideologies are sets of ideas, assumptions and images by which people make sense of society, which give a clear social identity, and which serve in some way to legitimize relations of power in society' (McLennan, 1991, p. 114).

Hypocrisies in this field – and many others – are reinforced on a gender basis. If widows with children are given social sympathy greater than that of non-widows, then widowers with children are given even more. Men who have separated or divorced and who retain custody of their child(ren) also receive much more positive attention than lone female parents. These beliefs are reinforced by the media, frequently one of the most determined agents in the socialization process. Hypocrisies and pre-conceived notions regarding deviance and traditional roles exaggerate the earlier inequalities spoken of. According to Letts: '... one-parent families are continuously subject to discrimination, and (that) this discrimination is intrinsically related to assumptions about women and men and family life which lie behind the formulation of social policy. In addition, discrimination against one-parent families is amplified by the existing inequality between the sexes' (Letts, 1983, p.5).

For women facing a future as a single parent, social security and housing are areas of legislation which may be completely alien to them. Even if these women have existed in relationships where there has been an overall reliance on social security provision, their male partner may have controlled the family finances and dealt with any conflicts between the family and the system. A woman who faces these political domains as a novice has additional dilemmas of inexperience and lack of confidence. She is entering an arena filled with people who have specialized knowledge – an arena replete with attitudes and assumptions which are largely structured around male stereotypes. While child benefit and maternity legislation is designed with particular emphasis on the sector of society which has a need for such policies, there is no helpful gender delineation in social security and housing. Any moulded polices take men as the norm, women as the deviators. Consequently, single women must not only cope with new areas of policy, but with a pervading atmosphere of exclusion. These are areas which they are not expected to deal with. Women can be seen as an outgroup who threaten norms and upset balances imposed by dominant groups. Their position in the social security and welfare benefits arena is consequently much more tentative – particularly if they lack the self-confidence and competence necessary to deal with the bureaucratic structure. Women's involvement in the external world of politics is frequently limited as is their subsequent development of confidence. Women possess neither pressure group status or uniform solidarity – as a result, they lack effective force and influence.

Discrimination and Democracy

Both men and women have to deal with administrative difficulties and bureaucratic problems within the welfare state – women however, have the additional uncertainty of coping with the political arena relatively unarmed, they have few of the skills and resources with which men are equipped, and their levels of competence are significantly lower. Although much more detailed analysis is required, there are a few tentative points we can make in relation to applying traditional political theory to this contemporary, and clearly gendered, issue.

The concept of civic competence as outlined by Almond & Verba (1963), proposes a method of analysis and consideration for the actions of the individual as a member of a wider societal grouping. They often ignore women as awkward disrupters of their theories, dismissing them abruptly, and consequently denying equality. Instead of integrating women's experiences and addressing the difficulties they face within the civic culture, they are expelled in a few brief paragraphs. They state in their Foreword: 'This book is about inequality, or more specifically, social inequality. In explaining what we mean by this we can take as our yardstick adult males in the prime of life ...' The authors describe the civic culture as a pluralistic one based on communication and persuasion, it is a culture of consensus and diversity, within which is the political culture – a term which involves the attitudes of citizens toward the political system and its various parts, as well as the attitudes toward the role of the self in the system. 'When we speak of the political culture of a society, we refer to the political system as internalized in the cognitions, feelings, and evaluations of its population. People are inducted into it, just as they are socialized into nonpolitical roles and social systems' (Almond & Verba, 1963, p.12). The process of socialization works in this political manner too. Just as girls are taught to be girls, and boys are taught to be boys, the people living within a political culture are taught to accept certain features of that culture. Almond & Verba studied five nations – Italy, Germany, Mexico, the United Kingdom, and the USA. Respondents were tested on their levels of political cognition by replying to the question which asked for their estimated degree of impact by national government on everyday life. While seventy-three per cent thought the government had a great effect or some effect on their daily lives, twenty-three per cent thought that there was no effect at all. Mexican citizens had comparable response rates of thirty per cent for great or some effect, while two thirds answered that there was no effect at all. Similar figures arose when respondents were asked of the effects of local government (Almond & Verba, 1963, p.46-47). The authors believed that if the respondent perceived that government influenced their lives, s/he was cognitively oriented to government action. The significance of government impact varies sharply with the level of education. Due to a lack of education, many of the Mexican respondents gave answers that suggested a belief that the government was corrupt and/or self-centred. The Mexican replies also suggested that many felt a great deal of alienation from their system. British respondents were much more aware of the links between themselves and government, but the results of the Mexican study are perhaps more germane to the position of women (certainly, single parents) and their interpretation of governmental effects.

In my study, many single parents stated that 'politics' had nothing to do with them. Almond & Verba asked respondents to consider two hypothetical situations. They were asked to imagine themselves in a government office with a problem that called for official action, and, they were asked to imagine themselves as having some minor trouble with the police. Responses which indicated that unfair treatment would be meted out, suggested output alienation. Again, educational achievement affected expectations strongly, but the authors found that the British expected serious consideration if placed in the situations outlined above. In comparison, the women in my study who I mentioned such a situation to would expect very little from 'the authorities', preferring instead to seek allies in welfare rights groups if necessary. If individuals considered themselves to be competent as citizens, they were defined as politically competent in the Almond & Verba study. Administrative competence referred to the level of competence felt by individuals as subjects. The number of female respondents who expect serious consideration was fifty-two per cent compared to forty-eight per cent of men. These figures relate to subject competence. Regarding citizen competence, forty-nine per cent of women said they could tackle unjust laws compared to sixty-five per cent of men (Almond & Verba, 1963, p.170-71).

> In every nation men are more likely than women to be politically competent, and in most cases the differences in frequency in this form of competence are quite striking. But the differences between the sexes in administrative competence are much smaller ... in the United States and Britain women are somewhat more likely than men to consider themselves administratively competent. (Almond & Verba, 1963, p.175)

'The civic culture is a male culture' (Pateman, 1980, p.71) and it ignores the specific problems of women in any culture. 'The findings show that women (in all countries) generally rank lower than men on all the indices of political attitudes and activity associated with the civic culture ... Nowhere in The Civic Culture is there an explanation of the nonparticipation syndrome, or the relationship among low SES, female sex, lack of civic orientations, and low levels of political participation' (Pateman, 1980, p.77-78). Pateman asks, what is democratic about the civic culture? How can a culture be described as a complete democracy when divided on the basis of sex and socio-economic status? Almond & Verba's theory of a civic culture combines the disparate elements of democracy and discrimination. Given a large amount of the latter, the existence of the former is in doubt. Traditionally, many authors have discounted as political activity the very acts which many women engage in, for example, Verba, Nie & Kim (1978) state that communal activity is not relevant to their study – but it is relevant to women. Women are frequently the ones who deal with basic problems of housing, education and other 'family' matters. It is typical of the male bias which permeates social and political research to treat this mode as peripheral despite the fact that it could be seen as a frequently-used approach by many women (Verba et al 1978, pp.53-54). Authors still negate one of the only areas of political activity which many women inhabit – those in my survey outlined experiences related to problems with housing, poll/council tax, and education, all of which were often linked to local campaigns. In the minds of these single parents, they may not be dealing with 'big' politics, but they are trying to affect the outcome of policy-making and influence decisions – it may be the only political participation they ever indulge in. To dismiss it as irrelevant is insular and exclusive. The demands of these women are being treated as unimportant because they are personal and trifling in the minds of politicians and analysts. Should women ever form a united pressure group, nursery-school closures and damp houses would quickly be accorded increased importance on the agendas of the day.

'Competence and personal satisfaction tend to be found together' (Barnes & Kaase, 1979, p.405.) Women who bear the brunt of unfair and overgeneralised welfare policies, bringing up children alone, living in poverty, and relying on state handouts, are unlikely to feel either satisfied or competent. Would such an individual feel that the government was responsive to her needs and demands as a citizen? She would have neither the time or energy to become politically active. With a strong lack of resources, her own perception of individual competence would be minimal – and probably never put to the test. In light of recent and continuing statements on issues of personal morality, it will be interesting to consider whether the socialization of women and their subsequent treatment by bureaucracy has significant implications for citizenship.

> 'I could never go to my MP and tell him all my problems and demand something was done! He'd surely laugh me out of the room. Anyway these people are very busy, you can't go bothering them.' (Personal interview with single parent)

Bibliography

P.Alcock, *Poverty & State Support*, Longman, 1987.

G.A.Almond & S.Verba, *The Civic Culture*, Little Brown, 1963.

G.A.Almond & S.Verba, *The Civic Culture Revisited*, Little Brown, 1980.

S.H.Barnes & M.Kaase, *Political Action*, Sage, 1979.

M.Bremner, *Dependency & the Family*, IEA, 1968.

K.Clarke et al, *Losing Support, Children & the CSA*, The Children's Society, 1994.

A.Garnham & E.Knights, *Putting the Treasury First*, CPAG, 1994.

C.Glendinning & J.Millar (eds), *Women & Poverty in Britain*, Harvester Press, 1987.

HMSO, *Children Come First* (CM 1264, volume 1), 1990.

HMSO, *Improving Child Support* (CM 245), 1995.

P.Letts, *Double Struggle – Sex Discrimination & One-Parent Families*, National Council for One-Parent Families, 1983.

G.McLennan, 'The power of ideology', in *Society & Social Science*, Open University, 1991.

J.Moore, *The End of the Line for Poverty*, Conservative Political Centre (0510/802), 1989.

C.Oppenheim, *Poverty – the facts*, CPAG, 1993.

C.Pateman, in Almond & Verba, *op cit*, 1980.

Popay et al, *One Parent Families – Parents, Children and Public Policy*, Study Commission on the Family, Occasional Paper 12, 1985.

S.Reinhold, 'Through the Parliamentary Looking Glass: "Real" and "Pretend" Families in Contemporary British Politics', *Feminist Review*, 48,/Autumn, 1994.

P.Townsend, *Poverty in the United Kingdom*, Penguin, 1979.

S.Verba et al, *Participation & Political Equality*, Cambridge University Press, 1978.

Political Utopianism

Lucy Sargisson
Nottingham University

'Contemporary Feminist Utopianism: The equality/difference dilemma'

Utopia is the good place which is no place. The word originates in Thomas More's scholarly pun, combining the Greek '*eu*': good, with '*ou*': not or non, and '*topos*': place. Nowadays the term is often used in a negative sense to depict the overly idealistic or optimistic. It is, in other words, conceptually opposed to the world of realism and rigour.

This paper takes a more positive approach as it is my belief that all social movements and all political ideologies needs utopias and utopianism to give them direction and aspiration. As with any contested concept there is more than one approach to utopianism and more than one definition of the concept of utopia. However, all commentators agree on two general features: that utopian thought is both critical and creative. Utopias and utopianism add creativity to political thought and activity – as well as being critical of the status quo, they express desires for something different and better. They explore alternatives.

The focal point of this paper is contemporary feminism and will be suggesting that it needs utopianism but not just any utopianism. I shall be suggesting that a certain utopianism can help feminist theorists to begin to work their way out of what we could quite legitimately call the mess that they are currently in. Illustrations will be drawn from the utopian theory of Hélène Cixous and Monique Wittig's fictional utopian text *Les Guérillères.*

Feminist theory faces a dilemma today which can be expressed partly by the question: Where do we go from here? And partly by the perceived tension in response to the question, between the need, on the one hand, for coherence and the need, on the other hand, for a respect for diversity. Women, it is said, need to unite, need to be able to speak 'as women' else feminism has no internal coherence – but also, feminism needs to articulate the differences between women. These are methodological and political problems which involve questions of intellectual and political rigour. I shall be referring to this dilemma of where to go from here as the sameness/difference or equality/difference dilemma.

For some years now I have been lecturing on feminist political theory to undergraduate students. One lecture that I have given to first year students in the past introduces some different branches of feminist theory which, I say, can be understood and differentiated in part by what they have to say on the topics of equality and difference. This gives the students a useful handle to grasp in the otherwise disparate theory with which I then present them. I tell them that liberal and socialist feminisms are, albeit in different ways, 'about' equality – and that radical and Black (and, if I'm feeling very brave, postmodern) feminisms are, again, albeit in different ways, 'about' difference. This has the advantage of allowing us to ask interesting questions about the goals and aspirations of feminist theory as well as deeper ontological questions about human nature and the differences between women and men.

What worries me about this approach to teaching feminist theory is that a frequently reached conclusion is that feminism is being pulled apart by the equality/difference debate and that feminism fails as a political ideology because it lacks coherence. I propose now to briefly rehearse some of these discussions before turning to utopianism as a potential route out of the theorists nightmare that this debate has become.

Firstly – thinking about feminist theory through the matrix of equality and difference is an instructive exercise. It allows us to identify differentiating features of different branches of feminist thought whilst also representing a dynamic of critique between different branches of feminist thought. For example, Liberal feminism argues for social, legal and political equality of opportunity on the grounds that women and men are potentially the same. Rationality and the exercise of reason are the privileged characteristics of liberalism and liberal feminists say that women possess the capacity to be *as* rational as men and so they should be treated equally. Equality (or sameness) of characteristic is the grounding for arguments for equality (or sameness) of treatment or opportunity. The liberal tradition takes a straightforward understanding of equality as sameness which is not problematised by liberal feminists. Difference, in this tradition, is seen as something undesirable and surmountable. Women and men are thought to be potentially the same.

Socialist feminists are critical of the individualism of liberal feminist calls for equality but do not generally challenge the equation of equality with sameness and difference with deviance. Socialist feminists calls for an equal *society*, arguing that it is not an essentially sex-neutral human nature which provides the grounds for this but rather an equitable environment in which our characters can be formed. Radical feminists criticize liberal feminist politics of equality saying that liberals are, in effect, trying to be *like men.* In arguing for equal access to the public sphere, in stressing people's rationality, liberal feminists are buying into masculinity. Radicals instead stress and celebrate sexual difference as both the root of and the rout away from oppression. Black feminists argue that radical feminist universalism is repressive of difference. By stressing sex as the root of universal oppression and by articulating universal answers/solutions to universal problems, radicals are silencing the diversity of women's experiences. Black feminists, then, stress the differences between women.

So far so good: looking at feminist theory through the matrix of equality and difference is a useful exercise. But if we continue these kinds of conversations, we end up with a vision of feminism that is fragmented and incoherent to the point of dissolution. Feminism ceases to exist as a coherent entity.

What *IS* important here, I'd like to suggest, is the way in which difference and equality are conceptualised. Without including consideration of this in our conversations, we will be led down a road of misrepresentation. We will be inevitably led to misrepresent the options open to feminists who are asking 'where do we go from here?' Our response is restricted by a framework of binary opposition that offers a choice: equality OR difference.

Equality takes its etymological root from the Latin word aequus which means level, flat, even, balanced and uniform. The word equality is associated in the western tradition with sameness and identity. To differ is to be unlike, to be non-identical or dissimilar. The problem, I'd like to suggest, is in the *opposition* of these concepts. Put another way: the problem is with the conceptual system or methodology in which they are situated and studied. The problem is in the approach which conceptualises equality and difference or sameness and difference as in opposition.

The same framework of thought restricts our approach to utopianism. There is an approach to utopianism that reads utopias as blueprints for perfection. Historically this has been the dominant approach to utopias. And of course, perfection is a universalist concept: the notion of two blueprinting utopias happily coexisting is, surely a logical impossibility. If this is the case, then the utopia, or goal, of liberal feminism is of course, in opposition to the utopia or goal of, say, radical feminism. If each movement believes in its own infallibility and in the idealness or perfection of its own particular utopia then competition will be the dynamic of relations between the different branches of, say, feminist thought. Likewise, taking the blueprint approach to utopianism implies that feminism as a whole needs a blueprint, a goal, a vision of the ideal polity, a universally applicable, perfectly theorised utopia.

Elsewhere I have taken issue at great length with this view of utopianism and with this view of feminism.[1] For now I hope these comments will serve to problematise this view and, more importantly, to problematise the conceptual system, the approach, the methodology, in which they are grounded.

For me, the interesting thing about utopias and utopianism is the new spaces that they allow us to create. These can be imaginative spaces in the form of fictional utopias which imagine and explore other ways of being, and/or they can be conceptual spaces that disrupt the ways in which we normally think. I shall focus on and privilege these latter in the rest of the paper as it is the utopian exploration of new conceptual space which, I shall argue, provokes the new paradigms that allow us to start to think our way past the equality/ difference dilemma.

By thinking about equality and difference in a non oppositional way that is outside of the tradition of dualistic thought, we can begin to see that feminism might have a future that goes beyond fragmentation and dissolution. Our thinking needs to be informed by an openended utopianism that is not affiliated to perfection or to the privileging of sameness that characterises the liberal tradition. Two of the many feminist thinkers and writers who undertake this kind of thought are Hélène Cixous and Monique Wittig and I shall spend a little time now on their work in this area. I shall

[1] L.Sargisson, *Contemporary Feminist Utopianism*, Routledge, 1996.

be looking to see what they tell us about equality and difference as political goals and also what they say about equality and difference as factors in the construction of sexual identity.

If we were looking at Cixous and Wittig through the oppositional equality/difference matrix we would have to place them on the side of difference. We would also have to point out that they were in opposition to each other within that category as Wittig is very critical of the *ecriture feminine* with which Cixous engages in much of her writing. Instead, I plan to engage in a more constructive approach. First a little background. Both of these women are French and most of the pieces to which I shall refer to were published in the 1970s. Hélène Cixous is associated with that 'branch' of feminist theory that is sometimes described as 'French feminism' and sometimes even more loosely described as 'postmodern feminism'. Monique Wittig is the creator of what she calls 'materialist lesbianism'. These are thinkers that come to the subject of feminism from quite different approaches but what interests me is that both of their approaches are transgressive of the dominant mode of thinking. This interests me because I have begun to formulate a theory of what I call 'transgressive utopianism' – this is an approach to the world that is transgressive of hierarchical and binary oppositional thought.

Equality and difference can be connected to other oppositions which form a cluster in a referential system which confers meaning. An example is the self/other relation, which is informed by reference to sameness and difference in the western tradition which privileges identity and which constructs difference as deviance. This can be schematically represented as follows:

Equality/Difference	Sameness/Deviance
Self/Other	Identity/Non-Identity

The dynamic of difference in such a system may vary according to historical and cultural context. Examples of things that have been taken to constitute so called 'relevant differences' are racial difference, religious difference, and sexual difference. These factors are conceptualised in such a way as to legitimise unequal (different) treatment. At different times in history, we might want to add different dynamics to the above set of clusters, examples are: Whiteness/Blackness, Christian/Jew, Man/Woman.

Both Cixous and Wittig are interested in sexual difference. They both see current dominant understandings of sexual difference as really being about sexual OPPOSITION. In her utopian novel *Les Guérillères*, Wittig depicts an imaginary world of women. Through dialogue with visitors from our world, they inform us about their world, and how it evolved or emerged from our own. This text is classically utopian, it offers a critique of the political present and a creative vision of an alternative. It also creates new conceptual space that allows us to engage in paradigm shifts in consciousness. Of sexual difference in our world, we are told, firstly, that it is a patriarchal construct:

> 'The women say, the men have kept you at a distance, they have stupefied you, they have put you on a pedestal, constructed with an essential difference. ... They say, oddly enough, what they have exalted in their words as an essential difference is a biological variation.' (Wittig, 19761, p.100).

So, sexual difference, as conceived in masculine terms is the exaltation, or rather, in practical terms, denigration, of a biological variation. It is, in other words, the product of an essentialist methodology: a trick, a sham.

Likewise, for Cixous, this sexual difference on which so much rests is a cultural construct and not an essential fact. She says:

> 'Of course there is the trap "man" and the trap "woman". These are denominations in language and on identity cards. They are only social indicatives, part of our role playing. In every individual there is a whole complex play of femininity, of masculinity.' (Cixous, 1986, p.4)

Man and Woman as universal categories of subjectivity are traps, tricks, and not inevitable. This speaks quite profoundly to a politics of sexual difference because although both Cixous and Wittig want to deny the essentialist approach to sexual difference, they *are* both interested in difference, nonetheless. They want to tell us HOW these constructs have been developed and WHY they have come to dominate our consciousness of what difference is. At the level of explanation, both focus on language. Wittig's women , for instance,

> 'say that there is no reality before it has been given shape by words rules regulations. They say that in what concerns *them* everything has to be remade starting form basic principles. They say that in the first place the vocabulary of every language is to be examined, modified, turned upside down, that very word must be screened.' (Wittig, 1971, p.134)

Much of the text of *Les Guérillères* is engaged in provoking these paradigm shifts: for example, it looks different to a conventional novel. It is written in a self-consciously transgressive way that disrupts the convention of a single 'straight' unified narrative. Pages of prose text are interspersed with pages on which women's names are recited in long capitalised lists, or pages which contain nothing but a large symbol: the letter O. The syntax is peculiar: disrupted and disruptive of easy reading.

Cixous' work is engaged in *deconstructive thinking* towards our linguistic system, for her, also, meaning is constructed by language and therefore sexual difference is treated as a linguistic construct. She also chooses a textual form in which to express this that is transgressive of narrative prose:

Where is she?
Activity/Passivity
Sun/Moon
Culture/Nature
Day/Night
Father/Mother
Head/Heart
Intelligible/Palpable
Logos/Pathos.

Form, convex, step, advance, semen, progress
Matter, concave, ground, – where steps are taken, holding-and-dumping-ground.

Man
___
Woman (Cixous,1976,p63)

This is beautifully expressive and sharply critical.

In terms of critique, then, both the fictional utopia of Wittig's guerillas and the theoretical analysis of Hélène Cixous perform the first function of what Tom Moylan has called the critical utopia (Moylan, 1986). The critical utopia is critical in the Enlightenment sense of critique, as well as in the nuclear sense of constituting a critical mass. For Moylan, the critical utopia contributes to what he calls an historic bloc of opposition which has transformative potential. Critical utopianism destroys, transforms and revives that which it critiques(Moylan, 1986). With regard to destruction: Cixous and Wittig both work to *destroy* the myth of sexual opposition on which gendered inequality has historically and conceptually been based. They also *transform* the notion of sexual difference and thereby allow its revival as an emancipatory concept. It is to this latter function of these texts that I shall now turn.

If sexual difference is not the essentialist opposition that we have been assuming, what is it? Both Cixous and Wittig begin to approach this question by focusing on points at which binary sexual relationships are transgressed. For Wittig, this is the category and practice of lesbianism, and, for Cixous, it is the category and practice of bisexuality.

For Wittig, the lesbian is NOT a woman and therefore she conceptually escapes the dualistic logic of the man/woman construct. The construct woman is defined in reference to that of man, the lesbian position, for Wittig is independent of man and therefore not entwined in this restrictive logic. The lesbian is a refugee form binary oppositional thought – this creates the kind of new conceptual space that I mentioned earlier for, if we can conceive of a subjective category that is not dualistically constructed, we might be able to begin to think about these things differently. This is a non-dualistic, *self*-defined third gender. This is transgressive utopianism at work.

For Cixous, conceptual bisexuality might allow us to open ourselves to the other. Here she is transgressing the opposition of self to other on which so many of our relations with other people are grounded. She does not talk of a *sexually neutral* bisexuality that merges femininity and masculinity, but rather, one that permits them to co-exist inside each individual. Here it is in her own words:

> 'To this self-effacing, merger-type bisexuality, ... I oppose the *other bisexuality* on which every subject not enclosed in the false theatre of phallocentric representationalism has founded his/her erotic universe. Bisexuality: that it, each one's location in self ... of the presence – variously manifest and insistent according to each person, male or female – of *both sexes*, non-exclusion either of the difference or of one sex, and, from this, "*self*-permission", multiplication of the effects of the inscription of desire, overall parts of my body and the other body.' (Cixous, 1976, p.254)

This, then, is a bisexuality that does not *annul* differences but rather permits them. This is not a sexually neutral androgyny which equality theorists might develop, but a sexually plural and multiple state of being.

What does this tell us about a revival of equality and difference as feminist concepts? It tells us that they are being reinscribed into our culture DIFFERENTLY. It tells us that an initial step in this process is through language. From Cixous we hear that:

> 'If woman has always functioned "within" the discourse of man, a signifier that has always referred back to the opposite signifier which annihilates its specific energy and diminishes or stifles its very different sounds, it is time for her to dislocate this "within", to explode it, turn it around, seize it; to make it hers, containing it, taking it into her own mouth, biting that tongue with her very own teeth to invent for herself a language to get inside of. And you'll see with what ease she will spring forth from that "within" – the "within" where she once so drowsily crouched – to overflow at the lips she will cover with foam.' (Cixous, 1976, p257)

We need to bring our long neglected bodies into this language, to transgress and deny the mind/body, emotion/reason dichotomies that underpin current theory-making. We need, in other words to engage in and practice transgressive utopian thinking. Thinking of this kind challenges many of the assumptions upon which political theory is built. Political theory has traditionally privileged reason and rational discourse. Thinking of this kind inscribes desire and emotion into and onto the political and cultural text.

What we do not need to do is to invoke another closure. Theory has traditionally sought answers and explanations which represent a certain closure. Utopianism, as traditionally understood, represents the full stop to progress and process. If a utopia inscribes a vision of the ideal polity, the perfect society, then it can be said to represent the death or end of politics. (Within Cixous' work perfection is often associated with death). Transgressive utopianism is a utopianism of process, the magic is in the moment, the activity of utopian thinking.

Wittig's guerillas are constantly working to avoid the kind of closures form which they have escaped. This is not an unproblemmatic exercise. I mentioned earlier in the paper that occasionally in the text of this book there are pages that are blank but for a large black circle and the letter O permeates this text and references to the vulva abound. The women have used it as a vehicle for the creation of an alternative symbolism to that which structures them as the universal construct of Woman. Their gynocentric imagery and symbolism is empowering. But, they resist fetishism and entrapment in their new symbolism. It was useful to them at one time in their society's development but is not their ultimate goal:

> 'The women say that they perceive their bodies in their entirety. They say that they do not favour any of its parts on the grounds that it was formerly a forbidden object.' (Wittig, 1971, p.57)

And this is despite all the references to O.

Every night before going to sleep in their O shaped sleeping cells they say 'This ordered must be changed.' A hangover from earlier days maybe, but I read this as also resisting the construction of ANY rigid, encoding, order. These women foster DISORDER. In a simple yet resonant phrase the guerillas say:

> 'If I take over the world, let it be to dispossess myself of it immediately, let it be to forge new links between myself and the world.' (Wittig, 1971, p.107)

And this, I'd like to suggest, is the key to real, sustainable change. This change is not a simple inversion of patriarchal values and symbolism. Rather it is an attempt to approach the world in truly new ways, ways that aren't restrained by the old paradigms.

For Cixous, hope lies in a gift economy that she characterises as 'feminine'. In the essay the Laugh of the Medusa, she outlines her utopian project as follows:

> 'The future must no longer be determined by the past. I do not deny that the effects of the past are still with us. But I refuse to strengthen them by repeating them, to confer upon them an irremovability the equivalent of destiny, to confuse the biological and the cultural. Anticipation is imperative. ... Thus, as there are no grounds for establishing a discourse, but rather an arid millennial ground to break, what I say has at least two sides and two aims: to break up, to destroy; and to foresee the unforeseeable, to project.' (Cixous, 1976, p.244)

To break up and destroy, and to foresee the unforeseeable. Not to evoke new closures. Elsewhere she talks of 'destroying the space of domination':

> 'It is not a question of appropriating their instruments, their concepts for oneself or of wishing oneself in their position of

mastery. ... Not taking possession to internalize or manipulate but to shoot through and smash the walls.' (Cixous, 1986, p.96)

She is talking here about a non-possessive cultural economy, in which relations with the other are not characterised by appropriation and opposition, but rather by openness and non-possessive love. She is, I think, occupying a new conceptual space of her own evocation.

We need to keep things openended if we are going to be able to join Cixous and Wittig in these new utopian spaces. We need an approach to feminism that does not seek one answer to the problems facing women today. An openended approach allows us to escape the binary opposition of either/or, so that we can call for equality AND difference, equality with a difference. This equality is closer in meaning to the word equity than to the old equality-as-sameness. Equality as equity is not a further inscription and affirmation of sameness. It permits difference, pure difference, and not difference as deviance.

Bibliography

P.Alexander & R.Gill (eds), *Utopias*, Duckworth, 1984.

L.Armitt, *Where no man has gone before: women and science fiction*, Routledge, 1991.

D.Baker-Smith & C.C.Barfoot (eds), *Between Dream and Nature: Essays on Utopia and Dystopia*, DQR Studies in Literature 2, Amsterdam, Editions Rodopi, 1987.

A.Bammer, *Partial Visions: Feminism and Utopianism in the 1970s*, Routledge, 1991.

M.S.Barr, *Future Females: A Critical Anthology*, Bowling Green State University Press, 1981.

M.Barrett & A.Phillips, *Destabilizing Theory*, Polity Press, 1992.

F.Bartowski, *Feminist Utopias*, University of Nebraska Press, 1989.

E.Bloch, *The Principle of Hope*volumes 1, 2 & 3, translated by N.Plaice et al, Basil Blackwell (written 1938-47, revised 1953 & 1959, English translation 1986), 1986.

H.Cixous & C.Clement, *The Newly Born Woman*, translated by Betsy Wing, Manchester University Press, 1986.

H.Cixous, 'The Laugh of the Medusa', in Marks (1981), 1981.

H.Cixous, 'Castration or Decapitation?', *Signs: Journal of Women in Culture and Society*, l7/11, 1981a (translated by Annette Kuhn).

P.H.Collins, *Black Feminist Thought*, Unwin Hyman, 1990.

V.A.Conley, 'Exchange with Hélène Cixous', Appendix in *Hélène Cixous*, University of Nebraska Press, 1984.

J.C.Davis, *Utopia and the Ideal Society: a study of English utopian writing 1516-1700*, Cambridge University Press, 1981.

M.Gatens, *Feminism and Philosophy: perspectives on difference and equality*, Polity Press, 1991.

B.Goodwin, *Social Science and Utopia: Nineteenth Century Models of Social Harmony*, Harvester, 1978.

E.Grosz, 'A Note on Essentialism and Difference', in Gunew (1990), 1990.

S.Gunew (ed), *Feminist Knowledge: Critique and Construct*, Routledge, 1990.

B.Hooks, *Feminist Theory: From Margin to Centre*, Boston, South End Press, 1984.

A.Jagger, *Feminist Politics and Human Nature*, Harvester Press, 1983.

F.Jameson, *The Political Unconscious: Narrative as a Socially Symbolic Act*, Methuen, 1981.

E.Kamenka, *Utopias*, Oxford University Press, 1987.

P.Kamuf, *A Derrida Reader: Between the Blinds*, Harvester Wheatsheaf, 1991.

J.A.Kourany et al, *Feminist Philosophies*, Harvester Wheatsheaf, 1993.

K.Kumar, *Utopianism*, Open University Press, 1991.

S.Lefanu, *In the Chinks of the World Machine: Feminism and Science Fiction*, The Women's Press, 1988.

R.Levitas, *The Concept of Utopia*, Philip Allan, 1990.

Frank Manuel & Fritzie Manuel, *Utopian Thought in the Western World*, Belknap Press, 1979.

F.Manuel (ed), *Utopias and Utopian Thought*, Souvenir Press, 1973.

M.E.Marks & I.de Courtivron, *New French Feminisms*, Harvester, 1981.

L.McDowell & R.Pringle, *Defining Women: Social Institutions and Gender Division*, Polity Press, 1992.

T.More, *Utopia*, translated by G.M.Logan, introduction by R.M.Adams, Cambridge University Press, 1975 (first published 1516).

T.Moylan , *Demand the Impossible: Science Fiction and the Utopian Imagination*, Methuen, 1986.

P.Murphy, *Women's Studies; An Interdisciplinary Journal* – special issue: 'Feminism Faces the Fantastic', 14/2, 1987.

A.Neustatter, *Hyenas in Petticoats. A look at twenty years of feminism*, Penguin, 1990.

L.J.Nicholson (ed), *Feminism/Postmodernism*, Routledge, 1990.

A.Nye *Feminist Theory and the Philosophies of Man*, Routledge, 1989.

R.Rohrlich & E.H.Baruch (eds), *Women in Search of Utopia: Mavericks and Mythmakers*, Schocken Books, 1984.

L.T.Sargent, 'Utopia: The Problems of Definition', *Extrapolation*, 16/2, 1975.

L.T.Sargent, *British and American Utopian Literature, 1516-1985: An Annotated, Chronological Bibliography*, Garland Publishing, 1988.

L.T.Sargent, 'The Three Faces of Utopianism Revisited', *Utopian Studies*, 15/1, 1994.

L.Sargisson, *Contemporary Feminist Utopianism*, Routledge, 1996.

J.Scott, 'Deconstructing Equality-versus-Difference: or, the uses of post-structuralist thought for feminism', in McDowell (1992), 1992.

S.Sellers, 'Hélène Cixous', interview in *Women's Review*, 7, 1986.

S.Sellers , *Language and Sexual Difference*, Macmillan, 1991.

M.L.Lyndon & C.Pateman, *Feminist Interpretations and Political Theory*, Polity Press, 1981.

M.Shiach, *Hélène Cixous: The Politics of Writing*, Routledge, 1991.

E.Spelman *Inessential Woman: Problems of exclusion in feminist thought*, The Women's Press, 1990.

D.Suvin, 'Defining the Literary Genre of Utopia', *Studies in the Literary Imagination*, 6/2, 1973.

J.Todd (ed), *Women Writers Talking*, Holmes & Meier, 1983.

H.Wilcox et al (eds), *The Body and the Text: Hélène Cixous, Reading and Teaching*, Harvester Wheatsheaf, 1990.

M.Wittig, *Les Guérillères*, translated by David Le Vay, David Owen, 1971.

M.Wittig, 'The Category of Sex', in Wittig (1992), 1976/1982.

M.Wittig, 'The Straight Mind', in Wittig (1992), 1980.

M.Wittig, 'The Point of View: Universal or Particular?', in Wittig (1992), 1980a.

M.Wittig, 'One is Not Born a Woman', in Wittig (1992), 1981.

M.Wittig, 'Homo Sum', in Wittig (1992), 1990.

M.Wittig, *The Straight Mind and Other Essays*, Harvester, 1992.

Historical Perspectives on Political Communication in Britain

Jenie Betteridge
University of Westminster

'Broadcasting the Post War Elections: Changing Media, Changing Rules, Changing Politics'

Introduction

To understand the developments in electioneering in post-war Britain it is necessary to study both politicians and broadcasters. The post war negotiations between these professionals amalgamated their separate agendas so successfully that today it is impossible to view broadcasting and politics as distinct activities.

Public Service Broadcasting required the BBC to inform, educate and entertain. To ensure that they were seen as serious informers and educators, broadcasters actively encouraged politicians to broadcast. The politicians actively utilised the media to reach larger audiences and previously inaccessible sections of the electorate. In these negotiations the BBC often acted as a referee between the parties, and had no real power to dictate the rules of political broadcasting.[1]

However, to ensure entertainment, broadcasters had to teach politicians new techniques. Politicians had to learn to employ them first for radio then for television. Here the broadcasters were aware that their superior knowledge gave them power over politicians. The techniques of public oratory were not appropriate to the new mediated politics.

Changing media

In 1945, the BBC monopoly and supremacy of radio were accepted. Broadcasting was limited to the BBC Home and General Overseas Services (GOS) and the Allied Forces Programme(AFP). Television resumed in June 1946 and by December the Light and Third Radio programmes had commenced.

BBC radio gained its reputation for serious broadcasting during the war. Television was considered a light entertainment medium. Vision broadcasters competed with sound to promote the seriousness of their medium, enticing politicians to appear. The unparalleled rise in licence numbers during the 1950s, also influenced politicians to accept television electioneering. The numbers were:[2]

[1] P.Scannell & D.Cardiff, *A Social History of British Broadcasting*, Basil Blackwell 1991 p.50.

[2] BBC T23/144.

1950	586,100
1951	763,941
1955	4,503,766
1959	9,627,657

After the 1955 Election, when the monopoly was broken, BBC sound and vision personnel combined forces to meet the challenge of the ITA. The BBC no longer deferred to Governments in the face of competition whose modus operandi was not based on a precedent of co-operation with politicians.

By 1959, not least because of the innovations of the ITA, television was the preferred medium for electioneering. Politicians were already convinced of the medium's efficacy.

However, Gallup Polls identified the preferred method of obtaining political information in 1955 and 1959 as:[3]

source	*1955*	*1959*
Newspapers	47%	41%
Radio	32%	12%
Television	15%	34%

Thus, although the positions of radio and television had been reversed, newspapers maintained top position. This, together with the evidence collected by the Parties indicating that broadcasting had little effect on voting, renders their concentration on political broadcasting in the 1950s, a curious phenomenon.

Changing rules

1945 saw the return of party politics after the wartime coalition, and set the pattern for subsequent elections. Broadcasts were based on arrangements made in April 1939, but shelved during the war. The arrangements allocated broadcasts between the parties, stipulated the closed period and agreed that minority parties had to nominate 20 candidates to qualify for broadcasts.[4]

The fortnight rule (FDR), under which nothing could be discussed on air if it was to be debated in Parliament in the coming fortnight, was adopted during the war. It was originally introduced in 1944 by a BBC Board of Governors' resolution with 'the object of bringing to an end a practice which appeared to be growing up of Ministers asking to broadcast in order to advocate measures which were about to be debated in the House of Commons.'[5] Thus, the closed period preceded the FDR, but the delay in its implementation led to a general assumption that the closed fortnight had been extended to the closed period during elections.

[3] BBC T23/144.
[4] BBC R34/536 4.3.49.
[5] CPA CRD2/20/12 12.1.51.

The distinction between formal and informal political broadcasting is crucial to understanding the importance of the FDR. For formal political broadcasts (FPBs) the Parties had editorial control and the BBC provided transmission. Informal political broadcasts (IPBs) were those in which politicians appeared or in which political issues were discussed, and over which the BBC had editorial control. As they were not arranged by the BBC, all FPBs were outside of the FDR.

During the 1945 election period, the Editor of Overseas News Broadcasts, Bernard Moore, issued a directive on IPBs. He stressed that coverage was dictated by commonsense and a strict adherence to objectivity, but a few rules could be laid down.

> 'No MP or candidate may be used in any programme ... It is our responsibility to know whether a speaker is a candidate or not. If one election address is used, all must be used.'[6]

The ban was not confined to News. The BBC took their obligation to refrain from influencing voting seriously. For example, a revised list of speakers, excluding candidates, was drawn up for the series *The Politics of Freedom*, and the *Sociology and Politics* series was suspended. Standard announcements were used during the election period. It was foreseen that stock announcements might cause some difficulty with the Conservatives, partly due to the 1939 arrangements referring to Government, not Conservative speakers, and partly to Churchill's insistence on the national rather than party character of his Government. However, as Richard Maconachie, Controller of the Home Service, pointed out:

> 'In the event, the Labour and Liberal speakers proved to be no more bound by the agreement of their Party offices to the formula ... generally speaking the speakers' own wishes were followed in the matter.'[7]

Politicians asserted their rights, both to control political decisions and to maintain editorial responsibility for FPBs. However, during the 1950 campaign when Churchill rang up George Barnes, Director of the Spoken Word, on the afternoon of his election broadcast to complain that it was followed immediately by a programme entitled We Beg to Differ, Barnes asserted the BBC's right to schedule programmes and reported:

> 'The matter was re-adjusted by the inclusion of a 60 second piano interlude – the BBC maintains its rights not to change existing programmes which had no political connection.'[8]

Clearly, power to control political broadcasting was being contested. When competition became a reality, the BBC having abided by the FDR and not competed with Parliament, now faced competition themselves. Thus in 1954, the Home Affairs Committee noted the BBC's request to abandon the FDR which stemmed:

---

[6]BBC R28/81/3 29.5.45.
[7]BBC R51/410 25.7.45.
[8]BBC R34/539 9.3.50.

> '... from a feeling that the advent of a competitive service would complicate the position. ... If the rule must continue, the matter should be taken out of their hands by the issue by the PMG of a Notice under Clause 15(4) of the BBC's Licence.'[9] 14.5.54

From its inception the FDR was seen as self-censorship, but the alternative had been a complete Ministerial broadcasting ban. The BBC were forcing the Government to take responsibility for its implementation. The Government were faced with a dilemma, if they imposed the FDR, the independence of the BBC would be challenged. The ITA and BBC publicly contested the FDR, and in 1956 it was suspended for six months and never reinstated.

Although the Conservative Party championed competitive television, and its immediate popularity prompted the other two parties to follow suit, political competition was less tolerated. In 1945 the BBC received 20 applications pressing claims to broadcast, 5 qualified: The Commonwealth, Communist, Scottish and Welsh Nationalist and Cooperative Parties.

In 1950, the Liberals protested that their allocation of one 30 minute broadcast was unfair.[10] Agreement could not be reached, and another meeting was called the following day. During these meetings the decision was taken to increase the number of candidates needed by a party to qualify for a broadcast from 20 to 50. This was the most dramatic development during the 1950 election, yet how it was reached is a matter of confusion.

After the meetings, the BBC Board of Governors received a paper stating the arrangements made by the BBC and confirmed by the Parties, including the arrangement to increase the number of candidates.[11]

However, the minutes of the Meeting reported:

> 'arrangements (1) to (8) made between BBC representatives and the Parties, including the rule, suggested by the parties, that the qualification for a 10 minute broadcast by any other Party at 6.15pm should be a minimum of 50 candidates.'[12]

So was the rule included in the arrangements made by the BBC and agreed by the parties, or did the Parties suggest it, as reported in the minutes of the Board meeting? After the Election a note by the BBC Director General, William Haley, confirmed the minutes:

> 'In 1945, the number was 20 – the BBC made the same proposal for the recent election. At the suggestion of the Parties it was argued the qualification should be raised to 50 candidates.'[13]

The minority parties were understandably furious. The Welsh Nationalists pointed out that, even if they stood a candidate in all 36 seats in their

[9]CPA CRD2/20/12.
[10]BBC R34/536 14.12.49.
[11]BBC R34/536 29.12.49.
[12]BBC R34/536 5.1.50.
[13]BBC R34/541/1 27.4.50.

Country they could not now reach the required minimum number. The Scottish Nationalists argued that they would need to stand a candidate in two thirds of Scottish constituencies to qualify. Along with the Communists, they argued that the decision was undemocratic, the scheduled time unfair, and that the new regulations denied the electorate access to a variety of political opinion. On nomination day the Communist Party had 101 candidates, and enquired if they could have a broadcast for each 50 candidates. The request was refused, and thereafter the BBC press announcement stated that any party with 50 candidates would be entitled to one, and only one, 10 minute broadcast. Barnes' post election report argued that the BBC were not responsible for the decisions to include or exclude parties, and the public should be made aware of the fact.[14] Regardless of responsibility, the requirement to stand 50 candidates effectively removed minority parties from the broadcasting frame. The Nationalists were excluded by the 50 candidates rule. The Cooperative and Liberal Nationals were included in the main parties, and the Commonwealth Party had disbanded.[15]

1949 saw the passing of the Representation of the People Act (RPA), Section 93 dealt with equal representation of all constituency candidates. Any broadcast which promoted or procured the election of a candidate was illegal. The BBC allowed no such broadcasts. In 1958, there was to be a by-election in Rochdale, and Granada Television took the unprecedented step of proposing television coverage. The Conservatives sought legal advice and were advised that while amendment of the RPA was technically simple, the Law Officers had considerable doubts about its advisability. It could prove highly controversial in itself and:

> 'Would leave the television people free to be grossly partial with really complete immunity ... It would mean that the candidate who did not wish to broadcast would be at a serious disadvantage and it would put a premium on candidates who were television stars.'[16]

So Section 93 remained, Rochdale was televised, and no action was taken. After Rochdale, all Parties agreed the presentation was without bias, the interviews almost ludicrously so. Television had not affected voting and could, once the novelty wore off, cause apathy. Nevertheless, Rochdale changed politics. Mr A Banks, North West Area Agent, sent a report to Conservative Central Office (CCO) advising that:

> 'By-election candidates will have to be given instructions at the CO in television techniques ... suitability for television will have to be taken into account when selecting a candidate.'

Against this suggestion the General Director had written 'Oh dear!' and added that he considered the idea erroneous:

[14] BBC R34/539 9.8.50.

[15] BBC R34/536 29.12.49.

[16] CPA CRD2/20/9 8.5.59.

> 'It would be quite wrong surely to select our candidates on glamour appeal and photogenic qualities. For instance had C Curran, whose best friends could not call him handsome, fought Rochdale he could not fail to have done much better than P(arkinson). The quality of our candidates particularly at a by- election matters; if they are telegenic that surely is a bonus.'[17]

So, by 1959, the two sets of professionals had negotiated the abandonment of the FDR, the effective elimination of minority parties, broadcasters had tested the RPA, and image had entered politics.

Changing politics

The 1939 agreement referred to speeches. All 1945 Election Broadcasts were in the form of straight talks, usually by prominent Party Members. All Conservative broadcasts were given by men. Labour and Liberals included a woman. After 1945, the Conservatives believed they had lost the election because of the Socialists' broadcasting ability, and reorganised the Party machine, appointing Lord Woolton as Chief Publicity Officer. Patrick Gordon Walker was appointed Labour Party Broadcasting Officer in 1946, prompting Haley to remind everyone of the BBC's complete independence in all programme matters including political broadcasting.[18] Haley, may have been fretting unnecessarily because, as Anthony Wedgewood Benn later asserted, Walker's appointment failed, responsibility devolved to Transport House.[19]

By 1950 CCO had developed a Radio and Television Department, whilst Transport House were still relatively unconcerned with broadcasting. The 1950 election, Barnes suggested:

> 'would be the first Election in which television would be used, and that when meeting the Political parties to negotiate sound broadcast, the BBC would have to inaugurate arrangements for television; the precedent will be important.'[20]

Barnes rightly assumed the radio rule, to revise schedules to exclude anything that might influence voting, would be applied to television. However, he had not anticipated that politicians too, were busy querying the role of television.

In preparation for the 1950 Election, Buchan Hepburn noted that:

> 'The Government may ask what we feel about using television in the Election, It is suggested that we resist this if we are asked.'[21]

[17] CPA CC0500/18/16 18.2.58.
[18] BBC R34/534/5 9.3.46.
[19] LPA GSP 201-301 19.2.53.
[20] BBC WAC R34/536 15.11.49.
[21] CPA CRD2/20/6 10.10.49.

The Parties declined the BBC's offer of television, officially because there were under 1 million sets nationwide. However, politicians still viewed television as inferior to radio. Barnes informed McGivern:

> 'The Parties unanimously rejected the idea of televising any of the Election broadcasts ... Every effort was made to interest them but the matter,in their view, did not even admit of argument.'[22]

The General Director of the Conservative Party, S.H.Piersenne, summarised the Parties discussions on the forthcoming election, thus:

> 'The radio is a greater vote winner than all other media of propaganda combined ... Representations have been made in many quarters that one broadcast should be by a woman and one by a working man.
>
> Women predominate among the electorate. They are showing a tendency to come over to our side. They would be pleased if we gave a place to a woman and critical if we did not, Miss Florence Horsburgh is strongly recommended ... She does NOT POSSESS A TITLE (Lady Davison or Lady Tweedsmuir would probably be very good but for this particular purpose the plain "Miss" would be a distinct advantage.)
>
> The psychological effect of an appeal by a working man, preferably a trade unionist, would be tremendous. It would have to be simple, genuine and entirely free from histrionics. It must not in any sense be a "turn" or a stunt. There must be a clear trace of dialect (preferably north-country) but it must not be exaggerated. Attempts are being made to find working men with suitable qualifications and to test their potential for broadcasting.'[23]

Politics was changing. Parties were adapting their election campaigns to the new medium. Speeches were less appropriate in the home, where broadcasts were received by ordinary working men and women. Speeches became broadcasts. Prominent Party members were replaced with a plain Miss and an ordinary working man. Miss Horsburgh did broadcast, but presumably the Trade Unionist with the right qualities could not be found, and his place was taken by Charles Hill, who also broadcast as The Radio Doctor. The Labour candidate in the same constituency complained of the use of The Radio Doctor in the election broadcast. The popularity of his series, and the publicity that this role had provided for Hill prior to his nomination, was perceived as an unfair advantage, which enabled Hill to be elected with a majority of 1,086.[24] Yet, officially, the Labour Party paid little attention to broadcasting.

[22]BBC WAC R34/866 20.12.49.

[23]CPA CRD2/20/6 12.12.49.

[24]BBC R34/539 9.3.50.

For Labour, Herbert Morrison had overall Government responsibility for broadcasting, and set up a technical sub-Committee of the Prime Minister's Committee. This committee had no official existence, and derived its status entirely from the fact that its recommendations went to Morrison. In view of the peculiar way it had been established, it operated almost in secret.[25] The Committee met only five times and, at the last meeting in May 1951, agreed Benn's appointment as Party radio adviser. However, despite the secrecy, this Committee did little. The Labour Party appeared less interested in broadcasting than their Conservative counterparts.

The Labour Party did not report on the 1950 election, but CCO undertook a review of every aspect of the campaign. The BBC also had a post mortem. Barnes stressing that television was becoming an important factor, said the BBC saw no difference between vision and sound, but evidence showed that the parties themselves saw a definite division between the two and had shown a reluctance to embark on political television.[26] That the BBC did not differentiate between the two media is debateable, and whilst the Parties were reluctant to accept televised FPBs, politicians were appearing regularly on the screen in IPBs, eliciting allegations that political personalities were being built up which did not correspond to their political status in the House. Television was primarily for entertainment.

In 1951, Haley was asked to outline what the BBC would consider practicable if the Parties decided to accept the Corporation's offer of television. He suggested: one broadcast each; the Parties to choose all participants; maximum length 15 minutes; format could be talk, interview or discussion. The Parties agreed. Grace Wyndham Goldie, Talks Producer, saw all three parties, and reported that 2 of the 3 wished to use 2 speakers and animated captions. The Liberal, Lord Samual, against Goldie's advice, decided not to be interviewed, argued that reading from notes would not seriously worry the viewer, and decided not to end the broadcast by saying Goodnight, but by putting his papers down. Goldie reported that, having overrun, Lord Samual:

> 'Fumbled with his papers and paused. I had to act instantly. He had in fact lost his place. This is the danger when the speaker can override the producer.'[27]

Lord Samual complained that his broadcast was cut short. Politicians were not yet expert in the television medium and producers were clearly unused to having their professional advice overruled. Barnes analysed the disadvantages of talking from notes, and the advantages of having two speakers in FPBs. He said:

> 'I think it would have been better if (Lord Samual) had had the notes in his hand in vision, so that so that the viewer did not see the strained movement of his eyes. Eden and Shawcross

[25] LPA GSP 201-301 19.2.53.
[26] BBC R34/541/1 31.4.50.
[27] BBC T16/141 16.10.51.

> were at a great advantage in being able to do what they liked with their eyes... The direct appeal by the single speaker, possibly with some visual aids may well turn to out to be the best electioneering, but that is not our business... in television such simplicity is alien to normal programmes and responsibility for the success of all programmes rests as much on the producer as on the performer or speaker.'[28]

Success being dependent on a producer was new to politicians. The political address could be adapted for radio, new techniques were required for vision. Broadcasters were not in the business of electioneering, but were aware that, in the interests of good television, politicians had to adapt to the medium and follow their professional advice. Politicians could no longer ignore media professionals, and vice versa. After 1951, Benn produced a report for the Labour Party stating that leaflets and meetings reached 15 million people. BBC figures showed each of the five radio broadcasts were heard by from 8 to 15 million and television broadcasts by another 3 million. He was keen to promote political broadcasting, and pointed out that virtually nothing was spent on Radio and Television work, as compared with £70,000+ on literature. Benn argued that equipment was needed, the financial implications of which should be fairly faced.[29] Labour was beginning to take the media seriously and William Pickles and Michael Young also produced a report on the broadcasts and suggested plans for the next campaign. Labour speakers, they said, excelled Tories, despite the latter's expensive and elaborate preparations. On the next occasion television would be even more important. They suggested: new speakers, as electors become bored with the same old voices; a mass of evidence suggested that 20 and 30 minute broadcasts were too long; talks were not as popular as other kinds of programmes. They concluded:

> 'It is probable that the straight talk will begin to lose its appeal in future General Elections. Television programmes, of the kind pioneered by Mayhew, will become more and more of a counter attraction.'[30]

Morgan Phillips, General Secretary to the Labour Party, acknowledged receipt of this report, and pointed out that the alternatives to the straight party talk were not allowed by the BBC.[31] This, of course, was for radio; television encouraged innovations.

By 1955 television and sound coverage of the election were equal. Leonard Miall, Head of Television Talks, produced a document entitled Sidelights on General Election Television Broadcasts 1955. It recorded humorous incidents during broadcasting, with considerable glee at the politicians lack of understanding of, and intimidation by, broadcasting. He mischievously noted that:

[28]BBC T16/141 19.10.51.
[29]LPA GSP 201- 301 11.3.53.
[30]LPA GSP 201-301 7.11.51.
[31]LPA Box 9 21-301 23.2.53.

> 'The Conservatives had planned an elaborate piece of "stage business" to bring movement into Macmillan's talk.'

He was to place a small money box on top of a larger one to represent the difference in personal savings under Labour and Conservative Governments. The party commissioned a firm to make the larger box 30 times the size of the smaller one. When it arrived two hours before the broadcast it turned out to be the size of a desk. The contractor had made it thirty times as large in each direction. The crisis was solved by shooting the large box from a great distance and the small one in tight close-up, skipping the business of putting one on top of the other.

Also Phillips, had suggested that the discussion between Dr Edith Summerskill and Harold Wilson, be interrupted by his voice off shouting 'what about pensions'? Miall said we:

> 'Explained that this not only broke all programme conventions but it would be necessary for us to issue a disclaimer in the Press that it not one of our cameramen who had interrupted the proceedings. Morgan Phillips was quite happy for it to be announced that it was his voice. It was pointed out that for the Secretary of the Party to interrupt the Chairman of the Party with this sort of interjection might not look good.'

The Liberals, with less air time, merited only the comment that

> 'Most of the rehearsal of this 15 min programme was devoted to preventing Lord Samual from taking 4.5 mins to introduce the speakers.'[32]

Clearly politicians still had a lot to learn, and broadcasters were not above enjoying their naivety. More seriously, Miall argued Macmillan's broadcast was a poor use of television. McGivern also commented, not on politics or content but on television use. The Labour broadcast was better than Macmillans, it was well composed and, at times, arty. He added:

> 'The Labour idea of having husband and wife, and a fireplace was excellent. Attlee was at ease. He made in my opinion, Macmillan look rather cheap. Mrs Attlee, even in her few brief glimpses, was charming. The opening and closing captions were good and dignified.'[33]

So, in ten years, electioneering changed from radio speeches to televised fireside scenes. Politicians had learnt that public speaking was no longer appropriate electioneering. Conversational styles suitable to the home environment in which broadcasts were received, coupled with the techniques and telegenic properties that made for good television were now electioneering requirements.

---

[32] BBC T16/510 25.5.55.

[33] BBC T16/510 12.5.55.

Conclusion

The 1950s altered British politics irrevocably. The business of politics is unthinkable today without the media, and vice versa. The negotiations that amalgamated the professions during the decade matured to become the slick media circus, controlled by spin doctors and reliant on sound bites, that the electorate will face in the 1997 Election.

In the 1950s, politicians were concerned that broadcasting could become a simultaneous debating forum with Parliament. Austin Mitchell, MP, now says:

> 'We have an alternative to Parliament created at College Green which is siphoning attention away from the real House and creating this fever about politics – a feverish, obsessive interest in politics which the electorate does not share.'[34]

Benn may regret having encouraged the Labour Party to spend more on broadcasting, today it is reported that:

> 'Whitehall spends more than 2 billion a year on information systems and technology, or almost 8 million every working day.'[35]

The legacy of Rochdale may well be that politicians are now chosen for glamour appeal and photogenic qualities. All Parties now take image seriously. Politicians now aim to entertain. Mitchell asserts that parties are anxious to wriggle out of PPBs:

> 'What we want to do is put on a piece of mood music and create image, and that is best done in two minutes. I think that parties should be made to do ten minute PPBs to prove they have something to say.'[36]

Yet despite the plethora of media literate politicians on our screens today, Section 93 of the RPA remains. Steve Perkins, Senior Programme Officer of the ITC, said:

> 'It ought to be repealed. But I bet it won't be. Because what this bit of the Act does is to give politicians a degree of power over broadcasting that they have at no other time ... If a candidate doesn't want to take part in any programme or item about a constituency, he or she can block the whole broadcast and prevent it going out'.[37]

Control of political broadcasting is still being disputed. The politicians can still dictate the rules. Broadcasters no longer have superior media

---

[34] *Serving the Citizen: Broadcasting and the General Election*, transcript of VLV One Day Conference, 28th March, 1996 p.16.

[35] *The Guardian Weekend*, May 11 1996, p.70.

[36] VLV Transcript, 1996 p.16.

[37] VLV Transcript, 1966 p.3.

knowledge, politicians have mastered the techniques. In the 1997 election control of broadcasting will be contested as much in the aggressive interviewing of politicians skilled in evading questions and manipulating broadcasters, as in FPBs.

However, despite the aggressive interviewer, the feverish activity on College Green, the vast financial implications, and the jockeying for power between broadcasters and politicians, evidence still suggests that voting behaviour is not significantly influenced by political broadcasting. Political broadcasting is indeed a curious phenomenon.

Historical Perspectives on Political Communication in Britain

Dominic Wring
Nottingham Trent University

' "Emancipation through Education" or Persuasion via Mass Communication: the Philosophical Debate over Labour Party Campaigning'

Introduction

Talk of the 1997 general election has once again focused British commentators' minds on the political role of the mass media and 'image-making'. This is reflected in the recent controversy surrounding the strategies being employed by the Labour Party to publicly promote its policies and leader. Opponents, notably Conservative Chairman Brian Mawhinney in his 1996 Party Conference speech, have sought to portray Tony Blair as a politician dependent on marketing research rather than principles. This argument has derived inspiration from earlier comments made by Clare Short, one of Blair's Shadow Cabinet colleagues. The senior frontbench MP, in making her feelings public, was careful not to criticise the leader himself but did make telling references to the marketing conscious aides around him. Her anxieties were summed up in the phraseology used to describe what she termed 'the people in the dark'. In developing her argument, Short questioned the wisdom of Labour's and these particular advisers' over-reliance on polling research. Far from being just a point of contention in the Labour Party of the late 1980s and 1990s, this paper will assess how similar sentiments have long informed strategic debate since the organisation was created at the beginning of the century.

Competing Philosophies of Political Communication

Traditionally a significant body of opinion within the Labour movement has objected to changes in electioneering which have appeared to involve the dilution of their party's commitment to converting people to its cause. According to Bernard Barker this is evidence of an approach to political communication governed by the philosophy of 'educational socialism'.[1] Labelled 'democratic rationalists' by another historian Timothy Hollins, adherents to this view found sympathy and support in a party which prided itself on a belief in utopian ideals designed to emancipate the poor and dispossessed.[2] Hollins uses the term in order to clarify the reluctance of many early Labour campaigners to engage in appeals built around anything

[1] B.Barker, *The Politics of Propaganda*, Ph.D York, 1972.
[2] T.Hollins, *The Presentation of Politics*, Ph.D Leeds, 1981, p.119.

but straightforward political education.[3] This educationalist conception of campaigning built on the pioneering work of J.S.Mill. Influenced by Aristotle, Mill was of the opinion that democracy would only properly function if it was based on solid reasoned debate amongst an informed citizenry rather than the populist appeals characteristic of mob rule.'[4]

Education was seen as both the opposite of, not to mention an antidote to, the shallow and emotive appeals of opportunist propaganda. To quote Robert Blatchford, founder of the *Clarion* journal, his and his fellow activists' mission was to 'Make Socialists'.[5] Coming as many organisers originally did from a background in the evangelistic Independent Labour Party or Nonconformist church movement, it was hardly surprising that some party servants saw their task in terms of 'converting' the apolitical.[6] Despite their sometimes emotive tones, Labour organisers saw the use of rational, fact filled discourse as a way of countering opponents' apparent reliance on fear and fiction.[7] This concern reflected the view of many in the party weary about the increasingly pervasive role of 'image politics'. Several organisers worried that their mission to educate and ultimately emancipate society would be hampered under a weight of propagandist distortion and subterfuge.[8]

In contrast to 'educational socialism' was what Hollins terms the 'persuasional' approach to political communication. Typically this was couched in language and symbolism primarily designed to provoke emotions rather than a reasoned response on the part of the recipient.[9] As Qualter notes such a perception clearly derives inspiration from the teachings of Plato.[10] Countering the Aristotelian belief in the potential for a democracy consisting of an informed populace, Plato feared this an imperfect state of affairs too prone to falling prey to the tyranny of an emotionally charged mob.[11]

An increasingly integral part of political discourse during the late 19th and early 20th centuries, persuasional propaganda began to gather support from advocates inside the Labour Party. This body of opinion gained influential endorsement from leading Fabian and early political scientist Graham Wallas who, in his seminal 1908 book *Human Nature in Politics*, argued that new forms of communication were helping to undermine the long held 'intellectualist assumption' of many democratic theorists.[12] Wallas believed the advent of manipulative mass propaganda offered a serious challenge to the notion that giving every person the vote would lead to informed, delibera-

---

[3]'Democratic rationalism' is not to be confused with Rose's concept of 'rational campaigning' as defined in his seminal study of media based electioneering in post-war Britain (R.Rose, *Influencing Voters*, Faber & Faber, 1967).

[4]I.McLean, *Elections*, Longman, 1976, p.29; V.Price, *Public Opinion*, Sage, 1992, p.5.

[5]*Labour Organiser*, 406, 1956.

[6]*Labour Organiser*, 30, 1923; I.McLean, 'Party Organisation', in C.Cook & I.Taylor (eds), *The Labour Party*, Longman, 1980.

[7]Hollins, pp.126-30.

[8]*Labour Organiser*, 29, 1923; A.White, *The New Propaganda*, Left Book Club, 1939.

[9]Hollins, p.122.

[10]T.Qualter, *Opinion Control in the Democracies*, Macmillan, 1985, p.11.

[11]Price, p.5.

[12]G.Wallas, *Human Nature in Politics*, Constable, (1908) 1948, p.87.

tive and stimulating public debate. Practical politicians, he argued, would inevitably develop the use of the 'image' based appeals in their attempts to win over the electorate: 'It is the business of the party managers to secure that these automatic associations be as clear as possible, shall be shared by as large a number as possible, and shall call up as many and as strong emotions as possible'.[13]

Wallas' sentiments found favour with several Labour veterans of the campaign trail. Faced with what he saw as a sad reality, agent Wilfred Hargreaves urged an abandonment of the party's adherence to educationalist methods: 'I infinitely prefer a convinced and thoughtful voter, but we must face the fact that many voters do not think very much, and many years will elapse before they cease to allow others to do their thinking for them'.[14] Others agreed and propounded the view that a substantial and critical mass of the public were fluid in outlook and probably disinterested in politics, particularly of the evangelical, intensely educative kind.[15] The acceptance of such arguments was a factor in the party's shift towards using more persuasional methods of political communication during the inter-war period. According to Hollins this was evidence of the party becoming 'as much electorally as educationally orientated'.[16] After the Second World War, and the arrival of mass television, modern polling and saturation advertising, the debate between strategists intensified with those holding educationalist and persuasionalist views coming into more open conflict.

The Rise of the Mass Media and the Prototype 'Modernisers'

During the 1950s Labour appointed David Ginsberg, formerly with Government Social Surveys, head of Research. Together with the leader's decision to take soundings from leading market researcher Mark Abrams, the choice of Ginsberg increased the likelihood that the party might invest time and resources in a programme of polling. At the 1957 NEC Publicity Subcommittee which met to discuss the matter left-winger Aneurin Bevan and his educationalist leaning allies took issue with Abrams' methods. The debate was heated with one participant likening polling research to the work of notorious Nazi propagandist Josef Goebbels.[17] Another adviser present, Professor R.H.Tawney, calmed the meeting before launching a defence of polling methods. The efforts of Tawney were, however, to no avail and further research was not commissioned until after the 1959 election though Abrams continued to be a discreet confidante of the leader. Then, having had his proposal to mount a survey post-mortem into Labour's subsequent defeat frustrated by elements within the central apparatus, Abrams formally linked up with the journal *Socialist Commentary* to conduct election

[13] *Op cit*, p.84.
[14] *Labour Organiser*, 63, 1926.
[15] *Labour Organiser*, 32, 1923.
[16] Hollins, p.133.
[17] D.Butler & A.King, *The British General Election of 1964*, Macmillan, 1965, p.67.

analysis.[18]

First published as a series of articles in the *Socialist Commentary* during the early part of 1960, Abrams' study gained greater notoriety when it appeared in book form later that year.[19] The volume, entitled *Must Labour Lose?*, proved to be an important source for political debate and made a notable impression on General Secretary Morgan Philips, Research Department head Peter Shore[20] and the Gaitskellite right-wing of the party who saw it as apparent scientific justification for their revisionist case.[21] In essence the research identified the basis of a move towards the 'embourgeoisement' of British society whereby growing numbers of working-class people began to aspire to and in some cases realise the comfortable lifestyle more commonly associated with the middle-class: such voters were thought unlikely to be impressed with a proletarian type party committed to a large-scale programme of nationalisation. It was an argument which gathered support in the party. Future Home Secretary Merlyn Rees, a candidate in the 1959 election, addressed himself to the potentially ominous electoral consequences for Labour of an increasingly 'atomised society' unfavourable to the collectivist ethos in organisations like the trades unions.[22]

Must Labour Lose? also modified the thinking of prominent figures such as Tony Crosland. Crosland was sympathetic to the idea that Labour needed to revamp its image in order, as he saw it, to place itself 'in rapport' with the public. In his 1960 pamphlet 'Can Labour Win?' he argued that the party ought to commission a programme of polls in preparation for the next election.[23] At least one motion to the Annual Conference of that year called for the integration of market research into electoral strategy.[24] Not long after the NEC appointed Mark Abrams as the party's official pollster. The advent of a coherent strategy for the supervision of opinion polling would not be the only organisational coup initiated by revisionist forces in the party.

The introduction of mass television created considerable interest, not least in the Labour Party. As former BBC producer and Tony Benn saw it: 'We must make it(television) serve us as surely as the pioneers made the leaflet and the soap box carry the message to the people of Britain'.[25] Prior to the 1955 campaign Benn had pushed for the party to take a more professional approach towards televised PEB production. Although his plans were not implemented, the new medium continued to hold his interest as he admitted in a 1958 article for political journal *Forward*:

> 'Just as one hydrogen bomb packs more power than the total load dropped in World War Two, so one television broadcast

[18] R.Worcester, *British Public Opinion*, Blackwell, 1991, p.24.

[19] M.Abrams et al, *Must Labour Lose?*, Penguin, 1960.

[20] Butler & King, p.67.

[21] Lord Windlesham, *Communication and Political Power*, Jonathan Cape, 1966, pp.86-88.

[22] M.Rees, 'The Social Setting', *Political Quarterly*, July 1960.

[23] A.Crosland, 'Can Labour Win?', in *The Conservative Enemy*, Jonathan Cape, 1962.

[24] F.Teer & J.Spence, *Political Opinion Polls*, Hutchinson, 1973, p.169.

[25] *Labour Organiser*, 398, 1955.

> more than equals a lifetime of mass rallies and street-corner oratory. Old methods of campaigning are as obsolete as conventional weapons.'[26]

Benn eventually got the chance to put his ideas into practice with the onset of the 1959 general election. Indeed the stylistic and much praised series of Labour PEBs he helped to produced were such that Lord Hailsham, the Conservative Party Chairman, felt obliged to attack them for being 'glossier than thou'.[27]

The most concerted and sustained appeals for a reorganisation of electoral strategy after 1959 came from senior Gaitskellites[28] and their rank and file supporters in the Campaign for Democratic Socialism(CDS). The Campaign, set up by several youthful supporters of the leader, organised itself during the critical period 1960-64.[29] Ex-MP Brian Magee, a founding member, later summed up the importance of group participants as the 'modernisers' of their day.[30] CDS activists engaged themselves in the organisation of a grassroots campaign designed to win support for the leadership amongst the 'quiet majority' of local party members whose views they assumed tallied with their own. If some have questioned the group's success in reforming policy, it is undoubtedly the case that the Campaign had an effect on the organisation of campaigning.[31]

Unlike other groups active in the party, the CDS excelled in its ability to pursue an informal public relations' strategy designed to promote the Gaitskellite case through quality and, on occasion, popular press coverage. Here the Campaign's work was facilitated by activists with media experience such as public relations consultant Denis Howell and political journalist Ivan Yates. These and other forerunners of what are now known as 'spin doctors' targeted sympathetic newspaper journalists in the ultimate hope of influencing the course of Labour Party debates. Consequently the CDS, as Lord Windlesham noted, was able to build up an influential network of opinion forming media outlets such as *The Times* and *The Guardian*.[32] By contrast, CDS opponents had few sympathetic contacts working in the print media prepared or able to use their position to further the Labour left's cause.[33] Despite the apparent imbalance in media publicity in favour of the right, the left did not suffer as greatly as it might have on account of the party's relatively strong horizontal structures, most obviously the Annual Conference.

Another CDS supporter, Bernard Donoghue, was greatly influenced by

---

[26] J.Adams, *Tony Benn*, Macmillan, 1992.

[27] I.Bulmer Thomas, *The Growth of the Party System 1922-66*, John Baker, 1967, p.249.

[28] M.Babaz, *Le Role de la Publicité dans les Campagnes Electorales Britanniques de 1964, 1966 and 1970*, Ph.D Lille, 1980, p.142.

[29] B.Brivati, *The Campaign for Democratic Socialism*, Ph.D London, 1992.

[30] B.Brivati & D.Wincott, 'The Campaign for Democratic Socialism 1960-64', *Contemporary Record*, 7/2, 1993.

[31] *Op cit.*

[32] Windlesham, p.102.

[33] M.Jenkins, *Bevanism*, Spokesman, 1979, pp.126-129.

his first hand experiences helping the Kennedy presidential campaign during 1960: 'that did have quite an affect on me. When you came back from America the Labour Party really did look like something out of a museum'.[34] Such a viewpoint did little but compound the notion that the work of Kennedy's team and, before that, the Colman Prentis Varley advertising agency's efforts on behalf of the Conservatives between 1957-59, had been crucial to the eventual outcome of the campaign. It was supported by a whole host of people with CDS connections in a range of publications including *Political Quarterly*, *Socialist Commentary* and a special Young Fabian Group report. As one advocate put it: '... the truth is that modern advertising is scientific – and no more. It is not by itself either good or evil', before admitting 'Of course, one doesn't try to promote the Labour Party like a soap powder ...'[35] Ultimately, perhaps, the most significant event during this period was the appointment of CDS activist and Gaitskell's former press aide John Harris as Labour Director of Publicity in 1962. In post Harris was able to oversee an intensification in the party's use of media campaigning.

The analysis and interpretation that followed the publication of *Must Labour Lose?* coupled with the efforts of Campaign for Democratic Socialism members and others helped provide an environment in which serious discussion of the future strategic direction of the party could take place. Even with such a well supported movement in favour of change, pioneering reform was not so easy in an organisation whose affairs were managed by a complex committee based system within which determined minorities could block transformations. Typically opposition of this kind was centred on two groups with differing motives: the passive, conservative traditionalists weary of spending money on expensive professional campaigns, and the activist, radical ideologues distrustful of what they perceived to be the leadership's investment in shallow, divisive and non-didactic methods of electioneering.

Dissenting Voices

Whilst groups on the centre-right tended to be in the 'revisionist' vanguard, not everybody on this wing of the party had the same aspirations when it came to the question of how party campaigning might be overhauled. This was not least because some Labour right-wingers held an essentially educationalist view of political communication and believed image management to be a dubious and misleading practice. Speaking in 1959 one of them commented:

> 'You see, I am a rationalist. I like to think that in a mature democracy people reach their conclusions mostly on the basis of actual evidence and argument. I do not like to think that they vote as they do because something appeals to their unconscious.'[36]

[34] Brivati & Wincott.

[35] *Labour Organiser*, 489, 1963.

[36] D.Butler & R.Rose, *The British General Election of 1959*, Macmillan, 1960, p.29.

Given that, in the main, it was revisionists who tended to favour less ideologically based and more professionalised, persuasional methods of electioneering it is perhaps surprising that the above observation was made by their guiding figure Hugh Gaitskell. A man ill at ease with certain aspects of modern mediated politics, Gaitskell initially held a low opinion of advertising, believing 'the whole thing is somehow false'.[37] By contrast with his policy pronouncements, the party leader's attitude towards marketing was initially more in keeping with those of the Labour left. This is perhaps because, unlike many of his youthful supporters in the CDS group, Gaitskell's background and earlier career had involved him in adult education rather than PR and journalism. During the 1959 general election the donnish disposition of the Labour leader made him appear uneasy on television, particularly when his performance was contrasted with that of his more polished Conservative opponent Harold Macmillan.[38] That said, Gaitskell's experience of leading the party during a national campaign converted him into a proponent of political advertising and market research.

Whilst Gaitskell was modest in his criticism of mediated politics, others in the party were not so restrained. Between 1955 and 1958 there were regular motions to the Annual Party Conference denouncing the political role of advertising and modern publicity techniques.[39] Even the apparently successful, highly stylistic series of Labour PEBs produced and shown during the 1959 election fielded criticism from party organisers, one of whom concluded: 'I feel that the clever television programmes perhaps fortified suspicions of our promises, instead of removing them. For this reason I think our television programmes may have lost, rather than gained us support'.[40]

Matters came to a head following the 1959 general election when several senior Labour MPs attacked the Conservatives' high profile relationship with leading advertising agency CPV. Speaking in the House of Commons in 1958, former party broadcasting officer and leading Gaitskellite Patrick Gordon-Walker denounced what he saw as the debasement of electoral debate through the introduction of the 'worst sort of Americanisation' into British political campaigning.[41] Of all the then opponents of political advertising within the party MP Alice Bacon was perhaps the most important. Reiterating the concerns of Gordon-Walker, Bacon used a parliamentary debate in July 1960 to give vent to her views, attacking the Conservatives relationship with an advertising agency as being 'alien' to British democracy.[42] A leadership confidante, Miss Bacon played an influential role as Chair of the NEC Sub-committee on Publicity. Her antipathy towards Conservative professionalism combined partisan reaction with a defence of educationalist campaign methodologies. Bacon's views were probably also coloured by a recognition that any imitation of the CPV approach by Labour might seriously erode party finances.

---

[37] Butler & Rose, p.20.
[38] G.McDermott, *Leader Lost*, Leslie Frewin, 1972.
[39] Teer & Spence, p.167.
[40] Butler & Rose, p.86.
[41] Rose, p.14.
[42] *Op cit*, p.63.

Amongst rank and file organisers there was evidence of some antipathy towards marketing techniques. This ranged from the dismissal of professional advertising and public relations as 'Fashions and Fads in Type'[43] to Ken Garland's more hostile denunciation of 'Ad Men' as 'Institute of Directors fellow travellers':

> 'all they know about is appealing to people's greed, whereas we are trying to appeal to their ideals ... we ruddy don't need (these) tricksters ... If you want a photo on let's say, Youth and Labour, you don't need a studio portrait of an impossibly smooth looking teenager wearing clothes that could only be afforded by a Mayfair call-girl. What you do need is a lively outdoor photo of the girl next door with freckles and a saucy grin, against a backdrop that could be your street or my street.'[44]

Despite disquiet within the grassroots' organisation and some on the Labour right, it tended to be left-wingers who voiced the most consistent dissent over moves to 'merchandise' the party. Speaking after the 1959 defeat one of them, Harold Wilson, attacked what he perceived to be the revisionists' obsession with ephemeral rather than substantive issues:

> 'There is a lot of talk about the image of the Labour Party. I cannot think it would be improved if we were to win, and indeed deserve, a reputation for cynicism and opportunism by throwing out essential and fundamental parts of a creed for electoral purposes.'[45]

The theme of Wilson's speech was taken up by another opponent of the Gaitskellites, Richard Crossman, in his pamphlet *Labour and the Affluent Society* (1959). Written by an expert in psychological warfare and promoter of the metaphor 'selling politics like soap', the publication related its argument with a characteristic mix of insight and invective. Attacking the Gaitskellites for their apparent lack of socialist conviction, Crossman warned against the creation of a British party in 'the image of the American Democratic Party' because, as he saw it: 'the Labour Party, if it is ever to return to power with a mandate from the people, must remain a socialist challenge to the established order'. Crossman continued his frank analysis in language which influenced the tone of subsequent debate:

> 'For politicians whose sole object, or even whose main object, is to regain office tend to be opportunists, to hedge and to equivocate in order to appease the voter ... Appeasement and equivocation are tactics essential to the great Tory tradition by which the British ruling-class has adapted itself to changing circumstances. But a left-wing party which adopts such tactics destroy itself.'[46]

---

[43] *Labour Organiser*, 417, 1957.

[44] *Labour Organiser*, no.488, 1963.

[45] A.Roth, *Harold Wilson: Yorkshire's Walter Mitty*, MacDonald & Jane's, 1977, p.233.

[46] R.Crossman, *The Affluent Society*, Fabian Society Pamphlet, 1960.

The thesis of *the Affluent Society* formed a counterpoint to *Must Labour Lose?* and the polling data it was based on. If Abrams' research created suspicion on the left it also offended those of a more traditionalist disposition such as Herbert Morrison. An early critic of polling and the 'election as game' ethos he believed lay behind it, Morrison scorned what he perceived to be artificial methods and argued the only reliable way to survey changing public attitudes was to go amongst the populace and talk with them.[47] Neither did polling impress trade unionist leader George Woodcock who bluntly dismissed the process: 'You get the answers you expect'.[48] As Butler & Rose noted these comments were representative of a significant body of opinion: 'Many members of the party were ideologically opposed to the PR approach to politics (and) felt it(the party) could express the needs of ordinary people without recourse to the findings of market-research experts.'[49]

The most sustained opposition to professional research methods (not to mention advertising) came from socialist intellectuals whose ideas influenced those of the Labour left. Invoking Aneurin Bevan's observation that polling is 'taking the poetry out of politics',[50] critics railed against what they saw as a vision of democracy ultimately driven by polling data. Questioning the premise underpinning the *Must Labour Lose?* study, left-wing historian Raphael Samuel attacked what he believed was Abrams' flawed approach to survey work:

> 'He sees people as consumers of politics, behaving in politics much as they would – in the motivational research imagination – when confronted with mass-marketed commodities: they "buy" political labels and allegiances as they would any brand associations it promises to afford. Thus Dr.Abrams leaves no standard by which to judge the relationship between Labour and its supporters, beyond the injunction that they must stand – as Mr.Crosland expresses it – in "rapport" with each other.'[51]

If some were suspicious about the means, others expressed scepticism about the possible uses of the ends. For Labour radical Michael Foot the notion of undertaking polling in order to inform strategy and possibly dilute the party programme sat uneasily with his and the left's commitment to egalitarian politics. In a passionate rebuttal of the public opinion conscious revisionist case, Foot articulated his position in uncompromising, educationalist inspired terms: 'In order to win an election, we have to change the mood of the people in this country, to open their eyes to what an evil and disgraceful society it is'.[52] Like-minded sentiments formed the basis of

[47] Worcester, p.14.

[48] R.Hodder-Williams, *Public Opinion Polls and British Parties*, Routledge & Kegan Paul, 1970, p.80.

[49] Butler & Rose, p.25.

[50] Butler & King, pp.50-51.

[51] R.Samuel, 'Dr.Abrams and the End of Politics', *New Left Review*, 5, 1960.

[52] D.Howell, *British Social Democracy*, 1976, p.229.

Samuel's conclusion to his attack on what he saw as the dubious practice of political polling and the work of Abrams in particular:

> 'If the Labour Movement were finally to abandon its traditional way of thinking about people – and that alone is truly fundamental – to lose the faith in the power of the word to move people, and of the idea to change them, if it were to let go its conviction in the capacity of human beings rationally to choose between the alternatives which face them, and purposefully to re-shape the society in which they live, then it would be finished, and would find itself trapped in that limbo of the political imagination whose features Dr.Abrams has so meticulously outlined.'[53]

Conclusions

The debate over Labour Party strategy has long been historically analysed in the context of the rivalries that have existed between different factions and bureaucrats within the organisation. This paper has attempted to show how the discussion has also had a distinctly philosophical dimension involving two contrasting views of political communication. Initially popular in the party, the 'educationalist' approach to the public was the hallmark of the early campaign work pursued by pioneering socialists in groups like the ILP. With the rise of a mass democracy during the inter-war period, the wisdom of such political methods was challenged and a rival school 'persuasional' school of thought emerged. Following 1945 and the intensification of mediated politics, this alternative approach began to gain wider acceptance within the party. Most dramatically it was the same opinion-formers who once adhered to educational methods, notably leader Harold Wilson and NEC chair of publicity Alice Bacon, that were central to the transformation of Labour into a more marketing conscious organisation during the early 1960s.

[53]Samuel 1960. It should be noted that there were also less ideological and more psephological criticisms of *Must Labour Lose?*. Analysis in the agents' journal *Labour Organiser*, used Gallup polling data to challenge the substance of report and interpretations affixed it by Gaitskellites, notably Abrams' co-author Rita Hinden (*Labour Organiser*, 462, 1960; 486, 1962).

Post-Thatcherism

Colin Hay
University of Birmingham and Harvard University

'No Left Turn? What to Expect from New Labour in Power'

Abstract

That the terms of political debate in contemporary Britain have been altered markedly in recent years is widely acknowledged. That this is not unrelated to Labour's self-styled 'modernisation' in the face of four consecutive election defeats is generally undisputed. More contentious, however, is the interpretation of this trend. Has Labour abandoned its socialist and social democratic traditions, re-projecting itself as an essentially Conservative, even Thatcherite, party, or has it managed to develop a novel, dynamic and modernising social democracy for new times? In this paper I seek to provide a bench-mark against which such propositions can be evaluated, assessing the extent of bipartisan convergence since 1992. On the basis of comparisons of policy commitments in 1992 and 1996, I argue that there has indeed been significant convergence between the parties, that this convergence has been driven principally by Labour, and that Britain is witnessing the emergence of a new bipartisan consensus. I conclude by considering possible alternatives to New Labour's politics of 'no alternative'.

Introduction: Towards a New Consensus?

The interpretation of the British Labour Party's self-styled 'modernisation' since its 1987 election defeat continues to divide commentators, analysts, and political scientists alike – as indeed it does many of the protagonists themselves. As Labour appears perhaps more electable today than at any other time since the mid 1970s, the stakes of this particular debate have recently been raised. At issue is our assessment of the very nature and trajectory of the British state and economy. Are we witnessing a convergence between the parties that is in fact symptomatic of the consolidation of a new political settlement, replacing the ascendant 'Keynesian welfarist' paradigm of the post-war years? Or does a certain stylistic convergence and the somewhat contrived novelty which has characterised New Labour's new-found appeal to the electorate merely serve to masquerade a basic divergence between underlying policy regimes? Alternatively, does a reorientation of the global political economy in an era of financial liberalisation, capital flight and an at least putative globalisation, usher in a new phase of capital accumulation, circumscribing the parameters of the politically and economically possible – constraints to which both parties are simply accommodating themselves?

In the context of such debates, the present contribution is a modest one. Its aim is neither to explain the distinctive character of political debate and competition in contemporary Britain (whether this is held to be consensual or adversarial), nor to engage in a normative evaluation of Labour's chosen electoral strategy. Rather my aim is to provide some basic parameters within which such a debate can occur. Accordingly, I assess the proposition that British politics is characterised by an emergent consensus, identifying the extent of the convergence between the parties since the last election.

On the basis of manifesto commitments, supporting policy documents and conference speeches, I identify clear policy differences between Labour and the Conservatives at the 1992 General Election in a range of policy areas. These provide an (albeit crude) baseline from which to assess the proposition that there has been a significant policy convergence between the parties *since 1992*, and that this convergence is largely the consequence of revisions *by the Labour Party* to pre-existing policy commitments. The full details of this analysis are presented and discussed elsewhere.[1]

Now, there are obvious methodological difficulties with this type of analysis. More accurately, there are methodological limitations to this approach:

(i) there is no neutral, unambiguous or privileged vantage-point from which to adjudicate the convergence proposition, and hence no neutral or unambiguous measure of consensus;
(ii) to produce evidence of policy revisions by one party to positions formerly associated with their political opponents need not imply convergence in a context of policy flux on both sides;
(iii) if, as has been widely noted, the 1992 election was itself characterised by an emergent bipartisan consensus, then an analysis which focuses upon issues where there was a clear policy difference between the parties in 1992 may serve to masquerade the full extent of any longer-term convergence; and
(iv) such an approach, by virtue of this same focus, gives limited attention to newly-emerging policy differences in what is a dynamic social, political and economic context.

For this and other reasons, considerable caution must be exercised in the intepretation of such evidence. Nonetheless, it is I think suggestive, and can be enlisted in support of a particular narrative – and a particularly surprising narrative at that.

For current purposes however I don't want to present this evidence in detail.[2] Because it is crucial to the argument that follows I will concentrate merely on economic and industrial policy.

Labour's industrial policy has undergone significant revision. Indeed it has effectively been rendered obsolete in recent years – a process accelerated since 1994 by the resolution of a growing conflict within the party

[1] See Colin Hay, 'That was then, this is now: The revision of policy in the modernisation of the British Labour Party, 1992-96', unpublished manuscript, University of Birmingham 1996.

[2] See Hay, *ibid.*

between the Shadow Treasury and Shadow Trade and Industry teams in favour of the former. Thus despite continued reference to the structural weaknesses of the British economy – the shortfall of dedicated capital and long-term strategic investment in particular – New Labour retains little (arguably nothing) in the way of concrete proposals that might address this distinctive British pathology. Where once the party emphasised the crucial strategic role that the Department of Trade and Industry would have to play in any rejuvenation of Britain's manufacturing economy, requiring its elevation to 'super-ministry' status, it has since undergone a complete *volte face* and now proposes to expand the role of the Treasury such that it will encroach significantly into the existing remit of the DTI. Proposals for a National Investment Bank that might provide investment capital on competitive terms to British industry have been dropped. Proposals for Regional Investment Banks introduced in 1994, and based on similar principles, have now been subjected to a similar fate. This leaves New Labour with no proposals to address what it still identifies as the principal structural weakness of the British economy – its investment shortfall. The sole remaining aspect of the industrial strategy developed under the tutelage of Robin Cook and Labour's Industry Forum is its commitment to regional development agencies. Yet insofar as these merely build upon and institutionalise existing arrangements, Labour seems effectively to have vacated the industrial policy arena emphasising instead macro-economic conservatism and fiscal stability.

Here too the general trajectory of Labour's reforms is one of convergence on an agenda increasingly circumscribed for both parties by the tenets of neo-liberal economics. Labour's current economic policy is a catalogue of abandoned commitments and political U-turns. Where as recently as 1992 the party identified the principal means of economic management as supply-side intervention in clear contrast to the Conservatives' fiscal conservatism and control of inflation, it now conceives of economic management as providing 'a robust and stable framework of monetary and fiscal discipline'.[3] Where competition policy was once justified principally in terms of its contribution in protecting employees from the consequences of unfair competition, it is now recast in terms of its role in protecting consumer interests and enhancing competitiveness. Where Labour previously identified increased public expenditure as a top priority it now chastises the government for an increase in welfare spending at a time of falling unemployment and pledges itself to no new public expenditure without corresponding reductions in existing departmental budgets. Where Labour sought significant reform of Britain's financial institutions and the development of, first, a National Investment Bank and, subsequently, a network of Regional Investment Banks as the means by which investment in the productive economy could be raised, it can now only echo the Conservatives' faith in public-private partnership. Where the party proposed an increase in the top rate of taxation to 50 pence in the pound and an end to the 'ceiling' on national insurance contributions (effectively raising the top rate of taxation from 40 to 59 pence in

[3]Labour Party, *A New Economic Future for Britain*, Labour Party, 1995.

the pound), it now advocates (albeit somewhat tendentiously) a reduction of the bottom rate of taxation to 15 (and ideally 10) pence in the pound, while quietly dropping any commitment to reform of the national insurance system. Where in short, in 1992 Labour's principal economic goals were to raise investment in the domestic economy, to boost productivity, and to reduce long-term unemployment, its primary aims now are to control inflation and to promote macroeconomic stability.

It would be difficult to interpret this as anything other than convergence, and convergence *by Labour* on the Conservatives' neo-liberal terms – there would appear to have been an economic paradigm shift.

Such convergence, however, is not restricted to economic and industrial policy. Of the 50 policy differences that I identified in 1992, on none of them had there been a policy divergence, on 4 of them policy had remained much the same, on 42 of them there were various degrees of convergence, and on 4 of them Labour has arguably 'out-trumped' the Tories (moving from one side of the Tories in 1992 to the other by 1996).

Now, we should of course be exceedingly wary of such crude aggregate statistics. Yet however much we might want to qualify such pooled measures, it would seem difficult to argue that there hasn't been a very significant convergence between the parties across the full range of policy areas.

So where does this leave the consensus thesis? Well, my argument would be that the only thing that could make us challenge the notion that there was a consensus in 1992 is the clear convergence that has happened since then! However, on balance, I think New Labour's trajectory since 1992 provides a powerful reminder that no consensus is ever absolute, and that policy convergence may continue in a context already characterised by underlying consensus.

Since 1992, then, itself regarded by most commentators as an election in which there was a rare degree of proximity between the parties,[4] Labour has undergone a significant and comprehensive review of policy in almost all areas. The trajectory of change for Labour has been overwhelmingly in one direction – that of convergence with the Conservatives on the basis of the dilution, weakening and selective abandonment of prior commitments.

The last vestiges of Labour's 'old' Keynesian, welfarist and social democratic sensitivities would seem to have been displaced by a pervasive spirit of 'new realism'. This has manifest itself in terms of macroeconomic conservatism, fiscal fortitude, and an increasing disavowal of both labour market re-regulation and consistent demand- or supply-side intervention. New Labour, like many of its former social democrat allies in Western Europe, and its Antipodean namesakes, has lost its former confidence in the ability to retain a comprehensive welfare state in an era of capital flight, financial liberalisation and burgeoning globalisation. On this understanding it must now accommodate itself to the task at hand – the more or less equitable

[4]See for instance Anthony Heath & Roger Jowell, 'Labour's Policy Review', in Anthony Heath et al (eds), *Labour's Last Chance? The 1992 Election and Beyond*, Dartmouth, 1994; David Butler & Dennis Kavanagh, *The British General Election of 1992*, Macmillan, 1992.

management of welfare retrenchment in the name of competitiveness.

It is this agenda that defines the new bipartisan consensus in Britain. It may have emerged in circumstances very different from that of the early 1950s, and the principal agent of revision this time around is clearly Labour and not the Conservatives, but in both contexts we see a re-projection, rethinking and internalisation of the new parameters of the politically and economically possible.

Towards a 'radical centrism'

If this is the context in which we now find ourselves, then the question is: *how did we get here*? In an attempt to provide some answers I turn to a very important piece published in *Politics & Society* towards the end of last year by Mark Wickham-Jones.[5] In the paper, the author presents an original and convincing periodisation of economic policy formation within the party after 1987. He distinguishes between the policy review period in which electoral considerations predominated, and the post-review period in which Labour sought to project itself to the City and the CBI as more representative of the interest(s) of capital. More contentiously, Wickham-Jones argues that in an era of globalisation and enhanced capital mobility, social democratic politics is almost synonymous with capital flight – the election of a social democratic administration will almost guarantee an exodus of capital. As a consequence, social democratic parties can no longer be elected without previously convincing capital that they have abandoned their social democratic credentials. This, he argues, is precisely the exercise that Labour has been engaged in since about 1990 – and it is an exercise born of necessity. In the now familiar language of the times, there is simply 'no alternative'.

Now, though I agree with Wickham-Jones that this is precisely the exercise Labour has been engaged in, *and* that it genuinely thinks there is no alternative (or at least Brown and Blair do ...), this is where I part company with his analysis. I simply do not believe that there is no alternative to internalising the perceived interest of capital and accommodating oneself to the neo-liberal spirit of the times – moreover, I think the consequence of so doing is to threaten to pile further social and economic derelication upon the accumulated debris that is the Thatcherite legacy.

There are I think two principle difficulties with Wicham-Jones' analysis: the first concerns the likelihood of capital flight; the second the implications of capital flight (whether real, threatened, or imagined) for social democratic politics and political strategy.

The threat of capital flight can be, and has tended to be, somewhat exaggerated. Though capital may indeed have a strategic stake in emphasising its mobility, and in playing up the likelihood of its immanent departure in the run-up to an election in which a genuine social democratic alternative is perceived to exist, this hardly guarantees a mass exodus of capital in the

[5] Mark Wickham-Jones, 'Anticipating Social Democracy, Preempting Anticipations: Economic Policy-Making in the British Labour Party, 1987-92', *Politics & Society*, 23/4, 1995.

post-election period. Indeed, New Labour's new-found macroeconomic conservatism would appear to demonstrate precisely the effectiveness of such pre-election bravado on the part of capital.

It is tempting then to conclude that Labour in power, and in preparation for power, should call the bluff of so-called 'footloose' multi-national corporations and investors, advocating say an expansive social democratic programme oblivious to the likely protestations from domestically-located capital. Yet there are at least two good reasons for holding back on such wilful antagonism. First, though capital is by no means 'footloose', financial globalisation has served to lubricate its flows – capital flight (however exaggerated) is a genuine threat. Second, and more significantly, *threatened* capital flight and the *perception* of its likelihood *in the event of the election of a social democratic government*, may militate severely against such an outcome. The lesson for Labour is that it must indeed take the interests of capital seriously – more seriously perhaps than it has (and has had to) in the past. In so doing, it must seek to persuade potentially mobile capital in particular that its economic policies, precisely by virtue of their departures from neo-liberal orthodoxies, will strengthen the productive capacity of the British economy thereby contributing to economic growth and securing higher rates of return on capital investment. The politics of persuasion and preference-shaping are thus placed at centre stage.

This in turn suggests a second line of critique. Wickham-Jones, and Przeworski and Wallerstein (on whom he draws) before him, simply assume that capital has a clear, unambiguous and singular interest, and what is more, that it is blessed with perfect knowledge of the conditions likely to maximise returns on its investment. Moreover, it is assumed that social democratic parties cannot act in the 'objective' interest(s) of capital. These are the three basic and explicit assumptions on which the thesis is constructed. Within this framework, what is required therefore of parties of the left is that they demonstrate – to the satisfaction of capital – that they will indeed act in its interest(s), while abandoning all (social democratic) measures that threaten to advance interests not held (by capital) to be conducive to profit maximisation (over capital's preferred time horizon). Yet as soon as we point out that

> (i) capital has no unambiguous or singular interest (as distinct from a series of divergent and conflicting interests projected over different time-horizons);
>
> (ii) it tends to act in pursuit of short-term gain often to the detriment of longer-term advantage; and
>
> (iii) representatives of capital, far from actively sponsoring major reforms in its long term collective interest, often provide the most vociferous opposition to such measures,

the argument that parties of the left should seek to accommodate the preferences of capital in economic policy formation appears less compelling.

Yet as Wickham-Jones powerfully demonstrates, this was precisely Labour's principal ambition in economic policy formation between the publication of the policy review in 1989 and the general election of 1992 (and one might argue, it has merely been confirmed as such since). Had Labour succeeded in winning the election in 1992, and should it win the forthcoming election, the clear danger is that it will do so merely to contribute further to the undermining of the long-term competitiveness of the British economy *in the name* of the parochial and conservative interests of capital.

This brings us to the question of what to expect from New Labour in power.

Today Labour presents itself to the electorate on the basis of its relative competence in the management of the Thatcherite legacy. Lacking a clear diagnosis of the British affliction and the confidence or vision to project a distinctive alternative, this might appear both expedient and unremarkable. Yet in accommodating itself to the terms of the Thatcherite legacy, the party has chosen to restrict itself to a repertoire of managerial techniques and resources heavily circumscribed by a neo-liberal economic imaginary. Though reinflected in more communitarian rhetoric, the ascendant paradigm of free-market liberalism has thus come to demarcate the boundaries of what is considered politically and economically possible for both parties.

Implicit in this paradigm is an understanding of the Major government as at worst incompetent in economic matters. For if Labour's macroeconomic policy is merely a variant on a Conservative theme, then to accuse the government of macroeconomic mis-management is, frankly, disengenuous. It is not surprising then that Labour shies away from the more dispassionate (and ultimately more convincing) analysis: that the Major government is attempting the impossible – the management and attempted consolidation of the structures of a deeply contradictory post-Thatcher settlement that is the Thatcherite legacy; and, moreover, that it is attempting the impossible with a range of strategic resources heavily depleted by the anti-statism of it economic convictions. Sadly, given the macroeconomic convergence between the parties, for Labour to admit this would be tantamount to an exercise in auto-critique.

The clear danger in all of this is that Labour may well achieve governmental power at the cost of consigning itself to futile attempts to manage the contradictions of a state and economic regime in an advanced state of decay. As the *Independent* recently suggested, drawing on the Treasury's own figures, '17 years of Tory taxing, borrowing, selling off and spending [have] cost Britain £3,204bn ... The Government is literally bankrupt – with net wealth declining from nearly £20bn in 1979 to *minus* £152bn at the end of 1995' (2 September 1996). In the light of such evidence, the level of budget deficit faced by any incoming Labour government is likely to be huge – indeed it is projected to rise to 5% of national income by the turn of the century. To protect against the capital flight likely in such a scenario, a Labour chancellor would be faced with the equivalent of a 7p increase in the basic rate of taxation, or the equivalent level of welfare retrenchment (and that, it should be noted, would only reduce the budget deficit to 2.5% of national income, a level outside the Maastrict convergence criteria). All of which merely points to the difficulties likely to confront the next government and the rather cynical nature of the pre-election skirmishes on taxation.

The point of this is that Labour seems destined to inherit not only the crisis-tendencies of the Thatcherite inheritance, but, by virtue of its own failure to identify and narrate such contradictions, responsibility for their management. Far from exorcising the 'ghost of winters past', Labour's pursuit of governmental power may merely serve to resurrect it, implicating the party in the disintegration of a deeply contradictory settlement. This may present a Tory opposition with an opportunity to reimagine, reposition and renew its political project, presenting itself once again as the only party capable of the degree of decisive intervention required in a situation of economic and political crisis. Although New Labour is anxious to present itself as the natural heir to the spirit of 1945, comparisons with 1974 would appear somewhat more realistic.

The challenge this presents for Labour in the run-up to the next election is considerable. If it is to avoid inheriting responsibility (and culpability) from the Conservatives for the looming crisis (as it did in 1974), it must not only offer a compelling diagnosis of the current British affliction (and its origins), it must also convince capital and the electorate alike that a resolution of this affliction (and Labour's chosen resolution at that) is an immediate concern overriding more parochial and short-term considerations of vested interest and material gain. In short, Labour must successfully recast the preferences and perceived interests of capital and the electorate (or at least broad sections thereof) on the basis of its assessment of the 'state we're in'. As yet it shows no signs of so doing.

But what might such an alternative conception consist in? In the brief concluding section that follows, I argue that Labour might in fact benefit from rediscovering the courage of its former convictions. Yet by this I do not mean a return to 'Old' Labour themes, but rather to the implicit growth strategy outlined most recently by Labour's Industry Forum and the Regional Policy Commission.

Renewing the British Left, Renewing Labour

In seeking to give voice to an alternative economic project, Labour need not return to an empty blackboard. For, though clearly underdeveloped, aspects of its former regional industrial policy might provide the basis for an alternative accumulation strategy. Labour's Industry Forum, particularly in its 1994 industrial policy manifesto *Winning for Britain* (now, sadly revised and diluted), developed an (albeit implicit) challenge to the ascendancy of macroeconomic conservatism and neo-liberal economics more generally, emphasising: (i) industrial strategy; (ii) supply-side intervention; (iii) the need to establish and sustain indigenous regional growth profiles; and, above all, (iv) the subordination of the interests of finance capital to those of industrial capital, and fiscal policy to an industrial modernisation strategy.[6]

[6] Labour Party, *Winning for Britain*, Labour Party, 1994.

The contradictions between such supply-side *dirigisme* and the fiscal fortitude so prominently expounded by the shadow Treasury team under Gordon Brown were not to go unnoticed – and, as we have seen, they have since been resolved in favour of the latter.

Such a vision must identify the conditions of existence of a renewed growth dynamic, the conditions for the restoration of structural competitiveness to the British economy. Indeed this is perhaps all that Labour's election manifesto *must* establish (and one thing that Labour's draft manifesto certainly doesn't establish). The conditions of national economic growth might here be conceived of not in terms of 'blunt' economy-wide instruments of macroeconomic demand-management, but rather in terms of 'sharp' local and regional interventions (principally on the supply-side) that are sensitive to institutional and cultural specificities and both adaptive to evolving regional trajectories of economic growth and responsive to changing external circumstances and conditions of competitiveness (national, European and global). Such a vision might thus project *regional structures of innovation* and *regional institutions of investment*. These would promote complementary, yet potentially highly differentiated, regional growth dynamics that, although centrally coordinated, would be *regionally sustained* through specific, adaptive and flexible regional institutions which might in time embody the principle of *regional stakeholding* (as opposed to regional quangocracy).

Behind this vision lies the basic premise that British industrial capital has to be encouraged to think long-term if its competitiveness is to be restored through modernisation, diversification and strategic investment in new technologies, 'human capital' and new management techniques. This requires a fundamental change in the mind-set of British industrialists *and* a transformation of the institutional contexts within which such a mind-set has arisen and become entrenched. This is a clear example of how a change in the perceptions of (domestic industrial) capital must go hand-in-hand with a programme of financial reform, (regional) institutional design and constitutional redesign. The vision is one of regional infrastructures of investment facilitating distinct, independent and indigenous regional growth trajectories. The role of the centre within this schema is to promote co-operation between regional economies, to militate against (and in certain instances outlaw) mutually destructive regional competitive strategies (such as regulatory undercutting to attract inward investment), and to facilitate the access of the British regions to European funds and to an emergent 'third tier' of trans-regional governance within Europe.[7] But to imply that ideas like these are likely to be taken up by New Labour would be to end on an unduly optimistic (and perhaps naïve) note. The contemporary context, like that of the late 1970s, is one of profound, protracted and widely experienced state failure, social dislocation and economic contradiction – in the *Independent's* memorable terms of 'looming bankruptcy'. This presents New Labour with a clear if unenviable choice: does it seek to offer itself to

[7] For a further elaboration of these themes see Colin Hay, 'Anticipating Accommodations, Anticipating Accommodations: The Appeasement of Capital in the Modernisation of the British Labour Party, 1987-92', *Politics & Society*, 25/2, 1997.

the electorate by projecting itself as the party of fiscal rectitude and managerial competence – the natural heir to the legacy of Major; or does it seek to diagnose and narrate the crisis of the British state, arguing the case for a decisive break with the strictures, practices and ideologies of a decaying state regime and an obsolescent economic paradigm?

The evidence of recent experience would suggest that in so far as it has recognised the choice, it has perhaps already chosen the former option. The cost may well be British social democracy itself.

Post-Thatcherism

Stuart McAnulla
University of Birmingham

'Fade To Grey? Symbolic Politics In the Post-Thatcher Era'

Introduction

My objective in this paper is to provide insight into the nature of British politics in the post-Thatcher era. However, a key aim is to suggest that this can only be achieved through a prior consideration of the Thatcher period. Dominant interpretations of the Thatcher period have emphasised the radicalism of government strategy during Mrs Thatcher's term in office.[1] On the other hand, revisionist accounts, based upon analyses of policy implementation, posit the view that Thatcher's radicalism was more rhetorical than real.[2] Recent work on the Major Government has demonstrated that in many ways the post-Thatcher period should be thought of in terms of a continuation *mutatis mutandis* of the Thatcher era.[3] My aim here is not to take sides in the existing debate on the Thatcher period, or to take issue with the aforementioned work on Major. Rather, I will highlight a neglect feature of the existing literature which can help us to distinguish the Major period from its predecessor. Specifically, I am concerned to demonstrate the importance of symbolic politics to an understanding of post-1979 Conservative politics.

I will seek to explain why the Thatcher period is commonly interpreted as a time of high radicalism and, partly in consequence, why the Major period is often viewed as a pale successor. It is argued that politics has transformed between the two periods at a symbolic level. Yet, this cannot merely be understood as superficial or ephemeral transformation. This paper proposes that symbolic politics are crucial not only to perceptions of a period but also have essential practical consequences. Most pertinently perhaps, recent transformations of symbolic politics can explain why the Conservatives' hegemonic grip on electoral power now appears to be crumbling.

This paper divides into three broad sections. The first reviews the Thatcher governments use of symbolic politics during the 1980s. The second studies the governing style of both John Major and his Government. The final section analyses the importance of public image and discursive strategy within contemporary party politics. Overall, my aim is to demonstrate that symbolic politics are crucial to an explanation of both the Thatcher and Major eras.

---

[1] A.Gamble, *The Free Economy and the Strong State: The Politics of Thatcherism*, Macmillan, 1988.

[2] D.Marsh & R.Rhodes (eds), *Implementing Thatcherite Policies : Audit of an Era*, Open University Press, 1992.

[3] P.Kerr et al, 'Charting Late-Thatcherism: British Politics Under Major', in S.Lancaster (ed), *Developments in Politics*, Causeway Press, 1997, forthcoming.

Thatcher and the 'Other'

Both the perception and 'reality' of radicalism in the Thatcher period can be best grasped if conceived of largely in symbolic terms. This is not to be confused with the merely superficial or rhetorical. As Bentham argued, non-existent or fictitious entities can have all too real effects.[4] It is important to be aware of the complex interplay between 'actual' events and what people percieve of as 'real'. The Thatcher Governments commited a number of different acts, presented in particular discursive terms, which have greater significance at a symbolic level, rather than in substantial short term or even medium-term, material change. Commonly, this symbolic change has been articulated against the 'Other(s)'. To name a period as radical is always a relative judgement and thus inescapably involves the Other.

For a politician who famously declared that 'There Is No Alternative', Mrs Thatcher spent a lot of time suggesting what in fact the alternatives were. Frequently, she drew upon images and experiences of the recent past under preceding governments, most particularly the Labour administration of 1974-9. The 'Winter of Discontent' was frequently portrayed as the 'other' of Thatcherism. More accurately, it was the dominant discursive narration of the 'Winter of Discontent' which Thatcher utilised.[5] The media portrayal of this period of industrial strife frequently distorted, or fictionalised, events. Thatcher and her Government were adept, with the complicity of the media, at 'speaking' the past in such a manner as to legitimise Thatcherism's use of state power.

To a large extent, this version of the 'Winter of Discontent' was bound up with a presentation of the 'postwar consensus' and how this had failed. This included 'Keynesian' demand management and social democratic and, corporatist practices which were alleged to have created an overweening state protecting the interests of 'producers' and government bureaucrats. Thatcherite discourse was particularly effective in simultaneously establishing a diagnosis of past illness and a prognosis for future cure.

Once again, the substantially fictitious nature of this presentation of events must be emphasised. Whilst the simplifications of Thatcher's popular epithets may be self-evident, other elements of Thatcherite discourse have more intellectual currency. For example, the periodisations and designations of 'Keynesianism', 'the Keynesian Welfare State', post-war social democracy and, the postwar consensus are regularly used within political science.

An interrogation of these concepts is beyond the scope of this paper. Suffice it to say that the notion of 'postwar consensus' is coming under increased scrutiny.[6] Many commentators have questioned the extent to which 'Keynesian' economics were ever implemented in this period. Similarly, it can be argued that there was never a social democracy in Britain worthy of

---

[4] J.Bentham, *The Panopticon Writings*, Verso, 1995.

[5] For a full account, see C.Hay, 'Narrating Crisis: The Discursive Construction of the Winter of Discontent', *Sociology*, 30/2, 1996.

[6] P.Kerr & D.Marsh, 'False Dichotomies and Failed Assumptions: Revisiting and Revising the Consensus Debate', in I.Hampsher-Monk & J.Stanyer (eds), *Contemporary Political Studies 1996*, volume 2, PSA, 1996.

the name. Another important point must be made regarding the chronology of a putative break in the course of British politics. Many authors who support the idea of a break or 'paradigm shift' in the 1970s following the oil crisis would assert that this led to a similar crisis in Britain which exposed the contradictions of the postwar settlement.[7] Certainly, there is clear evidence of a move to monetarist economic policy and a similar move from the rhetoric of expansionism within the welfare state. It would thus be a mistake to view the Thatcher Government as the instigators of a discursive break with the 'postwar consensus'. As much as actors such as Keith Joseph and Mrs Thatcher formulated a discursive strategy, they also drew on and incorporated different narrative and experiences which emerged from different sites during the 1970s. They were however, effective in constructing themselves as instigators of an authentic break with the past during the 1980s.

Just as Thatcherism recruited the 'past' as its Other it was able to sustain its radicality throughout the 1980s through reference to the malign presence of assorted 'Others'. The centralisation of state power away from local authorities was commonly legitimised by reference to 'high spending' or 'loony left' Labour councils. Again, the media was complicit with this strategy, – variously distorting, and crucially, moreover generalising isolated incidents of local government action. Frequently, cases were highlighted which could be easily narrated as being incompetent, wasteful or dangerously socialist. The overall message was that Marxists, crypto-socialists, self-interested bureaucrats and politicians were dominant in local government, thus they had to be stripped of power. Certainly, there were a few local councils willing to fulfil the role as outright antagonists to Thatcherite reforms and to use local powers to resist central government strategy. Militant councils were happy to confront and defy Mrs Thatcher in this 'play of opposites'; for example through refusing to comply with caps on spending. The discursive presentation of such events served to obscure the fact that nearly all councils adopted a strategy of accomodation to the Thatcherite reforms. Meanwhile, the Sun reader awoke to read that their LEA was likely to ban 'Baa Baa Black Sheep' from their children's schools as part of an anti-racist programme.

Having diagnosed union power as a key source of Britain's economic ills, the Thatcher Government's legislative restrictions on union activities were presented as a fundamental reform of United Kingdom industrial relations. However evidence of actual change in this area is mixed. Nevertheless, this version of events continued to resonate at a discursive level. The cries of 'foul' from trade union leaders to government demands for democratic ballots only strengthened Thatcher's position.

Of particular significance in this regard was the strike called by the National Union of Miners in 1984. The strike lasted almost a year, with high publicity for bitter clashes rhetorically and physically between miners and government. Thatcher was determined to mobilise every state resource necessary to defeat the strikers. Failure was a calamity for the coal industry

[7] C.Hay, *Re-stating Social and Political Change*, Open University Press, 1996.

and the mining communities. However, the broader importance of this strike lay largely in its symbolic significance. Through their victory over Heath in 1972, the miners had solidified an image as 'the shock troops of the working class'.[8] During the 1984 strike, Thatcher named them as 'the enemy within' and, hence, as a threat to parliamentary legitimacy and the prosperity of the nation. NUM leader Arthur Scargill was only too happy to participate in this 'play of opposites', invoking classic dichotomies such as workers/bosses, workerism/parliamentarianism, socialism/capitalism and so on. The miner's defeat set a context for future industrial relations; signifying an end to trade union militancy and delegitimising struggles against the baleful effects of economic restructuring. The event was therefore significant in marking a 'break' with the past and also as a portent for the future.

Commentators agree that the Thatcher Governments' privatisation initiatives had a radical character. Sales of council houses brought significant material benefit for many people. Studies have shown that this benefited the Conservatives' electorally . The privatisation of the monopolised utilities brought smaller, but no less significant, material and political benefits. Whilst there is disagreement about the governments' primary motivations in pursuing privatisation (ie, the relative importance of political, economic and ideological factors) there is little doubt that these changes became central to peoples' understanding of Thatcherism. Indeed, the phrase 'privatisation' was scarcely heard in popular discourse prior to the Thatcher era – previously, such reforms were couched as 'de-nationalisation'. Labour was greatly on the defensive on an issue which once again served a symbolic purpose as an 'anti-Labour' measure, which marked a complete break with the postwar period (eg. in government approaches to housing). Perhaps more than any other issue, the privatisation question invoked in the public mind the binary oppositions of 'individualism' (share-owning) vs 'collectivism' (state-owning) and 'individual choice' vs 'state control'.

Majoring in Grey

One of the dominant public perceptions of John Major is represented by Spitting Image's all grey coloured puppet of the Prime Minister. His seeming inability to sustain interest in his public persona has placed a question mark over his leadership capabilities. Major has variously been referred to as indecisive, weak, dithering and incompetent. This is not merely a popular view, or the opinion of Major's natural enemies, but also a view expressed by the 'Tory-friendly' press during much of his premiership. Young argues that Major has been a figure who, 'at best, people couldn't give a damn about'.[9]

---

[8] K.O.Morgan, *The People's Peace: British history 1945-1990*, Oxford University Press, 1990.

[9] H.Young, 'The Prime Minister', in D.Kavanagh & A.Seldon (eds), *The Major Effect*, Papermac, 1994.

Governing Style and the Appearance of Crisis

There are a number of episodes which can be used to suggest weakness in Major's style of governmental management. One relatively early example was the handling of the announcement of pit closures in 1992. This provoked public outcry; being seen as a ruthless measure which would destroy communities and decimate an industry which had already suffered enormously in the 1980s. The Government's establishment of VAT on fuel bills was another serious political miscalculation; a measure seen as harming vulnerable people for no morally defensible reason. In both cases, the presentation of policy was also bungled. Subsequent policy prevarication only added to public derision. The policy on VAT on fuel was defeated in the House of Commons after a backbench rebellion. Arguably here again, Major contributed to his own downfall as eight of the government rebels had been freed from the party whip in the lead up to the VAT vote after abstaining on European Community budget increases which Major had made a vote of confidence. The rebels inflicted a later defeat on the government over Common Fisheries policy. Yet, in a self-humiliating act, Major restored the whip without the need for apology for their previous disloyalty. Of course, it could be argued that such an unpalatable act was necessary to maximise party cohesion in the long-term.

Major has initiated two independent public enquiries into governmental and parliamentary behaviour; namely, the Scott and Nolan reports. In one sense, these initiatives may be viewed as decisive, politically sensible reponses to public concern over perceived government sleaze and corruption. However, in the case of Nolan, Major tarnished much of the credit he gained from this by subsequently refusing to accept the full findings of the report. This was particularly damaging as, to a large extent, it was his own ministers' behaviour which had generated public concern over standards. Worse still for Major, he suffered another embarrasing defeat on the subsequent Parliamentary vote on the Arms to Iraq enquiry. The issue created considerable anti-government publicity, thus fueling public perceptions of ministerial corruption and blatant hypocrisy on the part of the government. Such episodes have at times given the impression of Major turning form crisis to crisis unable to complete a good step forward. It is such imagery which has dominated the public mind during much of the Major period. There has been a virtual absence of the type of dramatic, ground breaking and confrontational theatre which characterised the Thatcher era.

Yet, given the unfavourable contexts Major has faced he has had considerable practical success for the Conservatives in both winning the 1992 election and maintaining a government with a small, now non-existent, parliamentary majority.[10]

---

[10] P.Kerr et al, 'Charting late-Thatcherism: British Politics Under Major', in S.Lancaster (ed), *Developments in Politics*, Ormskirk, Causeway Press, 1997, forthcoming.

Major's Partycraft

In particular, Major has demonstrated considerable 'partycraft' abilities in working with almost intolerable party divisions over Europe. Negotiations over Maastricht produced an outcome which, at least in the short-term, satified the party. He secured a British opt-out of the social protocol of the Treaty which could be used to re-inforce the neo-liberal position of the Conservative Party in the domestic political battlefield. Major also gained the right to opt-out of later moves toward a single, European currency, thus conveniently delaying a decision on an issue on which the party is entirely split.[11]

Whilst the European issue has been a persistent thorn in Major's side he has managed to maintain a successful balancing act between the pro-European and anti-European wings of the party. He has often appeased the Europhobes through expressing hostility to the notion of a 'federal' Europe. Yet, he has frequently struck a more pro-European note, stressing that Britain has no option but continued involvement at the centre of the European community. At various stages when required, Major has played up his Euro-sceptic credentials most notably with his one-man rejection of the Belgian pro-federalist Jean-Luc Dehane as the new European Community President. More commonly however, Major has attempted to send out sympathetic signals to each camp in turn. A classic example came in Major's statement to Parliament following an European Union summit in Dublin in December 1996. At one point Major condemned as 'delusion' the notion of a British withdrawal from the European Union, yet later argued that if mistakes occured over the single currency issue 'the damage to our membership of the European Union ... might well be fatal'.[12]

Various events have conspired to undermine Major's credibility as a competent leader. Yet, he has managed to persuade sufficient sections of the party that he is their best option as leader. He has appealed to the party's one nation left- wing as the best available candidate to tame the Thatcherite right wing, whilst maintaining enough Euro-sceptic credibility to maintain right- wing support against alternative leaders such as Clarke or Heseltine. Major's provocation of a leadership election in 1995 must be considered a political masterstroke. Major was able to defeat Redwood's challenge after forcing the hand of his internal enemies at a time which suited him rather than his opponents. This solidly secured Major's position as Prime Minister and party leader for the duration of the current Parliament.

Governing Competence in Perspective

The question of competence should perhaps be placed in broader context. Major has been rated the most unpopular Prime Minister in history partly because he has been perceived as incompetent in his management of government. Yet, it is worth asking what possibilities exist today for leaders

[11] S.Ludlam & M.Smith, *Contemporary British Conservatism*, Macmillan, 1996.
[12] *Scotsman*, 14/12/96.

to appear competent. We are very much aware of the importance of image and ephemerality to such appearances. Media perceptions are crucial. However, the media is constantly changing in the forms, scope and standards deployed in its consideration of the political field. Logically then, what is required of a politician to appear competent will also change with such changes in the media. It can be argued that transformations of the media, in both its penetration and presentation of public life, make it increasingly difficult for politicians to appear effective. Derrida argues that however competent political leaders may personally be, they tend, today, to become structurally incompetent.[13] The media through its interrogation of Parliament, political parties and institutions may undermine traditional forms of legitimacy and power. In this sense, we may view Major as, at least in part, a victim of structural trends which are affecting the political classes both in Britain and elsewhere. For example, the eruption of 'sleaze' incidents during Major's Government cannot be explained merely in terms a lack of professional integrity on the part of assorted Conservative ministers (though this is no small factor). These incidents have been exposed largely through journalistic endeavour. Crucial to such work is the media's perception of what it considers as (1) its own professional vocation and (2) in the public interest. In the past, some 'sleaze' incidents have gone uninvestigated because of journalists belief that the public interest will be better served if the matter remained private. In general terms, the media focus on those in public positions has never been more intense, thus making it ever-more difficult for political leaders to project and sustain an image of governing competence. There is insufficient space here to trace recent developments in the relationship between the media and the political classes, however, it would appear an important area for further research.

Public Image and Symbolic Politics Under Major

Structural factors aside, it is worth reviewing Major's attempts to create a positive public image for both himself and his Governments' initiatives. Major proved an effective campaigner during the 1992 General Election presenting himself as the more caring face of Conservatism without abandoning Thatcher's legacy in any substantial way. At a rhetorical level, Major began to incorporate sporadic one nation sentiments into a generally Thatcherite discourse; for example, in his call for a 'classless' society and 'a nation at ease with itself'.[14] However, following the 1992 election, Major's 'man of the people' popularity began to dry up. Contrasts between his own style and that of his predecessor, which had served him so well during the election campaign, came back to haunt him. Major appeared indecisive where Thatcher would, it was argued, have demonstrated strength in the face of adversity. However superficial such comparisons were, they contributed to various frenzies of speculation about whether Major could hold

[13] J.Derrida, *Specters of Marx: the state of the debt, the work of mourning, and the New International*, Routledge, 1994.

[14] See Evans & Taylor.

on to the leadership. Major has thus faced pressure to project a personal or political message which might resonate with the public in the way that some of Thatcher's initiatives did. Yet, numerous public 'relaunches' have failed to establish popular momentum. These initiatives have tended to be strongly Thatcherite in tone; for example, the 'Back-to-Basics' pronouncements. These stressed the need for traditional morality and standards in matters such as education, law and order, and the family. Once again however, the presentation of this initiative left something to be desired, as it was unclear for a long time in exactly which areas the government wished to see a return to 'basics' and what the practical implications of such a move might be. Both this project, and Major's other initiatives, such as the Citizen's Charter, have been undermined or overshadowed by political contingencies, for example, the call for traditionalist morality in 'Back-to-Basics' fell flat when several ministers became caught up in scandals involving extra-marital affairs or 'cash for questions'.

There is a clear difference between Thatcher and Major's public relations style manifest in the relative reluctance ot the latter to engage in ideological preaching. Certainly, this seems in part to reflect a difference of temperament between the respective leaders. However, changed contexts provide other explanatory variables. For example, public enthusiasm for privatisation has waned and initiatives such as rail privatisation have proved unpopular. Thus, Major may calculate that there is little point in campaigning over issues which may exacerbate government unpopularity. In addition, Major inherited a political context in which many of the central tenets of Thatcherism had become widely accepted and uncontested, even by the Labour Party. In this sense, there has been less need, and indeed, less opportunity, for an evangelising leadership style. Yet, this is a key reason for the image of dull greyness with which Major is associated. Moreover, Major has been unable to engage in the type of symbolic politics which, it was argued earlier was crucial to sustaining the Thatcher Governments' appearance of radicalism.

Crucially, Major has lacked the presence of 'Others' against which he can articulate and legitimise his programmes. Trade union militancy has been minimal and there has been little political radicalism emerging from local government, even though the Conservatives have been virtually wiped out as a national force in local council elections. Most importantly perhaps, 'New Labour' has sought, with large success, to avoid being constructed as Thatcherism's 'Other'.

The modernisation process continued by Smith and Blair can be understood as an attempt to evade the right's discursive tactics which were employed to such effect in the 1980s. While Kinnock moved Labour to the political 'centre' the Conservatives were still able to argue that at heart Labour was be a pro-nationalisation, anti-business, high taxation party. Smith and Blair both pursued reforming measures of great symbolic importance for public consumption. Smith won the argument for 'one member one vote' for selecting MPs indicating that Labour was distancing itself from trade union influence. Blair dramatically provoked the Clause IV debate –

purging from the party any notion that it might still, in some latent way, oppose the market and wish to extend public ownership of the economy. More generally, the Blair strategy may be seen as an attempt to avoid being drawn in to the type of binaries mentioned earlier such as public/private, and individual/collective. Thus, the aim is to evade, or usurp, attempts to narrate Labour as the Conservatives' 'Other' on unfavourable political terrains. this can quite clearly be observed in the construction of many key watchwords of New Labour. Blair's slogan 'tough on crime, tough on the causes of crime' seeks to evade a discursive presentation of Labour as 'soft' on crime because it raises the question of underlying social causes of crime. Phrases, such as the communitarian inspired 'the rights we enjoy reflect the duties we owe' and 'individual achievement, backed up by a strong community' are designed to emphasise the importance both of individuality and community to Labour's basic philosophy. Thus, Labour hopes to avoid being portrayed as 'against' individual achievement and choice as it was in the 1980s.

Of course, Major and the Conservative leadership have still sought to emulate 1980s tactics in presenting Labour as a high-tax party and in the pocket of trade unions. Yet, these jibes have achieved much less resonance following Labour's symbolic transformation into 'New' Labour. This was tacitly acknowledged during the Conservatives' recent strategy rethink. Realising that they could no longer credibly tie Labour to past policies they instead attempted to find 'new dangers' with which to frighten potential Labour voters. Overall then, Major has faced much less convenient opposition than his predecessor.

Conclusion

As we have seen, the Thatcher Governments were able to justify many of their actions through discursively de-legitimising resistence to their strategy. This use of real or fictionalised Others of Thatcherism served to profoundly shift politics at a symbolic level. This helped the Thatcher Governments sustain both an image of competence and radicalism, and the notion that there was 'No Alternative' to Thatcherism.

Working within some unfavourable contexts, Major and his government have been unable to engage in this type of symbolic politics. Consequently, they have been unable to maintain an image either of competence or radicalism, however competent or radical they may have been in a practical sense. In general terms, Major lacks the presence of Others against which he can articulate and distinguish his Governments' actions. Rather, Major has been forced into holding together his Government through his symbolic oscilations between Euro-enthusiasm and Euro-scepticism.

Crucially, Major has confronted an opposition adept at avoiding interpellation as the Other of Thatcherism. Labour, so long the loser in the discursive binaries of public vs private, individual vs collective now stands in a much more favourable political position. It has achieved this transformation in large part through symbolic, acts particuarly the transition to

'New Labour', and the reform of Clause IV which had for decades been the symbolic heart of British socialism.

In conclusion, it is clear that the course of post-1979 Conservatism can be analysed usefully, if by no means comprehensively, through a focus on changes in symbolic politics over the period. Such an approach helps explain the Conservative Party's generation-long tenure of power, and why this period is often understood as one of radicalism. Analysis at this level also explains why perceptions of competence, radicalism and coherence have waned during the premiership of John Major. Above all, transformations in the symbolic aspects of British politics over time may help explain both the rise of Conservative Party electoral hegemony and its seemingly immanent demise.

Public Sector Reform in Australia and New Zealand

Christopher Pierson
University of Nottingham

'Globalisation and the Changing Governance of Welfare States: Superannuation Reform in Australia'

Superannuation

It is forty years since Richard Titmuss drew attention to the importance of occupational welfare – that is, those forms of entitlement to welfare that derived from a person's work record and status – and, above all, to occupational pensions (Titmuss 1958). In the intervening period occupational pensions have become an ever more important source of income security in old age, now covering about one in four old persons in all OECD countries. They have also been an important source of income inequality in old age. The pattern of coverage varies considerably between countries but has everywhere tended to be skewed towards high-income groups (see World Bank 1994, pp.162-200). As growing attention has been focussed upon the 'problem' of population ageing and as increasing doubts have been raised about the capacity of states (and the willingness of their citizens) to fund adequate state pensions, so the salience of superannuation has risen for international policy-makers (witness, for example, the widely-influential 1994 World Bank report, Averting the Old Age Crisis).

The crucial date in the emergence of 'Super' (the inevitable Australian truncation) was the negotiation of the Accord Mark II between the ALP and the ACTU in autumn 1985. Previous trades union interest in superannuation had been quite limited, though it had been raised during Gough Whitlam's premiership and had played a part in a number of industrial disputes in the early 1980s (Shaw 1986; Mann 1993, p.36). Facing difficult economic circumstances in the autumn of 1985, Treasurer Paul Keating was anxious to secure a 2 per cent real wage cut in the 1986 wage round. The trade-off for this restraint was to be an income tax cut plus government support for an ACTU claim for a 3 per cent productivity increase for 1986-8 to be paid not as wages but as employer contributions to superannuation funds for their employees (Kelly 1994, p.206). In June 1986, the Conciliation and Arbitration Commission, responsible for setting general terms and conditions of employment under Australia's high-centralised wage setting system, agreed to incorporate superannuation payments (up to 3 per cent of ordinary time earnings) as a part of its award settlement. Thus 'Super' first emerged as a part of the awards process and as a means of increasing the rewards to labour without raising wages and salaries.

In the 1990 General Election campaign, again as part of its revised Accord with the ACTU, Labor declared its support for an increase in award-based superannuation to 6 per cent of ordinary time earnings. In 1991, the Industrial Relations Commission (inheriting the wage-setting responsibilities of the Conciliation and Arbitration Commission) declined to support the principle of superannuation contributions above 3 per cent. This, along with the failure of employers to honour award superannuation for as many as a quarter of workers so entitled, formed the prelude to the government's major initiative for compulsory superannuation – the Superannuation Guarantee Charge – introduced on 1st July 1992.

Compulsory Superannuation

In essence, the 1992 legislation required all employers to make a minimum contribution on behalf of their employees into appropriate superannuation funds. Employers who fail to make such payments become liable for a tax, the Superannuation Guarantee Charge (SGC), which will be used to purchase superannuation for their employees. Attendant provisions make it cheaper for employers to comply with their obligations rather than pay the SGC. In the first instance, the level of payments was set at 3 or 4 percent of ordinary time wages (depending on the size of the employer) but this is scheduled to rise by increments to reach nine percent by 2002/3. The legislation also anticipated the introduction of an employee contribution of 3 per cent of wages (Dawkins 1992). The latter measure was incorporated in the 1995/6 Federal budget which anticipated employee contributions reaching 3 per cent by 2000. The Budget also included plans for the government to 'repackage' previously announced income tax cuts as a means-tested matching contribution to employees' savings which would raise Super contributions for some employees to 15 per cent of earnings, (Willis 1995).

The 'Super' funds themselves (numbering about 1500) are heavily regulated but private. Most are trustee corporations with the trustee boards controlled equally by the representatives of capital and labour. Funds conform to three basic models: union-initiated industry-wide funds with members drawn from across a particular industry or occupational sector, single employer funds and master trust funds in which contributions form a variety of sources (the self-employed, small employers) are directly managed by insurance companies. In practice, the union-initiated industry funds have proved to be especially popular. Trustee boards generally meet no more than four times a year and day-to-day management of funds is usually devolved to private insurance companies or life houses (Olsberg 1995; Toohey 1995). The whole process is regulated (in some detail and at considerable cost) under the Superannuation Industry (Supervision) Act introduced in 1993.

There is now an element of bipartisanship in superannuation policy. In part, this relates to the 'private' nature of the rights acquired by superannuitants. At the same time, it reflects the incrementalism inherent in Australia's federal political institutions and the common interest that all governments have in off-loading some of the future liabilities for pension provision from the state. Nonetheless, the new Coalition government's first budget has put in doubt the idea of a 'matching state contribution' for employees' Super payments and it may not move any further towards Labor's eventual target of 15-18 per cent of earnings devoted to compulsory superannuation,(*Sydney Morning Herald*, 8/96).

Superannuation Assessed

This is the barest outline of the 'Super' story. A full assessment of the policy would require an account of the arcane changes in the taxation of superannuation benefits and the complex structure of fund regulation, as well as an investigation of the rather variable response of employers to Labor's reforms. Some of this detail we can legitimately avoid, since my interest is in the rather narrower question of whether Labor's Super policy can be seen as a new mechanism for securing social democratic ambitions or, perhaps a little more modestly, for maintaining the sorts of outcomes with which welfare states have traditionally been identified.

Just such a positive view of superannuation reform is indeed taken by the ALP and its sympathisers. Indeed, 'Super' has sometimes been presented by both its trades union and governmental initiators as the centrepiece of Labor strategy of the past decade, (see Olsberg 1995; Willis 1995; Kelty in Kelly 1994, pp.285-6). This account of 'Super as strategy' certainly owes much to the systematizing power of hindsight. But from its modest origins, as part of a deal to prevent a wages break-out, by the mid-1990s superannuation had come to be seen as a multi-purpose mechanism for meeting the governmental challenge of an ageing population, raising the retirement income of all Australians and increasing national rates of saving (and consequently) investment and economic growth. It was also celebrated as the most substantial product of the sustained Accord process between ALP governments and the ACTU. Above all, it was defended as a policy which managed to reconcile the ALP's twin (and seemingly irreconcilable) ambitions of opening up the Australian economy to international competition whilst maintaining a commitment to social justice. In the words of one sympathetic insider, the ALP's record could be seen as 'combining egalitarian social policies with economic policies attempting to enhance economic efficiency, within the framework of a consensual incomes policy' (Whiteford 1994, p.253).

There is a longstanding tradition in Australia of securing social security directly through the occupational structure, rather than indirectly through the state's social security apparatus. This has applied not only to the setting of wages by the industrial courts but also to the provision of work-related benefits as, for example, in the case of employer-provided sickness pay (see Castles 1992). In many ways, occupational superannuation corresponds to this model. It arose originally in sector-specific wage deals in, for example, the building and construction industry and amongst pulp and paper workers (Shaw 1986). It was then extended much more generally through the awards system of centralised wage bargaining (from 1986 onwards) and finally mandated as an employer responsibility under the Superannuation Guarantee Charge legislation in 1992.

In so far as the ambition of superannuation policy was to an extend a form of 'middle class welfare' enjoyed by an affluent minority to the rest of the working population, it can be said to have met with some success. In 1983, less than 40 per cent of employees (and fewer than 10 per cent of part-time workers) were covered by superannuation. By 1994, this proportion had increased so that 87 per cent of the workforce enjoyed superannuation cover. The advance was still more pronounced amongst women employees (who have traditionally been over-represented in part-time, low-waged and casual employment and correspondingly under-represented in superannuation schemes) with coverage moving from 24 per cent in 1988 to 72 per cent in 1991 and thence to 85 per cent in 1994. Once fully implemented (at a rather improbable point still some forty years' distant), the reforms would also have a very significant impact upon the income replacement function of the age pension. The government estimates that a person earning an average wage over a forty year period and in receipt of 9 per cent employer contributions over that time would enjoy a 68 per cent increase in retirement income compared with receipt of the aged pension alone, (Willis 1995, pp.20-1).

Breadth of coverage and adequacy of income replacement rates are important features of any satisfactory pension system. A social democratic pensions system might, in addition, be expected to institutionalise an element of redistribution in respect of contributions or benefits or both. Throughout the superannuation reform process, the Labor government argued that the major instrument of income redistribution in old age would be the flat rate, non-contributory but means-tested age pension. This has been described as 'an essential cornerstone of the Government's retirement incomes policy', (Willis 1995, p.9). There is a clear expectation that, as superannuation matures, a declining proportion (or even absolute number) of the aged will be entitled to the means-tested pension. The capacity to provide a 'generous' age pension is said to depend upon the declining number of eligible clients, (just as the 1980s saw some tightening of eligibility but some improvement in replacement rates). In its 1995 budget proposals, the government anticipated the introduction of employee contributions to superannuation (rising by increments to 3 per cent by 2000) which would trigger an element of matching means-tested government contributions. In essence, the government promised to match employee contributions to superannuation funds up to a maximum of 3 per cent of average weekly earnings. Support was focussed upon low and middle income earners, with state contributions tapering to disappear completely for a worker earning twice national average wages. In this modest way, the government proposed to introduce an element of redistributive funding into the superannuation process itself (the funding for governments' means-tested matching contribution was described as a 'repackaging' of delayed personal tax cuts originally promised in 1992!)

With the package of government measures fully implemented, lower-waged workers could look forward to replacement rates in excess of 100% although the income-related element of superannuation coverage means that, upon some measures, higher earners would gain much more from the policy. Nonetheless, the government was anxious to demonstrate 'the progressive nature of Australia's retirement incomes system':

> 'the lower pre-retirement income is, the higher the proportion of an individual's retirement income that comes from the age pension and the Government's superannuation initiatives. Furthermore, the bulk of retirement income for lower income groups comes directly from Government assistance (in the forms of the age pension, tax concessions and now the direct Government contributions). Conversely, for those on higher incomes, the bulk of their retirement income comes from their own (and their employers') contributions. Finally ... the Government's superannuation initiatives increase the real retirement incomes of individuals, relative to what they would have received had they relied solely on the pension, by more than 60 per cent.' (Willis 1995, p.14)

The Critics

Given the scale of the monies involved (with nearly $200 billion under management by the Super funds and with the expectation that as much as 12 per cent of income may come to be mandated for superannuation contributions), opposition to superannuation reform has been surprisingly muted. It was not a big issue in the 1996 election campaign and though the Coalition government has resisted further growth in the allocation of resources to Super, it has not yet sought to reverse the general direction of Labor policy. There have been critics from the right, who resent the state's earmarking of such a large element of individual's personal income, and from some sections of industry, who resent both the additional non-wage labour costs and the control of investment decisions by trades unionists which the co-management of Super funds implies (on the latter, see Mann 1993). Some critics argue that with 85 per cent of the Super funds $185 billion assets invested within Australia, superannuation has set up a new and surrogate form of Australian protectionism at the future pensioners' expense, (Pender 1995). In the context of this article, I am more concerned with criticisms that have come from the left and the poverty lobby, particularly those that focus upon the distributional consequences of the new regime.

One line of criticism – a longstanding 'minority' opinion in Australian left-of-centre thought- is that Labor's reforms fail to secure forms of social citizenship corresponding to those of the more progressive Western European states (see, for example, Beilharz et al 1992). Upon such an account, Labor failed to use its period of sustained incumbency to rehabilitate state welfare as something in which all of the population might participate, fashioning its reforms within the prevailing Australian tradition of low social expenditure and means testing. It coupled this with an 'economic rationalist' enthusiasm for micro-economic reform (presiding over flattened tax regimes and growing income differentials). Superannuation emphasises individual entitlement, leaving the state pension as a means-tested safety net for those without an adequate employment record.

Other critics focus more directly upon the distributional consequences of the ALP reforms. Whatever its other vices, the old Australian pensions regime, which combined strong tax progressivity with means-tested benefits, was quite strongly redistributive. The newer regime combines a much less progressive personal taxation system with a quite regressive pattern of tax expenditures used to subsidise superannuation contributions. Tax concessions cost about $5.6 billion in 1995. With the expansion of the scheme (and the introduction of matching government funding for some employee contributions), this figure will rise in coming years. The greatest tax expenditures go upon those who make the largest contributions, generally those with higher incomes. Even the government's own figures suggest that the gain for higher incomes earners (at twice the average weekly wage) may be twice that for below average earners (those at 75 per cent of the weekly average), (Willis 1995, p.10). Since it was the tax saving associated with the growth of superannuation which was supposed to give the federal government the scope to improve the age pension (and other benefits), this pattern of tax expenditures is likely to be a source of concern.

There is also a fear that private superannuation will tend to do least for those with a record of part-time or intermittent work at low wages – a group within which women are over-represented. The aspiration to extend the benefits of superannuation beyond a well-paid securely employed and disproportionately male population may be a worthy one. But there is a legitimate concern that low-waged workers cannot afford to give up 12 per cent of their present wages in superannuation contributions and that those with relatively little to contribute will find their payments eaten up by administrative and management charges (parallelling the position with personal pensions in the United Kingdom). For such workers, compulsory superannuation may be a dubious benefit, leading to the slightly improbable situation in which the replacement rate of their pension may exceed 100 per cent (that is, workers receiving more in age pensions that they earned as wages). Pensioners' groups giving evidence to the Senate's Standing Committee on Superannuation in the run-up to the introduction of the SGC in 1992 opposed the reform, favouring a tax levy to pay for a universal non-means tested age pensions payable at age 60, (Mann 1993, pp.47-8). They feared that, despite ALP assertions to the contrary, an age pension paid only to a (poorer) minority of the community would be vulnerable to erosion, leaving this pensioner population adrift of growing affluence elsewhere in the waged and superannuitant population.

There are also a number of complex 'knock-on' consequences of the compulsory savings involved in superannuation (though the equity consequences of these remain rather obscure). Clearly, the income foregone in superannuation contributions is likely to have an impact upon levels of private saving. If in the long run, returns to Super funds were comparatively low (which given the current conservatism of Super institutional investors seems possible), pensioners might have fared better by making their own investment decisions. There is also a potential trade-off between superannuation contributions and housing tenure. Castles & Mitchell (1995) draw attention to the possibility that greatly increased contributions to superannuation may impact upon existing high levels of home ownership. These high levels of home ownership (around 80% for pensioner households) have helped to lessen the costs of those on retirement incomes and have been an important source of income for those whose smaller income coincides with a smaller household. For some marginal households, the costs of superannuation may foreclose the mortgage route to owner occupation.

A 'Super' Social Democracy?

In the light of all this evidence, is it appropriate to see the ALP's superannuation policy as a surrogate form of social democratic politics – and one that is peculiarly appropriate to a society fully open to the impact of international economic forces?

A number of preliminary points are in order. First, we should not expect that superannuation policy would carry the full burden of Labor's claim to have been a social democratic party. Consideration of a range of other issues – including employment policy, policy on health and education, approaches to native title as well as the approach to the regional and international economy – would be essential to making such a judgement. Secondly, social democracy is a fairly generic term covering a broad range of parties, policies and practices. Even in its so-called 'Golden Age', international experience of social democracy was very varied and the Australian tradition has always, to some degree, been exceptional. Nonetheless, we are likely to think of a more equal citizenship and the moderation of economic inequality as normally being key objectives of social democratic politics. Finally, given that social democrats are concerned with that which can be done (and given that they hold to a rather unheroic vision of where the outer limits of the possible lie), it is probably more appropriate to measure their policies against existing or emergent alternatives elsewhere rather than against some more absolute criteria of a good social order.

Within these limits, 'Super' may seem to have much to recommend it. Critics have noted that Australia's welfare arrangements are stronger on redistribution than upon citizenship (a reflection of the means testing tradition). In some ways, 'Super' reverses this trend. It is not as strongly redistributive as the age pension but it is more inclusive (for the economically active). In a European context, the implication that income maintenance across the population in retirement may mean greater benefits for the more affluent has been widely accepted as the price of political support for universalism (Esping-Andersen 1990). Of course, this still remains a wage earners' welfare state rather than a citizens' welfare state – but it is run alongside policies whose ambition is to raise levels of economic activity and maximise employment.

In practice, social democrats have been concerned to raise incomes for the less well off, even if this has also benefitted those further up the income profile. They have also characteristically been concerned to promote economic growth as a way of generating positive-sum distributional gains, (with 'everyone a winner'). If fully implemented and sustained over the next forty years, 'Super' should generate a substantial improvement in the retirement income of those in the lower half of the wages profile. It should also raise levels of investment (and thus the rate of economic growth). 'Super' might also be amended to improve its redistributive capacity, as in the means-tested matching contributions proposed in the 1995 Budget or, for example, by crediting unwaged work, childcare or other forms of community participation outside the formal workforce. The fact that contributions are made to private funds and not to the state opens up the possibility that clients with similar records of contribution may end up with quite differing pension entitlements and may detract from the sense of shared citizenship that an entirely state-run pension system might encourage. But the boost thus given to domestic capital markets and the partial protection of pensioners' assets from state interference (and a corresponding willingness to pay the equivalent of an additional 10 per cent of income in social insurance contributions) may be a trade-off worth having. The alternative, in which a universal or near-universal basic pension is relentlessly squeezed, the benefits of the state earnings-related pension are constantly redefined (downwards), whilst the balance is to be made up by citizens subscribing to a wide range of (expensive and confusing) private savings instruments, is not very attractive. The commitment to allow the means tested age pension to do most of the work of redistribution in old age is, of course, extremely vulnerable to a change of political circumstances. But, in practice, even the most 'private' of pension systems are vulnerable to political change since almost every government (outside New Zealand) runs a regime which grants tax concessions to pensions premia and/or benefits. These are permanently vulnerable to substantial change (and have been repeatedly changed in the United Kingdom, for example).

One should not be too sanguine about what superannuation can do. Essentially, it is being funded out of a reduction in take-home wages. One may not wholly believe those neo-classical economists who insist that labour's remuneration is fixed in such a way that whatever is claimed as a deferred wage (paid into superannuation accounts) is simply foregone as take-home pay. But this is certainly the basis upon which the ALP sold its reform, (see, for example, Willis 1995) and it is clear that the principal redistribution effected by the reform is either between different employees or across individuals' life-cycle (from their working to their non-working years). Superannuation is not really a vehicle for redistributing wealth between capital and labour. We have also seen that even the redistribution amongst employees may be regressive – with tax expenditures benefitting the more affluent rather than the poorer, whose economic status might be more effectively improved through increased spending on public services and/or an increase in the basic age pension. Despite the private (though compulsory) nature of superannuation, its benefits are also acutely vulnerable to a deft transposition of the goalposts by a cash-strapped government.

Despite these reservations, 'Super' is likely to present an attractive option for social democratic (and perhaps other) politicians elsewhere. As Herman Schwartz has argued (forthcoming)Australia's unusual social democracy may have a few lessons for social democrats elsewhere, especially in Western Europe. This is, so he argues, because the Australian labour movement has long faced the sorts of circumstances (of internationally mobile capital and debt-ridden states) which define the 'new' circumstances of European social democracy exposed to global economic forces. Australia's social democratic strategies are seen to be peculiarly well adapted to these circumstances with a smaller but more distributive social state and much social protection delivered directly through the employment relationship. Whilst the threat of demographic disaster has been wildly over-stated, it is certainly the case that pensions' funding and reform represents an acute and deep-seated challenge for western Europe's social democracies in the coming decade. This problem is made still more difficult where politicians respond to the challenges of the international economy by bearing down on public deficits and public expenditure (whether at nation state or European Union level). Many European politicians will wish to transfer effort from a universal state pension towards some form of secondary pension (public or private) built upon some form of guaranteed minimum retirement income.

Yet for all its attractions, the Australian model may not travel well. First, the existence of social insurance in a European context means that citizens will feel that they have already contributed to their pensions (even though pensions are actually financed on a pay-as you-go basis). This means that a problem of 'double payments' (involving a generation that must pay for the pensions of both its elders and itself) arises in a much more acute and politically problematic way in Europe. Introducing Australian forms and levels of means testing in Europe would be difficult not only for cultural and political reasons, but also because of its interaction with existing areas of social provision, poverty and employment traps and so on. Australia is one of the lowest taxed counties in the OECD. It commits a lower percentage of GDP to public pensions than any other OECD country, including the parsimonious Britain (cited in *The Economist*, 30th November 1996). In countries with a much larger existing tax take and much greater financial commitment to public pensions, introducing additional charges of as much as 12 per cent of take-home pay is likely to be widely resisted. Putting 'Super' in place was very much a product of the Accord process, of the special relationship between the ACTU and the ALP, the nearly unique Australian system of awards wage setting and the capacity of the ACTU to deliver on its side of the Accord bargain. Levels of trust and compliance between the

ACTU and the ALP were similar to those that existed in the most successful days of Swedish SAP-LO co-operation. In fact, with the industrial relations reforms that are now imminent in Australia (and with the ending of the special union-government relationship that prevailed during the ALPs' years in power), it may be that the Labor decade represented a 'window of opportunity' for reform. Path dependency and inertia may sustain the process in Australia – but it may be much more difficult to introduce parallel reforms in a European context.

Conclusion

Even the successes of social democratic politics have been rather mundane and inglorious. In so far as there has been a process of globalisation in recent years it has tended to intensify or recast those constraints which are part of the birthright of the social democratic approach. Within these tight constraints an area for policy discretion and innovation remains. It is within this context, and in its contrast with other contemporary policy initiatives, that we should judge the ALP's superannuation policy.

Bibliography

Australian Bureau of Statistics, *Australian Social Trends*, ABS, Canberra, 1994.

Australian Department of Social Security, *DSS Clients*, DSS, Canberra, 1995.

P.Baldwin, *Beyond the Safety Net: The Future of Social Security*, Department of Social Security, Canberra, 1995.

K.Banting, 'Social Policy Challenges in a Global Society', in D.Morales-Gomez & M.Torres, *Social Policy in a Global Society*, Toronto, International Development Research Centre, 1995.

P.Beilharz et al, *Arguing About the Welfare State*, Allen & Unwin, 1992.

F.Castles, *The Working Class and Welfare*, Allen & Unwin, 1985.

F.Castles, *Australian Public Policy and Economic Vulnerability*, Allen & Unwin, 1988.

F.Castles, 'On Sickness Days and Social Policy', *Australian and New Zealand Journal of Sociology*, 28/2, 1992.

F.Castles, 'On the Credulity of Capital', *Australian Quarterly*, 68/2, 1996.

F.Castles & D.Mitchell, *Designing for the Future : an institutional view of the Australian Welfare State*, Australian National University, 1995.

P.Cerny, *The Changing Architecture of Politics*, Sage, 1990.

P.Cerny, 'International Finance ...', *International Organization*, 1995.

B.Chapman et al, 'Perspectives on Australian Unemployment', in F.Gruen (ed), *Australian Economic Policy*, Australian National University, 1991.

R.Cox, 'Global restructuring', in R.Stubbs & G.Underhill (eds), *Political Economy and the Changing Global Order*, Macmillan, 1994.

J.Dawkins, *Security in Retirement*, Australian Government Publishing Service, Canberra, 1992.

B.Easton & R.Gerritsen, 'Economic Reform: Parallels and Divergences', *The Great Experiment*, Allen & Unwin, 1996.

G.Esping-Andersen, *Politics Against Markets*, Princeton University Press, 1985.

G.Esping-Andersen, *The Three Worlds of Welfare Capitalism*, Polity Press, 1990.

G.Esping-Andersen, *Welfare States in Transition: National Adaptations in Global Economies*, Sage/UNRISD, 1996.

F.Gruen & M.Grattan, *Managing Government*, Longman Cheshire, 1993.

P.Hirst & G.Thompson, *Globalization in Question: the International Economy and the Possibilities of Governance*, Polity Press, 1996.

R.Jessop, 'The Schumpeterian Workfare State', in R.Burrows & B.Loader, (eds), *Towards a Post-Fordist Welfare State*, Routledge, 1994.

Martin Jones, 'Full Steam Ahead to a Workfare State?', *Policy and Politics*, 24/2, 1996.

Michael Jones, *The Australian Welfare State: Evaluating Social Policy*, 4th edition, Allen & Unwin, 1996.

P.Kelly, *The End of Certainty: Power, politics and business in Australia*, Allen & Unwin, 1994.

J.Kelsey, *The New Zealand Experiment: A World Model or Structural Adjustment?*, Auckland University Press/Bridget Williams Books, 1995.

K.Mann, 'Supermen, Women and Pensioners: The Politics of Superannuation Reform', *International Journal of Sociology and Social Policy*, 13/7, 1993.

D.Mitchell & A.Harding, *Changes in Poverty Among Families During the 1980s*, NATSEM, Canberra, 1992.

K.Ohmae, *The Borderless World*, Collins, 1990.

D.Olsberg, 'Australia's retirement income revolution: a Finnish system "down-under" ', *Scandinavian Journal of Social Welfare*, 4, 1995.

L.Panitch, 'Globalisation and the state', in R.Miliband & L.Panitch, (eds), *Socialist Register*, 30, 1994.

H.Pender, 'The Super Protectionism', *Australian Financial Review*, 22nd August, 1995.

J.Perraton et al, 'The Globalisation of Economic Activity', *New Political Economy*, 2/2, 1997.

C.Pierson, *Socialism After Communism: The New Market Socialism*, Polity, 1995.

A.Przeworski, *Capitalism and Social Democracy*, Cambridge University Press, 1985.

M.Pusey, *Economic Rationalism in Canberra*, Cambridge University Press, 1991.

P.Saunders, *Welfare and Inequality*, Cambridge University Press, 1994.

F.Scharpf, *Crisis and Choice in European Social Democracy*, Cornell University Press, 1991.

H.Schwartz, 'Social Democracy from Down Under', *Comparative Politics*, forthcoming.

D.Shaw, 'Trade union and worker participation in the control of superannuation funds', in E.Davis & R.Lansbury, (eds), *Democracy and Control in the Workplace*, Longman Cheshire, 1996.

T.Skocpol, *Protecting Soldiers and Mothers*, Harvard University Press, 1992.

B.Toohey, 'Super Politics', *Australian Financial Review*, 23rd August, 1995.

G.Therborn, 'Welfare States and Capitalist Markets', *Acta Sociologica*, 30/3-4, 1987.

R.M.Titmuss, *Essays on the Welfare State*, Allen & Unwin, 1958.

R.M.Titmuss, *Social Policy*, Allen & Unwin, 1974.

P.Travers & S.Richardson, *Living Decently*, Oxford University Press, 1996.

K.van Keesbergen, *Social Capitalism*, Routledge, 1995.

P.Whiteford, 'Income Distribution and Social Policy under a Reformist Government', *Policy and Politics*, 22/4, 1994.

R.Willis, *Saving for our Future*, Treasury of the Commonwealth of Australia, Canberra, 1995.

World Bank, *Averting the Old Age Crisis*, Oxford University Press, 1995.

Public Sector Reform in Australia and New Zealand

Jonathan Boston
Victoria University of Wellington

'Learning the Art of Government Formation under Proportional Representation: Recent New Zealand Experience'

Acknowledgements

The research upon which this paper is based forms part of a much larger three-year study of the impact of MMP on New Zealand's political system. This project – the New Zealand Political Change Project – is funded by the New Zealand Foundation for Research, Science and Technology. The other members of the project team are Stephen Levine, Elizabeth McLeay and Nigel S.Roberts.

Introduction

On 6 November 1993 – the same day as the general election – New Zealanders voted in a referendum by a margin of 54 per cent to 46 per cent to replace their long-standing first-past-the-post electoral system with a system of proportional representation. A variant of the German additional member system, the new voting system is referred to in New Zealand as mixed-member proportional (MMP). The first MMP election was held on 12 October 1996. As expected, but in contrast to every election since the 1930s, neither of the major parties – Labour and National – secured a majority of the seats in the unicameral chamber, the balance of power being held by New Zealand First (NZF), a relatively new centrist party with populist-cum-nationalist leanings. Accordingly, for the first time in several generations intensive inter-party bargaining was required in order to form a government. After almost two months of more-or-less parallel negotiations with Labour and National, NZF's leader, Winston Peters, revealed on 10 December that his party would form a majority coalition government with National. The dramatic nature of the occasion was magnified by the fact that the major parties were not informed of NZF's decision until the precise moment of Peters' public announcement on nationwide television. A rather inelegant 70 page coalition agreement was signed the next day and the first MMP government was sworn into office by the Governor-General on 16 December.

Drawing on the insights of coalition theory and the practice of government formation in comparable democracies, this paper explores how the key political actors responded to the new and uncertain dynamics of coalition building brought about by MMP. In particular, it considers the constitutional and political context surrounding the formation of the first MMP government, the preparations for coalition building, and the bargaining strategies adopted by the three main participants in the process (that is, Labour,

National and NZF). It also examines the outcome of the government formation process and reflects on how this initial experience may affect subsequent rounds of coalition bargaining. The paper draws upon a range of sources, including media reports of the coalition negotiations, published and unpublished coalition documents, and interviews with various participants in, and those connected with, the negotiations.

MMP and the 1996 Election

With a unitary state, a first-past-the-post (or simple plurality) electoral system, and a long tradition of majoritarian single-party governments, New Zealand was once regarded as 'a virtually perfect example of the Westminster model of democracy' (Lijphart 1984:16). This tradition ceased in late 1993 with the vote in favour of MMP. As in other 'mixed' systems, electors have two votes under MMP – a party (or list) vote and a constituency vote (see Boston et al 1996). But unlike most other mixed systems, it is the *party* vote which determines the overall share of seats won by each party in Parliament. Hence, if a party secures 25 per cent of the party vote, it is entitled to a similar proportion of seats. Under the new system, a party must win either 5 per cent of the party vote or at least one constituency seat in order to qualify for any of the 55 list seats in the expanded 120-member chamber. Of the 65 constituency seats, 60 are *general* seats and 5 are *Maori* seats. Unlike the German system, therefore, New Zealand has retained its previous system of dual constituencies.

The 1993 referendum vote in favour of proportional representation coincided with a very close election result (Vowles & Aimer 1994; Vowles et al 1995). The governing National party won 50 seats in the then 99-member Parliament, giving it the barest of majorities – a far cry from the large parliamentary majority it had achieved in 1990. Labour – the main opposition party – staged a significant recovery, winning 45 seats compared with only 29 seats three years earlier. The remaining four seats were secured by several relatively new political movements: two went to the Alliance (a left-of-centre grouping of five parties – the Democrats, Greens, Liberals, Mana Motuhake and New Labour); and two were secured by NZF (one of these being a Maori constituency, thus ending Labour's fifty-year hegemony within Maoridom). Under the previous first-past-the-post electoral system it would normally have been possible for a government, even with a one-seat majority, to retain effective control over the legislature for a full three-year parliamentary term. The impending introduction of MMP, however, prompted a significant political realignment. During the 1993-96 Parliament no fewer than 13 MPs shifted their party allegiance: National lost nine MPs and Labour four. Three new parliamentary parties – the Christian Democrats, the Conservatives and United – were formed from amongst the ranks of the defecting MPs. Hence, by the time of the first MMP election in October 1996 there were seven parties represented in the legislature, the most since the emergence of New Zealand's modern party system. Additionally, many extra-parliamentary parties were formed to contest the first MMP election, the most important being ACT – a strongly market-oriented liberal party with substantial backing from the business community.

Prior to the 1993-96 Parliament, New Zealand had experienced single-party majority governments for more than half a century. Yet within the space of three short years it witnessed four different types of government (several of them twice): majority single-party government; minority single-party government; majority coalition government; and minority coalition government (Boston et al 1996, pp.94-7). The first coalition emerged in September between National and the sole MP of the Right-of-Centre party (later renamed the Conservatives) and lasted for a year. The second, and more significant, coalition was formed in late February 1996 between National and United – a liberal/centrist party and the largest of the new political groupings with seven MPs – and continued until the election. But while the forms of government changed with remarkable speed, the transition to MMP was characterised by two underlying constants: first, throughout the period National retained the support of the majority of MPs; second, Labour, the Alliance and NZF adopted a consistent oppositional stance.

Table 1

The Results of the 1996 General Election

A	*B*	*C*	*D*	*E*	*F*	*G*
National	33.8	33.9	-1.2	30	14	44
Labour	28.2	31.1	-3.6	26	11	37
NZ First	13.4	13.5	+5.1	6	11	17
Alliance	10.1	11.3	-6.9	1	12	13
ACT	6.1	3.8	+3.8	1	7	8
United	0.9	2.1	+2.1	1	0	1
Others	7.5	4.3	+0.7	0	0	0
total	100.0	100.0		65	55	120

Key

A = *party* B = *party votes (%)* C = *electorate votes (%)*
D = *electorate: votes change since 1993*
E = electorate seats F = *list seats* G = *total seats*

Note: United and ACT did not contest the 1993 general election.

Source: Boston et al 1997

No fewer than 21 parties contested the first MMP election (Boston et al 1997). Of these, six won seats (see Table 1). While both major parties lost support, National, as expected, remained the largest party – winning 33.8 per cent of the party vote. Yet with 44 seats in the 120-member Parliament, it was 17 seats short of the 61 seats needed for an overall majority. Labour secured 28.2 per cent of the party vote and 37 seats – seven seats less than National and 24 seats short of a majority. Contrary to expectations, Labour strongly outperformed the other main opposition parties, the Alliance and NZF. Support for the Alliance, which had exceeded 18 per cent in 1993, fell to just 10 per cent of the party vote. NZF, by contrast, significantly improved its share of the vote – the only party of those to have won seats in 1993 to do so. Remarkably, it also secured all five of the Maori seats, no doubt reflecting the fact that both its leader and deputy leader (Tau Henare) are Maori. None of the three parliamentary parties formed since 1993 crossed the 5 per cent threshold. However, United managed to secure a single constituency seat and thus retained a presence in Parliament. Of the parties without MPs to contest the election, only ACT crossed the 5 per cent threshold, winning eight seats on a party vote of 6.1 per cent.

Preparing for Coalition Building

Following the referendum endorsement of MMP, senior politicians and public servants made every effort to prepare themselves, and the political system generally, for the advent of a multiparty Parliament. For instance, a group of senior parliamentarians conducted a study tour of five European countries in early 1995 to investigate the management of Parliament and the process of governing under conditions of coalition and/or minority government. Fact-finding trips to Europe were also undertaken during 1994-96 by senior public servants, including staff of the Cabinet Office, the State Services Commission and the Treasury.

At the most senior political level, the Prime Minister, Jim Bolger, took a particular interest in the formation and management of coalition governments during meetings with various political leaders, including the former Irish Prime Minister, Albert Reynolds, and the German Chancellor, Helmut Kohl. Also, of course, Bolger acquired direct experience of some of the issues of leading minority governments and coalitions via the turbulent political events preceding the first MMP election. Helen Clark, the Leader of the Opposition, was already familiar with policy making under proportional representation having studied in Sweden as a post-graduate politics student in the 1970s. Nevertheless, the move to MMP prompted her to take a renewed interest in the dynamics of multiparty politics. She was particularly attracted to the idea of single-party minority government, as practiced by the Norwegian Labour party and the Swedish Social Democrats. However, the prospect of her own party receiving sufficient electoral support to emulate these examples was never good.

All in all, by the time of the first MMP election there was a reasonable understanding on the part of most senior politicians and public servants of how coalition building was conducted elsewhere, especially in Ireland and Scandinavia. Indeed, copies of several recent Irish coalition agreements were in circulation during the coalition talks in late 1996. Interestingly, too, a number of people who were involved in advising the coalition negotiators were also familiar with some of the academic literature on coalition theory (for example, Laver & Schofield 1990). However, there is little evidence that any of the insights from this literature had a significant bearing on the conduct of the negotiations. Similarly, the unprecedented character of the new political environment and the unpredictable nature of NZF (see below) raised doubts about whether the experience of other countries in coalition building furnished many useful lessons for party negotiators as they sought to form the first MMP government.

Among the many issues to attract attention during the transition to MMP was the appropriate role of the public service during the government formation process. The State Services Commission, as the central agency responsible for the overall conduct and management of the public service, was keen to ensure that any assistance rendered by departmental officials to those involved in any inter-party negotiations did not undermine the principle of public service neutrality. To minimise this risk, detailed guidelines were issued by the Commission (1996) on how departments should respond to requests for assistance. In short, the guidelines required the negotiating parties (including ministers in the caretaker government) to submit any questions they might have to the Commission. Where it was deemed appropriate these were to be forwarded to individual departments for action. However, departments were only allowed to supply *information* and *analysis*; the tendering of specific policy *advice* was not permitted. Thus, while officials could estimate the costs of a particular proposal or comment on its practical implications, they could not evaluate the proposal's merits. In the event, these guidelines were closely adhered to after the 1996 election, with at least one of the party's involved in the coalition formation process (that is, National) making extensive use of the analytical resources of government departments.

Government Formation: The Context

By comparison with the situation in many other multi-party democracies, the bargaining environment for the formation of the first MMP government was relatively uncomplicated: New Zealand's constitutional rules are simple and straightforward; a single party – NZF – held the balance of power; and the policy divisions between the 'core' parties (that is, Labour, National and NZF) were not impossibly large.

Against this, none of the key political actors had extensive experience in coalition formation, the internal cohesion of the parties in the new political environment remained uncertain, and NZF was a relatively new and untested political force (only four of its 17 MPs having had any previous parliamentary experience). Moreover, it was recognised that the outcome of the inter-party negotiations could shape the structure of parliamentary politics for many years to come. Although NZF had campaigned on a slogan that it was 'the only party that can beat National', its leader had repeatedly refused to rule out a coalition with his main adversary. Accordingly, the stakes were high and there was considerable uncertainty surrounding the outcome of the negotiations.

As befits a country with no entrenched constitution, there are few constraints of either a constitutional or extra-constitutional nature on the process of government formation. Nor are there any formal rules governing the conduct of inter-party negotiations. For instance, unlike the situation in a number of other countries, there is no provision for appointing formateurs or informateurs, and the head of state, the Governor-General, is not expected to play an active role in the negotiations (Bergman 1993; Boston et al 1996: 106-7; Strom et al 1994; State Services Commission 1995). Rather, the process is left more-or-less entirely in the hands of the party leaders. They are thus at liberty to adopt whatever means seem appropriate in the circumstances in order to form a viable government.

Apart from the requirement in the Constitution Act (1986) for ministers to be MPs, there are no restrictions on the size, composition or structure of the cabinet. Nor are there any constitutional constraints on the timetable for forming a government. Admittedly, the Constitution Act requires Parliament to meet within six weeks of the return of the writs from a general election (in effect, around two months after the election). This, of course, does not mean that a new government must be sworn in by the time the House resumes. It does, however, place a strong political incentive on the relevant parties to complete the process of government formation before Parliament sits. In relation to the 1996 general election, Parliament was legally required to meet no later than 13 December. Without doubt, this date was seen as pivotal by the coalition negotiators.

Unquestionably, the most important constitutional principle is that a government must secure and retain the confidence of Parliament. However, a government only requires a simple majority to win a vote of confidence. This means that a minority government is perfectly able to retain the support of the House as long as a sufficient number of potential opponents abstain (an option which became available in 1996 as a result of changes to Parliament's standing orders).

This latter consideration was highly relevant to the inter-party dynamics following the first MMP election (Boston & McLeay 1996). As explained, both major parties needed the support of other parties in order to govern – whether as part of a formal coalition or as single-party minority governments. For its part, National could almost certainly rely on the support of ACT and United. This gave it 53 seats. Although this was eight seats short of a majority, it was three more than the combined support of Labour and the Alliance. Hence, if NZF supported National, or at least abstained on votes of confidence, National would be able to remain in office. Moreover, if NZF could be persuaded to enter a coalition with National, it would be possible to form a two-party majority government. Commanding 61 seats against a potential combined opposition of 59, this outcome would represent a genuine minimum winning connected coalition. In these circumstances, the support of ACT and United would be virtually irrelevant – unless, of course, one or more National or NZF MP were to defect.

Labour, by contrast, was in no position to form a majority government. For one thing, there were significant policy differences between its two potential coalition partners, the Alliance and NZF. For another, the Alliance (1996a) had categorically ruled out participating directly in a government unless a common platform had been negotiated (presumably with Labour) prior to the election and submitted to the voters. Labour had equally categorically rejected this approach, preferring to leave the process of coalition building until after the election. Nevertheless, the Alliance had also declared that it would support a Labour-led government in preference to a National-led government. Hence, Labour could more-or-less rely on the Alliance's 13 votes. Yet in order to govern Labour, had no choice but to seek the support of NZF. If the two parties could form a coalition, they would command 54 seats. While this was seven seats short of a majority, significantly it was one seat more than the combined votes of National, ACT and United. Accordingly, as long as the Alliance was prepared to vote with Labour and NZF, or at least abstain, the two parties would always be able to muster a simple majority.

Without doubt, then, the results of the 1996 election placed NZF in a uniquely privileged position. A 'strong' party (Laver & Shepsle 1996), it commanded the crucial 'median' legislator along the dominant socio-economic issue dimension (or left-right continuum). In New Zealand the control of this position is all the more critical because most of the other potentially relevant issue dimensions or social cleavages – ethnic, religious, urban-rural, foreign policy, postmaterialism, regionalism and gender – have only limited political salience (Boston et al 1996: 58-9; Nagel 1994). This was highlighted by the failure of certain parties based on these dimensions (for example, the Christian Coalition and the Aotearoa party) to secure parliamentary representation. Furthermore, while there has been the potential for issues relating to Maori cultural identity and reparation claims under the Treaty of Waitangi (1840) to become a major source of polarization along party lines, so far this has not occurred. Needless to say, if other issue dimensions had been more salient and if the parties' relative positions along these dimensions had varied significantly, then the bargaining environment would have been correspondingly more complicated.

With NZF holding the balance of power, and the Alliance having ruled itself out of participating in a government, there were relatively few politically feasible governing options. Assuming that both Labour and National were prepared to coalesce with NZF, there were effectively two issues to resolve: did NZF wish to be part of a government and would it side with Labour or National? Depending on its responses, there were four possible outcomes: a National-NZF majority coalition government; a National minority government (with explicit support from NZF, and possibly also from ACT and United); a Labour-NZF minority coalition government (with explicit support from the Alliance); and a Labour minority government (with explicit support from the Alliance and NZF).

Uncertainties

The core parties faced no shortage of risks and uncertainties as they sought to establish the first MMP government. For instance, there were the problems of predicting the likely bargaining posture of the other negotiating teams, deciding how far to compromise in the interests of reaching an agreement, and assessing the likely durability and electoral impact of prospective governing arrangements. Such problems are, of course, commonplace where government formation entails negotiations between two or more parties. Nevertheless, for the coalition negotiators in New Zealand in late 1996 such uncertainties were compounded by the novelty of the political dynamics generated by MMP and their relative inexperience in serious inter-party negotiations. In particular, the new environment raised questions as to whether previous political verities and assumptions could usefully be employed to predict the likely behaviour of political adversaries and potential coalition partners. There was, in short, much to learn.

Undoubtedly the principal source of uncertainty for the major parties concerned the policy orientation, cohesiveness, reliability and future electoral appeal of NZF. Established in 1993 by Winston Peters – a mercurial, ambitious, photogenic and relatively charismatic politician – the party was largely the product of personal conflicts and policy divisions within the National party following its return to office in 1990. Faced with a large budget deficit and under the influence of its powerful market-liberal wing, National embarked upon a programme of harsh expenditure cuts (including significant cuts in social welfare benefits); it also abandoned some its key electoral commitments, most notably the promise to abolish the unpopular surtax on National Superannuation (the tax-funded, 'universal' pension scheme) introduced by the previous Labour government. Although a cabinet minister, Peters publicly criticised some of the government's decisions, thus breaching the doctrine of collective responsibility. He was eventually sacked from his post as Minister of Maori Affairs and subsequently ejected from the National party caucus.

In founding NZF, Peters sought to create a party that would appeal to those disaffected by the failure of recent Labour and National governments to keep their campaign commitments and be well positioned to capture the middle ground under the new MMP electoral system. He thus put together a policy programme combining various ideological strands: an anti-monetarist and mildly protectionist economic policy (including opposition to the sale of state assets, stricter limits on the sale of New Zealand land and resources to overseas interests, and export incentives), greater universality in the area of social policy, a strong commitment to the public health and education systems, the advocacy of compulsory superannuation, and a firm approach to law and order issues. During the three years leading up to the first MMP election, he also campaigned vigorously against political patronage, cronyism and sleaze, the misuse of public funds, and tax evasion by big business. He later added an anti-immigration theme to his existing nationalistic, anti-establishment and populist political message. Given this platform, NZF not surprisingly attracted virtually no support from the country's political, bureaucratic and economic elites (Boston et al 1996: 39-40).

In policy terms, there can be little doubt that by the time of the 1996 election NZF was closer to Labour than National. This was particular so in relation to health care and education – both pivotal issues during the 1996 campaign. The main exceptions were industrial relations (where Peters' hostility to trade unions placed his party closer to National) and fiscal policy (where NZF was somewhat nearer to National in terms of overall levels of public expenditure, the appropriate rate of debt repayment and opposition to tax increases). There were also issues where NZF's policy stance placed it equidistant from the two major parties (for example, both Labour and National opposed the idea of compulsory superannuation and rejected the idea of repurchasing the Crown's recently sold forestry assets).

To the extent that a party can be expected – in line with the predictions of at least some theories of coalition bargaining (Narud 1996) – to choose a partner that is closest to it across a range of important policy dimensions, NZF seemed most likely to coalesce with Labour. Such an outcome appeared all the more probable in the light of opinion poll evidence showing that NZF supporters preferred a deal with Labour over National by a margin of five-to-one (Dekel 1996). However, it was also evident that NZF's campaign commitments might be an unreliable indicator of the party's eventual coalition preference.

First, Peters was bound to exercise a decisive influence on the party's choice of a coalition partner, even if the formal decision lay with the party's caucus and ruling council. As a former National MP, his natural sympathies were widely assumed to be conservative. Moreover, his commitment to some of the causes he had espoused was regarded by many as highly suspect. To critics, his selection of policy positions owed more to electoral considerations than genuine convictions. It was thus unsurprising to many that during the coalition talks between mid-October and mid-December 1996 NZF's negotiators readily sacrificed some of the party's central policy planks (for example, much tighter restrictions on foreign investment, the repurchase of the Crown's recently sold forestry assets, and a reduction in the size of the cabinet).

Second, in the months immediately preceding the election, the party's policy position on a number of issues – including housing and foreign investment – underwent significant modifications. Such changes were attributed to the influence of several ex-National MPs – Michael Laws and Peter McCardle – who joined the party in early 1996, and the subsequent demotion (or sacking) of a number of longer-serving party spokespersons. If policies could be changed with such ease before and during an election campaign, they could equally be changed after the election. To compound problems, many of the party's policy positions were poorly developed, amounting to little more than general expressions of sentiment rather than detailed commitments. They were thus amenable to a range of possible interpretations.

Third, as already noted, most of the party's MPs after the 1996 election had no previous parliamentary experience, many were relatively new members of the party, and most had never been involved in detailed policy formulation at the national level. Accordingly, their level of understanding of some of the more complex areas of public policy was limited. Nor was it clear how committed they would feel to policy positions that they had taken virtually no part in developing. Indeed, during the coalition talks, some NZF negotiators had little hesitation in advocating positions at variance with their party's election commitments. While the policies of NZF represented something of a moving target, another major source of difficulty for both Labour and National related to the party's longer-term cohesion, durability and reliability as a coalition partner. Electorally, the party drew support from a disparate and inherently unstable combination of interests. On the one hand, it had strong backing from generally conservative retired people (especially in Peters' Tauranga constituency) angered by the major parties' broken promises on superannuation. On the other hand, it enjoyed widespread support amongst Maori voters. Yet apart from their shared position as low-income earners and their preference for NZF to align with Labour, these two groups have relatively little else in common. Reflecting the party's diverse electoral base, seven of its 17 MPs are Maori; similarly, seven had previously been members of the National party while at least five had previous Labour party links. Given this situation, there was some doubt as to whether all 17 MPs would remain with the party during the full three-year parliamentary term. Also, notwithstanding its 13 per cent support at the first MMP election and its success in winning all five Maori constituencies, the party's likely longer-term electoral appeal was difficult to predict.

If there was uncertainty over NZF's programmatic commitments and long-term viability, there was much less over its interest in holding office. Peters and other senior party figures seemed genuinely keen to be part of a government rather than act as a support party. In some respects, this quest for office was surprising. As already mentioned, the party had only four MPs with parliamentary experience. In order to enter a coalition, it would therefore be necessary for a number of novice MPs to hold ministerial positions. In New Zealand such appointments are highly unusual, being seen as politically risky.

Both major parties also faced their own internal uncertainties. National's electoral performance in 1993 and 1996 had been disappointing, and its loss of support during both campaigns had been blamed largely on its leader's lacklustre performance. Bolger was thus aware that securing a deal with NZF would be vital not merely to his party retaining office but also to him remaining leader. Yet any coalition with NZF posed difficulties. Many National MPs had little but contempt for Peters, regarding him as an unscrupulous opportunist. More important, there was no desire to make any concessions that might undermine the economic policy framework painfully erected over the previous decade. Indeed, if National were to make significant concessions on economic policy it risked losing many supporters, and possibly several MPs, to ACT. And of course the loss of even a single MP would make the management of a coalition with NZF all the harder since the government would be dependent on either ACT or United to get its legislation through the House. There was also concern over the long-term electoral prudence of a deal with NZF. For instance, by going into opposition, the party would be better able to rejuvenate its leadership and frontbench and, given a normal anti-government swing, might be able to form a majority government with ACT at the next election. It would thereby avoid a potentially acrimonious and damaging relationship with NZF.

Labour had similar reservations about a deal with NZF. Yet having already spent six years in opposition, it had little option but to seek an agreement with its only viable coalition partner. In attempting to forge a coalition it was constrained not only by its need to keep faith with its key electoral commitments (especially in areas like education, health care, housing and industrial relations), but also by the need to retain the support of the Alliance. Unlike National, however, it did not face a serious risk of MPs defecting if it made some significant policy concessions. Nor was there a strong likelihood of a challenge to Helen Clark's leadership if the party failed in its bid to form a government.

Government Formation: The Process

Immediately following the election, Peters announced that his party would hold parallel negotiations with each major party, the aim being to see which would offer the best deal. Once the negotiations were complete, and only then, would the NZF caucus and ruling council be invited to make their choice between the two detailed coalition packages on offer. In effect, therefore, NZF was inviting both major parties to tender for the right to govern. Peters also emphasised that previous personal conflicts and anti-government campaign rhetoric would not prevent a deal with National – if this proved to be the best available. Additionally, he insisted that the coalition negotiations should be conducted in absolute secrecy, demanding that an agreement on confidentiality be signed by the major parties before serious discussions commenced.

Strategically, the decision to conduct parallel negotiations appears to have been designed to maximise uncertainty concerning NZF's likely coalition partner, thereby placing maximum pressure on Labour and National to compromise. To be successful, of course, both major parties had to agree to play according to NZF's rules. If either had refused, Peters' bargaining position would have been seriously weakened. In the event, both accepted the proposed approach. For its part, Labour believed that it had little choice but to do its best to secure a change of government. To have refused to negotiate on NZF's terms risked alienating supporters, condemning the party to another three years in opposition, and forfeiting the opportunity both to implement progressive social policies and expunge the taint of its enthusiasm for market liberalism during the 1980s. For National, the desire to retain office, together with Bolger's determination to remain Prime Minister, appear to have dominated the party's calculations.

Having agreed to the idea of parallel negotiations, the major parties spent the following two months constantly guessing as to NZF's true intentions and ultimate coalition preference. Within both parties there were those who believed that Peters and his team always intended to side with Labour and that the negotiations with National were simply designed to secure the maximum concessions from the Labour camp. Equally, however, there were those who believed the opposite, namely that the intention was always to go with National and that the purpose of the parallel negotiations was to wring concessions from the government. Yet whatever NZF's underlying game plan (if it in fact had one), its negotiators pursued their talks with both sides with equal seriousness for more than seven weeks and at no stage prior to 10 December indicated which way things were moving (or most likely to move). Peters, in particular, remained utterly inscrutable. In fact, he went to considerable pains to keep both sides guessing, socialising late into the night at Wellington cafes (as was his well-known passion) with Labour and National MPs and their advisers. Similarly, in his limited public comments and speeches during the talks he made various remarks which seemed deliberately designed to give each side cause for comfort and discomfort. Politically, it was a masterful performance.

Equally remarkable, the much maligned secrecy agreement was closely adhered to. At no stage did the NZF negotiators reveal to their Labour or National counterparts what policy concessions were being offered by the other side; a firm Chinese wall thus divided the two sets of negotiations. Similarly, there were relatively few leaks from the major parties' negotiating teams and caucuses. Hence, while it was possible to guess where Labour and National were likely to adjust their policy positions (for example, it was widely expected that Labour would forego its plan to increase the top marginal tax rate and that National would be prepared to delay its promised second round of tax cuts due in mid-1997), neither side had a good feel for what the other was prepared to offer NZF in order to secure a deal. This, of course, served to intensify the difficulties for the negotiators, making it all the harder to decide whether, and to what extent, to compromise on particular policy issues. There was a further problem: for the party which ended up in opposition there was the risk that its policy compromises would eventually be revealed (notwithstanding the secrecy agreement). Not only might this cause political embarrassment but it might also render it harder to oppose certain government policies.

Labour's negotiators were particularly concerned that the two major parties might make concessions that would ultimately prove unwise or excessively costly. They also wished to avoid a situation in which, in an endeavour to outbid each other, one of the parties might be prepared to offer Peters the finance portfolio, thereby giving him control of the powerful Treasury department. In an effort to minimise such risks, informal approaches were made to senior National party figures. However, these were rebuffed. As matters transpired, Labour remained resolute in its refusal to offer Peters a senior finance role. National, however, conceded at the eleventh hour, agreeing to split the finance portfolio – with Peters taking the senior economic role of Treasurer and Bill Birch, the existing Minister of Finance, retaining a role (as Minister of Finance) in the management and control of public expenditure. From all accounts, this concession was crucial to NZF's decision to coalesce with National.

As to the formal mechanics of the coalition negotiations, the procedures adopted were not unlike those used in many other countries (Budge & Keman 1990; Laver & Schofield 1990; Strom 1990). For instance, negotiating teams were selected by each of the parties (comprising senior MPs and party officials). Most attention, at least initially, focussed on issues of policy rather than the composition of the cabinet. Also, as often happens elsewhere, much of the detailed policy work occurred outside the formal negotiating sessions. Similarly, the respective party caucuses were briefed from time to time, and were given the opportunity to set the broad parameters within which the negotiations were conducted. They were not closely involved, however, in the negotiations surrounding the size of cabinet, the allocation of cabinet posts between the parties, or the determination of specific ministerial portfolios.

The parallel nature of the negotiations generated understandable difficulties for NZF. With few experienced MPs, a small caucus and few professional in-house advisers, the party was fully stretched in its efforts to negotiate more-or-less simultaneously with both major parties. Moreover, several of its senior members, including its deputy leader, Tau Henare, and the party president, Doug Woolerton, quickly lost interest in working through the full range of policy issues, and eventually withdrew from most of the formal negotiations. This placed an even greater load on the remainder of NZF's negotiating team. Not surprisingly in these circumstances, the major parties took responsibility for drafting the understandings which were reached on policy issues. However, NZF's legal adviser, Wayne Peters (one of Winston Peters' brothers), drafted the main text of the coalition agreement. This covered the obligations of the respective parties, the structure of the administration, the membership of the executive, and the management of the coalition.

The major parties adopted numerous tactics to secure the support of NZF MPs. At the policy level, concessions were deliberately made in areas known to be of interest to particular MPs. For instance, Peter McCardle, one of NZF's main negotiators and among its few experienced MPs, had a long-standing interest in employment policy. Both parties were thus quick to back some of his favoured schemes, notwithstanding their doubtful efficacy. Both parties also sought to accommodate Peters' passion for compulsory superannuation. Since neither was prepared to support his proposals directly, the solution adopted in each case was an agreement to hold a referendum on the issue.

Building up relationships with NZF MPs was another tactic employed by the major parties – partly as an intelligence gathering device and partly as a means of influencing the party's eventual coalition choice. Thus, various Labour and National MPs were assigned to strengthen their existing relationship with, or build a new relationship with, particular NZF MPs. Wider party and extra-party networks were also used for this purpose (for example, contacts were made with some NZF MPs via mutual friends, business associates or relatives). Consequently, a large web of informal contacts developed between the negotiating teams and extensive socialising became the order of the day. The Maori dimension received particular attention. Labour and National were mindful that seven of NZF's MPs were Maori and that the party had won over 40 per cent of the *party* vote in the Maori seats. Accordingly, both included a Maori MP in their negotiating teams. They also sought endorsement from various Maori groups and interests. Labour, in particular, used its extensive Maori networks to bring pressure to bear on the five NZF MPs in Maori constituencies.

The Outcome

By the end of the first week in December, and with Parliament due to meet no later than 13 December, substantive agreement had been reached by NZF with Labour and National on a wide range of issues. The relevant coalition documentation with both sides followed a standard format. For instance, under each policy topic, such as conservation or housing, there was a statement of general direction, a list of key policy initiatives, and a summary of the fiscal and legislative implications. Yet significant policy differences remained. Labour, for example, remained committed to its long-standing positions on such matters as accident compensation, housing policy, labour relations, and welfare benefits. Importantly, too, Labour wanted substantially higher public expenditure and a more redistributive focus than NZF. National, meanwhile, had moved its policy position on many issues, accepting NZF's pivotal demand for greater public expenditure, especially on education and health care (Boston 1997). It had also agreed to postpone its promised tax cuts, broaden the Reserve Bank's target range for inflation and abandon its controversial fiscal cap on the settlement of claims under the Treaty of Waitangi. In the final stages of negotiations – which continued during the crucial meeting of NZF's caucus and ruling council on 10 December – National offered further concessions, most notably on the structure of the public health care system. By virtue of these concessions, the policy differences between National and New Zealand had been significantly narrowed and, when taken as a whole, were not much greater to those which continued to separate Labour and NZF.

In deciding in favour of National, Peters and other NZF MPs subsequently argued that their caucus and ruling council were influenced by at least two major considerations. First, they claimed that a coalition with National offered a better chance of 'political stability' (Peters 1996). The problem with siding with Labour was that the government would ultimately be dependent on the Alliance in order to implement its policies. Although the Alliance – via a separate agreement with Labour – had offered to support a minority Labour/NZF government on matters of confidence and supply, it had reserved the right to withdraw its backing if the government acted in a manner 'significantly detrimental to the interests of the country' (Alliance 1996b: 2). For at least some NZF MPs, this opt-out provision was too open-ended and provided insufficient certainty.

Yet the claim that it was the Alliance which had destroyed Labour's chances is open to question. As already noted, a Labour/NZF government would have commanded more votes than the combined strength of National, United and ACT. Hence, only if the Alliance actively opposed a particular initiative by threatening to vote against the government would problems arise. But given the electoral risks of being seen to have brought down a Labour/NZF government, the Alliance was in a relatively weak position politically – and this was widely recognised. Moreover, if NZF MPs had been genuinely concerned about the potential risk posed by the Alliance it is strange that they made so little effort to influence the nature of the 'support agreement' reached between Labour and the Alliance; nor did they at any stage raise their concerns directly with Labour's negotiators. In any case, National's leader faced a restive caucus with several MPs publicly questioning the merits of a coalition with NZF. He was thus in no position to guarantee that none of his MPs would desert the party before the next election (thereby removing the coalition's parliamentary majority). Given these considerations, it is hard to sustain the claim that the 'Alliance factor' represented a decisive influence on NZF's coalition choice. It did, however, serve as a politically convenient excuse for rejecting Labour.

According to NZF, the second main reason for siding with National concerned the respective fiscal strategies of the major parties. Whereas National insisted on explicit and firm expenditure caps for three-years and a relatively rapid reduction in the level of public debt, Labour argued that the overall level of public expenditure was less important than the maintenance of budgetary surpluses. Labour's negotiators maintain that NZF's negotiating team, on having the technical issues explained, was prepared to accept the idea of a target range for the government's operating balance rather than an explicit expenditure cap. (The proposed target was for surpluses of 2.0-2.5 per cent of GDP, an extremely favourable fiscal position by international standards.) Yet, to the fiscal conservatives in NZF, National's approach seemed more prudent and convincing.

Of course, whether many NZF MPs actually understood the implications of what National was proposing is uncertain. For instance, the coalition agreement between National and NZF provides for only modest increases in public expenditure in nominal terms (around 2 per cent per annum), with no allowance for inflation. What is more, all the new policy initiatives outlined in the agreement are conditional on the government remaining within the designated fiscal parameters. Consequently, unless the economy performs strongly it will be extremely difficult to implement important elements of the coalition programme. Had the NZF caucus been fully aware of this, it may have been less inclined to back National.

Whatever the influence of the 'Alliance factor' and fiscal concerns on NZF's decision, other considerations most assuredly played their part. Despite the preferences of its supporters, some NZF MPs believed that it would be harder for the party to retain its distinctive 'brand' in a coalition with Labour. They also feared that Labour would take much of the credit for the new policy initiatives introduced by a centre-left government. By contrast, if the party sided with National, it would be NZF that could claim most of the credit for the government's 'softer' line in areas like education, health and social welfare.

Personal dynamics probably also contributed to NZF's decision. Notwithstanding the close relationship between Peters and Mike Moore (one of Labour's former leaders and a key negotiator), NZF MPs generally developed a better rapport with their National counterparts during the coalition negotiations. Whereas National's team appeared pragmatic and unthreatening, the NZF negotiators found some of their Labour counterparts arrogant, patronising, and inflexible. No doubt this partly reflected the strongly academic orientation of the Labour team (four of whom were previously university lecturers). From Labour's standpoint, few of the NZF negotiators had a strong grasp of the policy issues under discussion. Many of the informal negotiations were thus treated as 'tutorials' or 'training sessions'.

Finally, there was the issue of cabinet posts. As noted, National, albeit reluctantly, eventually agreed to Peters' request for a senior economic post. Labour, by contrast, refused. Similarly, National agreed to a greater representation of NZF within the executive than Labour. For instance, whereas Labour was prepared to support a two-to-one ratio within the executive (that is, with Labour having roughly two positions to every position held by NZF), National agreed to a formula under which NZF's share of positions will increase from eight (out of 26) to 11 by October 1998 (including eight within the 20-person cabinet). NZF will thus eventually hold 42 per cent of the positions within the government (despite commanding only 28 per cent of the coalition's seats), with almost two-thirds of its caucus being members of the executive. By international standards, this is a highly disproportionate level of representation (Budge & Keman 1990).

Conclusion

The introduction of MMP, as widely expected, ended the long-standing dominance of New Zealand's two major parties, thereby making necessary inter-party negotiations on government formation. Also, as expected, the balance of power after the first MMP election was held by a party – NZF – occupying the middle ground between Labour and National. Although centre parties often hold critical positions in multiparty parliaments (especially in a context of uni- dimensionality), the circumstances surrounding the formation of the first MMP government were unusual in several respects. For one thing, none of the party leaders had extensive experience in the dynamics of coalition building. For another, NZF – as a relatively new party with a populist bent – was not bound by previous coalition commitments or long-standing policy positions; it was also prepared to exploit its pivotal bargaining position in the new political environment to the full. Moreover, despite its consistent oppositional stance during the 1993-96 parliamentary term, it had deliberately left open the possibility of a coalition with its main adversary.

Given the particular configuration of circumstances following the first MMP election, NZF was able to secure the support of the major parties for a process of coalition formation via parallel negotiations. While it is not uncommon after an election for a centre party to hold discussions with parties both to its left and right, it is unusual for such negotiations to continue for several months. It is equally unusual for two detailed sets of coalition documents to be drafted employing more-or-less the same format (whatever their differences in content). But if NZF displayed remarkable skill in playing the two major parties off against each other in late 1996, its chances of doing so again are remote. Having formed a coalition with National, NZF will be treated very differently in the future by Labour. Equally, if NZF's electoral prospects have been harmed by siding with National, it may never again hold such a powerful bargaining position.

More generally, the events surrounding the formation of the first MMP government highlight the fact that considerations of policy space are by no means decisive in determining the coalition choices of political parties, particularly where a party has strong office-seeking tendencies and relatively weak programmatic commitments. NZF's decision to form a coalition with National also indicates that parties do not necessarily feel bound by the coalition preferences of their supporters, even when these are skewed overwhelmingly in one direction.

It remains to be seen how the first round of coalition negotiations under MMP affects the new electoral system's longer-term legitimacy and public support. On the one hand, the policies outlined in the National/NZF coalition agreement represent a shift back towards the centre of the political spectrum. This is bound to be welcomed by the 'median voter', as well as those who supported proportional representation on the grounds that it would put an end to the neo-liberal experiments of recent governments. On the other hand, the protracted nature of the coalition negotiations, NZF's eventual decision to support National, and National's willingness to trade so many cabinet posts to buy NZF's support, drew widespread criticism. Given that the introduction of MMP was prompted largely by public concerns over broken election promises by Labour and National, the spectre of NZF doing the same under MMP has done nothing to inspire confidence in the new system. Also, with the new coalition enjoying a parliamentary majority (albeit perhaps temporarily), there will be little evidence of the constraints on the power of the executive which some had hoped MMP might usher in. If the new coalition proves unstable and if it fails to deliver on its key commitments, public support for MMP is likely to be sorely tested. With a parliamentary review of the electoral system due in 2002, the long-term survival of the new system of proportional representation cannot be taken for granted.

References

Alliance, 'Statement on Coalitions and Other Arrangements', Wellington, September 1996a.

Alliance, 'Alliance Support for a Labour-NZ First Minority Government on Confidence Matters', Wellington, 10 December 1996b.

T.Bergman, 'Constitutional Design and Government Formation', *Scandinavian Political Studies*, 16/4, 1993.

J.Boston, 'Coalition Formation', in R.Miller (ed), *New Zealand Politics in Transition*, Oxford University Press, 1997.

J.Boston & E.McLeay, 'Forming the First MMP Government: Theory, Practice and Prospects', paper presented at the 1996 post-election conference,

Victoria University of Wellington, 6 December 1996.

J.Boston et al, *New Zealand Under MMP: A New Politics?*, Auckland University Press, 1996.

J.Boston et al, 'The 1996 General Election in New Zealand: Proportional Representation and Political Change', *Australian Quarterly*, 69/1, 1997.

I.Budge & M.Keman, *Parties and Democracy: Coalition Formation and Government Functioning in Twenty States*, Oxford University Press, 1990.

G.Dekel, 'Maori Voter Survey', Survey Research Unit, University of Waikato, 1996.

M.Laver & N.Schofield, *Multiparty Government: The Politics of Coalition in Europe*, Oxford University Press, 1990.

M.Laver & K.Shepsle, *Making and Breaking Governments: Cabinets and Legislatures in Parliamentary Democracies*, Cambridge University Press, 1996.

A.Lijphart, *Democracies*, Yale University Press, 1984.

J.Nagel, 'How many parties will New Zealand have under MMP?', *Political Science*, 46/2, 1994.

H.Narud, *Voters, Parties and Governments: Electoral Competition, Policy Distances and Government Formation in Multi-party Systems*, Oslo, Institute for Social Research, 1996.

W.Peters, 'An address to the people of New Zealand', Wellington, 10 December 1996.

State Services Commission, *Working Under Proportional Representation*, Wellington, 1995.

State Services Commission, 'Negotiations Between Political Parties to Form a Government: Guidelines on Support from the Public Service', Wellington, 1996.

K.Strom, *Minority Government and Majority Rule*, Cambridge University Press, 1990.

K.Strom et al, 'Constraints on Cabinet Formation in Parliamentary Democracies', *American Journal of Political Science*, 38/2, 1994.

J.Vowles & P.Aimer (eds), *Double Decision: The 1993 Election and Referendum in New Zealand*, Department of Politics, Victoria University of Wellington, 1994.

J.Vowles et al, *Towards Consensus? The 1993 Election in New Zealand and the Transition to Proportional Representation*, Auckland University Press, 1995.

Health Policy

Stephen Harrison
University of Leeds

'Evidence Based Medicine: Politics, Policy and Problems'

Introduction

Evidence-based medicine (EBM) is the doctrine that professional clinical practice ought to be based upon sound biomedical research evidence about the effectiveness of each diagnostic or therapeutic procedure ('intervention' hereafter). It is very much a common-sense aspiration for a health care system such as the National Health Service (NHS); after all, who wants to be the object of ineffective interventions? The argument that patients do not want care for its own sake but only for the improvement that it will bring to health has been put forward neatly by Evans as a thought experiment:

> 'Patients seek care in order to be relieved of some actual or perceived, present or potential, 'dis-ease'. The care itself is not directly of value; it is generally inconvenient, often painful or frightening. As a thought experiment, one could ask a representative patient (or oneself) whether he/she would prefer to have...a condition perceived as requiring care plus the best conceivable care for that condition, completely free of all...costs, or would prefer simply not to have the condition ... [C]are is not a good in the usual sense, but a 'bad' or 'regrettable' made 'necessary' by the even more regrettable circumstances of 'dis-ease'. It follows that patients want to receive *effective* health care, that is care [in respect of which] there is a reasonable expectation [of] a positive impact on their health!'[1]

EBM as Policy

The kind of reasoning which underlies Evans' formulation is now manifest in formal policy for the NHS; in 1993 health authorities were asked to begin to identify interventions of which they would in future purchase more and less, on grounds of effectiveness and ineffectiveness respectively.[2] Current official policy on EBM holds that

> 'The overall purpose of the NHS is to secure, through the resources available, the greatest possible improvement in the physical and mental health of the people ... In order to achieve this, we need to ensure that decisions about the provision and

[1] R.G.Evans, 'The Dog in the Night Time: Medical Practice Variations and Health Policy', in T.F.Andersen & G.Mooney (eds), *The Challenge of Medical Practice Variations*, Macmillan, 1991, pp.118-9, emphasis original.

[2] NHS Management Executive, *Executive Letter* EL(93)115, 1993.

> delivery of clinical services are driven increasingly by evidence of clinical and cost effectiveness, coupled with the systematic assessment of actual health outcomes.'[3]

This line of policy has been supported, at some expense, by two types of related development in the NHS. First, there has existed since 1991 a national research and development (R and D) strategy for the NHS, involving the creation of national and regional directors of R&D, the establishment of national and local research budgets to be the object of competitive bidding, and reorganisation of the flow of research fund through NHS hospitals.[4] According to the first national Director, the central objective of this strategy was to disaggregate the vast proportion (conventionally estimated at eighty percent) of health interventions stated never to have been the subject of proper evaluation into two categories: the effective and the ineffective. Second, a range of specialist institutions has been funded as the means of reviewing, collating and disseminating the findings of effectiveness research to the NHS; these include the Cochrane Centre at the University of Oxford; Effective Health Care Bulletins co-ordinated from the University of Leeds, the NHS Centre for Reviews and Dissemination at the University of York and the Outcomes Clearing House at the University of Leeds.

Theory and Politics of EBM

Two key theories underlie this whole strategy. The first defines 'sound evidence', that is, that which may be relied upon to contribute to the classification of an intervention as effective or ineffective, as evidence derived from studies conducted in a certain way held to be 'scientific'. This approach is typified in the influential 'hierarchy of evidence' (see Table 1) proposed by Canadian academics (and later modified in various ways) but widely cited as an authoritative definition of the soundness of scientific research purporting to demonstrate the effectiveness of medical and similar interventions.[5]

The principle which underpins this hierarchy is validity, that is the elimination from research findings of bias arising from any differences between patients treated by means of the intervention being researched and patients not so treated (that is, treated with other interventions or simply not treated). The pinnacle of the hierarchy is occupied by the randomised controlled trial (RCT) in which patients are conscientiously allocated randomly (and with informed consent) between the group who will receive the intervention under investigation and whatever group(s) with whom they will be compared: 'control' groups receiving perhaps placebos, or no treatment, and/or existing conventional treatment, as the case may be. Ideally, it is held, RCTs

---

[3]NHS Executive, *Promoting Clinical Effectiveness: a Framework for action in and through the NHS*, Department of Health, 1996, p.6.

[4]Department of Health, *Research for Health*, 1991; Task Force on R&D Funding, *Supporting research and Development in the NHS* (the Culyer Report), Department of Health, 1994.

[5]Task Force on the Periodic Health Examination, 'Report', *Canadian Medical Association Journal*, 121/9, 1979.

should be 'double blind', that is neither the treating clinician nor the patient should know which intervention they are receiving. This ideal cannot of course always be met; for instance it is hardly possible to conceal whether or not surgery is occurring or ethically to perform a dummy operation. Special methods, described as 'meta-analysis', have been developed in order to aggregate the results of several RCTs.

Table 1
The Hierarchy of Evidence

	Type of research
I	Strong evidence from at least one systematic review of multiple well-designed randomised controlled trials
II	Strong evidence from at least one properly designed randomised controlled trial of appropriate size
III	Evidence from well-designed non-randomised trials, single group pre-post, cohort, time series or matched case-controlled studies
IV	Evidence from well-designed non-experimental studies
	from more than one centre or research group
V	Opinions of respected authorities, based on clinical evidence, descriptive studies or reports of expert committees

Column 1 = *Level of validity of findings*

The second key theory upon which EBM is based is that the most useful, though not necessarily exclusive, method for disseminating sound research evidence as defined above to practising clinicians is the 'clinical guideline';[6] clinicians cannot be expected to read every research study relevant to their practice as it is published. The logic of guidelines is essentially algorithmic, that is, it guides its user to courses of (diagnostic or therapeutic) action, dependent upon stated prior conditions: 'if ... then' logic. The logic is also normative, that is, it tells the clinician what ought to be done. In general, guidelines do not claim to determine clinical action completely, and degrees of discretion are left.

The doctrine of EBM is by no means new and indeed the attempted popularisation in the United Kingdom of the notion that randomisation between comparison groups is a crucial means of avoiding bias in biomedical outcomes research dates from Cochrane's seminal Rock Carling Lecture of 1971, published the following year. As is often the case with ideas,

[6] NHS Executive, *Clinical Guidelines: Using Clinical Guidelines to Improve Patient Care within the NHS*, Department of Health 1996.

Cochrane's central insight took a long time to become officially, or widely, accepted and it seems likely that changes in social and political context were more important in allowing the widespread acceptance of the idea than any intrinsic 'rightness'.[7] In particular, EBM has strong appeal as a criterion for rationing NHS care at time of rapidly rising demand which coincides with a government agenda for tighter control of public expenditure.[8] It seems unlikely that in 1971, after a time when NHS resources underwent rapid growth in real terms, Cochrane had any concern to provide the tools to solve a policy problem of rationing. Indeed his main concerns were for what he saw as the genuine progress of science towards truth and for the avoidance of subjecting patients to ineffective (and therefore in his analysis, unnecessary) interventions. He was fiercely critical of the NHS in this second respect:

> 'I once asked a worker at a crematorium, who had a curiously contented look on his face, what he found so satisfying about his work. He replied that what fascinated him was the way in which so much went in and so little came out. I thought of advising him to get a job in the NHS, it might have increased his job satisfaction ...'[9]

But it is easy to see how Cochrane's ideas, twenty years on, serve both to provide criteria for health services rationing and to legitimate those criteria. First, the approach draws on 'science' and all its modernist trappings of truth, progress and so on; it can therefore be presented as rational and politically neutral. Second, the approach is one which leaves doctors in charge, albeit with a shift of influence away from the clinical practitioner and towards the academic/epidemiologist/health services researcher. This is important for the political acceptability of rationing; in line with the general occupational status of doctors and the high public esteem in which they are held; several studies have shown that the medical profession is seen by the public as by far the most legitimate actor in making rationing decisions.[10] Third, as noted above in relation to Evans' thought experiment, and despite the science, it can be presented as common sense.

Overall, then, EBM looks like an elegant resolution to the problem of matching demand for health care technologies to the level of resources available. Although it is logically possible, as advocates of EBM regularly point out, that EBM might reveal the effectiveness of interventions and thereby increase demand, policymakers do not in practice believe this to be likely; the retiring national NHS Director of R and D has been quoted as claiming that the implementation of research findings in clinical practice might save £1 billion per annum. The main argument of this paper is that EBM as official policy is based upon a number of naivities, both conceptual and

---

[7] J.W.Kingdon, *Agendas, Alternatives and Public Policies*, Little Brown, 1984.

[8] S.Harrison & D.J.Hunter, *Rationing Health Care*, Institute for Public Policy Research, 1994.

[9] A.L.Cochrane, *Effectiveness and Efficiency: Random Reflections on Health Services*, Nuffield Provincial Hospitals Trust, 1972 p.12.

[10] See for instance C.Heginbotham, 'Rationing', *British Medical Journal*, 304, 1992.

political, and the following sections review three that are current: the weakness of the assumptions which underpin the use of guidelines as the main mode of implementing EBM, the existence and advocacy of various criteria for rationing which rival effectiveness, and the existence of epistemologies (theories of knowledge) which rival that upon which RCTs are based.

Implementing EBM

The choice of clinical guidelines as the main vehicle for implementing EBM is, at one level, a logical one; as noted it is unrealistic to expect the average busy clinician to read and understand all research papers relevant to his or her own sub-specialty, discriminate between acceptable and inadequate research methods, interpolate findings with existing knowledge, and modify routine clinical practice accordingly. At another level, however, it is an assumption which is somewhat naive; it is hard to imagine another policy arena in which what amount to a set of bureaucratic rules (the phrase is used in a technical, not pejorative sense) would be thought to be self-implementing. Yet this is effectively the approach which has been taken in most research to date on this topic: essentially as an issue of communication, with studies mainly focused upon dissemination strategies.[11] Communication is, of course, a necessary condition for implementation of a policy such as EBM, but it is not a sufficient condition. Logically, other necessary, though individually insufficient, conditions are as follows ... [12]

Adequate resources

Implementation clearly depends on the clinician's access to the material resources required for conformity to the guideline: drugs, equipment and so on. But non-material resources are essential too. Critical examples are skill and time; there is a recurrent theme in the sociology of the caring professions which explains 'corner cutting' behaviour, such as hasty diagnosis or the 'labelling' of clients, as an inherent and inevitable response to scarcity of time.[13]

Incentives

It is clear that one cannot simply assume that communication of a guideline provides sufficient incentive for a clinician to comply with it. Intrinsic incentives might include the source of the guideline's being seen as authoritative; there is some evidence that locally-determined guidelines are more likely to be seen as such,[14] even though it might be expected that

[11]See for instance Effective Health Care 8, *Implementing Clinical Practice Guidelines*, Universities of Leeds & York, 1994.

[12]For the concept of 'perfect implementation', upon which this analysis draws, see L.A.Gunn, 'Why is implementation so difficult?', *Management Services in Government*, 33/4, 1978; for more detailed analysis, see S.Harrison, 'Knowledge into Practice: What's the Problem?', *Journal of Management in Medicine*, 8/2, 1994.

[13]M.Lipsky, *Street-Level Bureaucrats*, Sage, 1980.

[14]Effective Health Care, *op cit.*

nationally-determined ones would be the most technically expert. Otherwise, little seems to be known about intrinsic incentives, though there are a number of studies underway into the role of 'opinion leaders' and into the possible impact of 'academic detailing' (that is, marketing preferred clinical practice to individual doctors in much the same way that drug companies market their products by face-to-face contact). Extrinsic incentives such as economic rewards need also to be considered. Whatever incentives exist for compliance with guidelines may, of course, be wholly or partly offset by disincentives. Again there is little systematic knowledge, though covert organisational imperatives can often subvert ostensible policy; one United Kingdom study found that clinicians were prepared to manipulate audit results by modifying casenote entries to maintain the appearance of reaching targets.[15]

Co-ordination

A good deal of the literature about clinical guidelines makes the implicit assumption that what matters is the diagnostic and therapeutic behaviour of individual clinicians. Given the intellectual origins of much guidelines work in the puzzle of medical practice variations, this not surprising. Yet it may be misleading; in practice the success of health care can depend on whole teams or chains of health workers performing the correct tasks correctly. This particularly true in nursing care, where the twenty-four hour commitment multiplies the scope for error and omission, and community care, where multi-agency, multi-professional working has the same effect. The formal mathematics are gloomy; on the relatively optimistic assumptions that a chain of ten health workers is involved in following a guideline for a particular patient, and that there is 0.95 probability that each will fully comply, the total probability of the patient getting precisely the care specified is 0.95 to the power 10, or little better than evens! This calculation, however, departs from what occurs in the real world in that it assumes that the compliance probabilities for each individual worker are independent. This is unlikely to be the case; people's behaviour is usually affected by the social (in this case, workplace) context (or organisational 'culture') in which they find themselves.

Rival criteria for rationing

The attractions of effectiveness as a criterion for rationing are obvious; as noted, it can seem (or be made to seem) ludicrous to suggest that anyone might want ineffective care. However, it is a matter of fact that people sometimes do value care for its own sake, irrespective of its effectiveness. Any GP has the story of a patient who demands antibiotics for a viral infection despite being assured that it will do no good, and the public often value heroic but obviously vain rescue attempts, whether medical or at sea or

---

[15] N.Black & E.Thompson, 'Obstacles to medical audit: British doctors speak', *Social Science and Medicine*, 36/7, 1993.

on the mountains. Moreover, the use of effectiveness as a rationing criterion rests heavily on the ability of the relevant social actors to agree upon what constitutes a 'reasonable' expectation of a positive treatment outcome. Such agreement is not always forthcoming, as was graphically demonstrated in the much-publicised case of 'Child B' who was denied a second bone marrow transplant by her local health authority; NHS haematologists and a private consultant differed over the probable effectiveness of such treatment whilst her family felt that any positive probability was acceptable.[16]

A policy of effectiveness implemented through EBM promises authoritative answers to both kinds of dispute. Second, it allows the rationing process to be defended as the authority of 'science'. Third, it leaves the decisions in the hands of doctors which, as noted above, concords with public preferences. But there remain other rationing criteria which have their attractions too. Without any claim to be exhaustive the remainder of this section describes four: the 'rescue principle', entitlement, cost-utility, and equity.

The 'rescue principle'

The term 'rescue principle' was coined by Dworkin,[17] to refer to the belief that the moral imperative of medicine is to attempt to help those who are acutely ill or whose lives are threatened. The moral content of such action is in the process (hence 'attempt') rather than in the outcome. Although the application of such a principle clearly implies potentially significant opportunity costs (since others may suffer whilst resources are expended on hopeless cases) it is one which seems to receive wide support in public policy generally, underpinning as it does such services as air/sea rescue and mountain rescue. Whatever its internal incoherences or unsought consequences, the rescue principle is one to which people subscribe. It is also the formal moral basis of medicine;

> 'Resources are finite and this may ... infringe the ordinary relationship between patient and doctor ... The doctor has a general duty to advise on ... efficient utilisation (but this) is subordinate to his professional duty to the individual...'[18]

Entitlement

Strictly speaking (and in contrast to the detailed statutory provision for social security) United Kingdom citizens have no rights to publicly-financed health care. Rather, the legalities are accomplished via the Secretary of State's duty, originally contained in the NHS Act of 1946, to provide a 'comprehensive' health service. Litigation in pursuit of treatment therefore typically takes the form of an action against the Secretary of State (or

[16] For a different example, see N.Freemantle & S.Harrison, 'Interleuken 2; the Public and Professional Face of Rationing in the NHS', *Critical Social Policy*, 13/3, 1993.

[17] R.Dworkin, 'Will Clinton's Plan be Fair?', *New York Review of Books*, 13 Jan 1994.

[18] British Medical Association, *Handbook of Medical Ethics*, 1980, p.35.

his/her agent, a Health Authority) for breach of statutory duty. Whilst courts have been generally unsympathetic to plaintiffs in such cases, people do see themselves as having rights to treatment irrespective of calculations of effectiveness. Denied arterial surgery on the ground that his continued smoking increased the risks of treatment and reduced the probability of benefit, a 62 year old Wakefield man was quoted as saying

> 'I have worked since I was fourteen up until recently and paid a hell of a lot in taxes to the government both in income taxes and on the forty cigarettes a day I smoked. Surely it is not too much for me to ask to have an operation that might ease my pain in my old age and make me live a little longer.'[19]

Cost-utility

Unlike effectiveness, which provides no formal basis for making comparisons between different interventions for different diseases, cost-utility analysis both provides a lowest common denominator concept in terms of which the outcome of any intervention may be assessed and provides for the calculation of the unit costs of producing such outcomes. The best-known operationalisation of this outcome measure is perhaps the Quality-Adjusted Life Year.[20] Despite a number of technical problems,[21] this approach possesses a good deal of technical appeal for its culmination in a 'league table' of health care interventions, from which policymakers can in theory maximise the health outcomes from any given level of expenditure.

Equity

Equity may be defined as equal treatment for persons with equal need. In practice, equity can be extremely difficult to operationalise according to a single definition, since there are options about whether it is the distribution of resources, health care interventions or of health outcomes that are taken to be important, as well as options about the social dimensions of inequity (race, class, gender, locality) which are held to be policy priorities. However, there is a sense in which increasing the degree of equity with which health care is distributed in a society forms the rationale for any system of third party payment, whether tax-based, social insurance or private insurance. In other words, such systems pool resources and spread risks so that (to varying extent in different systems) people can receive health care when needed without immediate out-of-pocket payment of the full cost.[22]

---

[19] *Yorkshire Evening Post*, 26 August 1993, p.1.

[20] QALY; for a straightforward account of the basic calculation of which see Gudex 1986. This formed the core of the 'Oregon formula' applied to the determination of Medicaid priorities in the eponymous American state. The World Bank used the Disability-Adjusted Life Year (DALY) in its recent review of world health and there is at present increasing interest in the EUROQOL which aims to support cross-national measurement of quality of life.

[21] See, for instance, K.Gerard & G.Mooney, 'QALY League Tables: Handle with Care', *Health Economics*, 2/2, 1993.

[22] Harrison & Hunter, *op cit*.

Rival Epistemologies

The epistemological underpinnings of randomised controlled trials and meta-analyses which, as has been seen above, form the basis of the EBM movement are not necessarily identical with the way working clinicians think about evidence of effectiveness. This has recently been examined in a small-scale, but important American study of clinicians, in which the traditional biomedical model of research, based in laboratory methods, is contrasted with that entailed by RCTs.[23] This contrast is summarised in Table 2.

Table 2
Alternative Epistemologies in Medicine and Research

Traditional Biomedical/ Laboratory Research	*Outcomes Research/Randomised Controlled Trials*
Reveals cause-effect mechanisms (via aetiology, pathology etc)	Demonstrates statistical relationships from past experience
Provides knowledge of what *ought to be* effective, and why	Provides knowledge of what is *likely to work*, irrespective of why
Based on deterministic models	Based on probablistic models
Underpinned by realist/ naturalist epistemology	Underpinned by empiricist/ positivist epistemology
Espoused by working clinicians	Espoused by epidemiologists and health services researchers

For the sake of contrast the Table presents the two epistemologies as ideal types, though in the real world it seems unlikely that many clinicians are not influenced by elements of both. The point, however, is that in the last analysis it is the traditional model that predominates in medical decisionmaking. (In contrast, as Table 1 above makes clear, the health services research model places clinical observations at the bottom of the hierarchy of evidence.) The traditional model, taught to and espoused by clinicians, relies on the discovery of cause-effect mechanisms by the observation of the way in which disease processes develop over time and impact upon normal physiological processes. Treatment is therefore very much a logical process of intervening in the aetiology (natural history) of a disease so as to arrest, reverse or retard it. Expressed in more philosophical/technical terms, the model is deterministic (that is, it assumes that clinical events necessarily have causes which can be identified and, in principle, modified) and realist or naturalist (that is, it entails a belief in a world of objectively real entities whose nature can be observed).

[23] S.Tanenbaum, 'Knowing and acting in medical practice: the epistemological politics of outcomes research, *Journal of Health Politics, Policy and Law*, 19/1, 1994.

The outcomes/RCT model is the foundation of epidemiology and the relatively new discipline of health services research. It consists primarily of the inference of cause-effect relationships from past statistical relationships between treatment and outcomes. It is therefore less concerned with disease processes than with establishing what interventions are likely to be effective, irrespective of why. In technical philosophical language, the model is therefore probabilistic (that is, one where the cause-effect relationships are inherently uncertain) and empiricist (that is, one where knowledge can only justifiably be derived from past experience.

The practical consequence of these apparently rather abstruse observations is that clinical doctors are more likely to be influenced in their practice by their own (and close colleagues') experience with similar types of patient, and by their own reasoning about treatment logic, than by the publication of meta-analyses of large numbers of cases.

Concluding remarks

In the space available it is not possible to do more than reiterate what seem to be the main areas of naivity built into current policy for EBM. First, the attention so far paid to the problem of implementing EBM has been partial; it is clearly not sufficient to treat it as solely a matter of communication. Second, it is not uncommon to find disputes about what is the probability of an intervention's being effective, and about who is authorised to determine it; EBM is as much a social and political artefact as a scientific or technical one. Third, alternative criteria for rationing exist and have their supporters; it cannot simply be taken that the criterion of effectiveness which underpins EBM commands predominant support. Moreover, the different criteria are in many cases mutually incompatible. Thus there may well be a trade-off between cost-utility (which is concerned with maximising total health gain) and equity (which is concerned with distribution). Finally, it is not the outcomes/RCT model of knowledge, but rather the biomedical/laboratory one which is consonant with the individualistic ethic of the practice of medicine and to the habit of doctors of being influenced by their own experience of single cases, a habit that is reflected by the occasional column in the *British Medical Journal* entitled 'The Case That Changed My Practice'. All these add up to the assumption of a consensus where there is none.

Children and the Family

Elizabeth Brake
St.Andrews University

'Personhood and the Family: Hegel's Account'

Summary

A central achievement of the feminist movement during this century has been to promote the idea that members of families have rights against each other: spouses' rights, children's rights. This paper will present an account of the family which moves beyond rights, for while they are necessary in the family, it will be argued that family membership ideally takes place on a level at which rights are inapplicable. The first half of this paper will elucidate Hegel's theory of family relationships, the basic thesis of which is that family members are subsumed into an ethical unity. The second half of this paper will argue that some version of this thesis best describes the functional family. However, Hegel's thesis of the unity of individuals within a family prompts serious questions about the compromise of self and the role of individual autonomy within a family.

Hegel's account of the family

The family occupies a crucial position in Hegel's political philosophy: it is the immediate phase of ethical life (*Sittlichkeit*), which in turn is the third, and highest, stage in Hegel's system. In ethical life, freedom becomes actual, manifest; and it is only in ethical life that individuals are able to achieve substantial freedom, which is their essence and aim.[1] Duty is the key to this fulfillment: ethical life, that is, family, civil society, and the state, is the realm of duty, customary and habitual as well as moral. It is through the constraints of duty that the individual, though she may seem to lose her freedom, actually attains it, through the purification of the unchosen drives of the will and the firm acceptance of a particular self, a particular set of goals, motives, and values. One of the many achievements of the *Philosophy of Right* is to chart the individual's psychological progress from the unlimited freedom of the 'arbitrary will' to full personhood: in the former, she realizes that she has a limitless choice of actions, yet has no basis for choice; in ethical life, by assuming a social role – a nexus of duties – she is able to bring herself into the world, that is, to act in a manner which she endorses. And the family is the immediate, or spontaneous, phase of this process.

The family is the natural face of duty because its obligations are honored, when the family is functional, spontaneously; one does not simply fulfill

[1] G.W.F.Hegel, *Elements of the Philosophy of Right*, edited by A.Wood and translated by H.B.Nisbet, Cambridge University Press, 1991, 1995, p.189 or par.142, p.192 or par.149. All subsequent references will be to *PR*.

these obligations because they accord with one's self-image (as a father, for instance), but because on authentically desires to. As a family member, desiring to fulfill these obligations is part of one's identity. This notion obviously needs some qualification: a spouse may desire to break her pledge of fidelity, a mother may desire to spend her money on herself rather than her child. But the essential point, that the performance of family duties is motivated by feeling, survives these qualifications; there is a clear contrast between providing food and shelter for one's children and paying one's taxes. Both, according to Hegel, are species of duty; but in family life duty is encouraged by one's emotions, whereas in the state it is promoted by the law. Hegel explains the naturalness of performing duties within the family as an effect of the merging of selves which takes place between family members.

The chief assertion of Hegel's theory of the family is that 'one is present in it not as an independent person but as a *member*.'[2] The family is characterized by its dissolution of ordinary individual rights. This account is explicitly intended as a rebuttal to the purely rights-based notion of the family found in Roman law and the contractual explanation given by Kant: 'Marriage cannot ... be subsumed under the concept of contract; this subsumption ... can only be described as disgraceful.'[3] Instead, 'the substantial basis of family relationships is rather the surrender of personality.'[4] Hegel defines love, the emotion appropriate to the family, as the consciousness of unity.[5] This union is comparable to unions in other institutions, except that its basis is emotional. Citizens in a state work towards the same ends and have an identity with fellow citizens such that an injury to one of them is an injury to all; in a family, the same circumstances occur – shared values, shared goals, a sense of identity – but do so through a spontaneous feeling of unity rather than being enforced through law.

The problem with this basic account is that it is difficult to know how strongly to interpret it. If, on the one hand, we understand it to mean that family members are held together, unlike other sorts of social groups, by love, then we cannot attribute much originality, or indeed, much interest, to this thought. On the other hand, we may interpret it much more strongly, as claiming that personal identity is dependent, in a large part, on the family, and thus that, within the family, the differentiatin between persons fades. This account would be far too strong, as it would not allow for the possession of individual rights within the family.

It is therefore necessary to clarify in what sense Hegel means that members of a family are a single person. The routes to an answer differ greatly between the case of, on one hand, a married couple, and on the other, that of parents and children. Hegel does hold, in fact, that marriage originates in contract, but only '*in order to supersede it*';[6] 'its objective origin is the free consent of the persons concerned, and in particular their consent to *constitute a single person* and to give up their natural and individual personalities

[2] *PR*, p.199 or par.158; italics are Hegel's (throughout, unless otherwise).
[3] *PR*, p.105 or par.75.
[4] *PR*, p.71 or par.40.
[5] *PR*, p.199 or par.158.
[6] *PR*, p.203 or par.163.

within this union.'[7] A married couple becomes one person because, due to romantic or sexual love, they 'feel deficient and incomplete' on their own, and 'gain ... self-consciousness only through the renunciation of independent existence and through knowing [themselves] as the unity' of both.[8]

Hegel does not emphasize this line in his writing on children: the origin of the familial person lies in marriage, and children are merely an extension of this initial conjunction.

> 'The *unity* of marriage, which in substance is merely *inwardness* and *disposition* but in existence is divided between the two subjects, *itself* becomes in the children *an existence which has being for itself*, and an *object* which they [that is, the parents] love as their love and their substantial existence.'[9]

Hegel concedes the children's independent existence: they 'are free *in themselves*, and ... do not belong as things either to others or to their parents.'[10] They also have 'a right to be *brought up* and *supported* at the expense of the family,' and will ultimately 'become free personalities ... capable both of holding free property of their own and of founding their own families.'[11] Yet his account suggests that parents' feeling for their children derives from narcissism or their marital love; as far as it goes, this may be correct, but surely it ignores that part of parental love which respects and delights in children's difference.

Children are said by Hegel to be assimilated into the unity of their parents' marriage because they are its physical manifestation and symbol. But this claim surely is not right, first because it would exclude stepchildren, adopted children, and the like from the family unit in its highest ethical form. Second, and more crucially, this reasoning is insufficient: the fact that children issue from their parents' union does not prove that they immediately enter into this union, except in either a basic biological or a metaphorical sense. Hegel can give better reasons than this for a child's being in the family 'not as an independent person but as a *member*', and indeed he does. A careful examination of Hegel's notion of how and why family unity is constituted will reveal that his rationale for the single personhood of married couples applies equally to the subsumption of children into this unity.

Hegel describes two main senses in which members of a family are one person: first, as a unit in civil society, in terms of rights and property; second, psychologically and through shared identity. In the first sense, Hegel specifies that 'the family's resources ... are common property, so that no member of the family has particular property, although each has a right to what is held in common.'[12] Material wealth belongs equally to each family

[7] *PR*, p.201 or par.162.

[8] *PR*, p.199 or par.158. Roger Scruton suggests that this description of love is, in fact, at least partly of sexual love (Scruton, *Sexual Desire*, The Free Press, 1986, p.1).

[9] *PR*, p.210 or par.173. Words in brackets are translator's.

[10] *PR*, p.212 or par.175.

[11] *PR*, p.211 or par.174, and p.214 or par.178.

[12] *PR*, p.209 or par.171).

member, as if they were only one person: this does not mitigate against privacy, as Hegel is here concerned with financial assets, not particular private possessions. Equal ownership is possible because the rights-bearing individual who belongs to the sphere of abstract right is superseded in the family by the role-embedded person of ethical life.

This does not mean that individual rights are lost; in fact, family membership brings with it additional rights. Children possess a right to be supported, and family members have a right to the jointly owned property. But in a functioning family, the terminology of rights is unnecessary:

> 'the *right* which belongs to the *individual* by virtue of the family unit ... takes on legal form ... only when the family begins to dissolve. In this situation, those who ought to be members ... receive separately and in a purely external manner – [in the shape of] financial resources, food, costs of education, etc – what was formerly their due as a determinate moment within the family.'[13]

The performance of family duties is motivated by virtue or love, not respect for abstract right. Further, the concept of right is inappropriate because the child (for example) does not have an external right against the parents' resources; they are her own, as a member of a family unit. This analysis extends to other types of individual rights, the liberties required by personality to one's body and life.[14] These rights continue to exist in family life, but they are not relevant: Hegel assumes that in a functioning family a member does not think in terms of the others' right not to be harmed, but rather in terms of what they need, desire, and would benefit from, just as she thinks of herself. We do not usually consider our right not be harmed or killed as a right we hold against ourselves: this makes no sense. In short, a family is a single person in abstract right, in terms of property ownership and other rights.

The second mode of family personhood concerns psychology. First, members are conscious of their unity and experience it as love: 'The ethical aspect of marriage consists in the consciousness of this union as a substantial end, and hence in love, trust, and the sharing of the whole of individual existence.'[15] A marriage is an end, an endeavor, a commitment, and children, when they come, become part of this end. Children are not likely to conceive of their family as an end in the same way, partly because for part of their youth they do not even possess such ends, and partly because they learn, as they develop, that their long-term end is to leave the family and establish a life of their own. However, they are aware of the family as an entity – their parents' or parent's end — and their assured place within it: hence, they emotionally participate in the love and trust which, for their parents, arises from having committed themselves to their union.[16]

[13] *PR*, p.200 or par.159. Words in brackets are translator's.
[14] *PR*, p.71 or par.40.
[15] *PR*, p.202 or par.163.
[16] See *PR*, p.212 or par.175.

But the psychological unity which Hegel attributes to the family is deeper, and subtler, than its members' emotional involvement in their togetherness. Hegel's theory of personhood stresses the dependence of individual personalities on exterior sources. He claims that the realized self embodies Spirit through attaining freedom; without this freedom, the individual is either a bundle of natural inclinations, an empty and undirected consciousness, or forced to depend on isolated subjective judgments. Through taking on a social role, that is, locating herself in society, the individual realizes herself and overcomes these indeterminacies: 'he is liberated from that indeterminate subjectivity which does not attain existence or ... action, but remains *within itself* and has no actuality. In duty, the individual ... attain[s] substantial freedom.'[17] Hegel does not disallow individual subjectivity or particularity: 'The right of individuals to their particularity is likewise contained in ethical substantiality, for *particularity* is the mode of outward appearance in which the ethical exists.'[18] Hegel claims that identity can only be brought into being through seizing onto a restrictive, and hence educative, socially provided self-definition. In short, identity is not inborn, but the assimilation of a ready-made set of values and duties.

Hegel clearly sees identity as a malleable, interdependent phenomenon. Thus, he is able to hold with consistency that family unity does entail some merging of actual personalities. In one sense, self-description involves specification of spouse or parents or children as people deeply and unalterably related to oneself. In another sense, shared daily existence, over time, means that one's family does shape one's personality. Hegel's claim is stronger than these insights: family members are not ethically related through a contract, or rights against each other, but through deep identification with the other, renunciation of individual rights in dealing with the others, shared common good, and indivisibility.[19] And, a family member is incomplete on her own, until the ethical dissolution of the family.

The virtues of this account

Hegel's theory is an attempt to describe how a family works, when it is functioning properly. It provides an explanation for the deep nature of family membership, and the strength of its ties which differentiate it from membership in other associations. While love is the consciousness of this unity, the basis of family unity is not sentimental: 'for love, as a feeling, is open in all respects to contingency, and this is a shape which the ethical may not assume.'[20] The project is to explain family membership beyond contingency. This is more plausible in the case of children: for a child raised in a family structure, the relationship with her parent(s) is unique, irreplaceable, permanently etched into her identity. But Hegel includes marriage in his definition of family. Marriage is, first, an independent unit in civil

[17] *PR*, p.192 or par.149.

[18] *PR*, p.197 or par.154.

[19] Hegel recognizes the necessity of provision for divorce, but notes that the fact of marital contingency is at odds with its 'ethical substantiality'; see *PR*, p.213 or par.176.

[20] *PR*, p.201 or par.161.

society, more ethically significant than the extended family. But, second, Hegel's main references to shared identity concern the married, childless state. Hegel certainly intends that the physical intimacy of marriage is a route to, if not a prerequisite of, the merging of identities.[21]

Hegel's account seems useful for a number of reasons. First, the language of rights is insufficient to describe the family. This is not to say it is inapplicable: over the past decades, feminist activism and scholarship has drawn aside the traditional veil of privacy shielding the family from public scrutiny and legal jurisdiction. Rights are crucial to any description of the family, not least to protect family members from each other. But a rights-based account alone fails to differentiate the family from other types of institution; moreover, it fails to explain why the family is an end in itself, not a means to some other goal. Hegel's theory is able, unlike a rights-based or contractual account, to explain the strong and psychologically indissoluble bonds that characterize family membership, the deep sense of common good, the interpenetration of identity, and the internal nature of the relationship. His theory also helps to explain how a family holds us, and why it is worth ceding independence to belong, without resorting to the contingent factors of sex (in the case of marriage), contract (a notion applied by Kant to both marital and parental relations), or sentiment.

Hegel's account of why family membership is an ethical good is also appealing. This involves his concept of liberation through duty. By taking on a set of self-ascriptions yoked to a familial role, the individual is enabled to develop and experience in ways impossible outside this role. What seems like a limitation, then, is actually an expansion of self. Furthermore, by relinquishing one's atomistic identity, allowing the barriers between selves to dissolve within the family situation, the self is again enlarged: in virtue, since this merging promotes the performance of duty, but also in consciousness, since one's awareness of the world is thus supplemented by the awareness of others. Again, new forms and modes of self-knowledge, emotion, and thought become available to the family member.

Drawbacks

Hegel's treatment of children is brief, which is regrettable, as his theory of family personhood runs into particular problems when applied to children. Marriage, he assumes, is at least ideally a permanent arrangement, with no possibility of ethical dissolution; yet, as Hegel realizes, children develop out of the family. Their membership ceases, at least insofar as it comprises their primary identity: on the ethical dissolution of the family, children found 'their own families ... In this family they now have their substantial determination, and in relation to it, their original family recedes in importance as merely their original basis and point of departure.'[22] The mechanism of this transition is difficult to understand Hegel explains it as

[21] Hegel uses double entendres to refer to sexual intercourse, but his meaning is clear (for example, *PR*, p.200 or par.161, p.210 or par.173).

[22] *PR*, p.214 or par.178.

the result of their upbringing into 'self-sufficiency and freedom of personality, thereby enabling them to leave the natural unit of the family.'[23] But this means that, for children of a certain age, the family is only a transitional stage, and thus their feeling of unity may be weakened. Also, it is difficult to see how, as children develop towards self-sufficiency, they do not gradually become less a part of the family, rather than continuing to be a full member until they make a clean break.

Another difficulty in accepting the thesis that a family is a single person arises from the historical associations of such a view: for Hegel (though he is not alone in this) the single person who represents the family in the outside world and controls its resources is the husband.[24] To take the case of property, this means, in effect, that the assertion of shared ownership is a claim without consequences; the wife cannot access her property against her husband's wishes. She cannot cite a right to it, as rights are inapplicable in this context. Hegel fails to provide for the equality of which he ambiguously speaks as belonging to the members of the family: in this he is simply a man of his age.[25] Due to his absorption of contemporary prejudices, he conflates the single person which the family constitutes with the male head of household. This is obviously unacceptable, but it also proves inconsistent, for it contradicts the basic idea of the family as a single person, the idea that the welfare of each is the welfare of all.

Even after canceling out the biased generalizations which Hegel makes about the sexes, however, it is possible that the notion that family members compose a single person may, in its monolithic nature, its assertion of singleness over difference, intrinsically point to the conclusion that there must be a head of the household. In other words, is it really sustainable that the single unit which family members become is a composite, or a higher unity, or, rather, does it appear that family members are subordinated to a single person, that is, the head of household? This issue is probably the most significant difficulty for an exponent of Hegel's account; it is the accusation that, on Hegel's account, family members disappear into the larger ethical unit of their family, that their identities are lost to the head or to the family itself.

The solution to this problem will involve defining more closely what self-description is superseded by family membership, and what is left untouched. In order to protect individual rights, a revision or interpretation of Hegel must hold here that the juridical, purely legal, person is not superseded by family membership. Particular personality too is retained, as noted above; it is completely consistent for a husband and wife to have separate individual ends – one of which is their marriage – and a common good. And yet Hegel also says that we surrender our personalities in the family union: our personal inclinations give way to the claims of duty, and, to

[23] *PR*, p.212 or par.175.

[24] *PR*, p.209 or par.171.

[25] He does not in fact support actual equality because he believes the sexes have different abilities: man is volitional, woman emotional. 'Man therefore has his actual substantial life in the state, in learning, etc ... Woman, however, has her substantial vocation in the family.' (p.206 or par.166). These claims are extrinsic to his basic theory.

some extent, to the inclinations of others. So, while family members do not lose, forget, or suppress their identities, they acknowledge that something larger and more ethically significant, the family, takes precedence. The larger context of Hegel's work supports this interpretation: the concept of *Aufhebung,* or sublation, from Hegel's logic helps to make sense of the idea that the individual is superseded by the family yet remains. In Aufbehung, what is transcended is also preserved at the higher level.

There are pitfalls in Hegel's account which must be carefully avoided, most notably the neglect of rights and the threat to personality. However, these problems can be overcome by a careful description of the self-ascription which is superseded within the family, and the aspects of personhood which remain intact. The main benefit of Hegel's thesis is that it accounts for family membership without reverting to the external concepts of contract and rights: rather than thus emphasizing the ultimate separateness of family members, it concentrates on, and tries to pin down, their unity. Hegel ties this unity, very simply, to self-identity: it is not based on sentiment, which can fluctuate, or contract, which stresses separateness and self-interest. Though some qualifications must be made, Hegel's version captures the nature of family identity and begins to explain its unique character.

Jürgen Habermas's Discourse Theory of Democracy

Matthew Festenstein
University of Hull

'Habermas on Legitimacy and Rights'

Introduction

The question of the proper form of political association has pervaded Habermas's thought, and agitated his readers, while never receiving the full elaboration which the topic seems to merit. The publication of *Faktizität und Geltung* marked not only an important and wide-ranging contribution to thinking about legitimacy, deliberative democracy, and the sociology and philosophy of law, but the statement in political terms of an ideal of radical democracy which has fuelled excursions into pragmatics, systems theory, the philosophy of modernity, and historical polemic.[1]

The book involves the explicit articulation of the political significance of Habermas's developed theory of modern society and moral philosophy.[2] The core of this theory has been worked out at a very abstract level, in the theory of practical rationality. Habermas attempts to find a basic grounding for some core moral principles in an account of the presuppositions of the capacities of any competent speaker who possesses an understanding of reasons for action. This is the argument for his Kantian-sounding principle D:

> '[o]nly those norms are valid that meet (or could meet) with the approval of all affected in their capacity as participants in a practical discourse' (107).[3]

When we claim that some norm is valid, we presuppose that the claim for the norm's validity can be 'redeemed' in a process of 'practical discourse' or argument. Discourse is an idealised version of the more general activity of communication. In communicative action, participants search for understanding by offering arguments which could command the assent of their interlocutors. As opposed to strategic action, where participants are primarily interested in bringing about a desired behavioural response, participants in communicative action are interested in bringing about a genuine understanding. I may make you take part in some project of mine by threatening to punch you should you not agree. But in doing so, I have given you no

---

[1] J.Habermas, *Between Facts and Norms: Contributions to a Discourse Theory of Law and Democracy*, translated by W.Rehg, Polity Press, 1996. Page references to this appear in the main body of the text.

[2] This is not to say that this authorised version of this significance is the only interesting one, or necessarily the most coherent.

[3] J.Habermas, *Moral Consciousness and Communicative Action*, translated by C.Lenhardt & S.W.Nicholson, Polity Press, 1990, pp.65-66. For a contentious account of the philosophical context of discourse ethics, see M.Festenstein, *Pragmatism and Political Theory*, Polity Press, 1997, chapter 6.

reason independent of my threat to take part. In communicative action, I presuppose that I can give you inherently good reasons why you should take part in this project, independent of strategic considerations. Practical discourse is the sphere in which, if I am called upon, I actually attempt to give those reasons. The reasons offered in discourse are finite and fallible, aiming not a categorical certainty but agreement among the agents involved.

Between Facts and Norms is concerned to rebut charges of moralism: that the intention is derive an account of politics and legitimacy from an account of moral principle. Instead (like the recent Rawls), Habermas tries to articulate a distinctly political source of legitimacy, recasting some themes from traditional consent theory. He also seeks to overcome a dichotomy which recurs in the book, between 'liberalism' and 'republicanism'. The former emphasises the rule of law and the protection of individual freedom; democratic decisions are seen as constrained by rights which secure that freedom. The latter lauds the process of democratic deliberation which is thought to aim at a statement of the common good, and envisages freedom principally not as a protected private sphere but as participation in making the laws of the polity. Habermas sees this as a false dichotomy, arguing that 'private and public autonomy, human rights and popular sovereignty, mutually presuppose one another' (89; see especially chapter 3).[4] This paper explores these two claims: section2 outlines the basic argument for a 'democratic principle' of legitimacy, and the argument for the 'cooriginality' of rights and democracy; section3 describes a difficulty in his discourse theory of validity; section 4 traces this difficulty through the offered account of democratic legitimacy; section 5 describes the unease that liberals are entitled to feel at being reconciled with so-called republicans.

The basic argument

According to Habermas, the only grounds for legitimacy in a modern political association must be 'post-metaphysical': that is, they cannot rest on contentious ideas of the good life or of fundamental human capacities and interests (71-72, 94-99, 105, 443). Habermas takes it as axiomatic that modern societies contain a variety of conceptions of value and cultural perspectives. Within this diversity, he distinguishes between ethical and moral questions. The former concern what is good or appropriate for a specific community or individual, or what is required to live an authentic life; deliberation about ethical questions, in this sense, takes place within the framework of particular cultural traditions. Moral questions concern what is just or right for all, without restriction. Although sometimes appearing to confine discourse to moral issues, Habermas in his developed doctrine permits discourse in both spheres: the scope of ethical discourse is limited to those who share a particular community's perspective and traditions, while the scope of moral discourse is not limited in this way. Furthermore, there

[4] See also J.Habermas, 'Three Models of Democracy', *Constellations*, 1, 1994; J.Habermas, 'On The Internal Relation Between The Rule of Law and Democracy', *European Journal of Philosophy*, 3, 1995.

may be 'pragmatic discourses', which reflect upon the best instrumental means to achieve pre-given goals (95-99, 108-109).[5]

Distinguishing the discourse principle and its articulation as a rule of specifically moral argument allows Habermas to distinguish political legitimacy from morality, while analysing both in terms of his discourse principle. What he calls the democratic principle offers an interpretation of the general rule D for the sphere of lawmaking. D ii declares that 'only those statutes may claim legitimacy that can meet with the assent (*Zustimmung*) of all citizens in a discursive process of legislation that in turn has been legally constituted' (110). D ii is not understood as the application of the idea of a moral discourse. Although legal norms must remain open to moral argument, they both contrast with and complement moral norms: the contrast comes in legal norms' application only to specific legal communities, at the same time as they also provide a necessary decisiveness which complements the more open-ended character of moral discourse (128, 153-157). Although both legal and moral norms are ultimately grounded in the discursive account of validity discussed in the previous section, the abstraction of this account from the particular domain of morality allows us to distinguish the validity of legal from moral norms, and to detach our assessment of this aspect of Habermas's thought from criticisms of his conception of morality.

Apart from the discourse principle, the other crucial element in the account is the perspective on modern law, or what is sometimes referred to as the 'rule of law'. Accounts of the rule of law emphasise such features as the need for government to be subject to the law, and the openness and regularity of laws.[6] In brief, Habermas, following Kant, envisages modern law as a system of abstract rules which imply a sphere of personal liberty: 'there is no law without the private autonomy of legal persons in general' (83-85).[7] It creates the category of abstract, rights-bearing legal persons, demarcates areas within which private individuals may exercise free choice as they desire, and presupposes that what is not prohibited is permitted. The rule of law is not itself seen as adequate for the justification of prohibition of substantive practices (religious toleration or coercion, for example). The personal freedom that it implies is not a moral notion, nor, (as Kant believed) may it be derived from a conception of moral autonomy. Habermas agrees with Kant (and John Rawls) that the rule of law is a necessary but not a sufficient condition for the specification of basic rights; nor is it an empty form to be given content by independently generated principles of justice.[8] He is nevertheless guided by the Kantian idea that legitimate principles are those which we give ourselves, seeing this self-legislation as an intrinsically collective process, in keeping with his discourse principle. The democratic principle, D ii, then, is offered as the necessary supplement, which is distinctly political and not derivatively moral: practices are

[5] J.Habermas, *Justification and Application*, translated by C.Cronin, Polity Press, 1993, pp.10-16, 23-24, 88-91; W.Rehg, *Insight and Solidarity: A Study in the Discourse Ethics of Jürgen Habermas*, University of California Press, 1994.

[6] J.Raz, *The Authority of Law*, Clarendon Press, 1979, chapter 11.

[7] Habermas, 'Internal Relation', p.17.

[8] J.Rawls, *A Theory of Justice*, Oxford University Press, 1972, p.235.

legitimate only if they can meet with the assent of all citizens in a legally constituted discursive process of legislation.

Autonomy in the legal (as opposed to moral) domain is bifurcated into public and private forms: private autonomy is the sphere whose protection is implied by the form of modern law; public autonomy consists in rights to participate in authorship of those laws, according to D ii. The form of positive law guarantees equal liberty, but this refers only to the liberty of the abstract rights-bearing person. In order to gain content and legitimacy these rights must be the subject of discourse according to the democratic principle: 'individual private rights cannot even be adequately formulated, let alone politically implemented, if those affected have not first engaged in public discussions to clarify which features are relevant in treating typical cases as alike or different' (450). These rights can only be given content by a political sovereign, and this content can only be legitimate *ex hypothesi* if it is in accord with the discourse principle.

How then are democracy and rights related? He contrasts his conception with what he calls liberal and republican doctrines. Liberalism invokes the threat of tyrannical majorities and accordingly posits individual rights as prior to democratic decisions. Republicanism, by contrast, stresses citizens' public autonomy, and holds that individual rights are justified to the extent that they enable or are functional for capacities of collective decision-making. Liberals end up presenting rights as a 'paternalistic imposition' on a sovereign legislator. Republicans make rights merely instrumental requisites for legislative goals. There is a clear sense in which what Ronald Dworkin calls enabling rights may be justified from this latter standpoint; freedoms of speech and association, for example, like rules of debate, are better seen as conditions of possibility for democratic discourse, than as constraints upon it.[9] But this is a less plausible strategy for those classical rights held to secure citizens' private autonomy (property rights, for example, or rights to due process). Hence Habermas rejects the instrumental argument. At the same time, he opposes the liberal imposition of rights on the sovereign, as this would require some separate source of legitimacy for these rights, outside the democratic principle.

His ingenious resolution is to observe that when citizens exercise their public autonomy, and play the part of legislators, they are not free to choose the medium within which to work, so to speak. When they judge in the light of the discourse principle whether the law that they make is legitimate, they do so under discursive presuppositions which must themselves be institutionalised in legal form. For such an institutionalisation to occur, the form of modern law must be available. That is, to create modern law is to presuppose the category of legal persons who as bearers of individual rights belong to an association of rights-bearing individuals. As a result, without basic rights which secure private autonomy, there would not exist the medium in which legally to institutionalise the conditions under which public autonomy could be exercised. In this way, public and private auton-

[9] R.Dworkin, 'Constitutionalism and Democracy', *European Journal of Philosophy*, 3, 1995.

omy presuppose each other in such a way that neither rights nor popular sovereignty can claim primacy.

D ii and the legal medium do not suffice to generate the rights which liberals have traditionally been concerned to secure – 'to personal dignity; to life, liberty and bodily integrity; to freedom of movement, freedom in the choice of one's vocation, property, the inviolability of one's home, and so on' (125). These ways of working out the 'general right to individual liberties' necessarily remain subject to democratic determination, under D ii. To give specific content to these rights a priori would violate public autonomy. But such democratic determination is in part constituted by enabling rights (128) and the 'conventions of two hundred years of European constitutional law' (129).

The discourse principle

The general strategy of analysing validity in terms of a rational consensus attracts a familiar objection. The concept of a consensus based upon reasons, as opposed to any other motivation, presupposes the concept of a personal conviction based upon reasons; but then it is the strength of those reasons, and not of the consensus itself, that leads one to dub it 'rational'.[10] Who or what is the judge of whether or not the assent of a group of people has been given on good reasons? If it is each person herself, then the requirement is empty; if it is someone else, then the actual assent drops out as the decisive factor. The policy or norm N is said to be valid if, and only if, N is agreed upon after a process of rational discussion: but then N's validity derives from the reasons that we have arrived at, and not from the fact that we have agreed upon N.[11] To dramatise the point: that racial prejudice is wrong may be agreed upon by rational discussants; but the reason why people ought to agree is that it is wrong, and a failure of convergence even under the circumstances of well reasoned and open debate would not affect the validity of this judgment. This tension between 'facts' and 'norms' possesses, as we shall see, a counterpart in the discursive account of legitimacy.

The democratic principle

How can practical discourses act as critical standards within the complex and thoroughly strategic ecology of actual political practice? There seem to be two ways in which the ideal of legitimation through practical discourse may be seen as a critical standard for actual political agents. The first is to see some social or political arrangement, or the result of some negotiation, as legitimate to the extent that it models the outcome of a choice that the agents can be envisaged as making, if they were to adopt the rule D. But there are difficulties with the construction of such a counterfactual choice

[10] Cf. S.Benhabib, *Situating the Self*, Polity Press, 1992, p.57; A.Wellmer, *The Persistence of Modernity*, translated by D.Midgley, Polity Press, 1991, pp.157-159; N.J.H.Dent, *Rousseau*, Basil Blackwell, 1988, pp.176, 200-201.

[11] But compare J.Habermas, *Autonomy and Solidarity*, 2nd edition, Verso, 1992, p.160.

and with explicating its authority for actual agents. The problem of construction hinges on the amount of information allowed to the participants in the counterfactual discourses. If the agents are taken as they are, then the grounds for projecting that they will agree are correspondingly weakened. But if the agents are stylised in some way, then the agreement projected becomes an entailment of the theory of stylisation. Why should the projected agreements have any grip on agents who do not accept the stylising principles? If a person is presented with a policy with which she does not agree, with the rider that, if she were different (in ways specified by the counterfactual construction), she would agree, she is unlikely to be convinced: and the rider does not in itself provide a reason for her to become convinced. It is in order to avoid such difficulties that Habermas insists on an actual, and not counterfactual process of dialogue as the critical standard.[12]

The other way to conceive of practical discourses as furnishing a critical standard, which is presented as the official theory of the book, is to see them as offering a discursive ideal of fair procedure. This has the merit, which the first interpretation lacks, that it does not generate a requirement to formulate and justify a compelling counterfactual construction of an alternative social choice. Rather, to the extent that political argument and deliberation are concerned with rational debate, practical discourse and its standards are an 'idealising supposition' behind procedures which guide actual choice.[13] As Seyla Benhabib has it, 'the institutions of liberal democracies embody the idealised content of a form of practical reason'.[14]

Habermas envisages an 'ideal procedure' in which free and equal participants in a process of discussion attempt to arrive at a reasoned agreement (especially pp.304-308). What the democratic principle tells us is that the ideal deliberative procedure defines the democratically legitimate outcome: as Joshua Cohen puts it, outcomes of decision procedures are 'democratically legitimate if, and only if, they could be the outcome of a free and reasoned agreement among equals'.[15] Participants are free in the sense that they are bound only by the preconditions and results of such a procedure and take their deliberation as sufficient grounds for complying with its results. They are equal in that they have an equal opportunity to contribute to decision making, and that power and resources are not distributed in a way that decisively affects their chances to participate. They offer arguments that are reasoned in the sense that only the force of the better argument is exercised. Consensus on this basis is the fundamental aim of collective deliberation. Where this cannot be had, a decision must be made by majority rule. Provided that the debate has been competent and conducted under

[12]See R.Geuss, *The Idea of a Critical Theory*, Cambridge University Press, 1981, especially pp.45-54; J.Lear, 'Moral Objectivity', in S.C.Brown (ed), *Objectivity and Cultural Divergence*, Cambridge University Press, 1984, especially pp.150-158; Habermas, *Moral Consciousness*, p.66.

[13]Habermas, *Moral Consciousness*, pp.105-106; Habermas, *Justification*, pp.57-58.

[14]S.Benhabib, 'Deliberative Rationality and Models of Democratic Legitimacy', Constellations, 1, 1994, p.27.

[15]J.Cohen 'Deliberation and Democratic Legitimacy', in A.Hamlin & P.Pettit (eds), *The Good Polity*, Basil Blackwell, 1989, p.22. See also J.Cohen, 'The Economic Basis of Deliberative Democracy', *Social Philosophy and Policy*, 6, 1989.

the conditions described,

> '[m]ajority rule retains an internal relation to the search for truth inasmuch as the decision reached by the majority only represents a caesura in an ongoing discussion; the decision records, so to speak, the interim result of a discursive opinion-forming political process [....] [M]ajority rule justifies the presumption that the fallible majority opinion may be considered a reasonable basis for a common practice until further notice, namely, until the minority convinces the majority that their (the minority's) views are correct.' (179, 306)[16]

Unlike some proponents of a deliberative politics, Habermas does not stress that the citizenry must share certain 'active' virtues or a common ethos, which would conflict with his insistence on the diversity of conceptions of the good life and rejection of communitarianism. Instead he emphasises the importance of the institutional formats for public discussion (278-279).

Although the focus is now on procedures, D ii, like D, rests on the assumption that validity is conferred by rational consent. Indeed, some commentators (notably Albrecht Wellmer) have argued that the principle D is better understood as an interpretation of democracy than as a general principle of validity or morality.[17] The D ii account of legitimacy rests upon an assumption about the conditions under which it is acceptable to use political force or coercion, namely, the conviction found in liberal consent theorists that no one ought to be made to comply with norms the validity of which they cannot be brought to recognise through reasons.[18] Moral norms which we do not intend to use coercion to enforce do not require this sort of public justification; hence the discursive principle does not apply to them. But those which are political, in the sense that they are backed by coercion, are only legitimate for those whose rational consent they could receive. This ties the legitimacy of legal norms to what all could agree to in rational public deliberations which take the interests of each equally into consideration.

The model of ideal procedure guides the institutionalisation of those conditions necessary for public discourse, in guaranteeing rights such as the legal protection of free speech. But institutional arrangements are not sufficient for the production of a democratically legitimate outcome. For example, given the pluralism which Habermas emphasises, is it sensible to expect citizens who have differing moral and political outlooks and are given full range to express these differences regularly to arrive at a reasoned consensus about the common good? The response offered is that in the face of

[16] Compare Cohen, 'Economic Basis', p.33.

[17] Wellmer, *The Persistence of Modernity*, pp.145-188; Cohen & Arato, *Civil Society*, pp.350-351; B.Manin, 'On Legitimacy and Deliberation', *Political Theory*, 15, 1987.

[18] Cf. Cohen, 'Deliberation and Democratic Legitimacy'. On the liberal conviction, see J.Waldron, 'Theoretical Foundations of Liberalism', *Liberal Rights*, Cambridge University Press, 1993, and compare I.Kant, 'On the Common Saying "This May Be True in Theory but It Does Not Apply in Practice" ', in H.Reiss (ed), *Political Writings*, Cambridge University Press, 1970.

such disagreement, we shift to a higher plane of abstraction, resorting to procedures such as voting and majority rule. If those procedures are themselves accepted by all parties to the dispute, then the outcomes may likewise be accepted as legitimate.[19] In pluralistic societies, the best that we can usually hope for are broad agreements about basic rights, principles and procedures which live alongside a range of other disagreements.

This answer, however, only pushes the problem back. (1) There is an initial difficulty with the justification of majority rule. If the point of the ideal deliberative procedure is to reach a reasoned agreement, what justifies curtailing discussion in favour of some majoritarian decision procedure? Like other theorists of deliberative democracy, Habermas shifts attention away from the final act of voting toward the process of discussion which surrounds it. The position of being in a minority in some vote may no doubt be mitigated by a process of discussion, in which the grounds for the decision reached are debated: the minority does not then merely have the decision imposed upon it, but is given reasons for the decision and the opportunity to put forward its own point of view.[20] It may also perhaps draw comfort from the thought it may one day overturn the majority decision. But the reference to the 'fallibility' of majority decisions is misleading: neither of the foregoing considerations presupposes anything about the competence or fallibility of majority decisions. Consider a majority which votes for the public funding of floristry beating a minority which supports kick-boxing. If the sports fans eventually overturn the decision of the horticultural enthusiasts, they will not have shown that the earlier decision was wrong or false, and that the balance of reasons in fact favoured them, but only that it was alterable.

(2) A second difficulty for this procedural answer is the task of elucidating the sense in which procedures such as majority rule enjoy consent. For only if they do so can specific outcomes enjoy democratic legitimacy. A vote is only necessary (on the account described here) in the absence of rationally motivated agreement; that is, when discourse has failed to arrive at rational consent. But the losing side in the vote is compelled to submit to the outcome of the actual procedure, not of the process of public discourse. The empirical presence or absence of agreement is not central for Habermas, nor should it be: if the sports fans respond badly to their defeat, and decide that they can no longer put up with majority rule, this does not render the democratic decision illegitimate. He argues that his emphasis on the legal institutionalisation of public discourse does not eliminate the appeal to counterfactual idea of universal assent. He cites Wellmer (458-459):

> 'The concept of the legitimacy of the law also has a counterfactual application [....] Admittedly, it lies within the logic of the modern concept of legitimacy that the common nature of any decision-making process must as far as possible be realised in fact – that is, insofar as all those affected are ultimately to

[19]Compare T.McCarthy, 'Enlightenment and Public Reason', *European Journal of Philosophy*, 3, 1995.

[20]Cf. D.Miller, *Market, State, and Community*, Clarendon Press, 1989, chapter 10.

> be accorded an equal right to participate in the collective processes by which the common will is formed: this is the idea of democracy. But if legitimate laws are to be such that all those affected would have been capable of passing them collectively, and if all those affected are – in principle – to have an equal right to participate in the collective decision-making process, then it goes without saying that the settling of any normative questions by means of public argument must play a central part in any attempt to realise the possibility of legitimate law [...] and to ensure that the law is acknowledged as legitimate. To argue in favour of a legal norm – or system of legal norms – means in this case the attempt to provide reasons which convince all other affected persons why all people of good will and discernment should necessarily be able to deem it to be equally in the interests of all that this norm or these norms should prevail in society.'[21]

The issue then turns on this rational consent to underlying procedures. To say that the sports fans would agree with the horticulturalists under ideal circumstances does not in itself give them a reason to agree under actual conditions. But if we say that they should agree because under ideal circumstances they will come to see that the best reasons and arguments favour flowers over kick-boxing, then the issue hinges on the strength of those reasons and arguments and not on the counterfactual agreement. The same considerations apply when we consider the sports fans' consent to majority rule. Merely telling them that they would agree to this procedure if conditions were ideal does not give them a reason to agree now; so some reason must be given for them to agree. But what reason can be given to the dissenting group?

An alternative is to argue for the more permissive principle that what matters is what people could agree to; in effect ruling out only those measures which they could not agree to.[22] Here then a lot hinges on how the relevant agents are described. If kick-boxing fans would not remain kick-boxing fans if they gave up their beliefs about public funding and the worth of their sport, then there is a sense in which these people could not assent to victory of flowers. In other words, this course requires some account of what are citizens' more or less fundamental interests or commitments. Even this line of argument based on the bare possibility of rational consent,

---

[21] Wellmer, *Persistence of Modernity*, p.194; cf. O.O'Neill, 'Kommunikative Rationalität und praktische Vernunft', *Deutsche Zeitschrift für Philosophie*, 41, 1993, pp.329-332.

[22] Compare Kant, *Political Writings*, p.79: 'if the law is such that a whole people could not possibly agree to it (for example, if it stated that a certain class of subjects must be privileged as a hereditary ruling class), it is unjust; but if it is at least possible that a people could agree to it, it is our duty to consider it as just, even if the people is at present in such a position or attitude of mind that it would probably refuse its consent if it were consulted'. A very helpful discussion of Habermas's relationship to Kant is H.Williams, 'Democracy and Right in Habermas's Theory of Facticity and Value', *History of Political Thought*, 15, 1994.

then, requires an account of the reasons which can be given to the dissenter for acquiescing in a procedure or course of action with which she does not agree.

(3) The obvious candidate for such a reason suggested by the account of deliberative procedure is the underlying commitment to the process of discussion itself and to the public justification of proposed norms, which, at least for political purposes, takes priority over other interests, goals and ideals. Without this underlying commitment, there is no reason for a losing minority to assent to the procedures under which it has lost. On the other side, without this commitment to deliberation grounds the majority's continuing to respect the deliberative rights of the minority. But this is plainly a stringent and contentious commitment: it suggests that in politics my other fundamental interests must be disciplined by what can be publicly justified; the ardent kick-boxing fan must subordinate his passion to public justification. But some of my other interests may be so strong or inextricably tied up with my identity that I may find it impossible to abstract from them in this way: my sense of the urgency of the problem of pollution may override may be more important to me than the presumption that I must justify this sense to you before we legislate. This suggests, then, that this commitment may not be shared by everyone in the political community. Those who do not share it remain outside the scope of public justification, coerced into accepting norms which they could not validate: if my environmental ideals really are central to my identity, then I may have to put up with legislation (and procedures which create legislation) with which I not only do not agree but could not. At the same time, Habermas refuses to rest this commitment on some other basis, such as a view of the virtues of good citizenship or a common patriotic identity.

Liberal rights

It should be clear that, as I understand it, the argument for 'cooriginality' of rights and democracy is not an argument for the cooriginality of liberal rights and democracy. Rather, it suggests that democratic lawmaking presupposes the form of constitutional politics, while at the same time providing the only source of legitimacy for substantive laws made in that form. But it is silent on, for example, the legitimacy of decisions which permit religious diversity, including the freedom not to practice a religion, as opposed to those which impose religious uniformity. D ii is not then in itself an adequate account of legitimacy for liberals: from their point of view, it allows the paternalistic imposition of particular views and styles of life which should not be enforced by the state. What must be added to D ii, or how it must be restructured, is a complicated issue, which will be answered differently by different liberals. If the above sorts of criticism of the discourse theoretic approach are sound, what cannot be ducked is the obligation to describe and defend some particular conception of individual interests, an account which is not solely derivable from the democratic principle and the rule of law. But from Habermas's perspective, it should be noted, such a conception amounts to paternalistic imposition and political heteronomy.

Conclusion

I have argued that (1) the basic discourse principle is ambiguous, (2) that the democratic principle is subject to difficulties familiar to rational consent theory, and (3) that the promised reconciliation of 'liberal' and 'republican' views is not effected, at least in so far as the question of liberal rights is concerned. Habermas's is a rich and complex text to which, of course, I have not attempted to do full justice. But it seems to me that these difficulties lie at the core of his political project, and need to be addressed by those who wish to persuade the rest of us of the project's future.

Jürgen Habermas's Discourse Theory of Democracy

Maurizio Passerin d'Entrèves
University of Manchester

'Justice, Multiculturalism and Deliberative Democracy'

Summary

This essay examines the question of justice in democratic constitutional states from the standpoint of a theory of deliberative democracy. Its aim is to show that the validity of a conception of justice and the legitimacy of political institutions and public policies based upon it can be best defended on the basis of a normative theory of deliberative democracy. This theory, I shall argue, is superior to the two main normative models of justification that appeal to the ideal of neutrality (Rawls, Larmore, Nagel) or to the ideal of perfectionism (Raz, Galston).

Justice in Multicultural Societies

The problem of justice and legitimacy has become particularly acute in societies characterised by the fact of pluralism. Pluralism refers to the existence of a variety of competing and often antagonistic and irreconcilable conceptions of the good life held by individuals and groups in contemporary western societies. These competing conceptions of the good life have both an individual and a collective dimension, since they may refer to personal or to collective conceptions of the good, or be a combination of the two.

Although pluralism is not a uniquely modern phenomenon, it has assumed greater political salience in societies composed by a number of distinct cultural groups claiming recognition of their unique collective identities (or their collective conceptions of the good). The type of recognition claimed by cultural groups, based on their ethnic, religious, gender or linguistic identity, is a claim pertaining to their collective sense of identity and their collective conception of the good. It therefore differs from the standard claim about recognition of individual identity, which liberal theory from Mill to Rawls has attempted to incorporate, more or less successfully, in its normative framework of justification. The emergence and increasing salience of multicultural groups claiming recognition of their collective identities represents, therefore, a challenge to the standard liberal model of justification. In what follows, I want to examine briefly three responses to this challenge: the first is centred on the value of neutrality, the second on the value of autonomy and/or diversity, the third on the value of dialogue or deliberation.

Neutrality

Rawls is the most well-known advocate of the model of neutrality, along with Larmore and Nagel.[1] Given the fact of reasonable pluralism, the aim is to find a basis of agreement that is neutral with respect to competing conceptions of the good life, whether individual or collective. This aim is achieved by the creation of an overlapping consensus among the variety of (reasonable) comprehensive doctrines, whether moral, religious or philosophical, embodying different conceptions of the good. The strength of this model lies in the acknowledgment of the fact of pluralism, seen as both inevitable and ineliminable, and in the effort to find a basis of agreement that is least controversial, since it is restricted to constitutional essentials and basic questions of justice and does not appeal to contestable comprehensive conceptions of the good. This is what Rawls calls the 'method of avoidance'. The weakness of this model lies in the strong distinction between public and non-public aspects of identity and the difficulty of defining a non-contestable notion of the 'reasonable'. The model assumes that individuals, in order to achieve an overlapping consensus on constitutional essentials, are able to set aside their personal or non-public conception of the good from the public conception of justice or common good. For many individuals whose personal conception of the good is inextricably tied to the collective conception of the good of their group, this separation of private and public aspects of their identity is difficult to achieve. In effect, the individuals most likely to achieve and support an overlapping consensus are those for whom the separation of public and private aspects of identity is least troublesome, namely, liberal individuals. Liberal individuals have, as it were, a divisible conception of the self. But Rawls's theory aims to embrace non-liberal as well as liberal individuals, and there is some doubt as to whether his theory can successfully accommodate the former. Moreover, the very notion of what is 'reasonable' (reasonable doctrine, reasonable conception of the good, reasonable agreement) remains controversial, since its meaning varies in accordance with the different conceptions of the good (or reasonable comprehensive doctrines) held by various individuals and groups living in contemporary multicultural societies. Reasonableness thus remains a contested and contestable notion.

Perfectionism

Faced with these shortcomings of the neutrality model, some political thinkers have opted for a different model of justification, one based on perfectionist ideals, such as autonomy or diversity. They start by acknowledging the controversial, that is, non-neutral character of liberal principles of justice and of the conception of the self that underlies them, and go on to defend liberal principles by arguing for their superiority with respect to available

[1] John Rawls, *Political Liberalism*, Columbia University Press, 1993. See also Charles Larmore, *Patterns of Moral Complexity*, Cambridge University Press, 1987, and Thomas Nagel, *Equality and Partiality*, Oxford University Press, 1991.

alternatives. By doing this, they engage on the terrain set by the communitarian critics of liberalism (MacIntyre, Sandel, Taylor, Walzer), because they eschew appeals to neutrality and defend liberalism as embodying a superior or normatively preferable conception of the good life. This strategy has been advocated, among others, by Joseph Raz, William Galston and Will Kymlicka.[2] Joseph Raz, for example, has argued that a liberal state should protect and foster all those forms of life that encourage autonomy. He believes that autonomy is a precondition of human well-being, since the value of an individual's life is enhanced if it is freely chosen from a range of available options. He also thinks that membership in a community is conducive to human well-being, because it determines the horizon of one's opportunities and helps to shape one's identity. He defends value- pluralism on the grounds that many different and incompatible ways of life are good for their members. Traditional communities which do not put a high value on freedom of choice may still be valid sources of identity for their members, and should therefore be respected and tolerated, provided that they do not oppress their members and allow them the option of exit. The liberal state is to be particularly valued because it makes available the conditions for the free pursuit of, and participation in, all those forms of life that are capable of being good for their participants. By securing certain rights to individuals and groups, the liberal state makes available a range of valuable options that will permit every person to pursue his or her conception of the good, and thus secures the condition for human well-being. A similar argument has been put forward by Kymlicka in his liberal defence of group rights, which stresses the value of cultural membership and a secure cultural context for individual well-being. Other authors, such as Galston, have advocated the superiority of liberal principles by an appeal to the value of diversity, rather than autonomy. The liberal state accommodates diversity better than its rivals, since in its public principles, institutions, and practices it affords maximum feasible space for the flourishing of individual and group differences, constrained only by the requirements of liberal social unity. What is common to these defences of liberal principles and institutions is a rejection of the model of neutrality in favour of a perfectionist model based on the values of autonomy and/or diversity. The strength of this perfectionist model of justification is that it engages in a substantive debate with the critics of liberalism and argues for the superiority of the liberal conception of the good *vis-à-vis* its possible competitors. In doing so, it exemplifies what may be called a 'method of engagement' which sidesteps some of the difficulties of Rawls's 'method of avoidance'. It may indeed be a more straightforward way of defending liberal principles, since it disclaims any appeal to neutrality and enters self-consciously into a debate about the good. The weakness of this model, on the other hand, partly stems from its strength: it may allow for greater debate about competing concep-

[2] Joseph Raz, *The Morality of Freedom*, Clarendon Press, 1986, and *Ethics in the Public Domain*, Clarendon Press, 1994; William Galston, *Liberal Purposes*, Cambridge University Press, 1991, and 'Two Concepts of Liberalism', *Ethics*, 105/April, 1995; Will Kymlicka, *Liberalism, Community, and Culture*, Clarendon Press, 1989, and *Multicultural Citizenship: A Liberal Theory of Minority Rights*, Clarendon Press, 1995.

tions of the good life in the public-political domain, and will avoid claiming a spurious neutrality, but it will ultimately favour those individuals and groups whose conceptions of the good or well-being are predisposed toward the value of autonomy and/or diversity. The perfectionist model may be a more straightforward way of defending liberal principles and institutions, but is no less controversial or contestable than the model of neutrality. The aim of inclusiveness, of being able to accommodate the largest feasible range of competing and irreconcilable conceptions of the good, seems, in the end, unattainable on either model. But is this aim actually attainable? In what follows I will defend the model of deliberation or dialogue on the grounds that it is more inclusive than either the model of neutrality or that of perfectionism, but it is worth pointing out that such inclusiveness is a matter of degree. No model can achieve complete inclusiveness. Liberalism, as Taylor has put it, is also a 'fighting creed'.[3] The inevitable fact of exclusion of even the most expansive or accommodating forms of liberalism, such as that of Taylor, is what Donald Moon calls 'the tragedy of liberalism'.[4] The aim of complete inclusiveness is unattainable. There will always be tragic conflicts and tragic choices. But this should not stop us in our search for models of greater inclusiveness that will lessen the scope for tragic conflicts. The deliberative or dialogic model may provide for a greater degree of inclusion, or so I shall argue, than either the neutral or the perfectionist models.

Deliberation

There are several lines of entry to the dialogic or deliberative model of justification. I shall describe briefly those put forward by Charles Taylor, Amy Gutmann and Dennis Thompson, Joshua Cohen, and James Fishkin.

Taylor argues in favour of a dialogic model of justification based on the recognition of the uniqueness of collective identities. He calls this model the 'politics of difference' to distinguish it from the standard liberal model which he terms the 'politics of equal dignity'. He characterizes their difference as follows:

> 'With the politics of equal dignity, what is established is meant to be universally the same, an identical basket of rights and immunities; with the politics of difference, what we are asked to recognize is the unique identity of this individual or group, their distinctness from everyone else. The idea is that it is precisely this distinctness that has been ignored, glossed over, assimilated to a dominant or majority identity.'[5]

---

[3] Charles Taylor, 'The Politics of Recognition', in Amy Gutmann (ed), *Multiculturalism: Examining the Politics of Recognition*, Princeton University Press, 1994, p.62.

[4] J.Donald Moon, *Constructing Community: Moral Pluralism and Tragic Conflicts*, Princeton University Press, 1993.

[5] Charles Taylor, 'The Politics of Recognition', *op cit*, p.38.

Thus, while the politics of equal dignity

> 'fought for forms of nondiscrimination that were quite "blind" to the ways in which citizens differ, the politics of difference often redefines nondiscrimination as requiring that we make these distinctions the basis of differential treatment.'[6]

The example Taylor cites in defence of the politics of difference is that of the French speaking community of Quebec. They should be granted special rights and immunities so as to be able to preserve their unique collective identity, and to maintain their cherished cultural distinctness from the majority of English speaking Canada. Taylor's model of the politics of recognition is neither neutral nor perfectionist: it rests on the presumption of equal worth, namely, that

> 'all human cultures that have animated whole societies over some considerable stretch of time have something important to say to all human beings.'[7]

It is dialogic, insofar as it promotes cross-cultural exchange among different groups and collectivities. The aim of such an exchange is to enlarge our understanding of other cultures, so that we and they may learn something from the dialogic encounter. The aim, in other words, is to achieve a 'fusion of horizons', to use Gadamer's well-known formulation.

A similar stress on dialogue and deliberation characterizes the position of Gutmann and Thompson. They argue that controversial moral issues should not be excluded from public debate, but become subject of collective deliberation. A liberal state, they maintain,

> 'must permit greater moral disagreement about policy and greater moral agreement on how to disagree about policy.'[8]

The only constraints they advocate are procedural in character:

> 'Principles of accommodation [resting on the idea of mutual respect] govern the conduct of the moral disagreement on issues that should reach the political agenda.'[9]

In a subsequent article, Gutmann provides a more articulated defence of the model of deliberative democracy. She notes that deliberation

> 'may sometimes increase moral conflict in politics by opening up forums for argument that were previously closed ... Deliberation encourages people with conflicting perspectives to understand each other's point of view, to minimize their moral

[6] *Ibid*, p.39.

[7] *Ibid*, p.66.

[8] Amy Gutmann & Dennis Thompson, 'Moral Conflict and Political Consensus', in R.B.Douglass et al (eds), *Liberalism and the Good*, Routledge, 1990, p.125. This essay also appeared in *Ethics*, 100/October, 1990.

[9] *Ibid*, p.126.

> disagreements, and to search for common ground, but it begins by opening politics up to a range of reasonable disagreement that is restricted by less deliberative politics.'[10]

The advantage of deliberative politics over other models of justification (neutralist or perfectionist) is that

> 'in the absence of forums for deliberation mutual respect for reasonable differences is unlikely to be forthcoming and common ground is likely to be overlooked or devalued even by reasonable people since reason by itself, or reasoning by ourselves, rarely points us toward the conflicting perspectives of other reasonable people.'[11]

An even stronger defence of deliberative democracy as the best institutional mechanism for the adjudication of conflicting moral and political perspectives is provided by Joshua Cohen. By deliberative democracy he means an association 'whose affairs are governed by the public deliberation of its members' and where political debate 'is organized around alternative conceptions of the public good'. Such an association requires a broad and manifest equality among citizens and provides a basis for self-respect and the development of a sense of justice. Thus, when properly conducted, 'democratic politics involves *public deliberation focused on the common good*, requires some form of *manifest equality* among citizens, and *shapes the identity and interests* of citizens in ways that contribute to the formation of a public conception of common good'.[12] The idea is not to suppress difference, but to allow differences about competing conceptions of the public good to be debated in common deliberative fora that ensure the greatest degree of fairness to all participants. To this end Cohen sketches an ideal deliberative procedure that captures the notion of justification through public argument among equal citizens, and serves in turn as a model for deliberative institutions. We should seek, he says, 'to mirror a system of ideal deliberation in social and political institutions.'[13] He stresses the fact that

> 'the ideal deliberative procedure is meant to provide a model for institutions to mirror ... and not to characterize an initial situation [such as the Original Position] in which the terms of association themselves are chosen.'[14]

Cohen's model of deliberative democracy is strongly normative in character and is partly indebted to Habermas's discourse theory of democracy.

[10] Amy Gutmann, 'The Challenge of Multiculturalism in Political Ethics', *Philosophy and Public Affairs*, 22/3, 1993, p.199.

[11] *Ibid*, p.200. See also Amy Gutmann & Dennis Thompson, 'Moral Disagreement in a Democracy', *Social Philosophy and Policy*, 12/1, 1995. For a more extended elaboration of their model of deliberative democracy, see Amy Gutmann & Dennis Thompson, *Democracy and Disagreement*, Harvard University Press, 1996.

[12] Joshua Cohen, 'Deliberation and Democratic Legitimacy', in A.Hamlin & P.Pettit (eds), *The Good Polity: Normative Analysis of the State*, Basil Blackwell, 1989, pp.17, 18, 19.

[13] *Ibid*, p.20.

[14] *Ibid*, p.22.

The relevance of such a normative theory of deliberative democracy for our present purposes is that it articulates the conditions under which a fair debate among competing collective identities and conflicting conceptions of the good can be conducted. The outcomes of debates carried out under conditions of deliberative fairness are democratically legitimate, since they are 'the object of a free and reasoned agreement among equals.'[15] Cohen's theory of deliberative democracy embodies, as all normative theories tend to do, an ideal model of fair deliberative procedures, but its explicit aim is to explore ways in which to institutionalize such an ideal, so as to make our social and political institutions more open to free public deliberation. It is not an ideal thought-experiment, but an attempt to work out the fairest conditions for the adjudication of conflicting moral perspectives on the common good. Finally, the ideal of deliberative democracy is not a perfectionist doctrine, since it does not depend on a particular view of the good life (say, the life of active citizenship). Rather,

> 'it is organised around a view of political justification – that justification proceeds through free deliberation among equal citizens – and not a conception of the proper conduct of life.'[16]

The last contribution to a theory of deliberative democracy I want briefly to advert to is that of James Fishkin. Fishkin's contribution focuses on the kinds of institutions required for the ideal of deliberative democracy to be realised in large-scale and technologically advanced societies. Such institutions must embody both political equality and deliberation. In his book Democracy and Deliberation (1991) and, more at length, in The Voice of the People (1995), he defends an institutional design based on the model of the deliberative opinion poll, but also alludes to other institutional designs that embody both political equality and deliberation, such as the proposal of Philippe Schmitter and Claus Offe to give every citizen a 'representation voucher' and Bruce Ackerman's notion of a 'constitutional moment'. His institutional proposal centred around the deliberative opinion poll embodies political equality, since everyone has an equal chance of being represented in the national sample of participants, and deliberation, since a selected group of citizens is immersed for an extended period of time (say, one or two weeks) in intensive, face-to-face debate.[17] The results of such a deliberative poll

> 'have prescriptive force because they are the voice of the people under special conditions where the people have had a

[15] *Ibid*, p.22.

[16] *Ibid*, p.27. For a complementary paper to the one just discussed, focusing on the material preconditions of deliberative democracy, see Joshua Cohen, 'The Economic Basis of Deliberative Democracy', *Social Philosophy and Policy*, 6, 1989. See also Joshua Cohen, 'Procedure and Substance in Deliberative Democracy', in S.Benhabib (ed), *Democracy and Difference: Contesting the Boundaries of the Political*, Princeton University Press, 1996.

[17] James S.Fishkin, *Democracy and Deliberation: New Directions for Democratic Reform*, Yale University Press, 1991, p.2.

> chance to think about the issues and hence should have a voice worth listening to'.[18]

The topics under discussion in a deliberative opinion poll may vary: Fishkin suggests that deliberative opinion polls may be used to assess candidates in the 1996 American presidential primaries, but their more general purpose is to enable a selected but representative sample of people to evaluate and debate any issue that might be of public concern. The point of deliberative opinion polls is to allow people to engage in a reasoned debate and to find some common ground on disputed moral, political or ethical questions. By operating in a framework characterized by political equality, participation and non-tyranny, Fishkin writes,

> 'a collective process [of deliberation] occurs in which the group has a reasonable chance to form its collective, considered judgments – to give its public voice, if you will, to the topic in question. Arguments on rival positions get an extended hearing, and each side has a chance to answer the other. The same information is available to all. People are present and engaged by the process. They do not merely listen. They also participate, in a context which is small enough that each can credibly believe that his or her individual voice counts. And they discuss the issues in an atmosphere of mutual respect, attempting to find common ground.'[19]

The theories of deliberative democracy put forward by James Fishkin, Joshua Cohen, and Amy Gutmann, together with Taylor's dialogic model of recognition, should be seen as the first sketches of a model of normative justification that is more inclusive than the two alternatives I have examined at the beginning of my paper, based on the values of neutrality or perfectionism. Whether the emphasis is on the recognition of collective identities (Taylor), the adjudication of moral conflict (Gutmann), public reasoning on the common good (Cohen), or the evaluation of issues of public concern (Fishkin), they all stress the importance of dialogue and deliberation for a more inclusive and just form of liberal society.

---

[18] *Ibid*, p.4.

[19] James S.Fishkin, *The Voice of the People: Public Opinion and Democracy*, Yale University Press, 1995, p.34. For a related discussion of democratic deliberation in relation to the question of political legitimacy, see James S.Fishkin, *The Dialogue of Justice: Toward a Self-Reflective Society*, Yale University Press, 1992.

Britain's Post-War Institutional Decline

Jim Johnston
University of Birmingham

'Economic Decline Revisited: Challenging Idealist Fallacies Within the Literature'

Introduction

One of the major themes within British political discourse since the mid-1960's has been the nature and extent of Britain's political and economic decline. However, despite the enormous 'decline' literature which now exists, many of the principle issues within the debate remain unresolved. Consequently, the aims of this paper are threefold: to provide a detailed review of the existing literature; to analyse some of the theoretical and methodological difficulties within the literature; and to advance a novel perspective on the historical trajectory of the development of British capitalism.

Much of this literature is organised into two distinct and competing accounts. On the one hand, neo-liberal variants,[1] emphasise the rapid expansion of the state as being the principal cause of decline. In contrast, neo-socialist narratives[2] explain economic difficulties in terms of the failure to create a 'developmental state'. Yet, despite holding radically different normative positions, the similarities between these two historical narratives are remarkable. In particular, both mainstream and Marxist historiographers emphasise the cultural and ideological domination of an archaic ruling class as the principle factor in explaining Britain's economic decline.

In emphasising some of the theoretical and methodological difficulties within this literature we will attempt to provide a fuller understanding of the historical trajectory of the development of British capitalism. First, we will argue that much of the literature is too idealist. In emphasising the backwardness of the ruling class as the principle explanatory variable in explaining economic decline, there is a tendency to understate the influence of the peculiar structural development of British capitalism.

Second, many accounts tend to employ a rather vulgarised interpretation of the Gramscian notion of 'hegemony'. In particular, there is a tendency to interpret hegemonic domination as being relatively static and unchanging. As such, there is no attempt to demonstrate how the hegemony of the dominant class is historically reproduced. This leads to the development of a deterministic analysis in which economic decline is explained as the inevitable consequence of the continued cultural hegemony of the British

[1] For the purposes of this paper I will refer mainly to, arguably, the two principal neo-liberal historiography's on Britain's economic decline, namely Weiner 1981; Barnett 1986.

[2] The principal neo-socialist authors in this area are, arguably, Perry Anderson and Tom Nairn whose seminal essays in the *New Left Review* during the mid-1960's provoked a stimulating and often heated debate over the origins of economic decline, among both the Left and Right. In particular, see Anderson 1964, 1966; Nairn 1964.

aristocracy. Consequently, we will suggest the need to develop a more sophisticated understanding of hegemony in order to delineate the contours of economic progress. In conclusion, we will argue that, in identifying the 'exceptional' nature of British capitalism as a primary factor in the explanation of decline, we need to place a greater emphasis on the structural nature of this exceptionalism.

This paper will argue that two different narratives exist within most of the literature. First, we can identify a political narrative in which the character of the modern state and the principle causal factor of industrial decline (too much or not enough state intervention) are assumed from the outset. Consequently, it is necessary to locate much of the literature within the volatile political context in which it was written.

Many explanations of economic decline emerged during a crucial period in the trajectory of post-war British politics when Keynesianism was increasingly under threat from a renewed intellectual assault from neo-liberalism. As such, the decline literature itself forms part of the narrative; for example, Weiner's text in particular was published at an opportune moment for the New Right. Weiner's book, which gained a great deal of publicity within the media and formed the basis for two Granada TV, World in Action programmes,[3] arguably helped to legitimise the Thatcherite assault on the whole fabric of British society.

Second, we can identify a historical narrative which ostensibly aims to explain economic decline but is in reality preoccupied with the idiosyncratic nature of the British state. However, what is surprising about much of the literature is that despite radically differing political narratives, many authors draw on similar historical evidence to substantiate their normative positions. In particular, within the historical narrative, economic decline is primarily attributed to the 'exceptional' nature of British capitalism and the failings of a peculiarly backward-looking hegemonic class.

The Cultural Thesis

Neo-liberals have a vested interest in demonstrating that economic decline can be historically linked to the growth in size of the state. Indeed, Thatcherism emerges as a particular response to the perceived failings of a highly interventionist social democratic Keynesian state. Weiner and Barnett argue that, what they see as the continual expansion of the modern state has had a crippling effect on economic growth. They argue that Britain's economic decline is intrinsically linked to the rapid expansion of a modern state which is a welfarist legacy of the paternalistic panderings of a utopian ruling élite. Within this neo-liberal discourse it is no coincidence that Britain's decline from being 'the workshop of the world' to the 'sick man of Europe' parallels the profligate growth of the public sector. Consequently, the Thatcherite agenda becomes dominated by the need to strengthen the British economy through a return to the state/civil society relations which underpinned the zenith of Britain's economic power during

[3] Baxendale 1986, p.171.

the early nineteenth century. Following in the classical liberal tradition of Locke and Adam Smith, Thatcherism becomes the political expression of a theoretical belief in free-market economics and a minimalist role for the state.

Bolstered by Weiner's and Barnett's 'cultural thesis', many neo-liberals argued that a 'culture of dependency' undermined the entrepreneurial spirit essential to creating a successful economy. Indeed, the New Right's profound dislike of the welfare state is epitomised by Barnett's vitriolic attack on the New Jerusalem: '...a dream turned to a dank reality of a segregated, subliterate, unskilled, unhealthy and institutionalised proletariat hanging on the nipple of state maternalism'.[4] Armed with a sense of Christian justice, a paternalistic and anti-industrial élite sought to alleviate poverty through direct state intervention rather than through the strictures of the market. Furthermore, weaned on the nanny state the working class inevitably became less industrious and increasingly more dependent on social welfare. As such, it is argued that economic decline is primarily a consequence of prioritising state hand-outs over economic development. Rather than intervening directly within the economy it is argued that a minimalist state should facilitate (often through withdrawal or deregulation), an entrepreneurial culture in which enterprising individuals can realise their business ideas.

The Archaic State Thesis

In contrast, neo-socialists have a vested interest in demonstrating that economic decline is directly linked to the historical failure to create a modern 'developmental state' (See for example: Nairn 1964; Anderson 1964, 1987; Cain and Hopkins 1993; Gamble 1994; Marquand 1988; Ingham 1984; Hutton 1995). These authors view economic decline in terms of the failure of the British state to take a leading role in the development of the economy. Here, the focus is on the peculiar durability of the institutional settlement which was forged, in the aftermath of the 1688 revolution, between the landed gentry and the financial bourgeoisie. In many narratives the state is seen as being handed down almost intact from the seventeenth century; for example, Hutton argues: 'The Conservative Party has found itself in charge of a ruleless state, handed down almost intact from the settlement of 1688',[5] while Gamble also argues: 'The British state has not suffered a major break in the pattern of its development since the civil war in the seventeenth century'.[6]

It is argued that the survival of an archaic state has had a pervasive influence throughout Britain's civil society and has seriously undermined economic performance. As such, one of the principal reasons for Britain's economic decline is the absence of a modernising 'second revolution'. Unlike all her major competitors the UK never experienced a major period of social and political upheaval which would have radically undermined the outdated

[4]Barnett 1986, p.304.
[5]Hutton 1995, p.4.
[6]Gamble 1994, p.65.

institutions formed during the initial English revolution.

Britain's victory in the Second World War ensured that it was unique among all industrialised states in that it 'alone had now never experienced a modern 'second revolution', abruptly or radically remoulding the state inherited from the first'.[7] In contrast to the great social, political and economic upheavals which swept the European continent, Britain's victory ensured that her ancient institutions became even more revered. V-day marked the triumph of Parliamentary democracy not only over the tyranny of fascism but more importantly, though implicitly, the dangers of tinkering with historic state institutions. Ironically, at a moment when the modernisation of the state was crucial to economic development, the defeat of fascism ensured the continued survival of Britain's ancient institutions.

British exceptionalism

Despite arriving at the diametrically opposite conclusions outlined above, there is a considerable overlap between the 'cultural thesis' and many neo-socialist accounts of economic decline. In particular, both sets of literature emphasise the 'exceptional' nature of British capitalism. Both neo-liberal and neo-socialist authors argue that the unique survival of an aristocratic stratum led to the development of a peculiarly British 'gentlemanly capitalism', which was inherently anti-industrial. Through a historical alliance with a nascent financier class the traditional landed gentry was able to form a new historical bloc. In return, the financiers were assured that the state would forward their economic interests; for example, the continuation of Britain's imperial role which gave them access to lucrative foreign markets.

As such, the continuing historical ability of the aristocracy to retain its iron grip on power is explained in terms of its ideological and cultural hegemony. Economically, it is argued that this is disastrous for Britain as it results in the development of a pervasive anti-industrial ethos. Within both the neo-liberal and neo-socialist literature's we can identify a number of similar explanations for the historical dominance of this culture.

First, the industrial middle-classes failed to achieve political dominance during the Victorian period. It is argued that, despite being the first industrialised country, Britain has never had an industrial élite. Second, the emergence of financial capitalism provided a timely alternative source of income for the feudal élite, while the nouveau rich were content to mimic the culture and lifestyles of the aristocracy. Consequently, the latter were able to obtain an institutional settlement which restored much of their power and maintained many of their ancient privileges. Third, through an intricate web of élite institutions such as the public schools, university's and civil service the values and lifestyle of the leisurely gentleman were enshrined as being culturally superior to the vulgar materialism of the urban bourgeoisie. Fourth, the industrial middle-classes themselves, aspired to a gentlemanly status.

[7] Anderson 1987, p.47.

Both Weiner and Barnett argue that Britain has never had an industrial élite. British industrialists were never able to occupy a hegemonic position within the state and, therefore, their interests remained subordinate to a financier class, who had formed a cultural, political and economic alliance with the traditional landowning aristocracy. Similarly, Anderson argues that despite the extensive success which the industrial bourgeoisie enjoyed, they never managed to transform their economic dominance into political supremacy: 'Economically, English capitalism had triumphed completely; but no commensurate political advance by industrial capital had followed'.[8] This is a position which is also supported by economic historians such as Cain and Hopkins who argue that: 'Despite the growth of organisations such as the Anti-Corn Law League in the 1840's, provincial manufacturing interests were not in the political mainstream in the nineteenth century'.[9]

The English bourgeois revolution arrived too early so that the aristocracy were able to survive the opposition of a relatively weak industrial middle class and preserve many of the ancient institutions which underpinned their hegemonic position. Consequently, the Glorious Revolution 'transformed the structure but not the superstructures of English society'.[10]

Despite marginal political successes such as the 1832 Reform Act and the repeal of the Corn Laws (1846), the middle classes, fearful of the working class and awe-struck by the grandeur and prestige of the aristocracy, failed to fully challenge the hegemonic position of the latter. Buoyed by their economic success, the bourgeoisie were content to mimic the lifestyle and culture of the landed gentry: 'In return for accepting the values and lifestyle of the landed class, the most prominent manufacturers were to be admitted as full members of the status group of 'gentlemen''.[11] Consequently, 'The late Victorian era and the high noon of imperialism welded aristocracy and bourgeoisie together in a single social bloc'.[12] Rather than posing a threat to the hegemonic position of the landed gentry, the bourgeoisie were content to acquiesce within a political and cultural status quo which was fully compatible with their immediate economic interests. The middle classes were willing to piggyback on the landed gentry's political and cultural dominance which ensured both the continued legitimisation of a rigid class hierarchy and a commitment to an imperialistic role within the British state. Therefore, the acquiescence of the bourgeoisie strengthened the hegemonic position of the traditional British establishment through the formation of a new historical bloc which was anti-industrial.

As well as failing to transform their economic success into political power, British industrialists remained culturally subordinate throughout the nineteenth century to an aristocratic élite. The cultural significance of the finance and service sectors were that they provided the aristocracy with an alternative means of generating income which was still compatible with the leisurely lifestyle of the country gentleman. As income from these sectors

[8] *Ibid*, p.23.

[9] Cain & Hopkins 1993, p.40.

[10] Anderson 1992, p.29.

[11] Scott 1982, p.104, quoted in Overbeek 1990, p.44.

[12] Anderson 1992, p.29.

was largely invisible and indirect, a discreet distance could be maintained from the murky business of etching out a living:

> 'Gentlemanly capitalism was a formidable mix of the venerable and the new: it combined inherited and invented traditions with profitable enterprise in occupations which were compatible with gentility. The gentlemanly capitalist had a clear understanding of the market economy and how to benefit from it: at the same time he kept his distance from the ordinary demeaning world of work.'[13]

Equally, while the aristocracy needed to find alternative means of raising income than from the land, the emerging bourgeoisie aspired to a gentlemanly status. Unable to acquire the necessary acres and rural background, the growth of the public school system provided the urban bourgeoisie with the opportunity to imbue their children with the much vaunted characteristics of the country laird.

In this context, Weiner and Barnett locate the epicentre of Britain's peculiarly anti-business ethos within the hallowed halls of the traditional English public school. They argue that the raison d'être of such establishments is to help their pupils become 'gentlemen'; a process which is peculiarly detached from the vagaries of the modern world. Again, this is a position which is compatible with the neo-socialist literature:

> 'From the mid-century onwards, the public schools had provided a common education – not to speak of intensive intersocialisation – for sons of the gentry and upper bourgeoisie alike. The values of this education were markedly anti-industrial from the outset: a training for rule, not for trade.'[14]

Within the core curriculum an emphasis is placed on religious teachings and the Greek and Roman classics as forming the basis of a sound and moral education. In contrast, the teaching of the sciences was eschewed as being too closely associated with industry:

> '... science was linked in the public mind with industry, and this damaged its respectability in upper-class eyes. Industry meant an uncomfortable closeness to working with one's hands, not to mention an all- too-direct earning of money.[15]

As such, a definite line was drawn between a morally virtuous classical education and an inferior vocational education; a division which was reflected in the structure of post-war education. The former was seen as a necessary step towards a career within the great institutions of the British state or a position in the City, while the grimy world of industrial production was left to the 'lower classes'.

[13]Cain & Hopkins 1993) p36.

[14]Anderson 1987, p.41.

[15]Weiner 1981, p.18.

This bias against industry was continued within the University system:

> 'Victorian Oxbridge, too, followed the example of the public school, believing with John Ruskin that the purpose of a university was to provide a liberal education, and the purpose of a liberal education ... was to train young men to 'the perfect exercise and knightly continence of their bodies and souls.[16]

As such, a University education marked a continuation of the public school's emphasis on the cultivation of a gentlemanly persona underpinned by a grounding in the classics and Christian theology. The introduction of Civil Service entrance examinations in the 1850s which were heavily biased towards those candidates with the approved classical education reinforced the élite's grip on power:

> 'The move to meritocratic recruitment in the professions in the nineteenth century was intended both as a device to maintain and enhance gentlemanly status and as a method of rigging the markedly effectively once patronage had ceased to be a socially acceptable means of rationing.'[17]

Despite the introduction of an ostensibly 'open examination' recruitment process, the emphasis on the benefits of a classical education ensured that mainly Oxbridge graduates would continue to occupy senior civil service posts.[18]

However, at the same time it left the state poorly equipped to cope with a rapidly changing world:

> 'Thus in the early 1850s was born the Whitehall mandarin, able at a touch to transmute life into paper and turn action into stone.'[19]

The public school system may have produced the right sort of chap to defend sacrosanct English traditions and values. Unfortunately, it left successive Governments with many diplomats but little in the way of technical or scientific advisers.

Weiner also argues that the emergence of a professional class during the Victorian period also strengthened the dominance of the aristocracy within the state. He identifies a Victorian élite of administrators, professionals, financiers and landed proprietors who espoused a coherent set of values and aims which were born in the insular collectivity of the public school and universities and who were unimpressed, and even markedly hostile, about the merits of economic dynamism.

This marked hostility towards technological 'progress' was epitomised by a fetish for a mythological rural idyll. Weiner cites numerous pieces of Victorian literature and polemical articles to illustrate the tension which existed

---

[16]Barnett 1986, p.14.
[17]Cain & Hopkins 1993, p.28.
[18]Ingham 1984, p.140.
[19]Barnett 1986, p.215.

between England's schizophrenic existence as the 'workshop of the world' and a 'green and pleasant land'. Artists and intellectuals from both Left and Right warned against the infinite dangers of untrammelled scientific development, while emphasising the 'quality of life' over materialistic greed. The English garden became the principal metaphorical antidote to the horrors of the dark satanic mill. 'Our England is a garden' was a common refrain of those opposed to the growth imperative of industrial capitalism. This rural idyll symbolising peace and tranquillity was counterposed to the frightening insecurity of technological innovation.

The Disputed Character of the English Ruling Class

From the above, we have seen that both mainstream and Marxist historiography's have developed narratives in which the decline of British capitalism is attributed primarily to the failings of an archaic ruling class. However, within the literature we can identify an alternative position which rejects the notion of continued aristocratic hegemony and suggests that the industrial middle classes did indeed achieve a large degree of political power during the Victorian period. Indeed, much of the original debate on the origins of Britain's economic difficulties focused on the character of the English ruling class and its role in the development of English capitalism.

Perhaps the most (in)famous was the insightful, though often heated debate between Tom Nairn and Perry Anderson and Edward Thompson. At the heart of this dispute was the nature of the hegemonic class in Victorian Britain. On the one hand, as we have seen above, Nairn and Anderson argue that, due to the incomplete nature of the English bourgeois revolution, the industrial middle-classes remained subordinate within a new historical bloc, in which the landed gentry retained their historical, hegemonic position within the British state. In contrast, Thompson argues that Nairn and Anderson misinterpret the fundamental nature of the English ruling class. Although certain elements of the aristocracy retained some political influence, this was due to their metamorphosis into a capitalist class. Consequently, Thompson argues that the industrial bourgeoisie gradually became the dominant political class during the Victorian epoch.

Thompson argues that Anderson and Nairn 'mistake the true nature of our ruling class'. He argues that the Victorian middle classes formed a formidable ruling bloc as emphasised by Walter Bagehot's 'English Constitution'(1867); a 'locus classicus which Anderson and Nairn appear to have overlooked'.[20] Bagehot divides the British constitution into its 'dignified parts', including the monarchy and aristocratic institutions which were essentially ceremonial, and its 'efficient parts', principally the House of Commons where Government business was largely conducted. Thompson argues that Bagehot was clearly convinced that the latter was 'under the 'despotic' control of the middle-classes'.[21] Elaborating on Bagehot's view of the ceremonial nature of the aristocracy he argues that:

[20] Thompson 1978, p.53.
[21] *Ibid.*

> 'They were like the staff at an elaborate and prestigious hotel, who could in no way influence the comings and goings of clientele, who or at what time or with whom, but who could arrange the ball and appoint a Master of Ceremonies.'[22]

However, in a terse reply to Thompson's essay, Anderson argues that his and Nairn's thesis:

> 'was that the landed aristocracy of the 18th century blended with the industrial bourgeoisie of the 19th and thereafter, in the form of the modern British 'upper class', dominated the institutions and ideology of the single social bloc they formed.'[23]

In demonstrating the continued political dominance of the aristocracy, Anderson argues that 'two thirds of all Conservative Cabinet Ministers between 1868 and 1955 were from the 'traditional ruling class" '.[24]

As such, Nairn and Anderson emphasise the convergence between different fractions of capital into a single ruling bloc to such an extent that it is no longer possible to 'distinguish the opposing interests of a more aristocratic finance capital from a more bourgeois industrial capital'.[25] Additionally, Nairn has argued that the international investment portfolio held by British industrial 'giants' such as Unilever and ICI created an 'effective unity between financial and industrial capital'.[26] The international character of the leading companies within British industry means that they have similar interests to financial capital; for example, maintaining the value of the pound. However, this ignores the position of domestic industry whose interests often conflict with those of the financial sector. For example, an overvalued pound harms the competitiveness of domestic industry as it makes imports cheaper and exports dearer.

The Structural Basis of Hegemony: Challenging Hegelian Fallacies

As I have attempted to demonstrate above, one of the principle areas of controversy within the 'decline' literature is the nature of the hegemonic class. However, here I will argue that this debate has been crucially undermined by the concept of hegemony which has been employed by many of the authors within this debate. First, we need to develop a much more dynamic conception of hegemonic power which allows not only for a continual struggle between different social classes, but also between the different fractions of the ruling bloc.

[22] *Ibid*, p.55.

[23] Anderson 1966, p.16.

[24] *Ibid.* This is a position which is also supported by Paxman 1991 – 'For much of the eighteenth century British public life was dominated by a couple of hundred families, and the aristocracy's grip upon political power proved remarkably tenacious. In the 1833 Parliament, 217 MP's were either the sons of peers or themselves baronets. The comparable figure in 1880 was 170'.

[25] Anderson 1996, p.14.

[26] Quoted in *Ibid*.

Within much of the literature, there is a failure fully to identify the mechanisms and processes through which aristocratic hegemony is reproduced. Indeed, within the Marxist historiography's, it is arguable that the period from 1688 to the 1960s is viewed as a unified conjunctural moment. This leads to the development of a deterministic analysis in which economic decline is attributed to the historical hegemonic dominance of an archaic ruling class. This has led authors such as Fine and Harris(1985), to argue that Nairn and Anderson's historicist methodology leads to a 'curiously monolithic view of British history',[27] which understates the complexity and dynamism of economic, societal, cultural and political change. In particular, there is a failure to explain how the aristocratic class remains hegemonic.

Within Gramscian theory, hegemony is never static. Gramsci argues that there is a continual struggle to reproduce hegemony. Additionally, he does not necessarily associate hegemonic power with a homogenous class. In reality, at any one time there may exist a struggle between a number of small groupings within a wider class. For example, as Gramsci argues, there may be 'attempts by specific groups or sects to take over hegemony within the directive grouping'.[28] However, as Nield argues, Anderson, for example, views hegemony as a 'fixed and historically determined set of power relations'. Further, 'hegemony is not seen by Anderson as a terrain of conflict, negotiation, and consent requiring much political and cultural labour for its reproduction and renewal. Rather it is an adjectival shorthand for fixed, unchanging, and unequal relations of social and ideological power'.[29]

Second, we need to incorporate a structural element into our model of hegemony. To become a hegemonic class necessitates not only domination of the superstructures, but also a leading position within the economic base. For as Gramsci argues:

> 'though hegemony is ethico-political, it must also be economic, must necessarily be based on the decisive function exercised by the leading group in the decisive nucleus of economic activity.'[30]

As such, there is a need to contextualise the character of the dominant social bloc within the particular stage of the development of British capitalism. Hegemony necessarily incorporates a logic of social and historical contingency into considerations of the political.

In emphasising the role of the superstructures much of the literature understates the effect which the particular structural development of British capitalism had on the evolution of the state. The idealist nature of the historiography's identified above has led to an emphasis on the role of cultural and ideological factors in explaining the character of the British state. Moreover, in viewing hegemony as static and unchanging there is a tendency to develop a deterministic analysis in which economic decline is viewed as

[27] Fine & Harris 1985, p.63.
[28] Gramsci 1971, p.408.
[29] Nield 1980, p.498.
[30] Gramsci 1971, p.161.

the inevitable outcome of the failings of an archaic ruling class. However, in seeking to identify the role of the hegemonic class in Britain's economic development it is necessary: 'to locate actors within the broader contexts they inhabit.'[31] In particular, we need to account for the effect which the rapid changes which occurred within the economic base had on the superstructures of English society. For example, arguably it is the peculiar manner in which industrial capitalism emerges in Britain that is the primary factor in influencing the development of the state.

In contrast, as we have seen, both Marxist and mainstream historiography's explain the 'exceptional' nature of British capitalism in terms of the peculiar character of the ruling class. They argue that the unique survival of a hegemonic aristocratic stratum has led to the development of a peculiarly, 'gentlemanly' British capitalism which historically has been anti-industrial in character. As such, Britain's economic decline is attributed to the failings of an archaic and backward-looking ruling class which has blocked the creation of a more developmental state, in order to further its own narrow economic interests. In contrast, I would argue that the advantages which the British industrial bourgeoisie gained from being the first nation to industrialise manifested in a particularly vehement commitment to a minimalist state; a commitment compatible with the interests of financial capital which has also historically opposed any increased state intervention in the economy.

First, the industrial bourgeoisie had no real need for a modernising second revolution. Second, the character of early capitalism negated the need for any large-scale state intervention. Third, the early success of British businessmen further negated the need to develop the kind of corporate institutions which emerged in many European states.

A Capitalist State

Mooers argues that Britain lacks a second 'modernising revolution' precisely because the bourgeoisie were able to prosper without recourse to such a struggle:

> 'England's lack of a second revolution, should not be seen as a source of its own backwardness, but rather as an indication of the advanced character of its capitalist development when set against that of the continental countries.[32]

Whereas many neo-socialist authors argue that an archaic state has proved deleterious to the British economy, Mooers argues that the state performed a central role in facilitating the development of British capitalism. Contrary to the Anderson/Nairn thesis, Mooers argues that the state was not backwards but:

> 'In all its major respects – Parliament and the civil service, taxation, property and criminal law, foreign policy and war –

[31] Hay 1994, p.27.
[32] Mooers 1991, p.177.

> the British state in the eighteenth century was uniquely suited to the requirements of capitalism.'[33]

In particular, he points to the rapid growth in property laws during the early 18th Century; for example, the 'famous Waltham Black Act of 1724 which at a single stroke created fifty new capital offences governing poaching and game laws. The act itself had a wider significance though; it also expressed the special role of the 'rule of law' in mediating the separation of 'economics' and 'politics' which characterised the new social relations.'[34] Similarly, there was a plethora of enclosure Acts passed in Parliament throughout the 18th and early 19th Century. Both Mooers and Thompson argue that the law was a powerful ideological weapon in cementing ruling-class hegemony during the 18th Century.

However, although the state performed a crucial role in terms of legitimising the property rights of nascent capitalists, it had no direct role in the running of the economy. Arguably, it was the initial character of British capitalism which was the principle factor in influencing the hands-off relationship between the state and industry. For example, the majority of early industrial firms were relatively small, family-owned enterprises which were largely self-financing (Hutton 1995: 118). Any coherence within industry tended to occur at a regional or local level. The local factory owner would build up a personal relationship with the local bank manager with lending being conducted on a 'word of mouth' basis. Consequently, there was no need for the national industrial banks which developed on the Continent. As investment was largely met from retained profits, companies tended to borrow only small amounts of money from the banks and on a short-term basis. Consequently, 'the banks generally saw no need to take an equity share in firms or play an active role in their management.'[35]

In contrast, the higher start-up costs for nascent German and French companies necessitated the wider availability of larger, long-term loans, which, in turn, led to the development of massive investment banks. As long-term lenders these banks had a much greater interest in the financial soundness of their debtors, leading them to take a much closer involvement in the running of the companies to which they had lent. In Britain, the short-term nature of the financial relationship between banks and industry led to a much more hands off approach.

The key point here is that, although modern commentators such as Hutton may emphasise the economic disadvantages of the structure of British finance, it is a system which has been continually supported by British industry. The priority of British industrialists has historically been to minimise state intervention in the economy. It is this aim which has been the bulwark of its alliance with the aristocracy and financial capital.

---

[33] *Ibid*, p.171.
[34] *Ibid*, p.169.
[35] Hall 1986, p.38.

British Manufacturing: A Victim of its Own Success?

It is also arguable that many historiographical accounts understate the paradoxical effects which the remarkable success of early British manufacturers had on economic development. For, in many ways British industry was a victim of its own initial success. As the first country to industrialise Britain enjoyed a huge advantage in the initial staple manufacturing products. The early success of British manufacturers prompted them into ploughing most of their resources back into the areas in which they had a market advantage. Consequently, there was little interest in diversifying into developing markets which were much more science-based such as the chemical industry:

> 'In 1907 ... 70 per cent of Britain's exports and almost half her industrial output, came from three industries-textiles, coal mining and iron and steel ... Britain depended increasingly on comparatively unsophisticated markets, just as she depended on comparatively unsophisticated products.'[36]

Further, any attempt to analyse the extent of economic decline must account for the huge advantages which initial manufacturers enjoyed. As the first country to industrialise British manufacturers had an initial advantage in securing a large share of the world market which was unsustainable in the long-term. Some decline in manufacturing was inevitable; for example, as geographically larger nations with a larger indigenous supply of natural resources began to industrialise, Britain's share of the global market was bound to fall (Marquand: 121).

Marquand argues that there are two main interpretations of British economic development during this period. First, there is a 'pessimistic' interpretation which points to a declining share of world manufacturing exports. It is argued that this was primarily due to an over-commitment to the old staple industries and a corresponding over-dependence on markets in the colonies. Consequently, British manufacturers were slow to adopt new techniques and to diversify into new scientific industries. Here, the blame for the decline of British industry is placed firmly at the door of entrepreneurs.

In contrast, a more optimistic interpretation suggests that British capitalists were making rational economic choices in investing in overseas markets and the old staple industries. If they did not invest in the technologically advanced industries in which German and American companies dominated, it was because they were making sufficient profits from the old industries. The old staples still sold sufficiently well in the semi-industrial and non-industrial markets on which Britain was becoming increasingly dependent. From this perspective, economic decline becomes the inevitable consequence of the perfectly rational, in capitalist terms, short-termism of profit-maximising businessmen. The guaranteed profits which companies could command in the relatively unsophisticated but lucrative staple industries meant that there was no need to take risks in the developing science-driven industries.

---

[36] Marquand 1988, p.118.

Additionally, industrialists also had the option of investing their profits in the rapidly expanding financial and commercial sectors. By investing in these areas additional profits could be realised with much lesser risk and much more quickly than through risky and long-term investments in industry. This is a position which is supported by commentators such as Rubinstein 1993), Hobsbawm 1969) and, interestingly for the purposes of this paper, Anderson 1987). They argue that in moving their capital from industry into finance and commerce, British entrepreneurs were seeking to maximise the short-term returns on their investments while minimising the associated risks. As such, the development of British capitalism is attributed in Anderson's later work to:

> 'The sum of perfectly rational choices for particular capitals – to persist in traditional sectors in which investment had already been sunk, to move into those overseas markets where competition was least, to avoid extensive reorganisation of labour processes at home, or simply to shift from profit-making altogether into rent or interest – all together determined a creeping loss of competitive capacity for British capitalism as a whole, confronted with Germany or the USA.'[37]

So, in his later work Anderson now attributes Britain's industrial decline, not to the bewitching allure of a leisurely gentlemanly lifestyle, but to the consequence 'of perfectly rational choices for particular capitals'.

A Pervasive Liberal Individualism

This success which the early industrialists enjoyed led to the development of a strong tradition of laissez-faire liberalism within Britain which has historically constrained any political attempts to create a more developmental state. One of the primary reasons why Britain has failed to develop a more interventionist state is that nineteenth century market liberalism was more deeply ingrained within British political culture than on the continent. Within Britain, there was a greater emphasis on individualism, theoretically underpinned by Benthamite utilitarianism. As Crouch 1979) argues, in Britain:

> '... a lengthy development of industrialisation in a context of individualism and restricted state involvement imparted a deep liberalism to political, legal and economic institutions to which neither corporatist industrial relations nor state-regulated capitalism could be easily wedded.'[38]

In contrast, within European nations such as Germany where the state is historically more centrist, governments became more heavily involved in leading economic development.

[37] Anderson 1987, p.72. See also, Hobsbawm 1969, pp.187-92; Rubinstein 1993, p.40.
[38] Crouch 1979, p.17.

In attempting to demonstrate that the industrial middle-classes remained subordinate within a historical bloc which was dominated by the interests of financial capital, Anderson argues that the English bourgeoisie: 'produced no major political philosophy that became hegemonic in the society.'[39] However, arguably, liberal individualism was a major philosophical influence on the development of state/civil society relations within Britain. Bolstered by their initial economic success, the early industrialists did indeed pursue a political and ideological agenda. In seeking to protect their newly acquired wealth, the urban bourgeoisie vigorously advocated the virtues of social and economic individualism.

The spontaneous development of British capitalism meant that the state's role in the economy was limited from the outset. Following in the theoretical tradition of Locke and Smith, the industrial bourgeoisie sought to ensure that it remained that way. Therefore, in arguing that Britain's economic decline is due to the failings of an archaic ruling class, much of the literature fails to recognise that the industrialists were committed to a similar political and ideological agenda. The industrialists did not ally themselves with the ancien regime because they were dazzled by the aura of feudal grandeur but as it was in their own immediate economic interests.

Industrial Capital's Support for a Minimalist State

Within much of the neo-socialist literature it is argued that Britain's economic decline is primarily the consequence of a failure to create a more developmental state. Authors such as Nairn, Anderson, Hutton and Ingham have argued that a powerful historical alliance between the landed aristocracy and financial capital has continually blocked the creation of a more interventionist role for the state. However, this thesis ignores the fact that the historical priority of industrial capital has also been to support a minimalist state. In particular, there is a failure to recognise the historical opposition of the peak organisations of industrial capital to more state intervention. For example, Mercer argues that the principle opposition to the industrial modernisation proposals of the Attlee government came from the Federation of British Industries (FBI).

The Attlee government introduced various institutional initiatives aimed at improving industrial productivity. First, a number of bodies were established to promote increased productivity, notably the Productivity Efficiency Service and the Anglo-American Council on Productivity. Second, there was an attempt to introduce a number of Development Councils, aimed at co-ordinating development plans at a sectoral level. However, under strong opposition from the FBI these councils had little power and were all dissolved soon after the defeat of Attlee's government.

Therefore, at a theoretical level it may be plausible to argue that a more interventionist state would have been in the general interests of industrial capital. However, this ignores the inherent logic of capitalism. Individual firms are unlikely to sacrifice their own immediate interests in order to fur-

[39] Anderson 1966, p.17.

ther the interests of the national economy. Fearful of working class militancy and the creation of a centrally planned socialist state, industrial capital has historically allied itself with financial capital in order to preserve a degree of autonomy over its own interests, regardless of the insecurity of those interests. Consequently, they eagerly embraced classical liberal philosophy as the theoretical justification for their own economic autonomy. What is remarkable is the extent of their success in maintaining this autonomy and restricting the growth of the state.

The growth of the British state during the twentieth century has not, as is depicted in neo-liberal accounts, been an inexorably upward process. In reality, conservative forces have been remarkably successful in containing the state's growth. Cronin (1991) identifies two principal factors which have: 'been primarily responsible for limiting the expansion of the state: the anti-state logic embedded in the politics of taxation and the self-denying tendencies inherent in the unique structure of the British state.'[40] Any political party wishing to expand the state must not only convince the electorate of the benefits of higher taxes but must also counter fierce opposition from within the state bureaucracy itself.

In particular, the Treasury has historically opposed any greater economic role for the state. However, as Ingham (1984) argues, the Treasury has a vested interest in lobbying for minimal state intervention and low government spending. It is the Treasury's strict control over the public purse which is the basis of its own institutional power. Consequently, limited public expenditure increases its political influence over other state departments. Therefore, it is clear that any government wishing to create a more interventionist state faces a number of formidable structural constraints. In particular, they are likely to face vigorous opposition from both the financial sector and the peak industrial organisations, as well as from the Treasury.

Conclusion

Much of the existing historiographical literature argues that Britain's economic decline is primarily due to the failings of an archaic ruling class. However, this idealist approach understates the significance of structural factors in the evolution of the British economy. A principle factor in the development of the British economy is the initial character of its capitalism. As the first country to industrialise, British industrialists enjoyed a huge market advantage which lessened the need for a more active economic role for the state. As such, from the outset British capitalism was markedly liberal. Many of the institutions which evolved with the development of capitalism were also influenced by a pervasive classical liberal philosophy. Therefore, the liberal character of early British capitalism was an influential factor in the development of the modern state, which in turn influenced the development of the economy. The most significant continuity within this historical trajectory is not the continued hegemony of an archaic ruling class, but the priority given to maintaining a minimal economic role for

[40] Cronin 1991, p.5.

the state by British capitalism as a whole and key institutions within the British state.

Bibliography

P.Anderson, 'Socialism and Pseudo-Empiricism', *New Left Review*, 35, 1966.

P.Anderson, *English Questions*, Verso, 1992.

C.Barnett, *Audit of War: The Illusion and Reality of Britain as a Great Nation*, Macmillan, 1986.

J.Baxendale, 'Review of Martin J. Weiner's *English Culture and the Decline of the Industrial Spirit 1850-1980*', *History Workshop Journal*, 21, 1986.

P.J.Cain & A.G.Hopkins, *British Imperialism; Innovation and Expansion, 1688-1914*, Longman, 1993.

J.Cronin, *The Politics of State expansion; War, State and Society in Twentieth Century Britain*, Routledge, 1991.

C.Crouch (ed), *State and Economy in Contemporary Capitalism*, Croom Helm, 1979.

B.Fine & L.Harris, *The Peculiarities of the British Economy*, Lawrence & Wishart, 1985.

A.Gamble, *Britain in Decline*, 4th Edition, Macmillan, 1994.

A.Gramsci, *Selections From Prison Notebooks*, Lawrence & Wishart, 1971.

P.Hall, *Governing the Economy; The Politics of State Intervention in Britain and France*, Polity Press, 1986.

C.Hay, 'The Structural and Ideological Contradictions of Britain's Post-War Reconstruction', *Capital and Class*, 54, 1994.

E.J.Hobsbawm, *Industry and Empire*, Penguin Books, 1968.

W.Hutton, *The State We're In*, Jonathan Cape, 1995.

G.Ingham, *Capitalism Divided*, Macmillan, 1984.

D.Marquand, *The Unprincipled Society*, Jonathan Cape, 1988.

C.Mooers, *The Making of Bourgeois Europe*, Verso, 1991.

T.Nairn, 'The British Political Elite', *New Left Review*, 23, 1964.

T.Nairn, 'The Twilight of the British State', *New Left Review*, 101, 1977.

K.Nield, 'A Symptomatic Dispute? Notes on the Relation Between Marxian Theory and Historical Practice in Britain', *Social Research*, 47/3, 1980.

J.Paxman, *Friends in High Places; Who Runs Britain?*, Penguin, 1991.

W.D.Rubinstein, *Capitalism, Culture and Decline in Britain*, Routledge, 1994.

E.P.Thompson, *The Poverty of Theory*, Merlin Press, 1978.

M.J.Weiner, *English Culture and the Decline of the Industrial Spirit, 1850-1980*, Cambridge University Press, 1981.

The Global Development and Spread of Policies and Political Institutions

Rob Hulme
University of Central Lancashire

'Transferring Education Policies: a case-study of US-UK Policy transfer in the reform of further and higher education in the 1980s and 1990s'

Summary

This paper attempts to make a contribution to the debate on the international movement of policies, initially by offering a brief evaluation of the utility of the model of policy transfer generated by Dolowitz & Marsh (1996) and secondly through an application of this model to policy development in further and higher education in Britain, during the 1980s and 1990s. It finds that American policy goals, ideas and mechanisms were transferred in the process of reforming the system from an élite to a mass basis. Problems are identified concerning the explanatory power of the transfer model in a policy arena featuring strong central state control. The paper concludes by suggesting a future direction for transfer studies: a focus on the role of ideology in the process of changing policies.

Transferring Education Policies

There is currently burgeoning interest in the movement of policy ideas, structures and mechanisms between countries. That political scientists should focus on policy transfer can be explained in part because of the increasing integration of political and social systems coupled with the increasing tendency for policy makers to look abroad for responses to policy problems and perhaps in greater part to the need to transcend the pluralistic limitations of contemporary theories of public policy which present us with useful explanations for the continuity of policy in every significant policy arena but do not explain why and how policies change. The literature on policy transfer is undergoing development and even the most significant recent contributions – Dolowitz & Marsh (1996), Bennett (1991) and Rose (1993) – do not try to explain the transformation of public policy. They do, however, raise significant challenges for theorists of public policy. Many of the model's theoretical constraints are familiar from other meso-theories of policy making, in particular policy networks. Policy transfer seems to possess an almost universal applicability to any policy area, it lacks a satisfactory account of the role of ideology in shaping policy and it is as yet, unable to relate state theory to implementation studies. The literature suffers from a lack of terminological and theoretical clarity, the distinctions between policy transfer, diffusion, lesson drawing, learning and borrowing are far from clear and there is a tendency to focus on actors , processes and outcomes within policy sectors to the exclusion of analytical discourse.

Whilst the literature on policy transfer currently lacks the theoretical clarity and depth to offer explanations of why policies are transformed, it is distinguishable from other models of policy making through its concern for policy development rather than continuity. It is therefore, one of the most useful tools we have in accounting for developments in a complex policy arena like education. The range of influences on the transfer literature, particularly the influence of critical social theory through works such as Flora & Alber (1981) on policy diffusion, provides the field with a eclecticism which overarches the disciplines. Should policy transfer be linked to a model of policy development which provides sufficient scope for the role of ideology in shaping problem definition and the generation of policy responses, it could advance our understanding of the process of policy innovation and change.

Education policy in Britain provides an ideal case study for policy transfer due to the complexity of the educational state, its range of actors and networks and the centrality of education policy to all political and ideological projects. The model of transfer generated by Dolowitz & Marsh (1996) offers the best available framework for analysing the movement of policy in education, both within and between nations. It is premised on the idea that transfer is a process:

> 'in which knowledge about policies, administrative arrangements, institutions etc. in one time or place is used in the development of policies, administrative arrangements and institutions in another time or place'. (p.3)

The model distinguishes types and levels of transfer between various actors using a series of questions: what is policy transfer, who transfers, why is policy transferred, what is transferred and from where are lessons drawn? Below, the questions are considered briefly in turn and applied to recent developments in British education policy.

Attempting to provide an answer to the question of what transfer is in education policy reveals both the lack of terminological and conceptual clarity in the literature and the many variations in substance of scope in the nature of the policies transferred. Recent studies, primarily of 'United States'-Britain transfer in education policy by Finegold et al (1992), Phillips (1992), Robertson & Waltman (1992) and Raffe & Rumberger (1993) refer to appropriation, borrowing, diffusion, copying and learning. Borrowing is the most frequently used category in the comparative education literature; it is of some limited utility in explaining the appropriation of a reform mechanism or institutional form, student loans and city technology colleges for instance, but it over-simplifies the nature of transfer or diffusion and under-values the specificity of education policies to the political processes, economic conditions and cultural values of their host country (Phillips 1992). Borrowing might more usefully be understood in the context of a 'market' of ready made policy responses (Finegold et al 1992), brokered by 'policy entrepreneurs'.

Providing answers to the questions of who transfers policy and why it is transferred helps us to build a more complete view of the policy making process within the 'educational state'. Policy making in British education is conducted on a number of interlocking sites and levels, in short, a series of networks (Marsh & Rhodes 1993). Successful formulation and implementation of policy often depends on the effective transfer of policy goals between a series of networks in both policy formulation and implementation. The problems encountered by the British government in implementing the national curriculum illustrate this point. Furthermore, The cross-sectoral nature of education policy facilitates the transfer of policy options from related policy arenas, particularly employment on issues such as the national framework for vocations qualifications (NVQs). The transfer of policy ideas and goals in response to shared problems in education clearly has an international dimension, particularly between Britain and America over the past 10-12 years (Robertson & Waltman 1992, Raffe & Rumberger 1992).

Sabatier (1988) provides a perspective on policy development which sheds more light on who is transferring policy and why they are doing so. Sabatier perceives policy change as a process involving the interaction of various competing advocacy coalitions from within a policy community. Such coalitions comprise various actors including ideological groupings within political parties, elements of the media, some actors in government etc. They share a set of core beliefs which are translated into policy goals and set out to achieve these goals by influencing government at various levels. Conflicting advocacy coalitions are arbitrated by 'policy brokers' with an interest in stabilising the system. The educational policy community could be seen to divide in such a way in the late 1980s and early 1990s over schools reform. A coalition advocating 'cultural restorationism' (Ball 1994) sought to transfer policy goals on curriculum and schools organisation from Britain's past, while neo-liberal 'vocational trainers' (Ball 1989) drew policy lessons from the USA and Germany. Evidence of this conflict and its unsuccessful brokering can be seen in the 1988 Education Reform Act. The role of policy broker in Sabatier's model can be equated to that of policy entrepreneur in the model expounded by Rose and Dolowitz & Marsh. Such actors usually wish to see organisational change in their domestic system – see the case of the HMI in DES (1989).

Models of transfer and diffusion are therefore, of interest in clarifying the definition of policy problems. The transfer of policy options between nations most commonly occurs where there is commonality and compatibility in problem definition and a history of preferred solutions between the host and the borrowing systems. In the case of the United States-United Kingdom, transfer also occurs because the two nations are faced with similar structural problems, such as skills shortages and participation rates among the young and the need to reform educational institutions for a post-welfare era. Overwhelmingly though, ideological compatibility drives policy transfer. Policy makers in education seek to borrow symbols and political language in forcing the educational agenda, the 1980s witnessed two way transfer (USA-United Kingdom) on policy toward national curricular standards (Ball 1994) and Training and Enterprise Councils (Robertson & Waltman 1992, Dolowitz 1996). It can be argued that a global market in education policy options exists from which decision makers can engage in ideological mix and match in the search for quick responses to long-term problems (Finegold et al 1992), though such strategies run a high risk of failure as the transfer of American models of student loan to the United Kingdom demonstrated (McFarland 1993). The success of education policy transfer then depends on what is being transferred. Policy ideas and goals such as the American notion of a market have been transferred and adapted to host conditions (Gewirtz; Ball & Bowe 1996; Bridges & Mclaughlin 1996). Institutions, mechanisms and agents borrowed without sufficient regard for political, economic and cultural specificity such as Private Industry Councils, and the Assisted Places Scheme can be more problematic (Bailey 1993, Gewirtz et al 1996).

In assessing from where lessons are drawn in education policy, Richard Rose's maxim that policy makers are inheritors before they are choosers (Marsh & Dolowitz 1996, p.17) is apposite. The permanence of bureaucratic and professional interests within the networks and coalitions ensures that past practice and habit informs policy formulation before innovation. The borrowing of both positive and negative lessons across time from both domestic and foreign history is not uncommon. This process is not hindered by sectoral boundaries in national systems. The Dearing review's current deliberations on the American Community College model, devised in the 1960s is a case in point.

Policy transfer in education is constrained by many factors and the most salient are highlighted in the case study. The stability of networks in education determines very strong policy inheritance and undermines any attempt at innovative transfer. Ultimately, the political, administrative, economic and cultural specificity of education policies ensures that only general policy goals and symbols can be transferred in substance.

United Kingdom-United States Policy Transfer in the Reform of the System of Post-Compulsory Education in England

It is argued in this case study, that the British Government transferred policy from the United States in the late 1980s and 1990s in transforming post compulsory education (the primary focus will be higher education but the scope of policy development also involves the system of further education (FE) in England). The *Education Reform Act, 1988*, the *Higher Education Reform Act, 1991*, and the *Further and Higher Education Act, 1992*, along with intermediary legislation, had the effect of transforming the system from an élite to a mass basis by tripling the numbers in both sectors (Department of Education and Science 1991). To this end, the American notion of normalising full time education to 18 and mass participation in higher education was transferred as a policy goal, as was the basic model of a marketisation in higher education, mirroring in many respects competitive market for schools. Policy mechanisms to facilitate the operation of the market were also 'borrowed', student loans and through 'incorporation', certain organisational forms and management techniques for colleges and universities were transferred.

The transformation of these sectors of education though, was not simply a one dimensional process of appropriation from the United States. The shape and character of the post 1992 post 16 educational state was also determined by ideas transferred from Britain's history of educational policy making. Ending the binary divide and the process of 'massification', was in some ways the delayed fulfilment of the Robbins report from 30 Years earlier. Crucially, the notion of what was not transferred from the USA is as important as that which was borrowed as the Conservatives pursued their primarily ideologically driven agenda for creating a higher education and training system for the post-welfare state in creating the 'Learning Society' (CBI 1989) and creating a mass system which could be controlled.

Why was the System Transformed?

By the late 1980s the system of further and higher education was perceived by government to be unsatisfactory and failing to deliver due to the impact of structural changes and the need to mould educational institutions to the new post Fordist economy. The primary reason for action was the perception that Britain was failing to respond to the challenges presented by transitions in the global economy and thereby falling behind international competitors particularly in the USA, Germany and Japan. Further and Higher education had to be restructured in order to supply the demand for a generation of young people possessing flexible polyvalent skills for the emergent post Fordist industries in the services and high technology (Jessop 1989, Harvey 1992).

Britain's lag in the global skills revolution presented a two fold problem for the system of post compulsory education. First, the lack of participation both at 16 and at 18. Raffe & Rumberger (1992) indicate that in 1990 only 50% of 16 year olds stayed in full time education, with only 20% going on to full-time education beyond 18. Prior to the Dearing recommendations for FE in November 1995, and despite the doubling of the FE population in the period 1985-95 to 57.3 and the trebling of the post 18 population in higher at 33%, Britain was still third from bottom of the OECD world league tables on participation (Nash, *Times Educational Supplement*, 10.11.95). Secondly, and inseparable from the participation issue, Britain, suffered (and still does) from a 'low-skills equilibrium' (Finegold et al 1992), whereby, within an education system which encourages academic specialisation for a small percentage of young people preparing for higher education, there is a disincentive for the majority of low-achieving young people to seek further education and training. This disincentive, it has been argued (Ainley 1993), is encouraged by a tradition in Britain which is distrustful of German style planning on vocational and industrial training and which emphasises the virtues, for young people of the low-wage deregulated work which the government has created. Overall, the government had to respond to the fact that the new circumstances demanded higher skills and much greater participation yet its policies in education and training encouraged 'skill polarisation' and an unskilled youth labour market.

Allied to this was the need to create a new type of education system for the post -Welfare state. The expansion of further and particularly higher education in the post war period has been closely tied to the political management of the welfare state (Fulton 1990, Scott 1995). The last significant period of expansion in higher education took place in the 1960s in response to the Robbins Report in 1963 and sought(largely unsuccessfully) to develop a national system of post compulsory education through the 'nationalisation' of the Polytechnics and colleges. It was intended by Robbins and Anthony Crosland, that the resultant expansion in numbers and more open access would fulfil another central aim of the post -war social democratic welfare project. Reform produced an increase in participation from 8% in 1963 to 13% in 1981, rising to 15% by 1985 (Scott 1996, p.5).

During the 1980s, Conservative governments sought to develop in Britain the ideological and institutional foundations for the post-Welfare state. Partly in response to the problems indicated above this has culminated in the pursuit of a political project, fuelled by 'new right' ideology and intended to de-construct the welfare state and the social democratic/ neo corporatist institutions and techniques which sustained it. Bennett (1990, p.22.) encapsulates the aims of the post welfare strategy in a threefold maxim. Initially, the benefits of attempting to achieve equity through welfare are fewer than those to be gained by increasing efficiency, secondly, governments cannot interpret needs or allocate resources as effectively as the market and thirdly, that welfare produced a 'dependency' which undermined enterprise and individual achievement.

The government's response to such problem definition in dealing with the management of all public services has been , as Burns et al (1994) indicate to embark on a three fold strategy of extending markets, engendering a new managerialism and extending 'democracy' in the form of consumerism etc. This has resulted in the creation of 'quasi markets' throughout the public services. Within the educational state, a process of 'marketisation' was brought about by encouraging of competition, the development of contracts to deliver service, the separation of purchaser and provider and the development of the customer service model backed up by audit for the sector.

Two factors made the approach to post compulsory education distinct. First, the strategy was accompanied by shedding of the government's duty to provide higher education for purpose social justice, or indeed economic efficiency this meant that apart from the usual managerialist reform , new structures for self government should be generated. Second, and more significantly, in an era of contraction throughout welfare, the government intended to expand.

> 'The Thatcher and Major Governments, far more committed to rolling back the frontiers of the state than any other European government, nevertheless presided over the an expansion of

> higher education as remarkable as that undertaken in the high noon of the welfare state following the Robbins report of 1963.' (Scott 1995, p.222)

Thus the task of explaining the development of strategies to reform the system and from whence they were generated or transferred is more complex than in other areas where public services have reconfigured. The government looked to the USA for policy responses for two reasons. The United States system was facing comparable problems and could be relied upon for ideological and political parity.

The USA was facing similar structural problems in response to global change but with difference in terms of manifestation in the system of post compulsory education. The USA also had a need to respond to the new market for flexible labour and accordingly to increase participation but as (Raffe & Rumberger 1992 p.137) observe, the problem was inverted, where Britain had a 'staying on problem,' the American system had a 'drop out problem.'

In the USA participation rates were at a level that Britain aspired to. In 1986 Nine in ten Americans went onto the equivalent of further education and more than eight in ten stayed beyond 17. A significant HMI Report into the United States system of Higher education in 1989 (DES 1989, p.3) observed with some admiration the participation rates in post compulsory education in the USA:

> '55% of 18-19 year olds, 33% of 20-21 year olds, 18% of 22-24 year olds and 9% of those aged 25-29 years were involved in some form of education.'

The main focus in the participation debate in the United States is in the equivalent age range to FE in Britain, on the high school drop out rate from 16-18. Within the 'schooling to adulthood 'model operating in America, 50% drop out rate in higher education is regarded as acceptable. Mcfarland (1992) and Raffe & Rumberger (1992) comment that debate in the United States addresses broader issues such as the purpose of education beyond 16, this discourse tended to focus, and still does, upon those groups least represented in the system – particularly ethnic minorities, where dropout rates are highest.

Throughout the 1980s the administrations of Reagan and Bush followed programmes of public sector reform similar to those pursued by the Thatcher governments, described above. The reform movement was underpinned by shared assumptions about the proper role and function of welfare and similar interpretations of the state's role in solving these problems. Such ideological compatibility assisted in the establishment of f habitual communication of policy ideas through established networks throughout the eighties (Robertson & Waltman 1992).

In the field of post compulsory education there was a shared tradition of voluntarism in approaching the provision of training and a commitment to the market as a policy alternative to 'public service education'. The 'ideology of the market' (Ball 1996) was developed and refined much earlier in the

USA. There are however, significant differences in terms of the purpose of the educational market and the level of control and accountability exercised within it.

Prior to reform, efforts were made to gather information in the form of visits which produced a seminal report from the HMI. Two years before the publication of the White Papers *Education and Training for the 21st Century* and *Higher Education; a New Framework*, the DES commissioned a Report by Her Majesty's Inspectorate into the structure, funding and content of the American HE system. The resultant report, *Aspects of Higher Education in the United States* accounted for the Inspectorate's brief to:

> 'make comparisons between the two systems of higher education and to highlight those features of the United States system which have implications for higher education developments in the United Kingdom'. (DES 1989, p.vii)

The Report found much to commend in the United States system in terms of the broadly based curriculum with its emphasis on skills, on organisational form of American colleges with their 'responsive structures', quality assessment and 'sensitivity to the needs of the users of further and higher education'. Detailed and salutary lessons were drawn for policy makers on achieving higher participation rates for underrepresented groups and on the range and diversity of America's academic and vocational programmes. Significantly, recommendations were made about the structure and content of education in the American Junior Colleges(the nearest equivalent to FE) where modular structures and flexibility had been seen to increase access and raise participation. The 'important features of successful student loan schemes' were also observed. Negative lessons about 50% wastage figures and the absence of national standards balanced the good news.

Information and Knowledge had been gathered previously in 1987 with the three visits of Secretary of State for Education Kenneth Baker with the specific intention of studying the United States system of student loans (McFarland 1993). More structural knowledge about the operation of the American education market had been gathered through the visit of Baker the previous year to investigate magnet schools.

The tradition of commissioning visits by educationalists to facilitate policy transfer has continued in to 1996 with the Dearing Review's investigation into the relationship between American Community Colleges and local Universities. Local networks have also crossed the Atlantic in the form of College Managers seeking information about new organisational forms (Shackleton 1993). The extent to which such participants act as policy entrepreneurs or brokers open to debate.

What was Transferred from the USA?

Through the series of legislative reform referred to above, Britain transferred, at least superficially, a basis for the emulation of the American model of mass higher education, featuring in particular the Us notion of an educational market. The HMI anticipated legislative change in observing that:

> 'The United States has led the way in providing a system of mass higher education based on open entry to degree courses more broadly based than those in England.' (DES 1989, p.i)

In another act of prescience, prior to the government's White Paper of 1991 which set the target of 'nearly one in three young people to enter education by the year 2000' (DES 1991), HMI commented:

> 'If higher education institutions in England are to achieve the participation levels set by the government they will need to re-orient themselves in new ways to recruit not only more of the 18 year old cohort but also groups currently under-represented such as women and mature students.' (DES 1989, p.29)

The Government exceeded its own target inside five years. By 1995 the age participation index in higher education had become 32% (Nash, *Times Educational Supplement*, 10.11.95), surpassing the most rigorous definitions of a mass system Trow (1973) defines mass systems as those which enrol between 15 and 40% of the relevant age group and universal systems as those enrolling more than 40%. Britain it seems is en route to universalism. This direct emulation of the structures of the American system is all the more remarkable since as Scott (1995) observes, Britain only achieved 15% in the mid 1980s.

> 'Between 1987 and 1992 participation almost doubled from 14.6% to 27.8%. It was only yesterday, in that turbulent half decade, that Britain irreversibly acquired a mass system.' (Scott 1995, p.5)

In emulating the American notion of a mass system, there have been attempts to revise the notion of 'higher education 'in the creation of what Scott refers to as the 'multiversity', an institution which provides a full range of post compulsory qualifications ranging from the vocational to the post graduate. More open access and diverse modular structures are essential in realising this form.

> 'One of the main characteristics of post compulsory education in America is its diversity. A great variety of colleges and universities offer a wide range of vocational, recreational and leisure programmes of study which serve a wide range of individual needs and aspirations. This, together with the modular nature of many of the programmes on offer and the broad general, nature of ... degree programmes has made higher education much more accessible to all sections of the population.' (DES 1989, p.28)

Ideas on participation and institutional purpose were transferred across functional sectors, particularly, the community and two year Colleges. The Report suggests that consideration should be given to participation rates and strategies for retention in the Junior Colleges, 'which perform similar work to Colleges of further education in England' and suggests the coupling of statistics on participation from the English Further and Higher Sectors as an indicator of success. The primary impact such policy goals since the ending of the binary divide has been the emphasis, particularly but not exclusively on contractual or 'partnership' agreements with colleges of further education, further blurring the distinction between the functional sectors of post compulsory, further and higher education. In transferring such policy goals involves the re-conceptualisation of the purpose of the system. Such developments have only just begun with the extension of franchise arrangements. The Dearing review of higher education is awaiting the results of a report into the 'two plus two' partnership agreements common in the America between Community Colleges and local Universities (Meikle, *Guardian*, 29.10.96). Endorsement of this system would hasten the process of transfer and the fulfilment of policy goals set down in the late 1980s.

In drawing such lessons, the transfer the American model of mass education involved the re-conceptualisation of the purpose of the system. Primarily, the normalisation of school and college attendance to 18 followed by the transfer of as many as possible to university in an attempt to provide 'Education Without Jobs' (Ainley 1992, p.149). Jones & Wallace capture the spirit of this transition in identifying, 'training and education policies, backed by social security policies, moving towards creating just two groups of young people: trainees or students.'

True emulation of the American system demands the reversal of the proportions of these groups from a majority of trainees in the early 1980s to a majority of students in the 1990s (Ainley 1994). Negative lessons were also drawn. HMI compared the HE wastage rate of 50% in the USA with the 1988 figure for 80% success rate on English degrees. 'if participation rates in the United Kingdom are to reach American levels, wastage may become a more pressing problem than it is at the moment.' (DES 1989, p.30)

The influence of the American notion of a market for education has been pervasive in every aspect of British educational reform. The Government declared its intent in legislating the end of the binary divide and bestowing legal autonomy or incorporation on all institutions to:

> 'Increased competition among the present universities, polytechnics and colleges will promote the further efficient expansion which the Government wants to see'. (DES 1991, p.2)

The realisation of a post-16 market has led to the direct competition between colleges of further education and sixth form colleges, universities and colleges of higher education for students in search of demand-led funding allocated by the New funding Councils the FEFC and the HEFC, in an attempt to replicate the market in American HE.

Legislative reform of both sectors has hastened the development of new management styles and organisational forms in colleges and universities. This of course, represents the advent of the New Public Management , intended to deliver greater 'accountability' and 'democracy' referred to above (Burns et al 1994). The 'Responsive institution' had arrived with a United

States inspired customer orientation. HMI in 1988 advised that with the new corporate status bestowed upon Polytechnics, soon to be followed by the incorporation of FE colleges, institutions must become more 'responsive':

> 'The new governing bodies of our further and higher education institutions have much to learn from the American model, for this is based on directions from citizens rather than government'. (DES 1989, p.27)

The report highlights in particular, the importance of 'determining the mission of the institution' and the reviewing and appraisal of the work of managers. In carrying out such responsibilities they conclude that institutions, 'will need to be sensitive to the needs of users of further and higher education' (DES 1989, p.27) In further and higher education as elsewhere, this ethos has expressed itself as in attempts to audit and manage the output of institutions by measuring performance through new Quality Audit (QA) systems. Surviving competition in the new market where the relationship between funding and QA is so strong has become a critical issue.

What was not Transferred from the USA?

A number of aspects of the reform of further and higher education were not transferred from the USA. The influence of ideas from the past, and the transformation of American ideas when applied to the British circumstances, raise critical issues about Anglo-American policy transfer.

The contemporary American notion of mass post compulsory education was not the only model available to policy makers in the late 1980s. The massification of the system can be argued represent the transfer of the policy goals of the Robbins Report of 1963 into a contemporary context. Before Robbins was commissioned to produce a blueprint for expansion, the British system was highly selective and thus conformed to Trow's (1973) notion of an élite system. Fewer than 8% of the age range was enrolled. Crosland had briefed Robbins to produce a blueprint for the expansion of the university system (Fulton 1990, Silver 1990) and though in many ways the outcome of HE policy did not match its intentions, Robbins had succeeded in developing the notion of a mass system.

The Robbins Report was not fully implemented largely due the efforts of the University Grants Committee which provided a focus for élitist elements within the Higher Education policy Community. Thus the embryonic model of massification created in Robbins emerged as what Scott characterises as 'an extended élite system' in the binary structure (p.71), increasing the participation level from 8 to 28% in the period between the mid 60s and the 1990s but also allowing the retention the élitism and collegiality demanded by the university establishment of the 1960s, and which even now, characterises the 'exceptionalism of the British system'.

It is possible then, to see the renewal of expansion in the late 1980s and early 1990s as the transference of the goals of Robbins into the circumstances of the post welfare era. A consolidation of post war student growth, rather than a radical massification on the American model, underpinned by the New Public Management techniques of consumerism, managerialism and control. Developing this logic, it might also be possible to argue, that Britain is only now ready to transfer the original model of mass system of higher education- that developed in the 1960s in the United States. Scott observes that structural differences in the operation the American and British systems, forbids too close a comparison:

> 'too little attention perhaps has been paid, to the particularities of American political culture, with its paradoxical combination of extensive state regulation (the result of multi-layered federal-state-local government) and strong commitment to the market. The American system (of HE in the 1960s) was shaped by this culture. Planned stratification on the one hand; an open market on the other.' (Scott 1995, p.8)

Transitions in British political culture combined with a neo-liberal approach to welfare and public management have perhaps, finally prepared Britain for the American 'multiversity' of the 1960s.

Frequent reference has been made to the influence of the American notion of an 'educational market' in the reform of the British education system. However, due in part to the structural constraints referred to above and in part to the ideological project pursued by British Conservative governments a pure representation of the American market has not been created. Instead, a 'very British' pseudo or 'quasi market' (LeGrand 1990) has been imposed in education.

Since Britain lacks the market tradition in education, at HE as well as secondary level, long established in the United States (Burton Clarke 1993), and because no natural market exists in the sector, the government has been forced to intervene in an attempt to engineer the type of marketised public services referred to above. Thus as Felstead (1993) notes, policies and administrative mechanisms have been created in order to 'mimic the market'. The funding councils for further education , the FEFC and higher education HEFCE were created to stimulate the demand side of the market in post compulsory education. Both bodies were established with clear instructions to operate a system of funding which is irrevocably linked to student numbers. Within this mechanism, institutions receive a core funding based on a fixed percentage of their previous years income and bid for further students and courses against other institutions with agreed programme areas.

Other aspects of the United States model of the educational market have been 'filtered out' because they do not accord with the government's ideological project. Ball (1993) comparing the operation of the market in schooling in the United States and the United Kingdom finds that the United Kingdom's schools market is

> 'far more radical in the application of ideologically driven

> policy' but in terms of reproducing the American market orthodoxy (Chubb & Moe, 1990) the 'United Kingdom education system is organised as a very strange market indeed'. (p.8)

The fundamental difference is that the United States market systems in schools and in higher education have significant communitarian commitments to the 'social goals of equality or justice embedded within them' (Ball 1993, p.15). British Government's have rejected this aspect of market reform. Ball highlights the Chicago School projects with their focus on desegregation and the redirection of state funds to low income and special needs students.

Aspects of Higher Education (DES 1989, p.20) highlights one of the fundamental differences in market orientation.

> 'Equal access for all suitably qualified young people is a major goal of the American system One measure of progress toward achieving this goal is the participation rates of various groups such as women, blacks, Hispanics and mature students.'

It would be necessary, it suggested, to reorient the nature of higher education in the United Kingdom in order to transfer this goal. Such notions of equity have been absent in the transformation of Britain's system.

Finally, fundamental shifts in the character of the British state have served to determine the nature of policy transfer between the United states and the United Kingdom in post compulsory education reform. Due to the cumulative effect of public sector reform over the past 17 years, Britain now has a 'franchise' or 'contract' state (Hambleton, 1994, DuGay 1994, Herden 1992). Contracting responsibilities in the post compulsory sector allows the government to side-step the apparently empowering aspects of the market and to increase, rather than delegate its control of education. Government can then select those elements of the United States mass model which best suit its ideological purposes. As a consequence , government is more able to control the definition of policy objectives. In education, as with other areas this has meant the fragmentation of problem definition. Policy tends to be aimed not at generic problems such as the skills shortage but at individuals

It has already been noted that management of the new further and higher education market has involved the abrogation of the government's duty to provide public education and the delegation of public authority QUANGOs such as the FEFC and HEFCE, TECs etc. The 'contracting out' of regulatory, budgetary and auditing powers to such agents is defended by government as a means of decentralisation and a direct means of extending democracy through strengthening accountability and furthering individual empowerment (Burns et al 1994). For the post compulsory sectors this process has involved the tightening of government's control of the steering, formulation and implementation of policy. The use of unaccountable QUANGOs has allowed government to 'de-politicise' education policy by allowing the redefinition of implementation as a technical process and thereby marginalising those interests and voices within the educational networks, at all levels, who would be opposed to government policy, such as Labour controlled local authorities, lecturers and training providers. It also allows government to escape technical problems in implementing reform (that is, changes in employment status in further education colleges) by 'dumping' the problem onto a high profile public body such as The Colleges Employers Forum.

To conclude, the application of models of policy transfer to education policy raises many questions about the utility and future directions for work in this field. The model of policy transfer established by Dolowitz & Marsh provides a useful means of examining the recent growth of international policy transfer in education. Its simplicity and flexibility allows scholars of comparative education policy to explore the international movement of policy ideas whilst recognising diversity in structures, cultures and administrative systems.

There is a great need in the analysis of education policy, and indeed more generally, for a policy model which assists in explaining how and why policies change. The models most frequently applied to education policy, that is, policy networks, partnership etc, are extremely useful in explaining policy continuity, but add little to our account of change. Policy transfer assists in the explaining the development of particular policy platforms such student loans, but as yet it cannot fully account for the ideological factors determining changes in general policy movements such as the 'massification' of further and higher education.

One way forward could lie in an attempting synthesis of the transfer model with Sabatier's (1988) advocacy coalition approach to policy change. This model might help to explain shifting ideological patterns in policy by among other matters, the helping to distinguish the core and secondary beliefs of the competing advocacy coalitions in each policy sphere, exploring stability and change in advocacy coalitions such as those found in the education policy field and identifying shifts in ideological outlook determined by factors external to the policy field. In so doing, it might be possible to explain some of the problems raised by the case study examined in this work. In particular the means by which explicitly American policy goals were filtered and manipulated by ideologically driven policy makers in the transition of British post compulsory education from élite to mass basis.

References

P.Ainley, *Class and Skill, Changing Divisions of Knowledge and Labour*, Cassell, 1993.

T.Bailey, 'The Mission of TECs and Private Sector Involvement in Training: lessons from PICs', *Oxford Studies in Comparative Education*, 3, 1993.

S.Ball, 'Education Markets, Choice and Social Class: the market as a class strategy in the UK and USA', *British Journal of Sociology of Education*, 14/1, 1993.

S.Ball, *Education Reform*, Oxford University Press, 1994.

S.Ball, *Politics and Policy Making in Education*, Routledge, 1990.

D.Bridges & T.H.McLaughlin, *Education and the Market Place*, Falmer, 1995

D.Burns et al, *The Politics of Decentralisation*, Macmillan, 1994. J.Chubb & T.Moe, *Politics, Markets and America's Schools*, Brookings Institute, 1990

B.Clark, *The Research Foundations of Graduate Education: Germany, Britain, France , USA , Japan*, University of California, 1993.

CBI, *Towards the Skills Revolution, Report of the Vocational Education and Training Task Force*, CBI, 1989

Department of Education and Science, *Higher education: A New Framework*, HMSO, 1991.

Department of Education and Science, *Education and Training for the 21st Century*, HMSO 1991.

Department of Education and Science, *Aspects of Higher Education in the United States of America*, HMSO, 1989

D.Dolowitz & D.Marsh, 'Who Learns What From Whom?: A Review of the Policy Transfer Literature', Muirhead Papers 10, University of Birmingham, 1996.

D.Dolowitz, 'British Employment Policy in the 1980s : A Case Study in Policy Transfer', Muirhead Papers 18, University of Birmingham, 1996.

P.du Gay, 'Businessing Bureaucracy: Entrepreneurial Government and Public Management', ERU Conference, Cardiff 1994

D.Finegold et al, 'Something Borrowed, Something Blue?', *Oxford Studies in Comparative Education*, 2/2, 1992.

A.Felsted, *The Corporate Paradox, Power and Control in the Business Franchise*, Routledge, 1993.

S.Gewirtz, *Markets, Choice and Equity in Education*, Oxford University Press, 1995

R.Hambleton, 'The Contract State and the Future of Public Management', ERU Conference, Cardiff, 1994.

I.Harden, *The Contracting State*, Oxford University Press, 1992

D.Harvey, *The Condition of Post-modernity*, Blackwell, 1992.

B.Jessop, 'Thatcherism.The British Road to post- Fordism', *New Left Review*, 179, 1989.

J.Le Grand & Bartlett, *Quasi Markets and Social Policy*, Wheatsheaf, 1993.

D.Marsh & R.A.W.Rhodes, *Implementing Thatcherite Policies – Audit of an Era*, Oxford University Press, 1992.

D.Marsh & R.A.W.Rhodes, *Policy Networks in British Government*, Clarendon, 1993.

L.McFarland, 'Top up Student Loans: US Models of Student Aid and British Public Policy', *Oxford Studies in Comparative Education*, 13/1, 1993.

J.Meikle, 'Two-Track minds', *Guardian*, 29.10.96.

D.Phillips, 'Borrowing Education Policy', *Oxford Studies in Comparative Education*, 2/2, 1992.

R.Raffe & R.Rumberger, 'Education and Training for 18 Year olds in the UK and the US', *Oxford Studies in Comparative Education*, 3/1, 1993.

D.B.Robertson & J.Waltman, 'The Politics of Policy Borrowing', *Oxford Studies in Comparative Education*, 2/2, 1992.

P.Sabatier, 'An Advocacy Coalition Framework of Policy Change and the Role of Policy Oriented Learning Therein', *Policy Sciences*, 21, 1988.

J.Shackleton, 'US Community Colleges and Further Education in Britain', *Oxford Studies in Comparative Education*, 3/3, 1993.

P.Scott, *The Meanings of Mass Higher Education*, Falmer, 1995.

H.Silver, *Education, Change and the Policy Process*, Falmer, 1990.

I.Nash, 'Britain Comes Last in OECD Table', *Times Higher Education Supplement*, 10.11.95.

M.Trow, *Problems in the Transition From Elite to Mass Higher Education*, Carnegie Commission on Higher Education, 1973.

S.Vickerstaffe & P.Ainley, 'The De-politicisation of Vocational Education and Training in the Contract State: Will it work?', ERU Conference, Cardiff, 1994.

The Politics of Fishing

Mark Gray
Anglesey

'The Role of Fishermen's Organisations in United Kingdom Fisheries' Management'

Introduction

Fisheries policy has risen up the United Kingdom political agenda in recent years, for several reasons. One reason is that the current decline in many fish stocks has led to increasing conflict between fisheries managers (in the Ministry of Agriculture, Fisheries and Food – MAFF) and fishermen. Another reason is that Eurosceptic MPs have used the widespread criticism of the European Union's Common Fisheries Policy (CFP) as a stick with which to beat the European Union. A third reason is xenophobia: the media have hyped up the controversy by taking at face value the fishermen's and the Government's complaints against allegedly illegal fishing by foreign (especially Spanish) vessels and also against quota hopping (foreign countries such as Spain and Holland buying United Kingdom licences with quota allocations).

In this controversy, there are many difficult issues at stake and several solutions have been put forward to settle these issues. One such issue concerns the role of fishermen's organisations in fisheries management. Part of the anger that is felt by United Kingdom fishermen arises out of a sense of frustration that they are excluded from management decision-making processes. Some writers have suggested that the fishing industry would be much better managed if decision-making was devolved to the lowest level possible that is, if the principle of subsidiarity was adopted.

This paper is a contribution to the debate over the proper role of fishermen and their organisations in the management of the United Kingdom fishing industry. We begin with an account of the present structure of United Kingdom fishermen's organisations.

Structure of Fishermen's Organisations

Fishermen's organizations (FOs) in the United Kingdom have been formed to represent the common interests of local fishermen in activities such as: developing harbour activities, protecting fishing grounds from other marine activities (for example, aggregate dredging) and settling disputes between different fishing sectors (often arising from different fishing gear being used over the same ground). The majority of United Kingdom fishermen are members of fish producers' organisations (POs), first established in the United Kingdom in the early 1970s. POs are primarily concerned with marketing activities and distributing catch quotas amongst their member boats, overall quotas being allocated to them by the Government. In Scotland about 95% of all quotas are managed by the POs. The Government wishes to develop the managerial role of POs and give them extra responsibilities, such as dealing with member vessels committing over-quota landing offences, and additional marketing responsibilities including greater co-ordination of landings.

Some fishermen's organisations are concerned with a particular fishing sector (for example, shellfisheries and pelagic fisheries). Some of these are regional, concentrating on local issues such as pollution, protecting fishing grounds and avoiding conflicts with other fishing sectors. Others are nationwide (for example, The Shellfish Association of Great Britain) dealing with matters that affect the entire sector.

Recognised by the Government as the national fishermen's representative organisations in England and Wales, and Scotland are two federations; the National Federation of Fishermen's Organisations (NFFO) and the Scottish Fishermen's Federation (SFF) respectively. Their constituent associations comprise regional and sectoral FOs who remain independent in internal affairs. An executive committee in each of the federations is responsible for formulating a unitary response when, for example, asked to do so by the Ministry of Agriculture, Fisheries and Food (MAFF). The NFFO, established in 1979, is the representative body for fishermen not only in England and Wales, but also in Northern Ireland and the Channel Islands, representing over 1,000 boats in total. Established in 1973, the SFF comprises 7 member associations from the east and west coast, representing several hundred vessels (most over 15m in length). An executive committee in each organisation decides the federation's policy or position on a specific matter, and within each federation there are working groups comprising representatives of particular sectors of fishermen (fishery or region) focusing on issues of concern.

Present Role of Fishermen's Organisations

In accordance with the European Union's fishing strategy outlined in its Common Fisheries Policy, policy and management decisions affecting the entire European Union fleet are made by the Council of Fisheries Ministers. Such decisions include; restricting the fishing capacity of each Member State, allocating the total amount of fish each Member State can land each year and determining technical fishing measures every Member State's fleet has to abide by. Within this management framework, Member States are given a degree of autonomy to decide their own regulations to comply with those introduced by the Council, such as methods of reducing fishing capacity and distributing their allocated national fish quota amongst their fleet. The national fishermen's federations (NFFO and SFF) are formally consulted by the European Union and Government's fisheries departments – MAFF – in England and Wales and SOAEFD (Scottish Office Agriculture, Environment and Fisheries Department)in Scotland, on fisheries policy. Consultation also takes place with smaller FOs, often on policies that may affect a particular fishery or a certain area. Consultations may take the form of meetings or written communications. An annual meeting takes place between the industry, including the national FOs, and Government in early November, when the industry is told of the intentions of the European Union Council of Fisheries Ministers for the coming year; for example, their allocation of Total Allowable Catches (TACs) for particular species to each Member State.

At policy level, the Ministry frequently consults FOs over plans to introduce regulations and often asks the industry for its views on European Union and Government policies and for policies and regulations it would like to see introduced. For example, in 1993 the Ministry asked the industry to formulate a package of measures to address problems of stock depletion in order to meet European Union fleet reduction obligations. Both the NFFO and SFF duly replied. The Government has consulted the industry more extensively than usual during 1996, over issues such as decommissioning, regional management strategies,technical measures and modes of dealing with the problems of flagships (foreign-owned boats allocated United Kingdom quotas), as well as arranging a series of meetings between the fishing industry and the EC.

This unprecedented level of consultation during 1996 has seen the Prime Minister and his senior policy advisors meet with both national fishermen's federations. Pressure group tactics have been adopted by the industry to force decision-makers to take greater account of their concerns and incorporate their recommendations into fisheries policy. Such tactics have recently included lobbying European Union and United Kingdom Parliaments through demonstrations; targeting particular MPs particularly those with 'fishing' constituencies; conducting fringe debates at party conferences; and taking militant action such as disrupting merchant shipping and ferry services. Through lobbying, FOs hope to gain the support of both the public, and of MPs and MEPs who can air the industry's concerns at their respective parliaments, in the hope of influencing policy-makers.

One of the most effective forms of direct action in recent years occurred over the ill-fated 'days at sea' scheme introduced under the Seafish (Conservation) Act of 1992, which gave the Minister the power to restrict days at sea for vessels over ten metres in length. This Act provoked a furious reaction from fishermen's organisations, who were united in fighting it. Opposition to the Act took the form both of direct action, including blockading of harbours, and of legal challenge. In 1995, the NFFO's legal action managed to get the case referred by the High Court to the European Court of Justice and, although the Government won the case in 1995, it abandoned the scheme because of its unpopularity.

Sources of Tension between Fishermen's Organisations and Management

On six issues the FOs are in dispute with officials. First, FOs resent their lack of participation in decision-making processes. Until 1996, the degree of participation of FOs in management and policy-making can only be described as minimal, taking the form of either pre-arranged or crisis meetings with the United Kingdom Government, and gatherings in advisory groups within the European Commission. The annual meeting of the industry and Ministry representatives in November only serves to inform the industry of the European Union Council's intentions for the coming year, the industry having little prospect of influencing the advice given by the Ministry at this late stage. This kind of involvement has been described by the NFFO as merely 'cosmetic consultation'. Other meetings occur when the Government is faced with a crisis, for example after the industry's widespread condemnation over the Government's proposals to limit the number of days British fishing vessels were allowed to go to sea. Coming together in this way when there is a problem has been termed 'crisis management' by the NFFO. Greater participation during 1996, as mentioned above, has led to some agreements on policy being forged between industry and Government. However, such policies are ultimately decided upon by the European Commission and the European Union Fisheries Council, and many of the policies decided upon by the United Kingdom during 1996 appear to have had little influence. For example, technical measures proposed by the Commission have largely ignored the recommendations put forward by the 'United Kingdom Fisheries Conservation Group' (comprising scientists and industry representatives). Recently, the European Commission has fully endorsed the controversial 'Lassen Report' prepared by a group of fisheries experts with no direct input from the industry. The report recommends a 40% reduction in fishing effort within the European Union fleet which the Commission has translated into a 40% cut in fleet size which is being proposed for the next stage of the European Union's programme to reduce the size of the European Union fleet, known as the 'Multi Annual Guidance Plan' (MAGP). The United Kingdom industry and Government flatly rejected the Lassen Report's findings.The lack of consideration of United Kingdom recommendations by the European Commission has led the fishermen's federations to believe that despite improved relations with the United Kingdom Government and greater participation in national policymaking, they still have little influence over European Union policy.

Second, fishermen's organisations question the sincerity of the Government's objective to conserve fish stocks, when it appoints ill-qualified fisheries ministers for short periods of time, whose apparent aim seems to be to avoid short-term political problems (such as reducing fishing pressure) and to show fishermen that they are trying to help them. The Government's recent drive for greater industry participation could be seen as a ploy to appease Euro sceptic MPs (many of whom support United Kingdom withdrawal from the CFP) to avoid further aggravation in the run-up to the general election.

Third, dependence of the current quota management system on scientific advice based on estimating the size of fish stocks causes a great deal of contention amongst fishermen, not least because of widely fluctuating quota levels from one year to the next, which creates considerable economic and management difficulties. Scientists admit to a degree of inaccuracy in their assessments (reflecting uncertainties in marine science) thus compounding concern amongst fishermen over the general validity of such scientific advice. Fishermen occasionally experience a situation that contradicts scientific advice, such as the appearance of a species in a particular area in large quantities. In such circumstances, fishermen's reactions to scientific advice is naturally one of scepticism, claiming scientists are incompetent and their knowledge inadequate. FOs use such evidence to refute scientific findings and question management systems based on such arbitrary data. However, the industry generally agrees with the long-term predictions of the International Council for the Exploration of the Sea (ICES) that there is a declining spawning stock blomass for virtually all commercially important species; difficulties arise when reconciling the short-term predictions. A number of measures to reduce tension between the industry and scientists have been proposed by FOs. For example, the NFFO have suggested two measures; (i) attaching confidence ratings to scientific advice to be able to differentiate between those recommendations which are supported by a high degree of confidence and those which are not; and (ii) incorporating information and data from fishermen in ICES data.

Fourth, there is the vexed question of foreign vessels in waters around the United Kingdom. Following the declaration of exclusive fishing zones to 200 nautical miles by countries along the Atlantic coastline, for example, Iceland, Norway and Canada, in 1975, and by the European Community in 1977, fishing activity within European Union waters, particularly around the United Kingdom, has intensified. The accession of Spanish and Portuguese fleets into United Kingdom waters from 1995, albeit with restricted access in Western waters, has caused a furore within the industry resulting in a much publicised anti-CFP campaign. Many FOs, especially those representing fishermen working from ports along the southwest coast of England, vehemently oppose what they see as an encroachment by European fleets, particularly Spanish and Portuguese, on their fishing grounds. The anti-CFP campaign was initiated by the 'Save Britain's Fish' (SBF) group, whose supporters include many NFFO member organisations and some Scottish FOs. The sole aim of the campaign is for the United Kingdom fishing industry to relinquish its membership of the CFP, whilst remaining a member of the European Union, and to take control of its 200 mile exclusive fishing zone.

During 1996 the anti-CFP campaign has been fuelled by the European Commission's proposals to cut the European Union fleet by a further 40% (see above) and introduce specific technical measures, both totally rejected by the industry who feel their participation in developing such proposals has been futile. In response, the SBF group have been canvassing relentlessly, organising fringe meetings at political party conferences, holding open meetings at the House of Commons and arranging mass demonstrations in London. Consequently, they have acquired support from numerous MPs and MEPs who have lobbied their respective parliaments. Support for CFP-withdrawal appears to be gaining momentum in the north, including Scotland.

Fifth, the NFFO and SFF are concerned over current quota management arrangements, not least because inaccuracies in stock size assessments undermine the quota system (see above). They also highlight the difficulties fishermen face in trying to operate profitably when quota availability can vary considerably from one year to the next (up to 70%) which can lead to illegal over-quota landings (black fish) causing marketing problems and undermining scientific data and management advice.

Finally, there is tension over decommissioning. As we saw above, in 1992, the Government proposed days-at-sea restrictions in a bid to reduce fishing effort. The fishing industry decisively rejected the scheme claiming it to be an uneconomic measure not effectively addressing the stock depletion problem. Both the national federations recognise the need to address the current fleet over-capacity problem, and support the principle of decommissioning as the best way of reducing fishing effort. However, they have objected to the meagre level of funds provided by the government for decommissioning. They have also highlighted the socioeconomic drawbacks of the government's scheme which can threaten a port's infrastructure (as has happened in Newlyn). Moreover, the NFFO claim their members, particularly those in SW England, are concerned that United Kingdom fleet reductions could be allowing access to Iberian fleets. Faced with Governmental proposals to limit the days fishing vessels could spend at sea, the NFFO and SFF together presented an alternative approach in 1993 to meet the United Kingdom's fleet reduction obligations as set out in the European Union's 1992-1996 MAGP. Both federations provided a comprehensive range of technical measures (SFF also recommended certain days-at-sea restrictions) to achieve greater selectivity thereby reducing the quantities of undersized fish, unnecessary discards and nontarget species. However, the Government persisted with direct effort controls to meet MAGP targets, introducing a decommissioning scheme which compensated owners for terminating their boat's fishing activity. It was not until 1996 when the European Commission asked Member States for technical measure proposals (the Council of Fisheries Ministers intending to revise technical regulations in 1997) that FOs were consulted once again on these issues. But, despite this consultation, the recommendations put forward by the Commission were a far cry from the ones given by the industry.

Discord between Fishermen's Organisations

Although FOs were united in their opposition to the Government's days-at-sea scheme, they are disunited on almost every other issue (including the best way to fight the days-at-sea scheme: the NFFO mounted a legal challenge; the SFF launched a public campaign). Many of the disagreements that exist between the two national federations reflect the differences in fishing traditions and culture, as well as the differential threat of further competition from foreign fleets, between England and Wales, and Scotland.

One of the major divisive issues facing national and regional FOs is whether to support the withdrawal of the United Kingdom fishing industry from the CFP, or reform of the CFP. Support for CFP withdrawal is particularly strong amongst NFFO member organisations in SW England whose vessels are now competing with Iberian fleets in the same areas. The SFF on the other hand, does not support withdrawal of CFP membership, as the majority of their members believe they can cut a better deal within the CFP, and the perceived threat of Iberian fleets fishing their waters, particularly the North Sea, is far less than for their English and Welsh counterparts. However, there is some support for the SBF campaign in Scotland, and this has resulted in a minority of ex SFF members forming a separate organisation called the Fishermen's Association Ltd (FAL) whose primary aim appears to be campaigning for CFP withdrawal.

Other policy differences between the two national FOs include decentralisation and the setting up of regional management bodies; technical measures; and a non discarding scheme for a greater quota allocation. The NFFO support the establishment of regional management bodies comprising fishermen from each particular area using a particular type of fishing gear, scientists and managers, to formulate local management policies. The concept of decentralised management and policymaking has also been put forward by the SFF, but it emphatically opposes the idea of local or area fisheries management (such as sea fisheries committees in England and Wales) preferring to devolve management responsibilities only down to the level of states which have a legitimate quota share for a particular region, for example, the North Sea. Again, this policy difference reflects the different practices of fishermen in the two areas: there are no sea fisheries committees in Scotland.

These differences have led to irrevocable divisions between the national federations, particularly on the issue of withdrawal from the CFP. The implications of such disunity are far reaching; since it can only serve to weaken an already poor negotiating hand and allow the Government and European Union to impose their own policies. It undermines the aim of improving the role of FOs in the policy-making process; if FOs are to be taken seriously, it is critical for the industry to adopt a united position on a long-term strategy.

Future Role of Fishermen's Organisations

Fisheries organisations wish to play a more dominant role in fisheries policy formulation than the present fisheries management system allows. There are three ways in which they envisage their greater involvement. First, they demand far more involvement in policy-making and management responsibilities on a regional basis (together with scientists, managers and the rest of the industry) to formulate policies specific to particular fisheries. The suggestion of involving fishermen's representatives in management has been put forward by a number of key bodies: even the European Commission itself supports a more decentralised management regime. Most FOs support coastal state management in one form or other, whereby only those fishermen fishing a particular region are involved in the management of that area. The idea of such involvement is to legitimise conservation measures and to gain the fishermen's support to make these measures more effective.

Second, although FOs acknowledge the need for scientific stock size assessments on which to base a rational fishing policy, they call for greater participation in the collecting of relevant data. Incorporating information from fishing operations into stock assessment techniques would also help to authenticate scientific advice thereby gaining the support of fishermen. The Scottish fishing industry and the SOAEFD Marine Laboratory have already co-operated to determine actual landing data (used to assess the size of fish stocks), with further collaborative projects being discussed. The SFF believe there is scope for further involvement of fishermen in such scientific work, thereby improving both the quality of scientific advice and fishermen's confidence in the outcome. Third, the selectivity of fishing gear is viewed by FOs as paramount to fish stock conservation. They feel their members could be usefully involved in developing such gear,in coalition with the scientists. A limited amount of collaborative work between the two groups has already taken place and FOs hope further projects will be proposed by the Ministry.

In response to these and other demands, the Government set up a 'CFP Review Group' in January 1995, whose findings, published in July 1996,[1] confirmed the Government's position that the interests of the United Kingdom fisheries sector are best served within the CFP, together with a large number of improvements to it. Its findings were not wholly unexpected since the only representative of the catching sector was vice-chairman of the SFF (John Goodlad), which favours changes in European Union and United Kingdom fisheries policy from within the CFP.

One of the Ministry's recent objectives is to make fishermen aware that scientists are on their side and to give them an incentive to advise on policy. The Fisheries Minister instructed the Fisheries Research Establishment at Lowestoft to set up a new committee comprising 50% scientists and 50% industry representatives in order to improve communication between the two. The committee, formed in 1996 and called the 'United Kingdom Fisheries Conservation Group', has been very active in responding to European Commission requests to provide a United Kingdom response on technical measures.

The Government has also promised to raise the issue of flagships fishing off the United Kingdom fishing quota (one of the few issues on which the Government and the FOs see eye to eye) during the current InterGovernmental Conference, and has given an assurance to the industry that they will not sign up to any European Union MAGP agreements until the flagship issue is resolved. The Government has its own interest in the flagship problem as flagships undermine the historic rights agreement and increase the task of the United Kingdom meeting MAGP targets. If the Government succeeds in tackling the flagship problem then its credibility will increase

[1] Common Fisheries Policy Review Group, *Report*, 2 volumes, MAFF, 1996.

markedly, and this could make defending the CFP easier in Britain.

Conclusion

Fishermen's organisations play a critical role in the United Kingdom fishing industry – not least because they are the interface between managers and fishermen. They have both an executive and a representative function: their main executive function is to distribute quotas allocated by the Government; their main representative function is to communicate fishermen's views on fishing policies to the Government. In the eyes of many writers, the success or failure of the Government's fishing policy rests on the way in which it treats the fishermen's organisations. If it seeks genuinely both to devolve more powers to them and to give them a more important role in policy decision-making, the Government could regain the confidence of fishermen in the Common Fisheries Policy, and weaken the appeal of the Save Britain's Fish campaign. If, however, the Government ignores the demands of the fishermen's organisation, and pursues a policy of divide and rule, exploiting the divisions between them, the outlook for peace in the fishing industry is distinctly bleak.

It has to be said, however, that the fishermen's organisations themselves bear some responsibility for their current exclusion. Criticisms have been made that they are not capable of managing their members, and complaints that they turn a blind eye to breakers of fishing regulations – such as the illegal landing of over quota fish (black fish) – have led to calls that the Government should abolish them and take over quota management itself. If fishermen's organisations are to be given greater managerial and policy making status, therefore, they must demonstrate that they are capable of fulfilling these enhanced responsibilities.

The Politics of Fishing

Tim S.Gray
University of Newcastle upon Tyne

'Fishing & Fairness: The Justice of the Common Fisheries Policy'

Acknowledgements

I am grateful to Peter Jones, Derek Bell, Mark Bevir, Simon Caney, Ella Ritchie and Tony Zito for their helpful comments on an earlier version of this paper.

Introduction

This paper discusses the normative rather than the empirical dimensions of the Common Fisheries Policy (CFP). It focuses on the ethical or moral issues raised by questions of equity or distributive justice. The reason why I have chosen this topic is partly because (so far as I know) little or nothing has been published on it, and partly because fairness is a very important element of the CFP, highly relevant to its acceptability to fishermen. It is often argued that the equity of the CFP is a precondition of its compliance, but rarely, if ever, is that equity examined. The aim of this discussion is to help fill this gap in the literature.

There are three central questions that I wish to address.

First, what are the principles of fairness that drive the CFP?

Second, are they coherent in themselves?

Third, do they form a consistent set of moral priorities?

I will consider these questions in relation to the two main principles that comprise the CFP – the principle of equal access and the principle of relative stability.

The Principle of Equal Access

This is the primary principle of the CFP: the basic rule on which it is founded. What does the principle of equal access mean? It is a rule which arises out of the Treaty of Rome's principle of non-discrimination among Member States, adopted in 1970 at the inception of the CFP. Article 2 of Regulation EEC No. 2141/70 states that 'Rules applied by each Member State in respect of fishing in the maritime waters coming under its sovereignty or within its jurisdiction shall not lead to differences in treatment of other Member States ... Member States shall ensure in particular equal conditions of access to and use of the fishing grounds situated in the waters referred to ... for all fishing vessels flying the flag of a Member State and registered in Community Territory'.

What the principle of equal access entails is equality of access for Member States to Community waters, that is access on equal terms for all Member States - not freedom of access, that is unconditional access for all Member States. Member States retain the right to impose restrictions on access to their waters, 'providing that these measures applied equally to all Community fishermen regardless of nationality'[1]

In evaluating the fairness of the equal access principle, we may usefully distinguish between its procedural and its substantive fairness. First, is it procedurally fair? The manner of its adoption has been strongly criticised. According to Holden, it was rushed through by the original six members of the European Community immediately before accession talks began with Denmark, Ireland, Norway and the United Kingdom in 1970.

> 'All four applicants had major fisheries interests and much of the fishing by three of the original six Member States took place in their waters. If the 'six' did not agree a policy before the applicants joined, the new Member States would be able to influence its development, in particular the conditions of fishing and access to natural waters. With a policy in place prior to their accession, the new Member States would have to accept the acquis communitaire. The 'six' just managed to agree, almost literally at the eleventh hour ...' [2]

Such a process seems to breach natural justice, in that it was clearly designed to discriminate in favour of existing States at the expense of the new States.

However, it could be argued that since the 'new' States had not yet joined the Community, such last minute 'rigging' of the rules in the interests of existing States was not unjust, since it is entirely fair that the rules of a club should be determined by its existing members. The six were fully entitled to make whatever rules suited them, and so there was nothing procedurally improper about their decision. After all, the four new applicants were not obliged to join the European Community; they could have declined to join on grounds that they rejected the 'rigged' rules (indeed, Norway did just that). In joining, Denmark, Ireland and the United Kingdom consented to all European Community treaties and rules - including the principle of equal access. Hence, it could be argued that the principle could not be procedurally unjust: prior consent is a guarantor of procedural fairness.

On the other hand, it could be claimed that since the six knew that the four were about to join, the way they used the procedure may have been fair in letter, but not in spirit. Moreover, it has been argued that while it may be true that the United Kingdom Government consented to the equal access principle in 1970, United Kingdom fishermen did not. Indeed, Eurosceptics claim that the United Kingdom electorate did not consent: they

---

[1] M.Wise, *The Common Fisheries Policy of the European Community*, Methuen, 1984, p.91.

[2] M.Holden, *The Common Fisheries Policy: Origin, Evaluation and Future*, Fishing News Books, 1994, p.19.

were not even consulted by the then Prime Minister, Edward Heath. But such an argument opens up complex issues of representative versus direct democracy; suffice it to say that in a representative system (such as in the United Kingdom), on almost any question, a government's policy could be judged to lack majority consent, let alone unanimous consent, but not to lack electoral legitimacy.

Moreover, the equal access principle could be deemed to pass the test of procedural fairness in that, at least from 1983 to 1992, it was unchallenged by Fisheries Ministers. '... access has never once been the subject of debate in the Council .... The provisions on access were virtually unquestioned for ten years, from 1983 to 1992. The Council adopted them unchanged to continue another ten years, until 31 December 2002'.[3] However, it must be noted that the question of access is not the sort of issue that one would normally expect to be raised in the Council of Fisheries Ministers; debate on such a fundamental issue would be agendered for an Inter-Governmental Conference.

The equal access principle may satisfy the test of procedural fairness (it may have been introduced in a fair way) but it may nevertheless fail the test of substantive fairness (it may not be fair in itself). The substantive concept of fairness to be found in the equal access principle is, of course, the concept of equality. All Member States have equality of access to each others' waters, that is, (since 1977) within their 200 mile exclusive economic zones (EEZs). But on what basis is the concept of equality justified here? It may be justified on three grounds:

(a) the European Union depends on reciprocity – if fishermen of one Member State want access to waters of another Member State, they must allow reciprocal access by foreign fishermen to their own waters

(b) the waters of the European Union are a Community resource – a common pool – and as such ought to be open to all on equal terms

(c) the European Union is founded on the principle of a level playing field for all nationals of Member States.

However, all three justifications are controversial. Taking (a) first, according to Wise, there are three forms of reciprocity entailed in the equal access principle. First, there is reciprocity between fishermen. For example, if United Kingdom fishermen want to fish within the waters of France, as a quid pro quo they must accept that it is only fair that French fishermen should be allowed to fish in British waters. However, an objection to this argument is that the reciprocity here is very one sided; since British waters contain fish stocks which are approximately five times as abundant as the fish stocks in French waters, British fishermen are 'giving' to the French

[3] M.Holden, 'The Common Fisheries Policy: Origin, Evaluation and Future', Methuen, 1984, pp.117, 118.

much more than they are 'getting back' from the French. This does not seem fair.

Perhaps the second form of reciprocity redresses this imbalance? This is reciprocity between access to fishing areas and access to fishing markets. Was it not basic justice, argued its protagonists, that the free movement of fish products within the European Community be counterbalanced by equal conditions of entry to fishing grounds? Why should Britain and Ireland deny continental fishermen access to waters they had traditionally exploited, and then expect to export freely to other member states where there would be an increased demand for imports following decreased landings from domestic fleets cut off from fisheries around the British Isles?.[4]

On this argument, we cannot expect to be treated with good will by foreign consumers if we are perceived to treat their nationals discriminately. However, while this form of reciprocity is not one sided (the extent of the access to foreign markets will depend on the extent of the domestic product), it is a contingent rather than an ethical argument. That is to say, it amounts to saying not that we have a moral duty to allow foreign nationals access to our waters if we want to sell them our fish, but that we would be acting prudently to do so, in order to avoid a foreign consumer backlash.

The third form of reciprocity to which Wise draws attention may be summed up in the familiar injunction 'to refrain from doing to others what you object to others doing to you': For example, 'Why ... should continental fisherman be evicted from their traditional fishing grounds to make space for British distant-water vessels expelled from theirs around Iceland and elsewhere?'.[5] The point being made here is that it is unfair of one Member State to respond to discrimination against its nationals by a Third State, by itself discriminating against the nationals of a fellow Member State. Two wrongs do not make a right; to suffer injustice is not a justification for inflicting the same injustice.

This third form of reciprocity seems to be the strongest form. It can be broadened into the Rawlsian idea of asking people, 'how would you feel if you were in the other person's shoes?' It appeals to fishermen to take a detached, non-chauvinistic view of the issue. From the Rawlsian original position,[6] the equal liberty principle would be chosen in order to safeguard oneself from discrimination. This is a powerful justification for equality of access.

Turning now to (b) the second justification for the equal access principle – that European Union waters are a Community resource – we must note that the notion of a common pool of the waters of all the European Union Member States is anathema to many critics who argue that there is no other resource in the European Union upon which the idea of a 'common resource' is superimposed. The critics point out, for example, that the Common Agricultural Policy (CAP) does not assume that agriculture in

[4] M.Wise, *The Common Fisheries Policy of the European Community*, Methuen, 1984, p.165.

[5] M.Wise, *The Common Fisheries Policy of the European Community*, Methuen, 1984, p. 166.

[6] J.Rawls, *A Theory of Justice*, Oxford University Press, 1972.

Member States' land is a common pool resource of the European Union; so why should there be one in the waters of Member States? The answer to this objection is two fold, according to the CFP's defenders. First, fish do not confine themselves to national boundaries, and this justifies their designation as a common, rather than a national, resource. Second, there are other resources in the European Union that could be described as common pool – such as air and wild birds – 'access' to both of which the European Union regulates on an equal basis. However, even if European Union waters and the fish within them are legitimately designated as a common resource, the question remains open of whether or not equal access to that common pool resource is fair.

This brings me to (c), the third ground for equality of access, that of a level playing field for all European Union nationals - this notion is of course enshrined at the heart of the European Union, incorporated in the idea of a single market. However, critics have argued that there is not a level playing field in European Union waters, in that some Member States' fleets are stronger than others, and that the weaker Member States' fleets need special protection to enable them to compete on more equal terms. This is certainly the argument put forward to justify restrictions on foreign vessels in the Irish Box, since Ireland's infant fisheries industry needed protection. It is also put forward as a justification for the 1972 derogation from equal access in respect of foreign vessels in the coastal areas (6 and 12 mile limits) of all Member States – in order to protect small inshore vessels against large, distant-water vessels.

In other words, most of the exceptions (derogations) from the equal access principle could be justified on grounds that they were necessary to create conditions of genuine equality between Member States' fleets. On this argument, the egalitarianism of the equal access principle is preserved, not diminished, by the derogations. If, however, such an argument appears too paradoxical to be convincing (inequality guarantees equality), an alternative way of interpreting the derogations is to say that the inequalities were justifiable – ie, that the egalitarian content of the equal access principle has been diluted for good reason. One good reason for diluting the equal access principle might be the greater degree of dependence on fishing of the above areas. However, as Wise points out: 'Continental States ... resisted the argument that the "dependence" of certain British and Irish regions on fishing justified an abandonment of the national non- discrimination principles underpinning the CFP. They made the obvious, but often missed, point that all fishermen are "dependent" on fishing.'[7] All fisheries have a vital interest in fishing: how do we judge which interests are most important? (This issue will be explored later in relation to the 'vital needs' element of the principle of relative stability).

Another good reason for diluting the equal access principle might be the greater proximity of the Irish and British fleets to these areas. The concept of proximity entails that closeness to a resource generates a preferential right

[7] M.Wise, *The Common Fisheries Policy of the European Community*, Methuen, 1984, p.167.

to exploit that resource. On this view, because Ireland and the United Kingdom are closer than other Member States to the fish stocks in the coastal areas and EEZs around the British Isles and Ireland, they have a prior right to exploit those stocks. This right entitles them to special treatment of the kind that we have seen they have obtained.

However, the concept of proximity as a substantive principle of fairness is highly controversial. Why should mere closeness to a resource generate a moral claim to preferential access in exploiting it? 'Closeness' in itself, is simply a random physical fact, of no moral justification in itself. Being born, or living, near some resource is a purely accidental or contingent matter; how can such a physical fact generate a moral claim? This is to commit the so- called 'naturalistic fallacy' – attempting to deduce an 'ought' from an 'is'. Surely, the critics argue, it is only if and when someone actually does something to the resource that they generate a moral claim to it. Hence, for example, it is only when United Kingdom fishermen actually fish the stocks in the United Kingdom waters that they can be held to create a proprietarial right to those fish stocks. But, of course, on the same argument, when French fishermen fish the same stocks in United Kingdom waters, they too must be held to create a proprietarial right to those fish stocks. In reconciling these two sets of rights, some principle such as relative stability would have to be devised – ie, a principle which would adjudicate between them not on grounds of proximity, but on grounds of differential use – for example, by historic catch records (see below).

However, it could be argued that while proximity considered in itself is morally irrelevant, it may be less so if we regard it as an extension of national property rights. If we accept that each country has ownership rights over the resources within its territory, the question becomes 'what is a nation's territory?' If its territory is deemed to include the seas up to 200 miles around its coastline, it follows that it owns those seas and their contents. However, while such an argument might be persuasive in relation to inert products such as oil or natural gas or minerals on the sea bed, it is less persuasive in the case of fish, since, as noted earlier, fish move in an out of 'territorial' waters, spawning in one area and migrating to others. No single state could fairly claim exclusive ownership rights over migratory fish – they 'belong' to several states, or perhaps to none. So the argument of proximity is no more convincing than the argument of dependence in justifying derogations from the equal access principle.

Our verdict on the fairness of the equal access principle must, therefore, be conditional – that it is fair procedurally and substantively only up to a certain point. Perhaps fairness is secured when the equal access principle is combined with the principle of relative stability? This is the issue to which we must now turn.

The Principle of Relative Stability

This is the secondary principle of the CFP; the main restraint on the primary principle of equal access. What does the principle of relative stability mean?

It is a rule adopted in 1983 for dealing with the problem of scarcity of fish stocks. It operates by distributing shares of total allowable catches (TACs) largely on the basis of historic patterns of catches, adjusted for need and compensation.

> 'In 1983, Council Regulation 170/83 ... introduced the concept of relative stability (or fixed percentage shares) in quota allocation, within a TAC framework and on the basis of historic fishing patterns (modified as necessary by arrangements to protect fisheries dependent communities (Hague Preference) and compensation for lost international opportunities).'[8]

It differs from the equal access principle in that it was designed to regulate takes of fish stocks, not conditions of access to fishing areas; under the relative stability principle, the good to be distributed is the total fish catch, not the opportunity to engage in fishing. However, since the principle of relative stability regulates takes of fish stocks within each area, it effectively does control access to many areas, and in this sense it represents both a departure from, and a qualification of, the equal access principle.

The principle of relative stability was introduced, first, to avoid annual wrangling over the allocation of TACs; and second to provide a degree of security for all Member States' fishing industries by assuring them a guaranteed share of fish. Since, however, it was impossible to guarantee absolute quantities of fish, because of the wide fluctuations in the biomass from year to year, the Commission 'proposed that each Member State should be guaranteed only a specified percentage of the TAC for each stock, to which the term "relative stability" was given'.[9] These percentages were calculated on the basis of three factors; 'historical catches', 'vital needs' ('Hague Preferences'), and 'compensation for jurisdictional losses'. The main factor was the first one – 'historical catches' – and referred to the track record of catches during the period 1973-8:

> 'The year 1978 was selected as the end of the period because it was, at the time, the last year for which official catch statistics were available; the Commission was determined to use figures which were published ... and which could not therefore be disputed.'[10]

The second factor – 'vital needs' or 'Hague Preferences' (so named because they were set out at a 1976 Council meeting in The Hague) – referred to special allowances given to areas flanked by coastal regions which relied heavily on fishing. Regulation No. 170/83 states that relative stability 'must safeguard the particular needs of regions where local populations are especially dependent on fisheries and related industries'. These areas included

[8] Common Fisheries Policy Review Group, *Report*, 2 volumes, MAFF, 1996, II, p.4.

[9] M.Holden, *The Common Fisheries Policy: Origin, Evaluation and Future*, Fishing News Books, 1994, p.43.

[10] M.Holden, *The Common Fisheries Policy: Origin, Evaluation and Future*, Fishing News Books, 1994, p.43.

the whole of the Republic of Ireland (which had its 1975 catch quantities doubled) and the whole of Scotland, Northern Ireland and north eastern parts of England as far south as Bridlington (which had their 1975 catches by vessels up to 24 metres long, doubled).

The third factor – 'compensation for jurisdictional losses' – refers to losses suffered by Member States' fishing fleets by non-Member States extending their fisheries' limits to 200 miles in 1977. This compensation took the form of extra fish quotas in European Union waters.

In evaluating the fairness of the relative stability principle, again we may distinguish between procedural and substantive criteria of fairness. First, is it procedurally fair? The first procedural point to be noted about the relative stability principle is its general popularity. 'The [1992] review showed that the principle of relative stability has, for the majority of Member States, proved politically totally satisfactory. Only one Member State is wholly discontent . Spain voted against Regulation Number 3760/92'.[11]

This suggests that the principle of relative stability largely meets the test of procedural justice, since it is founded on the consent of all (but one) of the parties affected. However, this interpretation is open to question. For instance, Spain and Portugal argue that they should be given greater quotas for fish stocks, to take account of two factors. First, they had a large historic track record of large catches in, for example, Greenlandic waters, before 1977, for which they claim compensation under the CFP scheme for jurisdictional losses. Second, other Member States are not catching their full quotas in those areas and that the shortfall should be re-allocated to Spain and Portugal. However, both these claims were rejected by the European Court of Justice; under Article 2 of the Treaty of Accession, Spain and Portugal had accepted the acquis communitaire, which included the principle of relative stability as defined in Regulation No. 170/83, by which no account was taken of Spanish and Portuguese jurisdictional losses; and whether or not Member States catch their full quotas is irrelevant to the allocation of percentages. In any case, it could be argued that even if two countries are unsatisfied by some aspects of the relative stability principle, the vast majority of Member States are satisfied, and majority consent (not unanimity) is all that is required for procedural fairness.

However, each of these issues raises a deeper question of procedural injustice (and arguably also of substantive justice). First, is it fair that new Member States cannot claim any compensation for their jurisdictional losses resulting from the 200 mile EEZs adopted by the United Nations Convention on the Law of the Sea (UNCLOS) in 1977? Doesn't this mean that new Member States are treated differently from existing Member States for no good reason? Of course, it is true that Spain and Portugal knew these terms before they signed their Treaties of Accession, therefore there is no breach of one criterion of procedural fairness – consent. However, there does seem to be a breach of another criterion of procedural fairness that of natural justice – treating like cases in a like manner.

[11] M.Holden, *The Common Fisheries Policy: Origin, Evaluation and Future*, Fishing News Books, 1994, p.122.

In the eyes of the existing Member States, of course, such a procedure is perfectly fair, since they feel they should not be disadvantaged in any way by the accession of new Member States. As the CFP Review Group put it;

> 'United Kingdom interests have not been compromised by the accession of new Member States, since the principle of relative stability has simply been applied to the fisheries resources that they bring with them into the Community. There has been no question of parcelling out existing resources to new Members ... relative stability will continue to ensure that the national quota shares of all Member States (including the United Kingdom) are protected in the event of any enlargement of the European Union. For example, no Member State has suffered from the accession of Finland and Sweden'.[12]

However, such discrimination against new Member States, even if perfectly legal and tacitly consented to by the new States, seems morally dubious. Moreover, as Holden suggests, resentment by new Members against this procedural injustice could eventually destroy the principle of relative stability:

> 'The accession of new Member States to the Community will inevitably create pressure to abandon the principle of relative stability. These new Member States, no more than Spain and Portugal, will not be prepared to accept a system which benefits the 11 Member States which adopted the original conservation fishing policy and disadvantages all others. Sooner or later, the principle will be successfully legally challenged, even though Spain and Portugal have been unsuccessful to date'[13]

Second, is it fair to calculate allocations on the basis of a historic period of catches recorded in 1973 – 8? Why should that five year period be taken for all time as the source of a fair allocation? There are both procedural and substantive questions involved here, but the central issue is that the allocative criterion is arbitrary, not principled, in its application. For one thing, some of the records taken during that five year period may have been aberrant. For instance, the CFP Review Group drew attention to a United Kingdom grievance over the allocation of saithe. 'On North Sea and West of Scotland saithe ... there are complaints that the United Kingdom share, which was based on a very poor historical fishing performance during the late 1970s, is now far too low'.[14] For another thing, if a Member State is continuously catching less and less than its quota, why should its percentage not be re-allocated to other Member States? On this argument, there should be some procedural mechanism whereby adjustments can be made to reallocate unused quotas.

---

[12]Common Fisheries Policy Review Group, *Report*, 2 volumes, MAFF, 1996, II, pp.10, 49.

[13]M.Holden, *The Common Fisheries Policy: Origin, Evaluation and Future*, Fishing News Books, 1994, p.241.

[14]Common Fisheries Policy Review Group, *Report*, 2 volumes, MAFF, 1996, II, p.10.

However, there are two arguments for leaving the quota allocation system as it is. First, re-adjustment could re-open the entire debate about the allocation keys. But, of course, this is a political argument, not an argument from procedural justice. Second, there may be a good reason why a Member State fails to catch its full quota (eg poor weather conditions, lower biomass of fish, effort restructuring) and it would not be procedurally safe to permanently reduce its quota for factors which may be of temporary duration.

Interestingly, the CFP Review Group suggests an alternative way of addressing this problem – by bilateral deals with Member States who consistently underfish their quotas (such as France, in its North Sea saithe quota). On procedural grounds, there could be no objection to such bilateral deals, insofar as they were based on mutual consent. However, it raises the question of whether all other Member States should be given an opportunity to participate in such deals.

The final procedural issue raised by the principle of relative stability relates to 'quota hopping'. 'Quota hopping' is the term applied to owners in one Member State who buy vessels in another Member State and after obtaining fishing licences, can use these foreign-owned flagged vessels to fish against the quota of the home Member State. Quota hopping is a very serious problem in the United Kingdom, where about 20% of the tonnage is now foreign- owned, because much of the economic benefit of these flag ships flows abroad: many flag ships do not land fish in the United Kingdom; do not use British ship building or repair yards; and do not employ British fishermen.

However, there can be no objection to quota hopping on procedural grounds. Ownership of foreign vessels is perfectly legitimate within the European Union rules – indeed, it is unequivocally sanctioned by the right of establishment. Moreover, it satisfies the rationale of procedural fairness in the processes of market transactions; if people start with legitimate property rights and engage in voluntary exchanges of their assets, then the result of those exchanges must be deemed to be just, because it is the outcome of starting points and processes that are themselves just. Whether it violates any substantive principle of justice is, however, another matter, to which we now turn.

The principle of relative stability embodies within it two distinct concepts of substantive justice; entitlement (including compensation) and need. The primary concept is entitlement. This concept is at the heart of the principle of relative stability, entailed in the very notion of historic catch records. Fishermen who have built up a track record of fishing during 1973 – 8 in a particular area for a particular stock of fish, have created an entitlement or prima facie right to continue to do so, or to receive compensation if they are prevented from doing so. This historic catch concept of entitlement is also the criterion driving the United Kingdom's distribution of the quota allocations to Producer Organisations (POs) from the TACs awarded to the United Kingdom by the European Union Council of Ministers though the reference period here is the rolling previous four years.

It is worth pausing to consider the nature of this entitlement argument. It is based on the idea that expending labour not only entitles a person to the fruits of that labour, but also confers a preferential right to continue to expend that labour and reap its fruits in the future. But what is the moral justification of such a right? If the right is granted, it means that other fishermen who wish to expend their labour in the same way are disadvantaged, but is this fair? Why should preferential treatment be given to a fisherman who has built up a track record? Is it because he was there first, and can claim the right of first 'occupancy' on grounds of 'first come, first served' or 'finders, keepers' or 'possession is 9/10ths of the law'? None of these popular aphorisms seems morally persuasive, since the fact that a fisherman was first on the scene was a contingent matter of chance or accident, and not a matter of ethical significance. Perhaps the justification lies in the fact that since the fisherman has regularly fished in the area, he has 'used' it, invested his labour in it, mixed his labour with it (as John Locke put it[15]) and therefore, in some sense 'owns' it. But as Robert Nozick has said, why should mixing one's labour with a resource generate a right to ownership of that resource?.[16] Surely it might merely mean that one has wasted one's labour? In any case, Locke's argument was that since through one's labour, one made the land [more] productive, one was entitled to property ownership of the land one had worked on. But in the case of fishing, no such claim could be made – indeed fishermen arguably make the sea less productive. As far as fishing is concerned, the Locke argument applies only to aquaculture, where fishermen are responsible for 'growing' the fish.

Perhaps the answer is that expending one's labour on something means that one deserves reward for that effort? In other words, labour effort signifies desert. Desert is a strong principle of justice or fairness, embodied in familiar nostrums such as 'he got what he deserves'; 'just deserts'; 'you reap what you sow'. But it is also a very difficult concept to work with. It is easy to see how the desert concept can justify ownership of the fish that a fisherman has caught: he deserves to be able to sell the catch: it is a just (ie, well deserved) reward for his efforts. But it is not easy to see how desert can justify preferential rights over future fishing stock. Desert is essentially a backward looking concept: reward for some past effort. Why should that reward include a right to exclude others from making similar efforts in the future?

Perhaps the answer is simply that of tradition – a traditional or established pattern of use is one that doesn't need justifying: it is self-justifying. Simply because fishermen have traditionally fished in an area, entitles them to preferential rights to continue to do so. This is the argument of 'prescriptive rights' advanced by Edmund Burke. It is also the argument of 'established expectations' advanced by David Hume – that it is not unreasonable for people (and communities and governments) to form expectations on the basis of long established practice, and to organise their lives and make important decisions on the expectation that these practices will

[15] J Locke, *Of Civil Government*, Dent, 1962.
[16] R.Nozick, *Anarchy, State and Utopia*, Basic Books, 1974.

continue in the foreseeable future. It has considerable practical force, in that it recognises the important point that European Union arrangements cannot be constructed de novo, as if we were starting from nowhere; with a completely blank sheet. The fact is that European Union rules were not arrived at in a vacuum, but in the context of countries' long-existing fishing practices. So the European Union could not operate as if behind the Rawlsian veil of ignorance, since that would have done violence to established expectations. However, doesn't such a justification amounts to an assertion that whatever has occurred in the past is right? Moreover, how should these rights be transmitted from one generation of fishermen to another? Merely because X has fished for a long time in any area may entitle X to exclusive fishing rights in that area, but when X retires or dies, who is entitled to these exclusive fishing rights? Does X have the right to decide this? If so, on what grounds? Established expectation seems stretched rather far here.

Whatever the merits or otherwise of these arguments purporting to justify the entitlements generated by historic catches, it is important to note what sorts of entitlements are ruled out by the historic catches criterion. It rules out an idea of entitlement based on a crude form of egalitarian treatment of all Member States – ie an equal amount of quota for each fish stock in each area allocated to each Member State. Such an allocation would, of course, be absurdly unfair, giving land locked states like Luxembourg and Austria equal shares to the United Kingdom, Ireland, France and Spain, who have extensive fishing interests. An alternative rule of entitlement could be an allocation of quota proportionate to the populations of the Member States, but this would be almost as arbitrary and unfair, since population size has very little relevance to fishing industries as Member States. More relevant considerations would be the size of the country's population engaged in fishing, or the size of the country's fishing fleet, or the importance of fishing to the country's economy, and, indeed, such considerations are explicit in the nation of Hague Preferences, which I discuss below under the concept of need.

There is, however, another idea of entitlement – that based on differential national property rights in Member States' shares of European Union waters. Such an idea of entitlement is often advanced by some Member States (principally the United Kingdom and Ireland) when complaining about the low level of their share of the TACs. For example, the Irish South and West Fishermen's Organisation recently criticised the Irish Government for failing to address this issue in its current Presidency of the European Union. 'Despite appeals from the industry, the government has refused so far to address the basic injustices to Ireland caused by the CFP ... there is no mention of a revision of the deal that gives Ireland 5% of the quotas in mainly low value fish, even though we have 16% of European Union waters'.[17] Similarly, the United Kingdom has claimed that since it has 60% of European Union waters, it should be entitled to 60% of the quota of fish allocated under the European Union's CFP, instead of the 27% given to it.

[17]'Presidency Under Fire', *Fishing News*, 16/8/96, p.2.

A variation on this theme of entitlement through national ownership of resources is the claim, again put forward by the United Kingdom and Ireland, that since by far the majority (75%) of fish caught in the European Union are caught in the waters surrounding the British Isles and Ireland, so the majority of the fish quotas allocated by the European Union should be awarded to United Kingdom and Ireland. But on the principle of relative stability, such a claim is also rejected. So far as the CFP is concerned, both the waters of the European Union Member States and the fish stocks in these waters come under the jurisdiction of the European Union and whether or not Member States claim ownership or sovereignty over either these waters or the fish stocks within them, is neither here nor there, so far as allocations of quota are concerned. For the CFP, entitlement is related to labour mixing by fishermen, not to claims to sovereignty, territory or natural resources by Member States.

It is at first sight surprising, therefore, to read this statement from the CFP Review Group:

> 'The focus of relative stability is inescapably national ... without it, a scarce and finite resource could not be apportioned equitably ... In combination, relative stability and the derogation from equal access demonstrate the CFP's provision for what are essentially protected national assets'.[18]

But what the CFP Review Group means is that since fishermen belong to nations, when they build up track records of fish catching, these track records are attributed to the nations of which they are citizens. In this sense, the principle of relative stability does respect nations' rights, but the 'national' element here is purely incidental, contingent, and derivative; the claim is morally founded upon individual fishermen's efforts, not national sovereign ownership of waters or fish stocks. Assuming that this analysis is sound, is the CFP justified in prioritising a labour mixing criteria of entitlement over a national sovereignty criteria of entitlement? In my view, yes. It seems to me that of the two entitlement claims, although both are deeply flawed, the labour mixing claim is superior to the national sovereignty claim. The labour mixing claim at least has the moral weight that effort has been expended, and energy, initiative and investment have been used to achieve the historic fishing catch record, and this is at least a morally relevant reason for awarding preferential rights to future fishing opportunities. By contrast, the claim of national sovereignty seems morally weak, resting on little more than accidental proximity. But both claims face formidable objections from advocates of a less discriminatory allocative system.

Let us now turn to the concept of need. As noted above, the principle of relative stability contains within it two concepts of substantive justice: entitlement and need. What does the concept of need entail, and how does it relate to the concept of entitlement? The concept of need is explicit in the Hague Preferences – that is, the preferential treatment offered to

[18]Common Fisheries Policy Review Group, *Report*, 2 volumes, MAFF, 1996, II, p.9, I, p.11.

fisheries dependent communities in order to protect their 'vital needs'. How justifiable is this special treatment? One immediate criticism of the idea of 'vital needs' is advanced by free marketeers – that fisheries dependent communities do not need artificial subsidising: on the contrary, they need the discipline of competition so that they can make themselves economically strong, perhaps in another industry. The last thing they 'need' is to be lulled into a false sense of security: subsidies, in the form of privileged or preferential treatment, cannot be permanent.

In the discussion above on the equal access principle, we have already touched on another criticism of the argument for special treatment for fisheries dependent communities – that all fishermen are 'dependent' on fishing. To sustain a defence of the Hague Preferences, it would have to be demonstrated that the degree of fisheries dependence in the fisheries communities of the whole of Ireland, of Scotland and the North East England was greater than the degree of fisheries dependence in the fishing communities of, for example, Northern Spain. With over 22% unemployment in Spain such a case may not be easy to make out. As Wise says, the concept of 'dependence' is politically loaded:

> 'much is made in international fishery disputes, of how "dependent" a country – or region – is upon fishing. However, such notions of "dependence" defy precise objective definition. It is, for example, commonly accepted that Ireland is more dependent upon fishing than the United Kingdom. [But] ... in the process of political decision, it is the "importance" governments attach to the demands of fishing interests that is crucial, rather than some elusive measure of national or regional dependence on fishing'.[19]

Moreover, even if, on the need criterion, it was justifiable to give preferential treatment to Irish and United Kingdom fishermen over French and Spanish fishermen, that necessarily entails less consideration given to entitlement rights based on historic catches.

In a different way, quota hopping also raises the issue of tension between need and entitlement, according to its United Kingdom and Irish critics. As we saw earlier, there is nothing procedurally unjust about quota hopping. Indeed, it is a normal consequence of the freedom of capital guaranteed under the European Union single market legislation that a national of one Member State can set up in business in any other Member State. It is also quite consistent with the entitlement principle; according to (Nozickian) entitlement theory, quota hopping would not violate rights provided there was no coercion entailed, since any transaction carried out in a just (that is, uncoercive) way from a just initial distribution (of historic catches), must itself be just, whatever its wider social consequences. After all, no boat owner is forced to sell their vessel (with licence and quota) to a foreign buyer. Moreover, quota hopping, like the equal access principle, is consistent with

[19] M.Wise, *The Common Fisheries Policy of the European Community*, Methuen, 1984, pp.21-2.

the European Union's emphasis upon a single market and the rule of non discrimination between citizens of Member States.

However, many critics, especially in the United Kingdom, have argued that quota hopping completely undermines the intention of the principle of relative stability, which is to protect national needs. According to such a nationalistic interpretation of the relative stability principle (advanced by Prime Minister John Major, Fisheries Minister Tony Baldry and most United Kingdom Fishermen's Organisations (FOs)) quotas are allocated to nations for the benefit of indigent fisheries and any development which cuts the links between a quota and the nation to which it has been allocated, flies in the face of the whole rationale for allocating quotas. On this interpretation, entitlement is not an end in itself – fairness – but a means to another end – national need. So whenever the two concepts conflict, need overrides entitlement.

Although I have reservations about the nationalistic interpretation of the relative stability principle (for the reasons stated above), insofar as that principle does work to protect the needs of national fishing industries, it is threatened by quota hopping. Whether we choose to abandon the relative stability principle or to forbid quota hopping depends on the relative weight we place on the values of national need and equal freedom. However, on a practical level, if quota hopping is to be stopped, it can only be done by an unlikely decision of the European Union to amend the Maastricht Treaty and downgrade its commitment to market freedom within the European Union.

Our verdict on the principle of relative stability must be that it does not appear to solve the problems of fairness left by the principle of equal access. It lacks procedural fairness, at least in spirit, since it systematically discriminates against new Member States and ossifies 20 year old catching records. Nor does it entirely meet the test of substantive justice, since its element of entitlement and its element of need are both flawed.

Conclusion

The above discussion has revealed considerable doubt about the fairness of the CFP. One response to that doubt would be the cynical conclusion that the CFP is not about fairness but about economic and political considerations, and that considerations of equity are well down the list of priorities of CFP policy makers.

A more positive response would be to point out that the key to the problem lies in identifying the different categories of persons or groups to whom the CFP should be fair. Should the CFP be fair to (1) individual fishermen? (2) local fishing communities? (3) national fishing industries? (4) Member States? (5) European Union fish consumers? (6) fish species? (7) marine eco systems? In this paper I have been concerned only with categories (1), (2), (3), and (4), ignoring issues of fairness to consumers, fish species and marine eco systems. Confining our attention to the first four categories, we can see that different conclusions on the issue of the fairness of the CFP may be reached according to the different perspectives of the constituencies from which that issue is viewed. For instance, quota hopping would be viewed as fair by individual fishermen, and by some Member States, but not by fishing communities, national fishing industries, and other Member States. Similarly, the entitlement element (historic records) of the principle of relative stability would be regarded as fair by individual fishermen; the needs element would be regarded as fair by local fishing communities; and the compensation element would be regarded as fair by national fishing industries. In other words, there may be some elements of fairness in the CFP that each affected constituency can acknowledge. A third response would be to explain that an apparent breach of fairness by the CFP should be understood in the light of the wider context of rules of fairness operating between Member States within the European Union. For example, dilution of the derogations on equal access in order to allow Spain and Portugal a greater share of European Union fish stocks may be part of a complex balancing act in which fishing interests are traded off against other national interests, with a view to reaching an overall fair outcome. Such political deals are thus not devoid of fairness, but may incorporate within them a broader sense of fairness than that which is confined to fishing interests alone.

Whatever one's opinion on these different perceptions and levels of fairness, it is clear that the issue of the fairness of the CFP is much more complex than is generally acknowledged.

Democracy and Citizenship
Theory and Practice

Cecile Fabre
Worcester College, Oxford

'An Argument for Bills of Rights'

Introduction

The purpose of this paper is to argue that individual rights should be entrenched in the constitution of a democratic state, and to try to discriminate between those rights that could and should be constitutionally entrenched and those that could not and should not. For the purpose of this paper, I assume that we have moral rights against others that they do not do certain things to us. I also assume that rights are interest-based, in the sense that one has a right when an interest that one has is important enough to hold other people under lack of claim-rights, duties, disabilities and liabilities. I thus adopt Hohfeld's distinction between claim-rights, which correlate in duties; liberty-rights, which correlate in absence of claim-rights; power-rights, which correlate in liabilities; and immunity-rights, which correlate in disabilities, or lack of power.[1] Hohfeld thinks that the relation between these four rights and their correspondents is one of correlation, something which I disagree with. This thorny issue need not be addressed here. But it is worth mentioning that a clear example of a power-right, which is defined as the ability to change a legal or moral relation, is the power-right to make the law: if I have the legal power to make laws which affect you, it means that you are legally liable to your legal situation being changed by me through these laws. Correspondingly, the clearest example of immunity-right, which is particularly appropriate in this context, is a constitutional provision: if, say, the right to freedom of speech is constitutionally entrenched and if the constitution cannot be amended by the legislature, the legislature lacks the legal power to make laws which are in breach of the right, and the right-holders have a legal (or constitutional) immunity against the legislature

I also assume that we have a fundamental interest in having a good life, and that in order to have a good life one has to be autonomous. I take autonomy to be the capacity 'to form, to revise and rationally to pursue a conception of the good.'[2] I last assume that that we have a moral right against others that they respect our autonomy.

The Case for Bills of Rights

For someone to have a moral right to X means that other people are under a moral duty, a moral disability, a moral liability, and/or that they have no

[1] W.N.Hohfeld, *Fundamental Conceptions as Applied to Judicial Reasoning*, Yale University Press, 1919.

[2] J.Rawls, *Political Liberalism*, Columbia University Press, 1993, p.72.

claim right against the rights bearer. This as such says nothing as to who exactly these people should be. Should it be the state? Private individuals? If we set aside the case of special rights, such as the rights which arise out of promises and contract and which characterise relationships specifically between the parties in the promises or contract, the question remains as to who primarily has the moral duty to respect our moral claim-rights, is morally liable to our exercise of moral power-rights, has no moral claim-right against us that we do not exercise our moral liberty-right, and is morally disabled by our moral immunity-rights. It is my contention that if we take rights seriously, then it must mean that the state as well as private individuals stand under these complex relations with respect to our exercise of moral rights.

Let us assume, for example, that we have a moral right to freedom of speech. Such a right is a moral claim-right against others which holds them under a moral duty not to prevent us from speaking. Now if only private individuals, and not the state, were under this duty, we would weaken the right, because we would in fact allow the state, whose means for oppression far exceed those of private individuals, to harm this interest in such a way as to crush it. The moral right to freedom of speech is also a moral liberty-right to speak freely, and here again to say that private individuals have no moral claim-right against us that we refrain from speaking and that the state does have such a moral claim-right would make a mockery of our interest in freedom of speech.

Thus, if we were content to say that only private individuals are under moral duties, disabilities, liabilities and do not have claim-rights against us, if we were unhappy to concede that the state also stands in these relations with bearers of rights, we would thereby fatally weaken rights, and fail to accord decent protection to those interests that we deem so important. As Nagel puts it, 'the constraints of personal morality, which prohibit certain forms of direct harm to others, even as a means to valuable ends, apply in this way to the sate as well as to individuals.'[3]

Now, saying that states stand in such a relationship is too vague. For there are three kinds of state agents likely to be involved in rights relationships with rights holders: state officials, who apply the law; members of the legislature; and fellow citizens. Again, let us assume that we have a moral claim-right to freedom of speech against the state. This right grounds a moral duty on state officials to apply a law, voted by the legislature or by citizens in a referendum acknowledging this claim-right and not to apply a law imposing state censorship; a moral duty on members of the legislature not to vote for laws imposing state censorship; and a moral duty on citizens that they do not themselves vote in referenda for laws imposing state censorship. It indeed would not make sense to assert the importance of respecting individuals' moral rights and on that basis to hold the government under a moral duty to respect those rights, or to morally disable the government to violate those rights, but not to hold citizens under the moral duty not to vote, and/or the disability to vote, for laws which violate those rights.

[3] T.Nagel, *Equality and Partiality*, Oxford University Press, 1991, p.167.

Another way of putting it is this: in cases where P has an interest which is sufficiently important to hold that Q, as a private individual, is liable to P, lacks a claim-right against P, is under a duty to refrain from acting, or/and a disability to act in ways that are contrary to that interest, then this interest must also be sufficiently important to hold that Q as a citizen is liable to P, lacks a claim-right against P, is under a duty to refrain from voting for laws that violate this interest, and/or is under a disability to vote for laws.

The argument I have just put forward does not presuppose that it is possible to determine everything that citizens and members of the legislature cannot do simply by determining everything that private individuals cannot do. Holding the view that private morality in some cases forms the basis of public morality does not commit oneself to claiming that whatever private individuals cannot do the state cannot do either. Indeed, most of us think that there are things that the state can and ought to do and that private individuals cannot and must not do. We need then to distinguish between cases where an act performed by private individuals is considered a violation of a right and is therefore illegitimate, but is not considered as a violation of a right and therefore is legitimate if it is performed by the state, and cases where an act performed by private individuals is a violation of a right and is therefore illegitimate, and is considered as such if it is performed by the state. To bring this out with a concrete example, we need a criterion to decide why it seems acceptable on the part of the state and unacceptable on the part of private individuals to lock me up for twenty years if I commit a murder or to demand that I drive on a certain side of the road, and why it seems unacceptable on the part of private individuals and on the part of the state to prevent me from forming relationships with consenting adults, whatever their gender is.

It is far beyond the scope of this paper to tackle this issue in any detail, for it would require setting out a theory of political authority. I shall simply offer a guideline principle for distinguishing between these two cases. In the first case, I have either committed such an act that something must be done about it, or there is need for a policy regulating a particular practice. In the second case, what is at stake is a very important interest of mine which, if harmed, would diminish my autonomy. This interest is important enough to claim that it would be morally wrong for the state and private individuals to harm it. This, I think, is where the difference is. If the reason why a certain action is forbidden to a private individual is that this action violates the autonomy of someone who has not already forfeited his right to have his autonomy violated, then such an action should not be allowed to the state either; it should therefore not be allowed to this person when he acts as a citizen.

The fact that one has a moral right to X does not entail that one ought to have a constitutional right to X. Not all moral rights should be turned into constitutional rights (I shall come back to this later on.) However, there are grounds for constitutionally entrenching certain individual rights. Valuing autonomy means valuing the capacity to frame, revise and pursue a conception of the good. It follows that when pursuing our conception of the good life, we cannot encroach upon other people's pursuit of their conception of the good life. Autonomy is a fundamental value and gives rise to certain interests, which are protected by rights that we have and that other people must respect. But other people also have similar rights, so that I have rights to pursue certain activities only to the extent that my pursuit of these activities does not conflict with other people's rights to pursue their own activities.

Now, the right that I have as a citizen to have my preference satisfied if I am in the majority can be said to be derived from the value of autonomy. If it is important for people to pursue their conception of the good, then surely they should be allowed to advance it in the political forum should they so wish. However, private individuals, when pursuing their conception of the good life ought not to be allowed to harm other people's autonomy and thus to violate the rights others have which protect those interests the furtherance of which is necessary for autonomy, so that there ought to be a law preventing people from violating other people's rights.[4] Equally, citizens and members of the legislature, when seeking to further their conception of the good life in the public forum, should not be allowed to violate those rights either, and should be legally prevented from doing so. If we think, say, that private individuals ought not to be allowed to kill others or to infringe their right to freedom of speech, we must think that citizens and members of the legislature ought not to be allowed to vote for laws whereby others would be killed, whereby freedom of speech would be violated. If we take seriously autonomy and the rights which protect it, driving a wedge between people's duties qua private individuals and their duties qua citizens and members of the legislature seems arbitrary. Just as we think that there ought to be legal constraints on private individuals' pursuit of their conception of the good, there ought to be legal constraints on citizens' and members of the legislature's pursuit of their conception of the good. The constitution, and more specifically the bill of rights, thus serve as such legal constraints on citizens and members of the legislature in that they hold them under legal duties to respect individual rights and they disable them should they try to violate those rights.

So far I have focused on rights we have against private individuals and the state. However, some interests that we have can be harmed or furthered only by the state, and sometimes only by citizens or their representatives. For instance, my interest in voting can be furthered only by the state who is the only one to provide people with polling stations and to call for elections at regular intervals. If these interests are deemed important enough to be protected by rights, then those rights are necessarily rights against the state, and when appropriate against citizens. Note that the argument in favour of constitutional rights that I put above works for those rights as well. The interests protected by those rights, to wit autonomy and its derivative interests, are the same as the interests protected by the rights we have against private individuals as well, and there is therefore no reason to

[4] H.L.A.Hart, 'Are There Any Natural Rights', *The Philosophical Review*, lxiv, 1955.

think that they should not be afforded the legal protection that other rights are afforded, by way of the constitution. It would indeed seem arbitrary to say that such rights should be enforced legally when held against private individuals, citizens and members of the legislature, but that they should not be so enforced when held against citizens and members of the legislature only.

Entrenchable and non entrenchable rights

I said above that not every moral right should be turned into a constitutional right. For instance, I may have a moral right to spend my time cutting my lawn with a pair of scissors, and other people may be under a moral duty not to interfere with me, not to vote laws forbidding me to do it; yet there would be something odd in turning such a right into a constitutional right. For such a moral right protects a fairly trivial act, and it would devalue the constitution if trivial things of that kind were entrenched in it. Another example: constitutionally entrenching the right to free advertising would seem equally odd, because this right protects a specific type of expression. But, at the other hand of the spectrum, entrenching the right to autonomy, which protects a value which is crucially important and general, does not seem such a good idea either, because the right thus formulated seems to be too vague to be effectively protected by the courts.

How then can we discriminate between those moral rights that should be turned into constitutional rights and those moral rights that should not? The (very tentative) argument I offer ties in to the interest-based conception of rights. I suggest that we entrench in the constitution only derivative moral rights that protect actions and opportunities that we have a direct interest in, and which are general rather than specific, but which are not so general as to be hopelessly vague (such as the right to autonomy.)

Here, I make some distinctions between fundamental and derivative interests, and between fundamental and derivative rights. An interest is fundamental if it cannot be derived from another interest, while an interest is derivative if it can be derived from another interest. To say that interest B is derived from interest A here means that the reason why I have an interest in B is that I have an interest in A. If interest B were harmed, interest A would be harmed too. To give an example: our interest in having a good life is a fundamental interest, because there is no interest the possession of which could explain why we have such an interest, which could be harmed if this interest were harmed. The interest in autonomy is a derivative interest because the reason (or maybe one of the reasons) why we have it is that we have an interest in having a good life.

A right is fundamental if it protects an interest which is itself fundamental. A right is derivative if it protects an interest whose importance is asserted by appealing to the importance of another interest which itself is deemed important enough to be protected by a right. That is, a right is derivative if the reason why I have it is that I have another right.

Now, one should not entrench fundamental rights or very general derivative rights because they are too vague to be constitutionally entrenched. But the interests that they protect give rise to numerous derivative interests which, once they are spelled out, allow for the effective protection of the fundamental interests to be possible. For instance, autonomy gives rise to derivative interests in freedom of speech, freedom of association, private property, etc. Each of these interests is protected by a right which is clear enough to allow for constitutional entrenchment: the right to freedom of speech, to freedom of association, to freedom of movement, etc.

Thus, only derivative moral rights ought to be constitutionally entrenched. But one ought to distinguish between derivative moral rights which protect actions and opportunities people have a direct interest in, and derivative moral rights which protect actions and opportunities people do not have a direct interest in. The former, unlike the latter, are actions and opportunities the pursuit of which is necessary for the pursuit of our conception of the good. For example, the right to cut my lawn with a pair of scissors is a derivative right in that I have it because I have a right to private property, and ultimately (or so it could be argued) because I have a right to autonomy. But the action itself that it protects (cutting my lawn with a pair of scissors) is not a direct interest of mine, because I consider the action to be so trivial that it is not part of my conception of the good life. I could decide to do something else without changing anything significant to my life. Now, I suggest that we do not constitutionally entrench those moral rights which protect actions we do not have a direct interest in because these rights in fact protect trivial acts. A constitution which protects rights constitutes the framework for governmental action, as well as the solemn affirmation that certain things ought not to be done, or, for that matter, ought to be done, to individuals. Entrenching a right to cut the lawn with a pair of scissors, indeed entrenching any right protecting fairly trivial things, would introduce an element of triviality in the text, which then could not be taken very seriously.

The other kinds of derivative moral rights which I suggest should not be constitutionally entrenched are those which protect actions in which we have a direct interest in but which are fairly specific. Suppose that I love my garden to look in a certain way, and that being able to contemplate my garden when it looks that way is one of the elements of my conception of the good. And suppose that the only way for me to get my garden to look that way is to cut the lawn with a pair of scissors. In that case, being able to cut my lawn with scissors is not trivial, and I have a direct interest in it. But it is a specific action, in that it is part of my conception of the good, but not necessarily part of other people's conception of the good. What should be entrenched in the constitution is the right to private property, which protects an interest that everybody can plausibly be said to have if they are to be autonomous. Advertising is another of a specific action the right to which should not be explicitly laid down in the constitution. The freedom to advertise is an instance of freedom of speech, and it is specific in that it is performed by a limited category of people in the limited context of selling goods and services. Any other instance of expression (with the exception of political speech) would fall into the category of specific actions. Entrenching the rights protecting these specific actions, or indeed entrenching rights protecting very specific interests that are derived from interests we all have if we are to be autonomous, would be problematic for several reasons. First, the constitution must have some solemn character that it would lose if it included a whole list of rights protecting all sorts of activities and interests. Second, these activities might stop being performed, due to technological, socio-economic changes, so that the constitution would become obsolete and would lose some of its binding force or appeal. Third, if we protect certain types of activities and interests and not others, we run the risk of some people saying that those activities which are not explicitly protected are in fact not protected at all, or are less protected, with the effect that should conflicts arise between someone exercising a constitutionally protected activity and someone exercising an activity which is not protected, the former person might win the case even if there are reasons for saying that the latter person's interest should have prevailed.

This is not to say that these rights which I argued should not be entrenched could never be constitutionally protected. The moral right to spend my time cutting my lawn with a pair of scissors is derived from the right to private property. Should the latter be constitutionally entrenched, and should the government try to pass a law forbidding people to spend their time in such a way, the moral right thus attacked would in fact be constitutionally protected by the constitutional right to private property, and the law would be struck down on the grounds that it violates the right to private property.[5] But the point I am making still remains that entrenching it explicitly would not be wise.

Conclusion

To conclude, I hope to have shown that it is legitimate to entrench in the constitution of a democratic state those rights the respect of which is necessary for us to be autonomous, precisely because they are so necessary, and that it is legitimate to entrench in the constitution those rights which are uncontroversial, derivative and which protect general activities and opportunities we have a direct interest in.

[5]In certain legal systems, such as the American system, the moral right to cut one's lawn with a pair of scissors would automatically be turned into a constitutional right if the Supreme Court decided that a law violating it would violate the right to private property, which is itself a constitutional right. In fact, But this need not be the case. A decision of anticonstitutionality by the French Constitutional Council does not amount to adding new rights in the constitution. Suppose that the Council strikes down a law making homosexual acts illegal. The constitution will not thereby automatically be amended to the effect that no law forbidding homosexual acts can be passed. Another government could try again and risk being defeated again. So those who worry that even non entrenched moral rights in fact will be turned into constitutional rights might want to advocate a type of judicial review along French lines.

Democracy and Citizenship: Theory and Practice

Jane Freedman
King's College, London

'Can Women Transform Politics?
Women's Demands for Equal Representation as a Catalyst of Institutional Change in Britain and France'

Introduction

It could be argued that one of the major changes in the British and French political systems in the twentieth century was the granting of the right to vote and eligibility to all women in 1928 in Britain and 1944 in France. However, it seems to be a case of 'plus ą change, plus c'est la même chose': formal equality and rights of citizenship for women have not led to an equal participation by women in the political institutions of these two countries. Despite the suffragettes' hopes that the fact of women having the vote would lead to a gradual increase in the number of women members of Parliament, this has not been the case, and in both Britain and France, the progress towards equal representation of men and women in parliament has been slow if not non-existent. In both Britain and France the proportion of women in parliament and government is small (7.4% in the British Parliament and 5.9% in the French *Assemblée Nationale*) compared to most other member countries of the European Union. This under-representation of women in the highest decision-making institutions has led to a renewal of pressure from women's movements in Britain and France to find a way of increasing the number of women MPs and ministers. This article will examine the development of the *Mouvement pour la parité* in France, in comparison with the attempts to impose all-women shortlists in Britain, and then go on to examine presuppositions that if these movements were successful and women were equally represented in parliament and government in Britain and France, this would lead to a change in the functioning of these political institutions.

Le Mouvement pour la Parité

The *Mouvement pour la parité* is an increasingly large and vocal movement in France calling for parity between men and women in all areas of professional life and particularly in political representation. The movement has developed in the context of a general malaise of the French political institutions and in response to public disaffection with established political parties. The demand for change in political institutions and personnel stemming from an increasingly critical view of the traditional élites which dominate French politics and which are seen as increasingly unrepresentative of the French population, has led to renewed interest in the lack of women in parliament and government and a new campaign to achieve greater equality of representation of men and women in political institutions. The idea that the under-representation of women is a key element in the growing gap perceived between politicians and those they represent has become widespread.

The first impetus for the new movement in favour of parity came from a book published in 1992 by Francoise Gaspard, Anne Le Gall & Claude Servan-Schreiber, entitled *Au pouvoir citoyennes! Liberté, Egalité, Parité.*[1] The authors claim that the absence of women from political institutions and the exclusion of women from political decision-making undermine France's claim to be a democracy, and they call for an equal representation of women in all representative institutions, to be guaranteed by law. This demand has received strong support from, and could indeed be said to have revived, the French feminist movement which had been relatively inactive in the previous decade. Existing feminist groups have mobilised around the cause, whilst new co-ordinating bodies such as the *Reseau Femmes pour la Parité* have been organised and two regular newsletters, *Parité-Infos* and *La lettre de Parité are published regularly. The movement is lead and inspired mainly by women involved in politics or academia (or like Francoise Gaspard, ex-deputy and professor at the École des Hautes Études en Sciences Sociales*) both fields, and these women have succeeded in gaining a lot of media attention for their movement. A manifesto in favour of parity signed by ten women politicians including Edith Cresson and other ex-ministers was published as an exclusive by *L'Express* magazine in June of this year and was followed by articles in all the main daily newspapers and news magazines. The movement's appeal is not limited, however, to women who have previously been involved in politics or to feminist academics. It has also attracted widespread support from a range of women who had not previously been affiliated to any feminist movement, as can be affirmed by the large attendance at meetings and demonstrations organised in favour of parity. A demonstration in front of the National Assembly in October 1993 was attended by thousands of women and petition in favour of parity sent out to women's associations at the end of 1995 received 20,000 signatures within 10 days.

Nor has the support for the movement come solely from women. In November 1993, *Le Monde* published a 'Manifeste des 577 pour une democratie paritaire', of which 288 of the 577 signatories were men. Opinion polls suggest that a large majority of the French population is in favour of parity. A poll conducted by IFOP for *L'Express* magazine in May 1996 found that 71% of those interrogated responded favourably to the question

> 'Would equality of men and women in political life have a favourable effect on the equality of men and women in society in general?'

The pressure for 'parité' in France has thus come much more from the 'grass roots', from extra-parliamentary and extra-partisan sources than has

[1] Editions du Seuil.

the pressure for more equal representation of women in British political institutions. In Britain the initiative for all-women shortlists came from within the Labour Party and no movement or pressure group corresponding to the *Mouvement pour la parité* has developed in support of these all-women shortlists or of any other measures to increase women's representation in parliament.

The 300 group which was set up to campaign for equal representation of women in parliament never succeeded in mobilizing public support or attracting media attention in the way that the *Mouvement pour la parité* has done in France. This difference may be attributed to specificities of British and French political culture: the French have shown themselves much more ready to demonstrate publicly for many causes than their British counterparts, but perhaps the British women's movement has something to learn from the *Mouvement pour la parité* and its success in bringing the issues of women's under-representation to the forefront of public debate and forcing it onto the public agenda.

The *Mouvement pour la parité* has received widespread support in France but there has also been opposition both from outside and within the feminist movement. One of the most outspoken critics of the Mouvement has been the feminist philosopher Elisabeth Badinter, for whom the idea of parity runs counter to Republican universalism. The theoretical foundations of any system of quotas for women, as well as the practical problems involved in implementing such a system must of course be a subject of debate. There is no room here to go into the details of such debates, suffice it to say that although the theoretical and practical debates over the notion of parity have by no means been won by either side, the fact that there has been such widespread debate not only over the practical implications of parity, but over the theoretical foundations which support it, has brought the issue to the attention of a large sector of the French population, and has allowed a much fuller discussion of the issues and problems involved than has been seen in Britain.

The reaction of the political parties

The *Mouvement pour la parité* has been successful in attracting a lot of publicity and public support. The many public debates, demonstrations, newspaper articles and television and radio broadcasts devoted to the issue of parity have put the issue at the forefront of political debate, and have made it impossible for the major political parties not to react. The apparent depth of feeling in support of parity has prompted all the major parties with the notable exception of the Front National, to declare at least some degree of support for the idea of parity. The Communist Party and the Greens have gone the furthest in this support and formulated parliamentary bills in favour of parity, the Communists with a 'proposition de loi tendant à assurer une participation equilibrée des femmes et des hommes dans la vie publique'

(April 1994)[2] and the Greens with a 'proposition de loi constitutionnelle instaurant la parité Femmes-Hommes', April 1995.[3]

The Socialist Party has declared itself in favour of parity and in September 1996 the Conseil National announced that 164 constituencies (one third) would be reserved for women candidates at the 1998 legislative elections. The implementation of this decree has not, however, been without problems. In the department of the Allier, for example, designated to present a woman candidate in at least one constituency, the constituency that has been chosen by the local party is that of Montlucon, where it will be difficult for a socialist candidate to beat the popular Communist mayor, Pierre Goldberg. Moreover, the local party affirms that it has had difficulties finding a woman to be their candidate.

The RPR-UDF has been more restrained in its support for parité. Following the early dismissal of eight of the twelve women ministers from his government, Alain Juppé set up an *Observatoire pour la parité* headed by the RPR deputy Roselyne Bachelot, which is charged with preparing a report and propositions to increase the representation of women. Critics, however, have derided this measure, indicating that the Observatoire is merely a way for Juppé to salve his conscience, and to avoid any concrete action in favour of parity. Whilst Alain Juppé has confirmed that he is prepared to call a referendum on the issue of parity, the only concrete measures so far announced have been a promise that at least a third of the RPR-UDF candidates in the 1998 regional elections will be women. Whilst announcing this measure, however, Patrick Stefani, the deputy general secretary of the RPR admitted that the number of women candidates his party would present at the next legislative elections would not be greatly augmented as they intended to give priority in nominating candidates to those who already held a seat.

French political parties have thus been forced to take a much more positive line on equal representation of men and women than their British counterparts. The battle, however, is far from won. If the parties have been forced to acknowledge the public pressure in support of parity and to make some kind of reforms towards more equal representation of women, it is still not clear that this will be enough to greatly increase the number of women deputies after the next legislative elections in 1988. Behind the declarations of good intentions it is clear that there is still strong resistance to any measures in favour of parity.

Will more women make a difference?

Having examined the pressures in favour of a more equal representation of women in British and French political institutions, the question remains of whether a greater proportion of women in parliament and government would have a significant effect upon the functioning of these institutions and upon the British and French political cultures in general.

---

[2] Proposition of law tending to ensure an equal participation of women and men in public life.

[3] Proposition of constitutional law implementing parity between men and women.

One obvious effect of having more women in parliament would be a normalization of feminine models of political power. This could be seen as one of the strongest arguments in favour of some form of quota of women in parliament, for the current situation in British and French political institutions reveals a type of vicious circle whereby the absence of women from positions of political power makes it very difficult to construct positive models of feminine power, whilst the lack of such models presents a symbolic barrier to the access of more women to posts of political power. The quasi-total absence of women from positions of political power perpetuates the idea that women do not have a place in the political world, an idea that is even more powerful a factor of exclusion as it is interiorised by women themselves.

But beyond this possible symbolic modification in the political sphere, what effects would a greater number of women have on the functioning of political institutions. French and British women politicians interviewed for this study frequently commented that they thought women had a different approach to politics than men. This difference manifested itself in women's motivations for entering into politics, in their manner of conducting themselves in political debate and in their principal concerns and interests. The women interviewed often argued that they had chosen a career in politics not for the power and prestige attached to the role, but in order to achieve some concrete reforms. They generalised this observation to argue that women and men have a different relationship to power: women see political power as a means to an end whereas men see the obtention of political power as an end in itself. Edith Cresson is typical when she comments that,

> 'For me, and for most women ministers I know, power is the possibility of modifying something which you think is wrong. For a man, power is showing off, driving around with motorcycles accompanying your car, and saying I'm a minister.'[4]

A second element that many women commented upon was their perception of themselves as less aggressive than men. Diana Maddock, for example, remarked that

> 'I think we're less confrontational than men and we like to get some kind of consensus and bring people round to going forward with agreement and enthusiasm. And men seem to enjoy the combative method rather better.'[5]

There is thus the idea that more women in parliament would lead to a less confrontational style of politics with more consensus both within and between the parties. Many women interviewed felt that a positive improvement to the functioning of parliament could be effected through the advent of more women with their less adversarial style of politics.

As well as differences in style, the women interviewed pointed to a difference in the content of their politics. That is to say that they expressed the opinion that they were more in touch with everyday life than men,

[4]Interview 09.12.1993.

[5]Interview 01.11.1993.

and interested in concrete problems rather than abstract concepts like men. Huguette Bouchardeau, a socialist deputy, explains the origins of this approach by the fact that most women have another activity in life,

> 'they take a much greater role in bringing up children, housework, and they occupy themselves much more with the problems of everyday life. Which means that when women arrive in posts of political responsibility they have what could be called a culture of everyday life.'[6]

These few comments indicate a general perception that women have a different relationship to politics from men, and that a greater number of women in parliament and government could change the face of political institutions in Britain and France.

But how should these claims that women will radically alter the functioning of our current political institutions be interpreted? The question of the existence or not of a separate 'feminine culture' which would change the face of politics throws us back to the old division between those who emphasise the role of masculine domination and induce from it a 'poverty' of feminine culture, and those who perhaps underestimate the effects of masculine domination and claim the intrinsic superiority of feminine culture in what could be called a kind of 'feminist populism'. Pierre Bourdieu, who represents the first category, argues that the positive values to which women could lay claim are in fact an illusion, the product of symbolic violence which is accomplished outside the control of consciousness and willing, 'in the obscurity of the practical schema of the habitus'.[7] On the other hand, other theorists such as Carol Gilligan, for example, would argue that the specificity of feminine identity and culture cannot be deduced from the existence of masculine domination even if, in reality, the effects characteristic of this domination and the characteristics of a separate feminine culture overlap. A feminine culture which can even be considered superior to masculine culture[8] cannot thus be attributed merely to symbolic violence but exists independently of the structures of domination.

These two diametrically opposed approaches to the notion of a 'feminine culture' raise problems in our evaluation of women politicians' claims to a different approach to politics. Can we accept at face value the claims that women bring to politics a specifically feminine approach closer to the reality of everyday life, less concerned with the apparatus of power and more interested in practical and positive reforms. Should we, like Bourdieu, attribute these claims merely to the effects of masculine domination? Are women politician's affirmations that they view politics differently from their male colleagues merely an illusory component of the discourse of the dominated? Or can we accept a face value these claims of a different, and perhaps superior feminine approach to politics which could revolutionise and improve

[6] Interview 18.11.1992.

[7] P.Bourdieu, 'La domination masculine', *Actes de la Recherche en Sciences Sociales*, 84, 1990.

[8] For Carol Gilligan the feminine ethic of care is superior to the abstract, masculine ethic of justice. C.Gilligan, *In a Different Voice*, Harvard University Press, 1982.

the functioning and results of political institutions if more women were represented in these institutions?

Many of the claims for *parité* in France, or for all-women shortlists in Britain rest on the presupposition that women will bring to politics something new and lacking. It is thus important to see how far this claim can be sustained. Perhaps, however, the debate over the nature of women's supposedly different approach is a misleading one. It is clear that the processes of masculine domination must play a role in shaping women's approach to politics and whether or not there is an intrinsically 'feminine' element involved in women's political culture, it can be argued that women will have a specific input into politics.

In a study of women's and men's conceptions of politics in France, Janine Mossuz-Lavau observed that

> 'the essential point which distinguishes men and women in their relationship to politics is that women have above all a sense of need (besoins) whereas men have more of a sense of constraint (contraintes).'[9]

Through their long-term domination of politics, and thus a greater political practice, men have better integrated the institutional and economic constraints involved, which can lead them to depreciate the changes it is possible to effect through political reform. Whereas women will give priority to the satisfaction of the needs they see without such careful regards to institutional and economic constraints involved in the satisfaction of those needs. One of the criticisms often levelled at women politicians has been their naïety and absence of economic sense – women have traditionally been relegated to social domains such as education because these are seen to be within their capabilities. So to suggest that women do have an approach which concerns itself more with people's needs and ignores the economic and institutional constraints involved in politics may be seen as merely reinforcing the old stereotypes which have served to exclude women from positions of political power and to suggest that women are less able politicians than men (if by a good 'politician' we mean someone able to take into account the mechanisms and relations of power which authorise decision making, to have recourse to the abstract, to notions which permit a 'political' analysis of daily reality). It is natural though that if women have been so long excluded from political power and decision making they should be less integrated into this type of 'political' thought and action than men. This does not imply that women have less to contribute to political institutions and indeed their approach may be what our institutions are lacking.

It is clearly impossible to predict exactly how a more equal representation of women would alter, if at all, our political institutions, and any claim for quotas for women cannot therefore be based on any absolute claim that women will improve the functioning of political institutions. There is, however, a general perception amongst women politicians themselves, and in

[9] J.Mossuz-Lavau, 'Les conceptions politiques des hommes et des femmes', in M.Riot-Sarcey (ed), *Democratie et Representation*, Kime, 1995.

public opinion that women do have something different to contribute to our political institutions, and any reforms that helped to bring about a more equal representation of women in these institutions would be welcomed.

Political Communication, Globalisation and Techno-Populism

Mark Wheeler
London Guildhall University

'Multi-Mediatisation, Techno-Populism, Political Communication and the Citizens' Democratic Rights: The Netizen'

Qualification

Because there were problems with the ASCII-ing process the footnotes and references for this paper are not included. Copies of them will be available at the session itself.

Introduction

The traditional mass medias' (press, radio, television) role as a public watchdog has proved problematic. Instead of providing a check on the political system (or Fourth Estate), the media institutions, through the globalization of outlets, concentrated conglomeration of ownership , their reliance on commercial funding methods and close affiliations with the political élite, have been perceived as part of the political mainstream. Rather than there being a transaction of information and knowledge rights between the citizen and media systems, founded on public service values, mass communications have become private goods to be bought by consumers.

Therefore, Jurgen Habermas has argued that the mass media has eroded as a public sphere, becoming the site for ideological manipulation and the distortion of information. Effectively, rational public discourse has been overridden by power politics as major organizations have negotiated with one another and states to exclude the public. Rupert Murdoch's News Corporation's deal-making, across national, regional and global markets, demonstrates the extent to which it has been incorporated into the political élite, as politicians and media barons perceive the mutuality of their interests. As the media manipulates publicity, the political discourse has become state controlled, sensationalist and market-led.

In particular, electoral politics have been defined as a pre-digested 'spectacle'. Initially, American Presidential Election campaigns were fought through the mass media, principally on television. Now all manner of elections, throughout Western liberal democracies, are contested in the media. In Britain, the political parties' mass communication strategies appear to indicate that information has been manipulated by party mandarins as British politics has been Americanized during a period partisan decline. Moreover, critical political analysis has been suspended when the media moguls have become political actors. Silvio Berlusconi's use of his television channels to support his candidacy for Prime Minister provoked a debate about the safety of the Italian democratic process. Political communication techniques have also been blamed for the electorates' increasing cynicism and for promoting style over substance. Thus, it has been maintained that the mainstream parties control of political information, their usage of marketing techniques and campaign strategies which utilize television, have undermined democratic behaviour.

Alternatively, advocates of the new multi-media technologies argue that both general (the failure of the media) and specific (the anti-democratic nature of traditional forms of political communication) problems can be challenged through the emerging Information and Communication Technologies (ICTs). In particular, the Internet (the global web of computers on international telecommunications networks), has been popularized as a means to increase the citizen's participation. In this paper we will address the potentially liberating nature of the information technologies and consider electronic democracy.

To focus my study, I will refer to the Internet users' magazine *Wired's* online coverage, on its Hot Wired web-site, of the 1996 American Presidential election campaign. This initiative, entitled the Netizen, was designed to provide daily, weekly and monthly information. It was claimed:

> 'The Netizen is not about standard " horse race" coverage, it's about politics in a revolutionary context – one that questions whether politics itself isn't obsolete in the digital age, when the majority of the population doesn't even bother to vote.'

For this paper, I have taken a selection of the Netizen's coverage from the two weeks which preceded the Presidential Election. This content analysis is not methodologically rigorous, but is intended to give the reader a flavour of the web-site's political discourse. I have defined several basic units of analysis : the site's coverage and criticisms of the Presidential and Senate campaigns; the failure of the traditional American media ; and the technological agenda of the Internet's 'new politics'. I am aware of the potential pit-falls of such an approach, as I have introduced specific units of subjective analysis, however my principal concern is to utilize the material to test out the veracity of the arguments outlined above.

Consequently, we will analyze the arguments for democratic participation through the Information Autobahn, assess the worth of the Netizen initiative and address its impact on political communication. Moreover, such a study leads onto questions about whether ICTs can promote either individualistic or communal concepts of democratic behaviour. Thus, we will address whether the emerging ICTs will challenge political norms. Can the Information Superhighway provide an electronic landscape for a re-invented civil society? It is argued that the unregulated cyberspace of the Internet will allow information to by- pass the intervention of state controls and produce greater citizen empowerment. For some, the prospect of realizing a true Athenian democracy appears to be achievable. However, Athens was built on the back of slavery and its democratic principles applied to a few. Therefore, will the proliferation of communications networks increase the availability of political information?

Further, the theories of political participation, which make reference to the disparate nature of the information superhighway, would suggest that the multi-media evade institutional power to provide a truly anarchistic forum in which knowledge can be equitably distributed amongst individuals and user groups. However, as these multi-media developments have been orchestrated around market precepts such as private enterprise and individualism, can ICTs enhance democratic behaviour which has normatively been a collective activity? Therefore, will the information we receive on the Internet remain marginal, irrelevant and trivial if it continues to defy these institutional and collective traditions? In effect, will multi-media responses reassert or challenge Jurgen Habermas's concept of politics as a pre- digested spectacle in which information continues to manipulated for the purposes of social engineering? Alternatively, should we be looking at ways in which Information Technology can enhance collective methods of political association?

Information Communication Technologies and Democratic Rights

The technological revolution has produced major transformations within communications for business and domestic use. Interactive fibre-optic cable systems are developing alongside the widespread usage of personal computers and videoconferencing. A new generation of networks can promote low-cost broad-band communication. These developments provide access to greater numbers of communications links, permit the distribution of commercial and entertainment material, and advance telephony along the same highways. Moreover, new electronic services located around telecoms, computer and satellites have created a global electronic mail service. Integrated computer networks from universities, companies and the American military, generically entitled the Internet, have grown at a staggering rate connecting 1.3 million computers, eight thousand networks and over ten million users.

ICTs are applicable in three ways. First, computers increase the amount of data to be stored, retrieved and transmitted. Secondly, mass participation technologies, such as broadcasting, which distribute information from a central source to millions can be enhanced. Finally, they provide interactive communications flows among individuals and organized groups. For instance, there are thousands of on-line Bulletin Board Systems (BBS) and news groups. Thus, ICTs may have the following effects:

- They explode the limits on the volume of information that can be exchanged.
- They make it possible to exchange information without regard, for all practical purposes, to real time and space.
- They increase the control the consumers have over what messages are received and when.
- They increase the control the senders have over specific audiences who receive the messages.

- They decentralize control over mass communication.
- They bring two way or interactive capacities to television.

The advocates of the Internet argue that new forms of communication flow can challenge traditional political structures, institutions and methods of association. First, as the physical limits of time, space and geography have been overcome, the constraints over the volume of information available to the public have evaporated. Previously, as direct citizen participation was undermined by time, size, knowledge and access, élitist or representative models of democracy emerged. Alternatively, a wired world would stem the difficulties of time because communication and participation become instantaneous. Similarly, problems of size are solved because people do not have to be gathered in a single place. Concurrently, the distribution of knowledge is widely available through networks, which in turn removes the difficulty of access. Whilst the capacity of different interactive services to enhance participation varies, they are distinguished from the previous mass media as the information recipients are no longer passive.

Thus, Teledemocracy becomes a realistic possibility. Within this technological context, the current norms of political decision-making and information distribution are archaic and resistant to more modulated flows of communication from the grass-roots level. Andrew Adonis and Geoff Mulgan ironically demonstrate:

> 'On election days, modern citizens come home from offices and factories crammed full of computers, faxes and digital phone systems, to homes almost equally cluttered with telephones and videos, and on the way vote by scribbling a cross on pieces of paper which are then to be put into wooden boxes, to be counted by volunteers in a method that has scarcely changed since the introduction of the secret ballot in 1872.'

Moreover, even as a chamber or physical space, the Westminster Bi-Cameral Parliamentary system has become irrelevant, harking back to a pre-industrial form of decision-making. Whilst most people are familiar with PIN numbers, MPs continue to pass into the lobbies so that the tellers can record their votes. To this end, Graham Allen, a former Labour Party spokesman on the Media, has argued that the multi-media may establish a new political culture by removing the 'middle-man' of representational assemblies to allow the electorate to input their views within national, regional and local parliaments.

Lean Democracy and Techno-Populist Anti-Partyism

In turn, ICTs may significantly alter the future of democratic politics. Geoff Mulgan, founder of the Demos think tank, argues that political decision-making exists within a different multi-media universe:

> '... what makes our time so complex is that these shifts in media forms are now accelerating far ahead of the ability of political institutions to keep up, as new generations are brought up

> on computer games (and soon virtual reality) each of which carries with it quite distinct cognitive structures. It is not that they will displace the old media, or that linear logics of print culture will disappear altogether. It is rather that new generations will make much stronger demands on politics to deliver what they get elsewhere: not just monologues of 20th-century politics, but rather a politics that is much more personal, confessional and interrogative.'

This rationale has been developed by Demos under the broader umbrella of 'Lean Democracy.' The current arrangements of democratic behaviour have failed the citizenry as the political system is bureaucratic and unaccountable to the public. In order to transform this process, it will be necessary to make the democratic system more transparent, responsive, effective and accountable. Therefore, the governed will have greater control over the governors. Thus, Demos argues that there should be wholesale redefinitions of politicians' performances; a combination of representative and direct democracy; the creation of 'reflective' bodies such as voter juries and deliberative polling groups; the establishment of an independent election regulator Ofelect to scrutinize elections; a raft of reforms to ensure better training for politicians; and a constituent charter. Most specifically, ICTs will allow for '... a more participative, responsible democracy which will use the new technologies of push button democracy."

Mulgan further contends that political parties are irrelevant and stresses that new forms of political decision-making will offset partisan decline. He has argued that with the loss of ideological certainties and class identities, that the democratic process is fragmenting. The significant decline in party attachments has been accompanied by a reduction in party membership. These imperatives challenge the viability of representative democracy which is suffering from an irreversible decay. In the future, 'Party-Free' politics will reflect the changing nature of political activism and incorporate communications technologies to facilitate plebiscites, agoras, referenda and electronic town hall meetings.

Therefore, this thesis is interlinked with Baudrillard's conception of the 'Simulcrum' as there has been an implosion of virtual and real forms of political activism and institutions. This 'Virtual' democracy emphasizes the growth of post-modernist attitudes within politics , thereby allowing for new forms of democratic behaviour. In particular, Lean Democracy and Anti-Partyism place their core emphasis on individual rights over the promotion of collective forms of action. As Lipow and Seyd comment:

> 'If the allegedly inevitable death of the membership party ... has arrived, then , it is argued by these advocates of postmodern politics, there is still hope for democracy in the post steam-engine era: in modern technology which makes it possible for individuals to be empowered by the new forms of communication which link each person with an infinite universe of individuals across the world and provide access to information hitherto the

> preserve of the minority. New forms of participation are on the horizon – from teledemocracy and the deliberative opinion poll to citizen initiative and referendum. The age of the individual citizen, at last unshackled from the constraints of organizations, has dawned. He or she is able to participate in politics without the mediation of now outmoded institutions such as political parties.'

The Technological Revolution, Individualism and Libertarianism

On a broader socio-economic level, futurists such as George Gilder, Nicholas Negroponte and Alvin Toffler, maintain that a digital revolution or 'Third Wave' will increase individual citizen participation. Negroponte argues that the hardware is already available to effect significant change. Thus, letters and printed forms ought to be digitalized, virtual reality conferencing must replace business travel, and television should be transmitted by a digital signal (over cable, not the ether). There will be no choice but to switch from dealing with atoms to dealing with 'the DNA of information': binary digits or bits. Digitalization will lead to decentralization, globalization, harmonization and empowerment. Technology is an agency for change which cannot be denied or ignored.

The advocates of information technology have also been influenced by Toffler's concept of the 'Third Wave Prosumer':

> '... the 'productivity' of the consumer is (currently) seen ... only as a contribution to the production for exchange. There is no recognition as yet that actual production also takes place (in) ...(the) goods and services produced for oneself ... (which) may displace or substitute ... goods and services turned out (conventionally).'

Following upon this logic, individual enterprise is regarded as the principal source of economic wealth, social welfare and political activity. In turn, private preferences will be facilitated by competitive policies and minimal public regulation. Therefore individual economic liberalization is equated with societal benefit. The notion that political or societal élites can act for the greater good is rejected, as they qualify this freedom. By extension, state powers have to be limited and social communication should satisfy individual choice, rather than be an unprovable public service good.

In particular, Wired Magazine has maintained that the 'Virtual Economy' will establish a libertarian view of communications in which no 'fixed' societal order exists. It has developed on Toffler's view that there has been a transformation from an industrial to a service-based economy, arguing that there has been an even more inevitable movement to an information-based economy:

> 'The new economy becomes a sort of a manifest destiny for laissez-faire, in which government's role is to "encourage the new

economy to flourish while ensuring all Americans an opportunity to partake of its benefits'.'

According to the technophiles, this will have a number of beneficial consequences. First, as the technology flourishes there will be a removal of price controls and entry costs so that everybody can have their own web page independent of income. In common with the eighteenth century concepts of a press market, it is argued that a free trade of ideas will emerge through an open market of producers and consumers using the Internet. This means that information is decentralized and that electronic democracy may defy institutional order. Invariably, it has been posited that traditional collective forms of political association become irrelevant. Therefore, new forms of individualistic political activity become available as the Internet may serve a market of 'one'.

Thus, the Information Superhighway will provide the electronic landscape, or cyberspace, for a reinvented civil society so that citizens may participate in their civil, political and social rights. ICTs reform the flow of communication distribution as one-to one, one-to-many and many-to-many interactivity is achievable. In turn, a truly interactive discourse occurs which allows alternative ideas enter the mainstream, political organizations to emerge from the grass-roots and the agenda to be set by the electorate:

> 'The new electronic technology, in fact, has given opportunities for lots of spreading alternatives. ... (Information distribution) is much more diffuse and ... (defying) organized institutional forms. ... There are tens of thousands of people hooked into various networks on all kinds of topics and lots of discussion goes on and lots of information comes through. It's of varying quality, but a lot of it is alternative to the mainstream.'

As a consequence, the problems of political clientelism will be overcome. A common argument has been made, ranging from the anarchistic left to the market-libertarian right, that the political and mass media institutions have undermined the citizens' participatory rights. According to this view, the present media organizations have failed to provide free information and have been incorporated into the interests of the powerful. Electronic 'billboards' will circumvent the centralized, conglomerate and outmoded media structures.

Information technology and political communication

Therefore, as ICTs could make the representative process increasingly transparent, they can reform the nature of political communication. Margaret Scammell argues that new forms of marketing, and the growth in media and multi-media outlets, can significantly advance democratic participation by allowing the public to have a greater involvement in the electoral process. Thus, this new 'fourth estate' will educate the citizenry. As a consequence, the multi-media will not only advance information but also facilitate citizens' knowledge rights in a significant manner.

ICTs can enhance the normative, vertical top-down political communication between the parties and the electorate. The conscious utilization of Information Technology has only started to become an important campaign strategy for the established Western democratic political parties. Presently, ICTs have been used for storing damaging information on opponents. For example, the Labour Party will use the 'Excalibur' data-base to rebut allegations made against it and to find anomalies in the Conservative's platform. Interactivity between party-leaders and Internet users remains restricted to rather staid web-sites aimed at the floating voter.

However, these reforms do not really challenge the charges levelled against modern forms of political communication. Whilst a significant debate has ensued within British and American political science about the democratic distribution of information, a dominant literature has suggested that an 'illegitimate' relationship between the politicians and media relays has emerged. The principal criticisms have been directed at (i) the negative effects of election campaigning and (ii) the British Parliamentary Lobby system, which is dominated by specific interests, collusion between journalist and press officers, and replicates a fake discourse. Broadly, there have been two significant critiques of political communication:

> (a) That the political parties have become increasingly sophisticated in their usage of the mass media. In particular, commentators have suggested that an 'Americanization' of political communications has occurred as US Presidential marketing and advertising campaign strategies have become the political norm. This has meant that the political actors may set the agenda as 'Primary definers' and that the media simply act as relays (or 'Secondary definers') by distributing doctored information into the public domain. Bob Franklin has further argued that there has been a significant decline from a 'golden age' of politics when candidates fought over policies, addressed public meetings and directly canvassed the electorate. Therefore, as style has subsumed substance, the candidate's image matters more and political 'spin doctors' put the best available gloss on the news.
>
> (b) Alternatively, this distortion of political communication has been led by the media. Through their selection of material, support for partisan groups and distortion of events they may set the agenda (for example Rupert Murdoch's The Sun continually ridiculed the former Labour Party leader Neil Kinnock for his verbosity and Welsh background). In particular, the relations between ownership, advertising and output are vital . In this context, a sensationalist and anti-democratic mode of address has dominated the relationship between the media and the politicians.

Effectively, reforms to the vertical flow of communication suggest that the political parties and media élites will continue to determine the flow of information from a central set of sources to the public.Thus, ICTs may compound biases in the distribution of communications and sustain the power of the political and media élites. Moreover, ICT users suggest that technological changes go far beyond such limited reforms to the traditional dissemination of political communication. Therefore, through the creation of horizontal networks between different individuals, new communities and forums may emerge. For instance, political organizations, pressure groups or local users can create free-nets so that they can communicate laterally. Ideally, this means that different forms of democratic participation are available as ICTs can create a level playing field for a diverse range of interest groups.

The Netizen Website: 'Way-New Journalism"

Hot-Wired's Netizen initiative attempted to provide an interface between the two forms of political communication (vertical, horizontal). However, it would be incorrect to suggest that the site resembled anything approaching an agora for political debate. The information remained filtered and particular editorial judgements continued to dictate its output. To this end, a specific stacking of the information occurred which appeared to be at odds with the arguments governing the horizontal flows of communication.

Yet, whilst it maintained a largely one-way flow of written political coverage, the authors argued that the problems associated with the vertical flow of political information would be offset by the Net's principles of 'way new' journalism. Time reporter Josh Quittner, in his 1994 manifesto, 'The Birth of Way New Journalism", established several criterions for net-based reporting, comprising of 'sudden narrative,' 'voice,' 'hypertext links,' and 'instant reaction.' Indirectly, Quittner's ideas have been influenced by Jacques Derrida's deconstructionist analysis of Electronic Writing, when he argues that computer writing creates new relations between subject and object, thereby creating different cognitive structures of understanding and changing concepts of identity. Accordingly, the net acts as an alternative space for the dissemination of communication With regard to 'way-new' journalism, a diverse range of information sources would enable web journalists and users to circumvent the traditional flow of communications from a central source to the mass of the public. In effect, this narrowcasting and interactivity meant that the journalists would not fix the agenda, but respond to the specific needs of the readership who would e-mail their responses to further the debate.

Therefore, the website included daily and weekly e-mail campaign reports filed by the former Economist Washington correspondent John Heilemann on the campaign trail under the main section entitled 'Impolitic'. Jon Katz, Wired's media critic, hosted 'Media Rant' which was designed to spark debates about the daily topics surrounding the medias' representation of the presidential race. Both Heilemann and Katz could be e-mailed by Internet devotees. Further, alongside these written articles, the website provided daily issues to be polled upon by the HotWired users. However, this poll was rather more problematic than it may have originally appeared. On one level, the authors of the site determined the questions. On another level, the nature of the discourse was hardly enlightening as demonstrated by the poll from the 25th October :

> 'The Mickey Mouse Election
> – new: Scooby Doo won; let's celebrate with a Scooby Snack
> –
> – The poll is on –
> Netizens overwhelmingly chose Scooby Doo for president in a recent daily poll. Bill Clinton was a distant second, barely beating out Mickey Mouse, Pocahontas, and Bob Dole. How would you analyze the poll results?
>
> 1. I trust Scooby Doo more than Clinton or Dole.
> 2. It's a Mickey Mouse election year.
> 3. The results are meaningless.
> 4. These polls suck.
> 5. Rright, Rraggy!
>
> Ross Perot has refused to endorse Bob Dole for president. And, he told the National PressClub that he's, predictably, not going quietly: "Do I intend to campaign until the bitter end? Yes." What's your take on this?
> 37.6 (395) . . . Perot is in love with the sound of his own voice.
> 29.2 (307) . . . I'm not voting for him, but his efforts are admirable.
> 14.5 (152) . . . Perot's still campaigning?
> 13.9 (146) . . . Perot for president.
> 04.9 (51) . . . Perot should go quietly.'

Other areas of interactivity were similarly disappointing. There was Netizen TV, a short-lived and ultimately unsuccessful cable station , and 'Noise', in which audio sound bites ofthe latest promises and platitudes were chosen.

Theoretically, the web-site's diverse sources of information would make the Presidential race relevant to Internet users. However, the principles of 'way-new' journalism still focused the important information within the coverage of the mainstream politcal actors and media institutions. Therefore, the Netizen's principal purpose was to provide a critical coverage of the political élite's and 'old' medias' representation of the Presidential election

The nature of the political coverage

The 1996 Presidential and Senate Campaigns were to be 'the last campaign(s) of the unwired generation'. The moribund nature of the Presidential contest between Clinton and Dole led Heilemann to denounce the campaign as tedious bore. On the announcement of the result, 'Impolitic' commented:

> 'Clinton defeated Bob Dole decisively, if not in a landslide. Indeed, as I sit writing this at 9:30 p.m. CST, in a 12th-floor room at Doubletree Hotel looking down on the 100,000-strong crowd that gathered to celebrate in front of the Old State House, it remains far from clear whether Clinton, despite his convincing electoral college tally, will wind up with a majority of the popular vote.
>
> Which is to say: an eminently predictable conclusion to an interminably boring contest. Or, at least, this is the verdict the conventional wisdom – spouted both by the punditocracy and by the public at large – is certain to render.'

Effectively, the election had stopped being a meaningful contest in 1995, when the congressional Republicans tried to pursue a new agenda within US politics. At the core of their policies was an attempt to balance the budget founded on cutting taxes and curbing the expansion of Medicare. This combination of reforms, alongside Newt Gingritch's triumphal declaration that the GOP would preside over a 'revolution' and his subsequent inability as Speaker, made the Republican's agenda an easy target for an exceptional politician like Clinton. Further, the GOP's decision to shut down the federal government on two occasions in order to force the President to negotiate was misjudged. Thus:

> 'By the time Bob Dole won his party's nomination, all of this history was an albatross around his neck so fat and foul that it would have severely hobbled even a candidate of consummate ability and agility. Which Dole plainly wasn't. And so, instead of a race full of crackling spark, thrust and parry, charge and countercharge, what we witnessed instead was campaign as epilogue – in which Clinton was rebounding from a domestic political victory of Gulf War proportions, and one that had forced his team to come up with a set of arguments and strategies that – again, whatever you think of them substantively – were durable and potent.'

The site concentrated on the campaign's failure to encourage debate as Clinton was largely able to side-step issues on policy due to his opponent's weaknesses. Dole's ineptitude was criticized, although Heilemann provided an ironic account of the old curmudgeon returning to his former 'mean' glory in the last few days of the campaign. However, as Dole failed to give the Republican views a decent airing, Clinton presented dishonest representations of his own views. Accordingly, few alternatives were provided by either candidates as Clinton remained unengaged. Further, potential scandals surrounding the Democrats fund-raising activities were easily brushed aside.

The Senate Elections garnered equally unfavourable coverage. The limited political excitement of a contest for Senate control was offset by the fact that only one national figure, Jesse Helms, was running for re-election and incumbents generally retain their seats. Conversely, in 1994, Ted Kennedy was fighting for his political life in Massachusetts and the big-state incumbents, notably the Democratic pair in California, were running high- publicity races. Heilemann argued that only the Massachusetts race between Republican Governor Bill Weld and Democratic Senator John Kerry generated any significance as it was more colourful and could determine the eventual majority within the Senate.

The coverage of the media

Jon Katz's 'Media Rant' similarly pointed out the inadequacies of the traditional medias', in particular television's, coverage of the Presidential race. On one level, the mass media have set themselves up as illegitimate moral guardians. Consequenttly, the boundaries between investigative journalism and law enforcement have become muddied:

> 'The media is abusing its power. They routinely create the appearance of scandal when there often isn't much, or any. They suggest incompetence and malfeasance or brutality at every stage of public inquiries into crimes and tragedies, although these allegations are often later proven false or distorted, or the result of self-serving interests like lawsuits. Or just plain wrong.'

When this sensationalism was combined with the old medias' traditions of objectivity, the political debate was stymied. In turn, 'Media Rant', unsurprisingly argued that the self- serving media ignored the impact of the multi-media or turned it into a sideshow. However, according to Katz, the reality was rather different as web sites, newsgroups, and online news services disseminated polling information which the network news didn't receive for hours:

> 'When this era's media history is written, it will be noted in mainstream media's obituaries that however they tried to mask it, they never could give up on the idea that they had to be doing all of the talking all of the time. The 1996 election marked a great generational change – the final passing of that generation of leaders that has dominated politics and media in America for years. It marked as well the inevitable change from one information culture to another – a change we can see and grasp for ourselves.'

Thus, Katz suggested that the traditional democratic structures have failed the citizenry. Instead of the normative imperative of objectivity, he argues that diversity, argument and debate mark out the Internet and ensure the health of the democracy. Net culture provides a medium for individual expression akin to the eighteenth century pamphleteers in colonial America. Through bulletin boards, conferencing systems, mailing structures and web sites, political organizations, academics, and ordinary citizens can post messages, raise questions, share information, offer arguments and change minds.

The Ideology of the Netizen

According to the Netizen, the traditional American politicians were unreliable weathervanes who were out of touch with the views of the public, in particular the 'wired' generation. The 'Second-wave' government within Washington, comprising of power cleavages, unaccountable mandarins, and political actors obsessed with being re-elected, failed to acknowledge the virtues of the Virtual Economy. In the future, politicians would have to realize that the new generation would no longer look kindly on the old-style populist liberalism of social welfare provision. According to Heileman, the entitlement system has created an economic crisis which will detrimentally effect the new economy. Thus, only far- seeing potential Presidential candidates, like Al Gore or Richard Gephardt, have begun to utilize the rhetoric of the multi-media stressing that there has been a shift from the industrial to the information age and from the national to the global market. Concurrently, the mainstream media provided an unreliable account of the events as they had been appropriated by the political establishment which they had been set up to check. The authors of the site argued that the politics was a 'traffic accident' and claimed that radical new visions of participatory behaviour were required in the Information age to overcome the limits of the state.

The Critiques of the Netizen: the contradictions between Individualism, Techno-Populism and Democratic Association

The material demonstrates that the Netizen did not provide any real alternative coverage of the election campaign. The site had a limited amount of interactive connections and largely acted as a vehicle for the ideological views of its authors. It failed to engage in a different political discourse, as it continued to propagate the perceived wisdom of the electorate's cynicism toward mainstream politics. Moreover, it showed how another pressure group, using multi-media forms of delivery, attempted to shape the political agenda and develop issues for its own interests. In this respect, it mirrored rather than challenged the traditional mass media. It simply became another source of news information and part of the electoral propaganda which has infiltrated the modern political communication process. By its own criterion of the developing 'politics in the revolutionary context' , the Netizen must be seen as a dismal failure.

Some contextual reasons may be cited for this state of affairs. First, the moribund nature of the contest between Clinton and Dole meant that little excitement was generated throughout the coverage of the 1996 campaign. Secondly, the Hot Wired site was one of a series of expensive failures for Wired. The parent company has recently experienced financial difficulties as it attempted to float itself on the Wall Street amid allegations of poor and arrogant management. The site also has failed to attract users in sufficient numbers to be both economically viable and a force for political activism.

This is illustrative of the general problems which exist concerning the distribution of communication between an information rich and information poor. Presently, the medium of the Web remains too expensive, limited and complicated to sway a large amount of the electorate. Within America, only about twelve percent of the population are regular users, and most of these do not have the appropriate hardware to manoeuvre through the vast array of information cheaply or effectively. Even Jon Katz, in a rare moment of candour, admitted, despite his claims of the multi-media replacing the mass media, that the Internet remained a marginal force within the 1996 election:

> 'The Web, meanwhile, remains mostly stuffed with countless special-interest Web pages and big political sites looming out of the ether like rudderless ocean liners, offering slick graphics, static information, and worthless propaganda.'

More pertinently, the Netizen's 'Way-New Journalism' meant that site failed to really distinguish between vertical and horizontal flows of information. The areas of interactivity were largely limited to polls and e-mails to the site's authors. Instead of engaging the users in debate, the political stories continued to be framed by a central source to a specific section of the electorate. In many respects, the authors were writing to the converted and were not challenging the users' pre-held dispositions. As a progressive force for developing on-line political activism, the Netizen remained negligible. It failed to engage visitors to the site in any significant debates and certainly did not break any stories which could not be found elsewhere.

This returns our attention back to Jurgen Habermas's arguments concerning the erosion of the public sphere. Instead of providing alternative information, through which members of the public may become rationally informed, this usage of the multi-media continues to encourage a fake discourse. Whilst, citizens may believe that they are engaging in a broader political debate, the reality is one in which politics continue to be defined as a 'spectacle', information is trivialized, and the barriers to true grass-roots politicization remain fixed. This view not only questions whether the Internet can provide an electronic agora through which information may flow freely between many-to-many, but whether knowledge rights may be equitably bestowed through the web.

To this end, the study of the Netizen demonstrates that technology is not an agency of political reform. It may be utilized to promote change, but with regard to this web-site we have to be aware that certain types of informational flow and ideological presumptions underpinned its output. Principally, the individualist notions of political activism, which have been promoted in Britain by Demos through techno-populism and in America by 'Third Wave' zealots who have proclaimed the Virtual Economy, determined the site's viewpoint. Accordingly, the Information Superhighway must defy the previous institutional forms of political behaviour such as economic governance, welfare, political parties and representational assemblies. However, this type of individualistic anti-institutionalism promotes its own form of monolithic behaviour which undermines collective democratic activity:

> '... the Netizen is an obvious portmanteau of net and citizen, implying membership in a state (appropriately enough, 'the net") wherein rights are reserved for its members. What's interesting here is the use of the singular 'The Netizen' (rather than 'the Netizens"), speaking to a sole, idealized body politic, indicating a monolithic presence and stance, isolated from plurality and debate. The Netizen may attempt to illustrate itself with a clenched fist with lightning bolts, but the echoes of the anti-conservative movements of the 60s are just that – echoes.'

Thus, the Netizen's dissemination of communication was inequitable not only due to the limits on hardware, but because of the techno-populist ideologies it advanced. As long as the Internet and other forms of information technologies remain rudderless, built on concepts of individualism, they will continue to produce either meaningless 'sources of chatter ... (or) ... at worst (act as) the vehicles for demagogues and small, well-organized groups which rely only on themselves.'

Conclusion: Political Reform through the Web

The Netizen may be seen to have failed on several levels. Firstly, it did not impart any alternative political information. Invariably, it followed rather than preceded the traditional medias' coverage of the Presidential election. Secondly, it had a marginal impact on the electorate. The reasons were twofold. On the one hand, the majority of the American population remain unwired due to the market distribution of these information services. On the other, its reliance on individualistic concepts of political behaviour meant that it was only directed at and served a well-informed clique who were attempting to promote their own interests. Therefore, the Netizen draws our attention to the inappropriate forms of market- libertarian individualism which have underpinned Toffler and Mulgans' concepts of political activity in the information society. For labour, whether at work or at politics, power can only be drawn from organization. If aggregated power is dismantled in favour of 'Third Wave' market-liberalism, individual expression is undermined as people become powerless and atomized. Concurrently, élite control is consolidated. As Lipow and Seyd comment, the disaggregation of normative forms of political behaviour:

> 'makes individuals – citizens – weak ... whatever the democratic rhetoric about direct democracy ... Polls and juries substituted for legislatures and representative bodies are a means of élite manipulation – a goal which have obvious appeal to mediacrats or think- tankers for whom popular organizations, particularly those rooted in the needs of employees to defend their interests, are resistant to élite control.'

It would, however, be incorrect to perceive ICTs as being inherently monolithic or anti-democratic. The changes within the distribution of information can be positively activated if they are tied to 'organized publics' who will provide a meaningful social and political context for reform. Therefore, rather than the individualistic or post-modern notions of political activity , which have dominated the current development of the Internet, new ways should be sought out to utilize the information technologies so that they can allow for collective concepts of democratic behaviour. To this end, it may be suggested that on-line activism will only be successful if it is incorporated into appropriate forms of democratic organization such as trade unions, political parties or workers' councils. Moreover, local or city-level initiatives , rooted in communal traditions, may also successfully advance on-line activism. Instead of the top-down plebiscitarian democracy advanced by the techno-populists, ICTs could be employed to advance collective democratic organization by generalizing information and creating an informed citizenship.

Political Communication, Globalisation and Techno-Populism

Gary D.Rawnsley
University of Nottingham

'An Assessment of the 1996 Presidential Election Campaign in Taiwan'

Introduction

A truly comparative approach to political communication is in its infancy. With very few exceptions[1] studies which seek to advance our understanding beyond Europe (specifically Britain) and the United States are rare. And this is unfortunate, since such concentrated research makes it incredibly easy to overlook the rich diversity of experience and application which flourishes in other areas of the world.

1996 was a busy year for observers of elections, since we were presented with the unique opportunity to explore the structure and methods of political communication from a genuinely comparative perspective. Significant elections were held throughout the world – in the United States, of course, but also in Israel, Russia, Taiwan, Bosnia, Korea, India and many other places – and each offered a fascinating insight into how different states mobilise the electorate according to the defining political, social and cultural character of that environment. Of particular concern is the so-called 'Americanization' of communication, an issue which has deservedly received attention from several prominent studies. This is a term, often used in a pejorative sense, to refer to an apparent convergence of electoral practices (especially political communication and election campaigning) which transcend obvious differences in political institutions and cultures: 'The suggestion is ... that the nature of campaigning in democracies around the world is becoming more and more Americanized as candidates, political parties, and news media take cues from their counterparts in the United States.'[2] But as more comparative research is completed, the suggestion of a global Americanization of politics is no longer acceptable. Thomas E.Skidmore has centred his investigations on Latin America, and has observed a fierce resistance to the Americanization of that continent's politics due in large part to its association with cultural imperialism.[3] Most recently, Ralph Negrine & Stylionos Papathanassopoulos have addressed the issue from a

[1] In particular, see T.E.Skidmore (ed), *Television, Politics and the Transition to Democracy*, Johns Hopkins University Press, 1993; E.Fox (ed), *Media and Politics in Latin America: The Struggle for Democracy*, Sage, 1988; J.Blumler et al (eds), , *Comparatively Speaking: Communications and Culture Across Space and Time, Sage, 1992.*

[2] R.Negrine & S.Papathanassopoulos, *The "Americanization" of Political Communication: A Critique', Harvard International Journal of Press/Politics*, 1/2, 1996. A longer version of this article appears in Ralph Negrine, *Communicating Politics*, Sage, 1996.

[3] T.E.Skidmore, 'Politics and the Media in a Democratizing Latin America', in Skidmore (ed), *Television*, pp.1-22.

slightly different perspective. They warn that it is no longer possible to accept a definition of 'Americanization' which refers to the simple importation of American techniques. Rather it may in fact denote a process whereby a society or political culture recognises and adapts to the advantages of using modern communications technology: 'It is the practices of politicians and the media, exploiting technical innovations and marketing approaches, that have altered the appearance of elections.'[4]

This paper explores political communication and election campaigning in Taiwan's first ever direct Presidential election in 1996. This is part of a wider investigation of political communication and the media in democratising states which seeks to understand the transformation of communication practices in regime transition. Such research is crucial since political communication helps to structure the participation, competition which are associated with democracy, and can serve the consolidation of democratic procedure. Once we begin to view political communication and election campaigning as part of a wider political process, including the institutionalisation of democratic procedure, we can see how the idea of convergence or Americanization breaks down; emerging democracies will draw upon the experiences of many systems, and some are more compatible, both with each other and with the existing political culture, than others. Many global influences have inspired and formed every level of Taiwan's transformation, including its electoral procedure, as well as the style of communication and campaigning used.

This analysis draws upon our understanding of election campaigning in the west to demonstrate how the candidates responded to (1) the advantages of incumbency; (2) the requirements of the modern mass media; (3) negative campaigning; and (4) the growing importance of finance and professionalism. Observations of Taiwan's most recent elections (especially the 1996 Presidential contest) reveal that many of the methods of campaigning which are associated with American politics either did not work, or were rejected altogether. This includes the use of negative campaigning and an apparent hesitation to professionalise political communication. Explaining this phenomenon is a more difficult undertaking, but it appears to be culture-based; in Taiwan, rejection of American techniques seems to derive from the fundamental differences which separate oriental from occidental societies, and which theories of Americanization cannot ignore. So despite the growing relevance of the mass media in Taiwan, key features of the Chinese character remain influential, such as a deference to authority, and the continuing importance of the primary group and other traditional methods of voter mobilisation. The entire organisational framework has clearly structured the types of vertical and horizontal communication that has created a vibrant political society in China over many centuries. This reinforces the logic of the argument against a global Americanization of pol-

[4]Negrine & Papathanassopoulos, 'The "Americanization" of Political Communication'; D.Butler & A.Ranney (eds), *Electioneering: A Comparative Study of Continuity and Change*, Clarendon, 1992, p.4. See also M. Scammel, *Designer Politics: How Elections are Won*, Macmillan, 1995, pp.288-295.

itics, and allows for a more intelligible and sympathetic understanding of political communication in Taiwan.

Four pairs of candidates contested the Presidential election: for the Kuomintang (KMT), incumbent President Lee Teng-hui and his Premier Lien Chan; for the main opposition, the Democratic Progressive Party (DPP), Peng Ming-min and Hsieh Chang-ting; Lin Yang-kang and Hau Pei-tsun, both of whom were senior members of the government, decided to contest the election as a team of independent candidates and received the tacit endorsement of Taiwan's third largest party, the New Party (although their membership of the KMT was suspended as punishment for running against the Lee-Lien ticket).[5] Chen Li-an, another former senior member of the government and Wang Ching-feng (the only female in the contest) also ran as an independent team.

Incumbency

Incumbency has been identified as one of the more significant factors affecting an election, but is certainly not the single most important explanation for a candidate's success. Political history has repeatedly demonstrated that while incumbent candidates certainly possess a considerable number of advantages over their rivals, they are also in a potentially very vulnerable position. Their high profile, together with a very visible record of service and achievement or failure, mean that an incumbent's campaign must be carefully and professionally structured if it is to capitalise on the advantages and avoid being forced onto the defensive. Compare, for example, the disastrous campaigns of recent incumbent American Presidents seeking re-election – Gerald Ford in 1976, Jimmy Carter in 1980 and George Bush in 1992 – with those of successful incumbents: both Reagan in 1984 and Clinton in 1996 were very skilful campaigners with efficient and professional teams of advisors; in addition they were running against far less charismatic

[5]The New Party is largely composed of aggrieved former members of the KMT who balk at Lee's 'pragmatic diplomacy'. In simple terms, the New Party 'favours some form of eventual unification' with China 'whether it be achieved on the basis of dual sovereignty or other forms'. T.J.Bellows, 'The March 1996 Elections in the Republic of China', *American Journal of Chinese Studies*, 3/2, 1996. In the final two weeks of the campaign, the New Party became more active in its co-operation with the Lin-Hau camp (*China Post*, 9 March 1996). The *China News* (15 March 1996), described how important the New Party's contribution actually was: 'Lin decided to switch emphasis to media campaigns instead of sweeping the streets soliciting votes. He said the key to increasing support lies in frequent television commercials which present him as a better candidate than Lee.' The New Party had urged this change of style in order that the electorate might distinguish Lin from Lee more easily, and was characterised by a more aggressive personal criticism of Lee.

candidates,[6] and clearly benefited from a fortuitous 'feel-good' factor.[7]

Similarly in Taiwan incumbency has not been a guarantor of victory in the recent elections, as the result of the contest for mayor of Taipei city in December 1994 clearly illustrates. The campaign of the KMT candidate and incumbent mayor, Huang Ta-chau, depended on the party's established commitment to stability in Taiwan-China relations. In practice this had previously been a very appealing theme, and certainly contributed to the KMT's success in other elections. However, they were not sufficiently popular with the increasingly educated, cosmopolitan electorate in the highly volatile political arena of Taipei. The DPP candidate, Chen Shui-bian, decided to play down his party's traditional platform of independence and instead addressed problems confronting Taipei specifically – transport, pollution and corruption – and won the election.

At the national level, stability continues to be the most important consideration and tends to favour the incumbent KMT office-holder. The race to decide the Governor of Taiwan Province, which coincided with the mayoral election, was fought on this issue, and the DPP's defeat was partly due to its inability to fight the KMT on equal terms on such issues at the national level (the DPP's rallying cry of 'Taiwan for the Taiwanese', which reinforced the party's traditional independence platform, was not popular with voters). So provided a favourable set of circumstances are in place, an incumbent can assist his campaign by marshalling his record of service and experience, his guaranteed visibility, and his political competence. Thomas J. Bellows has drawn attention to how foreign policy and issues of national security can determine how an incumbent uses these advantages. He reminds us that such issues helped Presidents Roosevelt in 1940, Johnson in 1964, and Prime Minister Thatcher in 1983, but weakened Truman in 1952, Johnson in 1968 and Jimmy Carter in 1980.[8]

Observers do not hesitate to emphasise that national security and foreign policy helped secure Lee Teng-hui's stunning 54 percent victory in Taiwan's presidential election. The KMT's television advertising campaign juxtaposed images of Lee mixing with Margaret Thatcher, Nelson Mandela and George Bush with pictures of the President overseeing construction projects and the implementation of social welfare policies. For this reason, his opponents were prevented from competing with the KMT on a level playing field; their resources could not match his visibility as the incumbent President. Moreover, his advantages were sharpened by the develop-

---

[6]The Pew Research Centre for the People and the Press 'pointed out that a study of winning and losing presidential candidates since 1960 showed that the two with the lowest personal approval were the two men Mr Clinton was lucky enough to run against – George Bush in 1992 and Mr Dole this year'. 'Hedge: Voters Place Both Parties on Probation, Balancing Their Powers to Press Programs', *International Herald Tribune*, 7.11.1996.

[7]'Presidents, even presidents like this one (Clinton), mistrusted by the electorate, are unlikely to be cast from office in times of peace and prosperity.' 'Economy: Peace and Prosperity Helped the Incumbent to Win', *International Herald Tribune*, 7.11.1996.

[8]Bellows, 'The March 1996 Elections', p.248. This argument cannot explain George Bush's defeat in the 1992 election which, according to this theory, he should have won because of his successful prosecution of war against Iraq.

ing crisis with mainland China[9] which meant that he was the most familiar candidate, demanding news coverage as head of state.[10] Opinion polls repeatedly suggested that he was trusted by most voters as the most competent to handle the deteriorating relationship with China, meaning that the election was essentially transformed into a referendum on Lee's handling of cross-strait relations.[11] Together with the KMT's continuing influence over the mainstream media, especially television, the crisis enabled Lee's campaign strategists to project an image of their candidate as the 'most experienced, the wisest and most courageous'. Lee 'attacked those cowering at the threat of Chinese military force, saying that those candidates do not deserve voter support. He asked supporters to trust him in defending the island's security'.[12] Many prominent observers have claimed that what has become known as the Lee Teng-hui complex or mentality helped propel the president towards the 54 percent victory he secured. Lee had become popular among many traditional DPP supporters; his position on Taiwan's independence/ reunification was deliberately vague, and satisfied both extremes (in other words there was no longer any 'clear blue water' separating the KMT from the DPP).His position was strengthened by the fact that he is the first native Taiwanese to hold such high office which, together with the many political reforms he had introduced, distanced him from the old-guard of the KMT party itself. Many voters, including traditional DPP supporters, therefore cast their ballot in favour of Lee himself rather than the KMT.[13] In an interview with the author, Taiwan's leading political scientist, Professor Hu Fo concluded that 'many DPP supporters gave up Peng to support Lee under Taiwan consciousness or Taiwanism'.

As an incumbent, Lee had the most to lose and the least to gain from

---

[9]Since 1949, the People's Republic of China has regarded Taiwan as a 'renegade' province and remains determined to secure reunification. Military exercises have been China's preferred method of responding to Taiwan's efforts to solicit sympathy from the international community. In particular, China is determined to prevent Taiwan from making any moves towards independence. In the run up to the March election, China conducted missile tests near to Taiwan's coast-line, and mobilised its army. In response the United States sent two aircraft carriers to Taiwan.

[10]It has also been suggested that Lee was the most familiar because, in previous elections, he had mobilised support for KMT candidates at the local level. *United Evening News*, 24 March 1996.

[11]'Mainland Chin's military exercises have pushed other issues aside in this election', said Yu Mei-nu of the women's action group, the Awakening Foundation. Chi Hui-jung of the Garden of Hope Foundation, criticised the local media for not paying enough attention to the 'real issues'. *China Post*, 23 March 1996.

[12]*China News*, 13 March 1996. The benefit that Lee derived from his handling of the crisis was reflected in such newspaper headlines as Resisting Pressures Helped Lee-Lien'. *United Evening News*, 24 March 1996.

[13]Anomalies exist: Veterans of the military have strong ties with the KMT, and many do not like the way that Lee has 'destroyed' the party. However, he still enjoyed their support in this election. As one veteran explained: 'Every veteran in my village will vote for the [KMT]. But it's the party, not Lee Teng-hui, we will vote for ... After we came to Taiwan, the KMT took very good care of us veterans'. *China Post*, 23 March 1996. The Lee Teng-hui mentality was reinforced by news of his nomination for the Nobel Peace prize. The English-language daily, the *China Post* (2 March 1996), described this as god-send for the KMT. ... 'It gives him an aura that sets him apart from the rest of the pack'.

engaging in a televised debate with his opponents. In theory, debates allow the voter to see a candidate scrutinised about their individual platforms while under pressure and in competition with each other, and it is hoped that the increasingly superficial quality of media electioneering based on image and sound-bite, will give way to a more orderly exchange of ideas between candidates and introduce to the process a sense of accountability. As provided for in Taiwan's Presidential and Vice-Presidential Election and Recall Law, the hopefuls did meet four times in televised fora, but were denied the opportunity to openly challenge each other. Instead these fora were merely additional vehicles of political propaganda whereby each candidate could present their platforms to the viewing electorate. However, the China Times did sponsor a number of debates on cable television, although President Lee and Premier Lien Chan declined to participate. When confronted with this, the KMT party organisers candidly admitted that this was campaign strategy: Why, they asked, should they expose Lee, who is not a very competent debater, in this way? After all, the Election and Recall Law makes no provision for debates, and so they are not yet a formalised part of the electoral system.[14] However, the KMT went one step further and organised a broadcast of important press conferences with Lee to coincide with the televised debates on cable. Such is the power of incumbency.

Using the Media

All candidates in an election – but especially the opposition who must confront the advantages of incumbency – must maximise their visibility to survive, and this requires sensitivity to the requirements of the modern mass media. This can create its own problems, since it supposes the sacrifice of substance for image and personality. While one must remember that it is perhaps inevitable that a Presidential contest will be more personalised than other elections, one finds it incredibly difficult to dispute the fact that image has increasingly taken precedence over competence, and that this is considered to be yet further evidence of an Americanization of politics. In Taiwan, however, there is reason to believe that voters are not convinced by the commercialised packaging of personalities, and that the issues they must deal with – national identity, China's frequent sabre rattling, survival in the international environment, further liberalisation and democratisation etc. – determine that voters interpret politics on a far less superficial level than the theory of Americanization allows.

In Taiwan, opposition candidates are especially aware of the need for positive exposure to the electorate because the mainstream media – particularly television – remain heavily influenced by the KMT.[15] They also enjoy access to a much smaller resource base than the governing party, and must therefore ensure that every available avenue for generating further publicity

[14]The KMT even used Mrs Thatcher as its model, and quoted her insistence that debates were a bad campaign strategy. Interview with James Chu, Taipei, 5 April 1996.

[15]See Ming-Yeh & Gary Rawnsley, 'Political and Social Change in Taiwan: Television's Perspective', Nottingham University Institute of Asian-Pacific Affairs Discussion Paper 1, November 1996.

is explored. With the hindsight of defeat, critical elements within the DPP conceded that the party may have chosen the wrong candidate to contest the election. In part this was due to Peng Ming-min having been a compromise candidate who emerged from the DPP's commitment to primary elections. Research conducted in the United States suggests that such 'democratic' mechanisms may in fact sacrifice strong leadership for other less valuable performance criteria.[16] It was felt that Peng's many years in the political wilderness had distanced him from the electorate, while Thomas Bellows has described how many Taiwanese regarded Peng as 'a tedious academic', who was unable to compete with Lee's 'amazing energy and buoyancy': Lee, said Bellows,

> 'is a photogenic individual, invariably with a smile and a good word. His stature, energy and bearing make him a made-for-media candidate. He projected an aura of self-confidence and pleasantness which enlisted voter sympathy.'[17]

Voters could all too easily contrast Lee's image with that of Peng, and the DPP now accepts that in future contests it must select candidates who are either familiar to the electorate, or engage in a more aggressive effort to sell their candidate.

The DPP might learn from the deceptively simple campaign style of the independent candidate, Chen Li-an, who acquired positive media exposure by adapting the classic photo-opportunity 'to the presumed format requirements of television'.[18] This involved the candidate and his running-mate, Wang Ching-feng, taking an eighteen-day walking tour of the island to canvass votes. His advisers were most enthusiastic: this would demonstrate, they affirmed, that unlike his opponents, Chen was determined to take his campaign to the people and establish an intimacy with them. His image, captured by the television cameras and press photographers who accompanied him, was by the far the most positive and inspiring of the opposition candidates. He was promoted as warm, friendly and sincere, and unlike the others, he was rarely seen in a formal suit, preferring open neck shirts and casual jackets. In addition the tour confronted the perennial problem of how to finance an election. Free publicity was guaranteed because of the campaign methods which were used suggesting that, for all its simplicity on the surface, Chen's campaign team understood how to use the media in a relatively sophisticated and cost-effective way. The creation of pseudo-events such as walking tours provides candidates with free publicity. In this way, television has contributed to what has been described as 'the reinvention of publicness'.[19] The irony is that while Chen's advisors had every reason to

[16]See D.A.Graber & D.Weaver, 'Presidential Performance Criteria: The Missing Element in Election Coverage', *The Harvard International Journal of Press/Politics*, 1/1, 1996. Even the DPP's Vice-Presidential candidate, Hsieh Chang-ting, accepted that the primary elections must bear some responsibility for the party's defeat. See 'After set-back at the polls, DPP takes stock of the future', *Free China Journal*, 12 April 1996.

[17]Bellows, 'The March 1996 Elections', p.243.

[18]D.Kavanagh, 'New Campaign Communications: Consequences for British Political Parties', *The Harvard International Journal of Press/Politics*, 1/3, 1996, p.62.

[19]J.B.Thompson, *The Media and Modernity*, Polity Press, 1995, pp.243-9.

be proud of the fact that they had not matched their opponents' expenditure on such traditional campaign methods as the deployment of flags around the island, and had relied on the administrative support of a skeleton volunteer campaign staff, they conveniently overlooked that of all the opposition candidates, they had spent the most money on television advertisements. These were based on Chen's tour of Taiwan, and carried the message 'The reality of Taiwan is our responsibility'. They projected the sincerity of the candidate and were emotionally driven; they contained few references to what observers would consider to be Taiwan's most pressing problems (especially relations with China), and offered few solutions other than making Taiwan a better and more moral place to live. There were suggestions that Chen's style and message could not compete with the reality of politics, and that he was dismissed as an 'irrelevance' in this contest.[20] His morality was encouraging, but was not appealing to an electorate which considered ability to run the country the most important criteria by which to judge the candidates. One newspaper even suggested that most voters realised that when candidates visited temples, they did so only to canvass votes and to maximise the photo-opportunities such events provide.[21] Clearly the electorate is learning the techniques of electioneering extraordinarily quickly, suggesting the gradual growth of a modern (cynical?) political culture in Taiwan.

Chen's campaign was also significant because it seems to have used the 'new media' most effectively, especially cable television (legalised in 1993). Indeed, of the three opposition tickets, Chen-Wang spent the most on advertising on cable television.[22] The academic community is only just beginning to appreciate the need to study the impact of the new media on modern politics and several important studies have opened the debate.[23] Again, however, the validity of such research in a comparative context is restricted by its narrow focus on the United States, where it is felt that the new media have done little to stem the growing popular dissatisfaction with politics.[24] Moreover, John B.Thompson has questioned the non-dialogical character of such programmes as the radio and cable call-in shows, suggesting that the idea that the new media contributes to a greater level of popular participation is largely illusionary.[25]

In Taiwan, a systematic investigation of the new media is crucial. Many observers have prematurely announced that the 1996 elections put the 'fin-

---

[20] *United Evening Post*, 24 March 1996.

[21] 'Religion won't sway voters: poll', *China News*, 5 March 19.

[22] The Chen-Wang campaign spent a total of NT 44,550,000 (c. 1,113,750). While this does not match the KMT's expenditure of NT 77,000,000 (1,925,000), it exceeds the DPP's NT 37,970,000, and Lin-Hau's NT 34,940,000. *United Evening News*, 24 March 1996.

[23] In particular, see J.B.Abramson et al, *The Electronic Commonwealth: The Impact of New Technologies on Democratic Politics*, Basic Books, 1988; M.X.Delli Carpini, 'Voters, Candidates, and Campaigns in the New Information Age: An Overview and Assessment', *The Harvard International Journal of Press/Politics*, 1/4, 1996.

[24] See E.Diamond & R.A.Silverman, *White House to Your House: Media and Politics in Virtual America*, MIT Press, 1995.

[25] Thompson, *The Media and Modernity*, p.246.

ishing touches on democracy'.[26] However, it is difficult to be accommodating of such optimism when an external actor (the PRC) can have such profound influence on the political behaviour of a de facto sovereign state, and when the mainstream mass media remain politically constrained from fully participating in competitive politics. Taiwan's three network television stations are all dominated in either ownership or influence by the KMT. However, we should not overlook the fact that liberalisation has encouraged the growth of a much more varied media environment. The lifting of licensing restrictions in 1987 allowed for a greater diversity of press ownership, with many newspapers now openly supporting opposition candidates and their platforms. Taiwan boasts over three hundred daily newspapers, with one newspaper for every four citizens. Thus in one of the most literate societies in Asia, the press are fundamental to the structuring of a more pluralist socii-political system. Nevertheless, many voters are clearly turning to the electronic media for further opinion and information. For many, their convictions will simply be reinforced, but the growing numbers of undecided voters, together with the proliferation of parties and independent candidates, endow the media with an incredible influence over the direction of further political transformation. Moreover, the media industry itself is experiencing continuous structural and technological change, the implications of which were convincingly demonstrated during the presidential election when the full effects of the new media were most observable.

In the democratising systems, the new media open up exciting possibilities. John Keane has identified the need for the development of a 'plurality of non-state media' in democracies 'which both function as permanent thorns in the side of political power ... and serve as the primary means of communication for citizens situated within a pluralistic society'.[27] This plurality includes greater opportunities for competition among the opposition: as James Robinson has observed, 'Cable news coverage and talk shows did not make for notably more objective comment. They promoted competition in bias'.[28] The growth of the new media also presents compelling opportunities to the team with responsibility for structuring and managing an election campaign – the use of new technologies,[29] but also in allowing the candidates to explore the potential benefits of 'narrowcasting'. Narrowcasting enables a campaign to be developed in such a way that it will appeal to particular geographic and/or demographic groups. In Taiwan, such localism has been forced upon the cable television industry by limits on the range of frequencies available. Nevertheless, on an island where the social

[26] John F.Copper, *Taiwan's Recent Elections: Putting the Final Touches on Democracy*, Paper presented to the conference on Taiwan on the Move, Taipei, April 1996. An editorial in the *China Post* on 24 March 1996 was titled, Democratization of ROC Completed'. For an alternative perspective, see J.A.Robinson, 'Taiwan's 1995 Legislative Yuan Elections: Appraising Steps in Democratization', *The American Asian Review*, 14/3, 1996.

[27] J.Keane, 'Democracy and the Media – Without Foundations', in D.Held (ed), *Prospects for Democracy*, Polity, 1993, p.238.

[28] Robinson, 'Taiwan's 1995 Legislative Yuan Elections', p.112.

[29] A.J.Glass, 'On- Line Elections: The Internet's Impact on the Political Process', *The Harvard International Journal of Press/Politics*, 1/4, 1996.

and cultural differences between north and south, and between Taiwanese and mainlander, are extensive, narrowcasting can dramatically affect and transform the political climate.

In Taiwan, narrowcasting proved to be of most value to Chen Li-an. His whole campaign was structured around appealing to specific social groups (especially Buddhists) who were most sympathetic to his style and message, and his programmes on cable television allowed him to address such groups without having to resort to the often meaningless political rhetoric required by broadcasting. But Chen also experienced the problems associated with a heavy dependence on narrowcasting. Cable television does provide voters with alternative sources of information, but the programmes are generally so specific and one sided that they support the argument that political propaganda can only be effective in reinforcing already existing attitudes; that voters will seek out that information which most closely corresponds to their political interests.[30]

Nevertheless, in a political system where the interests of the governing party still exercise a profound influence upon the mainstream media, an equally biased 'new' media in favour of the opposition is considered a most welcome development. Thomas B. Gold has been particularly enthusiastic, and has observed that cable television has 'offered multiple opportunities for candidates and pundits to participate in politics'.[31] By the end of February 1996, between 65 and 67 percent of households in Taiwan subscribed to cable television. Moreover, subscription rates jumped by 5 percent during the Presidential election, suggesting that voters demand greater access to cable when their political interest and involvement are highest.

Negative Campaigning and the Professionalisation of Politics: An Americanization?

So far, this discussion of the style and content of Taiwan's election campaigns resonates with familiarity: The advantages of incumbency; the need to maintain visibility; the growing importance of image; and the introduction of media campaigns – all reinforce an apparently Americanized political culture. Moreover, there has been much discussion of 'campaign strategy' and 'campaign advisers' suggesting a professionalisation of election communications.

This section is intended to demonstrate how Taiwan has responded to this threat – Americanization is usually understood to be a threat – and suggests that powerful cultural and social forces inhibit the complete Americanization of election campaigning. Observers of western elections now expect

[30] See M.Harrop, 'Voters', in J.Seaton & B.Pimlott (eds), *The Media in British Politics*, Avebury, 1987, pp.45-63. For an alternative view, see W. Shieu-chi & S. Hsiu-hui, 'How Media Use Influences Voters' Political Knowledge, Party Preferences and their Voting Behaviour During 1994's Election in Taiwan', *Journal of Electoral Studies* (Chinese), 2/1, 1995.

[31] T.B.Gold, *Consolidating Taiwan's Democracy*, The Illinois-Taiwan Seminar Series 1, Centre for East Asian and Pacific Studies, University of Illinois at Urbana-Champaign, 1996, p.2.

negative campaigning to feature prominently in any election. Writing on British politics, Dennis Kavanagh has described how 'Campaign managers appear to believe that negative messages are electorally more effective that positive appeals' [italics added].[32] Whether in fact such negative campaigning is electorally more effective requires further investigation. Certainly in Taiwan's recent elections, the scale of negative campaigning has been extraordinary, yet its impact cannot be verified. It only further supports the suspicion that Taiwan's transition to democracy has not been complete, and that a mature political culture has not yet developed. Candidates and the media both see negative campaigning as an outgrowth of democracy's promotion of freedom of speech, but are not yet familiar with the responsibilities of democracy which would constrain a great deal of the personal, usually uncorroborated, and often anonymous attacks on rival candidates. Lee was linked to the criminal underworld, and was accused of having been a communist and selling out his party comrades.[33] In a full page advertisement Peng Ming-min was described as 'a false gentleman with a knife in his smile'. The advertisement suggested that it had been written by other members of the DPP dissatisfied with Peng, and that he would sell out his comrades to avoid taking any risks. He was accused of being a coward, unfaithful, and even of having raped a friend's wife. No data is yet available to allow rational discussion of the electorate's reaction to such negative campaigning. One campaign strategist told the China Post in language echoing that heard in the allegedly 'Americanized' political systems: 'One way to increase your chance is to blacken the name of your rival. If the voters buy it, then you win. As for the possible legal actions taken by the rivals, we will take care of them later. The most important thing is to win the elections.'[34]

However, media such as the China Times, which now regrets publishing an 'anonymous' advertisement attacking Lin-Hau, together with most political observers, and some campaign managers themselves all agree that negative campaigning is bound to be unsuccessful in Taiwan's Presidential elections. The Chinese culture tends to be more tolerant towards those in such high positions of authority and will not accept personal criticism of them (although the Taiwan electorate is very critical of 'legitimate' subjects – policies and records of service). The interesting factor is that during elections at lower levels, negative campaigning is used, accepted and expected, and it is this experience which inspired the negative campaigning in the 1996 election.

Of equal significance is Dennis Kavanagh's focus on campaign managers. In the same essay, he describes the growing importance of communications professionals, 'most of whom are recruited from outside the party. Within the party machine, those charged with responsibility for publicity

[32] D.Kavanagh, 'New Campaign Communications', p.62.

[33] Hsieh Chang-ting said: 'If Lee could sacrifice his comrades, he may sell out Taiwan, bowing down to the Chinese intimidation'. The Lin-Hau ticket planned to broadcast an advertisement on the most popular and potentially politically-influential cable station, TVBS, entitled: 'Betraying comrades yesterday, selling out Taiwan today'.

[34] *China Post*, 20 March 1996.

have moved up the pecking order, ahead of other party officials'.[35]

In Taiwan, those employed by the candidates to advise their campaign have experienced a different attitude towards their skill. The spokesmen for both the DPP and the Lin-Hau tickets were bitter at their treatment; their advice was solicited, but ignored despite being employed as professionals with vast political experience and broad knowledge of campaigning.

The problem seems to derive from the DPP's fragmented character, reflecting its evolution as a party from an amalgam of Taiwan's previously illegal opposition movements. In turn this factionalism has influenced the party's success at elections, and has determined how the campaign should address its commitment to Taiwan's independence. In the 1996 Presidential election, this theme opened up a wide and perhaps destructive gulf between those who recognised that a more professional and therefore responsive approach to campaiging was required, and those within the leadership itself who were determined to maintain the party's traditional focus on relations with mainland China. Campaign managers implicitly conceded that the Presidential candidate, Peng Ming-min, and other leaders of the DPP, exercised a decisive role in structuring the campaign, and had refused to listen to party-coordinators who warned that too much emphasis on the somewhat abstract and theoretical issues of independence-unification would cost the party votes.

The DPP reviews its performance after every election, and every time reaches the same conclusions: a need for party unity and greater professionalism, and less concentration on what is generally frowned upon as the 'burden of independence'. The problem is that once the party moves away from its tradutional platform, it alienates many traditional supporters and activists; it is not suprising that only a few days after the election, the DPP should suffer its most serious split since its formation, and the Taiwan Independence Party was established by disaffected activists. This is also confirmation of Otto Kirchiemer's deduction that the need to respond to the requirements of the modern mass media and attract new voters can reduce a party's ideological commitment.[36] Sissy Chen was the party's spokesperson before resigning after the election to take up a post with EMI's Taiwan subsidiary. Even before the election, she recognised that the DPP's organistion would affect its performance: 'The party must do more to appeal to the younger generation', she said, 'casting itself as the party of the future, not of the past. Policy-making and public relations in the party must also be upgraded.' She described how she was prevented from participating in the DPP's policy-making, rendering her the party's "flower vase", 'mouthing the party line, but not being allowed to voice opinion of her own'.[37]

Clearly the message has not yet reached the top of the DPP's hierar-

[35] D.Kavanagh, 'New Campaign Communications', p.63.

[36] For further discussion of Otto Kirchheimer and how his theories relate to British politics, see Kavanagh, pp.70-1. For further information concerning the development of the Taiwan Independence Party and its likely impact on Taiwan's political environment, see P.K.Yu, 'Another new party marks shifting of political sands', *Free China Journal*, 12 October 1996.

[37] *China Post*, 11 March 1996.

chy which remains divorced from its base of acadmic consultants and campaign managers. In particular there is an urgent need to reconsider the way campaigns are politician-driven rather than electorate-responsive, and to adapt the campaign message and style of delivery accordingly. This involves not only a greater understanding of modern communications, which is self-evident, but also 'an uprating of publicity priorities and campaigning, as the parties devote more energy and resources to media strategy and tactics'.[38] Some progress has been made: Although the advisers for each ticket denied the deliberate tailoring of the campaign to suit specific demographic and geographic audiences, there is sufficient evidence to suggest that strategies which would appeal to different audiences in different ways were developed. Lin Yang-kang's vice Presidential candidate, Hau Pei-tsun, concentrated on campaigning in the south of Taiwan where his popularity was lowest; in the first televised forum, the DPP's Hsieh Chang-ting spoke in Hakka, Ami and Taiwanese, the indigenous dialects of Taiwan which are most associated with opposition, to demonstrate what he called the 'Peng-Hsieh ticket's respect for Taiwan's minority groups'.[39] In the same forum, Wang Ching-feng appealed directly to women voters, while the DPP took advantage of Internatioal Women's Day to press home gurantees of gender equality. The aboriginal communities, military veterans, even fishrmen and farmers, were all carefully targeted by each campagn team's rhetoric. This may have been Taiwan's first truly national election, and China's military exercises may have created an agenda that was dominated by national issues, but the methods and themes used to appeal for the electorate's support were still very localised.

Conclusions

Does the 1996 Presidential election suggest that political communication and campaigning in Taiwan has been 'Americanized'? Clearly a more sophisticated method of examining comparative political communication is required to understand how convergence exists alongside an indigenous path. As Ralph Negrine & Stylianos Papathanassopoulos have remarked, 'to focus on specific patterns of importation and exchange of practices and to attribute them to a single source undermines the complexity of the modern world ...'.[40] Clearly the campaigns did incorporate many of the features associated with an American political campaign: an elaborate use of the mass media, a growing dependence on the projection of favourable image, negative campaigning, and the creation of an organisational structure which is responsible for managing the campaign. Rather than Americanization, the Taiwan experience demonstrates that political actors are growing ever more urbane in their adaptation to Taiwan's increasingly liberalised media environment. Further investigation of the new media will yield further

[38] Kavanagh, 'New Campaign Communications', p.61.

[39] *China Post*, 4 March 1996.

[40] Negrine & Papathanassopoulos, 'The "Americanization" of Political Communication', p.49.

evidence to support or destroy this thesis. However, we must also understand that indigenous methods of voter mobilisation, particularly primary groups and strong patron-client networks remain very important. What most influenced the public in the 1996 election were social, economic and political conditions – especially the daily threat from Chinese missiles – and the way these were transmitted in their every day culture. But the media are important in reminding audiences of these conditions, of presenting and interpreting them in easily-understood terms of reference. Thus future research must be mindful of Ralph Negrine's call for more attention to the implication of various forms of communication, especially any offering evidence of convergence of practices, 'for the future patterns of socio- political development which these countries are embarking on'.[41]

The record of negative campaigning, image and professionalisation in Taiwan is even more spurious: a review of the 1996 Presidential canidate reveals that many of these features traditionally associated with American style campaigns either did not work or were rejected altogether, even though they are extremely effective in lower level elections. The personalised nature of the Presidential election, with its focus on specifically national issues and national leaders, prohibits the successful application of such techniques; they simply do not 'fit in' with Taiwan's current political culture.

The need to professionalise is most urgent. The problem which the opposition face is to professionalise in order to confront the indisputable might of the KMT which remains a formidable campaign machine: its advantages as the party of government, including over forty years of experience; the incredibly large and efficient party organisation which permeates every layer of life in Taiwan; its continuing managerial and editorial influence over the three main television networks; and the enormous sum of financial and politival resources at its command. These advantages are all sharpened by the fact the opposition is in a state of apparent disarray. Traditional methods of voter mobilisation are still important as a way for the opposition to stage pseudo-events which demand news coverage and therefore to aquire the free publicity which is needed if they are to combat the strength of the KMT. It remains to be seen whether Taiwan will follow the likes Russia and Panama down the road towards political marketing and hire the service of professional advertising and public relations organisations.[42]

The KMT's victory in this election was always probable; the favourable conditions facing the incumbent created by Beijing's sabre rattling meant that success was virtually guaranteed. The Deputy Secretary-General of the KMT described President Jiang Zemin of the PRC as the party's most valuable campaign manager. The 1996 election forces one to question whether this was the joke he intended it to be!

[41] R.Negrine, *The Comunication of Politics*, Sage, 1996, p.146.
[42] R.Negrine, *Communicating Politics*, p.146.

Elections, Public Opinion and Parties

Mike Young
The Nottingham Trent University
Matt Henn
The Nottingham Trent University
&
Neil Hill
The Nottingham Trent University

'Labour Renewal Under Blair?: A Local Membership Study in Middleham'

Acknowledgements

We would like to acknowledge the help of David Jones, a former postgraduate student at The Nottingham Trent University, who contributed to many important day to day aspects of the operationalisation of the project. We wish to express our thanks to Paul Whiteley for allowing us to use some of his questions from the 1992 national study of the grass-roots Labour Party.[1]

A pseudonym has been used to disguise the city constituency parties studied because of the politically sensitive nature of the issues explored so close to the impending British General Election at the time of publication of this paper.

Introduction

After four successive election defeats and 18 years as parliamentary opposition to the Conservatives, the Labour Party looks set to regain governmental power at the next United Kingdom general election in 1997. Under the stewardship of Tony Blair, the Party has vigorously pursued a programme for organisational and political change, in an attempt to 'modernise' its values, priorities and image, unify the Party by marginalising internal dissent, and in so doing, gain a wider appeal and credibility amongst the electorate. At the same time, Blair's project has sought to arrest the decline in Party membership, and establish the grass roots infrastructure through which to conduct effective electoral campaigning at the local level to assist in the goal of winning national governmental office. In a number of respects, this programme appears to have achieved these important objectives: membership has increased steadily to over 400,000. The Party has formally united around 'new' Labour's pre-electoral programme with 95% support for the 'Road to The Manifesto' document in a referendum of the membership; the leadership won every vote at the 1996 Party pre-election conference (and

[1] P.Seyd & P.Whiteley, *Labour's Grass Roots: The Politics of Party Membership*, Oxford University Press, 1992.

importantly was seen by the electorate to do so); and the Party is demonstrably electorally popular, according to the record leads it has enjoyed in the opinion polls since Blair took over the leadership after John Smith's death in 1994.

Clearly, these indicators suggest that in the run-up to the 1997 General Election, 'new' Labour is in a qualitatively different league to the Labour Party of the 1980s when it comes to electoral prospects. But, to what extent has 'new' Labour been transformed from a party of opposition with limited electoral appeal, to a government-in-waiting? The Labour Party has traditionally exemplified a 'mass party'[2] or mass indirect branch organisation.[3] It might be argued that the current Labour Party displays some characteristics of a vote-maximising, centralised 'catch-all' party. Certainly 'new' Labour's recent organisational and policy changes appear to reflect the last two of the four factors underpinning the emergence of catch-all parties summarised by Ware as:

> '... the weakening of pre- existing cleavages in Western societies, the absence of new social cleavages ... , the reduced power of ideology ... , and the ability of parties to transform themselves organisationally'.[4]

There has undeniably been a substantial ideological shift in the Party's centre of gravity since 1983. The return to the centre-ground under Kinnock and Smith was reinforced by organisational changes[5] and changes to the focus of policy responsibility.[6] These processes have accelerated under Blair's leadership.[7]

Traditionally, the most difficult coalition of our established parties to lead, Labour's ideological centre of gravity has shifted several times during the post-war period and markedly since 1983. It is not the purpose of this paper to consider whether or to what extent Labour is moving from a mass to a catch-all party as it competes for an increasingly complex and dealigned electorate. However, given the changed relationships between leadership and membership implied by such developments, as the recruitment of new members has an increasing impact, how have grass-roots members responded to the changes that have occurred?

---

[2] R.Michels, *Political Parties*, Free Press, 1962, p.44.

[3] M.Duverger, *Political Parties*, Methuen, 2nd edition, 1959, pp.1-27.

[4] A.Ware, *Political Parties and Party Systems*, Oxford University Press, 1996, pp.87-88. This model is based upon a critique of the key work of particularly L.Epstein, *Political Parties in Western Democracies*, Pall Mall, 1967; O.Kirchheimer, 'The Transformation of the Western European Party Systems', in J.LaPalombara & M.Weiner (eds), *Political Parties and Political Development*, Princeton University Press, 1966.

[5] For instance, the expulsions of leftist members of the Militant Tendency throughout the period, and the introduction of One Member, One Vote in 1987, and its extension in 1993.

[6] For example, the establishment of policy reviews from 1987 and Policy Forums after the 1992 General Election.

[7] By, for instance, replacing Clause 4, conferring power to the Party leadership to call ballots of its membership on policy issues and the pre-election manifesto, and reducing the union bloc-vote at Party Conference.

The Roots of Party Membership and Activity

Labour has always actively sought to recruit members for fund-raising and electoral purposes. Ware[8] reports that the Party's 'individual' membership declined from one million members in the 1950s to less than 300,000 in the late 1980s. One of the achievements of the Party under Blair's leadership has been to reverse this, with a 56% increase from approximately 240,000 when Blair was elected Party leader in July 1994, to over 400,000 in January 1997. Of course, general political activism in Britain has traditionally involved only a small proportion of the population.[9] The rational actor theories of economists such as Olson and Downs[10] exploring the logic of collective action assert that rationally self-interested individuals will seek to maximise personal benefits while minimising costs. They stress the non-rationality of political activity when most forms of individual political participation are likely to have only a marginal impact on political outcomes. These approaches, when applied to party membership provide an explanation for parties failing to maximise their membership, since they offer largely 'collective goods' which can be enjoyed by citizens irrespective of party supported, and by party members irrespective of their level of activity. Consequently, purely rational self- interested individuals can minimise costs and maximise benefits from not participating in party politics and by free-riding[11] (but only so long as some individuals do participate and generate the collective goods).

In recent work, Seyd & Whiteley[12] discuss the narrowness of such approaches, and consider a range of general incentives for party membership in addition to the 'selective incentives' that Olson relies on to provide a logic for organisational collective action. They expand consideration of selective incentives to consider process as well as outcome pay-offs for the participant. They also consider, for example, the importance of any ideological and policy emphases expressed by political parties which can give collective rather than individual rationales for rank-and-file membership to be active. These can be both positive involving social norms[13] and altruistic desires[14]

---

[8] A.Ware, 1996, *op cit*, pp.87-88.

[9] G.Parry et al, *Political Participation and Democracy in Britain*, Cambridge University Press, 1992.

[10] M.Olson, *The Logic of Collective Action*, Harvard University Press, 1965; A.Downs, *An Economic Theory of Democracy*, Harper & Row, 1957.

[11] P.Seyd, & P.Whiteley, *op cit*, 1992, pp.56-59; K.Schlozman, et al, 'Participation's Not a Paradox: The View from American Activists', *British Journal of Political Science*, 25/1, 1995.

[12] *Op.cit*, 1992; P.Whiteley et al, 'Explaining Party Activism: The Case of the British Conservative Party', *British Journal of Political Science*, 24/1, 1993; P.Whiteley et al, *True Blues: The Politics of Conservative Party Membership*, Clarendon Press, 1995; P.Whiteley, 'Rational Choice and Political Participation – Evaluating the Debate', *Political Research Quarterly*, 48/1, 1995, pp.211-233; P.Whiteley, & P.Seyd, 'Rationality and Party Activism: Encompassing Tests of Alternative Models of Political Participation', The *European Journal of Political Research*, 29/2, March, 1996.

[13] Social norms include, for instance, influence of parents, spouses, children, friends and workmates (P.Seyd & P.Whiteley, *op.cit*, 1992).

[14] Altruistic concerns include, for instance, overarching ideological concerns such as 'a belief in Socialism or left-wing politics' and to create a 'more equal or compassionate

driven by affection, loyalty and ideals) and negative, for example, 'getting rid of collective "bads" '.[15] Ware[16] develops Olson's thesis by asserting that parties in European democracies can offer three kinds of incentive (material, solidary, and purposive) to attract members and encourage activism.[17] Each has allegedly declined due to external social changes. In particular, purposive incentives have declined as parties have attempted to become 'catch-all' organisations at the expense of ideology.[18]

It appears then that ideological emphasis is especially important in motivating party members to take an active role in party affairs in general, and electioneering in particular. It can be argued that the Labour Party shows clear signs of both reducing its reliance upon its ideological heritage and commitments, and de- emphasising its traditional sectional ties as a strategy for broadening its electoral constituency and maximising its potential for electoral success. Even if the thrust of the changes pursued by the Party to meet the needs of electoral campaigning is as much to do with image as reality, they pose an obvious contradiction for the Labour Party in that it has perhaps determined to take the risk of alienating its grass-roots membership, in favour of programmatic moderation. Our aim is to further explore this question.

Party Membership Studies

A number of studies have been conducted to reveal the nature of party members, their values and beliefs, and their response(s) to policy and organisational initiatives instigated by party leaderships. These include investigations of members from both the Conservative Party[19] and the Liberal Democrats.[20] Seyd & Whiteley's[21] work is arguably the most comprehensive national study of the grass-roots Labour Party membership to date. At the time of the study (1989/90), party members generally viewed the modernisation process pursued under Neil Kinnock positively.[22] However, the majority supported the 'socialist touchstones' of 'public ownership', 'the legitimacy of trade unions', 'reduced and non-nuclear defence spending' and 'high public expenditure'.[23] Subsequent research revealed decreasing sup-

---

society' amongst others. *Ibid*, pp.74-77. Also see J.Leighley, 'Attitudes, Opportunities and Incentives: A Field Essay on Political Participation', *Political Research Quarterly*, 48/1, 1995, pp.181-209.

[15] P.Seyd & P.Whiteley, 1992, *op cit*, p.63.

[16] *Op cit*, pp.65-92.

[17] A material incentive would be, for instance, payment or employment; a solidary one enjoyment of the political process or social life; a purposive incentive could be related to policy issues or ideological ones.

[18] *Ibid*, p.76.

[19] P.Whiteley et al, *op cit* , 1995.

[20] W.Rudig et al, 'The Membership Dynamics of British Centre Parties: From Liberals and Social Democrats to Liberal Democrats', in J.Lovenduski & J.Stanyer (eds), *Contemporary Political Studies 1995, PSA, 1995.*

[21] *Op cit*, 1992.

[22] *Ibid*, pp.240-244.

[23] *Ibid*, pp.44-45.

port for re-nationalisation, and a further decline in activism.[24]

There are also various case studies of local Labour parties.[25] Most of these studies have shown Labour Party members to be more politically heterogeneous than would be suggested by popular views of 'extremists' within the Party. Nonetheless, in a very recent survey of the members and ex-members of a Southern Labour Party constituency, Jones has asserted that the repositioning of the Labour Party beyond the 'centre-left' by the party leadership may be an important factor in reducing the commitment of left-wing activists, who retain an adherence to 'traditional socialist or labourist beliefs'.[26] However, because of the timing of the fieldwork, Jones was unable to assess any corresponding change in activism levels by newer members as a reflection of any possible 'Blair effect'.

Our study is concerned with examining how local Labour Party members (including those who have joined under Tony Blair) have responded to recent ideological, policy and organisational changes pursued and implemented at the national level under Tony Blair's leadership. Using both quantitative and qualitative research, it focuses on the political values of this grass-roots membership, and the extent to which these resonate with the restructuring of the ideological and policy positions of the national Party leadership. In particular, it seeks to throw light on the nature of 'new' Labour's membership, and whether there is any dissonance between them, the party and its leadership in terms of support for the modernisation programme, perceptions of the organisational changes recently set in motion, and priorities for any incoming Labour government.

The focus is on 'Middleham', a cluster of urban constituencies within the Midlands. Middleham has been chosen as the area for study specifically because of its post-war electoral history as a largely settled adversarial two-party political system, though it is nonetheless a predominantly 'Labour' area. With its municipal status, and comparatively middle class 'professional' electorate, the Party members in Middleham are likely to be more accommodating to the recent changes instigated under the leadership of Tony Blair than those in the traditional industrial heartlands of the North. The paper assumes that if there is some hesitancy amongst this local grass-roots to embrace these changes, then this is likely to be more marked amongst Labour's membership in northern constituencies and therefore may harbour significant difficulties for the Party's leadership in developing its current 'modernising' agenda.

---

[24] P.Seyd & P.Whiteley, 'Labour and Conservative Party Members: Changes Over Time', *Parliamentary Affairs*, 48/3, 1995, pp.457-471.

[25] See for instances: D.V.Donnison & D.E.G.Plowman, 'The Functions of Local Labour Politics: Experiments in Research Methods', *Political Studies*, 2, 1955; J.Blondel, 'The Conservative Association and The Labour Party in Reading', *Political Studies*, 6/2, 1958; A.H.Birch, *Small Town Politics*, Oxford University Press, 1959; F.Bealey et al (eds), *Constituency Politics*, Faber, 1965; D.Berry, *The Sociology of Grass Roots Politics*, Macmillan, 1970; B.Hindess, *The Decline of Working Class Politics*, Paladin, 1971; T.Forrester, *The Labour Party and The Working Class*, Heinemann, 1976; S.Goss, *Local Labour and Local Government*, Edinburgh University Press, 1988.

[26] B.Jones, 'Left-Wing Political Activism in a Changing Political Culture', *Sociology*, 30, 1996, pp.520-521.

Methodology and Response Rate

The aim is to provide an insight into how individual constituency memberships in politically significant areas are experiencing the internal changes instigated by Blair's leadership, rather than infer the views and experiences of the national Party membership as a whole. The study is based primarily upon a self- completion questionnaire survey of a sample of Middleham Labour Party members taken at the end of October 1995 (with a recall letter four weeks later for those who did not respond in the first wave) but also includes preliminary findings from a series of focus groups.[27] The usual concerns regarding confidentiality and anonymity were addressed in the covering letter, which also noted the support of the Middleham Labour Party for the project.

Stratified random sampling enabled the membership list for the three parliamentary constituencies of Middleham to be divided into 'new' and 'older' members,[28] and every fifth member of each of these two groups was subsequently sent a questionnaire. From a total membership of 2598, a 20% sample of 519 was drawn (99 'new' members, and 420 'old' members). Of the 174 completed questionnaires returned (a response rate of 34%), 17 were from these comparatively new members (a 17% response rate), with 157 from the longer-standing members (a 37% response). It should be remembered that the generalisations made within this report must be tempered by the knowledge that a significant proportion of members chose not to take part in the survey. They might be quite different from those who did respond. Furthermore, the Middleham Labour Party covers areas with comparatively high numbers of Black and Asian persons. Whilst we do not have details of the actual numbers of such persons within the Labour Party, the proportions of such members who participated within the survey at 8.4% may well be below the actual membership rate. The same caveat therefore applies as for the response rate of the full sample.

Labour Party Membership in Middleham: Main Findings

Traditionally, the grass-roots membership of the Labour Party has been perceived to be essentially comprised of male blue-collar manual workers from the heavy industry sector, dominated by trades unionists and left-wing activists, whose ideological and policy priorities are out of step with

---

[27] Three focus groups were conducted in November 1996 with 22 Middleham Party members comprising all those who volunteered from those respondents who had taken part in the questionnaire survey. The intention was to explore issues emerging from the survey in more depth, and to give members an opportunity to elaborate on and clarify responses given in the questionnaires.

[28] A 'new' member is defined here as one which joined the Labour Party within the 12 months prior to October 1995, and 'older' members before this time. This enabled us to achieve a sample with proportionate numbers of members who had joined approximately since Tony Blair had been elected leader of the Labour Party.

those of the parliamentary Party and its leadership.[29] Recent studies have suggested that, as with the other major British political parties, there is also a demographic crisis within the Labour Party in terms of its age profile. Thus, the average age of the national membership of the Conservative Party has been found to be 62, and 49 for the Liberal Democrats, which compares with 48 for Labour.[30] Furthermore, 19% of Labour Party members were aged 66 or over in Seyd & Whiteley's national study of the Labour Party, and only 22% were aged 35 or under.[31] This ageing of the political parties has led some commentators to claim that they are in danger of withering at the grass-roots.[32]

In many respects, Party members in Middleham are quite similar to this stereotypical view. They are characteristically more likely to be male (60%) than female, and can be classified as middle- aged (average 46.5 years old). The age range is 17 to 86, with 14% 65 or over, and only 18% under 35. Three-fifths of Party members are in paid employment, including 54% who are working full-time. Of those in paid work, over two-fifths (47%) report they work in the broader public sector (27% local and 5% central government; 10% public corporation; 5% NHS) with a third working in the private sector (37%). Furthermore, members are, by a margin of 2 to 1, significantly more likely than not to belong to a trades union. Generally, Party members in Middleham have been educated in the public sector, and appear to be highly qualified. Over 60% received their schooling in either a grammar school or a comprehensive school, and a quarter attended a secondary modern school. Nearly two-thirds (63%) report they have been to an old or new University; indeed half are graduates, and nearly a quarter (24%) report post-graduate qualifications, and 21% are teacher-trained. Middleham Labour Party members still largely recognise the concept of 'class', with nearly seven out of ten (69%) saying they belong to a particular social class. Of these, over half (52%) identify with the working class and over two-fifths (42%) with the middle-class.

Whilst the socio-demographic background of the Party members in Middleham appears to mirror the conventionally-held view of who comprises the grass-roots Labour Party, the level of activism falls far short of it. As in Seyd & Whiteley's study,[33] there were relatively few activists represented in our sample. On the basis of answers given to the question, 'which of the following political activities have you taken part in during the past five years and how often did you take part in them?', a typology of activism was devised.[34] We found that 28% of our sample could be defined as 'In-

[29] P.Seyd & P.Whiteley, 1992, *op cit*, p.1; A.Ware, 1996, pp.82-3; H.M.Drucker, *Doctrine and Ethos in the Labour Party*, George Allen & Unwin, 1979, p.44.

[30] P.Whiteley et al, 1995, *op cit*, p.42; W.Rudig et al, 1995, *op cit*, p.392; P.Seyd & P.Whiteley, 1992, *op cit*, p.32.

[31] *Ibid*, 1992.

[32] P.Seyd & P.Whiteley, *op cit*, 1995, p.459.

[33] 1992, *op cit*, 1992, p.99.

[34] Respondents were asked if and how often they took part in nine types of Party activity. They were then given a separate score for each, depending on how frequently they got involved (Not at all – 1; Rarely – 2; Occasionally – 3; Frequently – 4). Scores were then combined, so that the most a respondent could score would be 36, and the

active', 41% were only 'Occasionally Active', 24% 'Fairly Active', and only 8% could be considered 'Very Active'. Assuming that the non- respondents in the survey are, by their very act of not responding, largely inactive, then these figures probably substantially understate the degree of passivity amongst the membership of the Middleham Labour Party.

Furthermore, when we divide the sample into members who have joined since Tony Blair was elected leader of the Labour Party (post-Blairites), and those who joined before (pre-Blairites), the nature of the post-Blairites becomes clear in that they are significant in terms of their comparative 'inactivity'. Over half (53%) are 'Inactive' (which compares with only 23% of the pre-Blairites), and a further 43% are only 'Occasionally Active' (39% for pre-Blairites). Only one member who has joined during Blair's incumbency is 'Fairly Active', and none can be included in the category of 'Very Active'. Hence, all the activists are pre-Blairites, and 37% of these more established members can be classified as activists in this way. This suggests that, whilst Labour's membership drive under Blair's reign has paid dividends in terms of actual numbers recruited, the Party has so far failed to turn these into anything more than passive members. This may also be reflected in the relatively lower response rate of post- Blairites in the survey (as reported earlier).[35]

Why did Middleham's Labour members join? In an open question, respondents were invited to indicate up to three key factors encouraging them to join the Party. Interestingly, in relation to particular issue concerns defined by Seyd & Whiteley[36] as 'collective positive incentives', the most popular motive was an identification with the Party's policies on the public sector including the NHS (14%). The most significant factor of all, however, mentioned by 45% of the respondents, was a 'collective negative incentive' – getting rid of the Conservative government. More positive 'altruistic concerns' included a commitment to social justice and notions of equality (36%,), to support and become involved with the Party (21%), and a commitment to 'socialist ideology' (20%). As with Seyd & Whiteley's findings,[37] 'social norms' like the influence of family and friends on joining the Party, were not strong incentives and this factor was mentioned by less than 5% of members.

To what extent therefore do the priorities of the Middleham Party members correspond with the traditional, stereotypical view of Labour activism, that is, of prioritising exclusively class-based productivist concerns?[38] Our findings suggest that value orientations are changing so that both 'old' and 'new' Labour concerns are coexisting within the local membership. Local members demonstrated significant support for alternative issue positions

---

least 9. Inactives were defined as those with a score of between 9 and 15, Occasionally Active 16-22, Fairly Active 23-29, and Very Active 30-36.

[35] However, it must be remembered that some of these post-Blairites may in fact have joined too recently to have been able to assist the Party in its general activities.

[36] 1992, op.cit, p.74.

[37] *Ibid*, p.74.

[38] These include 'working-class' issues such as pay and income redistribution, public spending, full employment, conditions at work, industrial relations and workers rights.

that have been associated with post-materialist 'new politics'. Almost four-fifths oppose further development of nuclear energy. Furthermore, there is overwhelming support for animal rights, with 78% supporting legislation outlawing hunting with hounds and nearly seven out of ten supporting a ban on exporting live animals for slaughter. There is also substantial support for constitutional reform with 71% supporting the introduction of a Bill of Rights and 61% favouring electoral reform. There is also continuing endorsement by 94% of respondents for the long-standing 'old' Labour commitment to reform of the House of Lords (22% favour disenfranchising hereditary peers and 72% favouring its replacement by a democratically elected chamber). Furthermore there is substantial support for the idea of building alliances with other non-labourist/non-socialist political forces. For example two-fifths (40%) of respondents both favoured closer links with the Liberal Democrats as a means of defeating the Conservatives, and accepted the possibility of some form of coalition after the election if necessary. On the other hand, over half (53%) of the respondents thought defecting MPs from other parties require a 'quarantine period' establishing their commitment before gaining formal membership.[39]

When asked what they felt were the most important challenges facing a future Labour government, only five out of 16 suggested policy areas scored strongly; in order of frequency of mention they were full employment, education and schooling, the NHS, the economy, and crime/ law and order. Focus group participants clearly recognised the practical and budgetary limitations on a substantial enhancement of public services. In the questionnaire survey, two important current pre-election issues demonstrated significant support for what might be regarded as 'old' Labour policy positions over 'new' Labour commitments. On education, nearly three-fifths (59%) of respondents favoured the abolition of grant maintained status with opted out schools returning to governmental control, whilst only two-fifths (38%) preferred the 'new' Labour position of reorganising the system of equalised funding across all schools. Similarly, in relation to health-care, members expressed considerable dissatisfaction with the status-quo. Three-fifths (58%) of respondents favoured a return to the past by reversing Conservative NHS reforms (like the purchaser-provider split) and bringing independent trusts back under direct government control. However in line with 'new' Labour's current position, over a third (37%) favoured retaining the system but enhancing the sector's regulation and political control. Other responses revealed further support for what might be regarded as 'old' Labour priorities from a significant minority of the local membership. Whilst over half (55%) disagreed that the party should set a minimum wage before the General Election, two-fifths nevertheless would prefer to do so. Furthermore, more respondents disagreed than agreed (49% to 43%) that the Party's current commitment to ration universal benefits through introducing a means test would allow better targeting of benefits to those on

[39]The answers to this question may have been influenced by the controversy surrounding the resignation of the Conservative MP Alan Howarth and his taking of the Labour whip.

low-incomes. In addition, the vast majority of members (85%) supported special issue tax increases to invest in health and education. The tendency, therefore, amongst Middleham's local membership is of significant (but not universal) continued support for a Party which prefers the 'tax and spend' policies associated with 'old' Labour rather than the 'save and invest' policies associated with 'new' Labour.

How, then, have members received 'new' Labour and the modernisation programme? There is definitely some sense of disillusionment with the direction in which the Party has developed under Blair. In our questionnaire survey, the largest group of members (49%) considered that 'the Party has moved too far away from its traditional values'. This finding was confirmed in that 51% of members considered that Tony Blair's modernisation of Party values had either 'gone far enough' (41%) or 'too far' (10%), although a significant minority (42%) sought further changes. In addition, nearly three- quarters felt that his modernisation of the Party's organisation had either 'gone far enough' (51%) or 'too far' (23%). However, on this occasion, less than a quarter (24%) wished for further modernisation. Furthermore, whilst over a third (34%) agreed that 'the Party should stick to its principles even if it means losing the next general election', a larger group (46%) disagreed. Many seem prepared to suspend formally articulating their reservations until after the General Election since they recognise that 'new' Labour is likely to be an effective vehicle for winning governmental office. This fairly widespread view found particular expression in the focus groups when one member said, '... I don't necessarily agree with everything that Tony Blair says or does, but, if it means defeating the Tories then I'm all for it'. This rather generalised cognitive dissonance was best summed up by another focus group participant who stated that '... principles have been compromised, but it was necessary to compromise them in order to get the level of popularity'.

We were able to explore members' perceptions of 'new' Labour in more detail through the focus groups. Interestingly, members recognised that the modernisation process dated back at least as far as Kinnock's policy reviews but that it had definitely accelerated under Blair. They saw 'new' Labour as increasingly disowning its past by moving to the centre-ground to appeal to the middle- classes and voters in the South, dissociating itself from its socialist and trades unions roots and seeking to become, as one participant put it, '... everything to every man'. Nonetheless, in the questionnaire survey, respondents expressed some positive expectations of an incoming 'new' Labour Government. Sixty percent in the questionnaire survey expected it to 'keep its promises'. Over three-quarters believed it was 'quite' or 'very' likely to 'improve welfare services', more than seven out of ten thought it would reduce unemployment, and over two-thirds thought that it would help both to improve living standards (though expecting income tax to go up) and to project a 'strong voice in Europe'. On the other hand, only a quarter felt that Labour would be able to keep inflation down (about the same proportion who thought that they would fail).

The issue of the compatibility of the repositioned 'new' Labour Party with the views of its grass-roots was further explored through a number of questions asking members to 'place' themselves ideologically on a nine-point left-right continuum in comparison to their perceptions of 'other Labour Party members', of 'Tony Blair', and of 'British politics as a whole'. Perhaps, not surprisingly, on this last dimension, Middleham members considered themselves to be left of the centre of political gravity in the country. Over four-fifths (82%) of respondents placed themselves to the left of the perceptual mid-point of this scale. In view of the acknowledged rightward movement of the Party in recent times it is worthy of note that considerably more than a third of this group placed themselves in the two most 'left' positions. In relation to 'other Party members', respondents reported a fairly wide spread of positions with a tendency to the centre-left. Just under a fifth (19%) placed themselves at the mid-point and just over a quarter (27%) to the right of this (only 7% placed themselves in the two rightmost points). In contrast, well over half positioned themselves to the left of the mid-point (including 17% in the two leftmost positions). This suggests that, by a small majority, Middleham Labour Party members perceive themselves as more left-wing than other Party members, and nearly a fifth significantly so. Of particular interest, our survey revealed that a large majority (two-thirds) of Middleham Party members tended to place themselves to the left of Tony Blair's perceived position on this ideological scale, including 30% who occupy its two most-left points. In contrast, less than a fifth (17%) either place themselves at the mid-point (consistent with Tony Blair's position) or to the right of this. These results may be a product of the perception of some members that the leader has moved the Party too quickly to the right; the most trenchant version of this view was typified in the comment of one focus group participant that, '... Blair is desperate to lose the tag of being socialist'. As might be expected, therefore, a majority of Party members in Middleham consider themselves to be not only to the left of British political activity, but even to the left of other Labour Party members. Even more importantly, they perceive themselves to be significantly further left than the Party leader Tony Blair, who more than anyone is associated with the modernisation processes.

Another marker of the lack of full congruence between the views of the Party's leadership and its grass-roots membership is the question of public ownership which, of course, has both symbolic and policy significance for the Party. Since at least Hugh Gaitskell's leadership Clause 4 has been a matter of contention between the Party's right and left wings. It is under Blair's leadership that the Party has finally changed both its constitution and its attitude towards the relevance and extent of public ownership. The replacement of the old Clause 4 by a new statement of values was endorsed by a vote of 65% to 35% at a special Party Conference in April 1995. The level of support for this development amongst Middleham members was less substantial. Twice as many of our respondents identified with the sentiments of the new prescription compared to the older Clause 4 (54% to 26%).

Somewhat paradoxically, as a policy priority nearly four-fifths of local members (79%) favoured more public ownership compared to the one in five who were equally divided in being either satisfied with the current balance or wished to see less. When considering economic policy and its social implications in more general terms, the local membership strongly supported public ownership as a means of achieving social justice (by a margin of 64% to 22%). Focus group responses, however, help to explain this apparent lack of enthusiasm for the old Clause 4, in spite of members' strong attachment to public ownership. Participants' criticisms were aimed more at the inaccessibility of its 'outmoded' language, rather than the ideological sentiments embodied within it. A common view shared by participants was that the old Clause 4 sounded '... old-fashioned, wordy and complex' , and yet for many it was '... an ideal basis for changing society'.

What about the alleged 'Blair effect' on local party membership? Members' perceptions were explored concerning Tony Blair's continuing ability to lead an invigorated and electorally successful Party, and the extent to which this has (even if only temporarily) caused them to suspend judgement about the acceptability of the modernisation project for 'new' Labour. Middleham members overwhelmingly thought Tony Blair's leadership had been a good thing for the Party with nearly four-fifths (78%) indicating that he has had a positive impact. Respondents were then asked to rate him on a number of dimensions, allowing them to express both positive and negative views of varying strengths for each. Table One,[40] below summarises the results.

Table 1

Percent Thinking Tony Blair is ...

88	an election winner/ loser	7
76	a strong/ weak leader	5
72	good/ bad at getting things done	4
57	likeable/ not likeable as a person	18
51	trustworthy/ untrustworthy	21
44	moderate/ extreme	20
42	likely to unite/ divide the Party	19
59	right-wing/ left-wing	6
24	most likely to listen to ordinary members/policy advisers	38

We reported above members' views concerning Blair's attempts to modernise the values and organisation of the Party. Clearly, Blair is perceived, above all, as an election winner. He is also rated very strongly on his strength of leadership and also his effectiveness. Middleham members do not hold him in such high regard in terms of both likeability and trustworthiness (though there is a strong preponderance of positive compared to negative feelings). Interestingly, more than twice as many members rate

[40]The figures exclude the middle two of the six points in the scale for each dimension, that is those who held essentially a neutral or weak view. This allows a polarisation of member's views where they are expressed most clearly.

him as moderate rather than extreme, a similar split in relation to perceptions concerning his potential to unite rather than divide the party. Only on the last two dimensions might members disagree about which is the positive attribute for Blair to possess. In one case the vast majority of members who expressed a strong view defined Blair as right- rather than left-wing. In the other case, members were also more likely to think the leader listens more to policy advisers than to the ordinary membership.

As a final marker of members' confidence in and motivation for working on behalf of the Labour Party, we asked a series of projective questions concerning the effectiveness and electoral success of 'new' Labour, its shape and development, through to the millennium. There is almost total confidence in the Party's capability of winning the forthcoming General Election: 97% thought the party is in a condition to defeat the Conservatives and secure governmental office. Clearly, this is not an unexpected finding given, as revealed earlier, members considered Blair, above all, to be an election winner. However, is the Party's future electoral success, and the modernisation processes designed to secure it, dependent upon a continuing Blair leadership? There was less certainty about longer term prospects in that only just over half (56%) believed the Party would be capable of winning the General Election after next. There was strong agreement amongst the focus group participants that victory in 1997 was not sufficient. For their continued commitment, members felt strongly that the Party leadership must 'deliver' on some of the high-priority policy areas mentioned earlier. If Labour did not deliver, Blair, as Party leader, would most likely receive the blame, and that may lead him to either resign or else to be removed. If he were to be replaced, members' unprompted preference for a successor (by a substantial margin) was John Prescott (53 mentions from a possible 174) with over twice as much support as Robin Cook in second place (23). Other popular choices in order included Margaret Beckett (18), and Gordon Brown (17). Clare Short and Tony Benn each secured 6 votes, a local MP 5, Dennis Skinner 4, and Ken Livingstone 3 votes. Interestingly, all (with the exception of Gordon Brown) are generally seen as on the 'left' of the Labour Party.

Overall, these findings seem to suggest that Blair is perceived as a linchpin for electoral success in 1997, but not necessarily for a second term. The focus groups suggest that there may also be a preference amongst the membership for a modification of both the modernising agenda and the centralised style associated with the current leadership. These ideas were typified by participants who stated that, '... people with real personality and real views will come through', '... I think in five years ... it will throw up a new leadership' , '... the current supposed dictatorship will need to be toned down'. Focus group participants seemed sanguine about contemplating the prospects of a new leader even after electoral victory, although there were different ideas about whether the Party would become more authoritarian or not, or whether it would evolve into either a European-style 'social democratic' party or a clone of the Democrats in the USA. On the other hand, they were almost unanimous that a new leader would be needed in the event of a fifth successive defeat, and there was a fair measure of pessimism about what would then happen to the Party:

> '... it will lose its members'; '... a lot of the grass-roots members will disappear'; '... I think it'll just disintegrate';
> '... the Labour Party will end up exactly like the Social Democratic Party. It will break completely from the trade unions (sic)';
> '... it will set the Labour Party back something like fifty years and it will be hopelessly split. The centre-right will almost certainly join with the Lib Dems to form an anti-Tory administration. The rest will become like the old ILP or a neo-communist section.'

Conclusion

If Middleham Labour Party members were a barometer for the mood of the Party nationally, then this study suggests that in the crucial period of the run-up to the general election in 1997, Tony Blair's leadership team will face no major dissent from the rank-and-file. The results of this research indicate that despite the Party membership in Middleham considering itself fairly well to the 'left' of Blair ideologically, it is generally impressed with the Party leader's performance to date, particularly as a possible election winner. It is this latter factor above all else which will guarantee for the Party leadership a level of disciplined loyalty and high degree of pragmatism amongst the membership not witnessed in all the years of opposition since the demise of the Callaghan administration. This is not surprising, given that the most important reason cited for joining the Labour Party was to oust the Conservatives from governmental office.

However, on a number of crucial counts, the membership is hesitant about how the Party might achieve and then operationalise this parliamentary power. It is evenly divided over the questions both of forming pre-electoral alliances with the Liberal Democrats, and of seeking a coalition government with them after the general election. A large minority claim that the Party should stand firmly behind its principles, even at the expense of winning the next election – not surprising, given that the largest group of members consider the present leadership has moved too far away from its traditional values. Furthermore, members have a strong signal to send to the Blair leadership over the modernisation programme of organisational and policy changes that it has pursued, and that is that these changes have achieved their objectives, and should, by implication, now be stopped.

However, at the time of writing, all the indications are that the question of securing political power at the next election is virtually a rhetorical one. The Party has a long-standing and seemingly unassailable lead in the 'adjusted' opinion polls;[41] the Conservative party is beset by structural divisions over Europe, turmoil over allegations of sleaze, and has lost Members

[41] At the general election in 1992, the polls forecast a narrow Labour victory when in fact the Conservatives secured a 21 seat majority in the House of Commons. The

of Parliament to Labour and other parties, with others who have resigned the Whip; and at the October 1996 Party conference, Labour's leadership avoided defeat on all the issues debated. Government seems there for the taking. If this is so, then the key challenges for an in-coming Labour administration as far as the membership is concerned are (in order) full employment, education and schools, the economy, and crime. Large majorities of the membership want a complete reversal of the health and education reforms implemented by successive Conservative administrations, with well over three-quarters wanting the Party to pursue a programme for extending public ownership of enterprises generally.

There is an additional piece of the electoral jigsaw the Party may have to consider putting in place if it is to achieve its objective of winning governmental office: it needs to assess how important it is to turn a predominantly passive membership into one which is prepared to go out onto the streets and maximise the potential vote. To the extent to which modern electorates can be influenced directly through national political marketing techniques rather than constituency based direct campaigning this consideration by the Party leadership may be of central significance. It is certainly true, that under Tony Blair's leadership, the Labour Party has not just arrested the decline in its membership, but has actually increased it significantly. However, the dilemma for 'new' Labour is that whilst its membership is largely inactive, its new post-Blairite members appear to be much more so. Undoubtedly, in an election campaign period, members can more readily be persuaded to forsake valuable leisure time for the cause of Labour, but the Party should not be complacent about this, and members' goodwill should not be assumed. Our investigations reinforce the general picture provided in other research concerning the reasons for members' attachment to the Party, in that we found that ideological concerns remain crucial. If Labour either fails to achieve the expected victory at the forthcoming General Election, or else fails to deliver on its admittedly somewhat restrained policy commitments, then these ideological concerns held by grass-roots members in Middleham will become much more difficult to manage; this will become even more problematical, by implication, in some of Labour's more traditional northern heartland constituencies. Consequently, Labour's recent success in expanding its membership may well be reversed.

polls were criticised on a number of counts for this error, and a series of innovations and adjustments have since been implemented to eliminate what some have claimed as an in-built Labour bias.

Elections, Public Opinion and Parties

Alastair Jones
De Montfort University, Leicester

'The Classification of Electoral Systems: Towards a Multi-Dimensional Approach'

Introduction

Much has been written on the classification of electoral systems, with Lakeman, among others, leading the way. Yet most subsequent attempts at classification have failed to go beyond that starting point. The multi-dimensional approach offers a new perspective to the classification debate. There is no search for a 'best' or 'most proportional' system as this leads to the biases that have plagued classifications. Rather, this new approach is more functional.

This paper sets out to examine a range of electoral formulae. More specifically, it will examine how voters cast their ballot(s) and how these are translated into some form of representation. A critique of various categorisations of electoral systems will be developed and a new multi- dimensional approach outlined before examining specific systems. Detailed descriptions of the different plurality, majoritarian, and proportional electoral systems will not be undertaken since such detail is readily available elsewhere.[1]

The objective of this paper is to assess a range of classifications of electoral systems. Their strengths and weaknesses will be outlined, and from this a new multi-dimensional approach to the classification of electoral systems will be presented in Figure 6. One of the problems that will become apparent is that no previous classification is complete. In every case there are omissions – often the result of attempts to promote a particular type of electoral system as being the best, fairest, or most proportional system. The new classification that is developed attempts to step back from such subjectivity. No single electoral system can or should be promoted as the 'be-all and end-all'. It is impossible for any electoral system to be able to cater for the needs of every country, as evidenced in countries such as Bosnia and Northern Ireland. Thus the new classification attempts to form the basis of alternative ways for choosing an electoral system. Rather than reducing the debate down to the choice of a plurality system or a proportional system, alternative starting points are made available. These include

[1]See, for examples, E.Lakeman, *How Democracies Vote*, Faber & Faber, 1970; V.Bogdanor, *What Is Proportional Representation?*, Martin Robertson, 1984; V.Bogdanor & D.Butler (eds), *Democracy and Elections*, Cambridge University Press, 1983; A.Carstairs, *A Short History of Electoral Systems in Western Europe*, George Allen & Unwin, 1980; R.Newland, *Comparative Electoral Systems*, The Arthur McDougall Fund, 1982; D.Urwin, 'Choosing Representatives: Majority Electoral Systems', *Social Studies Review*, 2/4, 1987; D.Urwin, 'Electing Representatives: Proportional Systems', *Social Studies Review*, 2/5, 1987; A.Lijphart, *Democracies*, Yale University Press, 1984a. For a critical overview of the literature in the field, see A.Lijphart, 'Advances in the Comparative Study of Electoral Systems', *World Politics*, 36, 1984b.

the district magnitude and the type of ballot (single vote, multiple vote, ranking preferences, etc). The possible formula(e) and the classification then become secondary. At the same time, it is just as easy to use the formula or classification as a starting point.

However, prior to outlining this alternative classification of electoral systems, a range of different classifications are outlined and critiques developed. It is through finding and addressing the weaknesses in these classifications that the strengths of this new classification are derived.

Classification of Electoral Systems: An Overview

Superficially the classification of electoral systems according to electoral formula appears to be straight forward. The literature suggests two or three distinct categories: plurality systems; majoritarian systems (which may be integrated with plurality systems under either label); and, proportional systems. Not only is this a gross oversimplification because some electoral formulae are overlooked, but there is also disagreement about which systems should be entered under which label. This will become apparent as various classifications of electoral systems are presented. It is of far greater use to examine the different classifications, highlighting the differences and inconsistencies, and then to develop a new form of classification than it is simply to outline the various electoral systems per se.

Figure 1

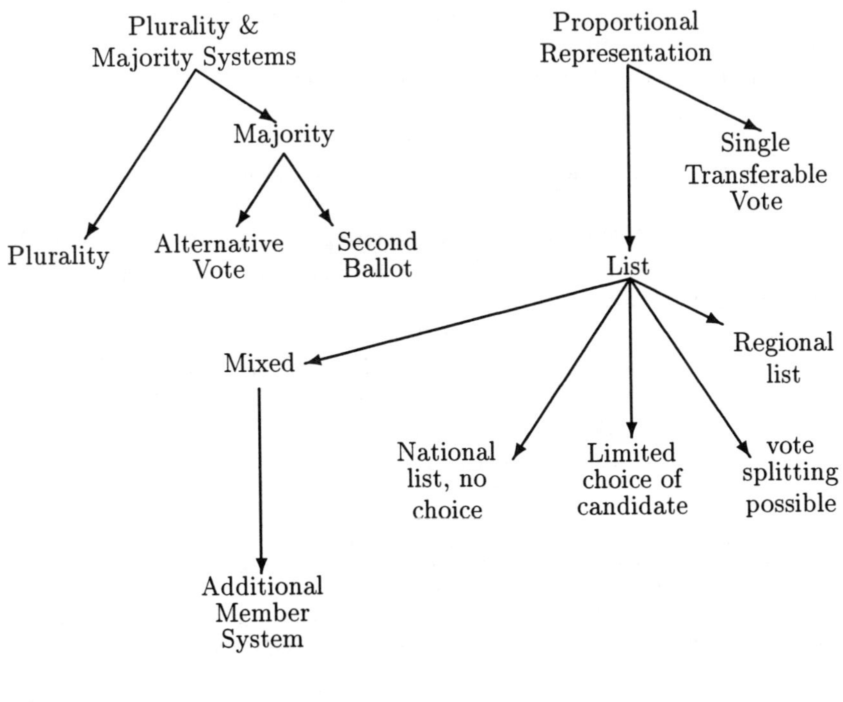

Bogdanor develops a very basic typology, presented in Figure 1, which is developed from the proportional-non-proportional divide.[2] However, his classification of the 'mixed' system is astute – and omitted by many others as will be seen below. The mixed system is based upon Germany's Mixed Member- Proportional (MMP) system. With each voter having two separate votes – one for a representative in a single member constituency under simple plurality, the second for a party list to ensure proportionality – the mixed system clearly cannot be presented under only one of the labels.

However, the actual placement of the mixed system as a separate entity under the list label must be questioned. This infers a different type of list to the others already cited. Bogdanor highlights four different forms of list voting, and then places the 'mixed' classification alongside them. Thus the label 'mixed' is inaccurately placed. It would have been far more appropriate to have the 'mixed' classification stemming from all of the list alternatives, using a dotted line to indicate that any of them could be used as part of the mixed system.

Although the specific placement of the mixed system is not a major fault, and is easily corrected, it does have the knock on effect of misplacing the Additional Member System (AMS). Bogdanor considers AMS a subset of the mixed system. In both cases, additional members are added to the simple plurality part of the election to ensure proportionality. Under AMS, this is carried out by using a top up of defeated candidates on a regional basis. A quarter of all representatives will be 'elected' in this fashion. The idea is to approximately equate the percentage of votes and percentage of seats in each region. It must be noted that AMS is purely hypothetical, never having been implemented. The Hansard Society Commission for Electoral Reform has been the organisation which has promoted AMS.[3]

The problem is that AMS is poorly positioned by the Bogdanor classification. While the mixed system has two votes, one of which is for a party list, the same is not so for AMS. As outlined above, there is only a single vote with the top up coming from defeated candidates rather than the choice of all voters. Possibly the mixed system should be cited as an independent category, and then divided into two groups based upon the type of format – one ballot or two.

Ultimately, the Bogdanor classification is very simple. Issues such as district magnitude and type of ballot are not fully addressed – although the latter is partially included under the list label. This flaw or omission is prevalent throughout most classifications of electoral systems.

Within the Bogdanor classifications, there are still a range of omissions. Some of these are evident in the subsequent three figures. These are developed from a range of other texts.[4] Lijphart has three sections: plurality and majority formulas; semi-proportional formulas; and PR. Each is followed by examples of specific formulae to translate votes into seats.

---

[2] V.Bogdanor, *The People and the Party System*, 1981, p.213.

[3] *The Report of the Hansard Society Commission on Electoral Reform Hansard Society for Parliamentary Government*, June 1976.

[4] A.Lijphart, *op cit*, 1984a, p.152; Figure 2, E.Lakeman, *op cit*, Appendix 1; Figure 3, V.Bogdanor, 'Introduction', in V.Bogdanor & D.Butler (eds), *op cit*, p.17.

A striking feature of figures 2 and 3 is the inclusion of the classification 'semi-proportional systems'. However, in Lakeman and Bogdanor there are also changes in the Plurality/Relative Majority classification to include multi-member constituencies. One feature missing from Bogdanor and Lijphart is the mixed system. This is to omit an important type of electoral system. Not only is it used in Germany, but has also been adopted by Italy and New Zealand, and is recommended for use in the United Kingdom by organisations such as Charter 88.

Figure 2

1. Majority Systems		
A Relative Majority	(i) single-member constituencies	– FPP
	(ii) multi-member constituencies	– BV
B Absolute Majority	(i) single-member constituencies	– SB
		– AV
	(ii) multi-member constituencies	– SB
		– AV

2. Semi-Proportional Systems
- A Limited Vote
- B Single Non-Transferable Vote
- C Cumulative Vote

3. Proportional Systems	
A Party Lists	(i) no choice between candidates
	(ii) choice of one candidate in a list
	(iii) choice of more than one candidate in a list
	(iv) panachage
B Mixed Systems	
C Single Transferable Vote	

key

FPP = first past the post BV = block vote
SB = second ballot AV = alternative vote

Lakeman, however, includes mixed systems as a subset of proportional systems, and thus to some extent ignores the majoritarian part of that specific formula as well as the potential for each voter having two separate ballots. Although mixed systems have a separate categorisation under the broad label of proportional systems, it does gloss over the idea of each voter having two separate votes and the single member constituencies.

There are also differences in the presentation of the proportional list systems, with Lakeman focusing solely upon candidate choice, while Bogdanor looks to both candidate choice and allocation. Lijphart points out: 'There are minor variations in list formulas, but they all basically entail that the parties nominate lists of candidates in multi-member constituencies, that the voters cast their ballots for one party list or the other, and that the seats are allocated to the party lists in proportion to the number of votes they have collected.'[5] The allocations to party lists could themselves be subdivided according to the mathematical formula used – largest remainder, highest average, etc.

What is most obvious about figures 2 and 3 is their starting point: the electoral formula classification; that is, the labels: plurality, majority, semi-proportional and proportional systems. Lakeman moves on to the issue of district magnitude for the majority systems – although it is difficult to imagine how there could be an absolute majority in a multi-member constituency. However, the same is not done for any other section. Lakeman also highlights the type of ballot for the party lists, but for no other systems. Bogdanor in Figure 3 develops much detail on the party lists, including the district magnitude and type of ballot. However this is not extended to any other system.

Figure 3

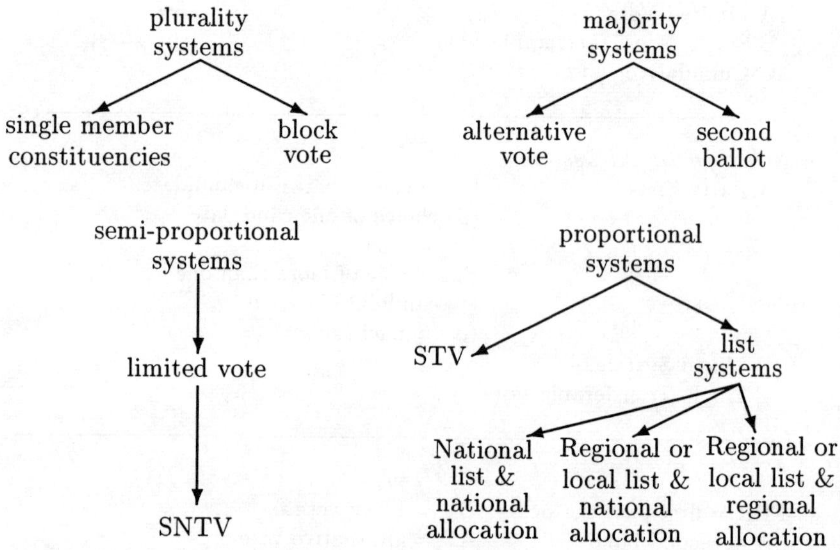

Note

In list systems the choice of candidate may be *closed; flexible; open; free.*

A slightly different perspective is developed by Newland[6] who, it must be noted, sets out to promote the Single Transferable Vote as the most appropriate electoral system to be adopted.

[5] Lijphart, *op cit*, 1984a, p.153.

[6] Newland, *op cit*.

Figure 4

Single place
- relative majority
- absolute majority
  - successive ballots
  - alternative vote
- condorcet pairs
- borda points

Single place constituencies
- relative majority
- absolute majority
  - successive ballots
  - alternative vote

Multi-place constituencies
- multiple vote
- multiple alternative vote
- repeated alternative vote
- limited vote
- single vote
- cumulative vote
- borda points

Party lists
- ordered list (no choice)
- ordered list with optional single vote
- unordered list (single vote)
- ordered or unordered with limited or cumulative vote
- mixed systems

Election of representatives
- STV

What is notable about Newland's classifications is the number of different electoral systems cited. Many of these are omitted by others in the field, as evidenced by the four earlier figures. A critique of the various systems is also developed by Newland, but is engineered towards promoting STV as the most appropriate system. Single place constituencies are rejected outright, as are many of the multi-place formulae. The Single Vote (often termed the Single Non-Transferable Vote) is seen as the most preferable of these but the non-transferability is considered a major handicap.

Figure 5

Plurality systems
- single-member constituencies
- multi-member constituencies
- weighted

Preferential systems

– single member	– AV
	– Double Ballot
– multi-member	– STV

List systems
- simultaneous list
- local list
- party list

Mixed systems

At the level of party lists the option of having a single vote for a single candidate, rather than the obligation of voting for a party list, is considered to be a viable option. The major problem is, again, the non- transferability of the vote. As stated earlier, the entire critique appears to be developed to present STV as the most appropriate electoral system. Voters choose their candidates in order of preference for multi-place constituencies, thus reducing the chances of wasted votes as should the first option be defeated then the voters next option may then take precedence.

Newland presents STV as a separate category under the peculiar label 'Election of Representatives'. Such a category could just as easily be applied to any of the other categories. Within each there are systems that elect representatives to a specific geographical area. STV should possibly be listed under multi-place constituencies. However, Newland would highlight the transferability of ballots within the system. Yet, at the most basic level, this is simply the ranking of preferences in a similar manner to the Alternative Vote.

Ultimately Newland starts with the district magnitude in his classification, and then moves on to the type of ballot. This is a different approach to the previous four figures. However as the figure is fundamentally engineered to promote STV, this categorisation must be treated with great caution.

Taylor & Johnston have developed a significantly different form of classification based upon three distinct characteristics: the number of votes for each elector; the way in which votes are allocated; and, the number of representatives for each constituency.[7]

Within this classification, the concepts of the majority system, the semi-proportional system, and the proportional system are discarded. Also what is of note is the placement of STV under the preferential systems. Taylor & Johnston have done away with the traditional typologies and have largely ignored the final outcome of an election.

STV uses a simple electoral formula, known as the Droop Quota:

$$\frac{\text{TOTAL VOTES CAST}}{\text{TOTAL SEATS AVAILABLE} + 1} + 1$$

This formula is very similar to that used to convert votes under a party list system into representation: Hagenbach-Bischoff.

$$\frac{\text{TOTAL VOTES CAST}}{\text{TOTAL SEATS AVAILABLE} + 1}$$

Hagenbach-Bischoff could be used at a regional level, with a totally flexible list system and would thus be almost indistinguishable from STV except in the redistribution of excess votes. For this reason alone, the Taylor & Johnston classifications should be questioned, if not discarded.

The Double Ballot (Second Ballot) system is also wrongly classified by Taylor & Johnston. There is no preference for voters under this system. Each voter has a single ballot in a single-member constituency. If the leading candidate has an absolute majority in this ballot, then that candidate is proclaimed the victor. If no one has an absolute majority then a second ballot is held at a later date. There may be prerequisites for standing in the second ballot but these are beyond the scope of the voter. Thus, again, these classifications must be questioned.

Blais has also attempted a different form of classification.[8] It is to some extent modelled on work by Rae and also Taylor & Johnston.[9] There is a section entitled 'The Rules' which pares to a minimum the issues surrounding voting. The ballot, the constituency, and the formula are all clearly interlinked. Yet the underpinning of this model appears to be the outcome and 'The Degree of Disparity'.

[7]P.Taylor & R.Johnston, *Geography of Elections*, Croom Helm, 1979, p.40.

[8]A.Blais, 'The classification of electoral systems', *European Journal of Political Research*, 16/1, 1988.

[9]D.Rae, *The Political Consequences of Electoral Laws*, Yale University Press, 1967; P.Taylor & R.Johnston, *op cit*.

The degree of disparity basically focuses upon the relationship between votes and representation. 'No specific rule dictates the degree of disparity of an electoral system but a given set of rules defining the ballot structure, the constituency structure and the formula will typically produce a given degree of disparity. So while it is entirely appropriate to characterize electoral systems as being more or less proportional, it should also be clear that the distinction ought to be made on the basis of the actual outcome and not on the basis of the rules themselves.'[10]

Blais appears to be highlighting the issue of the proportionality of an electoral system. In many ways such an objective hampers research in this field. Most writers when examining electoral systems demonstrate a desire to show the proportionality of each electoral system: underpinning this is normally the desire to demonstrate the inadequacies of non-proportional systems. This is to set up a hidden agenda. There tends to be a clear divide between those authors on the one hand who wish to demonstrate that proportional representation is poor, or bad, or problematic. On the other side are those who wish to highlight all of the benefits that a proportional system can introduce. Newland was overtly in favour of STV. A large proportion of the literature, although not as overt, clearly wishes to promote a particular electoral system. This is unfortunate; there is no 'best' system. Each has drawbacks as well as positive features. To fall into the trap of promoting a particular electoral system brings us back to Duverger's problem: the representation of wills versus the representation of opinion. It is largely a zero sum game.

In many ways Blais encapsulates the problem of assessing electoral systems as a whole, and not simply the formulae used although this is then subsumed in the debate over the degree of disparity. It is within the different formulae that there is scope for development.

What has become evident in all of the figures so far presented is that there is no agreement as to how electoral systems should be classified. There are no agreed criteria as to how some systems should be classified. The focus in most cases starts with the 'safe' labels – plurality, majoritarian, proportional, and others – before moving to list which system comes under which label. The district magnitude and the type of ballot are viewed as secondary, at best, or are ignored. When selecting an electoral system, or moving to change electoral system, the 'labels' or the specific systems are viewed as the starting point. Yet there appears to be no logical reason for such an approach. These starting points polarise the entire debate into proportionality versus non-proportionality, and eventually to the degree of disparity as outlined by Blais. If agreement can instead be reached on the issues of district magnitude and/or the type of ballot, many of the problems encountered under the choice of electoral formula are addressed and thus obstacles removed.

[10]Blais, *op cit*, p.105.

Figure 6

A Multi-dimensional Approach

Classification	*Magnitude*	*Type of Ballot*	*Formulae*
Plurality	single member multi-member	single vote multiple vote (votes = seats)	Simple Plurality Block Vote
Majoritarian	single member	single vote rank preferences multiple vote (votes = candidates) multiple vote (votes < candidates)	Second Ballot Condorcet Borda Alternative Vote Approval Voting Exhaustive Voting
Semi-proportional	multi-member	single vote rank preferences multiple vote (votes < seats)	SNTV Cumulative Vote Limited Vote
Proportional	multi-member	rank preferences (closed list open list flexible list panachage)	STV D'Hondt Imperiali St.Lague Niemeyer Hagenbach-Bischoff
Hybrid	single member (with top up) single and multi-member	single vote two votes – one candidate – one list	AMS MMP
Consensual	multi-member	rank preferences	Preferendum QPS

A Multi-dimensional Approach towards the Classification of Electoral Systems

Outlined in Figure 6 is a classification of various types of electoral formulae, while encapsulating the problems of district magnitude and the ballot structure. It is a more extensive presentation of the various electoral formulae, yet the formula is the end result. Rather than looking to the formula, it is more appropriate to examine the desirable district magnitude or the type of ballot as modelled from Blais.[11] Only then does the formula become important. The classification of systems, as a consequence, becomes somewhat less important. They are used simply as dividers, highlighting subtleties such as between plurality and majoritarianism.

The advantage of this multi-dimensional approach is that there is no fixed starting point to choosing an electoral system. If a state decides to change its electoral system why must it polarise opinion early on in the debate by looking straight to either classification or formula. It may be more appropriate to commence with district magnitude (single member constituencies, multi-member, single member with a top up, or a combination of single member and multi-member), or the type of ballot (a single vote, multiple votes, ranking of preferences). By starting at either of these points, specific formulae or classifications may be removed from the process indirectly. The final outcome of an election should not be the most important aspect, be it for a coalition or a single party in power. If elections are to enable the representation of the people, be it of will or of opinion, a system should not be chosen because it will engineer a specific result.

With this 'new' multi-dimensional approach to the classification of electoral systems presented in Figure 8, an explanation of each categorisation will now be outlined. Rather than working through each of the individual formula, which has been done exhaustively by a range of authors, the various classifications will be outlined, with reference to the type of ballot and the district magnitude. Where there are still a range of different formulae presented, the subtleties and intricacies of each will be outlined.

Although having criticised earlier tables for using the basic classifications as their starting point, the approach to explain the figure is adopted here for three reasons. Firstly, it is the most straight forward for explaining the figure. People tend to be quite comfortable with the labels, and are fairly secure in their meanings. Secondly, there is the problem of repetition. An explanation of the figure with the type of ballot as the starting point may need to some needless repetition. The district magnitude and the type of ballot need to be clearly separated rather than subsumed together under either classification or formula. Thirdly, there is the introduction of two new classifications: hybrid; and, consensual. These will be explained below.

[11] Blais, *op cit.*

Plurality

Plurality systems work on the simple hypothesis of whoever gains the most votes wins the election. In single member constituencies, it is possible – and frequently occurs – that the candidate who gains election has done so on a minority of the vote. In the British General Election of 1992, the MP for Inverness was elected on 25.94% of the votes cast in that constituency.

In multi-member plurality systems, voters may cast as many ballots as there are candidates to be elected. In British local government elections, for example, many wards elect two councillors. Each voter is permitted to cast two ballots – although they may only cast one if they so wish. The two candidates with the most votes then gain election.

Majoritarian

These systems work on the principle of a candidate gaining an absolute majority of votes to be elected. The reality here is that only single member constituencies can be used. It is mathematically impossible for two candidates to gain an absolute majority. Within this classification, there are a range of potential types of ballot: a single vote; a ranking of preferences; and, a multiple vote (with one vote less than there are candidates).

There are a range of variants under the single vote section, all of them derived from the sole electoral formula cited. The Second Ballot, as used in France, requires candidates to win an absolute majority of the votes cast in their constituency to gain election. Failure to do so results in a second ballot, held at a pre-determined date. There are normally prerequisites to be eligible to contest the second round. For example, in the French Presidential elections, only the top two candidates may proceed. At the elections to the French General Assembly, a minimum threshold of votes is required.

The ranking of preferences under the majoritarian classification still leaves the option of a range of formulae. The Alternative Vote, as used in Australia, is the only system that is actually employed. Voters cast their ballots by ranking as many of the candidates as they wish. Upon counting the votes, the leading candidate requires an absolute majority to be elected. Failure to do this results in the last placed candidate being eliminated and their votes being redistributed according to the next preference. This process of counting, elimination, redistribution and recounting continues until the leading candidate has over 50% of the votes.

The Condorcet system is based around pair-wise counting. If a candidate gains an absolute majority of the vote, then that candidate is elected. 'If there is no such candidate, then for each pair of candidates in turn all other candidates are excluded together and their votes are transferred to the preferred candidate of the remaining two candidates. A candidate who is preferred to all other candidates is elected.'[12]

However, there is the possibility that no candidate is preferred to all others. This is known as the Condorcet Paradox. In such a situation, the counting reverts to the Alternative Vote.

[12] Newland, *op cit*, p.15.

The Borda formula is a points based system, with voters required to rank all candidates. The preferences are weighted. For example, if the first placed candidate gains one point, the second placed candidate two, and so forth, upon tallying the points the candidate with the fewest is elected. Again, on the off chance that candidates tie, the Alternative Vote is then used.

An alternative to ranking of preferences is multiple voting. Approval Voting enables the voter to cast a single ballot for as many of the candidates as the voter wishes. '[E]ach voter can... 'approve of'... as many candidates as he or she wishes... Each candidate gets a full vote from each voter who votes for him [or her]. The candidate with the most votes, and presumably acceptable to most voters, wins the election.'[13]

Exhaustive Voting works on a slightly different principle. In many ways it is a combination of the ranking of preferences and Approval Voting. Voters have one less vote than there are candidates. There is a continual process of elimination, with the last placed candidate being eliminated and their votes redistributed until one candidate has an absolute majority of votes.[14]

Semi-proportional

Semi-proportional electoral systems use multi-member constituencies. As with the majoritarian classifications, there are a range of different types of ballots. Firstly, there is the single vote. Each voter has a single ballot and may vote for one candidate, even though there are multi-member constituencies. This is known as the Single Non-Transferable Vote (SNTV) and is used in Japan. As with the plurality systems, the leading candidates gain election.

The ranking of preferences alternative was used in the state of Illinois, USA between 1872 and 1954, and is known as the Cumulative Vote. Voters cast as many ballots as there are representatives to be elected. In Illinois, each district elected three representatives, and voters could cast their ballots in any of the following ways:

- one vote to each of three candidates;
- one and a half votes to each of two candidates;
- all three votes to one candidate;
- two votes to one candidate, one to a second.[15]

The final alternative under the semi-proportional label is where voters have fewer votes than seats, known as multiple voting or the Limited Vote. It works on the same basis as SNTV except that voters have more than one ballot.

---

[13] S.Brams & P.Fishburn, *Approval Voting*, Birkhauser, 1983, p.xi.

[14] D.Black, *The Theory of Committees and Elections*, Cambridge University Press, 1958, p.71.

[15] G.Blair, *Cumulative Voting*, University of Illinois Press, 1960, pp.v, 6, 127.

Proportional

Proportional electoral formulae can be divided into two fairly distinct categories by the type of ballot. The district magnitude is labelled as multi-member. Thus, even if there is a single national constituency, it comes under the label of multi-member. The type of ballot causes some overlap but there is by and large two distinct formats. The ranking of preferences, as used by the Single Transferable Vote (STV), enables voters to choose in whatever order they wish the ranking of candidates. To gain election, a candidate must reach a specific quota of votes (as outlined earlier) derived from the Droop Quota. The Droop Quota enables the specified number of candidates to gain election on the lowest possible number of votes.

The alternative proportional systems to STV are collectively labelled 'list' systems. Under such systems, voters cast their ballots for specific party lists. There are variations of types of lists, as outlined in many of the above figures: closed; flexible; open; and, panachage. Explanations of these variations are available in most texts on electoral systems.

The formula for translating votes into representation can be broken down into two sub-groups: i) highest averages; ii) remainder systems. 'The objective of the highest average systems is that as the process of allocation proceeds, the seat next to be allocated should go to the party which has the highest average of votes... The remainder system works by allocating the seats per constituency according to a quota, and then by allocating remaining seats according to the votes 'left over' after the quota has been applied. The remaining seats could be given to the parties with the greatest number of leftover votes, or the least number.'[16]

The highest average formulae include d'Hondt, Hagenbach-Bischoff, and St. Lague. Remainder systems include Imperiali and Niemeyer.

It is the redistribution of left over seats that discerns the remainder formula from STV. To make up any shortfall in elected representatives, STV reverts to the Alternative Vote idea of eliminating last placed candidates and redistributing their votes, as well as redistributing any excess votes in proportion to the ratios of second (or next) preferences of all the votes cast for the individual in question.

Within the proportional formulae, there is also the issue of thresholds, where a minimum percentage of votes cast must be obtained before any representation can be gained. Thresholds may be set at regional or national levels. The major consequence is that thresholds to some extent reduce the proportionality of results by often preventing smaller parties from gaining representation.

Hybrid

What is of note within this new range of classifications is the replacement of the 'mixed' label with that of 'hybrid'. The term hybrid is far more appropriate, referring to the potential integration of different types of electoral systems, rather than simply a mixture. It acknowledges that there are

[16] A.Reeve & A.Ware, *Electoral Systems*, Routledge, 1992, p.152.

two classifications or types of elected representative: one elected to represent a constituency; the other as a type of 'top-up' (to gain some degree of proportionality). The label 'mixed' tends to infer that the voter has the opportunity to vote for the 'top-up', potentially mixing votes, whereas in some examples there is no such opportunity. This is clearly the case under the theoretical AMS, but came into being in the direct elections to the Northern Ireland peace forum in 1996. The hybrid systems were outlined earlier in the explanation of Figure 1.

Consensual

A new classification has also been included: consensual voting. Consensual voting – through either a Preferendum or Quota Preference Score (QPS) – is still largely theoretical, having been developed by Dummet[17] and Emerson,[18] among others. The objective with consensual voting, as the name suggests, is to move away from the majoritarianism-proportionality debate towards consensus building.

In a Preferendum, the voter ranks the candidates in order of preference. It is up to each voter as to how many of the candidates are included in their preferences but voters would be encouraged to rank all of the candidates. Thus in a ten-option preferendum, 10 points would be given to a voters favourite option, nine points to the next favourite, and so on down to one point for the least liked option.[19] However, if a voter decides to choose only one option then that choice would get only one point. If two options were chosen, then the favourite would get two points and the other one point. Ultimately, the objective is to encourage each voter to rank all preferences.

With the counting of the votes, rather than finding a 'winner', the aim is to achieve a level of consensus, using the formula:

$$\frac{\text{Total points gained}}{\text{Available points}}$$

In a ten-option preferendum, each voter is able to cast a maximum of 55 points in total. There would also have to be a pre-determined acceptance level, possibly at the average number of preferences.[20]

QPS is loosely based around STV and Borda electoral systems but the emphasis is still upon gaining a level of consensus.[21] Each voter lists the candidates in order of preference. To gain automatic election, a candidate needs to achieve a target of votes derived from the following formula:

[17] M.Dummett, *Voting Procedures*, Clarendon Press, 1984.

[18] P.Emerson, *The Politics of Consensus*, Peter Emerson, Belfast, 1994.

[19] Emerson, *op cit*, p.12.

[20] For further details see Emerson, *op cit*, Appendices 2-5.

[21] Dummet, *op cit*, pp.284-296; Emerson, *op cit*, pp.69-70, and Appendix 9.

$$\frac{\text{total votes cast}}{\text{number of seats} + 1}$$

If the required number of candidates have not been elected, then the second step is to find any pair of candidates who can meet the quota neither of whom have elected. If there pairs who meet the quota, then the member of the pair with the higher preference is elected. If the required number of candidates have still not been elected, then the third step is to find any set of three candidates who meet the quota, with the highest preference of the trio being elected. This process continues until all seats are filled.

Conclusion

This paper has focused upon the vast range of electoral formulae that may be used to translate votes into representation. A number of classifications of these formula have been outlined, and a new multi-dimensional approach is developed in Figure 6. No formula has been presented as any better or any worse than any other. To do so would force value judgements upon each system. The objective has been to outline the various formulae in relation to each other. Within Figure 6, the relations between the different formula are clearly presented.

Elections, Public Opinion and Parties

David Chapman
Democracy Design Forum

'Condorcet Election of the Government Party'

Introduction

A new form of parliamentary democracy is put forward, designed to guarantee single-party government, and to provide strong incentives for both government and opposition parties to converge towards a moderate centre policy responsive to all sections of the electorate. It is argued that this system would provide government which was more stable and effective, and more equitably responsive to the needs of the different sections of electors, than either a coalition government under proportional representation, or a single-party government under a majority system.

Under this new system, the election serves two functions, not only the usual function of determining each party's number of seats, but also that of electing one of the parties to be the sole government party. The government party is thus elected by direct vote of the whole electorate, which votes preferentially, each voter placing the competing parties in order of his or her preference. Then, in order to enable the party thus elected to govern, the following two provisions are made:

- (1) if the government party has fewer than 30% of the seats, extra seats are created and given to it, equal to the number by which it fell short of 30%;
- (2) each of its MPs (Members of Parliament) is given a weighted vote, sufficient to provide the party as a whole with a 55% majority of the votes in the parliament.[1]

The method proposed for electing the government party is a variant of the Condorcet method.[2] This can be expected to provide the competing parties with the incentive to follow a moderate centre policy, equitably responsive to each section of the electors.

One possibility is to combine this scheme for the election of the government party, with some form of proportional representation, which would give each party seats in proportion to its first-preference votes. However, PR has the drawback that it tends to give parties the incentive to become

---

[1] For example, if there are 600 seats, and the government party has 175, then five extra seats are created, and given to it. Each MP of the government party is given a weighted vote in the parliament, equal to (425 x 55)/(180 x 45) = 2.886. Thus the government has 180 x 2.886 = 519 votes out of a total of 519 + 425 = 944, which is a 55% majority.

[2] A Condorcet method of election is one which elects the Condorcet winner, if there is one, the Condorcet winner being that party which is preferred to any other party by a majority of voters.

more sectionalist, and to diverge from each other in policy, as each party seeks the votes of and responds to a different section of the electors.

It is desirable that, in contrast, the electoral system used to give each party seats, should reinforce the incentive which is provided by Condorcet in electing the government party, for each party to be responsive to each section of electors. This paper therefore puts forward a new electoral system, All-Preference Representation (APR), which gives a party seats, not only according to its number of first-preference supporters, but also according to the rankings given to it, by all the other voters, the ones who do not give it first preference. Under this system, a party can lose up to one-half of its seats, by getting a low ranking from these latter non-first-preference voters. This gives each party the incentive to appeal more widely, to sections to which it did not appeal before, in order to obtain a higher non-first ranking from them. Thus the use of APR to determine each party's seats, reinforces the incentive provided by the Condorcet election of the government, for each party to be responsive to each section of electors.

The APR system as so far described, has done no more than determine each party's number of seats. But to qualify as a complete electoral system, it must also allocate the seats won by a party between its candidates, and allocate these candidates to the areas of the country for which they are to have responsibility. It would be possible to do this by means of party lists in multi-member constituencies, just as in the usual forms of Party List PR. However, this paper proposes an alternative scheme of party lists in single-member 'territories', which will be referred to as the Territorial List Scheme. The advantages claimed for this scheme are (1) that it would provide much better contact between the individual MPs and the electors each one represents, and (2) that it would help each party to develop as an integrated team, able if called on to form a strong and effective single-party government.

Incumbency Condorcet

To elect the government party, a method of election is required, which gives the government thus elected the incentive to be responsive to each section of electors. Perhaps the best way of providing this incentive to all-round responsiveness, is to use one of the variants of the Condorcet method. The incentives which Condorcet provides can be seen by considering an example where there are three parties A, B and C, in more or less equal competition. Then any one of these parties, let us say A, will need to appeal to the first-preference supporters of B in order to get a majority over C, and to the first-preference supporters of C in order to get a majority over B. Thus in order to get itself elected under Condorcet, party A will have the incentive to appeal to all sections of the electorate.

But although Condorcet gives very desirable incentives, it has the drawback that sometimes there is no Condorcet winner to elect. For example, if 39% of voters vote ABC, 31% BCA, and 30% CAB, then there will be a cycle of parties, where A beats B by 69 to 31, B beats C by 70 to 30, and C beats A by 61 to 39, so that there is no party which beats each other party. Thus Condorcet needs to be supplemented by some other rule of election, such as the Alternative Vote, to use when there is no Condorcet winner, so as to ensure that some party will be elected.[3]

However, this only leads to another problem. Consider the following example, where the percentages of votes are: 40 ACB, 25 CAB, 35 BCA. Then C is the Condorcet winner, and A is the party which would win under the Alternative Vote. This gives the supporters of A the incentive to vote strategically, by voting ABC, or just by voting for A alone and expressing no more preferences. This will create a cycle, where A beats B beats C beats A, so that the Alternative Vote comes into use, and A is elected instead of C.

This possibility of strategy has important implications. As a result, the fact that a party has become the Condorcet winner, genuinely preferred by a majority to each other party, is no longer a guarantee that it will be elected. There is thus no guarantee that parties will always strive to become the Condorcet winner, or that the system will give them the desirable incentives to all-round responsiveness which we originally associated with Condorcet.

What then can be done to modify the system, so as to guarantee these desirable incentives? The solution to the problem is to narrow down our focus, from the attempt to provide all parties with the required incentives, to the more manageable task of providing these incentives to only one party.

Now the party in which it is important to ensure all-round responsiveness, is clearly the government party, since it is on the actions of this party, not those of the opposition parties, that the welfare of the electors depends. And for such an incumbent government party, the election which provides it with these incentives to respond, is not the past one at which it was elected, but the future one at which it may or may not be re-elected. Thus in any election, what is important is the incentives which that election provides to that party which has been the government party in the immediately previous term. Let us refer to this party as 'the incumbent'.

A method of election is therefore put forward, which provides the required Condorcet-type incentives to the incumbent party. That is, the incumbent can be re-elected only if it is truly the Condorcet winner (in other words, it is sincerely preferred by a majority to each other party), and it cannot be re-elected if it is not the Condorcet winner. The rules of this method of election, which will be referred to as Incumbency Condorcet, are as follows.[4]

(1) The incumbent is defined as that party which contains the largest number of candidates who were MPs of the government party or parties in the term immediately preceding the election.

---

[3] By the Alternative Vote, the party with fewest first-preference votes is excluded, and its votes are transferred, each vote going to its next preference. The party then with fewest votes is similarly excluded, and its votes are transferred, and so on, until one party has more than half the total votes held by all the non-excluded parties.

[4] An alternative version of Incumbency Condorcet, which would have much the same properties, is as follows. If there is a CW, elect it. Otherwise, elect that one of the parties in the cycle which beats the incumbent, or which beats the incumbent by the largest margin.

(2) If no party beats the incumbent, then the incumbent is elected. (A is said to 'beat' B if more voters prefer A to B than prefer B to A.)

(3) If only one party beats the incumbent, then this party is elected.

(4) If more than one party beats the incumbent, then the party which beats the incumbent by the largest margin is elected. (The margin by which A beats B is defined as: the number of voters who prefer A to B, minus the number of voters who prefer B to A.)

(5) If there is no party which conforms to the definition of incumbent, then one party is elected as the government party by means of the Alternative Vote method.

It will be clear from these rules that if the incumbent is the Condorcet winner (CW), then the incumbent must be re-elected, and no strategic voting, or indeed sincere voting, by the supporters of some other party P, can prevent it from being re-elected, and elect party P instead. The reason is of course that the supporters of P are only a minority.

Similarly, if some other party is the CW, then the incumbent cannot be re- elected, and there is no strategy by which its supporters can prevent its defeat. For let us suppose that it is expected that, on sincere voting, a party P will beat the incumbent and will be elected. Only those who prefer the incumbent to P will wish to elect the incumbent instead, but as a minority they will be unable to bring this about.

But what if the incumbent is not the CW, not because some other party is the CW, but because preferences are cyclical, and no CW exists? In this situation, the party which beats the incumbent is elected. There is then no strategy by which the incumbent can be elected instead, because again, only a minority of voters prefer the incumbent. However, if not the incumbent party, but some opposition party, is the CW, the system cannot guarantee that the CW will be elected. This is demonstrated by the following example, where N is the incumbent, and A and B are two opposition parties, and where the percentages of votes are: 17 ABN, 19 ANB, 13 NAB, 17 NBA, 17 BNA, 17 BAN. Thus B is the CW, since B beats N by a margin of $51 - 49 = 2$, and B beats A by 51 to 49. But A is elected, since A beats N by a larger margin, one of $53 - 47 = 6$.

Similarly, the strategy-proofness which applies in respect of the incumbent, does not apply in the case of the competition between opposition parties. For example, if 3% of B supporters were to change from voting BAN to voting BNA, this would reduce A's margin over N to $50 - 50 = 0$, thus electing B.

How far then does it create a problem, that there is at least a possibility that, if the CW is an opposition party, it will not be elected, or that an opposition party can be elected by strategic voting? In this context, the following considerations should be borne in mind. First, strategy will be possible only between opposition parties, where supporters of one opposition party seek to get it elected instead of the other. Second, this strategy, or this non-election of the CW, is possible only if there are two or more opposition parties which beat the government party, which situation is not itself a very likely one. Third, if in fact an opposition party which is not the CW is elected to government, or if an opposition party is elected by strategic rather than sincere voting, this will do little or nothing to distort governmental incentives, since the only way that the new government party can get itself *re*-elected, is itself to become the Condorcet winner before the next election. Thus however the new government party won the last election, the need to win the *next* election will still provide it with the required incentives, that is, ones to be responsive to all sections of the electorate.

Thus the important feature of the system is this. The only way the incumbent party can get re-elected is to become, or continue to be, the CW, that is, the party sincerely preferred by a majority over each other party, and there is no strategy by which its supporters can get it re-elected if it is not the CW. In order to beat any one opposition party, and get itself preferred by a majority over it, it will need to appeal to the first-preference supporters of each other opposition party. Thus the system provides the government party with the incentive to be responsive to each section of the electorate.

Similarly, the system gives the government party the incentive, in order to have a better chance of beating each opposition party, to move towards the centre of the left-to-right policy dimension, or any other policy dimension which is of interest to the electors.

What then can be said in conclusion, about this device of electing the government party by means of Incumbency Condorcet? First, however fragmented the legislature has been before the system is adopted, the system will provide government by a *single party* with at least 30% of seats, and with a majority of parliamentary votes. Second, this government party will tend to be a moderate centre party, with strong incentives to be responsive to each section of the electorate. Third, even if the opposition has previously been extremely fragmented, it is likely that, probably by merger of smaller parties, one or more substantial opposition parties will be formed, in order to get a better chance of achieving a majority over the government party.

All-Preference Representation

As was explained above, APR gives a party seats, not only according to its number of first-preference supporters, but also according to the non-first rankings given to it, by *all the other voters.* The rules of APR are as follows.

If any party has more than 35% of first preferences, the value of each of its votes is reduced, so that it has 35% of what is then the total of first preferences.[5]

[5] For example, if the party has 51% of first preferences, each of its votes is given a value of 35/51 = 0.6863, and the other votes a value of 65/49 = 1.3265. The party will then have (51 x 0.6863))/((51 x 0.6863) + (49 x 1.3265)) of the first preferences. The intention of this provision is to give any large party with significantly more than 35% of first preferences the incentive to split itself into two smaller parties, to avoid losing seats. This is likely to achieve a party system where the parties are more equally competitive, and where probably there are three major parties rather than two.

Basically, APR is proportional representation, plus a correction for each party's lower preferences. Thus each party is given an initial allocation of a percentage of seats equal to its percentage of the first-preference votes in the whole country, just as under proportional representation. Each possible pair of parties is then considered, and for each pair, if one party is preferred to the other by more voters than the other is preferred to it, an appropriate percentage of seats is transferred *from* the party preferred by fewer voters *to* the party preferred by more voters.

This can be expressed more precisely, as follows. In any pair of parties, let A be the party which is preferred by more voters, and B the party which is preferred by fewer voters. The percentage of seats to be transferred from B to A, is calculated as follows. Let us call the percentage preferring A minus the percentage preferring B the 'preference difference' between A and B. (Note that these are not percentages of all voters, but only on those voters who are not indifferent between A and B.) The percentage of seats to be transferred from B to A is equal to whichever is less: *either* (1) B's % of first preferences, *multiplied* by A's % of first preferences, *multiplied* by twice the preference difference between A and B; *or* (2) B's % of first preferences, *multiplied* by A's % of first preferences, *divided* by twice the total % of first preferences of all parties other than B. In other words, (1) is transferred from B to A, except when (1) exceeds the maximum limit on seats transferable from B to A, which is (2).[6]

This APR formula guarantees each party a minimum percentage of seats, equal to one-half of its percentage of first preferences, however few lower preferences it obtains.[7]

Note that unlike Incumbency Condorcet, APR is completely strategy-proof, in that there is no way in which the supporters of a party can increase its seats above what they can obtain by voting sincerely. For example, if voters whose true preferences are ABC, instead vote ACB, this does not affect the seats of A, their first-preferred party, but only transfers seats from B to C, contrary to their true preferences.

What then will be the general effect of APR on a party's seats? First, let us suppose that all parties are moderate centre parties, responsive to all

[6] For example, if party B has 30% of first preferences, and party A has 35%, and 40% of voters prefer B to A, then the proportion of total seats transferred from B to A, is equal to whichever is less, either 0.3 x 0.35 x 2 x (0.6 – 0.4) = 0.042, or (0.3 x 0.35) /(2(1 – 0.3)) = 0.075. That is, the proportion of total seats transferred from B to A, is 0.042, or 4.2%.

[7] This can be shown as follows. The maximum total loss of seats a party B can incur, that is, the maximum amount of seats which can be transferred from party B to all other parties, is shown by the above formula (2), but substituting in it 'all parties other than B' for 'party A'. Thus B's maximum seats loss will be: B's % of first preferences, multiplied by the total % of first preferences of all parties other than B, divided by twice the total % of first preferences of all parties other than B; which cancels out to: B's % of first preferences, divided by two. In other words, the maximum amount of seats a party can lose by getting a low preference from the first-preference supporters of other parties, is one-half of its initial allocation of seats, the allocation in proportion to its first-preference votes. Thus whatever its performance in respect of lower preferences, the party is guaranteed to get a final percentage of seats which is at least half of its percentage of first-preference votes.

sections of the electorate. Then any one party will be preferred to any other party by about 50% of the voters. Thus few or no seats will be transferred from one party to another, and each party will get a percentage of seats about equal to its percentage of first preferences. But if one of these parties moves away from a centre position, let us say to the right (while the other parties stay at the centre), the percentage of voters preferring it to any other party will be reduced, and it will lose seats to the other parties.[8]

Thus in conclusion, APR gives each party the incentive to appeal to all electors, even to those who previously have given it their lowest preference, since if it gets a low ranking from enough of them, it could lose half its seats. Similarly, APR gives each party the incentive, in order not to lose seats, to move towards the centre of the left-to-right policy dimension, or any other policy dimension which is of interest to the electors. APR thus strongly reinforces the incentives provided by Incumbency Condorcet, to be or become a moderate centre party, and to be responsive to each section of the electorate.

The Territorial List Scheme

As was explained above, this is an extension of the APR system, to allocate the seats of a party between its candidates, and to allocate these candidates to the areas of the country for which they are to have responsibility. The rules of the scheme are as follows.

Shortly before the general election, each party registers its provisional list of candidates, which normally will include the party's MPs of the previous term. A candidate selection ballot is then carried out, under the auspices of the electoral authority. In this ballot, all persons on the party's provisional list are placed as candidates on the ballot paper, and only persons on this provisional list may vote, voting for as many candidates as they like. The ballot is secret. To be accepted on to the party's final list, a person must obtain votes from at least one-half of the members of the provisional list. Further persons may be voted on to the final list, by the assenting vote of a majority of those already on the final list, in secret ballot.

The final list of candidates is then placed in the order in which they are to receive seats, again by vote of the candidates on that list, in another secret ballot. In this, the voting is preferential, that is, the person votes by writing '1' for a first preference, '2' for a second preference, and so on, for as many candidates as they wish. The candidates on the list are then placed in order by successive applications of the Alternative Vote method. That is, one candidate is chosen by AV, to occupy the first place on the list.

[8]Thus a party which has 30% of first preferences will lose 0.84% of seats, for each 1% of reduction in the percentage of voters preferring it over the other parties. If a party has 31.7% or less of first-preference supporters, it can lose up to half its initial allocation of seats by not getting high enough non-first rankings from the other voters, and if it has 35% (the maximum possible) of first preferences, it can lose almost two-fifths of its initial seats. If there are two parties A and B, each with 30% of first preferences, and A moves up past B on the ballot papers of 1% of voters, who change from voting CBA to voting CAB, then this gains A 0.36% of seats, at the expense of B.

From the remaining candidates, one is chosen by AV to occupy the second place, and so on.

Similarly, the candidates of the party elect the party leader, in secret ballot, for a term of one year. All candidates of the party are automatically placed on the ballot paper as leadership candidates, without need for nomination. The method of election is Incumbency Condorcet, or AV if the person who was the leader in the previous year is not standing. In the leadership elections which are held every year during the legislative term, all the MPs of the party stand as leadership candidates, and only the MPs of the party have a vote.

Under the Territorial List Scheme, the country is divided into small electoral areas referred to as 'tracts', there being at least as many tracts as MPs to be elected. From these tracts, each party creates a number of 'territories', a territory being a cluster of tracts, as many as the party chooses, in which the party places one of its candidates. The party may not overlap its territories, that is, it may not put more than one candidate in the same tract. But the territories may be of any size, as is decided by the party. Presumably the party will choose to create a number of territories which is not more than the minimum number of seats it expects to obtain, and will create them of such size that they cover the whole country, so that every tract in the country can be the responsibility of one of its elected MPs.[9] The party can be expected to put on its list enough additional candidates without territories, to fill the seats it gets in excess of this minimum number, and to fill any vacancies which might occur during the course of the legislative term due to death or retirement.[10]

Thus the general effect will be that large parties will create small territories, and many of them, and small parties will create large territories and few of them. Each tract of the country will have an elected MP of each party to take responsibility for it, while the territory of each MP will not be any bigger than is necessary for the MP's party to be sure of covering the whole country. Thus this scheme would appear to maximise the degree of contact between the individual MPs and the electors each one represents.

What then is the likely effect of this Territorial List Scheme on the coherence and effectiveness of parties? The individual MPs will be fully aware that they will face a candidate selection ballot before the next election, at which the other MPs of the party can, in secret ballot, with no risk to themselves, and without need to explain or justify, expel them without appeal from the party's list, or place them so low down on the list that they are very unlikely to get a seat. Thus any MP who wants to be re-elected will

[9]A party could, if it so wished, create fewer territories than this, and allow its leading members to stand as non-territorial candidates, placed at the top of its list, so that when elected they would be free of responsibility for a territory.

[10]If they are elected, these MPs without territory will have a status analogous to that of the list MPs under some forms of the Additional Member System. If it did happen that a party over-estimated the seats it would get, and so had some territories in which its candidate was not elected, it could assign each tract of these territories to one of its elected MPs, as an additional responsibility, so as to ensure that its MPs covered all tracts in the country.

have a strong incentive to cooperate with the rest of the party team, whose objective will be to develop and promote the kind of policy which, responsive to all sections of the electors, can win more seats for the party and increase its chance of winning government office. Thus the provisions of the Territorial List Scheme are likely to produce a set of strong and disciplined parliamentary parties, each of which acts as a coherent and integrated team, and can offer effective opposition, or if it wins the election, form a strong and effective single-party government.

Conclusion

A new form of parliamentary democracy is proposed, which has the following properties. (1) It guarantees a single-party government with an adequate majority of parliamentary votes, however fragmented the legislature has been before the system is adopted. (2) This government party, and indeed each opposition party, is likely to be internally unified, functioning as a strong and coherent team. Thus the system can be expected to provide stable and effective government. (3) However uncompromising has been the political culture of the country which has adopted it, each party, and especially the government party, will be subject to powerful incentives to adopt a moderate centre policy, which is equitably responsive to the concerns of each section of the electorate. (4) Any party which consistently follows such a policy, can expect to achieve considerable stability in its number of seats, and so to provide relatively safe seats for its individual MPs. Thus this new system is put forward, as a means of achieving stable single-party government, one which may well prove to be highly acceptable to politicians currently holding office.

The Global Development and Spread of Policies and Political Institutions

David P.Dolowitz
University of Birmingham

'The Child Support Agency: where is it from?'

Introduction

Arguments about the Child Support Agency (CSA) since its establishment in 1993 have concentrated on the problems, or the perceived problems, of implementation which the CSA has encountered. These arguments have focused upon issues such as: the influence the Agency has had on the fathers ordered to pay maintenance contributions, regardless of their incomes; the difficulty of establishing paternity; and the negative effects child support orders have had on the relationship between ex-partners and their children. However, an analysis of the institutional design and structure of the Agency is a necessary prerequisite to any comprehensive understanding of why these implementation 'problems' emerged and whether the changes implemented in the 1995 Child Support Act, and subsequent administrative alterations, will solve these problems.

However, before considering the institutional structure of the Child Support Agency it is necessary to understand its origins. The analysis presented here addresses why the Government developed the Agency, providing an insight into its problems. Specifically, the origins of the Agency are to be found in policy transfer from the United States and to a lesser extent Australia. It is important to understand these orgins because the failures of the American Child Support Enforcement System (CSES) should have led the Government to develop structures to avoid similar implementation 'problems.'[1]

Briefly, in late 1990 the Government published a two volume White Paper, *Children Come First: The Government's Proposals on the Maintenance of Children* (Cm 1264), announcing its intention to establish a Child Support Agency. The White Paper's proposals were given effect in the Child Support Act 1991 and then dramatically rewritten in the Child Support Act 1995 and subsequent administrative alterations in 1996.

Why Transfer the Child Support Agency from the United States?

There were three key reasons the Government decided to transfer the structure of the Child Support Agency from the United States: the United States

[1]This is an important point because it can also help advance the policy transfer literature by demonstrating why their are implementation failures when ideas and institutions are transferred from one system to another, regardless of the political desirability of the transfer or the support mechanisms the original system required for its success.

and Britain were facing similar problems within their child support enforcement systems; the Reagan Administration and the Thatcher Government shared ideological values; and America's CSES had a long history of 'success' in operating Child Support Enforcement Agencies.

Similar Problems

In the United States, the passage of the 1974 Social Service Amendments, the 1984 Child Support Enforcement Amendments and the 1988 Family Support Act, were each inspired by the perceived need to enhance the consistency and accountability of America's child support system. These Acts were a response to the inability of court-determined support orders, with no guidelines or accountability, to produce similar child support awards, even for families in similar situations.[2] It was particularly worrisome to policy makers that families who needed help the most were the least likely to receive it. This occurred because low income families found the cost and delays involved in court cases difficult to overcome. As Irwin Garfinkel argued:

> 'Until recently child support was a state and local matter ... The establishment and enforcement of private child support was characterized by judicial discretion ... How much non-resident parents were required to pay in child support varied dramatically from case to case. Families in similar circumstances were treated quite differently.'[3]

While the problems just discussed were not as prevalent in Britain they formed the basis of the arguments presented in *Children Come First* to justify the development of the CSA. Specifically, the White Paper argues:

> 'The present system of maintenance is unnecessarily fragmented, uncertain in its results, slow and ineffective. It is based largely on discretion. The system is operated through the ... courts ... and the ... Department of Social Security. The cumulative effect is uncertainty and inconsistent decisions about how much maintenance should be paid.'[4]

In addition to the inconsistency of payments, both countries were also seeing a rise in the number of non-payment of child support awards. Before the passage of the Child Support Enforcement Amendments of 1984, the United States Census Bureau released figures revealing that, of the nearly 9 million eligible families in 1983, only about 4 million were receiving child

[2] I am using 'families' to refer to single women and men receiving child support and parents living with a partner but still receiving child support from the absent biological parent.

[3] I.Garfinkel & M.M.Klawitter, 'The Effect of Routine Income Withholding of Child Support Collections', *Journal of Policy Analysis and Management*, 9/2, 1990, p.156.

[4] White Paper, *Children Come First: The Government's proposals on the maintenance of children*, volume I, Cm 1264, HMSO, 1990, p.i.

support payments.[5] Of these only: 'half received the entire award, another quarter received partial payments, and one out of four received no support at all.'[6] Even after the passage of the 1984 Child Support Enforcement Amendments, the situation continued to be problematic, leading to the inclusion of Title I in the 1988 Family Support Act (FSA). Briefly, Title I of the 1988 FSA implemented a national Child Support Enforcement System based upon the uniform application of a State-developed formula to ensure absent parents were held responsible for maintaining their children.

Similar trends were highlighted in *Children Come First.* The White Paper indicated that in 1989 70 per cent of case families who had been awarded child support received none, or a limited amount, because absent parents had fallen into arrears. Moreover, only 5 percent of the payments which fell into arrears were fully recovered. The White Paper also highlighted that, as in the United States, many eligible families failed to claim child support in the first instance.

As a result of the problems highlighted above, single parent families in both the United States and Britain were relying on the welfare system. In fact, one of the main arguments used to justify the 1988 FSA was the need to reduce dependency amongst single parent families caused by the lack of child support payments. As noted by Casebolt & Garfinkel:

> 'Failure to secure economic support from the fathers in these cases contributes the economic disadvantages faced by these mothers as well as the fiscal burden borne by the public.' [In response the] 'United States Congress and state legislatures have enacted legislation designed to facilitate the establishment of paternity and child support awards.'[7]

Once again these arguments are replicated in *Children Come First.* For example, volume II begins:

> 'Lone parent families have become more depended on social security benefits and have become less likely to receive maintenance.'[8]

In summary, the similarity in the 'problems" facing the United States and British child support enforcement systems, when combined with the increased reliance of lone parent families on State benefits provided a strong catalyst for the transfer of the American child support enforcement system.

The dramatic rise in the number of single parent families within both the United States and Britain was associated with a rise in the apparent 'dependence' amongst single parent families. In fact, it was Congressional concern with this rise which lead them to include a mandate for every State to

---

[5] United States Bureau of the Census, *Current Population Reports, Child Support and Alimony*, 1983, Series p-23, number 148, Washington, DC, Government Printing Office, October 1986.

[6] T.Corbett et al, 'Public Opinion about a Child Support Assurance System', *Social Service Review*, 62, 1988, p.633.

[7] A.Nichols-Casebolt & I.Garfinkel, 'Trends in Paternity Adjudication's and Child Support Awards', pp.83-84.

[8] White Paper, *Children Come First*, volume II, p.i.

include Aid to Families with Dependent Children Parents Program (AFDC-UP) in its welfare-to-work program.[9] Prior to the 1988 FSA, States were given the option to, but not required to, operate an AFDC-UP program. For this reason only 27 States and the District of Columbia were operating AFDC-UP programs prior to the passage of the 1988 FSA. Moreover, during the Congressional Hearings numerous witnesses testified that States which had eliminated their AFDC-UP programs were discovering that families were breaking up in order to re-qualify for AFDC benefits.

This same pattern was repeated in Britain, though on a much smaller scale. As noted in the Social Security Advisory Committee's Seventh Report:

> 'In the 1980s the number of lone parents has risen more rapidly than at any other time ... Some two thirds of all lone parents reviving benefit receive income support. Of these, over half are divorced or separated and half have at least one child under five.'[10]

More importantly, the Committee used these trends to justify the need to improve the child support maintenance system. Specifically, the Committee noted that, while the number of lone parents claiming benefits was increasing, 'over the same period the amount of maintenance paid by non-custodial parents has been static'. They also noted: 'Many possible options are now being considered to resolve the problem of parents who default in paying maintenance.'[11]

Because both countries were facing similar circumstances, the ability to turn to a well-developed and tested system increased the attractiveness of the American child support enforcement system and, in particular, the Child Support Enforcement Agencies.

Similar Ideology

The decision to transfer the Child Support Enforcement Agency from the United States was also influenced by the ideological similarities between the Reagan and Thatcher Administrations. The Reagan and Thatcher Governments were broadly neo-liberal in their economic policy and neo-conservative in their social policy. In particular, one of the key ideological arguments underpinning the development of both the CSES in the United States and the CSA in Britain was the belief that parents should take responsibility for their biological children, regardless of the marital situation.[12] In the United States these arguments were forcefully represented in the 1974 Social Service Amendments, the 1984 Child Support Enforcement Amendments (PL.

[9]The AFDC-UP program was designed to provide welfare benefits to low-income two parent families as opposed to the AFDC program which only targeted single parent families.

[10]SSAC, *Seventh Report Social Security Advisory Committee*, HMSO, 1990, p.44.

[11]SSAC, *Seventh Report Social Security Advisory Committee*, p.44.

[12]For more information on the shared belief in neo-liberalism or New Right principles between the Reagan and Thathcer Governments see D.King, *The New Right: Politics, Markets and Citizenship*, Macmillan, 1987.

98-378) and the 1988 FSA. In fact, the opening statement of the 1984 Child Support Enforcement Amendment defines the purpose of the Act: 'To ... ensure ... that all children in the United States who are in need of assistance in securing financial support from their parents will receive such assistance regardless of their circumstances.'[13]

This same belief was apparent in Britain dating back to the Social Security Act 1986. Specifically, Sections 24 – 26 of the Act mandate that both men and women are liable to maintain their children to the age of 19, even if they are divorced, separated or the child was illegitimate. This requirement was repeated and strengthened in Section 5 of the Social Security Act, 1989, which mandated that fathers were liable to maintain 'any children of whom he is the father', and that both men and women were liable to maintain any children 'of whom the man or the woman is the father or mother', regardless of their marital status or relationship.[14] *Children Come First* reiterates these sentiments in its opening paragraph:

> 'Every child has a right to care from his or her parents ... Although events may change the relationship between the parents ... those events cannot in any way change their responsibilities towards their children ... The payment of child maintenance is one crucial way in which parents fulfill their responsibilities towards their children.'[15]

The Thatcher Government's strong attachment to the work ethic further attracted it to the American CSES. Briefly, the 1988 FSA was passed not only to ensure absent parents met their financial obligations to their children, but also to require parents to support their children through work. In the words of the Act's primary sponsor, Senator Moynihan:

> 'The primary responsibility for child support rests with parents ... there is agreement that whether children live with both parents, or just one, able-bodied parents have a responsibility to support their children by working. Toward this end we ought to remove the barriers to employment.'[16]

Senator Moynihan's sentiments were repeated in Children Come First: 'The Government proposes to establish a system of child maintenance which will ... ensure that parents meet the cost of their children's maintenance whenever they can without removing the parents' own incentives to work, and go on working.'[17]

---

[13] United States Government, *Child Support Enforcement Amendments of 1984*, PL 98-378, Washington, DC, Government Printing Office, 1984, Introduction.

[14] HMSO, *Social Security Act 1989*, HMSO, 1989, Section 5.

[15] White Paper, *Children Come First*, volume I, Foreword.

[16] United States Government, 'Welfare: Reform or Replacement', Hearings Before the Subcommittee on Social Security and Family Policy, United States Senate, 100th Congress, 1st Session, Washington, DC: Government Printing Office, February 23, 1987, p.3.

[17] White Paper, *Children Come First*, volume I, p.5.

Moreover, in July 1989 the SSAC released *Why Don't They Go to Work? Mothers on Benefit*, which found: 'evidence that lone mothers who receive regular maintenance at a reasonable level show a markedly increased propensity to work'.[18] This added a further justification for the adoption of the American child support enforcement systems as a way of drawing families back into the labour market.

The change in attitudes towards women in work was closely associated with the desire to maintain the work ethic. In both the United States and Britain the Social Security System was designed with the underlying assumption that women with children should not enter the labour market. In the United States this assumption gradually changed as women, even with young children, began entering the labour market. So, by the time of the passage of the 1988 FSA it was assumed that women with children as young as one, should work.

As noted in *Why Don't They Go to Work?*, similar changes occurred in women's working patterns and in the attitudes towards single mothers in Britain:

> 'the social security system was planned on the further assumption that it was not in the interest of children for a married woman to go out to work ... the large scale return to the labour force of married women with dependent children has raised question about this policy.'[19]

Historical Record

The Thatcher Government was further drawn to the American Child Support Enforcement System because it was a well established system which had been highly studied and publicised for over 16 years before the introduction of Children Come First.[20] So, in 1974, in response to growing concern over the lack of co-ordination and consistency in the awarding and size of child support, Congress passed the Social Service Amendments. These established the basis of the American CSES. For the next 14 years Congress continued to adjust the system developed within these Amendments until the passage of the 1988 FSA, which completed the development of the American CSES. As this indicates, the Thatcher Government had ample opportunity to study a highly developed system before introducing the British CSA.

While the above section has demonstrated some of the reasons the Thatcher Government transferred the American CSES to Britain it has not establish whether the Government was aware of the American CSES. Moreover, it has not established that the Government was interested in borrowing lessons

[18]SSAC, *Seventh Report of the Social Security Advisory Committee*, p.3. See also J.Brown, *Why Don't They Go to Work*, HMSO, July 1989).

[19]J.Brown, *Why Don't They Go to Work?*, p.1.

[20]For more information see A.Nichols-Casebolt & I.Garfinkel, 'Trends in Paternity Adjudication's and Child Support Awards'; A. Stuart, 'Rescuing Child Support Payment System'; I.Garfinkel & E.Uhr, 'A New Approach to Child Support'; C.Adams Jr et al, 'Welfare Reform and Paternity Establishment: A Social Experiment'.

from the American CSES. Both of these conditions must be demonstrated before it can be established that policy transfer occurred. In the following section I will show that the Government was both aware of the American Child Support Enforcement System and interested in adopting lessons from it.

Knowledge of, and Interest in, the American CSES

The process of borrowing the American CSES began at a Paris conference in 1986 when David Willetts, a member of the Downing Street Policy Unit, met Irwin Garfinkel. After their meeting David Willetts reputedly wrote to Prime Minister Thatcher about the American CSES. Upon receiving this report she was allegedly: 'rapturous: nail the guilty fathers and at the same time cut hundreds of millions off the Social Security budget – give the man a rise!'[21] Less then four years after the Paris conference the Government announced its intention to implement the CSA with the same guidelines and functions as its American counterpart.

More direct evidence of the Government's borrowing of the American CSES was provided in *Children Come First* which announced that the: 'Secretary of State and senior officials visited the United States to talk to the judiciary and officials involved in the operation of the child support systems there'.[22] The White Paper continues with a description of the Wisconsin child support system. In particular, it highlights Wisconsin's use of a formula to determine the value of child support awards and the use of wage-withholding to ensure absent parents make their payments.[23] Each of these elements were integrated into the British CSA.

The Security Advisory Committee's report, Why Don't They Go to Work?, also examined the alterations to the American child support enforcement system made by: the 1974 Social Service Amendments; the 1984 Child Support Enforcement Amendments; and the 1988 Family Support Act. Not only does *Why Don't They Go to Work?* examine America's CSES but it also reviews the AFDC program dating back to it inception as the Aid to Dependent Children (ADC) Program in the 1935 Social Security Act.

All this provides ample evidence that the Government was aware of the American CSES and interested in it. However, while the above section suggests that the Government designed the CSA on the basis of its understanding of American CSES perhaps the final word should rest with Government. On 12 February 1990 Gillian Shephard argued:

> 'We are particularly concerned about the number of lone-parent families on benefit here who receive little or no maintenance. We are therefor examining the whole maintenance system to establish how it can be improved. As part of this process we are examining maintenance arrangements abroad, including

[21] P.Popham, 'Down By Law', *Esquire*, May, 1994, p.124.

[22] HMSO, *Children Come First*, volume II, p.85.

[23] See HMSO, *Children Come First*, volume II, pp.85-86.

> those in the United States, to see whether there are any lesson to be learned from them.'[24]

The Child Support Agency

The United States

In the United States, concern over the operation and application of the child support system and the way the court's determined maintenance awards reached the political agenda by the early 1970s. This concern led Congress to pass the 1974 Social Service Amendments which required every State to establish a child support enforcement system.[25] As part of this system, States had to establish: 'special agencies for the collection of child support payments due to recipients of AFDC who were required to sign over to the state claims to child support as a condition of [AFDC] eligibility.'[26] Moreover, State child support enforcement agencies were given the authority and responsibility for 'locating absent parents, establishing paternity, preparing support orders, monitoring compliance with support orders, distributing collections, and periodically reviewing and modifying support orders.'[27] Furthermore, the Amendments required States to establish parent locator services: 'that could request information from the Social Security Administration and the Internal Revenue Service', on the location and income of absentee parents. Finally, States were required to: 'offer similar services to non-AFDC cases if requested'.[28]

Widespread dissatisfaction with the implementation and results of the 1974 Act, particularly within the Reagan Administration, forced Congress to amend the Act with the passage of the 1984 Child Support Enforcement Amendments. Specifically, Section 3 of the 1984 Child Support Enforcement Amendments required every State's child support enforcement agency to establish procedures for automatically withholding income from the pay and tax refunds of absentee parents, whenever their child support payments fell into arrears of over one month, without having to request court intervention.[29] Section 3 also required States, to establish procedures imposing:

> 'lines against real and personal property for the amount of overdue support ... [and] Permitted states to extend withholding

[24]Parliamentary Debates (*Hansard*) Official Record House of Commons, 10 February 1990, volume 167, column 82.

[25]These are often referred to as Title IV-D agencies for they were created under authorization contained within title IV-D of the Social Security Act. All the changes to be discussed in this section also fall under this or Title IV-A of the Social Security Act.

[26]S.Archibald, 'Rescuing Children: Reforms in the Child Support Payment System', *Social Science Review*, 60, 1986, p.203.

[27]C.Adams Jr et al, 'Welfare Reform and Paternity Establishment', p.668.

[28]S.Archibald, 'Rescuing Children: Reforms in the Child Support Payment System', p.203.

[29]Section 2 strengthened the requirement to provided help to non-AFDC parents by making it explicitly part of the Act that help must be provided to all families regardless of their financial situation.

to income other then wages, such as bonuses and commissions, or dividends.'[30]

Additionally, Sections 15 and 18 required States to establish a committee responsible for formulating child support award guidelines. Once established these were to be provided to: 'all judges and other officials who have the power to determine child support awards within such State, but need not be binding'.[31]

Title I of the 1988 FSA completed the development of the American child support enforcement system. Specifically, Section 101 requires every State to implement various procedures for immediate and mandatory wage-withholding for all support orders being enforced by the State's CSEA. The only exception to this is if either a judge rules there is a 'good cause' for not enforcing the rules or both parents sign an agreement specifying other arrangements.[32] Section 101 also requires the Agency to begin such procedures upon the request of either parent or the Agency. Section 102 strengthens the 1984 requirement that the first $50 collected in support payments does not count as income for benefit entitlement purposes. Section 103 mandated that child support award guidelines established by the 1984 Child Support Enforcement Amendments:

> 'must be applied by judges and other officials in determining the amount of any child support award unless the judge or official ... makes a finding that there is good cause for not applying the guidelines.'[33]

Section 103 also required States to: 'periodically review and adjust' all child support orders being enforced by the Agency. Finally, Section 111 strengthens and extends State obligations to establish paternity in relation to AFDC cases, so that the Agency can establish and enforce child support obligations. The only exceptions to this rule were for:

> 'a child who is receiving cash benefits by reason of the death of a parent, or a child with respect to whom a mother is found to have good cause for refusing to cooperate in establishing or collecting support.'[34]

As will be discussed below, each element of the American child support enforcement system outlined above was transferred into the structural design of the British Child Support Agency.

---

[30] 'Child Support Enforcement', *Congress and the Nation 1981-1984*, volume VI, Congressional Quarterly Press, 1985, p.606.

[31] See United States Government, *Child Support Enforcement Amendments of 1984*, Section 18.

[32] See United States Government, *Family Support Act 1988*, Section 101.

[33] United States Government, *Family Support Act 1988*, Section 103.

[34] United States Government, *Family Support Act 1988*, Section 111.

Britain's Child Support Agency

In *Children Come First* the Government specified the functions of the Child Support Agency:

> 'to identify and trace liable persons if their whereabouts are unknown; to obtain information on the incomes and circumstance of the parents of the child for whom maintenance is claimed ... to assess the maintenance to be paid ... to record and monitor the payments made where appropriate; to take appropriate enforcement action at an early date when payments are not made; to review the assessment at regular intervals.'[35]

The above quote reveals the basic similarities between the American child support enforcement system and the British Child Support Agency. However, it is worth examining some of the CSA's operational guidelines to illustrate the similarities.

The formula

The 1988 FSA required states to determine child support orders based on the formula develop in response to the Child Support Enforcement Amendments of 1984. Using American experience, the Government required CSA to establish maintenance obligations based upon a formula.[36] As described in *Children Come First*, the formula would be an: 'assessment of how much maintenance should be paid ... [and] will apply to all families where maintenance is an issue and therefore eliminate any scope for inconsistency.'[37]

Before moving on, it should also be noted that the Australian Child Support Enforcement System, itself based upon the American CSES, was also influential in the development of the CSA. As noted in *Children Come First*:

> 'as part of the survey of the maintenance system in Great Britain the DSS carried out a literature study to look at the way other countries enforce child support provisions. The maintenance systems studied included ... New Zealand, Australia and ... the United StatesA ... [In addition] Senior officers attending a social security conference in Australia in November 1989 were also able to learn first hand about the new Australian Child Support Agency.'[38]

Of more importance, *Children Come First* stresses that:

> 'Australia had many of the same concerns as Great Britain about the adequacy of their maintenance system and conducted

[35] White Paper, *Children Come First*, volume I, pp.31-31.

[36] For more information on the use and structure of the Australian child support agency, itself transferred from the United States, see White Paper, *Children Come First*, volume II, p.85.

[37] White Paper, *Children Come First*, volume I, p.6.

[38] White Paper, *Children Come First*, volume II, p.85.

> in depth research before choosing the present radical system' [based on the American CSES].[39]

Periodic review

As in the United States, the CSA is also under legal obligation to undertake regular reviews of support awards to ensure they are kept in line with the changing circumstances of the parents. As noted in *Children Come First*:

> 'The Government proposes to establish a system of child maintenance which will be equally available to any person seeking maintenance ... and which will ... allow for maintenance payments to be reviewed regularly so that changes in circumstances can be taken into account automatically [without recourse to the courts].'[40]

In addition, there are provisions in both the United States and Britain that, when assessing and reviewing child support awards, administrators must ensure that second families are not damaged by the amount of the award granted and that an absent parent has a basic minimum income protected within the formula. Specifically, Cm 1264 states that the CSA must:

recognise that where a liable parent has formed a second family and has further natural children, he is liable to maintain all his own children. A fair and reasonable balance has to be struck between the interests of the children of a first family and the children of a second.[41]

This was expressed within the regulations governing 'exempt income' which was to be maintained at the 'protected level.' In the United States this level was set at 55 percent of disposable income for fathers with a second family and 65 percent for those living alone.[42]

Automatic income withholding

As in the United States, one of the mechanisms available to the CSA to ensure payment of income support is automatic income withholding.[43] It must be noted that, while the CSA is not obligated to impose automatic withholding, this is not a true 'requirement' within the United States. While the 1988 FSA mandated the automatic withholding of support awards it also allowed parents to agree to other arrangements. Due to this provision many parents have developed alternative arrangements. Additionally, as in

---

[39] White Paper, *Children Come First*, volume II, p.85. It should be noted that in addition to discussing the American CSES 'Why Don't They Go To Work?' also examines the Australian model actually calling attention to its use of the American CSES.

[40] White Paper, *Children Come First*, volume I, p.5.

[41] White Paper, *Children Come First*, volume I, p.5.

[42] See White Paper, *Children Come First*, volume I, p.7-30; United States Government *Family Support Act 1988*. I want to stress that these provisions could be traced to necessity rather then direct transfer. However at very least it would appear as if the American experience inspired these regulations.

[43] White Paper, *Children Come First*, volume I, p.34.

the United States, payments can be made directly to the caring parent or through the Agency.[44]

Reduce welfare budget

In the United States AFDC recipients are required to help the child support enforcement agency determine the paternity of their children. Additionally, they are required to claim child support, unless they have 'good cause' to refuse. If an individual is found not to have a good cause, he/she, but not any children, face losing his/her benefit entitlement. These rules were transferred to the CSA:

When the caring parent is receiving Income Support or Family Credit, the taxpayer has an interest in whether maintenance is paid. In these circumstances, the parent will be required to make a claim for maintenance to the Agency ... There will be exceptions where this is not in the interest of the children. Where there is no such good cause for declining to seek maintenance, the allowance for the caring parent, but not that for the children, may be reduced.[45]

Reserved income

Both the 1984 Child Support Enforcement Amendments and the 1988 FSA required States to transfer the first $50 of any child support collected to the family. Moreover, the $50 was to be disregarded for the purposes of determining welfare eligibility. Though not as generous as American regulations, this was replicated in the rules governing the CSA. Specifically, the Act guarantees that: 'Caring parents who receive Family Credit, Housing Benefit or Community Charge Benefit will not have the first £15 of maintenance received taken into account in calculating their income.'[46]

Charge fees for non-welfare families

The 1974 Social Services Amendments, together with the 1984 and 1988 legislation, required all non-AFDC families seeking the services of the child support enforcement agency to be charged a minimal fee for its services. This philosophy was also transferred to the CSA. Specifically, the Agency must charge all clients not receiving income support: 'for the assessment and collection of maintenance.'[47]

Parent locator service

Finally, as part of the child support enforcement system, Federal and State Governments were required to operate parent locator services capable of accessing information from State agencies, the Department of Health and Human Services, the Internal Revenue Services and the Department of Labor. The Service was designed to provide information on the location of absent parents, their place of employment and their income, at the request

[44] White Paper, *Children Come First*, volume I, p.36.

[45] White Paper, *Children Come First*, volume I, p.ii.

[46] White Paper, *Children Come First*, volume I, p.iii. Note this can be linked to the desire that the benefit system did not act as a disincentive to work, discussed earlier.

[47] HMSO, *Child Support Agency Framework Document*, HMSO, September 1993, p.6.

of the Child Support Enforcement Agency. This service was transferred into the structure of the CSA:

> In some cases, the present whereabouts are unknown and, in still fewer cases, the identity is not known for certain. The Department of Social Security already has powers to use its own records of names and addresses and the Inland Revenue's records or names and addresses of individuals and there employers to help locate liable persons ... The Child Support Agency will need similar powers.[48]

Agency Revisions

As the above discussion demonstrates, the British CSA had its orgins in the American CSES. However while borrowing the design and operations of the American system many of the safety mechanisms built into the American system were either not transferred or muted in their translation to Britain. Moreover, many of the criticisms and failures of the system were overlooked in the process of policy transfer from the United States to Britain. Finally, the cultural setting on which the Americana system depended was absent in Britain. As a result complaints began mounting over the operation of the CSA. By 1995 the appearance of failure became so extreme that the Government was forced to introduce the Child Support Bill to try and correct some of these failures. Chief among its new measures was the 'departure system' which allows the Agency some discretion in the allocation of the formula. This alteration in the functioning of the formula is extremely important because it was one of the primary features always present in the American system but not established with the agency.[49] Moreover, the Bill provided the courts with some of the same powers the American system always provided to override the CSA in specified circumstances.

Conclusion

While most scholars examining the Child Support Agency discuss its performance this paper has analysed the development of the British Child Support Agency. I have emphasised why the Government decided to develop the Agency, rather than continuing the court-based child support award system. I stressed that similar 'problems' and changes in the structure of the labour market and the wider society had been occurring in the United States and Britain since the 1960s: more and more women were entering the labour market; there was a dramatic rise in the number of single parent families, particularly in the United States; more and more of these families

---

[48]HMSO, *Child Support Agency Framework Document*,, HMSO, September 1993, p.32. I should be noted that this was not necessarily transferred but resulted from the realities and goals of the Agency. However, seeing its use in the United States undoubtedly helped justify the Government's decision to include this aspect of the legislation.

[49]Not only has the American CSES always provided flexibility in the application of the State formula but different states have developed different formula. When establishing the CSA the most regressive formula used within the United States CSES system was used.

were depending on State benefits for their survival; the number of women receiving child support awards and the amount of those awards showed considerable variation, even in cases with similar circumstances; and a large number of women were not receiving child support, even when awarded. It was these similarities in demographic developments which led the Thatcher Government to be interested in, and then to borrow, the key elements of the American CSES.

It is important to examine the development of the CSA from a policy transfer perspective because this not only helps explain its development and internal elements but it can also begin to explain why it is or is not working. Once it is known that the Government borrowed the idea and structure of the Agency it is possible to begin examining whether its implementation and use was so different from the American CSES that it was bound to encounter the type of difficulties consistently discussed within the media and academic literature. Moreover, once it has been established that the idea was borrowed it is possible to see if similar problems were occurring in the American system to discover some of the causes and possible solutions. It can also help predict some of the future consequences of the system.

By analysing the Child Support Agency from a policy transfer perspective it is now possible to analyse some of the problems with the CSA and see where to go instead of mindlessly criticising it as a failure, without knowing why it was established and if it has fulfilled its founding objectives. It is particularly important to begin realising that the CSA was transferred by the Thatcher Government because it raises questions as to why the Government did not perceive or attempt to alter its design to prevent the problems arising within the American CSES from emerging within the CSA. This question is particularly important since the Government would have been aware of the criticisms and problems emerging in the American child support enforcement system and its agencies.

Children and the Family

S.Matthew Liao
The Queen's College, Oxford

'Do Rights Promote Children's Interests? A Theoretical Examination of the Communitarian Critique of Rights'

1.

There is a general presumption that rights can advance the interests of children.[1] This presumption needs to be re-examined, however, in light of the recent communitarian critique of rights, which claims that in certain close-knit communities, rights are not only not useful but can actually be detrimental for the individual members within such communities.[2] In this paper, I consider the communitarian critique of rights. My general conclusion is that the communitarian critique is not devastating for rights. However, as I will also demonstrate, not only does our analysis deepen our understanding of how and why rights do promote children's interests, it also points towards a possible limit of rights in promoting children's interests.

2.

For many, to claim that rights can promote the interests of children will not seem unusual. After all, one primary way of understanding rights, sometimes called the Benefit or Interest based accounts of rights, is that rights protect or promote an individual's interests.[3] As Neil MacCormick, an advocate of the Benefit or Interest based accounts of rights, writes, 'the essential feature of rules which confer rights is that they have as their specific aim the protection or advancement of individual's interests or goods'.[4]

---

[1] See for example *The United Nations Convention on the Rights of the Child*, 1989, and the debate that had begun in the 1970's regarding children's rights. F.Schrag, 'The Child in the Moral Order', *Philosophy*, 52, 1977, pp.167-77; Gross & Gross, *Children's Rights Movement*, Anchor/Doubleday, 1977; M.D.A.Freeman, *The Rights and Wrongs of Children*, Frances Pinter, 1983; B.Franklin (ed), *The Rights of Children*, Basil Blackwell, 1986.

[2] I have in mind here the communitarian and feminist critics who believe that rights are 'morally impoverished', 'individualistic', 'antagonistic'. See for example M.Sandel, *Liberalism and the Limits of Justice*, Cambridge, 1982, especially pp.28-35; A.MacIntyre, *After Virtue: A Study in Moral Theory*, London, 1981; Carol Gilligan, *In a Different Voice*, Harvard, 1982, especially pp.100, 136f, 149, 164f, 174; John Hardwig, 'Should Women Think in Terms of Rights?' *Ethics*, XCIV/3, 1984, pp.441-55; Robert Young, 'Dispensing with Moral Rights', *Political Theory*, VI, 1978, especially pp.67-8; Karl Marx, 'Critique of the Gotha Program', in R.Tucker (ed), *The Marx-Engels Reader*, Norton, 1978, pp.525-41.

[3] Contrast the 'benefit' or 'interest' based accounts of rights defended by such writers as David Lyons, Joseph Raz and Neil MacCormick with the 'choice' based account of rights represented by H.L.A.Hart, *Essays on Bentham*, Clarendon Press, 1982, which claims that the fact that rights confer benefits or promote interests is neither a necessary nor a sufficient condition for having rights. See a discussion of this debate below.

[4] Neil MacCormick. 'Rights in legislation', in P.M.S.Hacker & J.Raz (eds), *Law, Morality and Society*, Clarendon Press, 1977, p.192.

More specifically, rights can promote an individual's interests by conferring status on the rights holder and/or by allowing the rights-holder to feel dignified. As Bertram Bandman explains,

> 'Rights enable us to stand with dignity, if necessary to demand what is our due without having to grovel, plead or beg, or to express gratitude when we are given our due, and to express indignation when what is our due is not forthcoming.'[5]

Similarly, Feinberg writes,

> 'to think of oneself as the holder of rights is not to be unduly but properly proud, to have that minimal self-respect that is necessary to be worth of the love and esteem of others. Indeed, respect for persons ... may simply be respect for their rights.'[6]

Also, rights can promote an individual's interests by placing individual interests above an utilitarian calculation of social interests. Utilitarianism, to put it very crudely, suggests that an individual's interests can be weighed alongside social interests. Under an utilitarian calculation of social interests, it is therefore possible for an individual's interests to be sacrificed in the name of promoting greater social interests. However, by calling particular individual interests 'rights', rights in effect take these interests out of the realm of an utilitarian calculation of social interests. As a result, interests that are also rights become what Dworkin calls 'trump cards'; just as a trump card beats cards of other suits, so interests that are rights will now 'trump' ordinary considerations of utility or preference satisfaction.[7]

Given the fact that rights can promote interests in at least these two ways, it therefore does not seem absurd to assume that rights can promote an individual's interests in general and children's interests in particular. Indeed, even though the United Nations Convention on the Rights of the Child (1989) (henceforth, the Convention) speaks of the 'best interest of the child', the dominant language is rights. As John Eekelaar explains,

> 'the language of rights performs an important function. It acknowledges that there are certain things which we should provide for children, not just because adults think it would be nice if they had them, but because we are prepared to recognise that children want them, or can reasonably be assumed to want them.'[8]

Such endorsement of rights talk on the part of the United Nations indicates our current entrenched belief that rights do promote an individual's interests.

---

[5] Bertram Bandman, 'Do Children Have Natural Rights?' *Philosophy of Education: Proceedings of the 29th Meeting*, 1973, p.236.

[6] Joel Feinberg, 'The Nature and Value of Rights', *op cit*, p.27.

[7] R.Dworkin, *Taking Rights Seriously*, Duckworth, 1978, pp.90-4, 364-8.

[8] J.Eekelaar, 'Why children? Why rights?' in Alston & Brennan (eds), *The UN Children's Convention and Australia*, 1991, p.21.

3.

Yet, there are some who doubt that rights can promote an individual's interests. One group which warrants mentioning here in order to give a fuller picture of the different accounts of rights, but which is not the primary object of our concern in this paper simply denies the claim that rights can be rights if and only if they confer benefits or promote interests. According to the group's main spokesperson, H.L.A.Hart, the beneficiary of a duty is neither a necessary nor a sufficient condition for possessing a right. Rather, for Hart, a right is a form of choice; what is important is that the person to whom the duty is owed has the choice to control the performance of that duty. To have a legal right, for Hart, then, is to have a 'legally respected choice.' and it is the presence of that choice that gives point to our speaking of rights.[9] If Hart is correct that having a choice is what counts as having a right, then there is no necessary link between rights and the promotion of an individual's interests. Indeed, if having a choice is the sole criteria for having a right, then it is possible that we may have a right to do wrong, so Waldron points out, or a right to do something that is harmful to our interests.[10] The dispute of whether promoting interests is an essential feature of rights in fact features in one debate about children's rights. Since the 1970's, there have been a group called the children's liberationists which have advocated children's rights to such liberties as voting, sex, choosing one's guardians, and so on. Its opponents deny that children have such liberty-rights on the ground that it would not be in children's interests to have such rights. Some children's liberationists argue however that rights need not confer benefits nor promote interests in order to count as rights. According to these children's liberationists, rights should be seen as a form of choice; and children should be given the right to choose even if this might mean that children will choose actions that are not in their interests. It is beyond the scope and intent of this paper to go into the intricacies of this debate. As a last remark, I shall simply point out that one might still claim that it is in one's interests to have liberty rights. If this is correct, then it is not so clear that having more liberty rights bear no relations to promoting one's interests.

The group, which I have in mind, which put forth a strong challenge to the idea that rights promote interests is the communitarians. According to the communitarians, in certain close-knit communities it is not necessary to invoke the idea of rights because members are already constituted by higher bonds of love, generosity and affection. As Michael Sandel, one of the communitarian spokespersons, points out, justice is the first virtue only of certain kinds of societies; when we 'consider a more or less ideal family situation, where relations are governed in large part by spontaneous affection', individual rights 'are seldom invoked, not because justice is rampant but because their appeal is preempted by a spirit of generosity'.[11] Moreover, if one nevertheless tries to use the language of rights in such

[9] Hart, *op cit*, p.189.

[10] J.Waldron, 'A right to do wrong', *Ethics*, XCII, 1981, pp.21-39.

[11] Sandel, *op cit*, pp.30, 33.

close-knit communities, according to the communitarians, the consequence is that the bonds of love, generosity and affection may deteriorate. Indeed, Sandel describes how such close-knit communities can become 'wrought with dissension' when they begin to invoke the language of rights, and how the 'affection of previous days' may now give way to 'the observance of rights'.[12] If Sandel is correct that 'an increase in justice does not imply an unqualified moral improvement' it follows that there could be contexts where rights do not promote an individual's interests.[13]

The communitarian critique has serious consequences when applied to children's rights. The reason is that children are usually raised in the type of close-knit communities that the communitarians claim rights are inappropriate. If so, rather than promoting children's interests, rights may actually cause detriment to children's interests. In fact, Schoeman cautions along this line,

> 'The danger of talk about rights of children is that it may encourage people to think that the proper relationship between themselves and their children is the abstract one that the language of rights is forged to suit ... Emphasis on the rights of children might foster thinking about the relationship between parents and child as quasi-contractual, limited, and directed toward the promotion of an abstract public good.'[14]

Indeed, critics of children's rights often cite examples of children suing their parents, and so on, to illustrate the negative aspect of rights talk.[15] Again, if the communitarian critics of rights are correct, their critique could undermine the enterprise of speaking in terms of rights when dealing with children. It is this communitarian critique that I would like to consider for the remaining discussion.

4.

In pointing out that rights do not necessarily promote an individual's interests in close-knit communities, the communitarians make three distinct charges against rights; specifically, the communitarians argue that rights a) are inappropriate; b) are not necessary; and c) could cause antagonism in close-knit communities. Let us consider each critique in turn in the reverse order.

5.

One critique which the communitarians have against rights is that rights could cause antagonism among members in close-knit communities. This

[12] Sandel, *op cit*, p.33.

[13] Sandel, *op cit*, p.32.

[14] F.Schoeman, 'Rights of Children, Rights of Parents, and the Moral Basis of the Family', *Ethics*, 91, 1980, p.9.

[15] See for example Helen Jones & Jane Millar, *The Politics of the Family*, Avebury, 1996.

worry seems valid as rights do seem to have a built in antagonistic nature in them. As Waldron points out, 'To stand on one's right is to distance oneself from those to whom the claim is made; it is to announce, so to speak, an opening of hostilities; and it is to acknowledge that other warmer bonds of kinship, affection, and intimacy can no longer hold.'[16] Indeed, if we consider some of the articles in the Convention, for example, Article 16 (right to privacy), Article 13 (freedom of expression), and Article 14 (freedom of thought, conscience and religion) are clearly rights that directed 'against' others such as parents and the state. If such rights were acknowledged as the ground rules of the relationship between parents and children, it could cause antagonism if children were to claim them. To use the words of Waldron, children asserting their rights could 'be seen as a way blocking and preventing warmth and intimacy, replacing relatively unbounded and immediate care and sensitivity with rigid and abstract formulas of justice.'[17] Thus, the worry that rights could cause antagonism in close-knit communities is a valid one.

Though rights could cause antagonism, it does not mean however that rights will cause antagonism. For one thing, just because we have a right does not mean that we will claim that right. As Meyer and others have pointed out, we may never claim a right because our rights may have never been violated.[18] Further, we may not claim a right even if our rights are violated, either because we may not want to claim a right or because we may think that the situation is not appropriate for claiming a right or because of other reasons. In general, rights holders are not obliged to claim the rights that they have although they may be in a position to do so. In fact, Feinberg cautions us against those who always claim rights:

> 'A person who never presses his claims or stands on this rights is servile, but the person who never waives a right, never releases others from their correlative obligations, or never does another a favor when he has a right to refuse to do so is a bloodless moral automaton.'[19]

Thus, as long as we do not claim our rights, there is no necessarily link that rights will cause antagonism.

Secondly, even if we do claim a right, it also does not follow that antagonism will result. For example, a child may claim a liberty-right to study French rather than Spanish, or may choose to enforce her right to privacy. But it does not follow that therefore her relationship with her parents will now become antagonistic. The reason is that the parents may learn to respect their child's rights to privacy and liberty. If so, such observance of rights on the part of the parents could actually strengthen the bonds between the parents and the child, rather than cause antagonism. Moreover,

[16] J.Waldron, 'When Justice Replaces Affection: The need for rights', in J.Waldron, *Liberal Rights: Collected Papers 1981-1991*, Cambridge, 1993, p.373.

[17] Waldron, 'When Justice Replaces Affection', *op cit*, p.373.

[18] M.Meyer, 'Rights between Friends', *The Journal of Philosophy*, 1992, p.471.

[19] J.Feinberg, 'A Postscript to the Nature and Value of Rights', in Bandman & Bandman (eds), *Bioethics and Human Rights*, p.32.

it seems that usually it is not the act of claiming rights that is the source of antagonism. Rather, often things have already gone wrong first, and then subsequently one decides to claim a right. As Young, a communitarian, admits that 'It is frequently where there has been a breakdown in the caring or loving relationships that hold between people, that appeals to rights are made'.[20] If this is true, claiming a right also need not cause antagonism.

Finally, even if claiming a right does cause antagonism, sometimes this might be necessary in order to promote a greater good. As Feinberg notes emphatically, 'not to claim in appropriate circumstances that one has a right is to be spiritless or foolish'.[21] For example, children who are abused might legitimately claim a right to be separated from their parents even if claiming such a right will end their relationship with their parents.[22] Though claiming such right will mostly likely cause antagonism, it might be necessary in the greater interests of these abused children.

It must be conceded here that having rights does not tell the rights-holder how those rights ought or ought not to be claimed. There needs in fact what Meyer calls a 'theory of virtue' to go along with rights.[23] However, this concession does not amount to a critique of rights but merely that people need to learn how to use their rights appropriately. In any case, if causing antagonism is sometimes necessary in order to promote an individual's interests, it is difficult to see how the communitarian can denounce rights on the ground that rights could cause antagonism among members in close-knit communities.

6.

Communitarians' second charge against rights is that rights are not necessary in close-knit communities. Consider Marx's position:

> 'In a higher phase of communist society ... after labour has become not only a means of life but life's prime want; after the productive forces have also increased with the all-round development of the individual, and all the springs of co-operative wealth flow more abundantly – only then can the narrow horizon of bourgeois right be crossed in its entirety and society inscribe on its banners: From each according to his ability, to each according to his needs!' (my italics added).[24]

As Waldron points out, what is being suggested by Marx here is not that people in the communist society will have rights to what they need, but rather, rights will not be necessary as goods and services will be supplied

---

[20] Young, *op cit*, p.68.

[21] Feinberg, 'The Nature and Value of Rights', *op cit*, p.24.

[22] See for example David Archard, 'Child Abuse: parental rights and the interest of the child', *Journal of Applied Philosophy*, 7/2, 1990, pp.183-194.

[23] Meyer, *op cit*, p.479.

[24] K.Marx, 'Critique of the Gotha Programme', in David McLellan (ed), *Karl Marx: Selected Writings*, Oxford, 1977, p.569, cited in Waldron, 'When Justice Replaces Affection', *op cit*, p.383.

naturally based on needs alone. Sandel elaborates on such ideal community further:

> 'Nor does this generosity necessarily imply that I receive out of kindness a share that is equal to or greater than the share I would be entitled to under fair principles of justice. I may get less. The point is not that I get what I would otherwise get, only more spontaneously, but simply that questions of what I get and what I am due do not loom large in the context of this overall way of life.'[25]

In Sandel's formulation, we get a sense that rights have no place in such close-knit communities.

6.1

To assess this communitarian position, we need ask: what if resources do become scarce? or what if members are no longer as generous towards one another? or what if some members begin to feel oppressed by other members of such close-knit communities? Would rights be necessary again?

It seems that rights are not necessary if and only if the communitarian could guarantee that members of close-knit communities will always be provided for; they will always receive at least what they need; and they will always want to be part of such close-knit communities. Communitarians such as Sandel have gone a long way in trying show how such secure states of affair can exist in families, friendships, and so on. In the end, however, it seems that the communitarian position is an impossibility because the secure states of affair that the communitarians need in order to make plausible their claim can never exist indefinitely. For one thing, as soon as resources are not as scarce or members are not as generous, rights would become necessary again in order to guarantee that members of the close-knit communities are at least receiving what they need. More generally, as Waldron points out, all one needs to accept is that it is possible that individuals can 'fallout from social relations' that is, it is possible for close relationships to rupture and for individuals to be left stranded by themselves in order for rights to be necessary.[26] Given the fact that any state of affairs, including close-knit communities, can never be indefinitely secure for its members, it follows that it will always be in the interest of individuals to have rights, as rights would serve as a 'fallback' position or an insurance in cases of eventualities.[27]

Some children's rights are advanced, in fact, because it is thought that the family is not always a secure place for children. Many of the rights 'against parents' are also defended on such ground. As unpalatable as such rights may be, these rights may be necessary as fallback positions for children something to guarantee that children's interests will be protected in cases of eventualities. Waldron writes in defense of rights,

[25] Sandel, *op cit*, p.33.

[26] Waldron, 'When Justice Replace Affection', *op cit*, pp.388-89.

[27] Waldron, 'When Justice Replace Affection', *op cit*, p. 384.

> 'It is not that a system of rights is the only imaginable way in which needs could be dealt with in a caring society ... But even if [it is], I think we would still want to set up a system of rights as fallback – as a basis on which some assurance of support could be given, without risking insecurity, resentment, and indignity.'[28]

Thus, as attractive the communitarian close-knit communities may be, there is still room for having rights in close-knit communities; rights are necessary to protect at least one aspect of an individual's interests his interest in being guaranteed some sort of protection when things do go wrong. If so, it seems that the claim that rights can promote an individual's interests could always be sustained.

7.

Communitarians' third charge against rights is that rights are inappropriate in such close-knit c close-knit communities is that members in close-knit communities are trying to create close-relationships through love, generosity and affection. By invoking the language of rights in such contexts, however, members may begin to think individually rather than communally. Hardwig explains,

> 'Thinking in terms of rights ... does more than reflect an egoistic, atomistic situation: it creates such a situation or reinforces our tendency to move in that direction ... Because thinking in terms of rights rests on an atomistic picture of us as separate, thinking in terms of rights systematically denies the unity, the togetherness, the "we" that we are trying to create.'[29]

Given that rights 'evokes a picture of persons as atomistic, asocial, and primarily egoistic', communitarians such as Hardwig argue that rights are inappropriate as a model for understanding personal relationships in close-knit communities.[30]

The validity of this line of the communitarian critique of rights depends on what the communitarians mean by 'thinking in terms of rights.' It seems that communitarians would not be correct if one were only to 'think about' rights but does not actually claim one's rights. For example, in thinking that another family member ought to respect my rights, I could become more distant with that particular family member as a result of my thinking in terms of rights. However, my thinking about the fact that this other family member ought to respect my rights needs not cause me to become more distant with this other family member, because I may decide to waive my claim to a particular right.[31] If so, I can think about rights in close-

[28] Waldron, 'When Justice Replace Affection', *op cit*, p.382.

[29] Hardwig, *op cit*, p.449.

[30] Hardwig, *op cit*, p.449.

[31] See section 5 for the discussion that one needs not always claim one's rights.

knit communities without automatically becoming more distant with other members of these close-knit communities.

On the other hand, the communitarians could be correct if in thinking in terms of rights, one were also to be motivated by rights. For example, in raising a child, I begin to think in terms of the rights that the child has and how I should respect his rights. I then say to the child, I am raising you because it is your right and my duty to do so. Even if I have provided the child with more than what he is entitled to under his rights, the fact that I am motivated by rights rather than by love in raising this child does seem inappropriate because it seems to diminish the quality of this parent-child relationship.

It is important to note here that this line of the communitarian critique points in fact towards a serious limitation of rights discourses as a means of promoting an individual's interests. The reason is that as long as one is motivated by rights rather than by love, then the type of relationship that will result will be formalistic and impersonal ones. To use an example, if we say that a child has a right to be loved. But we are motivated only by the desire of wanting to fulfill our duty to give love to this child, rather than by love itself, then it seems that the type of love that the child receives cannot possibly be the type of love that she needs. If so, we must question whether claiming that a child has a right to be loved has really advanced the child's interests.

This critique needs, however, not to be devastating for rights. The reason is that though being motivated by rights excludes the idea of being motivated by love in close-knit communities, the reverse is not true. One can be motivated by love and at the same time be motivated by rights. For example, in friendship, as Meyer points out, we can expect our friends not to violate our right to freedom of expression or our right not to be tortured and we can be motivated to think of not violating our friend's right to freedom of expression or right to be tortured. If so, we can love our friends and at the same time respect their rights.

In fact, it seems that being motivated by love requires that we are also motivated by rights. That is, whenever we are motivated by love, we must also be motivated by rights. If this is true, it means that the communitarian concern that rights are inappropriate is in one sense unfounded because thinking in terms of rights is actually a condition for being motivated by love.

Still, the communitarian critique that if we are only motivated by rights but not by love, then relationships in close-knit communities do become formalistic and impersonal, does point towards a serious limitation of rights discourses. The lesson to be drawn from this critique in relation to children's rights is that though today we tend to emphasise the rights of children as a means of promoting their interests, however, we must also not neglect emphasizing the love and affection that are crucially necessary in order really to promote children's interests.

8. Conclusion

Our analysis shows that the general premise that rights can promote an individual's interests has not been defeated by the communitarian critique of rights, although the communitarian critique does point towards a limitation in rights discourses. Here we ask: How does this analysis of the communitarian critique contribute to our understanding of whether and how rights can advance children's interests? Our analysis yields several insights. First, children's rights need not cause antagonism between parents and children. Parents can learn to respect their children's rights without being antagonized by these rights. At the same time, children ought to be taught the difference between having a right and claiming a right, and when it is appropriate to claim a right. Secondly, children's rights are necessary even in close-knit communities such as the family because we can never be sure that any community will be secure for children. As long as this uncertainty remains, children need rights in order to have a fallback position in cases of eventualities. Finally, children's rights are appropriate in close knit communities such the family. In other words, rights and love are compatible even in close knit communities. In fact, as we have seen, children's rights will actually be most respected by those families that are motivated by love for their children. On the other hand, parents must be wary not to be motivated solely by respecting rights in their childrearing.

British Territorial Politics

Peter Lynch
University of Stirling

'Regional Party Organisations and Territorial Politics in Britain

---

Introduction

The study of British territorial politics has tended to emphasise the impact of territory on party attitudes to government structures and policies rather than its effect on party organisations. The argument of this paper is that because of devolution there is increasingly likely to be a need to understand parties as institutions experiencing centre-regional relations in which territorial factors shape intra-party politics in addition to traditional relationships such as the hierarchical relations between leaders and members. Just as the development of new tiers of regional government in Europe have generated discussion of 'multi-level governance' between central, regional and European government institutions, the growth of regional government can be seen to produce pressures for multi-level party organisation between the constituency parties, regional organisations and the central organisation. This paper will seek to develop a tentative approach to the impact of territory on party organisation through offering a brief sketch of the current territorial structures of the Conservative, Labour and Liberal Democrat parties and an analysis of the potential impact of devolution on party organisation in Britain through reference to European examples of state decentralisation bringing about change to party organisations.

The regional dimension to party organisation in Britain has been subject to very little analysis by academics. The most recent research on regional party organisations dates from 1975, largely because the regional dimension to parties has been seen as a moribund topic. Writing in the 1950s, Robert MacKenzie dismissed the regional structures of the Conservative and Labour parties as of little importance to the distribution of power within the parties, with each party's organisation concerned with increasing support for the party within the region rather than with autonomous policymaking. To a substantial degree, MacKenzie's sceptical view of regional party organisations remains the case today as they are largely administrative rather than policymaking structures controlled by the central organisation. However, the prospect of devolution to Scotland and Wales makes regional party organisation a potentially important area of study, as devolution has the capacity to transform weak regional party bureaucracies and representative structures into more effective policymaking and campaigning structures. Subsequent devolution to the English regions provides an additional impetus to the decentralisation of party organisation, though this is likely to be a much less predictable development than change in Scotland and Wales.

Devolution and British Party Organisations

Though British party organisations are predominantly centralised in nature (and have arguably become more centralised in recent years) devolution holds out the prospect of altering party organisational structures to produce a more autonomous and significant regional dimension to party politics. Both Labour and the Liberal Democrats propose to restructure the British state through the provision of parliaments for Scotland and Wales and some form of elected regional government for England. If instituted, such reforms can be expected to impact upon party organisation in substantial ways. The impact of devolution on party organisation can be most clearly seen in the case of the Labour Party, with demands for the establishment of more autonomous Scottish and Welsh Labour parties to take account of political devolution: with the party organisations able to select candidates independently of the NEC; fight election campaigns on their own policies and manifestoes; and act to control party organisation within their territory. Such a development has the potential to throw up situations in which the main parties have different policies or policy priorities across Britain. To a certain extent this situation already exists with Labour having a different education policy towards schools in Scotland and England, but the provision of more autonomous government arrangements (and the likelihood of a Scottish parliament being governed by a coalition rather than a single party) make such policy differences more likely.

The argument advanced in this paper is that the new devolved institutions of government will not merely alter centre-regional relations between Westminster/Whitehall and Scottish and Welsh parliaments, but they will also alter existing centre-regional relations within political parties in a number of ways. Political parties have often been defined as top-down organisations in which parliamentary leaderships and central organisations take precedence in policymaking and strategic decisions. Intra-party politics is seen to involve conflicts between the leadership and members over policy and ideology, manifested through conference debates, elections to executive bodies, factional politics and grassroots attempts to gain greater influence over policymaking and specific issues such as candidate selection. Devolution has the potential to change this situation through elevating and politicising the regional tier of politics and transforming regional organisations and representative institutions within the parties into new arenas of conflict within intra-party politics.

Decentralisation and European Party Organisations

The extent of territorial politics and constitutional structures in European states has touched party organisations more than in Britain. Examples of the impact of decentralisation on party organisation can be found in states such as Belgium, France and Germany amongst others. Regional and linguistic pressures were responsible for the fragmentation of the party system in Belgium from 1968 onwards, with the Christian Democrats, Socialists and Liberals progressively dividing into separate Flemish and Walloon wings, with their own organisations, leaderships and platforms, in advance of Belgium's transformation into a federal state. France offers an additional example of the impact of decentralisation on party structures. Though France can be understood as a political system in which parties have become centralised and presidentialised, the decentralisation reforms of the Socialist government in the 1980s have enhanced the power and autonomy of local and regional politicians at the expense of central government, with consequent effects on intra-party politics. Greater powers for local and municipal government and the creation of an autonomous sphere of regional government with direct elections from 1986 had the effect of enhancing the capacities of peripheral politicians against the centre. This situation was particularly influential in altering centre-local party relations within the RPR (which was ironic given the party's opposition to the decentralisation reforms). Local and regional government became an alternative career structure for party officials, who no longer had to depend on Paris for patronage and promotion, and the RPR's electoral success in local and regional government provided local power bases for ambitious politicians independently of the central organisation: a development enhanced by the financial independence of local parties.

Germany offers a final example of a party system in which constitutional structures have impacted upon party organisation. The extra-parliamentary organisation of the major parties such as the SPD and CDU have been substantially effected by the federal nature of the constitution, with Land parties holding important organisational and policymaking roles within the federal party and guaranteed levels of institutional representation on federal party structures such as the SPD's parteirat. The Land parties are not merely an important part of the federal party structure but they also offer career structures for party officials in themselves as well as a ladder for politicians into national politics. However, it is the autonomy of the Land party and its links to Land government that are most important here, as they offer some guide as to the impact of devolution on party organisations, with some tendency for party organisational structures to parallel patterns of governmental organisation. The relevant question here is whether changes in the structure of the British state to accommodate the territorial dimension will generate a similar effect on party organisations.

An Agenda for Studying Regional Party Organisations

Political science has taken a great interest in both political parties and centre-local relations. However, it has seldom married these two areas of interest to exam the centre-local or centre-regional relations of parties. The argument being advanced here is that intra-party politics and the distribution of power within party organisations can have an important territorial dimension. What is clear about regional party organisations in Britain, discussed below, is that they are highly differentiated. Some are strong power centres which can offer significant political challenges to central party leaderships, whilst others are merely weak branch-offices of the central organisation. However, the prospect of devolution and the creation of regional government bodies across different parts of the Britain has the potential to make regional party organisations more significant factors in intra-party politics.

There are a number of issues to be addressed in relation to the importance of regional party organisations and also to their future development under devolution. The first factor to address involves the adoption of a territorial perspective to intra-party politics. Regional party structures experience varying levels of control/autonomy within the national party organisation. They can be spheres of autonomous activity or alternatively almost completely dependent on central party structures. The level of control/autonomy is shaped by a number of factors: the party's formal and informal constitution, in terms of its definition of the division of powers and responsibilities between regional and national party bodies; the policymaking capacities of the regional party organisation; the administrative demands made on the regional structure by the national organisation; and the financial autonomy of the regional organisation from the centre. Finance is particularly important as an indicator of whether a regional organisation will actually have the freedom and capacities to operate autonomously as they will not be open to central office sanctions when attempting to adopt policies or initiatives that conflict with central directives. Very little is known about the aforementioned factors within British regional organisations.

Regional party organisations in each of the three main parties in Britain have representative as well as administrative structures. There are regional party conferences, regional executives and committee structures within the Labour Party and areas councils and area executives within the Conservative Party. Therefore, to some extent, the regional organisation can act as a career structure and also a power structure for party members, particularly amongst middle-level élites, with members using regional structures to participate in decisionmaking, develop a profile within the party and begin to network with other activists beyond their local party. Similarly, regional representative structures can offer opportunities for factions and tendencies within the party organisation. Within the Scottish Labour Party, for example, the combination of the devolution issue, the Scottish Labour's radical roots and the existence of distinctive Scottish policymaking structures has brought about a situation in which the Scottish Executive contains members elected at Scottish conference representing factions such as Scottish Labour Action, the Scottish Labour Womens' Caucus and the Campaign for Socialism. These factions have also been prominent in grassroots activities in the CLPs and making policy at Scottish conference. The regional executive and conference therefore became a forum in which factions could organise and pressurise the party. It is an open question whether other regions of the Labour Party have experienced a similar development, though something that should become clearer if studies of regional party organisations are conducted in the future.

A final issue to consider is the extent to which the existence of regional party organisations fulfil an integrative, rather than disintegrative, mechanism within parties. Lawson has argued that parties form a vital linkage function between citizens and the state. It could also be put forward that the party's regional organisations, in tandem with the constituency parties, act to integrate and involve members from the regions into national politics. This development can be examined through identifying the role of the regional party organisation in acting as a lobbyist or representative mediator with the central party organisation or leadership, channelling policy concerns or demands into the party itself. In this way, regional party organisation is not the slippery slope to a divided party in which conflict becomes the end- product of territorial politics, but rather a mechanism for integration and cohesion between region and centre within the party organisation. The linkage function opens up the question of how central organisations will cope with intra-party conflicts, in terms of designing executive and committee structures to take account of regional diversity.

The Development and Functions of British Regional Party Organisations

Regional party structures in the Conservative and Labour parties exist as a result of administrative decisions made by central party organisations rather than demands for decentralised party organisation in the regions. The Liberal Democrats are rather different, as their organisational structure owes something to history and a preference for organisational decentralisation. However, very little is known about regional party organisations in Britain, with regard to either regional representative bodies within the parties or the parties' regional offices. Wilson's study of British regional party organisations up to the mid-1970s outlined four specific tasks for regional offices: a regulatory function in overseeing the implementation of party rules, candidate selection procedures, etc; an advisory role assisting local parties in campaigning, organisation and policy; a conciliatory role in resolving disputes between local parties, council groups and constituencies and conducting inquiries on behalf of the central organisation; and a service function providing campaigning support for local parties over publicity, literature and membership recruitment. Each of the party's regional offices fulfils these types of functions to some extent. However, Wilson's study focused exclusively on regional offices, not on regional councils or area executives. Thus party management took precedence over policymaking and representative functions, stressing the limits of regional party organisation.

Conservative Regional Organisation

The regional dimension to Conservative Party organisation has existed since the formation of the National Union in 1886. However, of the three main political parties in Britain, Conservative attempts to marry party organisation with decentralisation have been the most disparate. Two separate party structures exist at the regional level: those of the professional party organised via Conservative Central Office and the voluntary party organised through the National Union. Similar to Labour, the Conservative Party's regional organisation owes much to the central organisation's desire to implement its administrative and campaigning functions regionally as well as centrally. Current Conservative organisation in the regions owes much to incremental decisions and post-1992 financial problems rather than to demands for regional representation and grassroots involvement. In the 1970s, Conservative Central Office organised its regional structure into 12 areas in England and Wales of varying size in terms of geographical spread and numbers of parliamentary constituencies. This structure was reduced to 6 areas in England in the post-1992 reorganisation of central office activities. However, the regional structure of the National Union retained 12 organisations in the regions, which are significantly different from central office.

Though grassroots autonomy, in terms of the independence of the constituency parties, is important within the Conservative Party, regional autonomy is not. To what extent this situation changes with devolution is a matter of speculation. Both the professional and voluntary sides of the Tories' regional organisation are viewed as unimportant and the informal nature of intra-party politics within the Conservative Party means that this is likely to continue. However, there are occasions when the weakness of Conservative regional structures is damaging. Scotland may boast a rather unique organisational structure within the party, with a Scottish Conservative Central Office and separate voluntary wing in the Scottish Conservative and Unionist Association, but these sections of the party are dependent on central office in London. The Scottish party's former deputy-chairman, Bill Hughes, once famously commented that 'we are only a branch office of the United Kingdom party and are centrally funded from head office in London. We do not account independently and are not even registered for VAT in Scotland.' Such organisational weakness and lack of a Scottish identity may have played a role in the electoral decline of Scottish Conservatism and the autonomy of the Scottish party is something that is likely to become problematic post-devolution. However, regardless of such developments very little is known about the functioning and autonomy of the central party's area offices or the National Union's areas.

Regional Organisation in the Labour Party

Labour's regional organisation can be traced to the NEC's creation of a Scottish Secretary in 1914, followed by the establishment of a Scottish Advisory Council in 1915. Though this new institution was criticised by Scottish activists as an example of NEC-inspired centralisation to curb grassroots autonomy, the NEC sought to establish an overall regional level to the party in the 1920s and 1930s. The party created 9 area organisations in the 1920s. However, these were very much central offices located in the regions for administrative purposes rather than autonomous regional units. This tendency was partly corrected in the late 1930s, with the establishment of regional councils to act as a representative mechanism for the party in the regions. These were extensions of the regional conferences which had been used to popularise Labour policies in the regions in the 1920s, and their establishment was completed by 1948. The regional councils were briefly in conflict with the NEC over control of the NEC's regional offices in the early 1950s, but they quickly capitulated to become fairly subservient and unimportant parts of the national party organisation. For many years the regional executives and conferences were barred from discussing national issues, which significantly narrowed their scope for activity and influence within the wider party. In the 1990s, regional councils remain rather truncated organisations with limited objectives which emphasise organisation and electoral campaigning rather than policymaking, with the Council being administered by the regional secretary appointed by Walworth Road and changes in the Council's rules and standing orders subject to an NEC veto.

Labour's regional offices (as opposed to its regional councils) play an important and more identifiable role within the party organisation on behalf of the central party apparatus. Regional organisers have operated as an intelligence network for Walworth Road and the NEC, providing information on regional organisation, membership recruitment and activity, and campaigning. Regional officials, as agents of the central organisation, had a significant role in membership expulsions in the 1950s and the compilation of the proscribed list. In addition, one former Scottish regional organiser recalled being asked to compile a list of Militant members in the late 1970s for the National Agent and being instructed by the former General Secretary, Larry Whitty, to prevent regional party conferences and executives from debating the issue of the Gulf War to prevent divisions within the party that would embarrass the leadership. These examples demonstrate one facet of Labour's regional structure: its use as a control mechanism by the central organisation. The fact that Labour's regional offices are populated by appointees of Walworth Road have made them useful for central party management. In Scotland, the Scottish General Secretary has not merely been responsible for party management within Scotland in terms of managing candidate selections in difficult seats such as Glasgow Govan and instituting NEC inquiries into Labour activities on Monklands District Council (the regulatory and conciliatory functions), but has a role in delivering support within the Scottish party for central policy initiatives. Good examples of this practice came with the regional office's role in galvanising support for the revision of clause IV at the Scottish Labour Party conference in 1995 and for the leadership's proposal of a two-question referendum on Scottish devolution in the summer of 1996. The regional organisation therefore has a key role in gaining regional support for central policies, though Scottish Labour representation on Walworth Road committees and the large number of Scottish MPs within the senior levels of the party do provide some channels of access and influence into the British organisation. However, the role and function of other regional offices and regional councils remains obscure.

Federal and Regional Organisation in the Liberal Democrats

Liberal Democrat party structure is most attuned to accommodating the territorial dimension to British politics and the prospect of devolution. The Liberal Democrats are a formally federal party, with a federal constitution and decision-making structures. The federal party exists above the autonomous English, Scottish and Welsh state parties, with regional parties within the English regions and constitutional provisions for the transformation of regional parties into state parties. However, this federalism has its limits. Whilst the Scottish Liberal Democrats are clearly separate from the federal party, with its own head office, staff, elected leadership and executive, sovereign conference, candidate selection procedures etc, the Welsh state party is relatively weak in terms of finance and personnel and the English state party doesn't seriously exist separately from the federal party.

The Liberal Democrat's federal structure does provide opportunities for guaranteed state party representation in key decisionmaking bodies, with English, Scottish and Welsh representatives on the federal executive, federal campaign committee and federal conference committee. However, as suggested above, the English state party is indistinguishable from the federal party organisation and the regional parties within the English state party have remained weak within the party itself. Significantly, none of the English regional parties have sought to become state parties, despite the regional strength of the Liberal Democrats in areas such as the Southwest of England. However, there is still very little academic analysis of the functioning of the Liberal Democrat's federal organisation and its impact on intra-party politics. It is an open question as to whether it exists as a model for Labour post-devolution.

Conclusion

One of the main problems in examining the role of British regional party organisations is the paucity of academic material dealing with both the regional offices of the central organisation and the regional representative institutions. Little is known about these structures now, let alone in the context of devolution. The establishment of devolved parliaments in Scotland and Wales has the potential to politicise and transform regional structures in those parts of Britain with a knock-on effect for the English regions. For, just as devolution will cause strains between Scottish and Welsh parliaments and central government, the process will cause strains for party management between different levels of party organisation. The Scottish and Welsh Labour parties can be expected to seek some organisational and policymaking autonomy that will alter the distribution of intra-party power and present a challenge to Labour's English regional councils. If devolution occurs, then party organisations will need to adjust to it. Overall, party organisation is likely to become more complex through the elevation of the regional tier: a development which may also challenge the centralisation of British parties.

British Territorial Politics

Russell Deacon
University of Wales Institute, Cardiff

'Trimming the Borders: A Study on the Wales Labour Party's Policy Process'

Abstract

There appears to have been no attempt to analysis the policy creating process of the Wales Labour Party prior to this study. This paper examines the policy making process in the Wales Labour Party in the past, present and future. It is evident that in the past, the party in Wales has been very closely integrated with the national party in its policy creating. Only around the margins has there been any distinctive Welsh policy. The advent of a more active Shadow Welsh Secretary in the form of Ron Davies has resulted in a slight increase in Wales Labour Party policy creation over the last five years. Although this has mainly been apparent in the field of devolution other distinct policy areas on issues such as education and agriculture have also emerged. This policy distinctiveness is likely to increase still further with the introduction of both a Welsh Assembly and New Labour's 'policy fora'.

Introduction

Although academics such as Pelling, Smith and Spear (who have produced significant studies on the Labour Party) make numerous references to the Scottish Labour Party, no reference is ever made by them to the party in Wales. The subject of the Wales Labour Party remains, to all intense and purposes hidden. Outside the area of Welsh devolution, academic studies on the Wales Labour Party are limited almost exclusively to those historical studies undertaken by the historian K.O.Morgan. Contemporary academic studies on the Wales Labour Party are therefore non existent. This study attempts to fill in a little of this extensive knowledge gap. It is split into four sections:

Part I examines the Wales Labour Party's administration and its current policy creation process

Part II assesses the extent of Wales Labour Party policy differences with British Policy and the restraints on the Welsh Party's policy creation.

Part III considers the breadth of policy change in the era of the current Shadow Welsh Secretary, Ron Davies (1992 to present)

Part IV looks at how the Wales Labour Party's policy making structure is altering and what it is likely to look like in the future.

The Wales Labour Party administrative machinery

The Wales Labour Party is not an autonomous part of a federal structure, instead it is a branch of a unitary organisation. The Party in Wales represents one of Labour's nine United Kingdom regions (HMSO 1994, p.21). The operations of the Labour Party in Wales are within Transport House in Cardiff. For a Party with 5, MEPs, 28 MPs and 723 unitary authority councillors, there is a relatively small administrative staff in Wales. There are nine full-time staff members in Wales, headed by a General Secretary. It is the General Secretary, Anita Gale, acts as the chief administrator whilst the Shadow Welsh Secretary Ron Davies is the effective head of policy issues (Davies to author). With the exception of one Assistant General Secretary, the majority of Wales Labour Party staff are concerned with Party administration and campaigning rather than any policy issues (Interview with Ron Davies).

The Committee Executive of the Wales Party is the governing body of the Party in Wales. It contains representatives from the Party's elected members and affiliated organisations such as the trade unions. From the Committee Executive also spring two important Standing Committees: the Organisation Standing Committee, and the Policy Standing Committee (Wales Labour Party, 1996a). As their names suggest these committees have direct responsibility for organisational and policy issues. The two committees mark a clear divide between operational and policy matters.

The Wales Labour Party's policy creation process

The process of policy creation in any political party can be torturous and lengthy process. Burch and Wood define three phases in the creation of this policy:

- 1. Initiation: the source, generation and early development of a policy proposal.
- 2. Formulation: the development of a policy in detail and its outline as a concrete set of proposals.
- 3. Implementation: the carrying out of the policy once formally agreed to or approve (Burch and Wood 1990,, p.15)

Since 1979, outside of Welsh local government, the Labour Party has only been involved in stages one and two of Burch and Woods policy creation process. Within stages one and two the Wales Labour Party is closely drawn into the British policy creation process. On the whole this means that a great deal of the Labour Party policy that applies to England is only at best altered around the edges to apply to Wales. In the Wales Party's 1996 policy pronouncements only the issue of devolution marked it out as being distinct from the English regions (Wales Labour Party 1996b).

Despite the apparent lack of policy differences between English, Welsh and British policy, the Party in Wales is affected by a number of factors that make it different from Labour's English regions. The significant differences evolve around the fact that Wales is a distinct nation. One consequence of nationhood is the existence of a Welsh Secretary and a Welsh Office. This means that the government of the day has a Civil Service department and Cabinet Minister set aside solely to deal with Wales. No English region is covered by a similar department or has its political influence so readily acknowledged. The Labour Party in Wales must take account of these differences and therefore act accordingly. This means that every issue within the remit of the Welsh Office can be dealt with by the policy creation process of the Wales Labour Party, as long as it has no United Kingdom wide implications (Brennen to author).

The Party in Wales, as part of the wider Party, evolved its own policy making apparatus whereby issues are collectively discussed (Davies to author). At the start of the electoral cycle the policy creation process is more complex and developed than when coming up to a General Election (Taylor to author). On controversial issues or complex ones such as devolution, the Wales Labour Party can take a number of years passing different policy ideas and motions through various committees and conferences. Currently the policy creation process is linked closely to the Annual Welsh Conference in May. This is the key body by which to endorse new policy. At this Conference two types of policy, from two different origins, are either endorsed or rejected. These are:

- 1. Constituency motions, which can originate from a individual ward branch. These motions mainly concern statements of support for various issues such as the Party's United Kingdom wide policies on Health or specific Welsh issues such as Welsh language policy.

- 2. Policy Standing Committee Reports to conference. This Policy Committee consists of representatives elected at conference. This Committee reaches its decisions via discussion – consensus, rather than any formal votes. The Committee's findings are also dependent on the Chair. Ken Hopkins, an Old Labour stalwart, has held this position for a number of years. The Policy Committee's reports have already been submitted to the Welsh Executive which has to agree to them being passed onto conference. At conference they are either be accepted or rejected as a whole (Brennen to author).

The Annual Conference does approves a small number of uniquely Welsh policies, for example Educational Excellence for All was approved in May 1995 and the devolution proposals preparing For A New Wales were approved in May 1996. Any specifically Welsh policies passed by the Welsh conference are then passed on to the party's National Executive Committee (NEC), which then puts its seal of approval on them. The NEC has never found any Welsh policy controversial enough to reject or even seek its amendment (Bold to author). Although the Party's Leader Tony Blair did request that the Welsh Party reconsider its devolution proposals in June 1996. The Welsh Annual Conference acts mainly, however, as an Annual

General Meeting, with Welsh Party Executive officers reporting back, than a policy creating forum.

The extent of Wales Labour Party policy differences

The Labour Party established a regional office in Wales in the 1920s. In the late 1930s Wales was acknowledged as a separate regional council within the Party. The regional office, however, remained a force of central office in Wales rather than part of the regional council for a large part of its history (Lynch 1997, p.9). There was increasing pressure from the nationalists, within the Labour Party in Wales, to regard Wales as a nation rather than just a region of England. The significance of Wales as a nation was finally recognised in 1949 with the establishment of the Welsh Council. This Council (made up of MPs, councillors and businessmen) advised the Government on a variety of matters relating to Wales. It was consulted and had the power to contact the Cabinet directly on issues that concerned Wales. The Council also had the effect of making the Party in Wales focus more clearly on Wales. In 1964 the Wales Party also had one of its MPs as a Cabinet Member, by right (Welsh Secretary). This put them on a par with Scotland and ahead of the English regional councils. It gave the more nationalist Labour members a permanent figure head of their own to champion Welsh issues.

Although the Wales Labour Party is integrally linked to the other eight regions of the Labour Party, it does have a number of autonomous actions which are not enjoyed by the English regions. It has its own Executive Structure and policy creation process just like the other regional councils but it also has two additional differences. It has a Shadow Secretary of State (for Wales) who can argue for the Wales region in Shadow Cabinet. In addition to this distinction, the Wales Labour Party as a regional council also draws up its own General Election Manifesto. It has done this at nearly every General Election since its first Welsh Manifesto entitled: Labour is Building a New Wales, in 1950.

During the 1960s and 1970s, a succession of Labour Welsh Secretaries had the opportunity to shape Wales Labour Party policy so that it differed, to a slight degree from that in England. This was often diluted, however, so that it did not make Wales too distinct from England. Cledwyn Hughes attempted to introduce a Welsh Assembly and reform Welsh local government into a system of unitary authorities in the 1960s but this came to nothing. John Morris's attempt to do exactly the same ten years later also failed. Apart from these endeavours at devolution Labour Welsh Secretaries only efforts at unique or differing Welsh policies concerned some elements of industrial policy such as the creation of the Welsh Development Agency and the support for the Welsh language via a Welsh Language Act in the 1960s.

As the Wales Labour Party is clearly different from the Party's English regional councils we can justly ask the question: how different is Wales Labour Party policy outputs from the British Party as a whole? The evidence tends to point to the fact that it is not very different at all. In their 1987 and the 1992 General Election manifestos, outside of the issue of devolution, any distinct Wales Labour Party policies did not differ to a great degree from that of the Party's British Manifesto or even to those contained in the Conservative Party manifestos for Wales.

In 1987 the Wales Labour Party's distinctive Welsh policy areas were limited to a few issues: (Wales Labour Party, 1987):

- 1. a Welsh Economic Planning Council;
- 2. encouragement of the use of the Welsh language;
- 3. a separate Wales Arts Council for Wales.

In 1992 Welsh issues revolved around (Wales Labour Party, 1992):

- 1. an Assembly for Wales within the lifetime of the next Parliament;
- 2. a Welsh arm of the Environmental Protection Agency;
- 3. a new Welsh language Act;
- 4. the introduction of unitary authorities into Wales.

These were mainly issues in which their main opponents, the Conservatives, could find little fault. By 1994 the Conservatives had introduced legislation or policies for all but two of Labour 1987 and 1992 uniquely Welsh Manifesto pledges. The Conservatives had ignored the issue of the Assembly and its forerunner the Welsh Economic Planning Council. The Labour Party on the surface had very few uniquely Welsh policy differences from Conservatives, who are regarded as the strong Unionist Party.

Restraints on Wales Labour Party Policy variation

A number of reasons seem to exist for the lack of Welsh policy variation. These can be divided into four areas:

- 1. The centralist nature of the Labour Party
- 2. Lesson from the past
- 3. The split between Welsh and British within the Wales Labour Party
- 4. The domination and conservative nature of the South Wales Labour Party which mitigates against radicalism

Each of these factors are dealt with in this section.

The centralist nature of the Labour Party

Although it is the NEC which is theoretically in charge of approving party policy, in reality it is the view of the Party Leader and his inner group which dominate the party's policy creation process. The power of the Leadership and the fact that the Labour Party is not a federal institution is made clear to the Party in Wales. The message is that 'policy can be different in Wales from England but must also be compatible with wider British wide policy' (Davies to author). In recent years the power of the leader has become evident to the Welsh Party. On the issue of devolution policy, Tony Blair directly overruled the Welsh Executive and the Standing Policy Commission on devolution when he asked them, in effect, implement policy connected to a referendum and proportional representation for an Assembly. Both the Welsh Executive and Policy Commission had dismissed these policies on numerous occasions. Yet the Chair of the Policy Commission, Ken Hopkins stated publicly that upon Tony Blair's request 'they unanimously agreed to pursue his policy suggested' (HTV 1/11/96). The lack of descent on the issue of a referendum, compared to the reaction of the Scottish Labour Party on the referendum issue, showed that the Wales Labour Party is much closer to the Party's centre.

Although the central party leadership holds a strong role over eventual policy outputs, Shadow Welsh Secretary Ron Davies has stated 'there are no directives from Smith House, policy is a bottom up issue' (Davies to author). Similarly his junior Shadow Minister Rhodri Morgan has declared that there is 'hardly any role for Smith House, although some issues are discussed with the experts there but there is no specific direction' (Morgan to author). Smith House may not need to interfere because central control is already operated by the Party's Leadership or that Labour's research department sees itself in more of a propaganda role than that of policy research (Theakston 1992, p.64).

Lessons from the past

Kevin Theakston's examination of Labour Party policy making whilst in Opposition indicated that they have a poor tract record in preparation for Government (Theakston 1992 pp. 61-72). In the past this lack of preparation has had a direct affect on Wales. The Party's slowness in accepting the need for a Welsh Secretary and Welsh Office in the 1950s, also their reticence over supporting the Welsh language in the 1960s and 1970s fuelled Welsh nationalism and promoted the rise of Plaid Cymru. Similarly the Party's split and failure to deliver devolution in the 1970s was seen as a result of the Party trying to combine the twin concepts of Welshness and democratic socialism. As Welsh historian Peter Stead noted:

> 'An able, attractive and inspired minority had tried something on, achieved some success but were defeated as they were forced to explain and justify what seemed a glorious opportunity to a very cautious and unimaginative electorate who saw

no connection between what was proposed and their own best interests.' (Stead 1985, p.121)

The Wales Labour Party of the 1990s is keen to ensure that it does not recreate these disasters. Thus caution often dictates policy. Joel Barnet (Labour's former Chief Secretary to the Treasury) summed up the problems of Labour's policy creation whilst in Opposition:

> 'The 1974-79 Labour Government had a difficult economic and financial task rendered impossible by pledges foolishly made without any serious thought as to where the money would come from.' (Theakston, 1992, p.66)

This factor has come home to Labour. Since the mid 1980s policy creation has also been dominated by expenditure politics, how much does it cost (Burch and Wood 1990 p.145)? Therefore the Wales Labour Party is restricted in the sort of policy it creates. If it cannot find the money for its policy then the policy cannot go ahead.

The split between Welsh and British

In the past Labour, politicians from Wales have directed huge influence over the party nationally. This factor has done much to direct the Welsh Party's focus towards national rather than specifically Welsh policies and consequently influenced the policy making process within Wales. In Peter Stead's history of the Labour Party in Wales he noted that:

> 'The party that developed in Wales rarely doubted that Welshness had contributed to its legitimacy and genius but was never sure whether this Welshness demanded in return some specific constitutional or administrative provisions. In fact, the Party was divided for there were some for whom socialism and nationalism came neatly together whilst others felt that the claims of Wales should be left to fade with the Liberal Party.' (Stead 1985, p.99)

The battle between Welshness and Britishness has meant that for every heavy weight politician the Party in Wales produced that supported nationalism it produced an equal counterweight that was against it. When James Griffiths [in the 1940s and 50s] fought for greater Welsh political and administrative devolution, Anuerin Bevan fought against it. In the 1970s John Morris fought for, and Neil Kinnock fought against political devolution. The fact that the national Party was led by MPs with Welsh constituencies also meant that the Welsh Party's focus was concentrated still further on British issues.

Such pro- and anti- nationalist politics had their inevitable effect on the development of the Party in Wales. Up until 1966 the Welsh Labour Party went from strength to strength. In that year at the General Election it secured 88 per cent of all Welsh Parliamentary Seats. But the same year also saw the rise of Plaid Cymru who took a Parliamentary seat of Labour in the Carmarthen by-election. This victory and Plaid Cymru's increasing threat in Labour's South Wales valleys heartland's represented the first 'significant challenge to the political and intellectual dominance of Labour' (Morgan 1995, p.184). It also caused the party to seriously re-examine its Welsh credentials. Today Plaid Cymru remains the main political threat in the Labour dominated South Wales Valleys. The fact that a political party dedicated to Wales is Labour's, main threat in a large number of authorities, has caused the Wales Labour Party to re-examine its own Welshness. A consequence of this review has been the Party's more active support for Welsh language and cultural issues.

Labour's Welsh dominance and its affect on policy making in Wales

The fact that the Wales Labour Party holds more elected seats in Wales than all of its opponents combined has a number of affects on the party's own policy creation process. These revolve around:

- 1. The Labour Party's awareness of its political dominance in Wales which means it seldom desires or seeks consensus with those outside of the Labour movement when compiling its policy agenda;

- 2. The dominance of the South Wales Labour Party which leads to policy construction around the interests of those in the South;

- 3. The division of the Wales Labour Party into different policy factions which battle over policy determination.

This section examines these factors in greater detail.

The dominance of the Welsh Labour Party

With the virtual annihilation of the Conservative Party in Wales at a local level after the 1995 unitary authority elections, local opposition became limited. In only two of Labour's local authorities did the party not control more than 60 percent of the seats (Deacon 1996 p.83). In 79 per cent of Labour councils the Party control more than 75 per cent of seats.

The total dominance of the Wales Labour Party means that Party does not often see the need to consult with those parties or organisations which are not directly linked to itself. On devolution, the Wales Labour Party refused to hold a Constitutional Convention which encompassed all of those willing to discuss devolution. The Party did not see the need to actively involve 'minority parties' (Bold to author).

The influence of South Wales Labour

In the mid 1970s the Welsh Labour Party, for a while, became dominated by Welsh nationalist and rural Labour MPs. It was these MPs who pushed for, but failed to obtain, the most significant Wales Labour Party policy of any national note, devolution. For the rest of its history, however, it has been dominated by the MPs from the industrial Valleys and cities of South Wales (Stead 1985, p.115). South Wales is where the vast bulk of the Welsh population live, it's where the administrative and cultural capital of Wales is, Cardiff. Control of this area is in effect control of the entire Welsh nation.

Some 66 per cent of the Executive Seats are held by representatives from South Wales Labour, with only 19 per cent being held by those from North Wales (Wales Labour Party 1996a pp 2-3).[1] This division partly reflects the fact that the Party's political strength is concentrated in the South. Although nearly a third of Welsh Parliamentary seats are in the North, only 36 per cent of these are held by the Labour Party. South Wales contains 71 per cent of all constituencies with 85 per cent of these being in Labour's control. Thus the power of the Welsh Labour Party is concentrated in South Wales. The majority of the National Executive, all of the Shadow Welsh Front Bench and the two Standing Committees are chaired by representatives from South Wales constituencies. This has the effect of concentrating Welsh Labour Party interests on South Wales thus ensuring that the interests of South Wales dominate any policy discussions. It is the South Wales Labour Party that is also traditionally the most pro Unionist. It wants to be part of the British party and to directly influence United Kingdom policy. It is therefore the least likely to desire distinctly Welsh policies.

Wales Labour's policy factions

With so much control concentrated in one party's hands it was inevitable that different faction arose within the party itself. These factions became self evident over the issue of devolution. Labour's devolution proposals have divided the party's MPs into three clear policy groups mainly centred on South Wales. These groups are:[2]

- 1. *Official New Labour.* Those who support the Party's present devolution proposals, mainly those Shadow Government 'payroll vote': Ron Davies (Caerfilli), Wyn Griffiths (Bridgend), Rhodri Morgan (Cardiff West) Jon Owen Jones (Cardiff Central), Peter Hain (Neath), Alun Michael (Cardiff South and Penarth) and back bencher Ton Touhig (Islywn).

- 2. *Old Labour.* Those who want no political devolution or as little as possible. These Old Labour politicians are headed

[1]The remaining seats are held by organisationsaffiliated to the Labour Party.

[2]These MPs have publicly put their support or lack of support for devolution on record (Parliament for Wales).

by: Sir Ray Powell (Ogmore), Allan Rodgers (Rhondda), Kim Howells (Pontypridd) and Llew Smith (Bleanau Gwent).

• 3. *Radical Labour*, some of whom are acknowledged thorns in Tony Blair's side. They want maximum devolution (an Assembly elected by proportional representation with full legislative and tax raising powers). Prominent members include: Ann Clwyd (Cynon Valley), Paul Flynn (Newport West) and the not so rebellious Dr John Marek (Wrexham).

In the past, the Old Labour of South Wales had dominated or restricted Welsh policy creation. Their desire was to keep Wales as a Socialist bastion, a state controlled by committees. Their victories came in the form of no change. In Education for instance there are no City Technology Colleges, no Grammar schools and only a handful of Grant Maintained schools in Wales (the later bitterly contested at every stage by the Labour Party). Wales Labour Party policy seeks to maintain these differences with England, despite New Labour Party policy shifts in England (*The Observer*,, 30/6/96, p.17). The Old Labour factions have fought hard to exert their influence over what little Wales Labour Party policy there is. MPs such as Llew Smith and Allan Rodgers are on the Executive Committee and the Policy Standing Committee. Ken Hopkins (Secretary of the Rhondda Labour Party) is the Chair of the Standing Policy Commission. He is one of key old guard representatives in the policy creating arena (*Western Mail*, 3/1/97). This Old Labour group makes regular pronouncements about the desire to maintain the status quo or the implement minimal measure of devolution.

The Official New Labour MPs mainly hold Shadow Government posts. Although bound by Cabinet Collective responsibility they make use of others to express their frustration with Old Labour. Shadow Welsh Secretary, Ron Davies' constituency representative on the Policy Standing Committee is Gareth Hughes. Hughes is leader of 'New Labour's' Wales Labour Action which pushes for a more powerful Assembly. Rhodri Morgan's representative on the Committee is Kevin Brennan. He publicly promoted the imposition of the Additional Member System of proportional representation in any new Welsh Assembly (Brennan et al 1996). The same system was preferred by Rhodri Morgan, his political master. It is through these spokesmen that New Labour battles with Old without the appearance of serious splits occurring within the Parliamentary.

The more 'Radical Labour' MPs have no representatives on the Executive or the Policy Standing Committee.[3] They are left to put out the occasional press notice or discussion with journalists advocating their views.

The changing sea – The Ron Davies era

The replacement of Barry Jones by Ron Davies in 1992 has led perhaps to the most proactive Shadow Welsh Secretary since Nicholas Edwards. Ron

[3] Although Paul Flynn does attend the Welsh Executive asSecretary of the Welsh PLP Group.

Davies (1992 -) has been acknowledged by his fellow Labour Party MPs as having created a distinctly Welsh Labour agenda on issues ranging from devolution to the Welsh rural economy (Morgan, Griffiths and Wardell to author). Ron Davies is aware that the Wales Labour Party has a great deal of scope to create its own policy initiates independent of the English regions. There is increasing evidence that it is beginning to do so. A more independent Welsh policy making process has been enhanced by three factors, of which he makes use :

Firstly, 'quite a lot of policy autonomy already exists in the Welsh Office. This makes Wales distinct from the English regions '(Griffiths to author). The fact that Welsh Secretaries such as Walker and Redwood pursued different policies to those in England (on issues such as health care and the economy) has encouraged the Wales Labour Party to also detail their own policies. Often this process as been reactive rather than proactive, as was the case with their Rural White Paper (1996) in response to Welsh Office's own version. Nevertheless the Wales Labour Party has created its own distinct Welsh alternative policy without the need to merely adapt policy from England.

Secondly, there is a history of forming a political consensus in the smaller Welsh political community. In the 1980s, Labour councils and the Wales TUC co- operated with the Conservative controlled Welsh Office over inward investment. Some of this co- operation or acceptance of good ideas continues today. On the environment for example, the Countryside Council for Wales originated the Tir Cymen environmental stewardship scheme. A variation of the Countryside Stewardship Scheme that occurs in England, it links environmental payments to the whole farm not merely a field or two as occurs in England (Welsh Office to author). The Wales Labour Party has actively supported this Conservative Government scheme and would expand upon taking office (Morgan to author).

Thirdly, the role played by the Shadow Welsh Office team. The Shadow Welsh Secretary is without doubt the most important figure behind policy creation in the Wales Labour Party. As a member of the Shadow Cabinet he is linked directly to the Party at the highest level. He sits as an Ex Officio member of the Welsh Executive Committee and helps determine the composition of the Policy Standing Committee. Although the Shadow Welsh Secretary must bide by the decisions of the Welsh Executive Committee whilst in opposition when in government he takes on a more autocratic stance in terms of policy creation (Davies to author). Although the Shadow Welsh Office Ministers do not sit on the Welsh Executive Committee or its sub committees they often act as the policy dynamos of the Wales Labour Party.

The role played by the Shadow Welsh Office Team is important enough for further consideration. In the matter of rapid policy creation it is the Shadow Welsh Office Team which is the most important. Although Wales Labour Party policy usually differs only between 10 -15 per cent in respect of that concerning England or the wider United Kingdom (Morgan to author) some issues are much more distinct. Clear examples of these differences can be seen in Welsh agricultural and education White Papers or unique endorsement of Welsh language issues or devolution issues. In education for example the Wales Party's Educational Excellence for All highlighted in service training for teachers whilst in teaching; the English document highlighted training before starting work (Griffiths to author).

Ron Davies' deputies, the Shadow front bench spokesmen, are appointed after consultations have taken place between the him and the Party Leader (Davies to author). Although the Shadow Welsh Secretary covers the whole of the Welsh Office within his remit he also apportions individual portfolios to the two Front Bench Spokesman (Davies to author). Just like Welsh Office junior ministers, these portfolios are often shaped around the interests of the individual MPs. When Wyn Griffiths moved from being an Education spokesman to Welsh Affairs, Education continued as part of his new portfolio. Wyn Griffiths thus had expertise on Education, but generally Shadow Welsh Spokesman cannot hope to master the full extent of their varied brief. They therefore tend to limit their expertise and input in policy issues to certain areas. Griffiths concentrated on Education and the environment whilst his fellow Shadow Minister Rhodri Morgan concentrated on Health and European issues (Griffiths and Morgan to author). Despite Rhodri Morgan having nominal control of Agriculture, Ron Davies with his previous expertise as Shadow Agriculture Secretary deals with policy creation concerning Welsh agriculture.

The policy making role of the Shadow Welsh Office Team is only limited by its size and remit. Due to the fact that it covers such a wide remit its members cannot hope to be there at the start of all English-Wales policy. Shadow Welsh Office Ministers therefore only cover some issues in 'a big way'. Rhodri Morgan covers Health whilst Wyn Griffiths covers Education. This means that much of the mainstream policy creation which affects Wales is headed by English Shadows Ministers (Morgan to author). Shadow Ministers also set up their own 'Welsh Think Tanks to report back to them on new policy ideas which they can put before the Welsh Executive. Rhodri Morgan MP has set up a number of Welsh Think Tanks on issues such as Health. These meet once every quarter and bring together doctors and administrators who are sympathetic to the Party (Morgan to author).

Wales Labour Party policy making in the future

We have seen that in the past there was little distinct Wales Labour Party policy. Since 1992, with the advent of a more proactive Shadow Welsh Secretary distinct Welsh Policy has increased. Three factors are likely to expand the amount of Wales Labour Party policy creation over the next decade. These are:

- 1. The example set by the Scottish Labour Party, which the Wales Labour Party is keen to follow.
- 2. The introduction of New Labour's Policy Fora as a method of policy creation.

- 3. The advent of a Welsh Assembly.

Influence of Scottish Policy Creation

The Wales Labour Party regards the policy autonomy of the Party in Scotland as a model of good practice which it is keen to follow more closely (Davies to author). The Wales Labour Party clearly accepts that Scottish Labour Party dominates its own destiny to a far greater extent in terms of policy creation. They cite the reasoning behind this as being Scotland's own legal system and a far greater history of administrative devolution. This means that they are not 'led by the nose from their English Shadows', as the party in Wales sometimes feels it is (Morgan to author).

The Wales Labour Party often takes note of events happening in Scotland and models some of its own policies on Scottish Labour's. In 1987 the Scottish Party proposed the establishment of a Parliament for Scotland, the Welsh Party followed suit with it plans for an Assembly in it's 1992 Manifesto. The 1992 Wales Labour Party Manifesto also planned to allow the Wales Tourist Board the right to advertise attractions abroad, which was a measure to equalise it with the Scottish Tourist Board (Wales Labour Party 1992, p.10). More recently it has taken note of what it regards as 'good ideas'. On Education for example, Scottish Labour Party plans for a General Teaching Council and a Good Research Council, would be integrated into any new Welsh Assembly (Griffiths to author).

The role of the Policy Fora and future Welsh policy creation

The existing Labour Party system of policy creation has been deemed to lack many of the elements of democracy needed by a modern political party. The system of referring policy creation from branch to constituency and then on to conference is both lengthy and often lacks accountability when delegates fail to report back adequately to those they are meant to represent (Harl to author). It is for this reason that the concept of policy fora have been introduced. Policy fora involves 'a process and structure which will allow both a more deliberative determination of policy and a wider democratic participation in its evolution' (Labour Party 1996a, p.4).

Recently a National (United Kingdom wide) Policy Forum has been introduced. The National Policy Forum was recommended at the Labour Party's Autumn Conference in 1990. The first one was held in May 1993. They are held across the United Kingdom mainland; one was undertaken in Cardiff in November 1994. Each forum is held over one weekend, opening at lunch time on Saturday and ending at lunch time on Sunday. They examines consultative documents and NEC statements. The policy cycle works as follows they initially examine draft consultation papers at their Autumn/Winter forum before putting them out for wider consultation. A draft policy document is then submitted to the Summer forum before being presented to the following Autumn conference (Labour Party 1996a, p.4).

The National Policy Forum deals with policy that affects the whole United Kingdom, not just Wales.

The membership of the Forum includes representatives from across the Party and its affiliates. The NEC stated that there should be 81, however, trying to aggregate discrepancies mean that there are 88. Members are selected from various affiliated organisations and from the regions, including Wales. There should be 4 representatives from Wales but for some reason there are 8 (Hurl to author). Theoretically the NEC and Conference have ultimate control over the National Policy Forum, but in practice they are presented with a fait accompli. Many members of the NEC are also members of the National Policy Forum.

The Wales Labour Party has its own Policy Forum during the Spring of each year. This is better than some regions such as the South and West and South East which have failed to hold regular meetings at all, but worse than regions such as London and the West Midlands which hold two Forums each year. The role of these Forums is to:

- 1. Comment upon policy documents (both directly to politicians and indirectly through the region's members of national policy forum and policy commissions). Comments are designed to focus particularly on the regional and local implications of policy proposals.
- 2. Cascade discussion and information about policy issues down into local constituencies, branches and affiliated organisation (Labour Party 1996a, p.8)

In the future, branch and constituency Forum are designed to filter their views onto the Welsh Policy Forum which in turn will transfer them onto the National Policy Forum. Where issues solely concern Wales they will stop at the Welsh Policy Forum.

A Welsh Assembly and Labour Party policy creation

When Tony Blair 'requested' the Wales Labour Party to consider a referendum on devolution and a system of PR for any new Assembly, he showed the limit of the Wales Labour Party's own independence. It was a request that an obedient Wales Labour Party readily complied with. Yet it is the issue of devolution and a new Assembly, if it comes, that will massively increase the opportunity and the need for Wales Labour to create it own distinct policies. The Wales Labour Party is advocating the running of a Welsh Assembly by 1 April 1999 (*Western Mail*, 21/11/96, p.2). Although this Assembly will not have primary legislative powers it will have considerable secondary legislative powers. Once the Assembly is established future 'legislation framed by Labour governments on matters such as Education or the Health Service will allow for maximum discretion at the Welsh level' (Davies 1996, p.19).

'Maximum discretion' at the Welsh level will mean that the Wales Labour Party will have to adapt its policy creation process in order to create policy on the vast majority of the Welsh Assembly's functional areas. If it is to develop the Welsh Assembly on a distinctly Welsh basis it will have to adapt its policy creation process to a far greater extent than currently exists. Leading members of the Wales Labour Party policy creation process mechanism have accepted that the entire process will have to be strengthened (Griffiths to author). It has been accepted within the Party that in the three and a half years leading up to a Welsh Assembly, a great deal more finalised policy creation would be established within Wales (Morgan to author). Undoubtedly the Welsh Policy Forum will play a crucial role in policy creation which is distinctly Welsh..

Conclusion

Distinct Wales Labour Party policy output is limited. Historically the Party in Wales has viewed itself as almost totally integrated with the Party in the rest of the United Kingdom. Those in Wales felt that they would be sidelined from important national policy creation and decision making if they allowed the Party in Wales to become more autonomous. Major Labour Party politicians with a Welsh base such as Callaghan, Foot and Kinnock saw both their own and the Wales Labour Party's future at Westminster and Whitehall not in Cardiff. Due to the desire to be British distinctly Welsh policy was very rarely allowed to occur.

The next decade will almost certainly see a dramatic increase in Wales Labour Party policy outputs. The exact affect of the policy fora is as yet unknown but another factor may have a more important influence upon policy creation in Wales. The advent of an Assembly will force many within the Wales Labour Party to consider their own policy creation process more seriously. To campaign for a Welsh Assembly means creating a manifesto which will have to be tailored specifically for Wales. They may avoid too much policy making by continuing to tinker around the edges of their own Party's British policies, as the Conservatives have done for the last 18 years. On the other hand they may seek it introduce and implement their own policy agenda. Whether this policy creation is governed by New or Old Labour or even coalition Labour is something only time can tell.

Bibliography

K.Brennen et al, *Voting the Visions: A fair electoral system for the Welsh Assembly*, Cardiff, 31/10/96.

M.Burch & B.Wood, *Public Policy in Britain*, second edition, Blackwell, 1990.

R.Davies, 'The tools for the job', *Agenda*, Winter 1996/7.

R.Deacon, ' "Labour Day": Wales' First Unitary Authority Elections', *Representation*, 33/3, 1996.

Labour Party, *Domestic and International Policy Committee: Building on Success – the future of the National Policy Forum*, PD3961 DIPC 4/11/96 (1996a).

Labour Party, *New Labour New Britain New Vision*, 1996b.

P.Lynch, *Regional Party Organisations and Territorial Politics in Britain*, PSA Conference 1997.

K.Theakston, *The Labour Party and Whitehall*, Routledge, 1992.

Wales Labour Party, *Wales Will Win*, 1987.

Wales Labour Party, *It's time to get Wales working again*, 1992.

Wales Labour Party, *New Labour – New Wales Report*, 59th Annual Conference 1996 (1996a).

Wales Labour Party, *New Labour New Life For Wales: What a Labour government means for you*, 1996b.

Interviews with:
Andrew Bold – Wales Labour Party Assistant General Secretary (Policy and Information)
Kevin Brennan – member of the Wales Labour Party Policy Standing Committee
Ron Davies MP – Shadow Welsh Secretary
Annabel Harl – Wales Labour Party Representative on the National Policy Forum
Wyn Griffith MP – Shadow Welsh Front Bench Spokesman
Rhodri Morgan MP – Shadow Welsh Front Bench Spokesman
Matthew Taylor – Labour Party Policy Executive
Gareth Wardell MP – Chairman of the Welsh Affairs Select Committee